Tales of Bayfield Pioneers

A History of Bayfield

by Eleanor Knight

Beedlow Media
Bayfield, WI
Web ∞ Print ∞ Video
Design & Production
www.beedlowmedia.com

Tales of Bayfield Pioneers

A History of Bayfield

by Eleanor Knight

Copyright ©2008 Scott K. Hale

Printed in the United States of America.
Published by Beedlow Media, P.O. Box 1333, Bayfield, WI 54814.

First printing: August 2008
Library of Congress Control Number: 2008932840

ISBN: 978-0-6152-3586-8

Table of Contents

About the Author

ELEANOR KNIGHT WROTE THE FOLLOWING about Bayfield, and it may be a fair description of what inspired her to tell the story about Bayfield's Pioneers and their contributions to the city as "movers and shakers:"

> *"After the stakes were driven, and the town named, the story of Bayfield becomes a story of people, their lives, their actions and reactions. It becomes a lot of things that the passing of time has labeled incidents, though, when they happened, they may have been for the moment the happiest, funniest, or most tragic incidents in the world."*
> *Eleanor Knight, March 1956*
> *Bayfield Centennial*

Eleanor is a third-generation member of a prominent pioneer Bayfield family. Paternal grandfather, William Knight, arrived on a cold winter's day by horse and sleigh from St. Paul, Minnesota in 1869. At the Episcopal Church in Bayfield, William married Jesse H. Williamson in October of 1886. Together the Knights built successful businesses and a personal life that was enriched by three children, Douglas, Anne, and Gladys (Hale). Eleanor is the daughter of Douglas and Marjorie (Findeisen) Knight and the sister of William (Bill) Knight.

Born February 7, 1913, Eleanor Knight was raised and spent the majority of her adult life in Bayfield. She attended the Bayfield Central-Low School and graduated from Bayfield's Lincoln High School in 1930. A lifelong member of the Episcopal Church, Eleanor remained faithful to the church of her ancestry. A bookkeeper and secretary, working for her father Doug Knight at the Bayfield Canning Company, Eleanor also provided similar services for Booth Fisheries. She retired from the Bayfield County Highway Department in 1983. For many years Eleanor was a correspondent for the Ashland Daily Press and her hometown paper, the *Bayfield County Press*.

Eleanor's heart and soul, however, seemed to yearn and remain forever in the search of and writing of local history. The William Knight family had played an integral role in the making of Bayfield history. Eleanor's pride in her family, her love of Bayfield and the Apostle Islands area was evident. She greatly enjoyed the stories of the pioneers, their humor, their hearty enjoyment of life, their acceptance of the challenges created by Lake Superior storms and the dangers provided on an ice covered lake. These true-life stories undoubtedly inspired many a fine article.

On June 9, 1956, the Wisconsin State Historical Society presented Eleanor with the Society's most prestigious "Award of Merit." The acknowledgement statement reads, "The State Historical Society of Wisconsin is pleased to recognize and commend the distinctive contribution of Eleanor Knight for her carefully researched and well-written newspaper articles on the history of the Bayfield area, which provided a new appreciation of local history to the citizens of the region during the Bayfield Centennial period."

Eleanor was a member of the Wisconsin Rural Writers Association and won honors and awards in the statewide group of amateur writers. Her last known recognition came when she tied for top honors in a writers contest sponsored by the *Chicago Tribune*. Her entry in that event was once again a wonderful Bayfield tale—the story of the Robert Inglis wedding, which took place October 26, 1891.

Eleanor Knight passed to eternity on December 23, 1994. Her departure concludes one more chapter of Bayfield's history-rich past. May Eleanor's inspirations documented here provide academic passage to future historians and citizens of this timeless little pioneer town on the shores of beautiful Lake Superior.

~Robert J. Nelson

Introduction

This book of Eleanor Knight's articles on Bayfield History began as a passionate dream several years ago.

Eleanor Knight left behind five notebooks filled with her fascinating writings about the history of Bayfield. These were stories she had spent endless hours researching and her work is backed up by letters and documents gained through her dedicated effort.

Eleanor's stories appeared in the local *Bayfield County Press* newspaper beginning in the early 1950s. This book has been compiled from her original typed copies of those columns. Sometimes she had written a little note to the readers and these comments are also included. The sequence of stories in this book differs from the chronological order of the stories as originally published. All of these newspaper columns are saved in notebooks entitled Bayfield History, Volumes 1- 5. The friendships and times spent working on this book have been rewarding for everyone involved. We came to realize how many other people supported publishing these revealing articles about Bayfield's history-making pioneers.

The final dream is now that you, the reader, will enjoy Eleanor's work as much as we have, and that these vignettes may lead to further exploration of the rich history of this community and its early inhabitants.

~Kathie Knight Bernico & Scotten (Scott) Knight Hale

Acknowledgements

The following people and organizations have provided valuable assistance in bringing Eleanor Knight's newspaper articles into publication in the form of this book, *Tales of Bayfield Pioneers—A History of Bayfield*.

- Scotten (Scott) Knight Hale, grandson of William and Jesse H. (Williamson) Knight; son of Gladys Knight (Hale); nephew of Annie Knight and Douglas S. Knight; cousin of Eleanor Knight.

- Kathie Knight Bernico, great grand-daughter of William Knight, daughter of Bill and Frances (Anderson) Knight; and niece of Eleanor Knight. Kathie provided and brought the writings of Eleanor Knight to computer-ready availability.

- Bayfield Heritage Association, Inc. (BHA), for access to the *Bayfield County Press* editions and use of time period Bayfield photos.

- The Burt Hill Family Photo Collections; Robert Barningham, Peggy Barningham Morris and Pamela Barningham Maki.

- Bill Bernico for his assistance with the formatting and printing of the first reproduction of the onion-skin articles, previously typed by Eleanor, so they were computer-ready and now provide the basis for this book.

- June Olsen, sister-in-law of Kathie Knight Bernico, for the many hours of typing from the original onion-skin manuscripts that now allow us to publish this book.

- The late William Douglas Knight, father of Kathie Bernico, for his enthusiastic encouragement and support.

- Ruth Moon and Marie Muhlke Nelson for insight into the life of Eleanor Knight.

- Robert J. Nelson for his work related to the text, the securing of photograph and caption entries, the configuration of chapters, and the general oversight of book development, publishing and distribution.

- Joseph Beedlow of Beedlow Media for final formatting and publishing of this book, his input of ideas, bringing photos to life, and the wrap around photo on the cover.

Mrs. Marietta DeMars

One of Eleanor's special resources for this book was Mrs. May DeMars, who gave her oral history of Bayfield. Below is an article from the Bayfield County Press to commemorate her ninetieth birthday.

Mrs. May DeMars, 90 Years Old on Saturday; Her Parents Came to Bayfield 102 Years Ago

Parents Came from La Pointe in Bayfield's Founding Year; Descendants Have Remained.

With some fear and trepidation, The Press opines that Mrs. May (Marietta) DeMars, who on this Saturday will observe her 90th birthday anniversary, is the oldest living native of Bayfield. She was born May 3, 1868, the daughter of Nazaire and Mathilde LaBonte, the latter being in her own right the daughter of Mr. and Mrs. John Bono, who came to Bayfield in 1856.

The LaBontes ran what was known as the La-Bonte House (it is now Greunke's restaurant, extensively remodeled during the last 10 or 12 years).

Marietta grew up in Bayfield. She moved at the time of her marriage—1889—to Barnesville, Minnesota, and later lived at various places in the Pacific Northwest. She had four children; Lila (Mrs. Einar Miller of Bayfield); Lloyd, Verne and Raymond Church. She returned to Bayfield in 1918 and took up residence in the old family home until about 1945, when she moved to a new home next door to the residence of her daughter

Mrs. DeMars is possessed of a prodigious memory of early Bayfield history and has been most generous in passing on to others the vast amount of information she has of her own knowledge and memory and what she heard from her parents and other early residents.

The Press is happy to join with others of the community to wish Mrs. DeMars, on the threshold of her ninetieth birthday anniversary, good health and happiness and the serenity of old age and happy memories.

Chapter 1

Movers & Shakers: The Captains of Industry

Captain R. D. Pike

Captain Robinson Derling Pike, son of Elisha and Elizabeth Kimmey Pike, Bayfield pioneer of the lumber milling industry. (Photo: BHA)

CAPTAIN ROBINSON DERLING PIKE IS the outstanding citizen of Bayfield's first century. Of course, there are two years to go before the town is 100 years old but can anyone surpass him in that short time?

As the record stands now, it is very safe to say that Captain Pike accomplished more for Bayfield than anyone who has ever lived here. His character was well summarized in a county booklet published in 1905 which said, "Captain Pike is a thoroughly progressive man in the fullest sense of the term. He believes that what is good for Bayfield is good for him, and it is not out of place to add that no citizen takes more interest in the up building of the community than he does."

Thanks to the late Harvey Nourse, we have a story about R.D. Pike's progressiveness that almost landed him in jail, for people then, as they sometimes are even now, were very suspicious of progress. It happened when the wire nail was first used. About the same time the nail came into use, there was an open winter and consequently a shortage of ice in Chicago. Captain Pike immediately saw an opportunity to put up some ice and ship it down there. He began building an icehouse, using the newfangled wire nail, instead of the old steel cut. When the building was going up, a strong windstorm blew part of it down, injuring one of the workmen. There was loud talk of having Captain Pike arrested for using this dangerous new nail, when, in fact, it was much stronger than the old.

Captain Pike was born in Meadville, Pa., and came to LaPointe with his parents in 1855 when he was 17 years old.

They built a homestead on Pike's Creek, operating the small water mill, which had been put up in 1845 by the American Fur Co. R.D. Pike was a member of the party which gathered on March 24, 1856, for the founding of Bayfield.

At the outbreak of the Civil War, he entered the Army and served with distinction to its close. He became a Captain, commanding a company of cavalry. He and his men fought to the last battle. Afterward he served with the Army on the Western plains. When he returned to Bayfield he helped organize and was commander of the Bayfield Rifles. It was Captain Pike who led them to Ashland New Year's Day 1873 to save the town from destruction by the rioting railroad men.

There can be no explanation of why he came back to Bayfield except that he loved the place. He was a Captain in the Army and could have made a career of it. His tour of Army duty took him through the south and West and he had lived the first 17 years of his life in the east, so he had seen most of the country and still he chose Bayfield. His father, Elisha, did not need his help with the little water mill and Captain Pike went into business for himself.

Bayfield offered no great financial opportunities. An account written by William Knight says: "In those days in Bayfield, money was very scarce and everybody was poor and nothing in the country had any value attached to it. Property and pine lands had no value. About the only resource money was tourists coming in through the summer to fish and some came for climate... Pike was like the rest of us, poor as a church mouse, but we all were rich in energy, good health and full of hope that the day would come when Bayfield would be a prosperous and growing city."

So it seems strange that Captain Pike with his terrific ambitions should return to a place with so little financial opportunity. We can only conclude that like the other rugged individualists, (pioneer and present day) he wanted to live in Bayfield, money or no money, and back he came.

Captain Pike had many good qualities. Loyalty was one of them. He never forgot his Civil War companions and in 1868 when General Grant was inaugurated as President of the United States, Captain Pike drove his team all the way through the woods to St. Paul, left the horses in good hands and went on to Washington to see his old chief sworn in.

In October 1905, just six months before his death, he attended a reunion of his Army comrades. *The Press* said: "Captain R.D. Pike returned from Lansing, Michigan the first of the week, where he had been to attend a reunion of the old soldiers contributed by Michigan to the Civil War. The Captain Says, 'What most surprised me was to see how old the boys appeared. Why, darn it, they were all gray and wrinkled, but God Bless 'Em, their hearts hadn't a wrinkle, and their battle cry as in the sixties was, "God Save the Union!"

After Captain Pike returned from the Civil War, he bought the shingle mill which Taff and Dunn had put up at Pike's Creek about 1860. When it burned down, it evidently left him broke, because he and Asaph Whittlesey built a shingle mill at LaPointe, Mr. Whittlesey furnished the capital and Captain Pike the ability. This mill blew up killing three men and injuring others, and was never rebuilt.

After that you might think that Captain Pike would be discouraged, that he would decide he had had enough of sawmills and do something else, that he might even pound his forehead, as business men do now and say, "There must be an easier way to make a living."

But persistence was one of his qualities and in the spring of 1869 he built a shingle mill in Bayfield. He began to build a sawmill here the same year, which started running in 1870. It was about 40 x 60 and had a capacity of 10,000 feet per day. This mill had one circular saw and a small edger. Dockage facilities were practically nothing. The capacity of the mill, however, was regarded at that time as something quite wonderful. It was said, on good authority, that the employees of Vaughn's mill, a little way up the shore, were in the habit of making almost daily visits of inspection, so incredible did it seem that one saw mill could turn out 10,000 feet of merchantable lumber in one day.

In 1871 Captain Pike built a planning mill and also a small steamer called the *Mocking Bird*. His mill was now the only one that could turn out dressed lumber and he was able to monopolize the trade all along the shore.

Left: The Henry Baldwin at the R. D. Pike lumber mill facility and dock. circa 1880's. (Photo: BHA)

Below: Schooner's Maple Leaf and unknown ship loading lumber at Pike's Bay. circa 1875. (Photo: BHA)

By 1889, Pike's mill was turning out 75,000 feet of lumber per day. And *The Bayfield Press* said, "Now, instead of only the little *Mocking Bird* winging its solitary flight from port to port with products of the Bayfield mill, a large fleet of boats carry lumber to the greatest markets in the country."

With sawmills springing up all over Wisconsin, trust Bayfield to have a sawmill with a personality. The mill, of course, was Captain Pike's *Little Daisy.*

On July 26, 1890, *The Bayfield Press* headlined a story, "Our *Little Daisy.* She is getting there with both feet." And continued, "We have several times had occasion to refer to the fine record being made by Pike's mills this season. The Captain is nothing, if not romantic, and in the early history of his mill he determined that he would always be prepared to make a record that would go ahead of any mill of her capacity on the bay. Hence he named the plant *The Little Daisy.* This name has stuck to the mill through thick and thin, and rarely has there been a time when she has not more than deserved it. . . "

"Since starting this spring, the mill has averaged to cut fully 80,000 feet per day, and is doing better all the time. . . It must be borne in mind that this mill has but a single circular saw, and the cut given is for the day run only. When these facts are kept in mind we believe it will be concluded by everyone that the *Little Daisy* is doing herself proud and will be hard to beat. In our trip through the mill we found the chief positions filled as follows: Charles Brooks, head sawyer; Arthur Jones and Harry Dora, setters; Ed Gordon as carriage rider. At the other end of the mill the old reliable Myron B. Conlin handles the large resaw."

And, of course, a progressive mill had to have docks, so Captain Pike built them. The *Bayfield Press* for June 20, 1891, says, "The most important dock improvements, however, are to be found to the south of Bayfield.

Drawing of Pike's downtown Bayfield Mill. The home of the infamous and record setting Little Daisy Saw Mill. (Photo: BHA)

Captain R.D. Pike, beginning years ago with his plant almost in a marsh, has year by year reached out into the bay, extending around Austrian's clearing until now his mill and yards are practically over the water. His docks may truly be said to form a system by themselves. They now extend from the foot of First Street away beyond the platted portion of the town, nearly to Holston's farm and embrace in the neighborhood of 20 blocks. By means of this far-reaching system he is enabled to secure a boom for his logs which can hold from three to five million feet and which is perfectly secure against all storms. He can also pile on the docks from 20 to 30 million feet of lumber and they are so arranged that an entire fleet of boats can load at once. This last week he has again had the pile driver at work, extending the dock at the foot of First Street about 50 feet into the water. The depth of the water is about 30 feet and the Captain never needs fear any deepening of the Soo [river] which is likely not to take place for a century or two."

With all these improvements we can find as much truth as humor in a little item which appeared in *The Press:* "Look out for a boom in these waters as soon as navigation opens!"

Captain Pike's sawmill, The *Little Daisy* was a mill that set records. On Oct. 20, 1870, *The Press* said, "Pike's mill has sawed eight miles of shingles this season." And that was more shingles than any other mill sawed. The cut that year was as follows:

Vaughn's 800,000 feet of lumber and 600,000 shingles; R.D. Pike's 300,000 feet of lumber and 1,000,000 shingles; Red Cliff mill, 200,000 feet of lumber; Elisha Pike's mill, 150,000 feet.

The boys in the lumber camps that supplied the *Little Daisy* set records, too. April 10, 1886. "The boys in Pike's logging camp are bragging over a "big day's work" performed by them in one day last week by the handling of three teams with 19 loads which scaled 87,000 feet in board feet. . ."

July 7, 1888. "Pike's saw mill with only one circular saw cut last week working 6 days, 11 hours per day, 459,617 feet of merchantable lumber. This was an average of 76,617 feet per day or nearly 7,000 per hour. If there is a mill of the same size in the northWest that has beaten this record, we would be glad to hear of it. Bayfield claims the champion mill!"

May 24, 1890. "Pike's mill made lumber of 930 logs for its Wednesday day run. This is a record that it is believed a one circular mill has never equaled. The cut at Pike's mill averaged 79,000 feet a day for three days last week. Contractor McCurdy says the boys who handle the machines deserve the credit. They are just hustling to make the *Little Daisy* out-daisy herself."

That same year, 1890, the *Little Daisy* had the honor of being the first mill to open the season on the bay, starting about April 13, and it was not until Nov. 8, that *The Press* said, "Pike's mill, *The Little Daisy* met with its first breakdown of any consequence for this season last Tuesday. It ran for six months and two days without stopping except for one or two holidays. The average cut has been over 70,000 feet per day. When it is remembered that this is a single circular saw with two resaws having no gang saw, or band saw, the record is something to be proud of."

The mill didn't shut down in 1890 until December, and *The Press* said: "The run this summer has been the most uniformly successful in the history of the mill. Captain Pike varied his usual plan of operations last season by leasing the mill on shares to Messrs. McCurdy and Higginson. . . The mill has this season run 172 days and cut 12,230,756 feet of lumber, making an average of over 70,000 feet per day, taking into consideration delays caused by temporary stoppage.

During all this time but one break down has occurred and that stopped operations for only one day. Of course the greatest vigilance has been necessary on the part of Messrs. McCurdy and Higginson to bring about this result, but it has also been caused by the fact that every employee has felt a personal interest in the success of the mill. In case of breakage you wouldn't go into the mill and find the men all sitting around, waiting for the boss to fix things up, but every man did his best to assist in the work of repairs.

Mac says his relations with Captain Pike have been the pleasantest imaginable, and he will swear by *The Little Daisy* until the last dog is hung. . .

Mr. Higginson will begin work on several new features for next season among them [a] band saw. Next season the mill will be run night and day and we may expect to see the sawdust fly as soon as the ice goes out in the spring.

And as the months passed away and the spring of 1891 came, *The Press* reported: "Following the usual custom, as observed for several years, the ice went out Sunday last, April 26. The clearing of the harbor was a little later than usual this season, but when the ice was once started, it did not fool around, but went out with celerity and dispatch. Business of all kinds promises to be unusually lively this season. A stroll through Pike's mills and yards reveals the fact that the Captain is hustling matters for the best summer's work ever yet attempted. . . As soon as it is practicable, the mill will run day and night. . . "

The mill did run day and night and to keep it running longer, Captain Pike, in his energetic way, got out and found more business for it. *The Press* , Sept. 12, 1891 said, "Captain Pike has contracted with Wright and Ketchum of Ashland to get out 1,000,000 feet of logs at once which will be sawed at the mill here. Were it not for this, the mill would be obliged to shut down about the first of October on account of the impossibility of getting logs down the streams. Under this new contract, however, it is expected that the *Little Daisy* will keep chewing up the pine trees until late in November. The gallant Captain always manages to keep things moving, however stagnant they may be outside."

When the need for outside communication became great, Captain Pike and William Knight financed and put up the first telephone line between Bayfield and Ashland with the local telephone office in Pike's business office. When the first phone was installed, an Indian walked in to see it. Captain Pike called Ashland and urged the Indian to satisfy his curiosity by talking over the phone. The Indian was not too sure he wanted to do such a rash thing, but finally risked it by walking up to the phone and shouting, "How's your grandmother?"

Captain Pike has to be line man as well as owner and operator and in 1882 *The Ashland Press* said: "Captain R.D. Pike of Bayfield was in town Tuesday and while here gave the several telephone instruments a thorough examination as they have not been working as they should. The Central office of the Bayfield and Ashland Telephone Company has been established at Moore and Hart's store. All messages for or from Bayfield will hereafter be promptly delivered."

And by October 20, 1883, *The Bayfield Press* could say, "The telegraph and telephone wires running through town give the village quite a citified appearance."

Bayfield ladies enjoying a fine summer day adjacent to the Frank Stark home, located on 6th Street and Rittenhouse Avenue. (Photo: BHA)

Communication by Capt. Pike's new telephone line was far from perfect for quite awhile. The telephone received more profanity than messages; but it never got so bad it was abandoned completely. One day Capt. Pike called Ashland to get some hardware sent over for his sawmill. The clerk at the store was apparently unused to this outlandish new instrument and Captain Pike's progressive way of ordering by phone instead of by letter, could not understand who the material was to be sent to. Capt. Pike finally lost his patience and shouted "Send it to Sawmill Pike! Pikepole Pike! Capt. Pike! R.D. Pike! Pike's Bay Pike! Pike will pay for it!"

"Pike will pay for it!" became a catch phrase around town, and is still heard occasionally, but it will do you no good in a bar room. A very true phrase it was at that time. Pike paid for many improvements in Bayfield.

Here is an item that is typical of Capt. Pike. It appeared in *The Press* March 7, 1891. "Just before Capt. R.D. Pike left for the south, he sent Mr. J. H. Nourse, the Treasurer of the Presbyterian Church, a receipt for $385 being the amount in full of all indebtedness due him for lumber furnished for the church. The church is now free from debt."

And though Currie Bell got a lot of credit for getting the Fish Hatchery for Bayfield, and rightly so, Capt. R.D. Pike's generosity played a role behind the scenes.

He, and his father, Elisha Pike, had a private fish hatchery on Pike's Creek. You might have thought that Capt. Pike would enjoy keeping his hatchery and his private trout stream, but when Currie Bell saw a chance to get a state fish hatchery here if the proper land could be found, Capt. Pike was all for it. He immediately donated between two and three hundred acres of his valuable meadow land at Pike's Bay, including part of Pike's Creek. Col. Wing and William Knight donated land adjoining it, and some land was purchased from Wright and Ketchum, C.P. Rudd and the Moore estate.

Capt. Pike helped to entertain the State Fish Commissioners when they came to inspect the site. Then, with the rest of Bayfield, he settled down to wait for their decision, as Eau Claire, LaCrosse, Superior and other towns were offering every inducement for the prize. When words came that the fish hatchery was to be built at the fine site at Pike's Creek, Capt. Pike was so thrilled that not trusting the news services of *The Ashland Press*, he just had to call them and ask, "Have you heard the good news?"

"*The State Fish Hatchery and grounds were dedicated Friday, September 10, 1897. Early in 1895, J.H. Sykes, was sent to Salmo to superintend the construction of the ponds and hatchery building. The sandstone used in the building came from Pike's quarry south of Salmo. The front section was used for office space. Living quarters were on first and second floors while all fish were reared in the rear of the building. Red clay soils were dug out with large scrapers drawn by horses. Willow trees were planted to stabilize the banks . Water for fish eggs and fingerlings came from a point on Pike's Creek known then as the Red Dam.*" Robert Sykes, son of first Hatchery Superintendent J.H. Sykes. Photo, BHA Inc.

They had, and they printed it.

Capt. Pike made a less valuable, but much enjoyed donation in 1888 when President Harrison defeated Cleveland. In jubilance over this fine Republican outcome, he donated 50 cords of slab wood to build a big bonfire of celebration on top of the hill. It was a good bonfire and could be seen for miles.

Capt. Pike was well known throughout the state and in February, 1884, this little item appeared in the Chippewa Falls Herald. "1,854,000 pounds of fish were handled at Bayfield last season," according to *The Bayfield Press*. Bayfield is emphatically a fish town. No wonder, when it is remembered that the most prominent citizen there is a Pike!"

Roads were a favorite project of Capt. Pike's. When the Bayfield-Superior wagon road was opened for travel in the winter of 1870-71, a company composed of R.D. Pike of Bayfield and J.A. McCluskey of Cottage Grove, Minn., was organized to run a daily stage over this road.

The Bayfield-Superior road coincided with the St. Paul road as far as Moose Lake. There the road took a Westerly turn to Superior, a distance of 70 miles. Stations for travelers' convenience were built at Pine Lake and Brule. In November, 1870, *The Press* said: "Capt. R.D. Pike has gone East for goods. He started via the Bayfield-Superior wagon road to Superior City. He went as far as Iron River with a wagon and the balance of the distance on horseback."

Of course the wagon road wasn't meant to be used when navigation was open, for the boats made regular trips then. But in case someone might want to use the road provision was made for the traveler. *The Press* March 18, 1871 reported: "The stage keepers of Brule and Pine Lake have returned home bag and baggage. The station houses are thus unoccupied, but we understand a cook stove has been left at the Brule house for accommodations of persons coming over the route."

The mail carriers used this road, traveling it on foot. *The Press* Nov. 11, 1871 said: "Last Thursday the mail carrier, a full blooded Chippewa, walked from Superior to Bayfield on the wagon road, a good 80 miles, in 22 hours with the mail, blankets, etc., about 40 pounds. Joe Baker, another Indian, made the same distance last winter with a large pack in 20½ hours."

And, in case you would like to know what the road was like, here is a description of William LaPointe's trip over it in May, 1872. "He left Bayfield on Thursday morning, May 8, taking the mail to Superior and returned here, with the mail from superior on Friday, the 10th. He therefore walked 160 miles over a road, swampy, hilly and rough in four successive days with a heavy storm lasting through the whole time and carrying a pack on his back of about 50 pounds.

In January 1871, Capt. Pike made the first shipment of fresh fish over the new tote road to Superior and Duluth. It totaled 20,000 pounds.

In February of that same year, "A monster lake trout was shipped to St. Paul by R.D. Pike. It was five feet long, 14" thick and weighed 75 pounds."

During that same month, Boutin Brothers shipped 50,000 pounds of fresh fish to Duluth. So the road was well patronized and provided a much needed outlet for Bayfield products. It had a slight drawback. "Wolves reported plenty on the new Superior wagon road."

In April the Hon. S.S. Vaughn and wife returned from Madison, having a very hard trip overland from Duluth. In February, 1872, Henry A. Sweet, a prominent citizen of Bayfield, became exhausted during a storm while he was walking from Brule to Pine station on the Superior road and was frozen to death. The road was not an easy one, but it improved each year.

In case anyone asks, "Why didn't they build a road to Ashland first?" It is because in 1871 Ashland had only one settler, Martin Roehm. In February of that year, our old friend Capt. T.J.L. Tyler, who had opened a quarry on Presque Island and was getting out rock for the Ontonogan breakwater, and Jim Chapman went to visit Martin Roehm reported "The King" well and hearty. In July, Sam Fifield "with Capt. Patrick and a jolly party headed by Capt. Vaughn visited the Ashland Townsite and took a picnic dinner on an old wagon box in front of Martin Roehm's house. Met Mrs. Roehm, the only living soul seen during our visit."

But, by 1875, after the railroad came into Ashland, there were quite a number of people there, and Bayfield history readers will probably remember that in August of that year, Capt. R.D. Pike, who was Town Chairman, Capt. T.J.L. Tyler and Jim Chapman, walked over the proposed Bayfield-Ashland wagon road, reported it almost feasible, and proposed to open it at once.

Another road improvement for which we are indebted to Capt. Pike, is the present road to Salmo. The previous one ran up past Charley Larson's farm and back through the hills. He planned the road as it runs today and worked hard to see it completed. He became Bayfield's first commuter, building the fine home at Salmo, now occupied by the David Nourse, and driving back and forth to his office in Bayfield with a pair of Bay horses named Prince and Jessie.

After the railroad came into Ashland, it was quite easy to go to Chicago. You simply took a boat to Ashland and got on the train. July 4, 1877 *The Press* said, "Captain Pike returned from Chicago yesterday. When he went down last week on the Wisconsin Central Railroad, he arrived in Chicago only 26 hours after leaving Bayfield. This speaks well for the officers of the Wisconsin Central Railroad."

July 20, 1872, the following item appeared in *The Ashland Press* : "R.D. Pike, the live and energetic lumber merchant of Bayfield has been in town several times the past week. R.D. is always a welcome visitor."

And *The Bayfield Press* once commented, "Capt. Pike is never so happy as when making improvements." Those two items sum up Capt. Pike's character quite well. He was a live, energetic person and he loved progress.

Naturally anyone as forward-looking as Captain Pike wanted electric lights as soon as they were available. *The Press* on April 30, 1887 said: "Capt. Pike returned from St. Paul on Sunday morning's train bringing with him sample burners of his new electric light plant which he purchased and will have in operation in a few weeks. He will not only supply power to light the streets of the town, but also residences, stores, etc., at a price that is within reach of all. In fact this light, taking everything into consideration, is cheaper than kerosene. It is absolutely non-combustible and its use, to the exclusion of other means of lighting, will reduce insurance rates."

And in June of that same year the paper said, "Capt. Pike, with characteristic public spirit, has placed an electric light at the junction of Rittenhouse Avenue and Second Street and will maintain the same at his own expense. *The Press* moves he be given a rising vote of thanks."

Before this time the streets of the village had been lighted by kerosene lamps placed at the corners. In 1883 there were 15 of these street lamps. About 1889 it was decided to have electric lights for the whole village and a company was incorporated under a charter from the state as "The Bayfield Lighting Company." The charter gave the company the sole privilege of lighting the village for a period of ten years. The power for running a small dynamo was derived from Capt. Pike's planning mill, but as more people wanted the new-fangled electric light, it was soon found that the quantity of electricity generated was insufficient to supply all the patrons and a large dynamo was installed. The monthly rate of the company for one light was 75 cents for saloons and 50 cents for stores and private residences.

By 1889 street lights were installed and the paper for July 6 said, "A few electric lights shed their beams on the streets the evening of July 1. . .Capt. Pike, the general manager of the company has sown a great deal of pluck in surmounting the obstacles that stood in the way, successfully completing the work, and is entitled to a great deal of credit."

But just getting the lights up and flashing them on briefly was not Capt. Pike's biggest problem. He had to keep them burning, and that gave him trouble. *The Press* for April 11, 1891 said, "President Pike of the Lighting Company informs *The Press* that it may be a matter of 30 days before the lights are started. He will have to purchase and put in place a new boiler and it will require time. Bayfield, however, is much more fortunate than many larger places, as we have had the lights nearly two years now, with practically no interruptions. Of course the month of April will be a dead loss to Captain Pike on account of power, and to the stockholders on account of the loss of business. They will be the heaviest sufferers.

Since that time Bayfield has made many improvements in the light system. Those improvements started four months after Capt. Pike got the new boiler installed and the lights running once more. *The Press* on Aug. 1, 1891 said: "H.O. Cook returned from the mines last Friday. He is very sanguine as to their future. He has been putting in five extra street light clusters this week for the Bayfield Lighting Company. The town at its last annual meeting said, "Let there be more light." And President Pike of the Lighting Company answered, "There is more light!"

Capt. Pike would certainly be pleased with the new streetlights installed in Bayfield this summer. It isn't hard to write about Capt. R.D. Pike, the outstanding citizen of Bayfield's first century of history, because so many people remember him well. But it is hard to separate the things he did into categories and write bout them separately, because he was always doing several things at once. People say he never strolled through town. He walked briskly, almost ran, and when he drove he always flipped the reins up and down impatiently, wishing the horses would go faster. His whole life was lived with vigor and enthusiasm. I doubt if he ever had a dull moment.

He was impatient with looking back at the past. The future was so full and interesting and the present was so busy. It is almost funny to read the article he wrote on Bayfield history when Currie Bell asked him to in March, 1903. He evidently did it as a favor for Currie, and sat down only long enough to record this: "The town of Bayfield was laid out by William McAboy March 24, 1856, and for many years we celebrated the day when Andrew Tate and James Chapman were alive, but of later years it has all been dropped. During the years of '55 and '56 there were large encampments of Indians along the shore from Pike's Bay to where the town of Washburn now stands. They were a peaceable lot, however, and nothing was feared from them. When I look back upon that scene, I can't help but wonder that the little city of Bayfield ever got its start from the erection of a frame building."

Not until he was ill, confined to his home, and death was close did he write a full history of Bayfield, which will appear in the final chapters of this story about him.

An item from *The Bayfield Press* , July 16, 1887 says: "The first of this week Capt. Pike commenced the work of constructing a mammoth new dock on the bay shore south between First and Second Streets. The enterprise of Capt. Pike is phenomenal and it is a very cold day when he is not planning to open a stone quarry, enlarge his mill, build a bridge, dock or something else that will furnish employment to a goodly number of men."

When there was a need for fish barrels Capt. Pike made them. *Ashland Press* , Dec. 16, 1876. "Capt. R.D. Pike has procured some new barrel machinery and intends to engage in the manufacture of barrels, principally for the fishing trade next season, in addition to the several branches of industry he has so energetically pursued heretofore."

And when a steam drill would step up quarry production, Capt. Pike got one. May 3, 1884. "Capt. Pike has placed a large steam drill in his quarry and is now turning out the rock by the wholesale."

Steam drill with operating team. This type of drill rigging was used in the sandstone pits located at Stockton, Wilson and Bass Islands as well as pits located south of Bayfeild and near Houghton Point. (Photo: BHA)

Capt. Pike's rafts broke records. One raft left Capt. Pike's dock in August 1896. Up until then it was the largest amount of sawed lumber, which had ever left Bayfield in one bunch. The raft contained 2,140,000 feet. It was towed by the tug *J. C. Morse.* The raft was 289 feet in length, 48 feet wide, and drew 13 feet of water at the back end. It projected out of the water about 5 feet.

Capt. Pike never hesitated to be the first to try something new. The *Detroit Free Press* Sept. 1875 said: "Twenty years hence it may be a matter of public interest to know that the first vessel built at a Lake Superior port to carry a cargo of lumber from Lake Superior through Lake Huron and the Rivers to Lake Erie was the schooner "*Maple Leaf.*" She is owned by R.D. Pike of Bayfield as was the lumber with which she was loaded when she passed down Tuesday night."

A special story should be written about the *Maple Leaf* and her brave and skilled Capt. Larson. The *Maple Leaf* was built in Bayfield by Pike and Larson in March 1872. Capt. Larson sailed the schooner, loaded with lumber to many of the great lake ports, but her usual run was to Chicago. One fall, in a terrible storm just before navigation closed, he came in through the Duluth channel in the lee of Bass Island with a broken rudder and the sails ripped to shreds, but he made it home. Who has more information about the *Maple Leaf* and Captain Larson?

When Captain Pike did not have the machinery he wanted he invented it. *The Ashland Press* for November 13, 1875, says: "R.D. Pike of Bayfield has invented a siding machine that is destined to work a complete revolution in the manufacture of this much used and valuable lumber. He has just placed in position at his mill the first one manufactured for trial and it works like a charm. It is simple, yet planes and saws the siding at the same time, saving one half the labor over any other machine in use."

An *Ashland Press* item for July 1872 said: "R.D. Pike is selling cord wood to steamboats at his dock, and good wood, too." And in February 1890, the Ontonogan, Michigan Herald wrote: "Capt. Pike of Bayfield is putting up 25,000 tons of ice to be shipped to Chicago in the spring time. Next summer cool drinks made of Lake Superior ice will be advertised in the Windy City."

Currie Bell replied, "Right you are Bro. Herald, and hereafter no ice will be considered good for internal use in Chicago unless it is stamped, "Frozen and Packed at Bayfield.""

The business activities of Capt. Pike were many and varied. His interests spread beyond Bayfield and he became one of the original stockholders of the Los Angeles Olive Growers Association. Sept. 6, 1902, *The Press* said: "August Turnquist has just received a consignment of olives and olive oil from Capt. Pike's olive grove at Los Angeles, Cal., which can be found in his store.

Local residents still remember going into Turnquist's to try the olives and feeling sorry for Capt. Pike because they were spoiled. Ripe olives were new in Bayfield and it was awhile before people were convinced they were a marketable product, that they weren't just spoiled green ones.

Capt. Pike did not accomplish all these things with no obstacles in his way. We already know that people were angry when he used a new-fangled wire nail to build his ice house. He had a tough time keeping the electric light plant running, he walked miles planning roads and servicing his telephone lines, his rafts broke, the *Mocking Bird* went ashore, the *Maple Leaf* went through terrible storms, his office was on fire twice in 1879 and it was only through the heroic efforts of the men working for him that it was saved.

R.D. Pike mill in full swing; circa 1890s. (Photo: BHA)

And it was September, 1871, when he was just getting started, going along on a shoe string, that a strange thing happened to one of his rafts. *The Press* reported: "the water in the bay receded at least 10 or 12 inches on Monday. It fell with such rapidity and force that it caused the fastening that connects the boom sticks at Pike's mill to break and let the logs out. Some 40 or 50 of them went into the Bay, notwithstanding every effort was made to retain them within the boom. But within a short time the water came back, and has since kept its water line. This must be sort of a tidal wave. Old settlers say it indicates a severe Northeaster."

Since Captain Pike kept putting his money into improvements in Bayfield it is not strange that he was sometimes pinched for cash. Fred Bloom remembers when he worked at the sawmill one season Captain Pike had to pay everyone in script. People accepted it, for by that time they undoubtedly knew that what Capt. Pike started, he would finish. The old distrust of a dashing young Captain, home from the Civil War, who dared to use a new wire nail, was gone. Through the years they had watched him bring in logging camps, sawmills, a telephone line, electric lights, good roads, better docks. The storekeepers took the script so everybody got fed, and as the lumber sold, Captain Pike redeemed it, as they had known he would.

Little has been said of Capt. Pike's work as a village official. Before 1872 he was a supervisor, and in April of that year was elected town chairman for the first time. He worked hard in that capacity. But then, just as today, the work done by village officials was apt to consist of drudgery rather than show, and got little newspaper recognition other than meetings recorded.

Capt. Pike was one of the attractive bachelors of Bayfield for many years. That he was popular we know, for in February, 1871 the ladies of Bayfield went with him on a sleigh ride to Red Cliff.

Twice that we know of on the Fourth of July, Capt. Pike took the whole town for a boat ride. In 1883 he started out to take all who wished to go on the tug *Favorite,* but then, realizing it might not hold everyone, he attached a barge to his already commodious boat and thus "everyone from the babe in arms to the gray haired grandsire was represented." It was a fine afternoon and everyone had a good time. As *The Press* said, "It is our hearty wish that the people of Bayfield may enjoy the hospitality of Capt. Pike for many years to come."

The wish of *The Press* came true and in 1885, the weather must have been good on the Fourth, for that year the tug *Favorite* towed Capt. Pike's large barge, *The Grey Oak.* Over 600 people got aboard and went on a tour of the islands. The barge was trimmed with flags and evergreens and the Harbor City Band went along. As the barge left the dock, Alfonse River fired a salute from the old brass Civil War cannon.

On March 23, 1906, Bayfield celebrated its 50th anniversary. The Commercial Club, organized only the month before, sponsored the affair. Two hundred people attended a lavish dinner, program and dance at the Island View Hotel.

Capt. R.D. Pike, who had been ill for the past few weeks, could not attend. But sick, or well, his heart was always in whatever good things Bayfield was doing, so, in spite of his illness he exerted himself to write the Club this letter to be read at the 50th anniversary of the town.

"I regret very much not being able to be with you at the celebration of the 50th anniversary of the town of Bayfield. As you may be aware, I have been ill for the past few weeks, but am pleased to state at this time I am on the gain and hope to be among you soon. If my health permitted I would take great pleasure in being present with you this evening.

I remember very distinctly that the first stake was driven in the town of Bayfield by Major McAboy, who was employed by the Bayfield Townsite Company to make a survey and plat same, the original plat being recorded at our county seat.

This Bayfield Townsite Company was organized with Hon. Henry M. Rice of St. Paul at the head and some very enterprising men from Washington, D.C. Major McAboy arrived here about the first of March and made his headquarters with Julius Austrian of LaPointe. Julius Austrian in those days being the Governor General of all that part of the country West of Ontonagon to Superior, Ashland and Duluth being too small to count.

The Major spent probably two weeks at LaPointe, going back and forth to Bayfield with a team of large Bay horses owned by Julius Austrian, being the only team of horses in the county.

I remember very well being in the office at LaPointe with father (Elisha Pike), I was then a mere lad of 17, and I recollect hearing them discuss with Mr. Austrian the question of running the streets in Bayfield north and south and the avenues east and West, or whether they should run diagonally due to the topography of the country. But he decided on the plan as the town is now laid out.

Mr. Austrian and quite a little party from LaPointe came over here on the 24th of March, 1856, when they officially laid out the town, driving the first stake and deciding on the name of Bayfield, named after Lt. Bayfield of the Royal Navy who was a particular friend of Senator Rice; and it was he who made the first chart for the guidance of boats on Lake Superior.

The summer of 1855, father was in poor health, filled up with malaria from the swamps of Toledo and he was advised by Mr. Frederick Prentice now of New York, and known by everybody here as the "Brownstone Man" (He is the Frederick Prentice who built Bark Cottage on Wilson Island.) to come up here and spend the summer, as it was a great health resort.

So father arrived at LaPointe in June 1855 on a little steamer that ran from the Soo to the head of the lakes, the canal at that time not being open, but it was opened a little later in the season.

Upon arrival at LaPointe, father entered into an agreement with Julius Austrian to come over to Pike's Creek and repair the little water mill that was built by the North American Fur Co. (in 1845), which at that time was owned by Julius Austrian.

He made the necessary repairs on the little mill, caught plenty of brook trout and fell in love with the country on account of the good water and pure air, and wrote home to us at Toledo glowing letters as to this section of the country. Finally he bought the mill, and I think the price paid was $350 for the mill and forty acres of land, and that, largely on time.

However, the mill was not a very extensive affair. Nearly everything was made of wood, except the saw and crank pin but it cut about two thousand feet of lumber in twelve hours. Some of the old shafting and pulleys can be seen in the debris at the old mill site now. Remember, these were not from shafts, as we used wooden shafts and pulleys in those days. This class of a mill at that time beat whipsawing, that being the usual way of sawing lumber.

Father (Elisha Pike) left LaPointe sometime in September 1855, for Toledo to move his family to Pike's Creek, which stream was named after we moved up here. Onion River and Sioux River were named before that time.

On father's arrival in Toledo from this country, we immediately began to get ready to move. We had a large, fine yoke of red oxen and logging trucks. He sold out our farm at Toledo, picked up our effects and boarded a small steamer, which took us to Detroit. Our family then consisted of father, mother, Grandma Pike, and my sister, now Mrs. Bicksler of Ashland.

We stayed in Detroit several days to give father time to buy supplies for the winter; that is, feed for the oxen and cow and groceries for the family to carry us through until spring. We then boarded the steamer *Planet,* which was a new boat owned by the Ward Line, considered the fastest on the lake. It was about 250 tons capacity.

We came to Sault Ste. Marie, it being the Planet's first trip through the Soo, the canal, as I remember, was completed that fall. During this year the *Lady Elgin* was running from Chicago and the *Planet* and *North Star* running from Detroit, they being about the only boats, which were classed better than sail boats of the 100 and 50 tons.

We arrived at LaPointe the early part of October 1855. On our way up we stopped at Marquette, Eagle Harbor, Eagle River and Ontonagon. We left Ontonagon in the evening, expecting to arrive at LaPointe early the next morning, but a fearful storm arose and the machinery of the Planet became disabled off Porcupine mountains and it looked for awhile as though we were never going to be able to weather the storm, but arrived at LaPointe the next day. There were some parties aboard for Superior, who left LaPointe by sail.

We remained at LaPointe for a week or ten days on account of my mother's health and then went to Pike's Bay with all our supplies, oxen and cow on what was known as Uncle Robert Morrin's bateau. Uncle Robert and William Morrin are now of Bayfield (Robert and William Morrin, who were both present when the first trees were cut on the Bayfield Townsite, were also present at this 50th anniversary dinner) and if I remember rightly, each of the boys pulled an oar taking us across. We landed in Pike's Bay just before sundown, hitched up the oxen and drove to the old mill. (This mill was located on Pike's Creek near where the north and West branches meet). Now this was all in the fall of 1855.

As I said before the town was laid out on March 24, 1856, and record made of same at LaPointe by John W. Bell, who at that time was the "Witte" of all the country between Ontonagon and Superior, Julius Austrian being the "Czar" of those days and both God's noblemen.

The territory now comprising the town of Bayfield was taken from LaPointe County. There were a number of very prominent men interested in laying out the townsite and naming our streets and avenues, such as Hon. H.M. Rice and men of means from Washington after whom some of our avenues were named

Very soon after this they wished to build a large sawmill in order to furnish lumber necessary for building up the town . The Washington people decided upon a man by the name of Caho, an old lumberman of Virginia, so he was employed to come up and direct the building of the mill.

A hotel was built directly across from the courthouse (where the dry cleaner's now stands) by Mr. Bicksler, who afterward married my sister. The sawmill was built about a block West of where my sawmill now stands. The mill had a capacity of five or six thousand feet per day, and I think the machinery came from Alexandria, Virginia. Joe LaPointe was the only man recognized as being capable of running a mill, from the fact that he could do his own filing and sawing.

While they were constructing the mill, they had a gang of men in the woods getting out hardwood for fuel, not thinking of using any of the sawdust, and they piled the sawdust out with the slabs as useless.

Charles Day, whom many of you will remember, was the party who got out the hardwood as fuel for the mill.

Time has wrought many changes in our midst. As far as I know I am the only white man living who was here at the time the town was laid out.

In conclusion, I wish to say that at a banquet given in Bayfield some two or three years ago, I made a statement that when the last pine tree was cut from the peninsula on which Bayfield is located, the prosperity of our town and vicinity will have just commenced. The pine has gone, and we are not cutting the hemlock and hardwood, which will last ten to fifteen years; and long before this is exhausted, the cut over lands will be taken up and farms tilled, as is the history of other sections of the country."

Just four days after Bayfield's 50th birthday party, on Tuesday, March 27, 1906, Capt. R.D. Pike died. The news, although not wholly unexpected, saddened the town. He had tried hard to live. He had been confined to his home at Salmo for about two months, during which time the ablest physicians of this section attended him. They held a consultation, and at Capt. Pike's earnest request, it was decided to send him to a Milwaukee hospital for treatment. A sleeping car was sent over from Ashland to Salmo. With his wife and a trained nurse he began the journey, but he didn't make it. He died on the train before it reached Milwaukee.

The remains were returned to his home the next day, and were met at Ashland and escorted by a delegation of Bayfield Masons, of which lodge he was a charter member.

A paragraph from the long, detailed obituary printed in *The Bayfield Press* says, "He was a man noted for his remarkable energy and force of character, was quick to resent an injury, and was just as quick to forgive. During the long time he lived here he was always identified with good causes, which had in view the upbuilding of the town and the development of the country."

Captain Pike was an enthusiastic and active Republican and "entered into political strife as the war horse entered battle." Firm in his convictions, and fearless in maintaining the same, as most of our pioneers were, he still had many friends among his political opponents.

During the time of Capt. Pike's funeral, all business was suspended, the schools were closed and the flags of Bayfield flew at half-mast.

And then, after Capt. Pike's death, changes came, as they always do. *The Press* February 12, 1909 said: "The roadmaster of the C. St. P. M. & O. Railway. was in Salmo a short time ago and ordered the section crew to cut down the willow trees along the right of way which were planted by Mr. Pike. The trees had grown so tall that they interfered with the telegraph wires. Slowly, but surely, that which was once in the name of Pike is slowly fading away. The Pike Estate is now the Nourse Estate. Pikeville is now Salmo. Pike's Bay is now Salmo Bay and they now wish to change the name Pike's Quarry to Whiting. Then all that will remain in the name of the Hon. Mr. Pike is Pike's Creek.

This item was followed by a *Press* editorial wanting the name of Pike's Bay restored immediately. But nobody needed to be concerned because the name of R.D. Pike might be forgotten. It hasn't been. Pike's Creek is still Pike's Creek, and it has never even been shortened to Pike Creek. It's still and definitely Pike's. Pike's Quarry is still Pike's Quarry. It never did become Whiting, even though Mr. Whiting, a fine and progressive fruit grower purchased it for the purpose of making a large cold storage warehouse out of it.

The warehouse was never made and it is still Pike's Quarry, in late years improved by the addition of a roadside picnic table.

Above the office of Dutch Stark on our main street the name R.D. Pike is carved in a block of sandstone. But strangely enough, this thin piece of paper, preserved by the State Historical Society, will keep the name of Pike and our other pioneers recorded much longer than the sandstone.

Capt. Pike, the outstanding citizen of Bayfield's first century of history will not be forgotten, not as long as Pike's Creek flows down to Pike's Bay, and new generations of barefooted boys go fishing there. But with Capt. Pike gone, it looks as though the field is wide again; who will be the outstanding citizen of Bayfield's second century of history?

The Nourse Family

T HE STORY OF THE NOURSE family is an interesting one, for they have been associated with Bayfield since it was founded in 1856. Joseph Nourse, of Washington, D.C., arrived in Bayfield in August, 1856. He came for his health, and in Bayfield his health improved so much that he spent many active years as a hotel keeper, express agent, store keeper, farmer and was one of the founders of, and outstanding workers for, the Presbyterian Church.

Mrs. Nourse was the daughter of a Presbyterian minister and their oldest son, Edward, became a minister. Harvey and Laurie Nourse farmed at Salmo and will long be remembered for their fine voices and the duets they sang. Isobel and Bessie were outstanding artists. Many of the beautiful Bayfield scenes painted by Bessie are enjoyed in Bayfield homes today. Louise was a teacher and became the wife of a minister. All were fine people, contributing much to their community and their church.

Thanks to Gladys Nourse Frankie, of Ashland, we have a series of reminiscences written by her father, Harvey Nourse. Some of these incidents, in slightly different form, have appeared in Guy Burnham's book, *The Lake Superior Country in History and in Story*. Others were given at the Old Settler's Club picnic in Ashland, in 1947, at which time Mr. Nourse was the oldest settler in the Chequamegon region. The reminiscences, which will continue in this column for the next few weeks are as follows:

"My father came to Bayfield in 1856. He was first employed to manage what was then a large hotel built on the hill where the Presbyterian Church now stands. This hotel burned shortly after, and my father went in partnership with Mr. Vaughn who had a general store."

(Mrs. Marietta DeMars recalled this hotel on the hill. One day a man drove up to the hotel and left his team of horses standing there untied while he went into the building. Something startled the horses and they began to run. Gathering speed, they went down Washington Avenue, off the end of the dock, and were drowned.)

The Vaughn's were married at our home in Bayfield and they lived in Bayfield until Mr. Vaughn sold his interest to my father and moved to Ashland. Then he purchased a small steam ferryboat named the *Eva Wadsworth*, which was used to carry the mail and passengers from Ashland to Bayfield, stopping also at LaPointe.

(Sam Fifield wrote: "S.S. Vaughn's new yacht, the *Eva Wadsworth*, arrives from Erie, Pa., August, 1872. This boat was the first steam craft to pass through the Portage Lake Ship Canal and entering the Bayfield trade was for many years a great favorite with Ashland and Bayfield people.)

There was no railroad service at that time and we depended on boats in summer and stage with team and open sleigh in winter. My oldest brother, Ed, drove this stage one winter. It required a day to go and one to return, stopping each noon at the Silvernail's farm on Sioux River for dinner. I remember one trip I took with him. They were then logging at what is now the city of Washburn, which was then called McClellan's. This was all pine forest then, hardly a tree had been cut.

My father, a victim of tuberculosis, came here primarily to regain his health. He told me when the steamer he was on came into the Bayfield harbor, the odor from the balsam and pines was so poignant and pleasant that he felt sure he was going to get well, which he did.

One solid belt of pine, hemlock, cedar and hardwood extended for hundreds of miles, with only Indian trails through it. Hardly a day passes that I do not regret the loss by careless lumberman and the fires that followed, of this wonderful belt of timber. One hundred years of reforestation can never produce another anywhere near like this virgin tract. Each variety of soil grew the timber suitable to it; pine and cedar on the clay soils, hemlock and hardwood on the lighter, and more elevated soils.

From Pike's Bay, in a rowboat, I have a number of times followed the timber line with my eye by the different shades of green between the pine and hemlock, which also meant the dividing line between the clay and sandy soils. It was a wonderful sight. No scenery anywhere could surpass it."

"The mail was carried by Indians from Bayfield to Superior. The Baker brothers, two big husky Indians, and William Morrin were employed. They went as far as Gordon, where Antone Gordon relieved them and carried on to Superior. William Morrin told me that many times he dug into a snowdrift with just a blanket to cover him for the night.

A stage was put on between Bayfield and Superior a few years later. Joe LaPointe with Jim Chapman's famous team, Chap and Judd, drove this route. Many is the yarn that Joe used to tell us boys about this wonderful team. And he hardly had to exaggerate, for I still believe that no team of their size has ever come to Bayfield that equaled them. (Stories of this powerful team, Chap and Judd, appeared in the Chapman story in this column in earlier issues of *The Press*).

Bayfield, in the early days, was called the Fountain City, because of the numerous fountains maintained by our towns people. The Haywards, Tates, Whittleseys, McClouds, Bowers, Jim Chapman and Capt. Smith all had fountains. These fountains were kept running all through the summer and were certainly beautiful and much admired by the tourists.

Brook trout were always kept in the fountains and the tourists especially enjoyed feeding them. Mr. Chapman had a wonderful lot of trout in his fountain, bringing them in alive from his fishing trips.

The water supplying these fountains was brought from a small reserve fed by a stream that flowed through the town. The water was conveyed in Norway pine logs, bored through lengthwise with a three inch auger, pointed at the ends and fastened together with iron clips. These logs were laid out through the town and furnished water to nearly everyone living on the flat. Robert Morran usually was employed to bore the logs and look after the water system generally. It was quite a task to bore a straight 3-inch hole through a 16-foot log and required considerable strength. But we had strong men in those days and skilled men, also."

(After the log water system was out of use, the kids used to pry the iron hoops off the old log pipes and roll them. I haven't seen a kid rolling a hoop for years. Maybe it's because they don't know how to make a hoop stick, with a nail pounded in the side, but it's more likely there aren't any hoops. The old flour barrels, apple barrels, pork barrels, and cracker barrels are gone. Now [1956] we get consumer packages wrapped in cellophane.)

"During the tourist season when the Smith Hotel was operating, Capt. Smith opened a barbershop, the first I can remember of in Bayfield. One Bill Caul was installed as barber. It soon became a place for some of the boys to hang around and, after giving the boys a few haircuts different than they had ever had before, he induced a few of them to have their heads shingled. Our genial Billy Morran that takes such good care of our city streets, water works, etc., was one of them. Well, Billy was a little fearful of going home, not knowing what the folks would do about it. So he waited until evening and about bedtime sneaked in. The next morning his mother called him, as usual, and then called again and finally proceeded upstairs with the broomstick. Billy heard her coming and ducked under the covers. The mother whacked away at the bedclothes, but with so little satisfaction that she finally grabbed the covers and uncovered his head. She then gave expression to one heart-rending shriek and fainted. She had never seen a newly shingled head before. No wonder she was frightened and thought something terrible had happened to her boy.

Colonel Wing took quite an interest in Billy and used to employ him some when he had the land office. Billy used to refer to his job as the position of teller – that is, he used to tell people that Col. Wing was out.

He had a large Indian dog that bothered Wing considerably, for whenever Billy was present, the dog was sure to be around.

One day after Wing had stumbled over the dog several times, he said to Billy: "How much do you want for that dog?" Before Billy could reply, he handed him $2.00 and told him to take the dog away, shoot him, or do something with him, but never let him be seen around the land office again. Billy got a rope and started off with the dog. He didn't like the idea of shooting him and hardly knew what to do. About this time, he saw some Indians coming in canoes from Odanah and a happy thought came to him. Perhaps they would want the dog. He waited on the lakeshore for them to land. Very soon the dog was loaded in one of the canoes and Billy had $2.00 more. A pretty good price for a dog in those days."

"LaPointe was quite a town in the early days and many Indians lived there. The government pay station was there and the Indians received certain monies from the government.

LaPointe with the American
Fur Trade Company on left.
(Photo:BHA)

The Austrians, a fine Jewish family, established a store and maintained a good Indian trade.

"Knowing the Indians lack of providing for the future, the Austrians always laid in extra supplies for the winter and these were doled out when necessary.

"There came a long, cold winter, supplies were running short, and they were finally reduced to but one sack of corn meal, which Mrs. Austrian decided to keep for the family. The day came when there was just enough left for one loaf of corn bread. She gave the children half of it for supper, but went to bed without tasting any herself.

(Photo:BHA)

"About midnight she was awakened by the cry of "Steamboat! Steamboat!" Looking out of the window she saw the lights of the *North Star* approaching the dock. She immediately went downstairs and ate what was left of the corn bread.

The Austrians later moved to St. Paul, but came back every summer for a vacation and to purchase wild raspberries from the Indians, shipping them to St. Paul in 12 quart wooden pails. Mr. Austrian made his store our headquarters. I was clerking in the store. The Indians called me 'don-way-we-nin-ne", meaning small storekeeper.

Mr. Austrian could talk Chippewa as well as any of the Indians and it has been a life long regret that I did not learn the language. I knew the Chippewa names for about all the articles we carried in the store.

One Christmas morning in St. Paul while driving a cutter loaded with Christmas gifts for the poor, he was struck by one of the heavy old beer drays pulled by a powerful team of horses, and was killed.

(Mrs. M. DeMars, who was in St. Paul at the time, recalls going to the Austrian home that Christmas morning and finding the whole kitchen filled with weeping people, the poor and the needy of St. Paul, who mourned the loss of the man who had been so kind to them.)

The Austrians owned a large building north of where the present bank now stands. In this building in 1858, the first public school was taught by Sarah Mahan of Cleveland. She used to keep the playthings she took away from the students in her waist pocket. She needed such a big pocket for this that the deep ravine near what is now Dunkel's farm, was named Mahan's Pocket. It kept this name for many years. When the railroad trestle was built across it, it was called Devil's Hole.

Mrs. Austrian sent a telegram of congratulations to Bayfield on the 50th anniversary of the town, but was unable to attend the celebration held at the Island View Hotel.

Andrew Tate kept the first drug store in Bayfield and when he had no doctor, he would administer remedies for the sick. His principle remedy was a croton oil plaster; it was rather severe, but seemed to do the business and sick people got well.

Mr. Tate was a rank Democrat, coming to Bayfield from the South. He had a wonderful memory, especially for historic dates. And in any political argument would invariably quote the year and date of some happening probably 40 years back that his opponent could not dispute and thus win the argument. Father was as strong a Republican as Mr. Tate was a Democrat and many were the arguments they had; but Father said it was no use for one could not offset those dates mentioned by Mr. Tate.

When Cleveland was elected president, Nels Boutin, who was assemblyman, was appointed postmaster. Boutin and Mahan had a store on the West end of what is now the Booth dock and the post office was in the store. There was a large glass front on the West side and on some summer afternoons, it got very warm in the building.

We had experienced an unusually warm day and the sun was in the West sending its heat unmercifully through the plate glass window. Late in the afternoon, Nels Boutin came out and remarked that he believed it was the hottest day he had ever experienced and further remarked that it was simply unbearable inside the building. Just bout this time the mail arrived and Nels went back to distribute it.

An old box stove that was used for getting rid of old papers was full to the top. Old Sol, brother of Nels, who was always up to some devilment, sneaked in and touched a match to it.

It was not long before Nels came out the back door and waving his arms, said, "Gentlemen, I have seen it hot many times in my day, but nothing like it is in the office this afternoon. A man can't live in there and you will have to wait for your mail until it cools off."

"Ashland, as well as Bayfield, catered to the tourist trade. Some of them came up the lakes by steamer and others by train. I often think of the wonderful passenger steamers that docked at Bayfield.

There was the *Nyack*, the *India, China* and *Japan*, the *Peerless* and several of the White Pipe Line, whose names I have forgotten, and the old *Manistee*. The *Manistee* was more of a freight carrier and well do I remember the stormy night she left Bayfield and never returned.

Mr. Ingles, the dock agent, begged Capt. McKay not to go, but his pride as one of the oldest captains on the lake would not let him down.

There were good hotels in Bayfield, the oldest being the Smith Hotel, which burned and there was the Island View, run by Charley Willey, which also burned but was rebuilt.

(The Smith Hotel was the first hotel built in Bayfield. It was built in 1856 by John B. Bono and was known as Bono's Hotel. It was purchased by Capt. P.W. Smith and burned in 1883.)

An account of the burning of the Smith Hotel, taken from *The Bayfield Press* Saturday, June 16, 1883, is as follows:

"Tuesday morning of this week between the hours of one and two, the Smith House in this village was discovered on fire. The alarm was speedily given and in a short time, a large force of anxious and willing workers was on hand, but all too late to save the building from destruction, and attention was at once turned to saving the furniture and other valuables in the house and adjoining property.

The Smith House was a rambling, two-story frame structure with numerous outlying buildings, laundries, icehouse and barn, situated on the corner of Second Street and Rittenhouse Avenue. It was separated on the east by a 15 foot alley from the jewelry store of

C.T. Andreas, James Chapman's storehouse being an extension of his store fronting on First Street and S.E. Mahan's residence and the residence occupied by the editor of *The Press*. To save these buildings appeared to be a hopeless task, but thanks to the cool heads, willing hands and our water works, which, although crude in some respects, rendered it possible to confine the fire to the building in which it originated and those attached thereto. It was accomplished after one of the severest battles ever fought with the fire king in the harbor city.

The loss to Bayfield is not easily computed. One of the great drawbacks to the place has been the lack of adequate hotel accommodations and our people have just begun to congratulate themselves upon the fact that this drawback was about to be removed by the completion and operation of Vaughn's Hotel, which, although a much larger structure, will now be found unable to accommodate the influx of summer visitors that is heading this way. . .

Among those who distinguished themselves at the fire was Frank Boutin, Sr., whose cool head and willing hands were a force in themselves. As usual, the man who tenderly picks up a feather bed, carries it down stairs to a point of safety and carefully lays it down then rushed back, grasps a marble-topped stand and several mirrors and tosses them out the second story window, was on hand.

One of the cool-headed citizens was discovered pouring water onto a pile of ice after its wooden protection had been destroyed. He didn't propose to have that ice burn if there was any virtue in water. Thieves got in their work to some extent and a number of articles of value turned up missing from a supposed place of safety to which they had been conveyed.

Captain Atwood lost a valuable Past Master's jewel, valued more for the manner in which it came into his possession than for its intrinsic value. Much of Captain Smith's valuable collection of curios is destroyed and some stolen. Parties who will steal from a man under such circumstances ought to be strung up to a lamppost.

The need of a thoroughly organized hook and ladder company has been thoroughly demonstrated.

Notice has been served on the editor of *The Press* that hereafter if he leaves town, he will return at his peril. The occasion for this being the fact that last week he visited the southern part of the state and returning, found the courthouse in ashes and Friday of last week, he again visited he southern part of the state, returning Wednesday to find the Smith house in ashes. Forewarned is forearmed, and parties residing at a distance who wish to interview us personally will find us at Bayfield.

James Chapman had a roll of money amounting to $75 in his pocket when the fire broke out. It wasn't there at the close, neither has it been seen since.

June 23, 1883. Capt. Smith's new building is rapidly taking shape. It is 20 x 40 situated on the east side of the old hotel site. He expects to have it ready for occupancy by the first of July.

July 14, 1883. Capt. Smith has increased the size of his new building by adding 20 feet to its length. When completed, it will be one of the finest restaurant buildings in the county.

"There were some splendid boarding houses in Bayfield, such as the LaBonte House and the Fountain House run by Mrs. Bono. The tourists delighted in staying at these places for they served such wonderful meals. The Bonos were just across the street from our store and traded considerably with us. Mrs. Bono was a friendly lady, but was somewhat inclined to prevaricate at times. I was waiting on her one day and for change, I gave her some of the large two-cent copper pieces that were in circulation at that time. I said something about giving her lots of money and she remarked that she had seen Col. Wing take a peck measure full of such coppers quite frequently and throw them off the end of the dock in order to keep them out of circulation. She certainly had me going. I could not conceive of her telling anything but the truth, so my mind was occupied for a number of days (and nights, too) in planning some scheme to recover those coins.

Throwing the coins from the end of the dock reminds me of another incident in the early days.

This was on the R.D. Pike dock near the sawmill. In those days the sawmill had no burner or refuse consumer so a great deal of the sawdust was dumped into the lake to get rid of it. On a calm day around the docks, the lake would appear like a vast sawdust field.

A lady tourist with a small frizzle-haired dog with a large red ribbon tied with a bow at his neck, came down to the mill and then walked out on the dock. The dog was here and there, much to the amusement of a number of boys that had been in swimming but a short time before.

The dog had been walking on sawdust for quite a while and I presume he thought all around was sawdust, so he jumped off the dock into what he thought was a field of sawdust below, but it happened to be the lake.

He was certainly some surprised dog and the way he pawed around trying to get his feet on that sawdust was a caution. The lady was frantic and thought sure her doggie was a goner. She cried and screamed and the dog whined pitifully.

She finally pleaded with the boys to do something to save her dog. One of them jumped in and, grabbing the dog by the ribbon, held him up so that another boy could reach down and rescue him. He was a sorry looking pup, and I am afraid the silk ribbon was ruined forever. The boy who jumped in the water was given a dollar, and remarked that he wished some more ladies would bring their dogs down to visit the sawmill.

At the time I was born, there were no trained nurses or hospitals and all must be taken care of in the home. There usually were several old ladies present, some to help and some simply out of curiosity. One of them told my mother that I could not live more than six weeks. Well, it has been a long six weeks—77 years (1947) and I am still quite a healthy baby.

There were privations in the early days that we know nothing about now. They were shut in easily for six months during the winter. If a spool of thread or a package of needles was forgotten, it meant go without until navigation opened in the spring. There was no doctor nearer than St. Paul when my parents first arrived, and Duluth had not been given her name.

When I was about seven years old, my mother took me on a trip to Ashland on the *Eva Wadsworth*. I was very much impress ed at seeing a mule team belonging to Capt. Tanner hauling water in pork barrels for the people of Ashland. I felt so sorry for the Ashland people having to drink this water when we had such quantities of good spring water in Bayfield. Most of the people living on the flat had fountains in their yards and running water in their homes. Now there is an abundance of good water for everyone, both in Ashland and Bayfield.

I well remember when hemlock lumber was first used for building purposes. Capt. Pike concluded to build some houses for his mill hands. One of our carpenters asked him for work and incidentally inquired what kind of lumber he was going to use. When he said hemlock, the man replied, "Well, that counts me out. I don't work with hemlock."

However, there came a day when this same carpenter and others like him were glad to take contracts for buildings where hemlock lumber was used.

"Going back to the earlier days, I am reminded of the sailing vessels we had in Bayfield. There was the *Alice Craig,* owned by the Boutins, the *Anna Maria,* owned by Col. Rudd, and sailed by Capt. Judd and Ben Judd of Ashland, and the *Maple Leaf* owned by Capt. Pike and used by him to transport lumber from his mill to the Chicago market.

The *Maple Leaf* was sailed by Capt. Nils Larson and working until the last minute, was nearly always late in making the return trip in the fall which, several times, was the cause of much anxiety on the part of our Bayfield citizens. As the time for the closing of navigation approached, and the good old vessel failed to show up, we would say to one another, "I wonder where the *Maple Leaf* can be. She should surely be here by now."

One fall, just before navigation closed and in a terrible storm, the old captain sailed in through the Duluth channel in the lee of Basswood Island with a broken rudder and canvas badly torn, but otherwise safe and ready to try another season.

Another time we were anxiously waiting for her return; it was very late, there had been bad storms and the bay was freezing. Nearly everyone was asking, "Will the *Maple Leaf* get in?"

The next morning, Father called me to look out the window, and there, some 200 feet from the dock, was the *Maple Leaf,* frozen in the ice. The old captain could get her no further, and the next morning, a channel was cut for her and she was pulled to the dock. I don't believe that men could be hired now to take the chance that some of our old seamen took in the earlier days.

(Mr. Nourse refers to Capt. Larson as "old." Actually, during the time he sailed the *Maple Leaf,* he was between 35 and 45 years of age. He first came to Bayfield in the summer of 1871 when he was 34 years old and, during that summer, this was his homeport as he sailed on Lake Superior. During the following winter he built the *Maple Leaf* for Captain Pike and commanded her for a period of ten years. He was old in knowledge and skill with boats and it seemed to be a knowledge and skill that is gone. Nowadays, who could build a schooner, and sail her, heavily loaded with lumber down to Chicago and back during November and December, with as few aids as they had to navigation then, or, in fact, with all the aids they have now. In 1875, the *Maple Leaf* was the first vessel built at a Lake Superior port to carry a cargo of lumber from Lake Superior, through Lake Huron, and the rivers to Lake Erie. Capt. Larson commanded the tug *Favorite* for two seasons and then took command of Capt. Pike's Gray Oak, the first large boat built on Lake Superior of native oak. He sailed this vessel for two years, much of the time freighting between Milwaukee and other Lake Michigan ports. He was for two years foreman of the Bayfield Brownstone Company's quarry, "in which position he displayed great ability and judgment."

During the summer of 1890, he spent some time in prospecting for available brownstone for a quarry at the northern end of Bass Island, which was projected by Capt. Homer Durand of Toledo, Ohio.

Late in the fall of 1890, he took the schooner *Annie Rudd,* to Two Harbors, Minn. While getting into port during a heavy sea, he was taken with a paralytic stroke induced by the excitement in saving the boat. *The Bayfield Press* commented, "His illness was brought on by an act of heroism such as few men possess." He was taken to the hospital in Duluth and brought home to Bayfield as soon as he could be moved. During the winter, he rallied enough so that he could go outdoors when warm weather came, but once outdoors he exerted himself too strenuously and had a relapse. His death was sudden and unexpected. "Old" Capt. Nils Larson died on Wednesday morning the sixty of May 1891, in the 54th year of his age.

"With the modern sawmills came the steam barges with their consorts for transporting lumber, and while some of them were full rigged sailing vessels, they chose to attach themselves to the tow line of a steam barge rather than risk it alone.

All of our fishermen depended upon their sail boats in the early days and were always subject to wind and weather. How different now with the dependable gasoline launch. But they were not so dependable at first.

I well remember the first one that came to Bayfield. It was owned by Nels Bachand and Herbert Hale and was nicknamed the *Crackerjack.* Both of these gentlemen were members in good standing of the Catholic church in Bayfield, but it must have tested their religion tremendously when they tried to get this boat started in the morning. They sometimes worked for hours. It would crack away for a minute or two and stop. Then they would try again and keep on trying. It made such a noise we could hear it all over town and when it did finally get away, it sounded like a Fourth of July celebration leaving town and turning out to be such a failure that the gasoline boat was condemned by most of us for all time."

"When we consider all the conveniences we have today as compared to what we had in the early days, we wonder. As for instance, there were no storm windows. My mother made little bags about two inches in diameter and the length of a window sill which she filled with beach sand and placed them at the bottom of the windows to keep the cold air out. There were no screen doors or windows to keep the flies out and nothing to kill them with, like the DDT that we have today.

The stores had no deliveries. Whatever purchases were made, you carried or wheeled home yourself. Every family owned a wheelbarrow for summer and a strong home-made sled for winter.

I have often thought of the wonderful opportunity there was to invent a ball-bearing wheelbarrow that would have wheeled so much easier and which would have obliterated the squeaks.

There was the whittling age. Every man and most of the boys possessed jackknives. Old men used to pass away the time whittling. It was customary for a number of them to congregate at Tate's drug store, sitting on a bench outside, swapping yarns and whittling. There was plenty of nice, soft pine in those days for this purpose.

(*Bayfield Press*—April 6, 1889—"A *Press* reporter saw a very neat sample of whittling recently being a set of pliers cut from a single piece of wood and complete even to joints without a pin or a screw.")

Another common sight in the early days was a 16 year old boy standing on the street corner playing a Jew's Harp and keeping time with his feet. We sold hundreds of these musical instruments.

The big boys, and men, in fact, played baseball on the city streets, for that was about the only place there was in the early days.

Capt. Tyler's residence was on Broad Street. All the boys stood in awe of Captain Tyler. He was over 6 feet tall, with long arms and with but two fingers on his right hand, and when he held up that right hand with the two fingers in evidence, something was going to happen. A ball game was in progress directly in front of Tyler's house. My brother, Ed, with the Cooper boys, Charley McCloud and others were in the game. My brother owned the ball. There were board fences on each side of the street. Some one of the boys struck the ball and it made straight for Tyler's front window. There was a crash of glass and then in about ten seconds there was not a boy in the street. They were over the fence, waiting for what they were certain must come. They only had to wait a moment when the long, lank form of Tyler appeared on the sidewalk with outstretched arm and those two fingers spread apart as he brought it up and down he would shout, "You! You! You!" It is needless to say that my brother, Ed, never called for the ball and that this ended the game.

Speaking of baseball reminds me of the time our Bayfield boys played Ashland some 45 years ago. Frank Holston was our pitcher and Frank Gordon, catcher. Rev. Beaty, a young Presbyterian minister was first baseman. Together with the Cooper boys and the Hofch boys, we had what we considered a crack team. Rev. Beaty was the star player and Captain. The game was well along when it was discovered that there was considerable betting going on. Someone mentioned it to Rev. Beaty. In a moment he was out on the diamond and with up stretched arm called for attention. "Gentlemen," he said, "I understand there is some betting on this game. Unless these bets are called off at once, the Bayfield boys refuse to play longer." It was said in such good conscience that in a few moments, the crowd called out, "Bets off. Go on with the game." It is needless to say that Bayfield won.

Mr. Leihy, one of our oldest settlers, first located in Odanah where he built a sawmill on what was known as Taylor's Fork, a branch of the Bad River. He also opened a store and purchased furs from the Indians, paying for them in trade from the store. He tells that one day Mr. Vaughn visited him, and while there, Mr. Leihy asked if he would be interested in looking at some furs. Mr. Vaughn said he would and then remarked, "You have some nice furs there, Mr. Leihy. How much do you want for them?" He said that he had in mind that $15.00 would be a fair price and when Mr. Vaughn offered $75.00, it almost floored him.

From then on, Mr. Leihy made a great deal of money dealing in furs. One day while at the mill he got a steel sliver in his eye. The only doctor in the region was Dr. Ellis in Ashland. After suffering intense pain for several nights and days, he concluded to see Dr. Ellis. The doctor gave him very little encouragement. He said, "You know, Mr. Leihy, we don't have the equipment for an injury of this nature and the only thing I can do is to try and extract it with a magnet." After days and nights of agony, he finally lost the sight of the eye.

Mr. Leihy finally moved to Bayfield and opened a store and butcher shop. He drove cattle all the way from St. Paul to Bayfield over very poor and uncertain roads. Beefsteak in those days sold for 10 cents per pound and cow's liver for 5 cents. What a change from now."

"In the early days we sold many things in the store that are out of date now. All the workingmen wore knee-high cowhide boots and softer, lighter weight for Sunday. The old gentlemen wore shawls, made of gray wool which they threw around their shoulders. This in cold weather, of course.

Many of the women wore hoop skirts and all wore bustles. We bought bustles by the barrel. The best ones were made of spring wire.

I remember one Fourth of July years ago, Captain Pike had his large scow decorated for the occasion and the tug *Favorite* was designated to tow it. A row of balsam trees were nailed around the entire scow and several clumps of balsams were arranged in the middle. The whole town was invited for the trip. The Bayfield city cornet band furnished the music. It was a beautiful day and a wonderful trip and was enjoyed as much as any auto trip could possibly be enjoyed in these days.

Passenger boats brought a great many tourists to Bayfield and they were taken care of at the Island View Hotel. Someone from the hotel met every boat. The hotel was managed by Mr. & Mrs. Charles Willey, and after the annex was built, if I am not mistaken, they would accommodate two hundred guests. They were usually full during the hot weather and very often were compelled to send word to the boats that they could accommodate no more. Mrs. Willey was a fine pianist and Charley played the violin. Very often they played for dancing parties in the large reception room of the hotel to the enjoyment and entertainment of the guests.

Island View Hotel–circa 1980s. (Photo:BHA)

The big attraction for many tourists in the early days was out fishing. The streams were full of brook trout and there was also splendid rock fishing.

Men were employed to take tourists fishing in row boats and often they would go as far as Sand River and return in one day. Others would take tents and camp for several days.

Hank LaPointe had a mackinaw boat 16 feet in length and he was employed constantly during the summer in taking out fishing parties. Hank could row a boat all day and not tire in the least.

The happiest pastimes of my life were the days my father and I went fishing. Father had a rowboat built after the pattern of Hank LaPointe's, strong and sturdy and about once in two weeks we would row down to either Pike's Creek or Sioux River for a fish. The timber along the streams had not been touched; the water was shaded constantly by the trees. The woods were full of game and the streams were full of fish. How wonderfully beautiful it all was.

The Boutins were engaged in fishing and in the wintertime hauled their fish in sleighs as far as St. Paul sometimes. Then they engaged in lumbering and built that fine tug, the N. Boutin to be used both for fishing and towing logs.

Dan Best was the notorious foreman that logged their Raspberry Bay timber, said to be the finest pine timber ever put in the bay. They had their crack teamsters, Jack Murfey, Jake Lawrence, Jack Benedium and Alex Butterfield, all vying with one another to put in the biggest loads. They used double wrappers for their loads and seldom went to the landing without a peeker.

Some of the Indians were splendid canthook men, crack top loaders and were employed in the same camp from year to year.

Jim Harbert and I were boy companions. We enjoyed many a day fishing together and going on fishing trips. Jim was always up to some mischief and one day in school, he and the principal locked horns and Jim quit school. He went immediately to Currie Bell's printing office and asked for a job. Mr. Bell started him to work for $1.00 per week. His uncle in St. Paul heard about it and wrote him and said now that he was earning money, he should save and buy a cow. Jim thought nothing of it until a few days later, the depot agent telephoned that there was a cow and a calf there for him.

There was no loading or unloading platform at that time, so it was a problem as to how to get the cow and calf out of the car.

They tried several ways, but the cow refused to move. Finally they lifted the calf out and the cow made a flying leap to the ground and together with her calf started for the woods. Jim was all day getting them back to town and into a barn.

The Nourse family has been in Bayfield for 100 years. Joseph Nourse arrived from Washington, D.C., in August, 1856. The annual census taken March 24, 1859, when Bayfield was three years old, has as its first entry, "J. Harvey Nourse, wife and child." The total population of the town at that time was 115, with 45 residents out of the town limits making a total of 160 in the whole community.

October 13, 1870 *The Bayfield Press* had this item, "Our neighbor, Mr. Nourse, presented us with a fine basket of potatoes, being part of a hill containing 94 potatoes, the largest measured nine inches in circumference."

June 22, 1872, this item appeared in *The Ashland Press* . "J. H. Nourse is the express agent at Bayfield. Persons desiring to send express matter can apply to him at his store opposite the Smith Hotel." There was no train here then and express went by boat or team.

Some of the hardships of winter are described in *The Ashland Press* article of March 27, 1875. "The Misses Isobel and Emma Nourse of Bayfield snowbound here for some days went home by special train on Tuesday. (The train was a team of four dogs pulling a toboggan type sled. Two guides accompanied them.) Letters from Bayfield inform us that our young friends, who expected to be but four hours on their journey had a very hard trip, being all day and the night following on the ice, reaching Bayfield at 7AM. John Ojibway brought word the night before that they had not reached Houghton Point and a party set out to rescue them taking dogs and provisions, but in the darkness, they passed them. The young ladies suffered from cold and hunger, but the night was unusually mild. Their feet, though wet, were not frozen."

One of the pleasures of winter enjoyed by Belle Nourse is described in the diary of Mrs. Andrew Tate for February 8, 1877. "After dinner Mrs. Cruttendon, Mrs. McCloud, Mrs. Herbert, Belle Nourse and myself went out on the ice. Mrs. McCloud had chairs tied to sleds. The boys pushed us on the sleds. Spent a very pleasant afternoon."

The Nourses have had long experience in making their maple sugar and syrup which is so well known here. March 29, 1890, over 66 years ago, *The Press* reported: "Harvey Nourse has been in the sugar bush this week getting in saccharine sweetness for the community."

June 28, 1890, *The Press* reported another Nourse item, which fortunately did not become a tragedy. "As the Rev. E.E. Nourse was driving in from the farm last Thursday, he met with what lacked only a little from being a fatal accident. Just below Third Street, the wagon tongue dropped, striking one of the horses. They immediately began to run and as the wagon tongue struck the ground, it turned the wagon completely over. Mr. Nourse was thrown violently between the horses and was run over by the wagon. One of his feet was severely mashed and he was generally shaken up. The horses ran up Third Street and were partially stopped by colliding with a tree. Mr. E. K. Brigham took them in hand. The wagon is a total wreck."

The Nourse Homestead located on the banks of Pike's Creek, three miles south of Bayfield. Circa 1900. (Photo: BHA)

A picture of the Nourse farm at Pike's Creek appeared in a magazine of Bayfield County about 1900 and was described as follows: "It has the reputation of growing the 'sliced strawberry' which has made the hotels at Duluth and Superior so famous, having been supplied from this farm for many years. One berry measured 7 1/2 inches around it. Besides the farm has produced garden truck of all kinds and as high as 100 tons of hay has been cut in a single season of fine quality."

The Nourses were well known strawberry growers. July 16, 1909, *The Press* reported, "There were 336 crates of strawberries loaded at Salmo Tuesday. Nourse Bros. had 298 crates picked from less than 3 acres. They employ 61 pickers and 6 packers. A number of boys and girls picking strawberries for them are camping in tents near the Nourse residence."

When cars came into use, Harvey Nourse had the first one in Bayfield. In June, 1908, *The Press* said, "Harvey Nourse received his automobile the first of the week and is now enjoying rapid rides over our country roads." In August 1908, another item appeared. "Harvey Nourse is now able to master his auto providing everything goes alright."

Harvey and
Emma Nourse.
(Photo: BHA)

The Nourse brothers, Harvey and Laurie, were known for their fine singing. January 15, 1909, *The Press* recorded: "Frank Miller, a former resident of Bayfield, was here a short time ago visiting Laurie and Harvey Nourse. While Mr. Miller lived here, he sang a great deal with the Nourse brothers and Mr. N. E. Carver of Bayfield invited the trio to his home where 16 phonograph records were taken of their singing. These three may never meet again, but their voices will be heard for years to come on the phonograph."

Myrtle Judd Nourse, wife of the late Laurie Nourse, who now lives in California, has written some reminiscences of Bayfield. "My father, Capt. C. L. Judd, was master of the good ship Anna Rudd, a two-masted freight carrier that plied between Ashland and Duluth. Col. Rudd, owner of the same, spent most of his time in Bayfield, but when in Ashland made our home headquarters. He weighed about 300 pounds and the articles in *The Press* about him brought back many memories of my childhood. It was awesome to watch him as he balanced food on his overloaded fork and got it safely to his mouth, a real achievement.

(Mrs. DeMars recalls that at one time Col. Rudd reduced, and though his size shrunk greatly, he wore the same clothes as when he was very stout, probably because a new suit was not easily obtainable in this pioneer country. As Col. Rudd walked past someone remarked, "If the Colonel isn't careful, he's going to catch the seat of his pants on a nail in the sidewalk.")

My nephew, Claude Page and I enjoyed the privilege of singing for Col. Rudd. His appreciation was expressed with a quarter for each of us. But alas, we fell from grace when we learned a new song and proudly gave him the benefit. He was an old bachelor with very white hair. Our song, *I'll Never Marry an Old Man, I'll Tell you the Reason Why,* forfeited our 25 cent income, as he never asked us to sing again.

I was perhaps about six or seven years of age when my first visit to Bayfield was made. I had persuaded my father to let me accompany him to Duluth. As we entered the slip at Bayfield, the old Barker was tied to the right hand dock, and as the *Anna Rudd* swung around the left hand dock, her bow struck the *Barker.* I was standing in the door of the cabin. A large pan of greasy dishwater was on the table to my left and in the middle of that water I landed. My poor father came to the cabin to get me to accompany him up town. I, in utter dejection, dripping with dishwater from heat to foot, waited for the explosion, but it did not come. He patiently changed all of my clothes, wiped my hair, bought me a pair of dry shoes and I was happy again.

When ready to set sail, long pike poles were brought out and the crew used them in pushing the schooner out of the slip and into open water where the sails were set to a fair breeze and we headed for Rudd's farm on Bass Island.

As soon as the landing was made, I was off like a shot to find amusement and came to a large flock of white leghorns scratching in the sand. I threw my large straw hat up into the air and cawed like a hawk. I laughed and enjoyed the old biddies consternation as they ran in all directions for shelter. My mirth was short lived, however, when a vice-like grip came down on my shoulder and I was nearly shaken out of my new shoes. When I looked up into Col. Rudd's huge face under shaggy brows, I wished I were at home with mother.

He said, "Never let me catch you scaring my hens again. It stops their laying." I meekly returned to the ship and father.

At noon next day while all were at dinner in the cabin, I discovered a scaffold leading from high up on the cliff to a floating landing or dock close to the ship. It had unplaned boards on top and was used to slide the huge chunks of bark down to the landing from which it was, by means of a pulley, hoisted to the deck of the schooner and then stored in the hold. I decided to use a chunk of bark for a toboggan and started down the incline. About half way down, the bark left me and went on ahead while I slid to the bottom on my petticoat. I had to sit awhile after landing to get my bearings. My feet were touching the water.

When my father learned of what I had done he said, "You might have been drowned, etc." He told Brother Ben to put me in a rowboat and take me out to the passenger boat City of Ashland, which was about due from Duluth. I was put in charge of Capt. Doherty, father of Capt. John Doherty of Mary Scott ferry days, and his good wife, who promised to see that I reached my mother in Ashland safely.

It was about 10 PM when we reached Ashland and the moment the gangplank was out, I was off up the east end mill dock headed for home in the West end of Ashland.

In those days our minds were filled with murders committed in Bay City in some of the many saloons that lined the streets in the logging camp days and I ran for my life until I reached Ashland proper.

I got home at last but found no mother. I decided she was at the theatre so went to the old skating rink near 9th Avenue West, where theatre companies used the stage for performances. John Prince was in the box office and told me my mother was there.

When she saw her child whose hair had not been combed, whose dress was torn and soiled and learned why I had been sent home, she thanked God I was safe and no scolding ensued.

William Knight

William Knight. Early wild West traveler and Bayfield pioneer mover and shaker. Father of Bayfield's apple and cherry industries. (Photo: BHA)

MANY OF THE READERS OF the column will remember my grandfather, William Knight, for he lived to the age of 97. Fortunately, in 1925 he took time to write his memoirs. That was a surprising thing, for he was engaged in so many activities and projects, that sitting down to write about himself seems like the last thing he would do. However, in the preface he explains, "I wrote it exclusively for my children, and at their request. . ." Maybe insistence would have been a better word.

William Knight was born December 7, 1843, on a farm in Delaware. He didn't come to Bayfield until he was 26 years old. Quite a few of the years between were packed with travel and adventure. I will record a little of it, for, although it has no bearing on Bayfield history, it reveals something of William Knight's character, and gives a clear, though unglamorous picture, of the early days in Wyoming when the Union Pacific tracks were being laid.

Like many young men of his day he went West in search of fortune and adventure. The fortune he did not find, but adventure was plentiful. In response to a letter from his brother, John, who was a Captain in the regular army, he went to Fort Sanders, Wyoming, to take a clerkship with the Fort Traders at $125 per month.

Here is how he describes it. "Fort Sanders was near Laramie City. At that time, Laramie City was a tent city of 2,000 people made up of gamblers, outlaws, bandits, and the most lawless people in the world, and not a decent woman in the place. These people made it a practice to keep ahead of the iron laying so as to be where nine-tenths of the work was being done by the graders and the ties were being laid. They got most of the money paid to labor either by gambling or robbery."

"I will mention one thing I saw take place after the track was in use as far as Fort Sanders. I was playing billiards in a tent, when a man from Kentucky, a desperado full of whiskey, with a revolver in his hand, was walking back and forth, swearing he was going to kill some one that day. Of course, the friend playing with me and myself said nothing, but kept one eye on him. In a few minutes, an engine came in front of the tent and stopped. The engineer got off, passed through the tent and went into another one where there was a collection of men carrying on an election for something. The desperado followed him, and at once I heard a loud exclamation of curses. I stepped to the door and saw several men facing each other, apparently trying to avoid a clash between the two men. I saw the desperado raise his gun to shoot, but in a second, I saw the engineer pick a little derringer pistol from his vest pocket and shoot him in the forehead. The desperado dropped and squirmed on the ground. The engineer walked to his engine, got on and moved off before the crowd had picked up the wounded man and put him aside, out of the way, where he died in a few minutes. That was the first man I saw shot while I was there."

"Everybody was a law unto himself and everybody went armed with from one to three revolvers strapped to his waist and a wicked looking knife in his sheath. I saw men shoot each other like dogs, and after they were killed, they were treated like dogs and left lying where they fell until someone got good and ready to pick them up, throw them in a cart, haul them a short distance from town, dig a shallow hole, throw the body in, throw a little dirt on it, and the wolves ate them the next night."

This whole congregation of outlaws had apparently dropped in from everywhere singly. No two men appeared to be friends with each other. Every man distrusted the other one and they were ready to kill each other on the least provocation.

One morning I saw there was no city in sight, so I got on my horse and rode out there, and all I found was one lone wolf chewing some bones. The tents and people had all gone and not one was left to tell of their going. They made a skip of about one hundred miles and pitched their tents on the bank of North Platte River, just where the railway survey crossed and named the new town Blackwell.

The reminiscences of William Knight of his early days in Wyoming continue as he writes: "The trader at Fort Sanders was looking for a market to sell his goods, but he was not inclined to follow this lawless murder mob of people. He had seen the crimes going on right under the nose of a U.S. Military post filled with soldiers, which made for restraint with this class of people, but it was not entirely effective. He asked me if I would take his goods and go to the North Platte River and sell the goods there where the Laramie City mob had camped. I told him yes, if he would send a man with me.

He finally got his barkeeper, Pete Lamon to go. We found the same old crowd that was at Laramie City, but more lawless than ever, as there were no soldiers within a hundred miles to curb their evil ways. I got some teams and men and went along the river bank and cut some cottonwood logs to build a house to store my goods and do business. In a few days, I had it up and a canvas roof over it and I got busy selling out my stock.

While in Blackwell, Pete and I would pile boxes of all kinds filled with goods in an open square on the floor and spread out blankets in the square and go to bed for the night. This was for protection from bullets in case one got through a crack between the logs of our house. It got to be quite a saying when bed time came, "Well, let's dig our grave." All night long we could hear the popping of revolver shots, some near, and some faint, mostly faint, as our house was on the outer edge of the city. If all the shots had taken effect, soon there would have been no one left to kill. Some innocent persons were killed in their tents.

Pete Lamon, my helper, was not the bravest man I ever saw, either. He stood the strain for about a month and could bear no more and fled the country and started back for God's country, as he said when we shook hands and said good-bye and wished each other good luck. I have never seen or heard of him since. I hope he found the land he started for. In about two months I sold out the stock. I sent the money back to my employer and that ended my career in that turmoil of hell.

About that time a company of infantry and cavalry passed through the town and went down the river about a mile and commenced to build Fort Steel. After that there was less killing, but the gambling and other hellish doings kept up just the same. I went to Fort Steel and put in my time there for a month or two. Most of the time I spent hunting antelope and sage hens.

One day Ed Hunt and I were about 4 miles from Fort Steel hunting along a river valley. He had a shotgun and I had a rifle, so he followed the valley looking for rabbits and I took the hills hunting for antelope.

I saw a horseman come out of some foothills half a mile away. I dropped down behind a prairie dog mound and watched to make out whether he was hunting or not. In a few minutes, 10 or 12 more came in sight. I watched them closely and by the way they rode and were dressed, I knew they were Indians.

I crawled back until I got low enough so I could stand up and not be seen by the Indians. I waved my hat to Ed. By my action, he knew something was up and came on the run. We crept up the side of the hill and peeked over and watched them. We saw they were not coming toward us, but were heading toward the railroad graders about 10 or 15 miles away. As they passed out of sight, we made quick steps for the fort. When we arrived, I went to Col. Dodge and told him what we had seen.

"Oh, hell," he said. "You civilians are always looking for Indians."

"Yes," I said, " and we find them, but the soldiers go out with clanking sabers and never find them."

"Come on in," he said, "and have a game of billiards."

"Yes," I replied, "and a bottle of wine, and if these men are not Indians, I pay for it, and if they are Indians, then you pay for it."

"That's a deal," he said.

We played our game and had our wine. Then I said to the Colonel, "I am sure you will have to pay for this wine, because Ed and I watched those men for 15 minutes at not over a half mile distance and you know in this high atmosphere a man can see very distinctly that distance.

"You ought to," he said, "if you were not nervous."

"Well, Colonel," I replied. "I have been in this wild country longer than you have. I am not indifferent to danger, but I have learned to keep a cool head and use horse sense, attend to my own business and not mix up with other people's affairs and get my head shot off to gratify my temper."

"Well," he said, "I am beginning to think you have seen something."

He sent out his assistant wagon master that night on one of his best saddle back mules I have ever seen and the Indians got him and the mule. Poor Wallace, I was very sorry to have him meet his death that way. I knew him well and mourned him as a dear friend.

Next day the logging teams got in and had not seen Wallace or the Indians. A search party was sent out to find Wallace, but found nothing. I afterward heard that the next spring, they found his long cavalry boot with his foot and leg bone up to the knee in on Pass Creek, where I used to hunt and sleep in the grass over night.

In the fall of 1868, William Knight and his friend, Ed Hunt, heard of a new mining camp where gold had been discovered called South Pass. They went there, although, as William Knight said, "Neither of us knew any more about hunting gold than hunting a road that led up to the moon."

They built a log house and got some lots, which they finally sold, to a newcomer for $400. Hunt thought it best to strike back to the railroad and find work. William Knight wrote: "I disagreed with him. I argued that while we were on the ground, I did not think it best to leave it before we had searched the country and found out for ourselves what the prospect looked like. We talked and thought over the situation for several days. Finally Hunt heard of a railroad being built called Southern Pacific. He did not know what state the work was being carried on it, but he made up his mind to go look for it anyway and took the stage out and left me, as I had determined to stay and go prospecting for gold.

After Hunt left, it was a more lonely place than that I never lived. Homesickness seized me. That disease takes all the heart and pep out of a man while it lasts as no other sickness does. I brooded for days. I thought over my boyhood days in the good little State of Delaware. I sat and dreamed and dreamed. I could see all the surrounding country of my past life, the trees, the brooks and rivers, all possessed a beauty I never saw before.

But what was the use of it all. It only made my homesickness more intense and I realized brooding would eat the heart out of me if I did not shake it off and get from under its bad effects. I realized I must be doing something to occupy my mind and body so I made an arrangement to prospect with a miner. He was living in a dugout in the side of a hill and I went to live and work with him and we batched together. Flour was high, $50 a barrel.

Cool weather came and my partner started out with others on a 3 or 4-day tour to prospect. While gone, there came a fall of snow 4 or 5 inches deep and the sun came out bright and he came back snowblind and I had to doctor his eyes for several days. I kept tealeaves over his eyes and that cured him. During his trouble, we talked a great deal about the prospects for gold in the country and we agreed the whole country would prove a fake.

I was thinking what course I should take, whether to strike down for Mexico and work my way down to the coast and take a boat for New York or take the back track for God's country, directly the way I came, but one day in came 4 or 5 double wagon mule teams and, as they passed through the street, I saw a friend sitting on one of the wagons. I called out, "Hello, Raison, where are you going?"

I climbed on the wagon and he said, "My, I am glad to see you. I want, if possible, for you to go with me."

I answered that I could go anywhere under the sun if there was any money in it. "Good wages for you if you will go," he said.

He told me that he had come from Fort Bridger and Salt Lake City and that the wagons were loaded with goods belonging to the settler, Judge Carter, and he was taking them to Camp Washkee, a military camp of about 100 cavalry men, who were protecting the Snake and Crow Indians. The camp was on the Little Proposer River near Wind River Valley. The goods were for trade with the Indians. I soon made a bargain with him to go.

We got an early start for Washkee Camp, about a 45-mile drive, and hoped to arrive late in the evening, which we did. Raison brought his pony with him, but did not ride her much, only when he wanted to give some orders at the head wagon, or ride ahead to inspect the road at the crossing of ravines or rough places. We found the road quite good and dry for a road that had never been made any better than nature made it.

Next day after our arrival, we unloaded our goods in a log house. About all we had to do after getting the goods opened was to divide a case of whiskey among the officers, as there were no Indians in sight—anywhere. The whole tribe was out hunting buffalo and other fur animals.

The trading goods consisted of beads, tobacco, brass and silver trinkets, cotton cloth, calico, flannel of bright colors, blankets, some flour, bacon, sugar, salt, and some ribbons, and a little of everything that was worthless in my eyes. . .We did not trade with the soldiers at all. We did not have much a soldier would buy, anyway, for the U.S. had provided for all their wants in the commissary. So I loafed and fished the creeks for trout and the creeks were full of them.

William Knight's job at Camp Washkee (correct present day spelling Washakie), was trading with the Indians. He wrote: "I bought all their furs with the goods I had and when I got through, I had my house stacked to the rafters with all kinds of furs, buffalo robes, beaver skins, muskrat, prairie dogs and all kinds of skins the country had. Springtime was with us again and the grass was growing. Freighters came in and took the furs to Fort Bridger and Salt Lake City. Raison went with them and promised to send in more goods. I told him when he left that I would stay until fall and then I was going to God's country."

During the summer, I think it was July, a patrol of 4 or 5 soldiers were out scouting. They saw a couple of grizzly bears playing on the edge of a swale of willow brush and attempted to get a shot at them, but they ran into the brush. One of the scouts got off his horse and followed them to get a shot. He hardly got a few paces into the brush when he came to a bear standing on his hind feet, ready for a charge, not 20 feet from him. He shot the bear through the chest, near the heart.

The bear made one charge and struck the scout with his forefoot on the top of the head and, with his claws, cut the scalp to the bone down over his shoulder and side to his thigh, knocking him over. The bear fell dead on top of the scout.

His comrades heard his cries and rushed to rescue him. They were about six miles from camp, but rigged up a blanket stretcher between two of their horses and brought him in and the army surgeon fixed him up and he finally got well. The bear's claws were as much as two inches long and they left bad scars on his scalp and the side of his face clear down to his thigh.

Not long after that, a band of Arapaho Indians struck a band of Crows and Snake Indians and they had a fight about 15 miles out. But before they hit the Crows and the Snakes, they picked up some people making hay and killed and scalped them along with a soldier who had deserted the camp about 3 days before. This was done within 4 miles of our camp. I presume they struck the Crows on their getaway. The Crows got the best of the fight and followed the Arapahos 2 or 3 days. Four days after this fight, the scouts found a Crow Indian 4 miles from camp with a broken thigh. When shot, he fell from his horse into the long grass and hid until the fight was over. He had dragged himself nearly ten miles toward the fort. The doctor fixed him up, and he got well, but lost the fall hunt with his band.

During the summer, I rode my pony from the fort to the mining camp several times all alone, and I do not think I missed seeing fresh trails of hostile Indians any trip I made, but never had the bad luck to come in contact with any of them. I had my plan all figured out what I should do in case I did meet with them. I intended to get off my pony and let him run loose, then I would dig in and stand them off and I expected they would get my pony, but would not take many chances to get my scalp after they got the pony. Horses were wealth to them and they thought more of them than they did of a scalp.

In December I mounted my pony and started for the mining camp to take the stage for the railroad. I went alone and the weather was pretty cold and I knew my feet needed protection. As I had no overshoes, I took two muskrat skins and slipped them over my boots and found them very comfortable.

When about 5 miles from the mining camp, I crossed a fresh Indian trail and I kept my pony in town that night, as I feared to picket her out in the hills on account of that trail I saw. About daylight next morning, I heard a great yelling and it sounded like Indian war whoops and I jumped up and saw about 100 Indians on their horses surrounding a herd of freighter's horses and mules. They were all on a keen run and swept around and started for the hills.

I heard afterward that the freights got about a dozen horses and started after the Indians, but all they found was two or three played out horses and a few dead ones. They followed for three days, but the Indians kept dividing the herd and branching off from the main body and the white men kept following the largest body. This dividing kept up until they were following a dozen Indians and a few horses and finally this trail took them up in the mountains and a dangerous country for ambushing and they turned back empty handed.

In 1869, after two years in the "hellishness" of Wyoming, William Knight was riding comfortably toward "God's country" in a train that ran smoothly along the recently laid Union Pacific tracks. At Rolling Springs, Wyoming, the train stopped for breakfast.

He wrote: "Everyone left the cars for the dining room and the platform was full of people. I was about the last to get off and I started walking up to the end of the platform to stretch my legs before I went in the station dining room. When at the end of the platform, I saw a man come out of the saloon 150 yards away and he ran as fast as he could toward the station.

After he got about half way, another man came out and started running after him and commenced shooting a revolver. The first man whirled around and commenced firing at the man following him. The people on the platform rushed to the dining room to get out of range, but I was too far across the danger line and I dropped behind some railroad car wheels lying at the end of the platform. As the bullets rattled around the car wheels, I thought, 'Am I going to get a bullet at last after spending two years in this hellish country?'

I could look through the cracks and watch the whole performance. The headman, by the time he got to the platform, had exhausted all the shots in his revolver and, as he jumped on the platform, I got to my feel and he asked me to lend him a revolver. I told him I had none (but I had one). He passed on asking every man he met to lend him a revolver, and as far as I saw, no one gave him one and he passed on into the dining room.

Then I heard revolvers begin to crack and I went back into the car and waited until the uproar was over. Those fellows were bad marksmen, for they fired shots enough to kill a dozen men, but when it was over, it was found an innocent bystander was shot through the arm, and a woman sitting in her room at the head of the stairway came near being killed from a bullet that went through her door and passed just overhead and lodged in the wall, and one of the original parties got a flesh wound in his side as he ran up the stairway to get away.

I think someone must have let the first fellow have a revolver and the second fellow must have had two, or he could not have continued the shooting as he did.

After the fighting was over, I went in and got my breakfast. The wounds of the men hurt were bandaged and the man shot through the arm got on the train when the rest of us did and the train pulled out, leaving the two fighters at the station. They must have been amateurs, as their marksmanship was far from being what I had been accustomed to see in that country.

For Wyoming readers, may I add that some 80 years later my grandfather left the state of Wyoming in disgust, I went there and found it a wonderful state filled with cordial, non-shooting people, with all the spectacular scenery intact and the comforts of civilization added. Noting that the roads of Fort Steel and Fort Sanders and the town of South Pass and Camp Waskee are well marked on the map, I hope to return, seeing the changes that have come to my grandfather's old trading post, Hunting grounds and the site of his first gold mining venture.

The buffalo are gone now, too. But it was not the Indians who destroyed them. My grandfather wrote this account of their hunting.

"In September, our Indians broke camp and started out with all their women and children and camp equipage for their winter's hunt and I saw no more of them. Early fall, they hunt buffalo first thing, and when they strike a herd of them, they ride all around them and use bow and arrow only and kill them that way, and they keep it up as the buffalo are in a stampede and if the buffalo are a large herd, they kill as many as they think they can care for. They pitch camp, skin and cut off what flesh they want to dry over a fire so that it will keep for winter and summer's supply. But they use it only when fresh meat from game animals of all sorts runs short, or when hunting they take some of it as a reserve in case of failure to get fresh meat to eat. As soon as the killing of buffalo commences, the women commence to skin them and the men return to them after the killing stops. Indians do not waste wild animal life, they only kill to supply food and not for the mere sport of killing. Of course, small animals they kill for both fur and food. Deer and buffalo hides they use for their clothing almost exclusively and they tan all buffalo skins with fur on and deer with hair off. Some small animals with fur on are tanned for trimming their own clothes."

For years my grandfather had a buffalo coat and a buffalo robe for his cutter. Where they went to I don't know, but knowing the durability of buffalo hides, I am sure they never wore out. If I could only find them, I'm sure I would appear "fashionable" this spring in a buffalo stole.

After leaving Wyoming, William Knight got off the train at a Mississippi River town and took a steamer to St. Paul. He planned to go from there to Bayfield to take over the post of his brother, Capt. John Knight, who was Indian Agent here in 1869.

Captain John H. Knight, early Bayfield Indian agent, founder of the Knight Hotel in Ashland, WI and Vice President on the National Board of Trade. (Photo: BHA)

William Knight became 26 years old on December 7 of that year. His youth, his wonderful constitution, which was to carry him to the age of 97, his sense of humor and his great interest in new things, were all very much needed the December day he started for Bayfield. The trip was so horrible that I wonder if sometimes he didn't wish himself back in Wyoming.

He wrote: "In St. Paul I took a day's rest and learned how I was to get to Superior. I took a train out to a small village; I have forgotten the name of it, on the Duluth and St. Paul

Railroad that was building into the head of the lake. There I took what was called a stage, consisting of a lumber wagon with seats fastened on the wagon box. We traveled all day and at dark, arrived at a stopping house and stayed all night.

In the morning there was six inches of snow on the ground, and still snowing a little. The stage man left the wagon and hitched up to a long runner sleigh (not bobs) and we started for Superior.

Before the snow fell, the road had been cut up fearfully and when it froze, it left the road rough. This old, long, two-runner sleigh had a canvas top stretched over wooden hoops and curtains at the side and hard seats without cushions or springs. Five passengers and the driver got in. He cracked his whip and away we went, a jolly crowd, but we had not gone many miles before we were not as jolly, and the conversation died down to groans and swears.

Every mile we went seemed to get rougher and more hellish than ever. At noontime we came to a log hut for dinner and we filled up on fried sow belly, potatoes, coffee and biscuits heavy as lead. When we got out of that sled, every muscle of our bodies quaked and ached and our joints cracked like a new fire kindled with dry hemlock. We could scarcely stand up and straighten as we walked. I did not dare look back at that old rig, for fear my eyes would burn holes in the canvas top, I hated it so. Our stomachs felt as though they had been scooped out with a coal shovel. There was nothing left in us, not even our spirit. That had left us soon after starting that morning.

After dinner we stood up on our feet until we had to start again, because the bones in the seat of our pants ached so we feared they would break. Well, when the time came that we had to enter that purgatory again, we put the palms of our hands on the seat of our breeches, eased ourselves down on that old board and sat on them for awhile to ease up the pressure of that old devil of an ache seat.

The driver was a good-natured fellow, and when he got squarely seated said, "Now boys, we are off for the happy home." He gave his horses a slam with his whip and they went off with a jerk.

We had not gone far before we found sitting on the palms of our hands was soothing in one place, but the back of our hands were chafing badly and we took them away, sat down on the board, set our teeth, braced our feet and took our punishment.

The driver kept cracking his whip and the horses would jerk and speed up, but it did not relieve the agony so I said to him, "Don't you hear our bones cracking? Stop the cracking of your whip. Let us do the cracking."

"All right," he said, "I will just crack the whip occasionally to let your cracks rest."

That brought a roar of laughter, but it did not make the road any smoother. About the middle of the afternoon I became seasick, my head got dizzy and my stomach sick and I put my head outside and lost my dinner. After I got over the pain and agony of it all, I felt better and we kept up the speed and finally arrived at Superior after dark and put up for the night and got our supper at the hotel.

I inquired about boats and I found that the boat had left for down lake points several days ago. My heart sank to my boots when I learned that there was no way to get to Bayfield unless I walked, and no road to travel over if I should walk.

Next day I looked around the village of Superior and the people pointed out across the bay to me the townsite of Duluth. All I could see was a half dozen houses sitting on the edge of the front of a hill. The people of Superior stated there never could be much of a town there as they had no ground to build it on, except a small strip at the edge of the marsh along the bay, unless they built on top of the high ledge of rock, and that would never be done.

On the second day after my arrival, the stage started back and I took passage for St. Paul and my experience going back was no different from that going to Superior.

From the above account it is easily seen that Bayfield never was a "covered wagon town." Right from the start it was a steamboat town, built by the lake traffic, beautified by its lakeside location and characterized by the marine knowledge of its inhabitants.

William Knight returned to St. Paul after his first attempt to get to Bayfield in December, 1869 had failed. He wrote: "When I got to St. Paul and registered at the Merchants Hotel, the clerk handed me a letter from Bayfield saying I probably would be too late for the boats at Superior and to stay at St. Paul and James Chapman would come by land for me.

Of course, I did not know who James Chapman was. I stayed at the hotel two or three days and was sitting in the lobby when I saw a man come in at the door who was dressed as though he had just got in from a journey. I got up and met him about half way to the registering counter and said to him, "Excuse me, sir, is this Mr. Chapman?"

"Yes," he said. Then I told him my name was William Knight. We shook hands and he said he was from Bayfield and had come to St. Paul to get me.

We talked a few minutes before he went to his supper and I learned that my brother, John Knight, had taken the last boat for the East, destination Washington. Next day I learned that Chapman had come through to Taylor's Falls and there left his team and took the stage to St. Paul, as there was no snow from there in.

The second day we took the stage for Taylor's Falls and arrived there during the afternoon. Next morning we started for Bayfield in a sleigh (a pair of bobs, this time). Three of us made the party, Chapman, Capt. P.W. Smith, the Bayfield hotelkeeper, and myself. They brought along plenty of buffalo robes, blankets and wraps to keep us warm.

We had a splendid team of horses. They were large, strong and good travelers, and the road was smooth with plenty of snow to make it slip good. The road was not cut up and any knolls or swales in it were made easy with the bobs, where a two runner sleigh would make miserable riding. The first night we stopped at a place owned by a man named "Busky" and the second night at Gordon's place. On the third afternoon about sundown when about ¼ mile from the post office (about where the Baptist church is now), we were stopped, as the road was blocked with saw logs and the loggers rolled them out so we could pass.

It was Sam Vaughn's crew cutting white pine logs for his mill to saw next spring. Vaughn had a little sawmill about two or three hundred thousand feet a year and the timber that mill made was fierce, some thick, some thin and the edges varied from two inches to one half inch thick. It was not all like that, but there was a large percentage like that.

On entering the clearing where the town was built, I can remember but three houses. One was opposite Dr. Merten's house, one on the corner below Stark's store, and two small houses on Broad Street, down toward the depot. There was a small house where the bank stands and a small house across the street where the Pharmacy (Iverson's store) stands and over the door was a wooden sign lettered in black letters, "S.S. Vaughn." Below it was a sign on a smaller board with smaller letters, "Post office." The Vaughn sign was about 8 inches wide and 3 feet long and the post office board about 2 feet. Both boards were nailed to the house over the door.

This was the principle store of the town and sold groceries, shoes, dry goods, clothing and hardware. On this street north there were two or three houses and the same number south and a few scattered buildings along the south lake front with but little attention to street location. Up on the hill near the Roman Catholic Church there were some dwelling houses. In fact, about the whole town was on about six blocks on the flat and those blocks were long from being full.

From memory, I can count but twenty families living in the city of Bayfield, and one family living on a farm outside, and that was Elisha Pike, father of R.D. Pike, living on the old homestead of Pike's Creek.

Nearly all of these families were intelligent, well educated people from the East and would be considered the best in any country.

It is hardly possible for people who never lived in a community almost entirely cut off from the world to appreciate the friendship and mutual sympathy and kindness that binds them so closely together and to understand the sacrifices they will make for the community.

It is a lovely spirit, yes, a divine one, that few people can conceive of, and not experience to the full sense of the spirit, except under such conditions and environment.

William Knight writes in his memoirs as follows: "I came to Bayfield at the request of my brother, John H. Knight. He was a Captain in the U.S. Regular Army and had been assigned to this Agency as U.S. Indian Agent. He wanted to go East to spend the winter and wanted me to look after the Agency while he was away.

I arrived in Bayfield the day before Christmas, 1869. Of course, on Christmas Day, I met some of the men in town and he said occasionally mostly eggnog.

January 1st was a great day, the celebration of the New Year's entrance. Everybody kept open house, with their tables loaded with every good thing to eat and drink. The men went in groups of 4 or 5 and visited every house and found the tables all set and decorated for the occasion with the best silverware and cut glass and pot flowers. The ladies of the house were dressed in their silks and satins, all ready to receive and offer their best eats and drinks. You were expected to at least sample everything and it was considered your bet foot forward to do so. Politeness required you to do so.

I was fully up to the game for the two years I spent in the City of Detroit (where he worked in the Mustering and Disbursing office for the U.S.A after the Civil War.) I had been through it all.

I knew how to eat and drink, to keep my feet under me throughout the day and get back home with my own legs to carry me there. It was a great day for me. I was introduced to every married and single lady in town and they wore their best smiles and were affable and exquisitely dressed and polite to a high degree. When the day was over, I felt I knew everyone in town who was worth knowing and in my experience afterward, I found them as nice and as good a bunch of ladies as I had ever met. Our friendships and respect for each other lasted for many years and I mourned the loss of many of them when they received their call to the home beyond.

I think it was sometime during January I received word from home that father had died in December at the age of 69 years. When I got this sad news, the home ties of youth began to draw their strings about me. I longed to be back again to see the loved ones at home and the veil of sadness pressed heavily upon me. I longed to visit the grave of my mother once more in the churchyard where I attended church with her and father in my childhood, where happiness and sorrow had been with me when I was but a little boy. But the energies and hopes of a young life soon smooth over these rough places, or this life would not be worth the living of it.

In the spring, my brother John came back and said he was to start up the Indian sawmill at Red Cliff and employed me to superintend the sawing and I did. He and Chapman had another scheme to build a dock at Oak Island and they wanted me to take an interest with them and the general store that Chapman was running in Bayfield and combine the whole business.

As I had not much to lose and was nearly out of money and owned no property, I thought this was a chance to make a start in life, so I fell in with their plans. That summer we built a dock on Oak Island and that winter we got out about 1,000 cords of wood which we sold to the down lakes boats plying from the down lakes ports, Buffalo, Cleveland and Chicago to Superior. They stopped at all Lake Superior ports and some of them even at LaPointe.

I was General Manager of all business outside of the store. The next winter 70-71 I got out 3,000 cords of four foot wood for the boats to use the next summer. The first trip up I sold them wood, but before the summer was over and not half of the wood sold, they all changed over and burned coal.

This was a great disappointment to me, for I saw all my hopes and expectations of making money out of cord wood go glimmering. As luck would have it, a stray boat would come along burning wood and I would sell to her. Then, sometimes a coal burner would run short of coal and they would take wood. There were no coal docks at Superior and Duluth, and none were built for several years after.

I was three years selling off those 3,000 cords and all this time I had to keep the dock in repair and a man and span of horses and a wagon to keep wood on the dock, which was quite an expense for such a small business. When I got through I was worse off than when I began, for I was owing debts, which I paid afterwards."

During the summer of 1871, most of the lake boats changed from burning wood to coal, which ended William Knight's hope for a successful wood yard on Oak Island. He was neither the first nor the last man to be put out of business by progress.

He wrote: "I got along somehow, holding town and county offices and working in the store (Jim Chapman's). In those days in Bayfield, money was very scarce and everybody was poor and nothing in the country had any value attached to it. Property and pinelands had no value. About the only resource money was tourists coming in through the summer to fish and some came for climate. 1872-73 were years that brought a rush of people from outside to enter pine lands and the U.S. Land Office was kept busy. After people bought pinelands, they had to pay taxes and that gave funds to improve streets and build a few roads.

The owners of the lands did not pay all they were assessed for and though the assessments were small, they would not pay even the small sum they were assessed. The county board supervisors would have to compromise with them and take what the taxpayer saw fit to pay. Our town and county books had been kept in such poor shape the records would not win a case in any court.

In 1872 and 73 the fishing industry sprang up. Fish was cheap, but it gave a modest living to the fishermen.

(Actually, the fishing industry had been given its biggest boost in August 1870 when the firm of N & F Boutin of Two Rivers, Wisconsin, located at Bayfield, bringing with them in a mass migration, 100 fishermen and their families, 12 pond nets, 650 gill nets, the schooner *Alice Craig* and other fishing boats.)

I think it was 1874 or 75 we concluded that we would open a new set of books and keep the records according to law, which was done. At that time, R.D. Pike was running his sawmill in a limited way, according to his limited finances, and that little mill and the fishing interests were the only resources of business we had to support the people. Pike was like the rest of us, poor as a church mouse, but we all were rich in energy, good health and full of hope that the day would come when Bayfield would be a prosperous and growing city.

August 28, 1875, this item appeared in *The Ashland Press*: "William Knight, Bayfield's worthy county clerk, was in town Saturday, looking up his many friends."

This was only one of the political jobs he held. Only recently H.J. Wachsmuth told me of my grandfather's victory in some long ago election, for what office he couldn't recall. But in celebration he jumped on his horse and led a triumphal parade down Main Street. The horse went up the stone steps and through the swinging doors of the saloon, which stood where the Hotel Bayfield is now. This particular saloon seemed to fascinate the men of the Knight family. At the age of three, my father made it there. He escaped from his baby sitter, crossed the dust filled street, and though somewhat hampered by the white tunic he wore, which was fashionable for children in those days, he managed to climb up the stone steps and under the swinging doors. Unfortunately, before he had time to order a drink, he was captured and taken home.

Not only civic jobs demanded William Knight's attention. Like most of the Bayfield pioneers, he took any job that came along. In June 1877, the Superior Times had this item. "General Bill Knight, proprietor of the popular Island Hotel at Bayfield is one of the jolliest and best natured landlords we ever knew. Bill has a novel way of advertising the hotel, too. He takes a piece of chalk and writes lengthwise on the sole of his boot the old and well known schoolbook copy, *A Man is Known by the Company he Keeps*. He then sits on the upper balcony and lets his feet hang down over the sidewalk. Strangers, as they pass under, look up and think it is the lettering on the awning. He sometimes rests his heels on the railing of the piazza and people see and read the sign from across the street."

Of course, his feet were not really that big, although he was a tall man. Within a few years he was in another business and no longer needed to use his feet for an awning.

April 14, 1888, this item appeared in the paper: "William Knight, general manager of the Ashland Brownstone Quarry Company's quarry on Presque Island, is preparing for an active summer's work. He has a number of men busy now and will send out more in a few days. His company has the contract to furnish stone for a new city hall at Cincinnati, Ohio, besides numerous other public and private buildings in various parts of the country. Mr. Knight is a hustler and his quarry promises to rank second to none on the lake."

For a time William Knight was in the fish business with Capt. MacDougal, buying fish and shipping them by boat to Ashland and then by the new railroad to Chicago. In 1875, he got into the logging business in a modest way, getting out 300,000 feet of lumber the first year, which was cut by R.D. Pike's mill, *The Little Daisy*. By March of 1882 he was doing better. *The Press* reported: "If nothing unusual happens, William Knight expects to finish getting in his 2,000,000 feet of logs on Buffalo Bay next week. Will has made a good thing this winter and we are all glad of it. It's just what he deserved."

The next year he had two logging camps and *The Press* reported: "William Knight recently put in a logging crew of 25 men at Frog Bay above Red Cliff. In his two camps, the other being on Pike's Creek, Mr. Knight gives employment to 50 men."

Logging was far from an easy occupation. The problems were many. In Harvey Nourse's memoirs, I discovered how my grandfather solved one of his problems. Mr. Nourse wrote: "About 70 years ago (sometime in the 1870's), we had a winter with no snow. Many loggers were left with their logs on skids. Mr. Knight was logging back of Bayfield. He was all ready to haul and did make several trips to the landing when the snow melted and no more came. So, in order to save his logs, he built a tram road, using straight Norway pines for rails and large flange wheels with which he built cars. The cars were pulled by horses and were equipped with brakes to hold them on the down grades. These logs were banked where the Pureair Sanitarium is located, then rafted and towed to the Pike mill in Bayfield."

In those logging days, genuine horsepower was used. Dec. 15, 1905, this item appeared in *The Press*: "The first of the week, William Knight and A.J. Mussell received a consignment of heavy draft horses, largest and finest ever seen here. Mr. Knight has one span that weighs almost 4,000 pounds. Skidding hemlock and hardwood logs called for heavy teams, and the day of the light weight horse for this class of work is over, if it would be done profitably."

William Knight logged for five years at Frog Bay and built his own sawmill at Roy's Point to cut the logs. In 1890, he started the first bank in Bayfield.

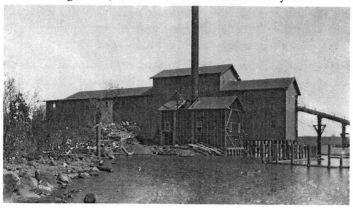

The William Knight Mill at Roy's Point Mill, approximately 1 mile north of Bayfield. (Photo: BHA)

In his memoirs he wrote: "Before I started the Lumberman's Bank, everybody was bellowing, "Why do we not have a bank where we could get a check cashed, anyway?"

Well, I thought I would see what could be done to start one so I called on every man who was doing business and they all said they would take an interest, so when I got all ready, I went around to sell all those who said they would take stock. I told them my object was to make it a home institution and have every one interested, even if it was but a small amount, and I would take what was left, much or little, but not a soul could I get to take a dollar's worth of stock. Col. Wing finally told me he would take $1,000 worth if I insisted upon it. By then my blood was up and I told them I was going to start the bank on my own responsibility and had hoped every man doing business here would feel pride in taking an interest in home affairs, but as they did not feel that way, I could not coerce them. I went on alone, started it up, and made it a personal bank instead of a state bank.

I soon found out what the trouble was. They all had stock in the Northern National at Ashland and she had put her foot down on their starting a bank here. I had no trouble getting deposits from the laboring class of people, but I had considerable trouble from the business men, who persuaded my depositors to take their deposits to Ashland and their bank would offer them more interest than I was paying.

Three percent was what they all advertised to pay, and did pay, except when they could steal my depositors away by paying 4%. But they could not get all of them at a greater rate of percent. After a few years they saw they were losing the fight so far as depositors were concerned and I was making them pay good rates of exchange and all other legitimate charges. They finally gave it up, as I was making money out of their meanness and they were paying the bills.

So in spite of all these obstacles, the Lumberman's Bank was founded. A picture of William Knight's little boy, Douglas, appeared on the checks as sort of a trademark. In 1904, the bank was sold to the First National Bank and it is now the Washburn State Bank, so Bayfield has had a bank for 68 years, ever since the Lumberman's Bank was started in 1890.

In 1890 Bayfield received by freight 4,067 bushels of potatoes and 723 tons of hay. *The Press* commented: "The items of potatoes and hay received show a condition of affairs that ought not to continue. The vast acres of pine, which are annually being cleared off, leave acres of stump land, which can be bought for a mere song. On these lands ought to be raised all the potatoes, hay and vegetables this community needs, with plenty to spare. Instead of importing such a large amount of produce, we ought to be exporting a much larger amount. What this country needs is more farmers."

Whether this item had any effect on my grandfather, I do not know, but he soon began to grow potatoes. The idea of growing them commercially evidently took hold, for Bayfield history readers may remember that in 1897, John Bjorge got tired of wheeling his potatoes to town in a wheelbarrow and built an airplane to fly them in.

William Knight oversees the ground-breaking of new apple orchards on the Bayfield highlands. Circa 1905. (Photo: Scott Hale Collection)

Potatoes were only the beginning. William Knight looked at the acres of stump land and thought, "Where these trees grew and were harvested only once, why not plant trees that will yield a harvest every year?"

He assembled men, horses and dynamite and began to work on the stumps. As fast as the land was cleared, he planted fruit trees. This was all an experiment, because up to this time no one thought fruit could be raised commercially here. Members of the State Historical Society did not believe it possible to raise fruit commercially so far north and had to be shown. There was plenty of evidence that fruit trees would grow here. There were cherry trees on Madeline Island believed to have been planted by the Jesuits in the 18th century.

In 1871, Mr. Pendergast, lighthouse keeper on Michigan Island, had a nursery there and experimented with many types of crops and trees.

Acting with faith on these bits of evidence he saw about him, William Knight planted his first trees in 1905, 20 acres in cherries and 20 acres in apples. The next year he planted 45 acres in apples and cherries. *The Press* reported on May 18, 1906, "William Knight is busy setting out 2,000 fruit trees this week. Mr. Knight has the land, the means and the disposition to make an orchard and he's going to do it." He did plant orchards so thoroughly that some are still bearing fruit.

Willam Knight was the father of the present day fruit tree industry in the Bayfield peninsula. Photo circa 1910. (Photo: Scott Hale)

By 1909 interest in horticulture was thriving here. Jan. 15, 1909, *The Press* reported: "William Knight, N.C. Carver and Carl Vollenweider attended the State Horticultural meeting in Madison, Mr. Knight going as a special delegate from the local branch of this society, which is the largest in the state, having more than 100 members."

Believing that Bayfield's future in agriculture was great and that marketing was one of the first problems to solve, William Knight became an incorporator of the Bayfield Fruit Association in 1910. Carl Vollenweider of Bayfield, and John Bissell of LaPointe were the other two. In 1912, this Association merged with the Bayfield Fruit Shippers Association and became the Bayfield Peninsula Fruit Association. This Association flourished and marketed fruit for farmers for over 30 years, became a Co-op in early 1940s and was liquidated in 1953.

Bayfield Fruit Association building. circa 1950. (Photo:BHA)

Just as he had been intensely interested in logging and banking, William Knight now switched his attention to agriculture and conducted experiments with all types of plants. I remember his blueberry project and only the other day one told me about the celery experiment. There were numerous other things tried and forgotten, but for his efforts in this field he was honored by the State Historical Society and was made an honorary member for outstanding work in the state.

In those pioneer days each household tried to put away a barrel or two of apples for winter. The market for them right in Bayfield was good. Nov. 8, 1884, *The Press* reported: "Winter apples are rolling into town at a lively rate. Last week there was received by boat upward of 200 barrels and as many more are expected. Twenty-two years later, boats were still bringing in apples. In 1906, "The steamer *Eber Ward* will be at the Dormer-Boutin company dock about next Monday with a carload of the finest apples at the loWest prices. When you hear her whistle, go down with your money."

In 1910 with the orchards planted and thriving, William Knight decided to run for State Assembly. N.E. Carner wrote the following letter to the Bayfield Progress urging every-one to vote for William Knight saying, "He has always been a man of action, of deeds and few words. He is not a man always going to do something and talking of what he is going to do. . .When chairman of the town board he built the city waterworks. . .When he announced today that he was going to do something tomorrow, you would see the work in progress. When the people were mourning that they had no bank in Bayfield, he announced one day that he would start one. In 30 days the bank was running. During the strenuous times of the '93 panic, not a man asked for money at his bank that did not get it forthwith, not being put off; no 30 or 60 days notice at his bank. No one knew he was going to build a sawmill until the machinery was on the ground and men at work on the building. No one knew he was to develop a farm and plant commercial fruit orchards until he was clearing land for that purpose. He has been an employer of men in this town for 40 years and never had a strike and all men were paid in full and I hear more good things said of him from the laboring men than from any other class of people."

That was natural. William Knight had been a laboring man. If he had not taken any job that came along and worked at it, he would have starved in the early days, and never lived to do anything.

He ran true to form in 1910. He announced he was going to run for assembly and was elected by a large majority, losing the vote only in the home territory of his opponent.

One day, Angus Defoe remarked about my grandfather, William Knight, "You know, I always remember him coming down the hill in a big blue cloud of smoke."

I remember him that way, too, and so do many others. But, so people who did not know him will not suppose he was a forerunner of Superman, I will explain that he wasn't exactly up in the air in a cloud, he was under it, driving a Willys-Knight touring car. Pale, blue smoke of a quality I have never seen before or since, poured from this car, wove itself around and above it until the car was almost invisible. But there was no danger of anyone being hit by an invisible car. The noise that came from the center of that cloud could be heard for blocks. Grandpa liked to drive in second gear. Sometimes he just forgot to shift gears, as he was preoccupied with his many agricultural projects and civic duties. Sometimes he drove in second because it was the easiest way to go up and down hills in those old cars.

It was an exciting time when he rolled over in the Willys-Knight on cemetery hill. The road was covered with loose sand, and was much steeper than it is now. Also, the wheels of that early make of car had no reverse strain, so if they were turned too far, they simply remained at right angles to the car and it would jackknife. That happened. The car jack-knifed in loose sand, rolled over completely and came up on its wheels again. There was nothing left of the top or windshield, or supposedly of William Knight. Horrified specta-tors ran up the hill as fast as they could. When they arrived, he was already out on the road. Blood from a cut on his forehead streamed down his face as he picked up scattered glass so no one else would get their tires cut.

When William Knight reached the age of 45, he had not married. One by one his friends had married, but he continued to live a comfortable bachelor's life at the LaBonte House. Mrs. DeMars, then Marietta LaBonte, remembers the evening in 1884 when the boarders were sitting around in the parlor after supper. William Knight was reading the Nov. 8 issue of *The Bayfield Press*. Suddenly he read aloud, "Miss Jessie Williamson of Edinburgh, Scotland, arrived in the village Thursday and will spend the winter with her sister, Mrs. Rev. St. George."

Jessie Williamson Knight with daughter Annie and son Douglas Knight. All children attended the Episcopalian Church as well as Bayfield Central "Low School" and Lincoln High School. Circa 1897. (Photo:BHA)

He threw down the paper and said, "That's my Jess and I am going to see her."

He did go to see her and in less than a year, they were married. October 8, 1885, *The Press* reported: "Knight-Williamson. The impressive ceremony of the Episcopal church was performed, Col. Cruttendon giving the bride away, and the solemn admonition, "Whom God has joined let no man put asunder" sealed a compact which *The Press* trusts will be fraught with peace and happiness for years to come."

As the years went on, William Knight continued his farming and civic activities with vigor. His civic duties extended from chairman of the executive committee to keep cows off the streets, through the vice presidency of the first Commercial Club organized in 1906, various city and county offices and the state legislature.

He broke his hip twice, but it only slowed him down a little. At the age of 87, he was one of the honored guests at the Paul Bunyan "Dinner-Out" held at Sebastian Feldmeier's wood lot. From the height of an old pine stump he addressed the crowd, telling them vividly of the days when forest covered all of Bayfield County.

At the age of 90 he was honored by the Masonic Lodge with a birthday party. He was a 50-year Mason, and no matter how many other activities he was engaged in, he found time for his Masonic work. This probably proves one of the old sayings, "The busiest people have the most time" or "As well have no time as to make no good use of it."

As his age increased and his twice broken hip bothered him, he decided to live at the Masonic home at Dousman, Wisconsin. The home has a long glassed porch where he could walk regardless of weather. At the age of 97, he had almost decided to give up physical labor for "brain work" and began, in collaboration with an elderly lady at the home, to write a book. Unfortunately they never finished it.

At his death, the legislature passed a resolution to be spread in the *Assembly Journal* as an express ion of respect for his memory and recognition of his services to his community and state.

I thank Hamilton Ross for summing up the character of William Knight in a letter written last April. He said, "I have noted with a great deal of interest the start of your articles about your grandfather Knight. I am very glad that you are doing this in order that the present generation may know something about the forward-looking work that he did for Bayfield and the whole Bayfield Peninsula.

"Where other people arrived, harvested the local resources and then moved on, your grandfather stayed to develop what looked like hopeless, cut over and exhausted land. As far as I am concerned, I believe he did more for the Bayfield community than any other one man or group of men. To me, he was the grand old man of the area."

The William Knight residence constructed circa 1890.
(Photo: Scott Hale Collection)

Currie Bell

Currie C. Bell: 1852-1921 (Photo) circa 1990. Bayfield County Press Editor "Devoted to the interests of Northern Wisconsin," was a weekly column from the editor that appeared in the Bayfield County Press every Saturday. Bell was a relentless promoter of kindergarten through high school education; he provided the editorial stimulus that roused the Bayfilders toconstruct Bayfield Central and Lincoln Hight Schools (1895). (Photo: BHA)

A GLANCE AT THE TOMBSTONE OF Currie Bell will tell you that he was born July 1, 1852, and died on Nov. 13, 1921. But it will not tell you of all the living he packed into those 69 years. For over 25 of them he was editor of *The Bayfield County Press.* 'nuff said, right there!

Thanks to Myrtle Judd Nourse we have the account of his arrival in the frontier Chequamegon Bay country. She writes: "When Currie Bell first came to the north woods he landed in Ashland. It had been raining, and on Second Street, a mere trail, wagons were stuck to the hubs in red clay. Mr. Bell went down to the waterfront and sat on a log while he debated whether to return home (to Waterloo, Wisconsin, where he had established and edited the Journal) or to go on over to Bayfield. He was feeling pretty blue and as he let one hand drop down to the ground, something cold touched it. He turned, and looked into the upturned face of a dog with a collar on. On the collar was the inscription, "I am Sam Fifield's dog. Whose dog are you?" He began to laugh, and went on over to Bayfield, where he remained the rest of his life."

Currie Bell was a natural born newspaper editor. The going was tough at times, as it is in most businesses, but his humor never seemed to fail. When he didn't write something funny himself, he picked it out of the exchange. This appeared in 1890: "An editor, who was evidently having a hard row to hoe, mused thusly: 'Lives of poor men oft remind us, honest toil has no fair chance; the more we work we wear behind us, bigger patches on our pants. On our pants once new and glossy, now are mends of different hue, all because subscribers linger, and will not pay us what is due. Then let them all be up and doing, send in their mites, though they are small, or when the snow and winter strikes us, we will have no pants at all.'"

During the winter of 1883, Currie made a serious mistake and violated an unwritten rule of the village. He shoveled his sidewalk! *The Press*, Dec. 23, 1883 said: "The editor of *The Press* has put his foot into it, and no mistake. Last Wednesday he had the temerity to violate one of the unwritten laws of the village by clearing the sidewalk in front of his residence of its covering of snow, and the entire community is up in arms, but most specially Sam Mahan and Major Wing, who join him on the right and left. They are massing their forces and threaten to take a summer vengeance on the author of his heinous offense. The editor, however, shows no signs of weakening and it is thought the Bayfield Rifles will be called out to preserve the peace."

Currie evidently was overruled, for it is still an unwritten law that sidewalks should not be shoveled, except on main street. You should shovel yourself a patch to the road and that's all!

But whether the sidewalks were shoveled or unshoveled, Currie Bell was for Bayfield, first, last and always, and commented, "Those individuals who persist in speaking ill of their home town ought to remember it is a filthy bird that befouls its own nest."

And though he would have gotten it for Bayfield if he could, he was forced to announce on March 1, 1890, "It is now definitely settled that Bayfield will not have the World's Fair."

Currie Bell wrote little about himself in the paper but he was in the habit of printing his own comments and bits of philosophy he picked up which revealed something of what he was thinking. From Dr. T. Chalmers he copies, "Every man is a missionary now and forever, for good or for evil, whether he intends or designs it or not." A German proverb: "Honor the old, instruct the young, consult the wise and bear with the foolish."

No telling who had been in *The Press* office just before these comments of his own appeared: "The kicker, like the poor, ye have with you always." No man who is ashamed to act as motor to a baby carriage has any business to butt into the matrimonial game." "Let those who tell us how to do things take us into their own grounds and show us; then will we listen in patience to their mouthings."

Feb. 16, 1884, *The Press* had this little story. "A certain lady, living not a thousand miles from Front Street, entered a closet a few nights since and on turning to come out hit her heel on the door jamb, bruising it severely. On complaining thereof, she was consoled by her companion with the remark that, 'It was supposed a woman of your age had more sense than to attempt to turn those feet in a three foot closet. You ought to have backed out.'" This will account for the rapidity with which one of our stately citizens was seen to make his exit to the street, rubbing the top of his head a few evenings since."

Who got hit on the head? We don't know, at this late date, but we do know that Currie himself was often described as stately.

A booklet about Bayfield and Bayfield County published in 1905 states: No man in Northern Wisconsin is better known than Currie C. Bell. . .In 1882 he came to Bayfield and purchased *The Press*, infusing into it a personality characteristic of himself, making it a dominant and powerful factor in the development of politics of this section of the state.

Mr. Bell was receiver of the land office at Bayfield for many years, has been chairman of his town for 11 years, and of the county board for nine. He has served as a member of the Republican State Central Committee for a number of years and also as a member of the State Fish Commission. To him, almost alone, is due the credit for securing the establishment of the fish hatchery near Bayfield, and many other marks of progress and advancement are the works of his untiring energy for the upbuilding of Bayfield, and the vicinity."

Securing the fish hatchery for Bayfield was one of the outstanding things that Currie Bell did for Bayfield. We have reviewed part of the story in the article about Capt. R.D. Pike. In a story published in the Bayfield Gazette April 7, 1904, "An Old Resident" says: "I know it to be a fact that Mr. Bell refused an offer of $2,000 a year and traveling expenses as a member of the State Board of Control, so as to accept a membership on the State Fish Commission, which pays nothing, so that he might work in the interest of Bayfield."

Let's just say that the good teamwork of Capt. Pike and Currie Bell made Bayfield put its best foot forward, and in October, 1895, came word that Bayfield, by a unanimous vote, had gotten the new fish hatchery which communities all over the state had been trying to secure for themselves. It meant that $16,000 was to be spent immediately, at what is now Salmo.

"An Old Resident" also writes about Currie Bell: No other man has ever been so long at the head of our town, serving twelve years on the county board, and for seventeen years as chairman of the town board, many years without opposition. . .In 1892 he build the first stone and brick building in the town, thereby setting an example for others to follow."

Does anyone remember who "An Old Resident" was, and does anyone have any copies of the Bayfield Gazette published from 1902 to 1904 and maybe longer? That "An Old Resident" was a great admirer of Currie Bell, there is no doubt, and his article gives Currie credit for serving three years more on the county board, and six years more as chairman of the town board, than does the county booklet. Who is right?

If any fault could be found with Currie Bell's paper it would be in the early days, when outside subscribers were probably few and everybody in town knew what happened anyway, as some stories were incomplete. For instance, "A good story has been going around town this week, but we guess everyone has heard it."

And in November, 1886, this item appeared: "Much credit is due Ed and Charley Herbert for the work they did in ascending the masts of the wrecked schooner *Lucerne* and cutting down the bodies of the dead sailors lashed thereto. To do it required a good deal of skill and nerve qualities, which the boys are not lacking in."

Naturally we immediately want to know more about the *Lucerne* and about the Bayfield boys who went out to the wreck that cold November day, climbed the shaking masts that stuck out of the icy water and cut down the bodies of the drowned or frozen men. But there is no story about it. Probably it happened just after *The Press* came out, and by the next week everybody knew about it, so only the information about the bravery of the Bayfield boys was published. In the summer of 1887, there was some salvage made of the wreck, but still no details were given of the sinking.

This item appeared on July 2, 1887. "Capt. Brown and his crew who have been at work on the *Lucerne* have secured all they could from the wreckage. It was ascertained that an effort had been made to anchor her during the storm in which she was lost last fall; her largest anchor weighing two and one fourth tons being thrown overboard and about 80 fathoms of chain having been dragged by it."

Does anyone remember how and where the *Lucerne* was wrecked? Currie Bell evidently believed that his first and most important editorial duty was to build up Bayfield and answer immediately anything that was said about Bayfield in any other paper.

On May 3, 1884, he replied to Sam Fifield, editor of *The Ashland Press*, "It is true, as *The Ashland Press* last week intimated, that the first of this week this harbor had a goodly supply of floating icebergs. But they all bore the marks of Ashland Bay, viz: Lots of mud on their hoary sides. Sam, the next time you send your icebergs up here to melt, scrape the mud off and they will not prove a give-away on that great "natural harbor" the bottom of which is so near the top."

On Jan. 5, 1906, the *Washburn Times* paid Bayfield this compliment: "Bayfield is reported to be one of the liveliest towns in the northern part of the state. We heard one person say that he had lived in Bayfield over twenty years, and that at no time during that period had business been as good as it is now. By the way, did you ever hear a knocker from Bayfield? We do not believe that you have. We have had occasion during the last few months to talk with hundreds of people from our sister city up the bay shore and have never met with one who has anything but good to say of his home town. . ."

Currie commented: "Up here, Bro. Oscar, if we find a knocker we treat him to a plunge bath off the end of one of the docks. . .We can stand a kicker, one who is always kicking to have things better, but a knocker is of no earthly use."

And *The Bayfield Press* got the last word here, too, back in 1883. The *Duluth Tribute* stated: "Eight or nine of the Ashland-Bayfield excursionists were left in this city Sunday night. The Steamer Barker returned without them. Perhaps they attended church, but it is more than probable that they were elsewhere when their boat whistled for departure."

Currie replied: "Just why it is more than probable they were elsewhere the *Tribune* man fails to state, but we presume he had the boys in tow, and is not disposed to give himself away."

The Currie C. Bell building, home of the Bayfield County Press. The press office is located at the far right of the building. The Bayfield Pharmacy occupied the Western three quarters fo floor space. (Photo: Burt Hill Collection)

The constant comment exchanged by Currie Bell and the editors of other papers made good reading through the years. Even a simple meal of parsnips was the basis of humorous exchange.

May 2, 1891 the *Colby Phonograph* said this: "Currie Bell of *The Bayfield Press* is bragging that he had a mess of fresh parsnips on the first of April. We noticed the commission merchants of Milwaukee shipping fresh parsnips about that time, and we consider it strong evidence of prosperity to be able to buy them."

The *Washburn Times* jumped in with this comment: "They were last year's parsnips, been in the ground all winter, Bro. Shafer. Don't be too envious."

Currie had the last word: "As evidence of the untruth of the above assertions the editor of this paper begs leave to state that he has had parsnips and other garden truck taken directly from his own garden for the last three weeks, a continual feast of it. What editor did the *Colby Phonograph* ever know who could afford to buy early garden sass at prevailing prices, and what human being ever lived who would let such succulent dainties stay in the ground all winter?"

On Aug. 16, 1884, the *Duluth News* said: "Bayfield, down the lake, is doing considerable bragging about her baseball club. Possibly after they have beaten every other club on the lake, a scrub nine from Duluth could be induced to wipe the field with them."

The Press said: "Trot out your scrubs; it's probably the best you have."

Here are a few of the numerous principals Currie Bell listed for building up a town. "Talk about it. Write about it. Help to improve it. Speak well about it. Beautify the streets. Patronize your merchants. Be courteous to strangers that come among you, so that they may go away with a good Impression."

It wasn't always easy to get out *The Press* as an item of Aug. 9, 1907 reveals: "During the past two weeks *The Press* has been issued under difficulties. The publisher's eyes are so poor he can't see a cat hole in a barn door. Foreman Hill has been confined to his home nursing several carbuncles on the back of his neck, and the work of the office has fallen on the shoulders of the editor and the devil, a combination equal to almost any emergency."

Currie Bell changed the name of his paper from *The Bayfield Press* to *The Bayfield County Press* in December 1882, the same year he purchased it. And that was not the only change he made. Articles began to appear in a new, humorous and sometimes sharply pointed style of writing that was purely Currie Bell.

He enjoyed kidding his good friend, Dr. Hannum.

Sept. 12, 1885: "Dr. Hannum has let the contract for the construction of his new residence on the corner of Washington Avenue and Second Street. It is said the contract calls for an iron roof, in order that Doc's genial laugh while entertaining his friends will not raise the shingles."

March 13, 1886. "Dr. Hannum has been on the sick list during the past week, but under the skillful treatment of the medical editor of *The Press* is rapidly regaining his old time vigor."

Feb. 23, 1889. "Mrs. Henry Hannum took the Tuesday morning train for St. Paul, where she will spend a couple of weeks visiting friends. The genial doctor will wear a long face till she returns."

Sept. 21, 1889: "Mrs. Dr. Hannum has gone to North Bloomfield, Ohio, where she will visit with friends for a space of several weeks. The haggard, careworn appearance, which our erstwhile sunshine making doctor presents as he wrestles with pots and kettles, would wring tears from a bone yard."

July 28, 1888. "Dr. Hannum dropped in just as we were closing the forms to tell us there was a new doctor in town. Office at residence, corner Second Street and Washington Avenue. Fighting weight 10 pounds. *The Press* extends most hearty congratulations."

Feb. 3, 1894. "Dr. Hannum has successfully secured a very fine flash picture of the interior of Bayfield's brownstone cave, located just north of Dalrymple's dock. The cave is easy of access this season of the year and will repay a visit. Go armed with torches. A guide is not necessary."

What happened to this cave? Is it still there, or did it collapse when the Bayfield Transfer Railway was built?

Editorials on many subjects appeared in *The Bayfield Press* . This appeared in the issue for March 14, 1891.

"Lift your hat reverently when you meet the teacher in the primary schools. She is the good angel of the public. She takes the bantling fresh from the home neat and full of his pouts and passions an ungovernable little wretch, whose own mother admits she knows her business, takes a whole car load of these anarchists, half of whom, single-handed and alone, are more than a match for both their parents, and at once puts them in a way of being useful and upright citizens. At what expense, patience, toil and soul weariness? Hers is the most responsible position in the whole school and if her salary were doubled she would yet receive less than she earns."

Currie Bell could point with pride, or he could point with scorn. May 19, 1900 he said: "Yes, the man who knows it all was in evidence at the fire."

And he did not hesitate to say, "A man well known in Bayfield, but not well liked."

Through the years Currie Bell kept kidding Sam Fifield, editor of *The Ashland Press* . On Jan. 19, 1884, he said: "One night the first of this week a sneak thief attempted to enter the residence of Bro. Fifield at Ashland, but a whack on the head induced him to decamp empty handed. Times must be getting hard when thieves attempt to make a raise in the residence of a country editor. But it is altogether possible that this thief was a new hand at the business and when he finds out his mistake he will hate himself to death."

Sept. 10, 1892. "Gov. Fifield brought over a pleasant party of high much-a-much and muchesses from Ashland last Wednesday on the Stella."

Dec. 18, 1897. "There is not enough ice in Bayfield harbor to make a cocktail for the mayors of Duluth and Superior."

The Press always boasted the Bayfield harbor and in June, 1883, said: "The question is frequently asked, 'Why do so many boats enter Bayfield Harbor in the night?' It is answered by vessel men, 'Because it is the only harbor on the lake which we can enter in the night with perfect safety.'"

Although Currie Bell published a weekly newspaper here for over 25 years, we find little in it about himself. He lived in Bayfield for 39 years, was married twice and had three children. That he didn't miss much, is shown by his weekly accounts of the town's activities.

In October, 1908, the Iron River Pioneer said: "*The Bayfield County Press*, the oldest paper in Bayfield County, passed its 34th mile post with the last issue. Like the essence of corn juice, *The Press* improves with age."

Subscriptions to the paper were solicited with humor: October 1906: "A man in Iowa was soundly thrashed last week by his wife for not paying his newspaper subscription after she had given him the cash to do it. May her crown be trimmed to order and her harp have an extra string."

Sept. 27, 1884 *The Press* drew attention to its advertisers by saying: "It is not polite to go where you are not invited. Look through the columns of *The Press* and trade with those who invite your patronage."

Currie Bell predicted a happy day in Bayfield's future on Aug. 23, 1907 when he wrote: "The town board has appointed a new cow catcher whose motto is, 'All cows look alike to me.' The day is bound to come when the streets of Bayfield will not be used as a cow pasture."

He was right, but the city cowcatcher cannot be given the credit. A new mechanical wonder drove the cows back to their lawful pasture – the automobile.

Currie Bell's son, Donald C. Bell, had become editor of *The Press* when this story was published in May, 1910. "The number of automobiles in this city is rapidly increasing. The new Ford machine of A. H. Wilkinson arrived and proves to be a dandy. F. Boutin, Jr. and William Knight both expect their machines in a week or so. When these arrive, Bayfield will boast of six machines as follows: H. Nourse 2, and one each of F. Smith, A. H. Wilkinson, F. Boutin and William Knight. The coming of these machines will undoubtedly be of a great benefit to Bayfield in more than one way, and especially in a new energy on the part of car owners for better roads which will undoubted have to come."

These new cars were hard enough to drive without cows standing around in the road, so the cows had to go and it has been many years since a cow was seen strolling along main street.

Over and over through the years Currie Bell enumerated the advantage of Bayfield. He had been in Bayfield for slightly more than a year when he wrote this. It appeared on Dec. 8, 1883: "*The Press* ventures that not another town in the northWest the size of the Harbor City can boast of being supplied with as many evidences of civilization and conveniences. Water works, street lamps, telephone exchange, fire apparatus, town house with fire proof vaults, hotel now the largest open in northern Wisconsin supplied with electric bells, bathroom, etc., churches of three denominations, schools, sidewalks and the only brownstone courthouse in the country outside the city of Milwaukee."

Currie Bell wrote this about the Christmas of 1906: "Christmas this year was one of the most pleasant days ever experienced by local holiday pleasure seekers. Even the sun, after taking one peek above the tree tops of Madeline Island decided to celebrate and rose amid a glory of colored beams to spread cheer and warmth and radiate a happiness of Christmas cheer and good fellowship among mankind. The air was warm and balmy and all day the merry tinkle of the sleigh bell was heard and the laughing and shouting of the young folks on the hill. . .There seemed to be no one who did not share in Christmas Joys."

People reading these stories of Bayfield's history have realized by now that at least half of what I write belongs to Currie Bell. It is his faithful recording of Bayfield events, touched with humor and plain speaking, that has made many of the stories possible. He is the one who knew where Jim Chapman was fishing, what Capt. Pike was building, who Dr. Hannum was bringing into the world. The old hackneyed phrases all shine with new truth when applied to Currie Bell. He was a "good judge of character," had a 'keen interest in human nature' and was a 'fine, outstanding citizen.'"

The *Washburn Times* in May, 1897 printed this item: "Currie Bell, who is known as the 'tall sycamore from Bayfield' represented his town at the board meeting last Tuesday. Just why he should be known as the 'tall sycamore' is a point we never could quite make clear. He has lived nearly all his life in Wisconsin, and it is a question whether he ever saw a sycamore. 'The tall pine tree' would be more appropriate. Currie has represented his town for years, the reason for it being that he always looks out for Bayfield first, the world afterward."

Perhaps that compliment paid by the *Washburn Times* best sums up Currie Bell's love for the town he had chosen for his home. Currie "always looked out for Bayfield first, the world afterward."

The New Year is a good time to catch up with unfinished business. But before I add to unfinished Bayfield history, I will ask a question about future history that Hi Hanson asked me.

"Is there going to be any dedication or formal recognition of the project in the ravine?" I don't know, so I'll ask the rest of you. Is there?

Also, we have one year left to get ready for Bayfield's Centennial. Walt Barningham reports that he is saving a horse for it and is looking for a fancy buggy. Are there any old cars around, like the 1909 model on Meyer's Drug Store calendar? Who has any suggestions for a Centennial program? Best question of all: Who has ideas for raising money?

Of all the stories that appeared in the *Bayfield History* series, the one about Johnny Sayles received the most comment. Maybe it's because so many people remember Johnny, but most likely it's because the people who remember him liked him so much.

Leo Casper sent a book of poems containing the French-Canadian dialect one Johnny used to recite so well, *The Wreck of the Julie LaPlante* by William Henry Drummond. It is the story of the sinking of the wood scow, *Julie LaPlante* with the loss of all hands, including Rosie, the cook. The last verse with the moral of the story is as follows:

> *"Now all good wood scow sailor men,*
> *Take' warning by dat storm*
> *An' go and marry some nice French girl*
> *An' leev on wan beeg farm.*
> *De win' can blow lak' hurricane*
> *An' s'pose she blow some more,*
> *You can't get drown on Lac St. Pierre*
> *So long you stay on shore."*

My brother Bill remembers going hunting with Johnny and his dog, Caleb. Bill shot the first bird. Caleb retrieved it and gave it to Johnny, and it was then discovered that Caleb would never give a bird to anyone else. As far as he was concerned Johnny shot and owned them all.

Caleb was probably the most famous retriever Bayfield ever had. He spent a good deal of his time picking up loose articles and taking them to Johnny. People got into the habit of saying, 'See if you've got my overshoes, will you, Johnny? I left them on the porch and I think Caleb got them.'"

Lloyd Church, now living in Los Angeles, wrote:

"You are probably right when you say nobody has forgotten Johnny Sayles, but it is likely that few remember him as I do. Johnny and I palled and worked together in the old "Opera House" for Archie Pine around 1905.

In addition to Johnny's duties as skating instructor and mine as skate repairman during the roller season, it was our job to convert the opera house from just that, with all its chairs fastened in groups of sixes placed on the floor from storage on the stage, to a ball room by restorage of chairs and waxing the floor, to a roller rink by scraping what was from the floor and chalking and again back to a theater.

The show season with the traveling theater personalities coming in was the most thrilling for us. The high spot of our excitement was the after curtain supper given by Mr. Pine for the cast and employees (Johnny and me) at the Rittenhouse. Anyone peeking into the opera house the next day when we were supposed to be sweeping out would probably have caught us reenacting some of the play of the night before. Johnny's later showmanship leaves little doubt that a good deal of the life rubbed off on him. For me it has left many pleasant memories and the thought that the Bayfield of today is missing something.

I didn't know Caleb, but the two beautiful spaniels Johnny had at that time were our constant companions. They did service as sled dogs for us in winter and swam with us in summer. It is quite apparent that his love of dogs never waned."

Well, Bayfield has not changed in that respect. It's still a great town for boys and their dogs. Just a few days ago I saw a fine hunting party of them heading up the ravine through the gap in our hedge. . .the gap we leave there especially for small boys and dogs to go through.

The Boutins

Nelson Boutin. (Photo: BHA)

THE ASHLAND PRESS FOR Nov. 16, 1872, had this item: "There is an old gentleman living at Bayfield who has nearly 100 children, grandchildren and great-grandchildren all living. He is the father of the Boutins of that place. The old gentleman is hale and hearty and is living with his son, Frank Boutin."

The Boutins had arrived in Bayfield in August, 1870, when the firm of N. & F. Boutin, Two Rivers, Wisconsin, located here, bringing with them 100 fishermen and their families, twelve pound nets, 650 gill nets, the schooner *Alice Craig* and a full complement of fishing boats, etc. They erected a store 25 x 80 and engaged in an extensive fishing business.

In December of that year the total amount of fish packed at Bayfield and LaPointe fisheries for the season was 15,000 halves. Number of men employed, 200. Value of product, $75,000.

In 1871, navigation opened on April 11, the ice cleared from the Ashland Bay on April 12, the light houses went on April 13 and the schooner *Alice Craig* departed for Ashland Bay with fish nets and crew. From that day to this present one, some member of the Boutin family has been in the fish business at Bayfield.

The next year one of the Boutins was caught by the hazards of winter fishing. The story appeared in *The Ashland Press* on Nov. 30, 1872, and is as follows:

"Benjamin Boutin, Esq. called upon us a day or two since and gave us a description of his late trip in a small boat from the north shore near Duluth to Bayfield. He started with his little craft with a fast wind, his boat being heavily loaded with gill nets, camp equipment and his family, consisting of five persons.

Edward Boutin Family: Top Left: Mrs. Kuntz, Solomon L., Henry W., Lydia (Mrs. Easton), Theodore, Estella (Mrs. White). Bottom: Mineva(Mr. Gonyon), Mary-Effie(Mrs. Hicks), Edward Sr., Mrs. Edward Sr. Edward Jr. (Photo, BHA)

The boat glided swiftly along with a fresh breeze from the northwest until within a short distance of Bark Pointe Bay when the wind shifted to northeast creating a heavy sea, compelling him to throw a portion of his load overboard to keep the boat from swamping. He endeavored to ride the heavy swells but the storm kept increasing and he was obliged to run for the beach.

When the boat struck the shore, he, with the assistance of his son-in-law, William Negette, and the breakers landed the craft high and dry. The boat was full of water and everything in it was wet through, the weather cold and ice making fast and his children nearly frozen.

A fire was made as soon as possible in the woods, where the trees were falling in every direction and the snow coming down thick and fast. Night was approaching and the cold wind blew a perfect gale, but Mr. Boutin knew he and his family had to grin and bear it.

Upon examination it was found that in lightening the little vessel in order to keep it from sinking, all of the provisions with the exception of a few pounds of sugar had been thrown overboard. This was an awful condition to be placed in, but not a word of complaint was made. The sugar was brought forward and all ate heartily and at a later hour enjoyed a few hours rest.

The next morning the wind came from the same direction and in order to make our account short, we would say that Mr. Boutin and family were wind-bound on that inhospitable shore for five days with nothing to eat but sugar.

When they left the place they were nearly starved and but for a cessation of the storm and a favorable breeze from the north which after a few hours sail brought them home, they would have undoubtedly perished, and only 40 miles away from their friends.

Such is a fisherman's life. They doubly earn every dollar received for their labor." Sixty years after Benjamin Boutin and his family were shipwrecked, with only a few pounds of sugar to keep them from starving; Allison and Wilfred (Manie) Boutin spent six days of severe January weather adrift on Lake Superior. A small can of sugar was their only food. They endured suffering and hardships that few men would live to tell about.

This newspaper account appeared in *The Ashland Press* on Friday, Jan. 15, 1932, in a story headlined *Extra* – Two Fishermen Reported Lost Among the Islands. "The Coast Guard Cutter *Crawford* and several fishermen from here were today on their way to the vicinity of Michigan Island, in the Apostle Group, to search for Allison Boutin and his brother, Manning...."

The boys were last seen on Wednesday, Jan. 13, two days earlier; but there is a reason for the gap in time before a search was started. Walter Parker, Benny Parker, Ulric Boutin and his sons, Allison and Manie, Joe and Cubby LeBel were staying at Michigan Island to fish. The afternoon of Jan. 13, Allison and Manie had been lifting and setting hooks. They returned to the island with their fish, and, as they had extra bait, went out again to set more hooks. They intended to come back soon, when the fishermen would all go in to Bayfield.

But after the boys left, the weather grew blustery. It was not until the next day that their father, Ulric and Walter Parker were able to launch a small boat and row to Madeline Island where they could reach a telephone to ask for help.

Capt. C. Christensen of the Coast Guard Cutter *Crawford* at Two Harbors promised to be on his way within the hour.

The story in *The Ashland Press* continued: "Fishermen in the vicinity have attempted to locate the men, but are not prepared to make a thorough search. It is feared the motor of the small boat may have stopped, and the men were driven upon the rocky shores somewhere in the vicinity of Michigan Island."

The story had the right angle. Their motor did stop. They were in a twenty-four foot, unnamed boat, covered with a canvas house. Water came in from the high seas and soaked the ignition so it would not start. They put out an anchor and went to work on the engine, while the wind and seas pushed them farther and farther away from the islands.

And then another frightening thing happened. The lamp they were using tipped over, exploded, and for awhile they did not know if they would be burned to death or drowned. They fought the fire and won, smothering out the last bits of it with their heavy oilers.

They worked through the rest of the night on the engine, and toward dawn it started. Taking a course for Michigan Island they ran through high seas until they could see the island, rising above the heavy steam on the lake. But even as they saw it the engine stopped. That time they knew it was no use to work on it. There was no more gas.

They tried to make a sail from some of their clothing, but failed. Their clothing was of ordinary weight. They had no extra heavy jackets or clothing with them. Once more the wind and waves pushed the boat toward the open lake, and there was nothing they could do to stop it."

On Jan. 16 *The Ashland Press* said: "The fate of Allison and Manning Boutin, about 25, who disappeared in a small open boat north of Presque Island last Wednesday was still unknown today as the *Crawford* and several island fishermen combed the island area for some trace of them. If the theory is correct that their motor stalled they may now be drifting helplessly about on the open lake, may be wandering about on one of the outer islands in search of shelter or food, or may be clinging desperately to the ragged rocks of one of the shores of an island.

The young men left Michigan Island with intentions of making a short cruise and then returning. They were reported to have little in the way of supplies, and no overcoats or other heavy clothing. . . ."

The Coast Guard Cutter *Crawford* docked at Bayfield Saturday night and left again at five AM. Boat crews were to be mobilized today to scour the area with a fleet of fishing tugs and other smaller ships in a last hope of finding the men alive.

Unless the boat beached itself on some portion of an island where there is a fisherman, the brothers have been without food or shelter since Wednesday afternoon. In the event that the boat was dashed upon the jagged rocks of one of the islands, where the rocky cliffs rise sheer out of the water for fifty feet or more, there is little possibility that the brothers saved themselves.

The Boutin Brothers, Allison and Wilfred (Manie) worked to save their lives with all the skill they had learned through their years on the lake.

They had a small airtight stove and broke up some fish boxes, which they burned as slowly and sparingly as possible. Allison remembers that Manie hesitated about burning the boxes, because they were new, especially strong ones their father had built himself. At that time they felt they would be rescued shortly. But they soon decided not to worry over what their father might say about the boxes. When the boxes had been burned they started on the floorboards of the boat. Finally, as the days passed, there was no wood left they dared to burn, for fear of weakening the structure of the boat. Then trying to keep enough heat so they would not freeze to death, they tore up old rags and a jacket, soaked them in crankcase oil and burned them as slowly as possible.

During the long, cold nights when they were tossed about, surrounded by thick steam rising from the icy water, they did not sleep at all. During the days they took turns sleeping, with one of them always on watch.

Once more the shifting gales took them back within sight of Michigan Island. They saw the top of it rising above the steam. The wind changed and took them out into the lake again. Twice they were in sight of the Michigan shore, and twice the wind took them away from it. There were hardly words enough to express their feelings as their hopes rose at the sight of land, and then were crushed as the wind and waves swept them out into the lake again.

They rationed the very small can of sugar, which they found tucked away in the bow of the boat, stirred it into water, managed to warm it a little on their small fire, and drank it. It was all they had for six days.

At one time while Manie was on watch he saw the *Crawford* coming toward them. He could see the spars high above the steam, then knew helplessly that the *Crawford's* course would carry them past. Though the boys shouted and waved, the crew apparently did not see them because of the steam and high waves. The feelings at seeing the *Crawford* pass them can only be imagined.

They shouted whenever they caught sight of land. Their throats became hoarse and sore, not only from the shouting, but from the oil fumes created by the slow burning rags. Their faces grew black, almost beyond recognition from oil smoke, and from fighting the fire on the first night out. Their hands were raw, and one of Manie's was becoming infected from frostbite. Ice had formed out from the sides of the boat, which steadied it some in the water, but they had to keep knocking off some of it to keep from sinking. As they knocked it off, icy spray dashed over them and their clothes became crusted with ice.

Allison says they suffered more from cold than from hunger. After the first two days, hunger seemed to leave them. But the cold bothered and pained them continually.

During the long hours they swore to each other that if they ever got ashore they would never go out on the lake again.

On Jan. 17, as they were trying to knock some ice off the boat they heard a dog barking. They answered, with what shouts they were able to. They could not see the shore through the steam, but the dog evidently heard the sound of them pounding off the ice, and was barking at the sound. Later they learned the dog's owner had come down on the beach to see what the barking was all about. The man looked out with field glasses, but could see nothing through the steam, and could not hear the distant sounds as the dog could. He had a boat and outboard at his cabin, and could have reached them in fifteen minutes. But seeing and hearing nothing, he turned and walked away.

Monday, Jan. 18, *The Ashland Press* said: **No Trace Of Lost Fishermen.** "The search continued today for Allison and Manning Boutin, but there was little hope of finding the two men alive, since they have been missing for six days. The *Crawford* traveled along the south shore of Lake Superior as far as Ontonogan, but found nothing, which might indicate the fate of the two men.

The theory is advanced that the boat might sink, due to heavy ice forming on the canvas top, which the men are believed to have put up when the weather got bad last Wednesday. Heavy snow made visibility poor on Sunday. But the *Crawford* searched regardless of weather conditions.

It was the morning of January 18 that something happened which Allison says he can never explain. The boys suddenly saw sheer cliffs rising ahead of them above the steam bank. High waves were forcing the boat right toward them. With what strength they had left they wrapped matches to keep them waterproof and prepared to try to jump to a place of safety when the boat crashed against the cliffs.

Then, as suddenly as though the boat was under power, it turned and bow first ran along the shore, parallel to the cliffs, a safe distance out. Allison says it might have been a strong current, running parallel to the shore, which caught and turned them. But he didn't know then, and he doesn't know now. He only recalls that the boat ran along, bow forward, just as though it was being pulled. It ran safely in this manner until the dangerous cliffs were passed and then, on the only strip of sand beach for miles, it was tossed up, bow first, at Union Bay, West of Ontonogan. They were saved, and just in time, for as Allison recalls they would not have lasted much longer and shortly after they landed, a strong offshore wind began to blow, a wind which would have carried them far out into the lake.

The men climbed out of the boat and Manie, reaching the sand, stumbled and fell over a tiny piece of wood. He lay on the beach and laughed. When he was able to get up the boys found that walking was almost a forgotten skill. They stumbled and tripped over every small stick and stone. In this struggling way they managed to travel a full mile to a cottage they could see in the distance.

When they knocked on the door a man looked out at them. Allison told him their names, but the sight of their oil-blackened, unshaven faces, caused the man to shut the door. Allison, with a last bit of strength managed to cry out "Wait!" and to keep the door partly open with his foot.

The man hesitated, then repeated their names. "Say!" he said. "Are you any relation to Ed Boutin? I used to fish with him here at Union Bay."

They told him that Ed Boutin was their grandfather, and at that the man, Louis Cook, threw open the door and asked them in.

Mr. Cook quickly set the table and in the center of it put a big kettle of rabbit stew. Suddenly he looked at them. "Did you tell me you hadn't eaten for six days? Then you don't get any of this!"

Allison and Manie sat there, too weak to fight him about anything, and watched him clear the table. Then he took the boys to the house of a doctor.

The doctor did not feed them either. He gave them some brandy and put them to bed. Manie remembers it was a feather bed. He sank down into it for his first rest in almost a week. He was sound asleep when he heard a voice calling his name over and over. When he managed to rouse up and answer, there was Glenn Scott, editor of *The Bayfield Press* , wanting the story of their shipwreck.

When Manie was weighed, it was discovered he had lost 16 pounds. By then he was able to joke enough to recommend going adrift to anyone who wanted to reduce quickly.

The next day the boys began to eat slowly, and after the first square meal, went out to look at their boat. Forgetting their vows to stay on land the rest of their lives, they began to repair the motor so they could go home.

One of the first people who saw them at Union Bay was Jack Supple, of Bayfield, who owned some property near there. Not knowing the boys had been rescued; he was walking along the beach, looking for traces of wreckage.

The south shore fisherman gave the boys help and food and their father, Ulric, wired them money. When the boys started home, they took an orange crate full of food. They ate all the way home, finishing the last of it when they came to the stick at Madeline.

The Ashland Press reported: "The Boutin brothers arrived here (Bayfield) about 3 o'clock this morning after they had repaired their boat and engine and had driven their boat from Union Bay to Bayfield. The two men said this morning that they wanted never again to endure the hardships and experiences of drifting on Lake Superior in a small boat for six days and six nights."

That last sentence must belong in the department of understatement.

Manie recalled another last line in a newspaper story: "Only a Boutin could survive." Said as a joke, perhaps, it is nevertheless a tribute to the Boutins, who came to Bayfield in 1870, earned their living from the lake by fishing in small sailboats and grew healthy and strong from hard work.

Another tribute to the Boutin brothers appeared in the Squibbers column of the *Ashland Daily Press*: "Congratulations. The citizens of the entire Chequamegon Bay region unites today in extending congratulations to two men who though lost have been found, Allison and Wilfred Boutin, Bayfield fishermen. Very few of us will ever pass through privations of the nature visited upon these men during the last five days. For that we can be thankful. Adrift on an open sea, little food, light clothing and high waves, the brothers often must have despaired of ever reaching shore again. But they did not let their despair carry them away. They kept on fighting, and now, after a terrible experience, once more they are safe.

The world would be a better place in which to live if we all could learn the lesson this harrowing trip has taught these two men. Regardless of how small their chances, they kept on fighting, and at last they won through.

To them for their indomitable spirit, which kept them going against, overpowering odds, are congratulations due. While to those of us who remain safe on shore a lesson has been learned. The Boutin family moved to Bayfield in 1870 and by 1873 they were taking an active part in the upbuilding of the town. Five of them were members of the Bayfield Rifles. Duffy Boutin was Second Lt., Sol Boutin was 2nd Sgt., Edward Boutin Sr., was 1st Cpl. and Edward Boutin Jr. and Nelson Boutin Jr., both twenty years old, were members of the company.

Two Boutins, Nels and Sol, served as sheriffs of Bayfield County in the early days.

In 1870, the Boutin fish business supported 100 fishermen and their families.

Many news items appeared about the Boutins. Duffy was evidently a civic leader. And among the stories it must be noted that two Boutins were on the basketball team when

Bayfield beat Washburn in 1909. On the team also was Paul Johnson, the only member who still lives in Bayfield.

The story is as follows: "In one of the most exciting and hotly contested games of basketball ever played in this city, the Washburn basketball team went down to defeat at the hands of the local team, which consisted of Allen and Francis Boutin, Nelson Brigham, Harrison Mussel and Paul Johnson. The game throughout was replete with brilliant plays and despite the fact that the teams were evenly matched in weight, the superior skill of the Bayfield lads was in evidence many times. The game was perhaps the roughest ever played in this city and in many instances the mix-ups resembled a football scrimmage. An extra large crowd was in attendance. In fact the hall was crowded to its capacity. The final score: 23 to 15 in favor of Bayfield."

The wedding of Mr. John Holahan and Miss Lucille Boutin, daughter of Mr. and Mrs. Frank Boutin, was the social event of 1905. A long account of the wedding appeared in *The Press* and the next week on Oct. 13, this item appeared: "An error crept into *The Press* last week which, of course, is something very unusual, and for which we are sorry. In the wedding announcement of Mr. John Holahan and Miss Lucille Boutin, we stated that the father of the bride presented her with one thousand dollars. Instead of one thousand dollars, it was eight thousand dollars."

Generous with his children, Frank Boutin was also generous with his church. One of his gifts is still used and heard by us today. In April, 1909, the four bell chimes he gave to the Holy Family Church were installed. Bishop Schinner of Superior said Mass. Fr. Casimir delivered an excellent sermon in Chippewa and Fr. Patrux of Odanah delivered a sermon in English.

Many beautiful parties were given in the Boutin home, now the new Sister's Convent. Here is a newspaper account of one given in 1910. "Miss Meta Boutin entertained at a very pretty lawn party. . .The party was one of the social successes of the season and most unique in plan of entertainment. The invitations were in poetry and each gentleman was requested to bring a light, owing to the absence of the moon. The array of lights, which finally assembled, included ordinary lanterns, torchlights, auto lights, launch lights and jack-o-lanterns. According to arrangements, the gentlemen were to use these in searching for their partners, who were hidden about the grounds, and, who wore corresponding cards. The menu, which was very delicious, was served on the large veranda, which was decorated with Japanese lanterns. Frank Hannum won the prize for the best written acceptance in poetry."

One of the first cars in Bayfield belonged to Frank Boutin. July 10, 1910 *The Press* noted: "The new automobile of Frank Boutin's arrived. It is a 30 h.p. Packard and carries 7 passengers."

One of the most interesting of the Boutins was Frank Boutin, Sr., sometimes called "Uncle Frank." Lloyd Brigham wrote this story about him. "The whaleback steamer, *Christopher Columbus*, brought an excursion party down from Duluth during the time the lilacs were in bloom. It was a large crowd and took over the town. After awhile they started picking lilacs and being boisterous stripped everybody's bushes they could lay their hands on.

Old Frank Boutin had a store across the street and to the north of what was known as Baldwin's corner, across the street to the West of where the Booth Fisheries office now is.

He stood there at the head of the dock, plumb disgusted. Finally he took out his keys and said, 'Boys, there are several cases of rather old eggs in the back room.'

The crowd on the boat were a fair target before they could let the lines loose and get away."

In case this seems like a blot on the well-known hospitality of Bayfield, remember that we wait through a long, cold winter before lilacs bloom here. I'd say Frank Boutin gave those lilac thieves a sporting chance by letting them start for the boat before he turned the boys loose with eggs.

In that same spirit one of the Boutin boys of this generation performed a good deed for our community. Last deer season he was taking an out-of-town party to one of the islands to camp. They had been drinking before they got on the boat, and, though he warned them to stop, they continued drinking as the boat headed out into the lake. Finally they reached a state, which could only be described as drunken. When Mr. Boutin saw they were far too irresponsible to be put ashore on a strange island in Lake Superior, he told them he was taking them back. This brought forth violent protests. One man pounded his hands on the net lifter and demanded to be taken to the island. But it was no use. Ignoring their protests, Captain Boutin turned his boat and took them to Bayfield.

For that he should have a good citizenship award. He knew that turning a group of drunken men loose in the woods with high powered rifles not only endangered their lives, but the lives of others. There was also the danger of them falling into the lake and drowning as they swung a bucket off the dock for water. Wandering only a short distance into a strange and thick woods they could fall and freeze to death.

I heard the story several times last fall, and everyone who was standing around to put in their two cents worth seemed to agree that Mr. Boutin did exactly the right thing. Like old Frank, this modern Boutin had a pride in and a sense of responsibility toward his own community. He knew that hospitality has its limits. Guests are welcome. Vandals are not.

The boats owned by the Boutins have their own special place in Bayfield history. The first one was the schooner, *Alice Craig*, which came to Bayfield with the Boutins in 1870. The *Craig* was originally built and used as a revenue cutter and was purchased by the Boutins in Chicago in 1867. At that time she was considered the fastest and handsomest sailing craft on the lake. Capt. Thomas Henry Bunker, one of the old time lake captains, commanded her.

The *Alice Craig* sailed through all kinds of weather, had many adventures, and it was only when the weather beat her up badly that any notice of it was taken in the papers. On June 17, 1871, *The Press* reported: "In a squall off Sand Island last Saturday, the sails of the *Alice Craig* were badly torn and she, with difficulty, reached this port, running under double reefed main sail. She had on board nearly 400 halves of fish at the time and stood the storm nobly."

When *the Craig* wasn't fishing, she worked at something else. Nov. 25, 1871, *The Press* noted: "The schooner *Alice Craig* took a cargo of shingles to Duluth for Pike."

That same year on Dec. 2, the *Craig* started on another trip to Duluth, but was caught in a terrible northeast storm. Capt. Bunker managed to run to Bark Point for shelter, and there the crew and several passengers had to abandon her and walked all the way through the woods to Red Cliff, nearly perishing from cold and hunger. Ice formed solidly around the *Craig*, but a south wind broke it up and a crew of fishermen succeeded in bringing the vessel into Bayfield on Dec. 16."

The *Alice Craig* met her final storm in November 1887. On Nov. 26, *The Press* reported: "Frank Boutin's schooner, the *Alice Craig*, is no more. She left this port Friday with a cargo of supplies for his camp at Siskiwit. She was caught in a gale on that night and went ashore near Eagle Bay. Her crew of five men succeeded in reaching shore in the morning and walked through the woods to Bayfield. . .Capt. Bunker is now quite ill from the effects of his experience. Mr. Boutin's loss will run into the thousands."

In 1909, *The Press* said, "Arthur Soper is exhibiting a curiosity in the shape of a copper spike, taken from the remains of the schooner *Alice Craig*, which was wrecked at Eagle Bay some 18 years ago. *The Craig* was a staunch schooner owned by Frank Boutin and used in the fishing and freighting here. At the time she was wrecked, she was commanded by Capt. Bunker, who died at Red Cliff last year."

The life of Capt. Thomas Henry Bunker, the *Alice Craig's* captain, was an interesting one. He was born in Johnstown, N.Y. on June 13, 1820. He commenced sailing at the age of 8 years, which, in this day and age we would consider a little young. He was employed on an Erie Canal barge at the age of 10. We would consider him a little young for that, too.

He came to Lake Superior in the schooner Mary in 1844 and landed at the canal at Sault St. Marie with a load of stone for the government docks. He was Captain of the *Alice Craig* for 18 years. After the wreck of *the Craig*, he was ill for several weeks in the Ashland hospital. He stayed off the lake one year and cooked for Irwin Leihy. He went to buffalo and brought the tug Boutin back to Bayfield and was captain of her the first year she ran in the fish business for Nels Boutin and S. Mahan.

The last five years of his life, Capt. Bunker lived at the home of John Soulier at Red Cliff. He died Nov. 29, 1908, at the age of 88, and *The Press* said: "He was respected and mourned by the many who knew him. He was an interesting old man, and had scores of friends in this vicinity."

The tug *Boutin* was a fast one. In the 80's and perhaps later, the fastest boat was entitled to carry a broom, straw end up, fastened to the pilothouse. On August 16, 1884, *The Press* said: "The tug *N. Boutin* carries her broom very high these days and shows a clear pair of heels to everything in the boat line that sails these waters. It is reported that on Tuesday she laid the *Waubun* on the shelf in a race from Ashland to Washburn. Capt. Nels says he has failed to hear from his Duluth challenge, but that the same will remain open during the season."

Apparently the Duluth boats did not want to compete with the *Boutin*, for on Sept. 13, 1884, *The Press* said: "The tug *N. Boutin* still carries the broom, Duluth wind to the contrary notwithstanding."

"Which Bayfield boat would be entitled to carry a broom nowadays?"

The *Boutin* was still going strong in 1889. On June 15 *The Press* reported: "There was quite an exciting race at this place Saturday afternoon of last week between the tug *Boutin* and the steamer *Emerald*. It is needless to say that the *Boutin* outdistanced her competitor."

The *Boutin* was working hard in 1890. We learn that: "The tug *Boutin* of Bayfield came into port this morning with a raft that looks as though it would cover several sections of land. It was sixty rods wide and one hundred rods long and contained about three million feet. It took ninety-two four-foot boom sticks to hold the boom. F. Boutin and son of Bayfield own the tug. This is the crack raft of the season and the largest tow that ever entered this harbor" – *Ashland Press.*

Dec. 14, 1906 *The Press* said, "The tug *Fashion* of the Dormer-Boutin Fish Co., did a great stroke of business in the Ashland harbor Sunday and Monday. The *Fashion* acted as icebreaker for two large ore boats which cleared from Ashland. The *Fashion* broke through eight inches of solid blue ice and received for its work $20 an hour."

The Fashon (Photo: BHA)

On July 10, 1910, one of the Boutin boats had a new job. "The gas boat *Superior* of the S.L. Boutin Fish Co., left today with 230 cases of strawberries from local fields."

Eighty-five years have passed since the first Boutin boat came to the Bayfield harbor, and Boutin boats are fishing here today. Quite a record.

Bayfield's Waterfront

Northern View of Bayfield, circa 1887-1895. (Photo: BHA)

The A. Booth Dock , circa 1906. (Photo: BHA)

The New Brunswick Hotel before the city dock was built, circa 1900.(Photo: BHA)

Booth fish tugs, under Captain Harry Brower, not only picked up the daily catches of commercial fish products and supplied the island fish camps with fresh groceries and supplies, but also served as tour boats for summer visitors to the Apostle Island. (Photo: BHA)

Left: The C. W. Turner served A. Booth & Sons from circa 1900 to 1938.

Right: The Apostle Islands. Captained by Elias Hendrikson, and crewed by engineer Elvis Moe and deckhand Lloyd Wicksten, the Apostle Islands spent nearly twenty years on duty and departed finally in 1958. (Photo: BHA)

The A. Booth and Sons longshoremen harvesting ice. Three by five foot blocks of ice were harvested as indicated, trolled up the ice slide, deposited in the ice shed in the background.(Photo: BHA)

Bayfield, Circa 1900

(Photo: BHA)

(Photo: BHA)

(Photo: BHA)

(Photo: BHA)

The City of Bayfield, Circa 1910

The southwestern edge of Bayfield. (Photo: BHA)

The central southwestern section of Bayfield. (Photo: BHA)

The central eastern section of Bayfield. (Photo: BHA)

The eastern section of Bayfield looking towards Bass Island. (Photo: BHA)

The tracks of the Bayfield Transfer Company run parallel to the beachhead and along Archie Pine's famous Bayfield Opera House, since replaced as Memorial Park. . (Photo: BHA)

Photo taken north and west of 205 North 5th street prior to 1913. (Photo: BHA)

Photo taken near Washington Avenue and 10th Street. Circa 1900. (Photo: BHA)

Photo taken from the "old Wooden Bridge." Circa pre-1913. (Photo: BHA)

The Solomon Boutin-Jacob Johnson Dock. Circa 1900. (Photo: BHA)

Chapter 2

Pioneers & Settlers

Alexander Henry

BAYFIELD WAS FOUNDED IN 1856, but in 1765, over a hundred families spent the winter on the site of this city. An account of that winter appeared in The Bayfield Press in 1871.

"In August, 1765, Alexander Henry, a trader, landed at what is now Bayfield and built a house just below Chapman and Company's store, and above Col. Banfill's house, occupied by F. Boutin, Esq. He called the place Chagawamig and says he 'found 50 lodges of Indians' there. These people are almost naked, their trade having been interrupted first by the English invasion of Canada and next by Pontiac's War."

"The Chippewa's of Chagawamig are a handsome, well-made people and much more cleanly as well as much more regular in the government of their families than the Chippewa's of Lake Huron. Adding the Indians of Chagawamig to those I brought with me, I now have a hundred families, to all of whom I was required to advance goods on credit.

At the expense of six days labor, I was provided with a very comfortable house for my winter residence. My winter food supply was the next object and for this purpose, with the assistance of my men, I soon took 2,000 trout and whitefish, the former frequently weighed 50 pounds each. We preserved them by suspending them by the tail in the open air. These, without bread or salt, were our food through all the winter, the men being free to consume what quantity they pleased, and boiling and roasted them whenever they thought proper.

After leaving Michilimackinac, I saw no bread and I found less difficulty in reconciling myself to the privation than I could have anticipated. On the 15th of December the bay was frozen entirely over. After this I resumed my former amusement of spearing trout and sometimes caught a hundred of these in a day.

My house, which stood on the bay, was sheltered by an island over 15 miles in length between which and the main shore, the channel is four miles wide... On the 20th of April, 1766, the ice broke up and several canoes arrived filled with women and children who reported that the men of their land were all gone out to war against the Sioux."

There were other settlers here before Bayfield was founded, but who they were, or why they were here, is beyond human discovery. All we know about them is contained in this article from *The Press* in August 1888.

"While digging the foundation of a house on north Second Street, a pine box was found which contained the skeleton of an Indian. It was wrapped in blankets and in the coffin were found a tin pail and spoon, thus proving that the body was not that of a white man. Who he was, or how long he had been buried, no one knows, but doubtless 40 or 50 years.

Father John says there is no record of anyone being buried there since the church on the mainland was started.

On the same lot, farther back, were two graves, which were surrounded by a fence in a good state of preservation. Whose bodies they are, and who built the fence, is a mystery. That the graves are old is proven by the fact that a poplar tree over six inches through grew upon the graves. The bodies were encased in good coffins placed in rough boxes and well trimmed, thus showing them to have been whites.

Verily this shore abounds in the mysteries of buried facts and histories to as great an extent as the storied castles and tombs of ancient days.

Admiral Bayfield

Admiral Henry Wolsey Bayfield. By it's name the city of Bayfield honors Admiral Henry Bayfield who prepared charts of Chequamegon Bay area from 1823-1825. (Photo: BHA)

WHEN I NOTICED THE CANADIAN flag flying below the stars and stripes on Greunke's new flag pole, I realized it was intended as a welcoming gesture for Canadians visiting our town. But the flag might have a greater significance, for Bayfield is named after one of the finest Canadian citizens, Admiral Henry Wolsey Bayfield.

In 1938, at the request of Mrs. Laurie Carlson, the life story of Admiral Bayfield was compiled by Deputy Archivist, Mr. William Bradley, of Prince Edward Island. Mrs. Carlson used the story in her booklet of Bayfield history.

One hundred and sixty years ago, Henry Wolsey Bayfield was born at Hull, in Yorkshire, England. He was a descendant of a very old English family, the Bayfields of Bayfield Hall.

From earliest childhood, the boy showed his love of the sea and ships and when he was ten years old, enlisted as a Supernumerary Volunteer in the Royal Navy. This was the beginning of a career that lasted until he had served under four sovereigns, George III, George IV, William IV and Queen Victoria. From the time of his enlistment at ten, until he died at the age of ninety, he either served at sea or lived close to it.

His bravery and intelligence led to rapid promotions. He first took part in actual warfare while serving on the ship, *Duchess of Bedford,* his ship, unsupported having engaged and defeated two Spanish feluccas. He was severely wounded in this battle. For his great bravery he received promotion and was placed on the staff of *H.M.S. Beagle.*

Here again he saw action, assisting in the rescue of a British merchantman and the capture of three privateers. When Lord Cochrane attacked the French in the Basque, Officer Bayfield proved himself to have such great courage and ability that his King presented him with a medal.

During the war of 1812, Bayfield served in Canadian waters and on proclamation of peace was appointed to assist Captain William Fitz-William on a survey of the Upper St. Lawrence. Here again he did such a good job that he was promoted in June, 1817, to the position of Admiralty surveyor.

During the war of 1812 the British had had trouble in navigating the Great Lakes. Admiral Bayfield's orders were to survey Lake Erie, River St. Clair, Lake St. Clair, Detroit River, Lake Huron, St. Mary's River and Lake Superior.

That sounds like quite a job for a man only twenty two years old, but he did it, and afterward came down to Quebec and began his charting of the waterways from Montreal to the coast of Newfoundland. And that was far from a simple little task, for it included the St. Lawrence River, Gulf of St. Lawrence, Anticosti, Strait of Belle Isle, Labrador, Prince Edward Island, Magdalene Isles, Cape Reton, Sable Island and all the coast of Nova Scotia from Canso to Halifax.

The charts of these regions by Admiral Bayfield were recognized as the most accurate and the standard charts of the Royal Navy as late as 1937, and as far as I can determine, they still are tops.

The vessel used for the survey was a small schooner, the *Gulnare.* For part of the survey he employed Indians with canoes and during this time he learned to speak at least five distinct Indian languages.

Bayfield is fortunate in having a photostat of the original map drawn by Admiral Bayfield in his survey of the Chequamegon Bay region in 1823-25. This map was secured for us and donated to us by Leo Capser of LaPointe.

Henry Wolsey Bayfield was promoted to the rank of Commander, Nov. 8, 1826, was raised to Flag Rank on Oct. 21, 1856, which was the same year that our town was founded and named after him. He was named a Vice Admiral in April, 1863, and Admiral in 1867, when he was 72 years old.

Henry W. Bayfield was married to Fanny, the only daughter of General Charles Wright in 1836. They made their home in Charlottetown, P.E.I. The roadway to his home was called Bayfield's Lane, but is now called Admiral Street. A good suggestion for a Bayfield, Wisconsin street if we ever have a new street to name.

Admiral Bayfield lived for almost 50 years at Charlottetown and during the time, published many works on navigation. When he died there on Feb. 10, 1885, at the age of 90, he was deeply mourned. When the solemn funeral processions wound its way to the railroad station, the train, at the orders of the superintendent, had been draped in mourning. In Sherwood cemetery in Charlottetown, you can find his tombstone, which says, "Faithful to his God and his Country."

Bayfield County was naturally named after the City of Bayfield, and in 1943, the name Bayfield went to sea again. The keel for *USS Bayfield,* attack transport, was laid on Nov. 14,

1942, and she was launched on Feb. 15, 1943. And again the name *Bayfield* made a proud record at sea. The *USS Bayfield* earned four Battle Stars during World War II, and just recently was in the news again for a rescue of survivors from a plane crash off the Pacific coast. A story about the *USS Bayfield* also appeared in a recent Reader's Digest.

Admiral Bayfield was informed that a new little town on Lake Superior had been given his fine and honorable name. On May 11, 1857, he responded to this information with a letter to Henry M. Rice, Bayfield's founder, saying, "I have received with much pleasure your letter of the 9th of April and the accompanying map of the town on Lake Superior to which you have done me the honor to give the name of Bayfield. I little thought when encamping there among the Indians 33 years ago that my tent was pitched near the site of a future town that was to bear my name. I trust that you will believe me to be very much gratified by this mark of your kind consideration and appreciation of my labors in those early times and that you will accept my sincere thanks with every good wish for the prosperity of your town. . . "

Henry M. Rice

Henry Mower Rice (1816-1894) Minnesota territorial Senator. Businessman and land developer of the Chequamegon Bay Area. Rice, along with businessmen from the Washington DC area formed the Bayfield Land Company and on October 9, 1854 filed for and was granted on March 21, 1855 a "land patent" for the present site of Bayfield. The Town of Bayfield, County of La Pointe, Wisconsin was commenced and "set out" on October 25th, 1858. Access to the vast pine and hardwood forests of northwest Wisconsin begins in earnest. (Photo: BHA)

SOMETHING OF THE CHARACTER OF Henry M. Rice, founder of Bayfield, is revealed in a letter he wrote to Col. Cruttendon here when he heard of the death of Paul Soulier. Paul died on Wednesday, Nov. 4, 1891, and is buried in the Catholic cemetery at Red Cliff. He was about 85 years old and was well known to all early Bayfield residents and visitors.

Dear Colonel: The sad news of the death of my old and faithful voyageur, Paul Soulier, was unexpected, for but last summer when I last saw him he looked in good health. Nearly half a century ago he accompanied me from LaPointe, via the St. Louis River, Sand Lake and Crow Wing, via the portage route to Leach Lake, thence via Cass and Winnebegoshish, back to Leach Lake, thence down Leach Lake River and the Mississippi to Crow Wing. From Crow Wing to Leach Lake we made a forced march in order to head off opposition to thwart our making a treaty with the villages, consequently we traveled without tents and otherwise as light as possible.

One night it rained until the next morning. What we had was wet and consequently heavy. We had a long portage to make, with four canoes and our baggage, all of which had to be carried on the backs of our men. Thinking I would be of some help, I took a small pack on my shoulders–when looking around, I found my men all sitting down. I asked in some surprise the cause. Paul got up, taking off his cap, and said that if I was to turn voyageur they would quit, and not one moved until my pack was put down. Then he added it to his own and all moved merrily on.

Although he had no book learning, he was brave, kind and courteous, a man of the woods and lakes, but a gentleman and one of the last of the old school. He has crossed the last portage. May his burdens be lighter in the next than they were in this world."

Yours truly,

Henry M. Rice.

On Saturday, Feb. 10, 1894, after the death of Henry M. Rice, this article appeared in *The Bayfield Press* .

"Vincent Roy, who had known the late Henry M. Rice, of St. Paul for about half a century says that his old friend was practically a god among the Chippewas and other Indians and one of the best and most generous men he ever knew. Vincent Roy had 146 acres in 1854 where Bayfield now is. It was high, dry ground and he thought it would make a good fishing station. He paid $200 for it. A few weeks later he sold it to Mr. Rice for $500 and bought 40 acres of land adjoining, for a few dollars, which he subsequently sold for $7,000, Mr. Rice having platted a city.

For many years Mr. Roy was the chief interpreter for Senator Rice in making treaties and participated in making many final treaties and removals of several tribes of Indians. "Indians would do almost anything," said Mr. Roy, "that Senator Rice told them was alright." He had a wonderful influence with them. I think it was because he was always kind and never lied to them. No Indian ever went to him for help without receiving it. I recollect once that Chief Hole-in-the-Day wanted a team of horses. Mr. Rice had a fine team with a double rig which he offhandedly gave to Hole-in-the-Day as though it were a match or a chew of tobacco. I think the rig must have been worth not less than $600. He was a perfect god with the Chippewas who called him "Wah-be-ma-no-min" which means White Rice.

A few days before he died, Henry M. Rice wrote Vincent Roy a rather lengthy letter in which he said, "I so often think of you and of the days and times of 1847, days of excitement with good appetites and nights that gave restful sleep. It is probable that I can start for home by the 20th of April and go to Bayfield early in June. Grand old Lake Superior still has charms for me. I wish you would write occasionally and let me know how you are and give me some news... Remember me to all your household.

Truly your friend,

Wa-Be-Ma-No-Min

Elisha Pike

Judge Elisha Pike and wife Elizabeth Kimmey Pike. (Photo: BHA)

Pike's Greenwood cemetery lot probably has the oldest tombstone in the cemetery. It is the one marking the grave of Mrs. Elisha Pike Sr., who was born in 1779, the time of the Revolution, and died in 1864, the time of the Civil War. She was undoubtedly buried in the old cemetery at Pike's Creek and later moved to Bayfield. Her son, Elisha Pike, his wife Elizabeth, his son Robinson Derling and other children are buried there, too. Among the tombstones is the one for R.D. Pike's baby boy, who died the same day he was born in 1890. His stone says consoling, "One Hour on Earth, Eternity in Heaven."

Elisha Pike and his family were here before Bayfield was founded. They came to LaPointe in 1855 and from there, crossed to the mainland in a rowboat, bringing in several trips their cow, oxen, tools and provisions. The oxen transported their goods up a trail through the woods to where the North and West branches of Pike's Creek meet. There Elisha Pike had a mill, a water mill, that had been built by the North American Fur Company in 1845 and later abandoned. He put up a log house and the family settled down to stay. They repaired and operated the little water mill in which nearly everything was made of wood except the saw and the crank pin. The shafting and pulley were all of wood.

The late A. H. Wilkinson had a fine collection of pictures of the early Bayfield settlers. When I looked at them he asked, "Don't you notice anything special about these people?"

When I said I did not, he explained, "Not one of them looks afraid. There isn't a scared looking one in the bunch."

He was right. The Bayfield pioneers were a sturdy, fearless and strong looking group. But just to be contrary, I went through the pictures again and managed to find one man who looked a little uneasy. When I showed it to Mr. Wilkinson he laughed, for the man was a national political figure, who used to visit here during the summer. It's too bad he didn't have his picture taken after a nice, restful vacation in Bayfield. He probably would have looked a lot better.

Certainly Elisha and Elizabeth Pike were among the sturdiest of our pioneers. Their picture shows that he had a square face with a short beard and dark, direct eyes. She was calm looking, relaxed, her hands folded on the lap of her best, black dress. A small neat bonnet covered her hair.

There was never any doubt that Elisha Pike was a man of courage, and age did not lessen his courage at all. When he was 57, unarmed, he took a loaded revolver away from a man who threatened him. The story is told in *The Ashland Press* , October 19, 1872, headlined, "Shooting Affair at Bayfield." One day last week a man by the name of McGillis, under the influence of liquor, created quite an excitement at Bayfield by flourishing a loaded revolver and threatening to shoot or fight everybody he chanced to meet. He finally had some words with Mr. E. Pike, who happened to meet him near Mr. Ley's store, and it seems he abused the old pioneer and pointed his revolver at him, whereupon Mr. Pike caught hold of the pistol and, in an endeavor to wrench it from McGillis' hand, it was discharged, taking off the ends of two of Mr. Pike's fingers, the ball lodging in the hand of another man who was standing nearby.

"McGillis dropped his weapon and attempted to escape, but was arrested by Sheriff Boutin and put in jail. He was brought before the Justice the next day and after a spirited trial was fined $50 and bound over to keep the peace."

To make a long, detailed story much shorter, it turned out that McGillis did not have the $50, but he thought he could get it in Ashland, so the authorities put him in charge of a deputy and sent him over there to get it. Nobody in Ashland would loan it to him, so he remembered a friend down near White River, who might be an easy touch. He and the deputy, whose assignment must have seemed endless by then, started off. Darkness overtook them and they camped in the woods for the night. As soon as the officer fell asleep, McGillis jumped up and ran away.

The newspaper story ended, "McGillis is evidently a dangerous man, and should be made to leave the country. His revolver has a sharp blade between two of the barrels which can be used as a dirk knife. We believe no attempt has been made to capture him and he is now probably exhibiting his muscle somewhere between here and Penokee Gap. Mr. Pike has his revolver, which he proposes to keep as a token of McGillis' friendship and brotherly love."

Elisha Pike, who came to Pike's Creek in 1855, the year before Bayfield was founded, was an old-fashioned man. His son, R.D. Pike, who was to become Bayfield's outstanding citizen, was a modern one. Perhaps this contrast can be shown in a small way by the sides they took in a Lyceum debate in December, 1870. "Resolved: That the right of suffrage should be extended to women. Affirmative: William Knight, R.D. Pike, B.B. Wade. Negative: N. Pike, T. Carrington, F. McElroy." As usual, there was no report of who won.

When Elisha Pike had his 59th birthday, his friends considered him a very old man, and honored him accordingly. *The Ashland Press* says on January 25, 1873, "Hon. Asaph Whittlesey of Bayfield sends the following to *The Press:* 'A resolution adopted at the Bayfield Club House Jan. 22, 1873–Whereas we understand that Judge Elisha Pike has this date attained the age of 59 years, it is therefore wished, hoped and earnestly desired that the Honorable E. Pike may live to enjoy many more years of happiness and pleasure and that his gray hairs may be associated with the memories of the past at Bayfield with joy and pleasure. James Chapman, President. B. J. Cooper, Secretary.'"

Elisha Pike may have seemed old at 59, but three years later he was still farming enthusiastically, and keeping accurate records of the crop yields. This item appeared in *The Ashland Press* , Oct. 7, 1876. "Elisha Pike Esq. planted June 10, 1876, 1 1/4 pounds of the king of early potatoes, and on September 30, dug from that planting 163 pounds of potatoes. He got

53 pounds out of two hills in which were planted six eyes of the potato. He got 53 large potatoes from three eyes. T.J.L. Tyler planted at the same time quantity and the same variety and got 136 pounds of potatoes. Where can that yield be excelled? We challenge the world. The above facts are vouched for by several reliable witnesses.

They may have wished "the old pioneer" Elisha Pike a happy birthday in 1873, when he was 59 years old, thinking that his days were in small numbers. But he fooled them. In 1885, when he was 72, he and his wife had a wonderful celebration of their golden wedding anniversary. It took place at their old homestead, three miles from Bayfield, on Pike's Creek. The Pike's had a nice farmhouse by that time, but their first log cabin on the creek was still standing to remind them of their pioneer days together. Looking at the log house that now seemed so small, they could recall their arrival on the sandy shore of Pike's Bay in a rowboat in 1855, the journey with their household goods hauled by ox team along the bank of the creek, the building of the little house itself, for the beginning of their new life in the Wisconsin wilderness.

One hundred twenty five of their friends were present on that beautiful New Year's Eve in 1885. Four generations of the Pike family were there, too. The bridge over the celebrated trout stream, Pike's Creek, was spanned by an arch, decorated with the large inscription, "Golden Wedding 1835-1885." (*The Bayfield Press* had a drawing of it.) Friends arriving in their horse drawn cutters passed under the arch and came upon a scene brightly lighted by the dazzling headlight from a locomotive. Chinese lanterns were hung in the snowy evergreens around the house.

The Press noted at that time that Elisha Pike was born Jan. 22, 1813 at Malta, Maine. His wife, Elizabeth Kimmey Pike, was born June 6, 1811 at Meadville, Pa. Thirty years of their fifty years together had been spent on their homestead near Bayfield, and they had almost two more years together, for Elisha lived until Oct. 20, 1887, when he was nearly 74 years old. Elizabeth survived him, and died in 1892, at the age of 81.

Bayfield Kitsteiner — The Mark of Affection

Wanted: Information About Bayfield Kitsteiner, Ex-Resident

Eleanor Knight Asks the First of Many Questions Concerning Bayfield"s First Hundred Years.

W HATEVER BECAME OF LITTLE BAYFIELD Kitsteiner? We can tell you this much. Little Bayfield was the first white boy born here. At the time, the Hon. Henry M. Rice, founder of the city, said to Mr. Kitsteiner, "If you will name your son Bayfield, I will give you a town lot."

Mr. Kitsteiner did, and received a choice lot, located near the town hall.

When a second white child was born in Bayfield, Mr. Rice said to the child's father, "If you will name the child after me, I will give you ten dollars."

The father agreed, got the cash, and the boy began life under the name of Henry M. Rice Hochdanner.

What became of Henry M. Rice Hochdanner?

This much we do know about Bayfield. It was founded on March 24, 1856. The Hon. Henry M. Rice located the land, selected the site, and financed a large part of the deal. Bayfield was to be the terminus of a railroad to the lake. A party of nine men, in charge of John C. Hanley, landed here on that date. The first stake was driven by Major McAboy, and the town was named Bayfield, after Lieutenant Bayfield of the British Royal Navy, who was a particular friend of Mr. Rice.

After the stakes were driven, and the town named, the story of Bayfield becomes a story of people, their lives, their actions and reactions. It becomes a lot of things that the passing of time has labeled incidents, though, when they happened, they may have been for the moment the happiest, funniest, or most tragic incidents in the world.

The "Hermit" Wilson

BURIED TREASURE HAS A LURE and mystery that few people can resist. Yet, in spite of searchers, the hidden gold of Wilson, the Hermit, has never been found.

It is ninety-two years ago this month since Wilson died alone in his island cabin. But his treasure is still talked about. Nobody can quite forget it. Wilson and his treasure are mentioned in the September issue of *Better Homes and Gardens* this year. The magazine article described Wilson Island as one of the points of interest on a trip through Wisconsin. And in Bayfield, we acknowledge the story telling ability of the boat captain who took that reporter around the islands. You got us some nice national publicity, Captain!

The story behind the treasure is an exciting one. If every detail was known, it would make a book of history and adventure almost unbelievable. Unfortunately, time has erased all but the plain facts, and even the "facts" contradict each other at times. The first name of the man who hid the treasure has been forgotten, and his last name may have been assumed. But during the final fourteen years of his life he was known as Wilson, the Hermit.

His name, his treasure, and the man himself made such a powerful impression on the Chequamegon Bay area of Lake Superior that the Island is still called by his name locally, and is shown on government charts as Hermit Island. After Wilson took over that island all other names were discarded. The Indian name, Ashuwaguindad Miniss, The Further Island; Schoolcraft's name for it, Minnesota Island; and another name, source unknown, Askew Island.

Wilson was born in Canada of Scotch parents in 1792. Nothing special is known of his life until he reached 18 when he ran away from home, deserting a young French girl he was to marry. He got a job with John Jacob Astor's company and shipped out on a sailing vessel, making the hazardous voyage around Cape Horn and landing at Astora, the famous fur trading post on the west coast.

He spent six years there as a voyageur and hunter, a job that suited him exactly. During those years he traveled through the wilderness which is now California, Oregon, Washington, and British Columbia.

In his youth Wilson was a dark, unusually strong, handsome man. When he lived at LaPointe on Madeleine Island in later years he was described as a man of medium height, powerfully built, with keen black eyes and a heavy iron gray beard and hair. He was lithe, quick in all his movements. Fear was unknown to him, and because of this unusual quality he was a useful man at a frontier trading post. Nothing was too hazardous for him to attempt. And the things he did attempt, and succeeded at, grew into legends. These legends traveled through the country with the voyageurs, persisted all his life, and still do, ninety-two years after his death.

Wilson went into the wilderness whenever he felt like it. He lived with the Indians, fought them, and took part in various wars until his name became a terror to some of the western tribes. He learned every trick of woodcraft, warfare and frontier survival so well that he went where and when he pleased in the great American and Canadian wilderness. He had one good friend, his rifle, and he felt that was the real friend he needed.

But even in the midst of adventure thoughts of his Canadian home, his aged parents and the girl he had deserted so heartlessly must have pressed on his mind, because he decided he wanted to see them again. So, in 1817, when his term of enlistment with the fur company expired, he joined a party of six and started overland across the Rocky Mountains, crossing some of the same territory Lewis and Clark had explored in the years 1804-1806.

The journey was a terrible one. It took two years. The little group clawed their way over the mountains, lived off the land, dodged hostile Indians and finally arrived exhausted and thin at a trading post somewhere near the present city of Duluth.

Wilson rested there, but not for long. Once his mind was made up to go home he kept going. He joined a canoe expedition for Sault St. Marie and began another hard journey, filled with narrow escapes and long, tedious days of paddling.

When he reached home at last there were familiar scenes, but when he walked up the path to his parents' house there were no familiar faces to greet him. His mother and father were dead. His deserted sweetheart, instead of languishing heart-broken, had married a well to do farmer and was the mother of a large family.

He learned that his parents had longed for his return and had believed he would come back. Because of their strong feelings they left what property they had for him in care of the parish priest. It was a large sum of gold.

We find that, even with a fortune in gold to spend, civilization did not tempt him, and could not hold him for long. He returned to Lake Superior in 1821, enlisted in the service of the Hudson Bay Company and resumed the life of frontier roving he liked so well. He made trips to the far flung posts of the company throughout the interior of British America.

And here is where some of the "facts" contradict each other. One says that Wilson had a wife and daughter, whom he left at a camp near the Columbia River while he was on one of his lengthy trips. When he returned to the camp he found that they had both been murdered.

Another says he had a wife and daughter at L'Anse whom he took out to the Columbia River and there deserted them. Later, repenting of this cruelty, he sought to reclaim them and found they had been murdered.

Grief over this is supposedly what drove him to his final hermitage and a life of remorse. But later stories of his life at LaPointe indicate he had another reason for severing his ties with what little civilization there was here. And if he was remorseful about anything, he didn't show it.

Reading through accounts of his life it seems as though the girl he really deserted is the one at his boyhood home. But desertion might have become a habit with him, and there is no way of finding out now. His supposed daughter has no name or age recorded anywhere we know of.

At any rate, Wilson continued to move through the wilderness as easily as an ordinary man walks through his own back yard. And again, legends began to build up around his daring exploits and his proficiency with a rifle. His courage was unquestioned, and he had a name and fame among the rough, brave men who spent their lives in the wilderness, surviving by their strength and wits.

When Wilson's enlistment with the Hudson Bay Company expired he returned for the third time to Lake Superior and entered the service of the American Fur Company. He was stationed at LaPointe, and at last stayed in one place long enough for people to learn of his past, to hear the legends about him from passing voyageurs and to discover he owned a fortune in gold. A fortune which Wilson and his rife kept well guarded.

But Wilson was getting old. What had been a determined, self-confident, headstrong disposition in his youth, turned into quarrelsome, bullying traits as he grew older. He still had wonderful strength and endurance and openly considered himself the best man on Lake Superior. But at LaPointe he met a better one.

The better man was John W. Bell, called Squire, or King Bell in his later years. He, too, had great strength and endurance, but unlike Wilson, he never used force unless imposed upon.

Wilson worked in Bell's cooper shop for a period of 18 months. One day Wilson was abusing a smaller man, who was doing his best to escape and avoid trouble. At last the small man went to Mr. Bell, asking protection. Wilson went right after the man, threatening him, or anyone else who interfered. But John Bell ignored his threats and just stood there, waiting. The small man found a place of safety behind him, and there is no doubt that the other men in the cooper shop moved back along the walls, giving these two giants plenty of room. But room wasn't needed. Bell hit Wilson with one powerful blow, knocked him flat on the cooper shop floor, and that was it.

Wilson could not stand to see a better man than himself live on the same island with him, so he moved to an island of his own. These are the Apostle Islands. One day in October, 1846, 106 years ago this month, he got into his heavily laden canoe, paddled to his uninhabited island, built himself a cabin and began his lonely hermit's life.

Wilson, after moving to his new isolated home, found plenty of room to be alone in. The island is 2 miles long, ¾ miles wide and has about 560 acres.

He began to make barrels which he sold to fishermen and this money took care of his simple wants so he had no need to spend his gold.

The one room cabin he built for himself was of pine logs finished with a rough, clay plaster. It contained a home made easy chair, two large, iron bound chests, a rough board bunk with a mattress, a few blankets and a bag filled with duck and loon feathers which served as a pillow. There was a broken looking glass, one or two pictures tacked to the mud lined walls, a few books and special pegs for his rifle and other guns. One small, dingy window let in some light. A rude mud and cobblestone chimney and fireplace furnished warmth in winter and a place to cook his plain meals. He had a garden directly in front of the cabin and for company, a few chickens, a dog and a cat. Game, fish and wood were abundant. Whatever the season, he did not lack food or warmth.

Even though Wilson lived alone, finally monarch of his own island kingdom, quite a lot is known about his life there. He was a mystery to the Indians who lived along the shore of Chequamegon Bay. He was mean to them, and they were afraid of him, calling him Muji Manito, the evil one. He was a terror to their boldest warriors, just as he had been to the western tribes. When some adventurous braves intruded on his island, so it could be said among their friends that "they were not afraid of Wilson", he punished them so severely that they were lucky to get off alive, and never came back. Once he seized his gun and shot two Indians, who, with whiskey bravery, tried to enter his cabin. That island was all his. He guarded it with his best and only friend, his rifle, and few people were welcome beyond the canoe landing.

He seldom left his home except to get a few supplies at LaPointe and to get whiskey. As age began to conquer him, to take the physical strength he had always been so proud of, he drank more. He had no intimate friends. He allowed some visitors. But if he thought they were staying too long, he would firmly invite them to depart. He would never allow anyone he disliked to set foot on the island.

Once a sheriff with a warrant for the collection of unpaid taxes attempted to see him, but was unsuccessful. There was one accessible boat landing. Wilson and his rifle had it covered. The sheriff valued his life more than county tax money.

Yet, it was taxes that tripped up Wilson, just as they trip up the biggest and toughest ones in this day and age. Wilson did not believe in paying taxes where he received no benefits, and certainly he was receiving no county benefits on his island. There were no roads for the county to improve. He needed no law, because he was the law. In order to avoid being served with legal papers, he always went to LaPointe, the county seat, on Sundays, and then only infrequently, to transact necessary business.

But on one occasion he made a mistake. Living alone, where one day faded into the next, with no special marking, he confused Sunday with Monday and when he pulled up his canoe on the LaPointe beach that particular Monday morning, the waiting officers arrested him. He stayed in jail several days, declaring he would not pay. But solitude in jail did not compare favorably with solitude on his island, so he finally changed his mind and settled his tax bill. There had never been any question about his having the money to do so.

Apparently while Wilson, the Hermit, was in jail no gold seekers searched his island. Fear probably stopped them. There was no knowing what minute Wilson would be released and would head for home. And, if he found anyone on his island...!

Wilson often read an ancient little book entitled, *The Whole Duty of Man*. This, he said, was his guide, and affirmed that future happiness would be assured to all who lived by it.

In 1856 Bayfield was founded. Probably that spring, as Wilson paddled his canoe to LaPointe, he glanced at the mainland, saw the new little clearing, the 4 or 5 log houses and the beginning of a dock. If he did, he undoubtedly gave this new sign of civilization a sour look, and hoped it wouldn't amount to much.

And as he went to LaPointe only on Sundays, except for the one time he got his days mixed, he probably encountered James Peet, first resident minister in Bayfield, who preached at LaPointe every Sunday afternoon that he could get there. But the encounter couldn't have been much more than a glance. Wilson, with his whiskey and his little book on how to live, would not likely have been attracted to James Peet's small sincere congregations. Yet, if they had stopped to talk, they would have discovered something in common. Both of them had the determination, the courage and the endurance to go wherever they wanted to go and to do exactly as they thought they should.

One bright October day in 1861, when Wilson was 69 years old, Ar-ti-cho, a Chippewa Indian, who, with his wife, was paddling to the mainland from his fishing grounds on Presque Island, decided to stop at the Hermit's and propitiate him with some whitefish. He paddled up to the landing and hesitated, not wanting to get out of the canoe until he was invited. But Wilson wasn't around. His dog came down the path, but before he reached the dock he stopped, and gave a dismal howl.

Ar-ti-cho got out of his canoe then, went cautiously up the winding path with the dog following him, knocked on the cabin door, but heard no sound. He called loudly, but got no answer. Except for squirrels and birds the forest was silent. He looked out on the lake, but could see no canoe. Finally he had the courage to open the cabin door. And when he did, he saw that Wilson, the Hermit, was dead.

After making sure he was dead, Ar-ti-cho, with a natural, human curiosity, took time to look around the forbidden cabin. He found a purse with some coins in it which he and his wife took to LaPointe and gave to Squire Bell. The Squire sent men for the body and then he acted as coroner at the inquest over Wilson, the second best man on Lake Superior.

It was evident that Wilson died of delirium tremens, for he was found in a position that would convince almost anyone that "whiskey did it."

So Wilson died as he had lived—alone. Whether death came by night or by day, no one knew. But right to the end he was fighting; his last fight against the terrifying hallucinations that come with delirium tremens. As misshapen monsters appeared against the mud lined log walls of his lonely cabin, he forced his trembling old body to go after them until life was wrenched from it in a final, violent convulsion.

Squire Bell had Wilson given a decent burial in the quiet, hillside cemetery at LaPointe, the Protestant burying ground near the old Mission House.

After Wilson's death, treasure seekers went bravely and frequently to his island. If, as some said, Wilson's ghost haunted it, they paid little attention, gold being more important than ghosts. They dug around the cabin, poked holes in the walls and ripped up the floor, but found nothing. There were persistent rumors after Wilson's death that some Indians were seen with a large number of Mexican silver dollars. But it was recalled that Wilson's original fortune was in gold, and it did not seem likely he would have traded gold for silver. Also, Mexican dollars were in common use by the traders.

And then, with Wilson gone, changes came to the island. It was logged, of course. The timber, which Wilson had walked through, fell and was hauled to one of the sawmills that were being built around Chequamegon Bay.

In the spring of 1891, the Prentice Brownstone Company opened the "Excelsior" quarries on the southeast end of the island. The quarries yielded a fine, light colored stone, "as handsome as could be desired."

Wilson (Hermit)
Island quarry
production.
(Photo: BHA)

A pamphlet, published in 1892, has this to say about the Wilson Island quarries: "The island is spanned on all sides by solid ledges of brownstone many feet high, which the waves have washed for years. The large stones seem almost chiseled into perfect shape, and no better proof need be required than this, as to the durability of brownstone. The quarries area admirably located for shipping stone direct to all lake ports and Eastern markets. As the quarry is located very close to the water's edge there is considerable economy in handling very large blocks. It is from these quarries that the Wisconsin monolith, to be furnished the World's Fair Commissioners by F. Prentice Esq., president of the company, is to be gotten. It will make an imposing feature of the great Colombian Exposition. It will be 106 to 110 feet in height, exclusive of base. The base of the monolith will be 9 to 10 feet square, tapering to 2½ to 3 feet square. It will be higher than any Egyptian or other obelisk known." When the obelisk was complete it was too heavy to be moved and had to remain right where it was. Eventually, the obelisk was cut up into small building stones.

Frederick Prentice of New York, president of the Brownstone Co., was as pleased to have the island as Wilson had been. In fact he was so delighted with it that in the early nineties he built what was known as Cedar Bark Cottage there, using only materials found on the island for its construction. The house was large, impressive, three stories high, with an observation tower facing the lake. Behind it was a barn almost as large as the house, with a high, peaked roof. The grounds were landscaped and well kept. The fireplace and chimney, made of fine island brownstone, were especially beautiful.

Rumor has always said that Mr. Prentice built the house as a surprise for his wife, but she was more surprised than he had expected her to be. She was shocked. They took one look at the large house, isolated, surrounded by wilderness on an island surrounded by rough water and left. Caring more for his wife than his cedar bark house, he followed her, and for quite a few years the island was uninhabited again.

Then in 1910, a Minneapolis land company bought the place, fixed up the bark cottage and started a summer hotel, hoping to build the place into a thriving tourist center. On the strength of this bright future, the company sold ten lots of ten acres each, where summer homes were to be built.

But maybe the customers were like Frederick Prentice's wife. They took one look and ran. Anyway, they didn't build. But nature did. She built new trees, bushes, grass and fine moss for the abandoned quarry rocks. The island went back to the same, wild state in which Wilson had found it.

The bark house, with its tall observation tower, began to collapse. The wind blew the shingles off the roof, rain came through and rotted the interior. Windows were broken. A bush began to grow through a hole in the floor, reaching out toward the broken windows for all the sunlight it could get. Sometime in the thirties, Jack Brautigan bought the place for wrecking. Carl Carlson bought the beautiful sandstone fireplace, carried it to his home at Salmo with the pieces well marked and rebuilt it there, exactly the way it was on the island.

With the house out of her way, nature finished up her work and restored the island to complete wilderness. The heavy growth discouraged any lingering gold seekers and gradually the search stopped.

But ninety-two years have passed since the Hermit died. Gold is still gold, even though it might have tarnished a little. And civilization has changed, though Wilson Island hasn't. Civilization has brought one new thing, one more new hope for the treasure.

Anybody got a Geiger counter?

More on Wilson The Hermit

T HE STORY OF WILSON, THE Hermit, which appeared in the history column of The Press, brought the following letter from Mrs. R. D. Goodwin, of Mattoon, Illinois, formerly Eva Mason.

"I read every word of the Wilson Island story three times. As you described him, old Wilson was ruthless. My father's mother was young when this happened. My grandmother was orphaned early, her mother dying at her birth and her father, a traveling peddler, was killed when she was about eight years old. She was cared for by her grandparents and lived in L'Anse, Michigan. They moved to Wilson Island after her father was killed. Her grandfather was a kindly old man, who would have harmed no one.

One day two strangers came onto the island, which was so zealously guarded by old Wilson when he was sober. They arrived unbeknownst to him, were hungry and caught a couple of the chickens which were roaming around, built a fire and had some chicken stew. What happened to them was never known, but it was assumed that after eating and resting, they left as quietly as they had come.

Wilson came upon the remnants of the dinner and campfire and jumped to the conclusion that my great, great grandfather was to blame. He made up a batch of cookies in which he put poison. When the old man came in the next day, as was his habit, Wilson offered him the cookies. Since it was considered an insult to refuse food in those days, the old man accepted. Shortly afterward he became violently ill and soon died.

His wife, in fear of her life, buried all the household equipment, consisting of several large copper pots and other utensils used in making maple syrup and cooking, and marked well the spot, so that they would be able to find them again. They fled the island and went to live on the mainland. Years later, my grandmother returned, but the markings had been obliterated by nature and man and she was never able to find them."

Pioneers and Jim Chapman

Jim Chapman, Bayfield early founder arrived in La Pointe to clerk for storekeeper Julius Austrian—1855. "Big Jim" worked as clerk for Samuel S. Vaughn, was second postmaster behind Joseph McCloud, stage coach & cutter line owner, proprietor of general store (Corner S. Rittenhouse Ave and 1st Street). (Photo: BHA)

T HIS STORY WILL BEGIN A series of stories about our pioneers. If any are omitted, it's because I don't know anything about them. If you do, tell me, and we'll write about them before the series ends. Most of the graves of these pioneers are in the Bayfield cemetery; so next month, when you clean up and decorate your lot for Memorial Day, why don't you walk around and see some of them.

Why did people come to Bayfield in the first place? The answer is easy—money. Bayfield was to be the terminus of a railroad from St. Paul to Lake Superior. People rushed in, bought lots, and everything was set for a big boom, until the money panic of 1857 blacked out the dream. People left then, just as fast as they had come, and bad as it sounds, it was a good thing for Bayfield. It was good because the gamblers, speculators and riffraff who generally follow a boom, drifted off, and left only the true pioneers here to build our town.

These pioneers stayed because they liked Bayfield, and for no other discernible reason. They liked it here, and they liked each other. They were poor, and had to work hard, but they had a good time. There was gold on the western frontier that they could have rushed for. There were large homesteads in the west for the claiming, but they stayed in Bayfield and enjoyed life.

Maybe that isn't so different from the situation in 1954. Once in awhile you'll hear someone complaining about Bayfield. But it isn't long before some citizens say, "Why don't you get out of here then? Go on. What's holding you?"

Actually nothing is holding the complainer. Certainly there are milder climates, certainly there are jobs with more money, there may even be greener pastures. But who wants them? None of the rugged individualists of Bayfield. . . and they didn't want them in 1857, either.

Let's start recalling our pioneers with Jim Chapman. There is so much to be written about him it is hard to know where to start. And the story won't be just about Jim. A lot of other people will appear in it because he had so many friends. Probably his two best friends were Col. Isaac Wing and Captain T.J.L. Tyler. If any three people ever had a good time living, they did.

Just for the record, James Chapman was born in May 1834 at Mackinac, Michigan. When he was in his teens, he located for a time at Marquette, Michigan, and it is said he cut the first tree on the site of that now thriving city. About 1855, when he was 21 years old, he came to LaPointe and clerked for Julius Austrian, who kept a store there. He probably came over here the day Bayfield was founded. For several years he worked for S.S. Vaughn as clerk, and later formed a partnership with him in a store at Bad River. In 1857 he was appointed postmaster at Bayfield by President Buchanan. He was our second postmaster. Joseph McCloud was our first. He was best known as proprietor of the general store on main street, on the site where *The Press* office is now located.

No story about him would be complete without mentioning his beautiful team of bay horses, named Chad and Judd. They were undoubtedly the finest, most powerful team ever owned in Bayfield. Joe LaPointe drove them, and thanks to the latter Harvey Nourse, we have some stories about them.

At one time Col. John Knight had to make a business trip to St. Paul, and had to be in Superior at six o'clock in the evening. He hired the team from Chapman, and told Joe LaPointe what was expected of them. Usually the trip to Superior took two days, but according to Joe they got an early start in the morning, were at Gordon at noon and at six PM exactly, they drove up to the hotel with the lines strapped around Joe's shoulders, as he held the team in with all his strength. The horses were as fresh as when they started. Col. Knight had offered to relieve Joe as teamster for awhile, but his arms got so tired he had to give the lines back to Joe.

Joe LaPointe had many harrowing experiences with this team. They broke through the ice several times, and on one occasion, Chap was in the water for over an hour, before Joe, who was all alone, could get him out. When they got ashore, Joe spent the whole night in the barn, working over him, and Chap came out of his chill as good as ever.

One day when Jim Chapman wished to drive to Red Cliff he asked Joe to hitch Chap to a cutter. Joe warned him against this, told him it was a risky thing to do, and that there would probably be a smashup; but Jim was determined to go. Joe gave in, hitched up Chap and drove him around to cool him down before he stopped at the store. Just as Jim was getting into the cutter, Captain Tyler came down the street and was invited to take a ride.

Joe held the horse's head until the men got a robe tucked around their feet, then handed the lines to Chapman. Joe said afterward, that he knew they were doomed from the first.

They took off at full speed, with snow flying up in clouds from the runners. Joe LaPointe ran to an upstairs window in Chapman's store where he could watch a break in the Red Cliff road. As the cutter approached the spot, he saw Tyler come flying out of it, and pretty soon Chapman followed. The horse, at full speed, kept on to Red Cliff.

After a while Tyler appeared on Main Street, cursing the man who would keep such a beast as was hitched to that cutter. Chapman came limping in, too. Joe LaPointe went out to try and bring back what was left of the outfit. He finally did recover it, but there wasn't much left of the cutter.

Jim Chapman & Captain Thomas Lewis Johnson Tyler

HERE IS ANOTHER STORY of Harvey Nourse's about Jim Chapman and Captain T.J.L. Tyler. One summer evening, when there were services in the Episcopal Church, Chapman suggested to Tyler, that they attend. It was rather unusual, but Tyler consented, they made hasty preparations, and started.

Chapman, who had been a dark, powerful man in his youth, had gotten overweight, and had to take his time climbing the hill. They were late. The minister was preaching when they arrived. The door was closed, so they hesitated about walking in. Tyler turned to Chapman and asked if they should knock. Chapman said it was so long since he had attended church he had forgotten, but just to be on the safe side they had better knock.

So they knocked on the door. The minister slowed a little in his address and the congregation were at attention, but such a thing was so unusual no one answered. Not getting any response, they knocked again. Mr. McCloud, who always took up the collection, went to the door. When he opened it, Chapman and Tyler bowed, said "good evening", doffed their hats and were escorted up the aisle, to the amusement and consternation of the minister and everyone present. They gave good attention to the balance of the sermon and at the close of the service said they had enjoyed it and would come again. They were told to do so, but the next time not to knock.

James Chapman's store was where *The Press* building now stands. Behind it, facing on Main Street, was his beautiful flower garden with a large fountain. He kept the fountain filled with trout, which he caught during his many fishing trips. Summer tourists used to spend pleasant afternoons and evenings strolling in Jim's garden, sitting beside the fountain, and feeding breadcrumbs to the fish.

Jim and Col. Isaac Wing often went fishing in Chapman's boat, and would take Joe LaPointe or Louis Job along to row. As they always had plenty of whiskey on their expeditions, the next day Louie or Joe would surely be drunk.

Captain Tyler died on January 10, 1879. Needless to say, he was missed by his friends, and they did not forget him. Philip Boutin remembers when Col. Wing and Jim Chapman would go fishing on Pike's Creek, they always walked up to the cemetery to visit Tyler's grave. At that time the cemetery was on the bluff north of the creek. They would sit by his grave awhile, talking about him and to him, as though he was right there, recalling the good times they had and insulting him affectionately. They carried a demijohn of whiskey with them and kept a glass on Tyler's grave. Before they left they always poured Tyler a drink.

Fortunately the account book Jim Chapman used in his store and in the post office for years between 1862 and 1874, has been preserved. The book is mostly financial transactions, but there are some interesting personal entries and the names of the people who lived here during those years are recorded over and over.

Here are some of the entries.

Set. 29, 1863. Paid Yellow Beaver for carrying mail $5.00.

Nov. 17. By my mistake in footing up like a dam fool, lost $12.25.

Nov. 19. L.E. Webb (who was the first Indian Agent in Bayfield) $20 in gold to sell.

Commenced board at T.J.L. Tyler's Tuesday, Nov. 10, 1863 at dinner. (He had been boarding at the home of John Banfill since January 15, 1862.)

To Mrs. T.J.L. Tyler, cash, for board, $25 Christmas Day.

Captain T.J.L. Tyler was charged with three dollars which he lost to James Chapman in a card game at Banfill's, and also charged with $3 which he bet on corn meal, probably how much was in a certain sack. Then Captain Tyler is credited with 50 cents which he won from Chapman in a bet about a pig. So you can see they didn't have much money to throw around, and if they didn't happen to have the cash to pay their bets, it didn't make any difference, they just ran the transaction through Jim's books. Our pioneers were poor in money, but they had a lot of fun.

Dr. Vespacian Smith. Bayfield's first medical doctor. Photo: BHA Inc.

Dr. Vespasian Smith bet on General L.E. Webb arriving some place before the 20th of March and lost $1, which was charged to him on Chapman's books. Incidentally, Dr. Smith was Bayfield's first doctor. He came here in 1858 and served as government physician to the Indians of the Bayfield Agency. He was here for eight years. He was known to have traveled forty miles in an open boat to visit a sick Indian. He was never known to have refused a call, no matter how hard it was, or what the circumstances were. Does anyone know anything more about him? We hope someone does.

Eventually Jim Chapman switched back to his first boarding place. "Commenced board at Banfill's Monday, April 10, 1865, at breakfast."

"Paid William Morrin for Brown for services carrying mail. All settled up in full to this day, Sept. 22. 1865. And don't intend to pay another ____ cent. This is the second time the same has been paid. Selah"

March 31, 1866, Paid. J.B. Bono, raffle on boots, 50 cents.

J.W. Webb, by cash, $4, draw poker."

"May 7, paid Tyler by bet that Captain Smith would not go to Ontonogan, $1.

"Left Bayfield to go to St. Paul Wed., Nov. 27, 1867. Arrived at Bayfield from St. Paul December 19, 1867. Was gone 23 days."

"Joseph LaPointe (driver of Chap and Judd) commenced services as government teamster Nov. 24, 1869, at 25 dollars per month. Whittlesey pays 15 dollars making 40 dollars per month."

"Martin O'Malley—Dr. Schooner *Mary Ann Hulbert* with all tackle, sails, etc. for $600, half to be paid down and balance in June, 1874.

"A. Whittlesey, April 1, 1874 Turkey red silk elastic, beads, etc. for wife's order, also halves on one keg of ale from St. Paul."

(The Ale, no doubt, was his own order.)

And on and on the entries go. They would be the despair of a bookkeeper today, for the post office accounts are mixed in with the store accounts, the bets on pigs, the corrected mistakes, some kind of a land business, where deeds and mortgages were recorded, and the accounts of the good old schooner, *Mary Ann.*

Harvey Nourse used to recall that occasionally Jim Chapman, S.S. Vaughn, Captain Tyler, Col. John Knight and Col. Isaac Wing used to meet in the rooms over Chapman's store to cook a pot roast. So you can see that times in Bayfield have not changed in that respect. Other men, with other names, have taken their places, that's all. Whether their cooking is up to the Chapman, Wing and Tyler standards is a question that cannot be answered.

One evening, when the pioneer group met to cook up something, it was suggested that Captain Tyler bring a few chickens, as he had been bragging about some blooded poultry that had been sent to him. Tyler refused, but after a few drinks of Chapman's whiskey, it seemed like a good idea to go out and get some chickens. He said he would go if Sam Vaughn would go with him. It was dark, and soon Vaughn had Tyler confused and led him around to his hen house where he robbed himself of his fine chickens.

Mrs. DeMars remembers something special about Jim Chapman. Susan Morrin, who lived in a house in the big ravine, and was "so merry and full of fun" used to hang the biggest stocking she could find on the door of Jim Chapman's store every Christmas Eve. When she went down to get it Christmas morning it was always filled with small gifts.

No story about Jim Chapman would be complete without a report on his brook trout fishing. There is no question but that he was the champion brook trout fisherman in these parts, and if there had been any country wide competition of that sort he would probably have been a world champion. Currie Bell reported in *The Press* that he had watched with envy while Jim Chapman hooked and landed a fourteen pound lake trout with light, brook trout equipment. *The Press* for May 25, 1871, said, "James Chapman has our thanks for some nice speckled trout. May your shadow never grow less, Jim." There is no doubt that James Chapman cast a fine shadow. He was overweight, but still a good looking man, with a mustache and thick, white hair that was cut almost crew style, which was unusual for that day and age. But it was probably a practical style for him, as during the course of his fishing expeditions he sometimes fell into the water. The first *Press* record of one of his dunkings was on Saturday, June 3, 1871. "Our fellow townsman, James Chapman, Esq., was thoroughly inundated in the bay this morning. The immersion, we hope, will do him no harm."

From the time Bayfield was founded, brook trout fishing was one of the most popular sports. Just a short jaunt to a stream and back was not enough for the enthusiasts. All day expeditions were organized, and Jim Chapman was usually one of the leaders. On July 7, 1883, *The Press* said, "Col. Knight, James Chapman and I.H. Wing went to Sand Island Wednesday on a trout fishing excursion. They reported capturing one of the largest strings of trout ever caught in this section. Among them was one which weighed 4½ pounds. Of course, it is needless to say that it was James who caught the whopper.

Sand Island was a favorite brook trout fishing spot. In July 1885 "Captain Pike, Major Wing, Commodore Chapman and Admiral J. E. Glove with a full fleet in tow of the tug *Favorite*, visited Sand Island Wednesday and engaged in a great naval battle with the brook trout fleet. They came out of the conflict victorious.

There is evidence that the sportsmen of Ashland and Bayfield competed fiercely in brook trout fishing, for on June 20, 1877, *The Press* said, "Mssrs Chapman and Tyler went fishing last Saturday and brought home among their catch 19 trout that weighed 23 pounds. Let Ashland beat them or give up the belt."

In July 1877 *The Press* reported, "The biggest catch of the season was made last Monday by Mr. Chapman. He went out in the morning and returned in the evening with a string of 32 brook trout which weighed 38 pounds. The largest fish weighed 3½ pounds."

By the next spring there could be no doubt of Jim's championship, for *The Press* stated boldly, "Mr. James Chapman, champion trout fisherman of two counties."

What percentage is skill and what percentage is luck in catching brook trout is a good subject for debate. But as far as Jim Chapman was concerned, skill was the great essential. He had skill, and he proved it. *The Press* , Sept. 3, 1881: "Several parties had been trouting last week and returned with a meager catch and reported that trout were becoming scarce. When Captain Chapman heard the rumors, tears filled his eyes and he donned his fishing suit and with pole and basket started for Pike's Creek, muttering, "I'll show them there is plenty of trout in any Bayfield stream." At night the Captain returned and as he spread out his catch, numbering 69, he remarked with a smile, which was child-like and bland, "If you want trout, always send a man."

The town had a great affection for Jim Chapman, and the same affection was felt by the people who visited Bayfield, sat beside the fountain in Jim's beautiful garden and fed crumbs to his fish, some of which were so tame that they would come to the surface and take crumbs almost from the hand of the feeder.

Sometimes his friends tried to show their affection with gifts. Here is one account of it. July 31, 1878: "Mr. James Chapman, the boss trout fisherman of this northern county, has been presented by Hon. H.M. Rice of St. Paul with a most appropriate gift consisting of a complete fisherman's rig of fine poles, reels, hooks and lines of all kinds and everything that an experienced fisherman could possibly need. The cost of the rig is something over a hundred dollars. Jim is as pleased as a schoolboy over a new jack knife, and well he may be, for certainly a finer and more appropriate gift could not have been bestowed on a person who deserves and appreciates the same more than he does. Ho! Besides the above, other St. Paul friends left Mr. Chapman valuable tokens of their esteem and regard which he will always cherish."

It was natural that when a fish warden was to be appointed in this district that the Governor should pick Jim Chapman for the job. Everyone approved of his selection, for there was hardly another person in the territory, who knew more about fish than Jim did.

The Chippewa Falls Herald said in 1885: "Governor Rush made a splendid selection when he appointed Mr. James Chapman of Bayfield, Fish Warden for the Lake Superior District. The artistic old bachelor will see to it that those elegant white fish up there are properly protected, (and properly cooked.) Whenever there is any doubt about it, his partner in marital views, Ike Wing, will act as referee."

Jim was naturally such a good man for the job that he kept being reappointed. General George C. Ginty said this, when Jim had a reappointment in 1889: "A superb angler, it's worth a fortune to see him handle a rod. . . of Jim Chapman it can be said everybody loves him because he knows all about the finny tribes, their habitations and where they lay off for a vacation. . . There is no record of what Jim was doing when he was on earth the first time, but history is complete and accurate as to what he has been engaged in for the last ten decades. He's been making his friends happy. He knows how. He's master of the art."

He did make his friends happy, and also did everything he could to make the town happy and a better place to live in. *The Press* referred to him in minor items as Genial James, Jolly James, and for some reason, Truthful James, which is a great compliment to such an ardent brook trout fisherman.

At the time William Knight was in business, *The Press* reported on May 13, 1871: "Truthful James and William Knight have planted quite a large garden adjoining their place of business with all kinds of vegetables. They did it with their own precious hands." By June 10 that garden had grown so well that, "Chapman has corn in his garden nearly a foot high."

And Jim had the distinction of owning the smallest Apostle Island. *Press*, July 15, 1871: "Madeline Island has 14,804.73 acres, being the largest of the Apostle group. Chapman's island is the smallest, containing only 00.17 acres. "Jim" is nearly as large as his island."

Like most of the Bayfield pioneers, one business was not enough for James Chapman. He had a lot of irons in the fire. The first boat to go on a regular run between Bayfield and Ashland was the J.C. Keyes, owned by Chapman and Knight.

And on October 28, 1871, *The Press* said: "Steamboat men will do well to procure their wood at Oak Island as it is on the regular steam boat channel with good dockage facilities, the water being twenty feet and upward at the landing. Chapman and Company have a large quantity of dry wood for sale at reasonable rates. Steamboat men will please bear these facts in mind."

James Chapman was public spirited, and he enjoyed being public spirited, which are two different things, if you stop to think about it. Every occasion that could be celebrated was celebrated by him. July 11, 1877, "Mr. Chapman celebrated the arrival of the *Little Maine* last Sunday evening by firing off several fine skyrockets." He saved a few of them until December 1877 when *The Press* said, "Mr. James Chapman had the misfortune to fall and dislocate his shoulder last Thursday evening while setting off fireworks in honor of the last boat."

And in case anyone should ask why the early Bayfield settlers had titles such as Captain, Col., and General, it is because some of them kept their Civil War rank, but most of the people in Bayfield had titles just because they like titles and for no other reason. Every man who wanted to be a Captain, was a Captain, in fact, according to the *St. Paul Dispatch* for Dec. 1877, a man was a Captain whether he wanted to be or not.

The *Dispatch* reported: "At Bayfield, Wisconsin, (so we are told by a traveler) no man is allowed to go without a title. When a stranger comes there to reside, he is at once waited upon by a committee of villagers, desiring to know by what title he shall be designated. If he has none, he is required to purchase a fish boat, upon which James Chapman issues him a commission as Captain, and his name, with the prefix of Captain, is then enrolled upon a village record book."

Anything that would make Bayfield more attractive and interesting to people was right down Jim Chapman's alley to accomplish. July 10, 1878, *The Press* said, "Mr. James Chapman, one of our most public-spirited citizens is preparing his yard for the reception of a few deer. The park is located on a distance of a hop, step and jump from Smith's Hotel. This will be a great attraction for persons visiting our village. Score another for Bayfield."

Jim Chapman, William Knight, R.D. Pike, Col. Isaac Wing and Thomas Bardon were gay and happy bachelors for many years. The first of the quintet to succumb to matrimony was Thomas Bardon in November 1884. Currie Bell wrote, "News reaches *The Press* to the effect that Thomas Bardon Esq. long and favorably known in these parts, has departed this state and has gone to join the innumerable tribe of benedicta, from which no bachelor ever returns. Carry the news to Bill Knight, break it gently to Bob Pike, and whisper it softly on Chap's corner, that Isaac and the Commodore, hearing may take council together as to the proper steps to be taken to avoid a like fate. *The Press* , being "one of those gone before", extends heartiest congratulations to the noblest Roman of them all, and doffs his chapeau to Mr. and Mrs. Bardon with warm wishes for their future, as well as present, happiness."

Later William Knight married, and Captain Pike was married twice, but Jim Chapman and Col. Wing remained bachelors to the end.

Chapman's store was his biggest and favorite enterprise, and in it he sold the best goods available at the time. That included local products. His ad on May 4, 1889 said, "I have just opened a pit of fine potatoes and will sell the same at a reasonable rate. Remember, these are home raised, and are as sound as a dollar. James Chapman."

His store on the corner was where people expected to find him, and they missed him if he was not there. Dec. 20, 1884, "James Chapman has been quite seriously ill during the past week, but is now improving slowly. The "little store on the corner" is lonely without the Jolly Commodore."

June 15, 1889. "Commodore Chapman is again doing business at the old stand on the corner after a weeks' illness that resulted in slightly diminishing his avoirdupois, but not his usual good spirits."

Jim's weight, and his good spirits, were two things he never did lose entirely. When James Chapman died on Sunday, December 8, 1890, it is not surprising that the whole town mourned his passing. *The Bayfield Press* had this to say: "Mr. Chapman had been a sufferer from heart disease for several years, and has known the last year that his days were numbered. About three weeks ago he was seen on our streets alive for the last time. His sufferings during his final illness were of the most acute nature. During that time kind friends ministered tenderly to his wants and everything that money and care could do to alleviate his suffering was done.

For several years he has been engaged in mercantile business and his store was always a favorite resort for prominent people temporarily here for health or pleasure. Among them the familiar form and quaint sayings of Jim Chapman will be missed when they return to us next summer, equally as among his fellow townsmen. He never married, and his only surviving relatives are a brother and several nephews. (This probably accounts for the reason Jim Chapman's grave has no tombstone. Does anyone know where the grave is?)

The funeral services were held at the Presbyterian Church Tuesday afternoon Dec. 9. The Rev. E.C. Freeman, pastor of the church, gave an appropriate and feeling address. The remains were borne to their last resting place by the following pallbearers: Ervin Leihy, Captain Pike, E.K. Brigham, William Knight, Fred Fischer, and Currie G. Bell. The Ashland Quartette furnished the music and rendered several hymns, all of which had been selected by the deceased before his death. In accordance with his wishes, the services were of the simplest nature. A sheaf of wheat rested on the casket.

From the time of Mr. Chapman's death until after his funeral the flags were displayed at half-mast, and during the progress of the exercises, a general suspension of business occurred.

Many of his warm friends, who were not here at the time of his death will drop a tear when they learn of it, as they think of the many pleasant hours in the old store where Jim delighted to meet his friends. These men are the most prominent of Bayfield's citizens, and many of the most important measures for the good of Bayfield have originated in that store about the big box stove.

There is no doubt that the pulse of Bayfield could be felt in that corner store of Jim Chapman's. Twelve years after his death they were still missing Jim and his store, and *The Press* wrote: "The old settlers of Bayfield, as they pass down First Street south of Rittenhouse Avenue and view Chapman's old store, recently moved from the rear to the front of the lot, instinctively recall to mind the many happy hours spent therein. In winter groups around the old box stove, and the quaint humor of the genial Commodore, now in that quiet city on the hill. Here railroads, docks and elevators were constructed and the future of the Harbor City most satisfactorily settled. Many a scheme was hatched here with an eye single to Bayfield's future good. This structure was erected in 1857-8 and has in days gone by frequently entertained men of note from all parts of the U.S., among whom have been vice-presidents, U.S. Senators, and noted Army and Navy men. In summer it was headquarters for all lovers of the rod and line and the fish stories reeled off in the shade of the old brown porch would fill a good sized volume. Like the old settlers, it is one of a very few left to tell the tale of bygone hopes and disappointments.

In those days, it was customary for the minister to deliver a long, extemporaneous eulogy of the deceased. Mr. Freeman had been in Bayfield only a short time, so he was not well prepared to speak about Jim Chapman, but he did his best, telling everything nice he knew about him. Among his remarks he mentioned how well-dressed Jim always was as he sat in a chair in front of his store on fine summer days, with his clothes so neat and his shoes well-shined. This was true enough, for Jim Chapman was always a clean, well-dressed person.

Bayfield people, knowing the minister was new, appreciated his efforts on Jim's behalf, but they joked a little, too, for the character of Jim Chapman was so much greater and more important than his physical appearance, which was all the minister had time to learn of him.

Mrs. DeMars remembers how her father, Nazaire LaBonte, came home from the funeral and walked in the front door of the LaBonte House (new Greunke's). As he headed for the kitchen he remarked, "Well, I must go and black my shoes, so when I die, the minister can say, "He was a nice old man. He always kept his shoes shined."

Captain T. J. L. Tyler

Captain Tyler, wife Jane Eliza, daughters Harriet and Nellie arrived from near Buffalo, New York in 1861. Tyler was assistant Indian Agent for Bayfield & Ashland County, Surveyor (surveyed the Penokee Range. Tyler's falls on Bad River near Mellen is namesake), operated a carpenter shop & assisted in the building of most early Bayfield buildings and bridges. He installed the earliest water system and lived near the big ravine stream in the Drakenberg home.(Photo: BHA)

"The Life of the Party" is a familiar phrase, and in this sense it could be said that Captain T.J.L. Tyler was the "life of the village" of Bayfield. Nobody who knew Captain Tyler ever forgot him. Hank Fifield spent two years in Bayfield, yet, twenty years after Tyler's death, he wrote about him in the Menomonie, Michigan *Herald*, describing him as a man "who furnished considerable amusement for the village folks."

That he did! And since it is almost impossible to separate Tyler from his many friends, and put him in a story all by himself, a number of his jokes and stories have already appeared in these columns. A phrase heard in this area many times must have been originated by Tyler, for on Aug. 26, 1871, *The Bayfield Press* thought it was so funny that it printed, "Captain Tyler claims he was in this section when Madeline Island was a hole in the ground."

And *The Bayfield Press* said on Sept. 23, 1871, "A hat of the first water cut" is being worn by the Captain and gives him the appearance of the "last rose of summer."

Fortunately Captain Tyler had his picture taken in this hat of "the first water cut." Sam Vaughn is in the picture with him. Tyler is staring into space, probably trying to convey the impression of a "last rose." He was a dark haired, good looking man, with an interesting, hard-to-describe face. But we know from the things he accomplished that he deserves the best of the adjectives: Talented, versatile, learned, adaptable."

When the Lyceum held a debate in March 1871, on the subject, Resolved: That the sexes are equal in intellect, "who do you suppose was on the dangerous, negative side? T.J.L. Tyler, of course, and with him were William Knight and Asaph Whittlesey. The affirmative was taken by two diplomatic bachelors, B.B. Wade and R.D. Pike with W.L. Portlock to assist them. Who won was never recorded, so maybe it should be debated again. In this day and age, are there any men brave enough to debate this subject on a public platform?

Thanks to Captain Tyler's granddaughter, Mrs. Victor Solberg of Stone Lake, Wisconsin, we know something of the serious side of Captain Tyler's life. First of all, those initials of his stand for Thomas, Johnson, Lewis, all family names.

Captain Tyler and his wife, Jane Eliza Tyler, were born and raised in New York State near Buffalo. They were married on October 29, 1849, and had two daughters, Harriet Lane, who became Mrs. H. L. Pratt and Nellie, who married M. Ryder. The family lived in LaCrosse for a time, but when Gen. L.E. Webb was appointed to the post of Indian Agent at Bayfield, he persuaded Captain Tyler to accompany him as his assistant. General Webb was the first Indian Agent here. Does anyone have any more information about him?

Captain Tyler's property happened to be in the way of the first recorded Bayfield flood.

There are a number of people (myself included) who said, "There never was any trouble with the creek when they let it run a natural course through town." Sounds good, but it isn't true. They had a bad flood back in 1876 and Captain Tyler lost his garden.

At that time there were no farms along the bank of the ravine, probably to a tree in it had been cut, and there couldn't have been much erosion, but the floods came anyway. A Bayfield item appeared in *The Ashland Press* , May 20, 1876, reported: "The northeast storm did us considerable damage. The rain caused a freshet in Bayfield Creek and it rushed through the village, tearing away gardens, fences, wood sheds and outbuildings and washed considerable real estate into the lake. Captain Tyler lost 25 feet of his lot. (His house and lot were where Drakenberg's Tailor Shop now stands.) Captain says he don't care so much for the land, but he hates to lose the garden seed he had put in. The water came close to the courthouse, capsizing all the outbuildings. (The courthouse was where the Bayfield Cleaners is now.) The damage done is estimated by many to reach $2,000."

Well, Captain, 78 years later, we can say that we don't care so much about the loss of the land, either. It's the redistribution we object to.

Captain and Mrs. T.J.L. Tyler came to Bayfield by boat in 1861. In addition to being assistant Indian Agent, Captain Tyler was a surveyor in Bayfield and Ashland counties, as far south as Mellen. Tyler's Forks are named for him. He operated a carpenter shop and assisted in the construction of most of the early buildings in Bayfield.

In fact, item after item in the old *Bayfield Presses* tell of work done by Tyler until it almost seems as though he built the town single-handed; and after he got through building the town, he started on the roads and bridges. Nov. 18, 1871: "Tyler has finished the bridge on Washington Avenue and made a good job of it."

Eight years later he had gotten around to the sidewalks and *The Press* reported on June 27, 1877: "The industrious Tyler is laying a sidewalk on the south side of Rittenhouse Avenue, between Second and Broad Streets." Perhaps this was the sidewalk reported in an earlier story, where Tyler kept track by marks on a fence of the "fools" who came along and asked, "What are you doing?"

But work was not all that the Captain did. Sam Fifield, editor of *The Ashland Press* , paid a visit to Bayfield and on May 30, 1874, reported: "Captain Tyler has taken to painting, and is now one of the village artists." Does anyone have a picture painted by the Captain?

And when Tyler decided to get up and talk, people listened, then asked for more. *The Ashland Press* for April 24, 1876, said: "T.J.L. Tyler Esq. lectured before the Bayfield Lyceum last week and we hear his lecture very highly spoken of." Praise for his talk must have been wide-spread, for the Ashland citizens immediately wrote to Captain Tyler as follows: "Dear Sir: We respectfully solicit you to deliver a lecture upon any subject you may choose before the Ashland Reading Society at whatever time you may designate."

Tyler replied promptly: "If the roads are passable, I will try and entertain you for about twenty minutes on Friday evening, April 30."

The Press remarked: "Captain Tyler's lecture will prove a rich treat and we trust he will have a full house to hear him."

There was no further comment or review of Tyler's talk, so perhaps the roads were impassable. Anyway, that same year, in August 1875, Captain Tyler and his friends started out to do something about the roads. Under a headline "Bayfield and Ashland Wagon Road" *The Ashland Press* reported: "Captain R.D. Pike, Chairman, James Chapman, and T.J.L. Tyler, Supervisors, acting in the capacity of road commissioners for Bayfield County, went over the recently surveyed wagon road between Fish Creek and Bayfield this week arriving here on Wednesday. They report the route a most feasible one and propose to open it at once, that it may be used the coming winter. The new road follows the old Bayfield and Sioux River road to Onion River then strikes across on the shore line to the mouth of the Sioux River avoiding all the big hills on the old road; from thence, across the peninsula to McClellan (Washburn); from thence around the bay shore to Boyd's Creek where it turns to the westward and running southwest strikes Fish Creek in the SW quarter of Sec. 2, T.47 R5 about ½ mile below Charlie Days' farm. Here it connects with the road running from Ashland, upon which work is already progressing, our town proposing to make their end in good shape before snow flies. We are glad that at last the long needed road is to be opened. It will do away with the necessity of traveling on the ice in winter, at all times disagreeable, and often unsafe, and give to these two settlements a connection that can be proved mutually beneficial. It should be worked every year, until it is a good buggy road when besides being useful, it will give to both villages a fine drive, something needed in order to make the towns attractive to our summer visitors. Ashland should do her part thoroughly and well and work hand in hand with Bayfield as far as possible in this good work."

And with Jim Chapman in the party, you can bet they didn't spend all the time looking at road possibilities on their long walk to Ashland through forest and swamp. They went fishing. When they dropped in at *The Ashland Press* office for a visit with Sam Fifield, they presented him with a "fine mess of trout, taken from their hiding places among the rocky caves of Houghton Point and along the coast."

A one way walk to Ashland was enough for them, too. They rode home. *The Ashland Press* said, "The tug *Wadsworth* made an extra trip to Bayfield Wednesday night, taking up the Bayfield Road Commissioners and several passengers."

The grave of Captain T.J.L. Tyler is marked with a tall gray monument. It has a large Masonic emblem, and still legible are the facts that he war born Nov. 30, 1821, and died Jan. 10, 1879. He was first buried in the Pike's Creek cemetery, in the grave so often visited by James Chapman and Col. Wing, when they went trout fishing on Pike's Creek. When the cemetery was moved, Captain Tyler and his tall monument were taken along.

There is a nice tree close by, and Captain Tyler would like that; for his granddaughter, Mrs. Victor Solberg, of Stone Lake has written: "Even in those early days he was interested in civic beautification, and the beautiful maple trees which adorn the streets of Bayfield were planted by my grandfather, assisted by my mother when she was about twelve years old. A very gorgeous memorial it is in autumn."

"He had a very keen, brilliant mind, and was very capable in many occupations. He had operated a sawmill, built railroads and bridges, edited newspapers, (he was editor of the LaCrosse Republican), installed water systems in LaCrosse, Superior and Bayfield. (In those days they used logs with holes drilled through the center for pipes.) He was a very well read man of the better books of the day and a daily reader of the Bible. My mother told that he would take a lighted candle when he went to bed, place it on his bedside chest and read the Bible until he went to sleep and the family had to watch to be certain the candle was out."

Unfortunately, no local newspaper for January 1879 can be found; therefore, we can only guess at the lengthy obituary and eulogy which must have been given to a citizen as beloved as Captain Tyler. We do know the date of his funeral, for on Jan. 13, 1879, the diary of Mrs. Andrew Tate says simply: "We attended the funeral of Captain Tyler this afternoon."

Mrs. Tyler outlived her husband by 34 years. Mrs. Solberg has written of her: "My grand-mother lived on in Bayfield in the same house until she was 87 years old." (This house is still standing, though it has been remodeled. It is the building now used by Andrew Drakenberg for a tailor shop.)

"She too was a very capable person, and had very good health, considering that vitamins, hormones, etc., were unknown in those days. She always had a large garden, fruit trees and bushes and a flock of chickens." (Bayfield history readers will remember that this flock was slightly depleted the night Captain Tyler and S.S. Vaughn went chicken hunting.)

Mrs. Tyler's fine garden impressed Sam Fifield, editor of *The Ashland Press*, for after a visit to Bayfield, he wrote on Sept. 21, 1872, "We saw the largest sunflower stalk in the garden of Mrs. Tyler at Bayfield a day or two since, that we have seen in a long time. It was nearly 12 feet high and had flowers as large in diameter as a half bushel measure."

Mrs. Solberg says of her grandmother: "She did her own housework, laundry and sewing and was well informed on the topics of the day, as she always read the daily papers. She died Feb. 13, 1913, from gangrene, which had set in, following hardening of the arteries, but was ill only a few days. She had been brought up as a close communion Baptist, but joined the Presbyterian Church when it was first organized in Bayfield. She was baptized in a room above Leihy's store (where the Standard Oil station is) which was used as the first Presbyterian Church, and was a very faithful member of the church until the time of her death."

The sentence: "She did her own housework, laundry and sewing and was well informed on the topics of the day" seems to sum up all the pioneer women of Bayfield. Other articles describe them as charming and hospitable, but nowhere have I found any information about a pioneer woman at Bayfield who was outstanding for accomplishment, beauty, or as a heroine. The town apparently was planned, built and run by men. There is no doubt, of course, that the women were coaching from the sidelines, but for that they got no credit. Doesn't anyone know of at least *one* outstanding pioneer woman?

A Delightful Tale Of Bayfield"s Early "Rugged" Men

By Eleanor Knight

From *The Bayfield County Press*
Circa 1953
Yes, But Think for a Moment
Of Some of the "Characters"
That Inhabit Bayfield in 1953

YOUNG BAYFIELD HAD A GOOD collection of "rugged individualists."

There was Frank Boutin, for one. Not Frank Jr. (though he would qualify, too) but his father, old Frank the lumberman, who had a thick, square beard. He hated concrete, as any good old lumberman would, and fought against the installation of concrete sidewalks. But in spite of his opposition, the old boardwalks went and the concrete ones were laid.

Joe O'Malley remembers the morning old Frank came up the street with a package under his arm. As he stepped up the curbing, the new concrete curbing, on the corner where Meyer's Drug Store now stands (1st South Second street and Rittenhouse Avenue), he tripped. The package he was carrying—a liquid—fell to the sidewalk and broke. Joe says he can still see him point down to the sidewalk and still hear him holler, "See, I told you these things were no good!"

And of course there was Captain T.J.L. Tyler. Before coming to Bayfield in 1861, he was editor of the LaCrosse Republican. His daughter, Ms D.L. Pratt, wrote this about him for Guy Burnham's book; "He had no enemies except for himself. He was well educated, good company and a good drinker."

He certainly had no enemies. He had lots of friends and lots of fun in Bayfield. People still begin to smile when his name is mentioned, because Tyler stories have been repeated for years. Here are the two of the best known, most repeated ones.

One morning a friend of Captain Tyler's saw him coming down the street with his hands held out about three feet apart. He looked neither to right nor left, but as he approached his friend said, "Good morning Tyler."

"Don't bother me!", Tyler snapped. "Can't you see I've got the measurements of a door?"

And one fine day Captain Tyler was building a sidewalk. As his fellow townsmen passed they paused to ask what he was doing. Instead of answering them he made a pencil mark on the board. Finally one man came along, said, "Hello Captain What are you making?."

Tyler made another mark and replied loudly. "There! That is the ninth fool that has passed by here this morning."

And here is the late Harvey Nourse's story about his father (Joseph Harvey Nourse) who ran a general store in Bayfield (J.H. Nourse, Dry Goods, Shoes, Clothing and Provisions).

One Sunday morning when my father went to the store to check the stove, Colonel Wing knocked at the door and rubbing his hands nervously said, "Now Mr. Nourse, I know it is against your principles to sell anything on Sunday, but I have some friends coming to see me today and I find I am out of cigars. Surely you will let me have a few for the occasion." But my father said, "No, not today, Mr. Wing", and he went away, very angry. However, he was the first customer on Monday morning and purchased a whole box of them.

"Another time when father went to the store on a Sunday morning for the same purpose, William Knight knocked at the door and said he needed a pair of overshoes, or arctics as we called them. (And he did too). There was a winter thaw and he had just walked in from his logging camp at Frog Bay through a mixture of slush and mud.

Father told him he would have to wait until the next day.

"Go to hell," Mr. Knight said and pushed the door open. He walked to a new box that had just been received, selected the one pair of number twelves which he knew would be there, and walked out. Like Mr. Wing, he came the next day and paid for them."

Judge Joseph McCloud

Joseph McCloud. Judge, first postmaster, Quarry caretaker. (Photo: BHA)

J oseph McCloud has a very small tombstone. You might have to look awhile before you find it. But Joseph McCloud would not have been hard to find when he was living, for he was governor of Bass Island. He was also a judge and Bayfield's first postmaster.

On July 4, 1891, he presented the local post office with his commission as our first postmaster. It shows that the appointment was made Nov. 3, 1856, but so slow were the methods of communication between Lake Superior and Washington, that the bond was not issued and the commission signed until April 27, 1857.

When he was judge here he wrote a letter to his brother in Philadelphia and, thanks to Hamilton Ross of LaPointe, we know what the letter said. It was written on March 6, 1859, and slightly condensed is as follows: "On Monday I grant naturalization papers in court and there are 40 applications. The fee, $2, which is divided between myself and the clerk, is awful to the Dutch and the wife of one of the applicants who has just brought me two dozen eggs at 50 cents per dozen to pay for her husband's papers. So you see there can be a trade in citizenship, as two dozen eggs is equal to a motion and a hearing and two dozen more equal to a certificate of full citizenship and an American citizen is equal to just four dozen unhatched chickens."

June 29, 1872 *The Ashland Press* said: "Judge Joseph McCloud will soon open a law office in this place. He is a gentleman of ability."

In the spring and in the fall of 1857, Joseph McCloud and his brother drove over the new tote road from Bayfield to Yellow Lake, and from there over logging roads to St. Paul. They made the trip in a light buggy. In 1858, he was a real estate agent in Bayfield and later had a hardware store here.

Judge McCloud is best remembered now as caretaker at the Bass Island Quarry. He lived there alone for years, why, nobody knows exactly, for he was a lawyer, district attorney, businessman and real estate agent. But he didn't stay as isolated as the hermit of Wilson Island did. He came to town when he could. July 30, 1881 *The Press* said, "Judge McCloud, Grand Khedive of Bass Island, spent Wednesday in Bayfield and his many friends were glad to see him feeling so well after his long imprisonment enforced by a severe attack of rheumatism. The judge was the first post master of Bayfield, built the first frame house and in early days, was editor of *The Press* and at all times a brilliant conversationalist."

Credit for building the first frame house in Bayfield has been given to John Hanley in most accounts of the founding of Bayfield. But it is possible he built it for Judge McCloud.

Wednesday seemed to be his day to come to town, for nine years later, on July 26, 1890, *The Press* reported: "Judge McCloud, Governor of Basswood Island, was in town Wednesday."

One thing Judge McCloud had in his shack on Bass Island was a parlor organ. He composed and liked to play his original compositions for friends who dropped in to see him."

Shortly before his death in November 1900, a reported from the *Washburn Times* interviewed him and said, "Perhaps very few people know who Judge McCloud is, whose life is slowly ebbing away. Thirty five years ago he was one of the most prominent men in Northern Wisconsin, and was one of the first district attorneys of LaPointe County. LaPointe County was then pretty much everything in Northern Wisconsin. Later he held other county offices and was for a long time county judge. Now he is a very old man, and has for many years lived alone on Bass Island, near Bayfield, holding the title it is said for certain property holders, who have furnished him with provisions about once a week. Here the old man lives a hermit life, shut off from the outside world and all alone on the little island. Very few boats stop over at Bass Island. But occasionally, a private yacht or sailboat goes to the place. Two or three times the writer has visited the place and met the venerable old judge. . . He is a feeble old man. . . his sight is almost gone, yet he managed to do his own cooking and take care of his own house. The old man has an organ and a cat, his only companion. Upon the approach of visitors, the cat takes to the woods, and to all appearances is almost wild, except to the caresses of the feeble old man." He is one of the last of the old men who in the early days was prominent in the affairs of Northern Wisconsin."

John C. Hanley

(Photo: BHA)

Excerpt from *The Bayfield County Press*

"If He Were Living Today, He'd Be In The Movies"

J OHN C. HANLEY–MARCH 24, 56. So reads the inscription. The Reverend W. B. McKee, Presbyterian minister who lived in Bayfield in 1858, wrote in 1906 of John Hanley—on the occasion Bayfield's 50th anniversary—that Hanley had the best proportioned physique of all men in Bayfield; that he was of an erect stature, over 6 feet tall, of commanding presence, with pleasing physiognomy.

He taught the first vocal music class in Bayfield and had a strong bass voice. He was the first law officer of the new community, and came in later years to be commonly addressed as "Sheriff" Hanley. (There is no evidence at hand stating that he was formally elected to office). Mrs. Hanley is described by the Reverend McKee as a "pious, cultured, handsome wife." The couple had "two interesting children."

Mr. Hanley drove his team of horses over the ice from Superior and landed on the mainland point about midway between the present Lakeside Pavilion and the East dock bathing beach. (near the foot of Manypenny Avenue) The Historical Atlas of Wisconsin lists Mr. John Hanley as first in the group of men who literally came to build Bayfield. The first family to arrive in Bayfield was the John Hanley family. The date given in the Historical Atlas is May 8, 1856. That date is probably correct. It is substantiated by the Census of Bayfield, under the date of March 4, 1858.

"The first family (J. Hanley) came from Superior in the schooner *Algonquin* and landed at the pier May 8, 1856 which was the first boat at the dock . . . Mr. Hanley erected the first frame house July 16. This house is said to have been erected on the present site of the Bayfield Bank. (1st North Second Street and Rittenhouse Avenue). Mr. Hanley was the first Director of the Town of Bayfield, La Pointe County, School Board.

Andrew Tate

B 8-23-1823 in Washington D.C. Tate arrived in Bayfield on May 25, 1857. He was admitted as lawyer in the County Court-1858 and Circuit Court-1861. He served as County Judge, District Attorney and first Superintendent of County Schools. Tate was a charter member of the Masonic Lodge in Washington and Bayfield Lodge 215. In 1886 Tate served as president of the Bayfield Hydraulic Company. Nellie Hall from Bayfield became his bride in 1866 and daughter Lillian married Bayfield notable, A.H. Wilkenson in 1902.(Photo: BHA)

ANDREW TATE WAS BAYFIELD'S PIONEER druggist. He built and lived in the house now owned by Mrs. E.R. Mitchell and his drug store was close by—right where the Odd Fellows building now stands. To say merely that Andrew Tate was a druggist is doing him an injustice, because for many years he was lawyer, doctor and general advisor to the whole village.

He came here in 1857, and like most of our pioneer men, undertook many civic jobs and did them well. Through his efforts the first school was organized. For many years his services as legal and medical advisor were in demand and were given to all, usually without price. He was County Judge, District Attorney, County Treasurer, member of the Town Board, President of the Water Company and held other minor offices, all with honor to himself and profit to the community.

One of his jobs in 1859 was Deputy Collector for the Port of Bayfield. He kept the record of boat arrivals and departures, and when the steamer *Lady Elgin*, which left Bayfield on Sep. 3, 1860, was lost five days later, he wrote in the port records:

"The steamer *Lady Elgin* lost Sep. 8, 1860, on Lake Michigan. She ran regular between Chicago and this place, and was commanded by Captain Jack Wilson. She was run down by the Schooner *Augustin* of Oswego. It occurred at half past two o'clock in the morning. Number of passengers and crew lost, supposed to be over 300. The Captain lost."

This terrible lake tragedy has been immortalized in the once popular ballad, "Lost on the *Lady Elgin.*"

Andrew Tate owned the first flag to fly over Bayfield. It was made in 1858 by the "deft fingers of a native Indian woman" from material he purchased in Superior. It was a good sized flag, 4½ x 8. It flew above Bayfield for the first time on July 4, 1858, and from then on, through the years there were little notations in *The Bayfield Press* that Judge Tate was the first to have his flag flying on the Fourth of July. And in March, 1891, *The Press* said: "Tuesday was the 34th anniversary of the birth of Bayfield. Judge Tate had his flag up on the occasion. A book of early reminiscences of the town would read like a novel."

Today Judge Tate's flag still exists, and is in the possession of his son-in-law, A.H. Wilkinson.

In 1885 Dr. Hannum was working in sort of a doctor-druggist partnership with Andrew Tate, both sharing the drug store as their place of business. For some reason they placed a very large stone in front of the drug store and painted it red. Of course, it was no sooner in place than everyone who walked down the street stopped, looked at it, and said something about it. Fortunately, a reporter from *The Bayfield Press* recorded the comments made by the following people:

"That ought to have been set in farther."–William Knight.

"That's the painted rock, isn't it?–Henry Conley.

"What are you going to put on it? White letters?–John Gonyon.

"What did you put that stone there for?–Joe McCloud.

"Did you know that stone was in the street?–Pat Howley.

"Now you want to drill a hole in the top and fasten a ring in it to hitch horses to"–J. H. Nourse.

"Why didn't you paint it white?–W. McLain.

"Hello! You're going to paint the town red?–John McCloud

"Going to paint all your rocks?"–John Collar

"That stone is changing color."–Ed Boutin

"That is a good color."–S. E. Mahan.

"What is that thing there?"–A stranger.

"You ought to have the wide side that way."–Col. McLain.

"Is that a tombstone?"–Fred Fischer.

"Hello! Is that the rock of ages?"–D.L. Pratt.

If Fred Meyers should decide tomorrow to place a totem pole in front of his drugstore, we would discover that times in Bayfield have not changed much. People would like it, they wouldn't like it, it would be too bright, not bright enough, too close to the street, too far back, but one thing sure it would not be greeted with indifference. Just as they did back in 1885, everyone would be interested enough to comment.

By the way, whatever happened to the big red rock that Dr. Hannum and Andrew Tate put in front of their drug store? When the Bayfield pioneers were not sitting around the old box stove in James Chapman's store to exchange the news of the day, they were spending a few moments of relaxation in Andrew Tate's corner drug store. Currie Bell wrote about him: "He was a walking encyclopedia of early events here, full of quaint sayings that made his place of business a favorite resort."

When there was no doctor, Mr. Tate would give remedies for the sick. Harvey Nourse used to say that the remedy he usually offered was a croton oil plaster. It was a severe remedy, but it seemed to work, or else pioneers were very hearty. Anyway, the people who used it, got well.

In appearance, Andrew Tate was a very tall, thin man, and usually had a bad cough, though it was not "a cough that carried him off," for he lived a full and interesting 77 years. He was enthusiastic about patent medicines and pills. When people came into the drug store to get his advice on patent medicine, he would give them something with the remark, "This is good. I've used it."

And, as Harvey Nourse said, "The customer would then choose something different, figuring if the product didn't do any more for him that it had for Mr. Tate, it couldn't be much good."

And here Captain Tyler comes into the story again, as he does into most of the early history stories. He used to tell this one about Andrew Tate. Mr. Tate, as has been mentioned, was tall and very thin, just skin and bones. One day he was on a ladder painting his store, when the ladder broke. Captain Tyler came down the street just as it happened. Without the ladder, the thin Mr. Tate was balanced in the air until an updraft struck him and started him skyward. Tyler, with quick thinking, grabbed a brick and threw it to him. With this added weight, Mr. Tate managed to drop to the ground:

Like the other Bayfield pioneers, Andrew Tate had a beautiful yard and garden and one of the numerous fountains that gave Bayfield the name, "The Fountain City." An item of Bayfield news taken from *The Ashland Press* of May 27, 1876, says: "Andrew Tate Esq., as usual, has the nicest, neatest and most cozy place in the village. His garden is a model of neatness and his beautiful fountain sends up its silvery jets and sings sweetly among the evergreens that surround it. Mr. Tate and his excellent wife show good taste in the management of their beautiful home and its surroundings."

Andrew Tate loved the study of history. He was an authority on the history of Bayfield and also branched out into other historical fields. In October, 1881, *The Ashland Press* said: "Andrew Tate of this village (Bayfield) has in his possession a section of the cane which Brooks used when he attempted to assassinate Charles Summer in the U.S. Senate Chamber. The piece in Mr. Tate's possession is the lower end, and has an iron ferule, and was presented to him by John P. Hamlin, who was one of the Capitol Police on duty at the time the assault was made. What historical associations cluster around the relic of the days when the slave dealers tried to crush out the onward march of the free men of the North."

And it took Andrew Tate to prove that Bayfield is the home of the planked whitefish. March 17, 1894, *The Bayfield Press*: "Ashland papers are indulging in a slight controversy over the originator of planked whitefish. Andrew Tate of this place, who is an authority on historical events, informs *The Press* that the first whitefish planked on Lake Superior was in the summer of 1862 at this place, under the direct supervision of Joseph Hamlin of Washington, D.C., who was spending a few weeks here and who was recognized in the East as an expert in the line of cooking planked shad. Ashland has robbed Bayfield of her Indian Agency and the U.S. Land Office, and Washburn has gobbled up the county seat, but the man or men who attempt to rob her of the honor of being the identical spot where the first planked whitefish made its appearance on the festive board, will have to fight or take a back seat. As a hint to those who might be so rash as to take the matter into the courts, *The Press* would state that Uncle Andrew is prepared to show portions of the original skeleton of the first planked whitefish."

When Andrew Tate died in Bayfield on May 14, 1900, the community lost a devoted citizen and it was the end of Tate's corner drug store, where people had gathered for years, where Uncle Andrew had offered them advice along with the pills and patent medicines he liked so well. It was the end of his quaint, humorous sayings, and with him went his personal knowledge of the history of Bayfield.

Currie Bell wrote him a fine and proper obituary, but at the end he cast form aside and wrote simply, "Uncle Andrew, we miss you. Requiescat in pace."

And then, an obituary didn't seem to be enough for the passing of such a beloved person as Andrew Tate, or the corner drug store, now so empty without him. Currie took more space in *The Press* and wrote: "Boys old in years with silvery locks, yet with hearts as young as in the days of auld lang syne, there's a corner down town where we were wont to gather. It is vacant now. Soon, ah! too soon, other corners will be the same, and the place that knows the old boys of today, will be filled with the new boys of tomorrow. There's a gap in the ranks: close up!"

Mrs. Andrew Tate

Tate's Drugstore, c. 1895, At corner of 1ˢᵗ. N. 1ˢᵗ Street & Rittenhouse Ave. The Family consisted of Andrew, Nellie & Daughter Lillian. (Photo: BHA)

Mʀꜱ. Aɴᴅʀᴇᴡ Tᴀᴛᴇ ᴡᴀꜱ ᴀ fine person. Some of the best adjectives apply to her for she was talented, capable, and gracious. Mrs. M. DeMars, who lived across the street from Tates, remembers her well. Alec Butterfield attended her Sunday School class and still recalls her many kindnesses.

The diaries, so fortunately kept by Mrs. Tate, reveal interesting sidelights on pioneer life in Bayfield. It is easy to picture that life, for the Tate family lived in the house now owned by Mrs. E.R. Mitchell and outwardly the house has not changed too much since Andrew Tate built it.

The Tates certificate of marriage is written on a ruled piece of paper by L.H. Wheeler, pastor of the mission church at Odanah. He states: "This certifies that Mr. Andrew Tate and Miss Nellie Hall, both white citizens of the town of Bayfield, county of Bayfield, Wisconsin, having requested to be united in marriage, and I, having examined one of the parties on oath, and being satisfied that there was no legal impediment thereto, did, in the town aforesaid at the house of O.K. Hall in the afternoon of July 1, one thousand and eight hundred and sixty six, unite the said parties in marriage, in the presence of O.K. Hall and his wife Fannie, parents of the bride, as witnesses. I further certify that the said Andrew Tate was born in Washington, D.C. and is by profession and business an attorney at law and that his wife, Nellie, was born in Michigan and was living with her parents at the time of her marriage and that her father is now engaged in business as a merchant in town and village of Bayfield, aforesaid.

Mr. Wheeler also wrote: "Credentials of my ordination are on file in the office of clerk of the circuit court for LaPointe Co."

This is the first entry made by Mrs. Tate in her diary on Jan. 1, 1872: "Another New Year! How the time flies. Altogether the day passed very pleasantly. I wonder if the whole year will glide by as happily, with so little to ruffle or mar our tranquility."

Jan. 29, 1872. "Sewed some. Finished the skirt and overskirt of my new alpaca."

This is a typical entry. Hardly a day passed when she was not sewing, knitting or mending. Mrs. DeMars recalls the old Howe machine Mrs. Tate used with the needle and threader on a high plate.

Feb. 6, 1872. "In the evening attended a dinner party at Mrs. Vaughn's. Had a very pleasant time, as we always do at her house. It was settled that a party of us go down the Bay Thursday on a sleigh and fishing excursion."

Feb. 7, 1872. "The day was spent in busy preparations for our trip tomorrow and now I believe everything is in readiness. Bob (Pike) and (Wm.) Knight have been in and out many times during the day and evening to talk about the trip."

Feb. 8, 1872. "A lovely day, most charming for our excursion. About eleven of our party of 14 started with a four horse team. The sleighing was grand on the ice, the shore beautifully robed in white, fleecy snow and frost and ice glittered on the rocks. We stopped at a cave which was very beautiful. After we arrived at the house, we made preparations for the night and got our supper, after which we danced, played cards, talked and laughed until 12, then all retired to our beds on the floor.

Feb. 9, 1872. Awoke in the morning much refreshed from the little sleep we got and found the sun streaming in at the window. Soon our party were all stirring and such a babble of voices and laughing and raising of heads and so much confusion, but after we had finished our breakfast, (which, by the way, was excellent) we all went to Fish Creek and fished from there to Ashland and then back to the creek and here; part returned to camp and part remained and fished, but soon we got cold and started out on foot, but met the sleigh. On arriving found a delightful meal awaiting us. The evening was spent as before, dancing, etc."

Feb. 10, 1872. "Our last day together. On rising, we found another pleasant day dawning. We dressed and ate breakfast and collected our things and then started for home. Felt quite bad owing to a fall, but soon felt better. Our ride home was charming and everyone was delighted with the trip. Last night we heard wolves howling. They made the woods sing. It was with feelings of regret that we parted on arriving home, so attached had we become and never were three days more pleasantly spent, days never to be forgotten. Bob ran in for a minute in the evening and we talked it over and enjoyed it almost as much as though we were going through it again."

Truly they were "days never to be forgotten" by the people who had enjoyed them, for my grandfather, in a letter written 68 years later, recalled the same camping party.

The house where they camped was a small one on a hay farm owed by Asaph Whittlesey, founder of Ashland. At that time, very few people lived on the Ashland townsite. The party went down from Bayfield in two sleighs, with a third sleigh bringing their food, cooking utensils and blankets. My grandfather, William Knight, wrote: "Mr. Hayward was with us and brought his fiddle and at night we would dance until 12 o'clock then we would stretch a sheet or blanket across the room in the middle and the men made their beds on one side and the women on the other side. In the morning after we got up, everybody went to work putting to rights, making fires and getting breakfast. In the day we would go fishing in Whittlesey Creek and Fish Creek and play cards and tell stories.

It was not an expensive trip, nor a long one, but those three days spent with a company of good friends were so rich in companionship that the memory of them lasted a lifetime.

Naturally in the diaries of Mrs. Andrew Tate we find reference to "northeasters." February 12, 1872. "A fearful northeast storm. Still, I have enjoyed it."

Sometimes she enjoyed them; sometimes they got on her nerves, which is still true in Bayfield life today.

Feb. 28, 1872. Very favorable news of our railroad grant today."

Bayfield was trying hard to get a railroad, and although they rejoiced at the prospects in 1872 the first train would not arrive until 11 years later.

Then comes March, the month that was hardest on the pioneers. The sweetest dispositions cracked and with reason. The town was completely shut in on itself. A miserable rough road through the forest to St. Paul was the only way out. The snow was deep, mail was uncertain. It was cold. Mrs. Tate wrote: "Have been blue today, that is nothing new. I am beginning fairly to hate myself." March was not too bad when each citizen sat and hated himself, but when they began to hate each other, there was usually trouble.

March 23, 1872. Have been feeling wretched today, however, kept up and did my usual Saturday work and Andrew invited a gentleman for dinner. Several called after dinner, but when I was at last left alone and had given Lilly her bath, I lay down with my book, "*Stepping Heavenward* to read, but soon fell asleep and was awakened by Matie and Mrs. Hayward, but before being fairly awake, Hasey and Miss Walker came for a book of plays. I was as short and cross as I could be, made myself thoroughly disagreeable, consequently, am out of sorts for being so and I think I had better retire."

Things were a little more cheerful on March 27, 1872, when Mrs. Tate wrote: "A beautiful spring day, and my little Lilly's 5th birthday. Dear child, may she live to see many and may they also be as bright and lovely as this."

Lilly was the only child the Tates had. Their daughter, Ida, had died in childhood.

March 31, 1872. "Have felt much happier for a day or two. Have returned my book and concluded it is much better to be my own self and not strive to be something more than nature designed me to be."

April 2, 1872. "(Wm.) Knight came in and invited us out sleighing. Quite a party went. We called on Mary Warren (at LaPointe), made a fire, snowballed and had a nice time."

In early April, a group planned an entertainment for the benefit of the Lyceum. They apparently had a nice program, but their tempers had not yet recovered from the miseries of March.

April 2, 1872. "Went to church to practice. We got quite indignant and I got so nervous I was almost sick. Went again in the evening.

April 8, 1872. "Found it raining this morning and damp and cloudy, although a dreary prospect for our entertainment tomorrow night. However, our committees and all interested braved the rain and met at the church this evening and afternoon for rehearsal."

April 9, 1872. "Has been cloudy, but not very unpleasant. Spent most of the day in preparing for the great event this evening, and now at last it is all over and was certainly a perfect success in every respect. Our proceeds amounted to over $70.00."

April 10, 1872. "Found myself tired after so much entertainment. I have had so little time to think lately, that now I feel that I shall really enjoy settling down."

April 28, one of the biggest events of the year for the pioneers–"ice breaking up."

May 4 brought further good news–"A sail vessel arrived from Duluth."

May 31, 1872. "Dr. McCormick, Lou, Mrs. Hayward and Hasey visited Ashland. Took the tug *Keyes* and were gone all day. Found the *city* full of mud, stumps, and brush; one street cleared and probably a dozen new buildings, and this is to be a great and flourishing city!"

Later she wrote: "some excitement about Ashland, but it doesn't seem to affect us much."

It is true that Bayfield was not affected much by the sudden prospects for Ashland real estate with the railroad coming in. However, in the winter of 1872, when the railroaders turned on the Ashlanders during the Ashland War, the Bayfield militia, which later became known as the Bayfield Rifles, had to go over there to put an end to it. An account of the "Ashland War" was given in these columns earlier.

Here the diary of Mrs. Tate ends for 1872. No reason is given. Most likely, she was too busy living to write about it. The diaries do not begin again until 1876.

However, we know that the summer of 1872 was a good one for tourists. The paper said: "Quite a large number of pleasure seekers have been with us this week and our hotels are overflowing. Parties who have recently come over the old St. Croix road report it is in most excellent condition and travel over it is constantly increasing.

The diaries of Mrs. Andrew Tate skip from May, 1872 to January, 1876. During those years, Bayfield was going along at a steady pace with the citizens enjoying life and not getting too excited about anything. There were innovations, of course. The Bayfield news column of *The Ashland Press* reported in July, 1872, "A pop factory has been started here and is doing a good business this warm weather."

Other items stated "Several bridal parties are making Bayfield their headquarters during the honeymoon."

"Whiteside's photographers tent is pitched on Front Street and is being well patronized."

Since Front Street at that time was the same short length that it is now, it is easy to picture the tent somewhere between the present Booth Fisheries dock and the city dock with tourists strolling up single or in groups to have their pictures taken. Whiteside's and Baldwin Photographers were located "opposite the reading room" in Duluth. In summer, they took their cameras and tents and went to the small towns where they photographed the pioneers and the adventurous tourists who had made the journey across Lake Superior.

July 27, 1872. "There have been 71 arrivals at the Smith Hotel within the past three days. The hotel is a popular one, a credit to the town. Captain Smith and his wife know how to keep it."

Presidential candidates were becoming conscious that there were many voters in the midwestern wilderness. The paper said, "Horace Greeley is expected here soon when he will tell us what he knows about whitefish. He is a candidate for president."

Aug. 24, 1872. "Our town is free from sickness and is by far the healthiest place on Lake Superior."

Dec. 1873. "The Christmas Tree entertainment was the finest ever gotten up in Bayfield. Over $1,600 worth of presents, some of which were elegant, were distributed. It was a complete success."

June, 1874. "The Bayfield Hydraulic Company has leased from the owner, the Hon. H.M. Rice, the right to use the water with which the village is now supplied, for 20 years, and the town authorities are arranging to lay down new logs with a 3" bore carrying the water through all portions of the village. For this purpose a new dam will be constructed above the old one, increasing the volume of water. At the corners of the principle streets, fire plugs will be put in, hose purchased, and other apparatus furnished which will provide for the future safety of the village from conflagration. The whole improvement will cost about $2,000, which will be money well expended."

Bayfield Waterworks reservoir and dam, located in the "big ravine" on Bayfield Creek and also abreast of the Lincoln High School. The reservoir supplied the old log water system to many homes and sawmills. Circa 1880(Photo: BHA)

The waterworks provided fine fountains in the yards of the residents, which gave the name "Fountain City" to Bayfield.

Sept. 4, 1875, the paper reported: "James Chapman Esq. has some very fine trout in his new fountain, one of which weighs 2½ #. He also has a sturgeon and a turtle keeping them company."

Jan. 5, 1876, Mrs. Tate wrote: "Mrs. Hayward brought down her comforters this morning and spent the day. We tacked three for her."

This was a common and neighborly task in the pioneer days. The diaries of Mrs. Tate are very concerned with domestic affairs. Since the first article about them appeared in this column, many women have told me how much they liked to read them. It seems that with all the modern household equipment we have now, women still feel a strong kinship with the pioneer housewife and her problems.

Jan. 7, 1876. "Mr. Pike and Knight went fishing. Brought home a nice string of fish."

Jan. 8, 1876. "Mr. & Mrs. Baird came from Bad River. First team on ice from LaPointe."

This entry is a reminder of Junior Civic League activities of today.

Jan. 17, 1876. "Went around to hotel with others to make arrangements for a party to be given next Wednesday evening for the Library Association."

Jan. 19, 1876. "Spent the morning preparing for the party which took place this evening and which proved quite a success, our profits being about $35.00. We had a nice time preparing the supper."

"We had a nice time preparing the supper" is one of the lines, which makes the diaries so appealing. In 1957, the same thing is true. Groups of women still gather in Bayfield kitchens, cooking, laughing, tasting, seasoning, and then appear in the dining room with trays of lavish and delicious food and pots of wonderful coffee, compelling everyone who gets up from the table an hour later to gasp happily, "That was the best meal I ever ate."

Jan. 28, 1876. Mrs. Tate wrote in her diary, "I received a note from Matie asking me to go a-fishing. About half past eleven, Bob called for me. We had a nice time, fishing until after four. Caught 23 trout among us. Snowed quite hard before we reached home."

Feb. 1, 1876. Sewed and baked preparatory to having company tomorrow night. Afterward, Hasey and I went out and gave invitations, then went up to Mrs. Cruttendon's and spent the evening."

Since there were no telephones, it was necessary to deliver invitations and messages in person. The Cruttendons, good friends of the Tates, lived in a house since torn down located between the residence of Nettie Wilson and the Presbyterian church.

Feb. 2, 1876. "Very cold. 24 below. I finished my preparations and not feeling very well, did little else. We had a pleasant evening dancing and card playing. Everyone seemed to enjoy it. Grandma Sutton spent the night."

Feb. 3, 1876. "Mrs. Hayward gave the children a party and early in the evening, sent for us to come up so we drew Mrs. Sutton on a sled."

The Haywards lived in a house about opposite the present W.W. Moon residence, so it was no great task to draw Grandma Sutton on a sled that far."

Feb. 5, 1876 appears another line that could equally well apply to a housewife's routine in 1957. "Spent the day in performing the many duties Saturday always brings."

However, the duties were harder in 1876. The old log water system brought running cold water into the house through hand pumps, but the washing was done by hand on a board in a tub with a hand wringer. Clothes that were especially dirty were put into pounding barrels. The barrels were not large and a pounder, made of wood with four small legs on the bottom, pounded the clothes up and down until they were clean, or at least, cleaner. Mrs. DeMars told me about these pounders. She is blessed with a clear and accurate memory and a fine sense of humor and I am greatly indebted to her for the many incidents and the background I have used in the stories of Bayfield history.

Mrs. DeMars, nee Marietta LaBonte, lived across the street from the Tate home. She was a year younger than Lilly Tate, but the two little girls were close friends. They ran across the street to play without giving much thought to traffic, which was usually a plodding team drawing a wagon or sleigh and only occasionally was a fast stepping horse pulling a buggy or cutter.

Occasionally, as the children played, they would dart into Tate's basement for a quick snack of pickled peaches. Mrs. DeMars remembers that the long shelves there were completely stocked with jar after jar of canned fruits and vegetables. Mrs. Tate did all of her own cooking and canning and was well known for the delicious ginger snaps she made.

Mrs. DeMars' mother was married at 14 and, at that time, had never cooked a meal of vittles or sewed a dress, but today she would rate as a "modern" woman. No sooner were they married than she and her husband both went to work, becoming a "modern" two-income family. Mrs. LaBonte ran the LaBonte House for roomers and boarders. Mr. LaBonte worked in the mill. In addition, he had a fine garden, raising an abundance of fruit and vegetables, which were thriftily canned by his wife. He also cut all of his own wood. Mrs. LaBonte learned to cut hair and did so, charging 25 cents for a haircut.

They saved by making their own soap, as most people did. Mr. LaBonte made it by the barrel, using kitchen grease and ashes. This soft soap was dipped out of the barrel for washing clothes and scrubbing, but cake soap, for face washing, was available in stores.

Light was furnished by oil lamps and candles and it was little Marietta LaBonte's task to clean the lamp chimneys, trim the wicks and fill the lamps.

They also had a version of the modern deep freeze. During cold winter nights, bread froze solid in the pantry.

Then, as now, fish was popular on the family table. When summer came and tourists jointed the steady boarders at the LaBonte House, fish was served three times a day.

Recently, Mrs. DeMars gave me the old dining room table from the LaBonte House. (For which, again, I thank her). It stretches to banquet size and a fifth leg holds up the middle so it will not sag if a load of good food is placed on it. My grandfather, who was a steady boarder, and a tall, thin young man at that time, always sat at the end of this table, probably so he would have enough elbow room.

The weather accounts for many entries in Mrs. Tate's diaries. Feb. 13, 1876, she wrote, "Wind increased during the night, a real northeaster. How much I enjoy a storm now and then."

Feb. 14, 1876. "Helped Mary make a handkerchief box." The handkerchief box was a popular item for handwork. Along with home made pin cushions, it accounted each year for a large number of Christmas gifts.

The entry for Feb. 20, 1876, is so agelessly human, composed of contentment, shadowed by a long look ahead. She wrote: "Read and sang a little with Lilly. How monotonous life is here, and yet how happy I am in my little home. I tremble at the thought of change ever creeping into it."

It is especially poignant, for Mrs. Tate's life was to be so short. It is ironic, for she was to die of the disease which today is so effectively cured at Pureair Sanitarium. At that time, it was called "galloping consumption" and was rightly named, for until it was checked, it took human life at a gallop.

Nellie Tate wrote in her diary on Feb. 22, 1876, "Sewed. Went to office for mail, as Andrew is not well. Has grown bitter cold. Some of our people have gone to Ashland to attend party."

Bitter cold! What of it? The party loving Bayfielders simply hitched a team to a sleigh and spent a few hours jogging across the ice to Ashland.

And the Ashland people, also party-minded, were not slow to return the visit. Feb. 25, 1876, "The Ashland people are coming to have a party this evening, so I spent the day baking. Began storming about dark. However, two sleigh loads came. Went to court house and assisted with refreshments, then came home."

Feb. 26, 1876. "The storm raged all night, an old-fashioned northeaster, and still blowing and snowing."

"Old-fashioned" can hardly date back far enough to describe a northeaster, for these respected and interesting storms were undoubtedly raging for centuries before man appeared in the Lake Superior region.

Feb. 27, 1876. "The storm still continues. Huge drifts are everywhere and are increasing."

Feb. 28, 1876. "Still storming, but abated some. Mr. Knight came for us to go to the hotel and dance awhile in the evening, as the Ashland people are there, detained by the storm."

The enthusiastic *Ashland Press* version of this gay, four day party appears in this column some time ago.

March 1, 1876. Went to Mr. Bracken's funeral.

March 2, 1876. "Spent the day in a strange manner. Andrew said being a Mason's wife I must assist in packing his (Mr. Bracken's) things for his children, so went to his house, with others, and remained nearly all day."

March 5, 1876. "Mr. Patrick came for me to go to Ashland to make a visit. Shall probably go tomorrow, if pleasant."

March 6, 1876. "About noon, Pat and I started for Ashland. Pleasant ride. Mrs. Vaughn had a tea party. Met quite a number of the Ashland people. Enjoyed the evening."

After she had been in Ashland a few days, Mrs. Tate, apparently was getting homesick. March 10, 1876, she wrote: "Mrs. Vaughn gave quite a dinner company. Met some pleasant people, but not quite like our Bayfield people. Was invited to dinner next Tuesday, but think I shall be home."

March 11, 1876. "Intended going home today, but a heavy wind is blowing, so must wait. Just as we were going to bed, a fire was discovered on the next street. We stood and watched the flames consume a two-story building. A fearful, but grand sight."

March 13, 1876. "Pat and I started home. All expressed regret at my departure and kindly urged me to remain. Arrived home safely."

March 16, 1876. "A terrible northeaster. Snow blowing and drifting so one cannot see across the street. Kitchen and dining room windows entirely hidden by a huge drift. Did my work by candle light."

March 17, 1876. "Cloud broke away at noon. Everyone busy digging paths."

March 18, 1876. "Never saw such immense drifts as are everywhere about town." (Just change the date and that entry is appropriate almost every winter.)

The entry for March 20, 1876, is written with typical motherly pride. "Lillian went into the Fourth Reader."

Finally it seemed as though spring was coming. April 19, 1876. "Lillian went to the sugar bush."

April 20, 1876. "Ice very poor. A team was drowned this afternoon."

Every housewife will thoroughly understand the entry for May 6, 1876. "Cleaned, baked some and did a little of everything but sit down."

May 7, 1876. "Found upon waking this morning a cheerless northeast rainstorm had set in. The wind broke up the ice this afternoon and the *Mary Croch* left the dock to assist the *Mary Ann* which was being carried away with the ice. At dark she had reached LaPointe."

The spring of 1876 brought a series of bad northeast storms on lake and on land. Reading about them in the diaries reminded me of "the old timer's" remark quoted by Captain Eliel Hendrickson, "It don't make no difference which direction that old Northeaster comes from, she's always cold."

On May 9, 1876, Nellie Tate wrote in her diary, "Another pleasant day. *Groch* left for Duluth. Just as we left the breakfast table, Mr. Hayward came in for us to go down and see the tug launched. It was a pretty sight."

But by May 16, 1876, bad weather had returned. "A gloomy, cheerless day. Bay full of heavy lake ice. *Manistee* still lying at dock. The water logs were torn away yesterday by the rising stream."

This was the first damaging flood to be recorded since the town had been built around the stream and the citizens had harnessed it with water logs. This flood overturned the court house outbuildings, which were near the site of the present depot, and washed out a wider bed for itself, taking some gardens along with it.

May 17, 1876. "Mrs. Hayward and I went around and looked at the damage done by the water."

May 18, 1876. "Tug attempted to go to Ashland. Was prevented by ice.

May 20, 1876. The *Groch* came in. Reported seven boats between here and Duluth locked in the ice.

By May 23, spring housecleaning had begun. The reward for this annual effort was the same in those days as it is now. "Spent the whole day cleaning Andrew's office. Was very tired, but everything looked nicely and that paid me."

May 25, 1876. Boat in from Buffalo.

May 27, 1876. Boats are still troubled with ice. *Manistee* came in from Duluth.

May 28 brought a weather phenomena familiar in Bayfield. "A very warm morning, but this afternoon as we came from Sabbath School the wind changed and the thermometer fell 26 degrees in 15 minutes."

May 29, 1876. "Strong northeast winds, quite cold all day. Some ice floating in." Even the month of June did not bring relief from the ice.

June 2, 1876. "A cold northeast rain. Bay full of ice. Tug attempted to go to Ashland, but came back."

June 3, 1876. "Bob (Pike) went to Ashland on horseback as tug could not get through the ice."

June 4, 1876. Bob came home late this afternoon. *Maple Leaf* left during the night. Some ice formed near the dock. This was really an "old fashioned winter", cold enough so ice formed near the dock in June.

June 6, 1876. Strong northeast wind. Ice coming in again.

June 7, 1876. A cloudy, gloomy morning. This afternoon settled into a cold rain, from the northeast, of course. It is so discouraging. . . Gardens are suffering from the cold. Bay *full* of icebergs and more coming. Almost sick with a headache.

Of course, it is unusual to have the bay full of ice in June, but it has happened at least twice in our recorded history. The *Duluth News Tribune* of June 7, 1917, started: "Jammed in the ice about a score of great lakes freighters were forced to spend the night about half a mile from Duluth while their decks were lashed by a 60 mile gale. The only known parallel is 1876, when on June 11, eleven boats were caught in the ice 10 to 15 miles from Duluth. The ice blockade of that year lasted until July 3."

In spite of the gloom caused by having the waterfront full of ice during June, the pioneers attempted to enjoy themselves. June 9, 1876, Mrs. Tate wrote: "Mr. Colley and Knight called and invited me to go to the observatory with a party tomorrow."

The observatory was a high wooden tower built near the present site of the fire tower and the party evidently hiked up there to look at the ice situation, and see if there could be an end to it.

June 10, 1876. "A little cold and damp this morning, but sun shone out warm about 10 AM and we were startled. Had a nice walk, but rather tiresome. Ate our lunch at the observatory and arrived home about teatime. Altogether a delightful day."

"Tea time" described the evening meal. A hearty breakfast was followed by a large dinner at noon. About six o'clock "tea", a light meal, was served.

June 15, 1876. Although so warm the bay has ice still.

June 17, 1876. "Still raining and cold. Have kept two fires all day. Worked as usual. It seems that everyone is discouraged and everything seems to have come to a perfect standstill."

June 18, 1876. "Rain, nothing but rain, a real fall storm from the northeast and cold. Considerable sleet fell last night."

A bay full of ice and a sleet storm in June is a little unusual, but actually nothing a Northeaster brings surprises Bayfielders too much.

Strangers, who wish to identify a northeast wind may be told:

"You'll know it is a northeast wind,

When straight back your ears are pinned."

And I am also convinced that:

"When the wind is from northeast

It's best to be outdoors the least."

June 26, 1876, Nellie Tate wrote in her diary, "We went to see a sort of magic lantern in the evening." The magic lantern was a forerunner of the slide projectors used today. The old stereoptic slides were shown on a screen and most elegant parlors contained a wooden hand viewer for them.

July 1, 1876, was an important day in the lives of the Tates. She wrote" This is the 10th anniversary of my marriage. How time flies. Spent the day baking and making ice cream as we had a few of our friends in to spend the evening."

July 3, 1876. "A strong southwest wind has blown dreadfully all day. I decorated the house with cedar and it took me most of the day, as I worked under great disadvantage, owing to the wind."

The decorations were for an important day in the life of the United States, the Centennial Fourth of July. The United States of America was 100 years old and the people of Bayfield, joining in the celebration, no doubt marveled over the fact that in only 100 years the United States had grown from a few states on the Atlantic coast to include a state named Wisconsin in the midwestern wilderness.

July 4, 1876. "The Centennial fourth. Mrs. Cruttendon and family spent the day with us. We went and listened to the Declaration of Independence in the morning, then attended different amusements in the afternoon. We had quite a display of fireworks, but a rain came up just before dark, which interfered somewhat. The town looked very pretty. Most of the buildings being decorated with cedar and flags."

July 6, 1876. "Spent most of the day trimming my hat." In those days, a hat was not to be discarded after one season of wear because of changing styles. A good hat could be trimmed over and over and sometimes lasted for years.

July 19, 1876. "Mary read aloud in the evening and I mended." This was long before the coming of radio, TV, or even the wind-up phonograph. Reading aloud was a common and pleasant form of entertainment. Fortunate was the housewife who could sit and do her mending while someone read aloud to her."

July 25, 1876. "Warm and delightfully pleasant. Ironed and got ready to go to Ashland. Worked myself into a perfect fever. Mrs. Cruttendon and Lillian and I are to be gone until Saturday. Had a nice ride down and found a hearty welcome awaiting us."

July 28, 1876. "Still delightfully pleasant. Quite a large party of us went out to Ponoka. Mr. Vaughn took us to the depot in a wagon. We spent a delightful day. In the evening, Mr. Chysoweth took Mrs. Cruttendon and I out for a boat ride. It was charming."

July 29, 1876. Mrs. Tate was evidently subject to the typical "after vacation" feeling. She wrote, "We bade our friends good bye this morning and returned home after a delightful visit. I went out with Andrew after tea. Feel a little restless tonight and dissatisfied, and yet am very grateful for the enjoyment of the past few days."

July 29, 1876, brought another event, not recorded in Mrs. Tate's diary, but in *The Ashland Press*, under the headline, "Heavy Bet."

"When the *Peerless* was at Bayfield two weeks ago, Captain MacIntire, who is a staunch Democrat, came ashore and was warm in his expression for Tilden and Hendricks, backing his words with offers to bet on his men. James Chapman, Esq., immediately thought to test his fate and told him to put up or shut up. The Captain happened to own 160 acres of pineland in Bayfield County and offered to put it up against a like amount, which offer Mr. Chapman immediately accepted. The deeds were drawn and deposited with a stakeholder and the parties separated, each feeling that he was sure to win. The land in question is valued by its owners at $1,000, it being good pineland. This is the first wager we have heard of on Lake Superior. 'Rah for Hays and Wheeler.' The bet was on, but it took a long time to find out who won.

In 1876, communication was poor and a month after the election, there was still uncertainty; but finally it seemed sure that Hayes was elected President and Jim Chapman of Bayfield won the pine land.

On December 16, 1876, the paper stated: "On receipt of the recent telegrams relating to election returns from Louisiana and Florida, many of the citizens desiring such a result gave way to the loyal enthusiasm which had been suppressed by the more doubtful prospects and indulged in a display of fireworks (which were seen in Ashland) firing of cannon and some degree of hilarity, with no greater harm than the shattering of windows and sprinkling one or two faces with burned powder.

"The electoral college vote on December 6 gave Hayes 185, Tilden 184. Reports from Washington state that everything is quiet and it is generally believed that Hayes will be inaugurated without trouble."

Aug. 11, 1876, Mrs. Tate wrote in her diary, "Mrs. Hayward, Matie and our family went down to Bob's dock to see a vessel load with ice." Each winter Bayfield put up a good ice harvest and shipped it boat to boat during the summer to cities in need of it. Since the Tates had lost their daughter, Ida, in childhood, and had only the one child, Lillian, she got a great deal of attention. On August 24, 1876, Mrs. Tate wrote, "Sewed for Lillian's doll all day."

Sept. 4, 1876, she was still sewing, but was now preparing clothes for the long winter ahead when washing and drying them would be difficult. She "cut out six shirts for Andrew this afternoon." Now days there are not many (if any) women who make all of their husband's shirts, but then it was necessary. Since Mrs. Tate was skilled at sewing there is no doubt that Andrew had six nice looking shirts to start the winter of 1876.

Sept. 12, 1876, came the event that is still an annual one, "School commenced today."

Oct. 2, 1876. Matie came for me after dinner to have her dress fitted. While there, the *Manistee* came and the ladies came to go to the boat with the Carringtons. Went with them. Mrs. Willey took tea with us, after which we all went down to the boat again and stayed until she left.

Oct. 5, 1876. "A terrible snowstorm, enough to give one the horrors." The "horrors" is probably an exact statement. Since the ice blockade had lasted until July 3 it was frightening to see winter appear again on October 5. It was far more disheartening than it would be now, for at that time they needed another month for the boats to run and bring in supplies, which they were counting on for the winter.

Oct. 9, 1876. "We expect to buy a cow, which has been quite an event in our family."

The Tate residence, being so close to the dock, was very handy for their friends who arrived by boat last night. It seemed that no one hesitated to call on them at any hour. Oct. 11, 1876. Mr. and Mrs. Vaughn returned last night about 12. Spent the remainder of the night with us. I went home with them and found that my dear friend, Hasey, is soon to be married and I am to go and assist in the preparations."

The next night there was more company. Oct. 12, 1876. Was awakened by Mr. Chysoweth and Mrs. Cooley, who arrived during the night. They stopped with us until this afternoon. After they left I went up to Mrs. Hayward's and assisted with her lambrequin."

Since the ladies made "lambrequins" for their homes quite frequently, I went to my good advisor, Mrs. DeMars and asked her what they were. She explained they were a shelf with a rather complicated drapery hanging from it and the whole thing was put on the wall with brackets for a decoration. They took a great deal of time to make.

October 22, 1876. Mrs. Tate was overcome with the feeling, which so often attacks Bayfielders at the beginning of winter. She wrote, "Another somber sky and a slow drizzling rain. Have just been reading a description of the lovely climate of the Bermudas and feel that I should love to go there."

Nov. 3, 1876. "Bob (Pike) started for Buffalo with a cargo of lumber." When Bob left it meant the mill had shut down for the season. Bayfield, as far as lumbering was concerned, lived on a seasonal routine. In the winter the lumber camps were used, as many as 2,000 men moved into the camps, logs were cut and in the spring, they were floated down to the lake when the water was high in the streams. Then the mill started. As soon as the lumber was cut, schooners sailed up the lake to haul it to the cities. They continued to haul as late in the fall as possible. When the logs were cut, the mill shut down and the whole routine started over.

Nov. 23, 1876. The *Wadsworth* made her last trip. By Nov. 29 they expected Bob Pike back from Buffalo and Mrs. Tate wrote, "Have been looking anxiously for the *Maple Leaf* all day." Nov. 30, "The Hayward family ate Thanksgiving dinner with us." Dec. 1, Tug *Amethyst* was in. Ashland bay closed."

Then on Dec. 3, the *Maple Leaf* came home. She wrote, "*Mary Ann* came in from Duluth, also the *Maple Leaf*, bringing Bob. He was in this evening and we had a little chat."

It was exactly a month since the *Maple Leaf* had left for Buffalo with her cargo of lumber. She was a sturdy vessel, with good sails, but heavily loaded and had November weather on Lake Superior to contend with so the time of arrival was always uncertain.

Dec. 5, 1876. Thermostat stands at 16 below tonight. Some ice formed in bay. Dec. 10, Bay nearly filled with ice." It had been a short season with the bay free of ice only from July 3 to Dec. 10.

Dec. 11, 1876. We all went up to Mrs. Cruttendon's and sewed for the Christmas tree in the evening. Wind during the night broke the ice up."

Then began the drama played every year since man decided to inhabit both Madeline Island and the mainland. Dec. 15. Boat crossed to LaPointe this afternoon. Dec. 16. Bay closed last night. A man crossed this afternoon. Dec. 18. "The first team from LaPointe."

Dec. 31, 1876. "New Year's Eve! How rapidly the year has slipped by. I wonder if the one to come will pass in like manner."

Jan. 1, 1877. Mrs. Tate wrote: "Another year has departed and again we welcome a new year. Nothing around us indicates the change. The day dawned as brightly and the snow fell as silently as on other days and people come and go, little heeding that something has passed from us beyond recall, and as I write, I question what these pages may contain, ere another new year dawns."

Jan. 3, 1877. "We organized a whist club, something that has been long talked of.'

In 1877, when you wanted mince meat you made it, and it was not too easy. Mrs. Tate wrote: "Have spent the whole day working with mince meat and attended to other household matters."

Jan. 15, 1877. "Andrew just entered, saying the Mercury has fallen to twenty-two below, the coldest night this winter, but it is perfectly quiet so we do not notice the cold very much."

Jan. 16, 1877. "I went to Mrs. Hayward's to sew, but we coasted most of the time. Went around for Emma Nourse and had a nice time sliding. It made me feel that my childhood days were not far gone after all."

Jan. 25, 1877. "A lovely moonlight night, and many enjoying the coasting."

Then, as though to apologize for the short summer and the ice blockade of June, the weather gave Bayfield almost a month of spring in the middle of winter. It all began on Jan. 26, 1877 when Mrs. Tate wrote: "A charming day, as soft and balmy as a spring day and scarcely a cloud to be seen. A lovely sunset and a beautiful night. The noise of the coasters reaches me as I write."

The coasters were probably sliding down Washington Avenue to the lake. As Mrs. Tate sat in her home it was easy for her to hear their laughter and voices on that still winter night.

Jan. 28, 1877. "Very warm and delightfully pleasant. Thermometer had indicated 48 above. Jan. 29, "Still delightful weather. This fine weather would almost cheat one into believing that spring has come, but I fear we shall make up for it with a storm." Jan. 30, "It settled into quite a rain about four this afternoon and is still raining quite hard." Jan. 31, Very unpleasant, but mild. Snow very soft and walking bad."

Feb. 6, 1877. "Another lovely spring day. This weather is positively wonderful. The snow is nearly gone and work has been abandoned." Feb. 7, "A charming day. Spent a busy day baking cake and making ice cream as whist club meets here." Feb. 8, "Still this charming spring like weather continues. It is most remarkable. Today people have been using wagons about town. Feb. 14, "Very pleasant indeed. Some work is being done outdoors and with wagons. It is wonderful. Such spring like weather was never known here at this season. The Indians are making some sugar. Feb. 20, "Another lovely day. The ice is getting poor in some places. Clear water has been seen in the north channel today."

But this appearance of spring in the supposed middle of winter was a little unnerving, perhaps even a trifle frightening to the pioneers, for Mrs. Tate wrote: "Feb. 21, 1877. Still this lovely weather continues. I feel it would be a relief to have a real old-fashioned snow storm. Ice is said to be gone the other side of the islands.

Feb. 22, 1877. Much colder this morning and snowing. It raised my spirits considerably.

The ice must have remained in good condition between Bayfield and Ashland, for on Feb. 27, "two sleigh loads of ladies from Ashland came."

March 6, 1877. "Went out in the ice boat with several others this afternoon. Had a pleasant ride."

The life lived by ladies of the 1870's so often pictured as quiet and domestic with no effort made at outdoor activities, completely fades away in Mrs. Tate's diaries. Nellie Tate and her friends, who were in their 30's, or older, lived at a pace that the modern woman could hardly keep up with. Their household duties were uncountable, and were all done by hand, from making their husbands neckties, to canning food for the family all winter. Yet, they found time for fishing trips, coasting, ice boating, skating, rowing, hiking and frequently they took tents and went camping.

The devotion to her only child, Lillian, is expressed over and over by Mrs. Tate and especially on March 27, when she writes "Lillian's tenth birthday. The time has slid along so noiselessly that I pause, hardly able to credit it. The happy years, may they always be filled with happiness for my darling child."

April 3, 1877, Mrs. Tate wrote in her diary, "Considerable excitement has been manifest over election. Bob came in to a very late supper, completely tired out. I am thankful the day is over. There is so much ill feelings, always."

In those days, ladies took no part in politics and, of course, did not have the right to vote. April 4, she wrote, "Mrs. Cruttendon and Mrs. Knight spent the evening with me. Gentlemen all attended a town meeting. Over and over the same pattern was followed. Election day came "there was so much ill feeling, always", and then the following evening the ladies stayed home alone and all the gentlemen attended a town meeting, where, presumably, they argued some more, or else patched up their differences for another year.

April 8, 1877, "Ice is getting very poor indeed. Several broke through yesterday."

This too, follows a pattern, and has been since civilization arrived in Chequamegon Bay. The ice absolutely must be walked or ridden on until someone falls through, then spring is on the way.

April 13, 1877, The ice broke up near LaPointe this afternoon and open water was to be seen nearly across the bay."

The Bayfield Rifles, since their defense of Ashland during the "Ashland War", had kept well-organized, entertained at military balls, sponsored Fourth of July celebrations and generally enjoyed themselves. April 14, 1877, Mrs. Tate wrote: "The Bayfield Rifles drilled this afternoon. They made quite a show and certainly speak well for our little town."

April 16, 1877. "The birds sang as gaily as in May this morning. Andrew is busy taking away storm sheds and working in the yard."

The first boat from LaPointe is always an event of the year. In 1877, it occurred on April 17. "Slightly cloudy and windy. Ice broken up and water almost clear. Boat crossed from LaPointe this afternoon. Quite an eventful day."

April 20, 1877. Bob (Pike) was in this evening. We have had so little snow or rain that the streams are very low, greatly impairing the logging. He is complaining, as others are, I suppose."

High water in the spring was very necessary. The streams were the highways through the forests and if there was not enough rushing water in the spring to float the logs to the lake, the logger was in trouble. There were no bull dozers, trucks or even roads which he could use as a substitute.

April 23, 1877. Some cooler than yesterday. Fires not uncomfortable. Worked and cut out my gray dress and ripped up my striped silk preparatory to make over. Tug came from Ashland. A strong southwest wind has cleared the bay of the floating ice."

April 24, 1877. "Had a present of a large bouquet of flowers from one of my Sabbath School scholars. The first of the season."

Picking arbutus was a regular spring affair. Parties went out to gather bouquets and in the fall, went out to gather colored leaves.

April 25, 1877. "Clear, mild and very pleasant. Andrew planted some peas and did considerable work in the garden."

April 27, 1877. "Still this cold northeast wind is blowing, chilling on through and through. Bob went out duck hunting."

Ducks, deer and fish were part of the daily food supply of the pioneers. Hunting regulations were simple: When game was available, get it.

April 28, 1877. Cold and wind still blowing, threatening snow. Bob came in to a late tea, having been obliged to camp at Pike's creek. Left the tug and walked in. This is by far the heaviest wind storm we have had for a long time. Tug has not been in for two days, so we are without mail."

April 30, 1877: "Bright and pleasant. Wind nearly gone down. Tug came bringing the mail. Received a long letter from Mary Warren. *Manistee* came in from Duluth this morning, quite early."

The *Manistee*, captained by John McKay, was usually the first boat into Bayfield in the spring. And on May 6, there were "two boats in from Duluth."

May 7, 1877. Bob (Pike) met with quite a misfortune, that of losing the diamond from his pin." In those days it was high fashion for a gentlemen to wear a diamond stickpin in his neck tie.

Mrs. Tate's diaries were not secret. Other people read them, and on occasion, wrote in them. May 8, 1877, Bob Pike wrote: "The day I think a steamboat will arrive from Duluth."

Mrs. Tate wrote an answer: "The St. Paul in from Buffalo, so Robert, a slight mistake after all."

May 9, 1877 the arbutus were blooming in the woods around Bayfield and Mrs. Tate wrote: "I, with some others, went out for mayflowers. Had a pleasant walk, but got very tired. Bob came in the evening with some samples of wallpaper for me to select from." (Naturally, Mr. and Mrs. Tate did their own wallpapering.)

May 12, 1877. "Warm and delightful. Atmosphere filled with smoke. The sun looks as it does in Indian Summer. The same red appearance. Bob went to Red Cliff with the *Mocking Bird.*"

On May 14, 1877, Mrs. Tate started her springhouse cleaning. This was no casual affair. It lasted for ten days or two weeks each spring and fall. They always "took up the carpets" which were wall to wall and tacked down. I could not understand why until I consulted Mrs. DeMars. Now I know there was a very good reason for doing so.

The carpets, in those days, were what was called "ingrain." Mrs. DeMars still has a small one. They are loosely woven, about the texture of burlap, with a raised patter. Straw was used to cover the floor, then the carpets were stretched over it and tacked down. Naturally, dust sifted through the loose weave into the straw, which was being completely shredded by people walking on it. By the time spring came, a stifling cloud of dust must have risen every time anyone crossed the room.

In the midst of taking up carpets, wall papering, unsettling and resettling rooms, Mrs. Tate was understandably tired. Then, it started to storm northeast and lasted until May 21 when she wrote" Cloud broke away for a little while and cheated us into the belief that it was going to clear off, then gathered again and the storm increased, wind rising and rain falling, not in large drops, but misting. I have been exerting myself to ward off the "blues" all day. No wonder people commit suicide in London on account of gloomy weather. We have done little. The storm would not permit."

But the weather changed, as it always does, and on May 22, the "sun shone out brightly, but wind continued blowing very hard, increasing about noon. Cleaning was resumed again and we have the pantry and kitchen in pretty good order."

That spring, in spite of the weather, the cleaning took only ten days. May 24 she wrote: "A lovely day. Nearly completed the cleaning, only a few little things remaining too be done. Am pleased with my work, and very thankful it is done."

June 2, 1877. "Andrew went to Ashland. The first train from Milwaukee coming through tonight. Quite a party went to receive the officials."

This was a great event for Bayfielders as well as the people of Ashland. The train made it possible for Bayfield to receive supplies during the winter by hauling them across the ice from Ashland by team.

June 3, 1877. "Tug came in bringing home the Bayfield people and a party of gentlemen."

June 4, 1877. "Cool and cloudy. It seems almost like weather we have in September. After finishing my work, I sat down to write a few minutes, while waiting for the irons to heat, when who should call but Col. Knight and Mr. Spaulding. I was much embarrassed to be caught in my working clothes."

Since the advent of blue jeans, ladies are no longer "much embarrassed to be caught in working clothes. However, the entry brings to mind the difficulties of ironing in those days. Mrs. Tate had to wait for irons to heat on top of the kitchen range, iron with one until it cooled off, take another one, being sure it was not too hot to scorch, and keep on this way until the ironing was done. Thirty years later, the Ladies Home Journal carried a helpful ironing hint–number the irons and use them in rotation. These irons were also called "sadirons" and were well named, for I know I would feel sad if I had to use them.

June 10, 1877. Again company arrived during the night, and, as usual, Mrs. Tate was delighted. "Had a most delightful surprise during the night. My uncle, William, came and made us a short visit while the boat was lying at the dock."

June 12, 1877. Mrs. (John) Knight came for me to go to the boat after tea. (They went to see the City of Duluth, which had been loading lumber all day.)

June 14, 1877. Mrs. Knight sent for me to advise her about upholstering a sofa. After dinner, Matie came down and I went up there and helped make a carpet.

This was truly the day of "home-made" things, some of which are treasured now as antiques. For a time, skills were abandoned in favor of "book-learning", but now with "how-to" books and workshops, we can again turn out articles that a pioneer would be proud of.

June 16, 1877, Nellie Tate wrote in her diary, "Mr. Patrick called and invited me to go to Silver Creek fishing with him and Matie tomorrow."

Matie Hayward was a popular young lady, and Mrs. Tate evidently acted as chaperone for the trip to Silver Creek.

June 17, 1877. "Bob (Pike) took dinner with us. Was feeling quite low-spirited on account of a raft near the island which has broken up twice already, and he fears it will be again."

June 18, 1877. "A strong wind from the southwest, but very warm. After dinner took the tug and had a very pleasant ride to Ashland. Mrs. Fifield invited us to stop with her. After tea we went out and made a few purchases."

June 19, 1877. "Arose very early and took the train at seven for Silver Creek found the weather cold and cloudy and a heavy northeast wind blowing. Thought the first thing of poor brother Robert and his raft. We had a pleasant day fishing and returned at half past ten tired out."

June 20, 1877. "Found a very cold, rainy, disagreeable day had dawned when we awoke and found ourselves nearly sick. However, we took the tug and came home. After getting a cup of tea I lay down, thinking I was paying dearly for my pleasure with an aching head and limbs."

June 21, 1877. "Cleared up this morning. Felt much better so took up my usual duties again and got the house in pretty good order and sewed some on Lilly's dresses."

June 23, 1877. "After dinner took my hat up to Mrs. Haywards and we trimmed hats all afternoon. She invited us to remain for tea. Bob was over to the island working on his raft, which has again gone to pieces. It does seem that he has more than his share of trouble."

"It does seem that he has more than his share of trouble" is indicative of the character of Bob Pike. When I referred to him in this column sometime ago as the outstanding citizen of Bayfield's first century, I noted the achievements of his life. In our slang nowadays, "He had it made." Reading the diaries of Mrs. Tate, it is easily discovered that he made it the hard way. There were no government loans for small businesses; there were very few banks in this part of the country. He had to save what money he could from shoestring operations, fight the weather, his rafts broke up, his mill at LaPointe blew up, low water in streams delayed the logging. He took his own lumber to Buffalo on a sailing vessel in November, after the mill was shut down. His office caught fire. His youthful struggles to make logging and a small sawmill pay, are real Horatio Alger stuff. His persistence and skill won. He achieved the flourishing sawmill, the beautiful home at Salmo, and the right to be an outstanding citizen.

One small triumph is noted on June 25 when Mrs. Tate wrote: "Bob successful in getting his raft over this afternoon."

June 29, 1877, Mrs. Tate was busy with a lambrequin again. Made a lambrequin for Lilly's room. It took me nearly all day."

July 1, 1877. "Attended Sabbath School. Afterward read the *New York Observer* by the open window. Spent several hours reading and thinking, hours much enjoyed, so quiet and peaceful."

That is a rare entry. Most of the time, Mrs. Tate was extremely busy and the house was full of company.

Fourth of July, 1877. "The tug came bringing quite a number of Ashland people. Mr. Vaughn took dinner with us. Afterward attended a sack race. Had a fine display of fireworks."

Again, on July 18, 1877, the Tates offered their hospitality. "The Good Templars from Ashland were here on a picnic. As weather was threatening rain, they made their coffee here."

When the boats came in from city ports, they not only brought passengers, but music to the town. July 19, 1877, "During the evening, the *Annie L. Craig* came in and we all went down and listened to some very good music."

July 24, 1877, the music was even better. "The *Manistee* came in during the evening. We went down and heard some very fine music."

Mrs. Tate was an accomplished pianist. Their parlor contained one of the old, square Hallerton Davis pianos, and with all the other things she had to do, Mrs. Tate managed to give lessons to those who were interested in music.

July 29, 1877. "Little Charley Flanders (a member of our Sunday school) fell from the dock and was drowned this afternoon."

The heartbroken Flanders decided to return to Iowa and left Bayfield on the last boat that fall. But in spite of the sad memory, they missed Bayfield and returned again, on the first boat in the spring and became lifelong residents.

July 31, 1877, Nellie Tate wrote in her diary an entry easily understood by housewives today. "Something is wrong with me. I cannot accomplish anything, yet am busy all of the time. Is it the weather."

Like the hats, which were trimmed and re-trimmed, the dresses had to be made over and over. August 2, 1877, "spent most of the day planning and cutting my dress. (She was making over the striped silk) These old dresses require a good deal of brain work."

August 6, 1877. "Received invitations to attend a party at Red Cliff tomorrow night."

August 7, 1877. "At seven we started for Red Cliff in a large sailboat which was towed by Mr. Pike's tug. The evening was thoroughly enjoyable."

August 8, 1877. "After dinner Andrew, Lou, Lilly and I went out boating. (They rowed, of course.) Stopped and gathered berries. Had a pleasant time."

August 11, 1877. Andrew, Lou, Lilly and myself went to Pike's Creek and Onion River. Spent the whole day and returned late."

August 12, 1877. "Cloudy morning. Arose late, hurried through my work in order to go to the Catholic church and see a number confirmed."

August 13, 1877. "Spent quite a busy day. Helped Lou make raspberry jam and went with her to make some calls. About tea time, the *Keweenaw* came, bringing Miss Warren and a little girl from Duluth to visit Lilly."

With every boat bringing her company, with the summer canning, the usual household chores and entertaining guests by taking them on picnics in a row boat, it is no wonder Mrs. Tate became exhausted. On August 14, 1877, she wrote: "Very warm. Nearly the whole day passed in working about the house and I have felt so miserable that I am almost discouraged. However, I try to keep up. I wonder if a day of rest will ever come to me. Lou and the little girl left this afternoon, late. Lou is a very nice girl, promises to make a fine woman. We have enjoyed her visit very much indeed."

On August 15, 1877, she was still exhausted and wrote: "Another warm day. Worked all morning, tried to get the house in a little order, but have been feeling so bad that I ended getting in a good cry over my dishpan. Lilly went and got Kate, so I am once more relieved from the kitchen drudgery for a time."

Kate Bullard frequently came to help Mrs. Tate, but even with her help, Mrs. Tate did not regain her spirits immediately. August 16 she wrote, "Warm again. I am so tired of writing this, and tired of awakening morning after morning and finding the sun shining so bright and hot. I am dreadfully oppressed by the heat this year."

Part of the reason she was oppressed by the heat was the necessity of spending the day fully dressed in the tight-waisted, full, heavy skirted style of the day. It was a chore just to carry those clothes around, as so many ladies found out during our Centennial celebration.

August 24, 1877. General Fuller came for Lilly to go to Red Cliff. Poor child, she was so happy. I wish I could give her more pleasure."

By August 27, things were cheerful again and Mrs. Tate was ready for more rowing and picnics. She wrote: "We have spent a most delightful day at Pike's Creek with the Col. Cruttendon family, Mrs. McCloud and family, the Nourse girls, and Matie. The sun shone out bright and clear this morning and we had a pleasant row. Arriving there we found a shady spot and spread down blankets, making ourselves comfortable. We spent the entire day fishing, walking and talking. Of course, Mrs. Cruttendon and I had our quiet little chat, which added much to the enjoyment. After lunch, who should drive up but General Fuller and Bob. We, of course, gave them a cordial welcome. Returned home feeling tired, but feeling better for the day's enjoyment.

The summer of 1877 was pleasant and quiet in Bayfield. *The Bayfield Press* returned after an absence of five years. When activity began in Ashland about 1871, *The Bayfield Press* printed Ashland news. When Sam Fifield moved *The Press* to Ashland in 1872, *The Ashland Press* printed Bayfield news. But on July 4, 1877, *The Ashland Press* reported: "*The Press*, after a retirement of five years, made its appearance again at Bayfield, up the lake. The paper is now issued by an association, and its managers seem to know what's what."

Morris Edwards was business manager of *The Press* that year. In the spring of 1879, D.L. Stinchfield became editor and remained until April 1, 1880, when Col. Isaac Wing purchased the paper. Currie Bell bought it in 1882.

No news may be good news, but a newspaper must be filled with words. July 11, 1877, the new *Press* said, "The only local news we could pick up yesterday morning was a dog fight, which took place near the Island House."

Fortunately, the cow situation was, as usual, so bad that an editorial about it always got a satisfactory reception. July 11, 1877, "There is nothing in Bayfield cows love to do more than to get near to someone's sleeping apartment at the still calm hour of one o'clock in the morning, when all of nature's creatures save herself sweetly repose and there to jingle her bell until morning breaks."

The pioneers of Bayfield enjoyed their wilderness. Living in a small village, with plenty of space around them, was not quite enough. They went out camping, winter and summer. Sioux River, where they evidently had some sort of house to stay in, was a favorite spot.

August 28, 1877, Nellie Tate wrote" A very pleasant day. General Fuller invited me to go to Sioux River with a fishing party. We took the tug from here and were landed at the river in a small boat. We fished a little while, but soon returned to the house, determined to rest in order to be fresh for the sport of tomorrow."

Of course, the stream fishing in those days was wonderful. There were no conservation laws and the streams were fished only by the local residents, although tourists took to it occasionally. *The Press* that summer said, "Robert Morrin was out at Sand River a few days this week, showing some tourists how to fish."

Aug. 29, 1877 Nellie Tate says: "Were awakened by the sun shining brightly through the windows, arose and dressed and started out to catch fish for breakfast, but only succeeded in getting very wet from the heavy dew that lay upon the grass and brush. After breakfast we started again to fish toward the lake. I was intending to return home, but found the tug had passed. However, Mr. & Mrs. Hayward came and after spending a pleasant day we returned home in a small boat."

Though the women went along on that trip, the men decided to have a stag party next week. That very evening, Mrs. Tate wrote" "Bob (Pike), Mr. Wing, Mr. Hayward and Andrew went to Sioux River late this evening to spend a few days fishing."

It is evident that in those day men were men and women were poorly informed, for Mrs. Tate did not seem to know just when Andrew would return from this fishing trip. Aug. 30, 1877, she wrote: "Slightly cloudy, but cleared off pleasant. After Kate and I had got everything in nice order, I took my dress once more and made fine headway. After tea, Mrs. Hayward, Mrs. (John) Knight and I called at Mr. Whittleseys and Mrs. Willeys. They went to Mrs. Cruttendon's, but I returned home to see to the chickens, which I had forgotten. Then read to Lillian and afterward read myself to sleep, waiting for Andrew, who has not come, so I think I shall retire."

August 31, 1877. "Spent the night alone for the first time in my life. Andrew did not come until I was seated at my sewing, then the party drove up decorated in autumn leaves and in fine spirits, having had great success."

Sept. 3, 1877. "Andrew, Mary and I went out to Mr. Roath's this afternoon, a distance of seven miles. I was delighted with the country, and was surprised to see such a lovely place so far out of town."

Roath's farm was an unusual and attractive place. It was located on the Star Route, as nearly as I can describe it now, at the top of the "big" hill. There is nothing left except lilac bushes and the outline of a house. It seems incredible that he could clear so much land in that rough, hilly country with only the aid of horses to pull stumps. But perhaps, in this day of tractors and bulldozers, I am underrating the horse. However he did it, Mr. Roath cleared the land so completely that even today large clearings remain. Does anyone know the history of the Roath family?

Though September had come, the days were getting cooler, and there was a "strong north-east wind" camping at Sioux River was still popular when on September 5, 1877, Nellie Tate wrote: "Mr. Vaughn came and invited Mary and I to go to Sioux River to meet Mrs. Vaughn and Matie, who are camping there. We took the tug and were landed at the river in a small boat. Found the party sitting around the camp fire talking We joined the group and after partaking of a hearty supper, spent a pleasant evening and then retired between two feather beds."

Sept. 6, 1877. "The sun shone out clean and bright this morning. After partaking of break-fast, we departed in various directions to fish. I returned with three at noon, found camp broken and all ready to go home. Mary and I returned with Mr. Cooper, leaving the rest of the party on the beach, waiting for the tug. Had a delightful ride through the woods."

In 1877 a trip to Duluth was not made as easily as it is now. On Sept. 10, Mrs. Tate decided to take the boat and go there for a visit. She wrote: "A lovely day. After breakfast I hastened to pack and by ten, Mary, Lillian and I took the Atlantic for Duluth. We had a pleasant trip, arriving here at tea time. Found Mrs. Smith and Lou at the dock with the carriage and glad to see me."

Sept. 12, "Wrote to Andrew in the evening."

By September 15, she was feeling her usual slight homesickness, even though she was having a good time with her friends, "Met some strangers, some very pleasant people, but do not think them quite as genial as our own Bayfield people."

Fishing excursions were just as popular in Duluth as they were in Bayfield. September 21, 1877. "A warm, pleasant day. After breakfast, Mrs. Smith sent for a team and we all started on a fishing excursion. Spent a delightful day on a beautiful sand beach. Some fish caught among the party. I spent most of the time playing in the sand with the children, who enjoyed it very much."

By Sept. 23, she was anxious to get home. "Cloudy and gloomy. I almost fear we are going to have a storm, but I hope not until we reach home. I had hoped to be there today."

Sept. 24, 1877. "Packed some of my things, as I expect to take the boat in the morning."

Sept. 25, 1877. "After breakfast, Lou, the Doctor, and I rode down to the boat, but the Captain informed us that he would not leave until tomorrow morning."

This is something that seemed to happen continually. The boats, apparently, did not run on any schedule. People had to go down to the dock to find out if, or when, they were going. Boats landed at midnight, and regardless of the hour people got off to visit. There was no certainty when the boat would leave again. When hotels in Bayfield were full incoming boats would be met and passengers told not to get off and get left, as there were no accommodations available. When boats arrived, letters were mailed and eventually reached their destination. It was a little confusing, but certainly not dull, for prospective passengers never knew just when their trip would begin or end.

On September 26, the storm Mrs. Tate had feared was coming arrived, and that was the day the Captain chose to leave. She wrote: "Found upon wakening this morning, that a strong northeast wind was blowing and the sky was dark with clouds. While at breakfast, the Captain sent me word that the boat would leave in an hour. So, again, we collected our things and went down to the boat, bade our dear friends good-bye, and soon started. Had a rough day, Lilly sick all of the time. Reached home about seven this evening in a rain storm. Andrew was waiting for us. Met Bob and he walked home with us, carrying my umbrella for me. Received invitation to lunch at Mrs. Willey's tomorrow."

Although she had enjoyed her visit in the village of Duluth, September 27 found Mrs. Tate, delighted, as usual, to be home again. She wrote: "A rainy morning, but cleared bright and pleasant about noon. Surely there is no place more lovely than this same little Bayfield and I never felt it more fully than when I stood on Mrs. Willey's porch this afternoon as the clouds broke away and the beautiful sunlight burst forth, falling brightly on trees and shrubbery."

Undoubtedly this view was spectacular, for Dr. Willey's house stood where Nettie Wilson's now stands. When Col. Fuller built the present house on that site, the Willey house was moved up the block, toward the Presbyterian Church and was made into a double house.

The entry in Nellie Tate's diary for September 28, 1877, gives a typical illustration of how to mail a letter when you saw a boat coming. "A lovely day. Spent the morning making ketchup and preparing pickles. After tea, I went up to Mrs. Haywards, but saw the "Pacific" coming, so hastened home to write to Lou. As I finished writing, Bob (Pike) came in and offered to carry my letter to the boat, as we were having a shower, but what does he do but bring it back with him, forgetting to mail it."

This brings us to the question. "Are men any better at mailing letters now than they were in 1877?" The 1877 scene is easy to picture. Bob Pike walked down to the dock, talked to the Captain of the Pacific, was told something very interesting about lumber prices down the lake, and never gave the letter another thought. Although his memory was faulty that day, he must at least be given credit for his bravery and honesty. He went back and told the lady he had not mailed it, instead of simply hiding it until another boat came along.

For the next few days, Mrs. Tate was very busy getting ready for winter: "Sept. 29, 1877. Spent a busy morning baking and making pickles. Went with many others to get autumn leaves."

Oct. 1, 1877. "Busy all day making apple jelly and marmalade."

Oct. 2, 1877. "A cold northeast rain storm, wind blowing very hard and bay very rough. Made pear preserves this morning."

Oct. 3, 1877. "Still blowing and raining. Three boats lying at the dock this evening."

Oct. 4, 1877. "Rain ceased and the sun struggled hard to appear, but clouded over again and a few flakes of snow fell."

But the weather was nice again on October 6, and "Quite a number of us went out for leaves. Spent the whole afternoon in the woods. Bob went to Outer Island today."

By October 14, the winter pastimes, such as reading aloud, had begun. "A dismal, rainy day. A real northeaster. Bob spent the evening and I read aloud to him and Andrew."

Oct. 18, 1877. "The *Peerless* aground. Mrs. Vaughn and I went down to see her, then called at Mrs. Knight's. Several ladies from Ashland here."

Oct. 20, 1877. "The tug returned to Ashland today and the Ashlanders went home."

Mr. Nourse had evidently just recovered from a long illness, for on October 21, 1877, she wrote: "Mr. Nourse was at Sabbath school for the first time in many months. It was very pleasant to have him back in his old place again."

Oct. 25, 1877. "Received a package from Mollie, a present of a collarette and a bow."

By November 2, winter had really begun. "The first snow fell today, has been falling and melting all day, making it most unpleasant."

Nov. 3, 1877. "The *Wadsworth* made her last trip."

Nov. 8, 1877. "A damp, disagreeable morning, snowing and raining together. Storm sheds are being put up. It seems only yesterday they were taken down."

Although storm sheds are not generally used in Bayfield any more, due to improved heating and insulation, the same feeling prevails, expressed now as we see snow fence going up along the highways. "It seems only yesterday they were taken down."

Thursday, Nov. 29, 1877. "It being Thanksgiving, I wonder if I am as grateful as I ought to be for all the many blessings we have enjoyed during the year."

In 1877, as now, the ladies went out to collect money for worthy causes. Dec. 3, Mrs. Tate wrote, "After dinner, Mrs. Cruttendon came for me and we went out to see if we could raise the money to pay off the debt on the church stove. Our efforts were unexpectedly rewarded, for which we were very thankful. In the evening, we met at Mrs. Cruttendon's to make arrangements for our Christmas tree."

Dec. 5, 1877. "After dinner worked on Christmas presents. Ladies met here in the evening to sew for trees."

Dec. 6. "*Manistee* was in today for last time."

On Dec. 8, 1877, is another entry in Mrs. Tate's diary that has a very familiar sound today. "I worked until nearly 12 midnight. There is so much to be done before Christmas."

On December 10, 1877, Mrs. Tate wrote in her diary: "A lovely day, mild and spring like. This being my birthday (her 31st), Lilly and Andrew surprised me with a present at the breakfast table."

Dec. 16, 1877. "We met at the church and decorated with evergreens."

That was the year Bayfield was to have a wonderful "green" Christmas, enjoyed by the pioneers, and shortening the winter considerably.

Dec. 22, 1877. "Pleasant, wonderful weather. Snow all gone and air as warm and delightful as in May. School closed today and they had some interesting exercises in the evening. We all attended.

Dec. 24, 1877. "Very pleasant, indeed. Today we had our Christmas dinner and tree in the evening. The Haywards enjoyed it with us. We had a Merry Christmas, indeed, and all received pretty presents from friends. It made me half sad to be so kindly remembered, and very happy at the same time. We had on our dinner table a bouquet of pansies that I gathered from the garden this morning."

December 25, 1877. "Looked like rain, but none fell. I almost forgot that this is the blessed Christmas Day, it has been such a busy one. We went to the church early, and worked most of the day, trimming the tree and getting things in readiness for evening. Then came home and made a pair of mittens for one of my Sabbath school scholars, with Matie's help, then ate a hasty supper and repaired to the church again. The exercises passed off nicely, and all of the scholars received presents. We felt well paid for all the labor."

By now, after reading the diaries, and understanding Mrs. Tate's kind disposition, it is evident she discovered one of her Sunday School scholars was not going to receive a present. This was something she would not tolerate. Still, it is incredible, that even with Matie's help, she could come home in the late afternoon and make a pair of mittens before supper, though it was a "hasty supper."

December 31, 1877. "This day finishes my journal for this year. I thought at the beginning of the year to have kept such a nice diary, but what a failure it has been. My time has been so much occupied, that I have never had leisure to write as I wished. It is with regret that I look upon its pages."

After the passing of 80 years, it is with pleasure, not regret, that we, in 1957, look upon the pages of her journal. Without it, much of the humor, love, kindness and general activities of early Bayfield would be lost to us. We would not have had these glimpses of their enjoyment of Christmases in Bayfield. We would not have realized how much they enjoyed all the camping, fishing, sliding, skating and boating. We would not have realized how skilled the women were at preparing many varieties of food for the winter or how much of their time had to be spent sewing.

Mrs. Tate called her journal a "failure." Actually, it is a triumph that her short life was so filled with family, friends and activities that she had little time to write in it.

Surely, the diaries have brought one thing to light. Though the inventions of modern civilization have been added to Bayfield, the "personality" of the town has changed very little in 80 years.

On Jan. 11, 1878, The *Amethyst* came from Duluth and returned again.

During the quiet winter days, Mrs. Tate made the less necessary articles of clothing for her family. On Jan. 19, 1878, she "spent a quiet evening making a necktie for Andrew." That same day, the *Amethyst* was still going strong, making a trip to Raspberry Island.

By January 23, there was some ice between here and Ashland. It apparently wasn't too strong, but Bob Pike had to take a chance on it to get his freight from Ashland. He got back to Bayfield safely, but lost some of his load through the ice.

It was a strange situation, for the Amethyst was still running out north among the islands, while Bob Pile was trying to haul freight by team on the poor ice between here and Ashland.

Naturally, Bob Pike did not give up because his freight was on the bottom of Lake Superior. He grappled for it and got it. On January 25, 1878, Mrs. Tate wrote: "Bob recovered the lost load, but some articles in bad condition."

January 28, 1878. "Nearly twenty of our friends came in giving us a pleasant surprise. The bay frozen over, but the *Amethyst* went out this morning."

It was not until January 29, 1878, that Mrs. Tate could write finally and definitely, "Bay closed."

Jan. 1, 1878 brought an event that became an only twice-fulfilled tradition in the Chequamegon Bay area. Ashlanders came to visit Bayfield by boat. Captain Patrick of the *Eva Wadsworth* brought about 30 Ashland citizens and the Ashland Silver Cornet Band on the beautiful, warm New Year's Day, 1878. The Bayfield Guards, under the command of Captain R.D. Pike, met the *Wadsworth*. The old cannon was fired in salute. A line of march was formed at the dock and headed up Washington Avenue to the Smith Hotel for dinner.

As *The Ashland Press* described it, "Bayfield never looked better than it did reclining on the snowless hillside, basking in the sunshine smiles of 1878. We noted bright pansies in the gardens and fountains were spouting freely, and this pleasant resort looked as in midsummer."

Mrs. Tate wrote about the event briefly, as she was very busy taking part in it. "Tuesday, Jan. 1, 1878 Warm and pleasant. No snow. The *Wadsworth* came from Ashland bringing a party of gentlemen and a brass band. The were received by the Bayfield military company and the firing of cannon. They returned in the afternoon. We attended a ball in the evening, a Military Ball."

It was not until 1932 that this visit could be returned. And though the weather at that time was horrible, Bayfielders were determined to go. As *The Ashland Press* said, "Despite a northeast gale and a snowstorm such as has not visited the region before this winter, the boats *Nichevo* and *Byng II,* bearing some 50 residents of Bayfield, Washburn, and LaPointe, arrived here about 2:30 PM New Year's Day to repay the visit made to Bayfield 54 years ago, and to make a page in the history of Chequamegon Bay such as may not be made again in 54 years more."

A.W. Bowron, of Ashland, was the only man who made both of those trips. He had come with the Ashlanders in 1878, and in 1932, in spite of the terrible weather, came to Bayfield and got aboard the *Nichevo* to make the trip to Ashland.

A gala dinner was held at the Elks Club and H.H. Fuller, president of the Ashland Chamber of Commerce, gave the greeting for Ashland and promised a return trip as soon as the bay is open again on New Years Day. Looking to the future, he added that when the first Atlantic liner lands in Ashland after the opening of the St. Lawrence Waterway, all of Bayfield and Washburn will be invited to Ashland again.

Twenty-four years have passed now and Ashlanders have never been able to make the trip. Each year that the ice seems late in coming, there is hopeful talk, but it is truly something that "depends on the weather."

Though this visit was an exciting event actually, in 1878 the mild weather and lack of snow was not desirable for lumbermen and fishermen. However, the town settled down to the quietness of January and the simple, home parties. On Jan. 3, 1878, Mrs. Tate wrote: "We attended a candy pull at Mrs. Willeys in the evening.

By Jan. 7, the ice was beginning to form. "The tug *Amethyst* was caught in the ice at the foot of Front Street."

January 8 the *Amethyst* broke loose and started for Duluth.

Bob Pike, intent on his logging, didn't pause to worry about the lack of snow. He let no lack of roads stop him either. Jan. 9, 1878, Mrs. Tate wrote: "Bob started to lay out a road to Bark Point this morning." That is how simple road building was in those days. If you wanted a road to Bark Point, you built one.

The lack of ice was good business for the tug *Amethyst.*

January 30, 1878 the Indian Agency building at Red Cliff burned during the night.

By February 4, 1878, the ice was good enough so that Mrs. Tate could write: "After dinner we all went out skating. Mrs. Herbert and I made our first trial."

It was an erratic winter. The old sayings did not hold true. "As the days grow longer, the cold grows stronger" did not apply to the winter of 1878. Nor did "January thaw, February freeze." The thaw came in February, after a relatively mild January.

February 6, 1878, Mrs. Tate wrote: "Bob went to Bark Point this morning. Snow nearly gone and ice very poor indeed."

Feb. 7, 1878. "Rain nearly all night. Birds flying about and chirping as in spring."

Feb. 9, 1878. "Ice broke up during the night."

But by February 15, there was enough ice to skate on, for she wrote: "After tea we all went on the ice and skated until quite late in the evening. I am beginning to learn and feel quite interested."

There was always sewing to be done and Mrs. DeMars has corrected my impression that Mrs. Tate had one of the old Howes. She had a Wilcox Gibbs and this same type of machine with the high plate and needle is on display at the Old Indian Agency House at Portage, which was built in 1832, and is now restored and open to the public.

Feb. 20, 1878. "Matie came in and found me fitting my calico dress, so insisted upon my going home with her and getting her mother to do it for me. I spent the afternoon and helped her on her dress. Attended a surprise party at Mrs. McCloud's during the evening."

Feb. 21, 1878. "We attended a dramatical entertainment (given by the Pleasant Hours Club) this evening. Quite a storm of sleet."

Feb. 22, 1878. "Washington's birthday. We played two games of whist in the evening and then went over to the hotel to a party for a little while."

Feb. 23, 1878. "Bob returned from Ashland this evening. Has had some difficulty getting hay, as ice is very poor."

It seems that very little hay was raised in Bayfield at that time, and hay for the many horses in the lumber camps had to be imported. It was not until about 1890 that hay fields became a profitable operation here. That year, *The Bayfield Press* noted, "A. Buffalo, of Buffalo Bay, harvested upwards of 75 tons of timothy hay on his place last fall, for all of which he has found a home market. . . . " How's that for farming in Bayfield?

Feb. 26, 1878. "Bob came for me and Matie. He and I skated until dinner. We went to Austrian's clearing and found fresh, delicate spears of grass among the old, dried leaves of last year."

Austrian's clearing, a very popular picnic spot, and a delightful camping spot, too, stretched between Bayfield "city limits" sign and the old coal dock. Tourists used to pitch tents there and remain for long vacations.

Feb. 27, 1878. "A lovely day. As I sat by the window this afternoon, I saw flies and insects lazily flying about in the sunlight as in summer. How wonderful at this season!"

But you can't really count on spring in February. On Feb. 28, "All the summer brightness of yesterday has vanished and a furious storm has raged all day with a heavy wind which has broken up the ice."

March 3, 1878. "The wind carried most of the ice from the bay during the night."

But by March 6, spring had come to stay. It was "warm and delightful. Went out in the garden and found flowers sprouting."

Then, as now, it was a popular pastime to take a walk "down to the dock." The dock, at that time, was at the foot of Washington Avenue.

March 7 was "A delightful spring day. Mrs. Cruttendon and I took a delightful walk. Sat awhile on the dock and there had such a pleasant talk. Bob is busy getting his boats ready for the water."

By March 16 the boats were running again. It had been a short winter. The last boat (the Amethyst) had gone out on January 28, The ice came and went quickly. Seven weeks later the boats were running again. "March 18, The *Wadsworth* came bringing the band and quite a party."

H.O. Fifield, who with his brother Sam, established *The Bayfield Press* in 1870, later wrote the following article about Bayfield in the Menominee, Michigan *Herald.* "At the close of the late rebellion, many southern people sought homes in the Lake Superior region, and a few of this class located in Bayfield. They were poor, but honest, and it was not unknown to meet a dozen Colonels, Majors and Corporals engaged in serious conversations in the public houses or upon the street corners. They were quite aristocratic, but were trying to earn a living by hard work and strict economy."

This accounts in part for the many friends of Mrs. Tate being referred to by their Civil War titles.

On March 20, 1878, Nellie Tate wrote in her diary." Bob (Pike) spent the evening and we worked examples, then played a game of cribbage."

No doubt that Bob Pike, young lumberman with complex financial problems, was good at working examples.

March 23, 1878. "A lovely morning, like May or June. Hurried through my work and prepared lunch, as quite a number of us went to the sugar bush. Before we returned, began to snow and we returned in quite a storm. However, we had a delightful time, but the sudden change in weather is very strange."

April 1, 1878. "Lilly brought in a few mayflowers."

April 5, 1878. "The first boat of the season, the *Manistee*, arrived this morning. A beautiful spring day. Andrew making garden."

April 6, 1878. "Went with a number of ladies to Austrian's clearing and found quantities of mayflowers."

April 16, 1878. "Went down to see the *Maple Leaf* launched, but she was not ready. After waiting awhile, returned to Mrs. Hayward's."

April 20. "After dinner helped Lilly with Easter eggs. Bob is again unfortunate with the *Maple Leaf.*"

April 21, 1878. "Bob worked with the *Maple Leaf.*"

Living in Bayfield makes me quite sure that Bob Pike was not working alone to launch the stubborn *Maple Leaf.* He no doubt got advice from the whole town, and on April 22, he got some practical help from the *Manistee*. Mrs. Tate wrote: "*Manistee* tried to pull the *Maple Leaf* off. Unsuccessful. Bob late for tea, nearly sick."

He might have been nearly sick but he kept working, and eight days after he started the launching, he triumphed. On April 24 Mrs. Tate wrote: "*Maple Leaf* is launched at last."

The reason Bob Pike is mentioned so often in the diaries is because he boarded at the Tate's during the winter, when the hotel, apparently, did not serve regular meals. He would come home to meals bringing lots of news about what was going on around town, and Mrs. Tate usually put the interesting items in her diary.

By May 2, 1878, the boats were arriving from down the lakes. On that day, the "India came in, bringing a few passengers."

And May also brought baseball games. On May 11, the "Baseball Club went to Ashland."

May 25, 1878. "Ashland ball Club came here. In the afternoon we went to witness game of ball."

On May 29, 1878, Mrs. Tate's little daughter, Lilly, was evidently watching her mother write in her diary. She wished to write also and, with a pen in round childish letters wrote, "And Mama, I love you so much."

When spring came, Mrs. Tate began to think of the delightful hours she loved to spend fishing at Pike's Creek or Sioux River, and then, as now, a fishing hat was very important. On May 30, 1878, she wrote: "Spent the evening trimming fishing hat."

By June, the summer picnics had started again and on June 12, 1878, she "worked all morning preparing for picnic. After dinner took boats and went to Austrian's clearing. Spent afternoon and took tea there. Had a pleasant day."

June 27, 1878, "*Manistee* came, bringing an editorial party of 200, went out among the islands with them."

This was not an uncommon occurrence. Several times in the history of Bayfield, large parties of editors of magazines and news papers arrived to make a grand tour of the region and later to write about it in the publications to encourage settlers to come here.

July 4, 1878. "The Glorious Fourth. A beautiful bright day. The military had an excursion to LaPointe and a dance this evening. We went to Mrs. McCloud's this evening and had fireworks."

July 12, 1878. "Several arrivals (of boats). The town quite lively. Attended Swiss Bell Ringers this evening, which I enjoyed very much."

The Swiss Bell Ringers made annual tours of the country. Mrs. DeMars remembers attending their program one summer in the large building that is now the Hotel Bayfield. At that time there was a saloon on the west end of the building and a hall upstairs where the Bell Ringers gave their program. Naturally, this once-a-year entertainment attracted a large crowd. They packed themselves in, and with all this weight, the floor began to sway. Everyone kept as quiet as possible and left one at a time. When the hall was emptied, the props on the stage fell down from the floor springing back into place.

July 18, 1878: "Another melting day. Thermometer reached 100 at one time. Tried to sew on my linen dress. After tea Mrs. Hayward, the Nourse girls, Andrew, Lilly and I went out rowing."

"After tea," would mean, of course, in the cool of the evening, and if the exercise was not too strenuous, they undoubtedly cooled off rowing about on Lake Superior.

July 20, 1878. "Two or three boats in. Town filled with strangers. Heard some good railroad news."

"Good railroad news was what Bayfielders longed for. Every bit of encouraging news was repeated over and over. But we know now, looking back, that they had five years to go before they got their railroad. Mrs. Tate would not live to see it.

There were some interesting items in *The Bayfield Press* during July 1878. "The town authorities have built a large fountain at the foot of Washington Avenue, near the dock. The basin is octagon in shape, with a diameter of 16 feet, by six feet in depth and will throw a stream of water some 20 or 25 feet high. This fountain is to be stocked with brook trout and other fish and will prove a great addition to the attractions of our little village. It can easily be seen from the steamboats, and will, no doubt, aid in drawing visitors to our town. Let the town provide a deer park now, and our attractions will be complete."

In those days, Bayfield was known as "The Fountain City." Almost every yard had a beautiful fountain, and now there is not one left.

By August they had their deer park, too, for on August 7, 1878, *The Press* commented: "Bayfield has at least got a public fountain and deer park and our citizens feel happy."

Among other interesting newspaper items during that nice summer of 1878 are these: "It is asserted that new islands are being formed from the rocky points projecting into the bay and that Bayfield, in the distant future, will become separate from the mainland and set upon an island."

The mild winter, with only a few weeks of ice, made it hard on the ice houses, since the electric refrigerator was more than 50 years in the future. The paper stated: "Ice houses in Bayfield are now almost depleted. All our ice cream factories have been compelled to shut down on account of the scarcity. That next winter will be a cold one is earnestly hoped by all Bayfield."

Two of our pioneer residents were married that summer: "Leihy-Stark. At the residence of the bride's parents at Red Cliff on Saturday, June 29, 1878. Mr. Charles Leihy to Miss Bell Stark. Justice Flanders officiating. "Charles has for a long time been one of the boys in Bayfield, and his action is much regretted by some of his friends. *The Press* , however, extends congratulations to the happy couple and wishes them a long life of happiness."

The summer of 1878 was a delightful one for camping parties and picnics. Nellie Tate, with her love of outdoor activities, kept a very happy diary that summer.

July 23, 1878. "Went to Pike's Creek berrying and fishing in the afternoon."

July 31, 1878. "Slightly cloudy and altogether a lovely day and delightfully spent with a picnic party at Pike's Creek. Bob kindly took the *Mocking Bird* and towed us down, which greatly added to our comfort and pleasure. A very happy day, long to be remembered."

Aug. 1, 1878. "A bright, beautiful day. After dinner Bob invited us to go to Buffalo Bay on the *Mocking Bird*. Took five boats in tow and were out until after ten."

Aug. 5, 1878. "Spent the morning working and preparing for a camping party tomorrow at Pike's Creek. In the evening went to the lighthouse with a party on the *Mocking Bird* and did not return until one o'clock at night."

Aug. 6, 1878. "A beautiful day. Spent the morning getting things together for the camp. We started about 3 in the afternoon, the Mocking Bird towed us. Went to Pike's meadow (I think this is the meadow which used to be across from the old Red Dam) got supper, put up tents, and got ready for the night. Spent a delightful evening."

Aug. 7, 1878. "After eating breakfast we took a ride on a hay rack to the bay, where we found a canoe, which we took possession of and paddled around in it. Then Matie, Bob and I went fishing. Met Mr. Pike on horseback. He kindly permitted us to ride. Visited a lovely spring. Returned home in the evening."

Aug. 8, 1878. "Dr. Simington gave us the pleasure of looking through his telescope."

Undoubtedly, the moon looked further away then, than it does now. In 1878, it was a great privilege to look at the moon through a telescope. Now, only 80 years later, people are planning to go there.

Aug. 9, 1878, brought one of the outstanding marine events of the summer. "The *U.S.S. Michigan* came in. Attended a party at Mrs. (John) Knight's where we met some of the officers, who kindly invited us to go out and look at the ship tomorrow morning."

Aug. 10, 1878. "Bright and pleasant. After hurrying through the usual duties we hastened to the small boat sent ashore for us. Went on board the *Michigan*. Were invited to go to Ashland. Spent a delightful day on the Man-o-war visiting every nook and cranny of the ship, the officers doing all they could to make our visit enjoyable."

Aug. 14, 1878. "Hastened through breakfast and took a small boat for Sioux River. Bob kindly towed us down. Spent the whole day fishing."

Aug. 15, 1878. "After dinner Andrew got boat and we all spent the afternoon at Basswood Island."

Aug. 22. "The *Peerless* came in with music." Aug. 23. "Attended a corn bake on the beach in the evening."

Mrs. Tate's enjoyment of her life, her family and friends in Bayfield is expressed over and over. She loved the outdoors with the camping, fishing, skating and was equally happy at home, entertaining the Whist Club and was always interested in the weather and the change of season. She loved to go away for short visits, yet, in spite of the good times, was always a little lonely and was delighted to come home again.

But in 1878 the Minnesota State Fair in St. Paul was such an outstanding event that she decided to take her daughter, Lilly, and go to see it. The trip would not be easy. She would have to change from boat to horse and buggy to train to streetcar. But it was worth it. Even the President of the United States, Rutherford B. Hayes, and his wife attended. Why this particular fair was important enough for the President to attend is not made clear in the diaries. It may be that the President went to extend a welcome to Minnesota since 1858 was the year it became a state. It may have been the first big fair held in the midwestern wilderness.

On September 1, 1878, Nellie Tate and her daughter, Lilly, started for the great Minnesota State Fair in St. Paul. She wrote: "Took the steamer Japan about 7 this morning. Met Uncle George on board. We had a nice visit and a pleasant trip to Duluth where we were welcomed by our friends."

Sept. 2, 1878. "Took the train at 7. A pleasant trip as regarding company, but warm and dusty. Kindly received by our friends in St. Paul."

"Warm and dusty" is exactly the right phrase. The train was undoubtedly one of the old timers, so often seen in western movies now. The seats were stiff and covered with red plush. Cinders and dirt flowed through the windows, but even so, it was better than the slow ride on poor roads with a horse and buggy, which was the way the McCloud brothers had gone to St. Paul only twenty years previously.

Sept. 3, 1878. "After breakfast, Louise, Jule, Lilly and I took the street car. Went around to Mrs. Austrian's and made a call, then did some shopping. After dinner attended the state fair. Saw many beautiful things."

Sept. 4, 1878. "Very warm and dusty. Spent the whole day at the fair, except an hour or so with Mrs. Carrington. Returned tired and very much soiled from the dust, which arose in clouds, and the sightseeing."

Another thing that probably added to her exhaustion was her clothes. Naturally, no lady would attend this event without being stylishly clothed in long-sleeved, high-necked, full-skirted style of the day with a proper hat, gloves, and the right number of petticoats.

But in spite of the pounds of clothes, the dust and the heat, she had gone to St. Paul to see the fair and back she went the next day.

Sept. 5, 1878. "Uncle William and George and I started for the fair again. Saw President and Mrs. Hayes and many distinguished people."

Sept. 7, 1878. "After breakfast Uncle William brought the carriage around and we drove down for Lou and started for Minnehaha, Fort Snelling and Minneapolis. I can never ex*Press* the perfect pleasure and happiness I enjoyed this day. The lovely country, the beauty of Minnehaha, and the pleasant company all combined to make it one of the most enjoyable days ever spent."

Sept. 8, 1878. "Aunt Nell and I attended church at the House of Hope. President and Mrs. Hayes also attended. We caught a glimpse of them. We had a lovely ride to Lake Como and back."

Sept. 9, 1878. "We separated from our kind friends this morning and took the train for Duluth. Were invited into the business car, had delicious lunch provided by our friends, and a pleasant ride home."

From Duluth, Lilly caught a ride back to Bayfield on the boat with Bob Pike. The little girl had had enough traveling and wanted to get home to her toys and her friends. Mrs. Tate remained in Duluth and on September 13, "Spent the day at Superior with Mrs. Brooks, an old friend."

Sept. 18, 1878. "Bell and I made a grass receiver."

This has me puzzled, and it has even stumped Mrs. DeMars. Does anyone know how a "grass receiver" was made, and who wanted to receive grass, anyway?

Sept. 19, 1878. "Uncle William called before we were through breakfast, then he got a carriage and took me to the *Nyack* where I bade him good-bye. Had a pleasant trip home. Found Andrew and Lilly waiting to receive me."

Sept. 22, 1878, found Bob Pike facing one more problem. "Bob came in. His ice house blew down this evening."

Oct. 8, 1878. "Attended Dr. and Mrs. Mahan's wooden wedding this evening."

Oct. 26, 1878. "*Maple Leaf* started for Eagle Harbor with cargo of lumber."

Nov. 5, 1878. "Election day, therefore one of considerable excitement."

The summer had gone quickly past and on November 20, 1878, she wrote: "*Wadworth* made her last trip today."

But the quietness of winter brought time for many things at home, and on November 30, 1878, appears an entry that is still easily understood today. "After dinner went to work on a pile of mending that has been accumulating for some time."

Again, it was winter in Bayfield. Dec. 5, 1878, Mrs. Tate wrote: "Some snow fell during the night. Cold today. Andrew went to Red Cliff in a wagon, there not being sufficient snow. Worked on Christmas work all day. *Manistee* in this morning for the last time."

Dec. 1, 1878. "Very pleasant. It being my birthday was surprised by some little remembrances."

Dec. 12, 1878. "School girls met here to practice dialogues in the evening." Which proves that then, as now, schoolgirls must have meetings, whatever the reason.

And, winter or no winter, the *Maple Leaf* kept going until the last minute. Dec. 13, 1878. "*Maple Leaf* left this morning for Duluth."

Dec. 18, 1878. "Very cold. Some floating ice in the bay. Thermometer only 10 above most of the day. *Maple Leaf* came in about 8."

By Dec. 19, Nellie Tate and Matie Hayward were busy making Christmas presents. This year they would not have to make mittens at the last minute. Each Sunday school scholar was to have a gift from Mrs. Tate. She wrote: "Matie helped me on cuffs and collars for my class."

But this Christmas was not as merry for them, as the previous years. Dec. 21, 1878. "As I sat at work in the evening, Mr. Hayward came for Andrew and I as Grandma was very ill indeed."

The Tates were always ready when a call for help came. Andrew Tate was a druggist. Mrs. Tate was skilled in nursing from first hand knowledge acquired during her small town pioneer life.

Dec. 22, 1878. "Very cold. We found Grandma unable to speak or hear. Andrew remained until 12, and I sat up all night."

Then her child became ill. Dec. 23, "Lilly quite sick all day. Mrs. Knight and Emma Nourse spent the afternoon and we dressed dolls for the tree. Bell and Emma spent the evening and we finished them."

Dec. 24, 1878. "Lilly still quite sick. Spent most of the day finishing off Christmas work for Lilly. In the evening received some pretty presents from friends. Andrew and I got our tree up and dressed it, while doing so Bob came in, bringing us all a pretty present."

Dec. 25, 1878. "Christmas Day, but a sad one in many respects, and very quiet. Matie and Mrs. McCloud were in. I worked most of the day. Went to see Grandma a little while after dinner. Spent the evening along with Lilly, Andrew and Bob having gone to the Christmas tree. Bay closed today."

Dec. 26, 1878. "Lilly some better. Spent the evening alone. Read to Lilly and worked for her."

By Dec. 27, Lilly was well enough so her mother could leave her and she wrote: "In the evening attended an entertainment given by the Blue Ribbons."

When New Year's Eve arrived, everything looked a little brighter. Lilly was well again, Grandma was feeling better, and the memories of the past year were mostly happy ones; the camping parties, the fishing trips, the visit to St. Paul, all crowded into her mind. She wrote: "The last of the old year, only an hour or so and the dying year will have departed, to be remembered in the past. This has been a year of pleasure and happiness, intermingled with very little pain. What will be next... ah, who can tell?"

As the year 1879 began, Mrs. Tate was happily busy with all winter activities in the small town. Jan. 8, "Mite Society went sleighing this evening." Jan. 17, "Mrs. Herbert came for me in the evening and we went coasting." Jan. 30. "Charley McCloud came for me to go skating. Bob gave Matie and me a delightful sleigh ride."

Feb. 3. "Attended an entertainment at the reading room."

Feb. 21. "Went fishing for Siscoes, caught 2."

Feb. 25. "Mrs. McCloud and Bob came for me to go to a 'pancake' party." The days were clear, cold, but filled with pleasant activities. On February 27, 1879, Mrs. Tate wrote: "The coldest morning of the year—thirty below."

When March 1879, came Mrs. Tate began to get her spring and summer clothes ready. March 11, she wrote: "Sewed all day and thought my dress was completed, but was obliged to do most of it over again."

Mar. 29, 1879. "Bob went to Ashland early this morning for his engine."

And again Bob Pike faced another loss. Mar. 30. "Bob returned, but lost part of his engine through the ice."

April 1, 1879. "Election day. Some excitement." This was followed by the usual after election entry, Apr. 2. "Spent a quiet evening alone. All gone to town meetings."

As we have seen in this column previously, Bob Pike never let himself be defeated by high winds, breaking rafts, burned buildings, blown down buildings, stubborn boats or cracking ice. April 3. "Bob started early this morning for his engine. Worked all day and returned late this evening."

Again, Bob Pike succeeded. "Bob returned late tonight with his engine. Has accomplished quite a feat."

Naturally everyone wanted to see the engine which had been brought up from the bottom of the lake. April 5, "After dinner went with Andrew to see the engine. Bob went for the things used in raising the engine."

Apr. 7, 1879. "Bob went to Ashland for freight. Ice very poor, team broke in."

Apr. 8, 1879. "Bob took teams from ice today."

Apr. 13, 1879. "A lovely spring day. Ice broken up, but no wind to carry it out."

On April 16, there was a great, modern event for the Tate family. "Mr. Whiteside put up a telephone between here and Mrs. Haywards." Of course, only the two houses were connected but since Mrs. Hayward was the person Mrs. Tate most wanted to call it worked out very well.

Apr. 20. "Mrs. Harbert and Bob were here this evening talking through the telephone, which works like a charm."

Spring was coming, to be followed by all the wonderful outdoor activities, which Mrs. Tate enjoyed so much. Apr. 21, she wrote: "Began my camping suit."

Apr. 22, 1879. "Worked on my suite all day, but accomplished little. Went to bed thoroughly out of sorts."

Apr. 23, 1879. "Sewed all day and got along nicely, a little sleep having done wonders for mind and body."

Apr. 16, 1879. "Wind has carried all of the ice out of the bay." April 29 navigation was opened when "The *Manistee* arrived from Duluth."

With the coming of spring, hopes for the railroad revived. May 3, 1879. "Railroad news very flattering."

On May 19, 1879, spring housecleaning began at Tates. Progress was as follows: May 19, "Began cleaning the office. Worked all day." May 20. "Finished the office, took up the carpet in the end rooms and nearly papered it." May 21. "Papered the front room." May 23, "worked as usual. Have the front room nearly settled." May 24, "Worked very hard, have the dining room nearly settled."

Sunday, May 25, she did not work, but reported "A cold northeaster. Two boats in during the night."

May 26, "Worked all day cleaning." May 27, "Worked hard all day." And at last on May 28, "Worked very hard. The cleaning is nearly completed." She made good time that year; allowing her the Sunday off, the whole job was completed in nine days.

As a reward for completing this strenuous housecleaning, she went on a camping trip to Sioux River with her friend, Matie Hayward. June 5, 1879, "We went to Sioux River in the afternoon. A pleasant ride. Will not return home until Saturday."

June 6, 1879. "A lovely day. I did not mention we saw a deer at Onion River yesterday. We spent a delightful day fishing, caught 32, saw two bear traps and plenty of deer tracks."

June 7, 1879. "Pleasant again. After breakfast we went fishing again. Caught 33. Mr. Hayward, Andrew and Lilly came for us. We returned in quite a rain."

On June 17, 1879, the annual summer event was reported. "The mill started today."

June 26, 1879, was a festive occasion for Mrs. Tate. She went to Ashland and "took tea with Mrs. Fifield at the Chequamegon."

The Chequamegon was the large, luxury hotel of Ashland, located on the site of the present courthouse, famous for its elegant parlors, dining room and spectacular view of Lake Superior.

The August 7 entry is a familiar one today. "Was obliged to make a fire this morning, so cold and windy."

Aug. 24, 1879. "Went to church and listened to a minister from a vessel, *The Glad Tidings*."

Does anyone have any more information on this minister or the route of the "Glad Tidings" as he made his way around the lakes, preaching at local churches, or perhaps from the deck of his ship?

Aug. 29, 1879. "We all attended a theater in the evening. Saw Rip Van Winkle."

Sept. 11, 1879. "Was invited to Mrs. Hayward's to a "Hen party." Could not go on account of rain."

Sept. 15, 1879. "Andrew and I worked on chairs, upholstering."

Sept. 23, 1879. "A few friends spent the evening and ate watermelon."

In 1879, as now, Bayfield was without a dentist. On Sept. 24, 1879, Mrs. Tate and Mrs. Hayward went to Ashland to see the dentist and enjoyed taking tea at the Chequamegon. It was necessary to take two days for this trip and on Sept. 25, she reported, "Returned home after having tooth filled."

By Sept. 26, the beautiful fall weather had arrived and she wrote, "Went out with ladies for leaves in the afternoon."

On October 2, 1879, Bob Pike was having trouble again. Mrs. Tate wrote, "Pleasant, but strong wind from southwest. Bob had a raft broken up. Railroad men arrived. Left the same day."

Of course there were no drycleaning establishments in Bayfield in 1879 and on October 3, in her preparations for winter, Mrs. Tate "cleaned Andrew's clothes."

On October 4, Bob Pike had hardly gotten back from rescuing his broken raft when his "office took fire, but was saved by the exertions of the men."

Oct. 7, 1879 was one of those wonderful indian summer days with the "thermometer above 80."

October 8, 1879 brought the beginning of the fall house cleaning. Mrs. Tate "cleaned the front room, took up the dining room carpet. Helped Lilly with her examples."

Oct. 9, 1879. "Settled the dining room and began the pantry. Nourse girls were in. Bell takes the school at LaPointe."

Oct. 20, 1879. "Strong winds from the south. Bob's office was nearly consumed by fire again. Poor fellow!"

Oct. 23, 1879 brought more hope for the railroad. Mrs. Tate wrote: "The railroad officials came. Went out this afternoon to look over the survey."

Oct. 24, 1879. "Gentlemen met the officials and talked railroad. They left this afternoon."

Oct. 25, 1879. "A dreadful wind from the south." This wind brought Bob Pike one more small problem. "The *Mocking Bird* went ashore."

By the end of October, preparations for winter were being completed. October 29, "Andrew put up the stoves." Nov. 4, "Sewed on Lilly's snow boots. Election day passed quietly." Nov. 10. "Andrew put up the storm sheds."

By December 1, 1879, the Ashland harbor was frozen and there was no chance of a New Year's Day boat trip. There was a "heavy northeaster." *Hurd* came in, last trip. Landed Ashland freight on ice, their harbor being frozen."

On Dec. 2, 1879, a heavy northeaster was blowing. The *Hurd* made a second attempt to get to Ashland but failed. But Bob Pike was putting the sails of the *Maple Leaf* in good condition, preparing for a first trip to Duluth before it freezes up.

Mrs. Tate was engaged in quiet, domestic matters. Dec. 4, 1879, "Emma Nourse was in. She spent the evening. We began pillows for the sofa."

Dec. 6, 1879. "The *Maple Leaf* has favorable weather."

Dec. 7, *Maple Leaf* came in this evening. Dec. 8, Bob laying up the *Maple Leaf.*

During the fall Mrs. Tate had not been feeling well. There were events, which she "did not feel well enough to attend." Some days she "worked, as usually, but feeling badly."

Dec. 9, 1879. "Concert in evening. I did not think of going. Mr. Warner came for me with a sleigh and very kindly drew me to the courthouse."

Dec. 15, 1879, "Bay full of floating ice."

Dec. 17, 1879, "Bay fairly closed today."

By Dec. 19, the bay was evidently solid, for Bell Nourse, eager to get home for Christmas, walked over from LaPointe, where she had been teaching school.

Dec. 23, 1879. "Thirty below this morning. Finished up most of my Christmas work."

Dec. 24, 1879, "Spent most of the day preparing a few things for Christmas. Feeling badly, as I always do now. Oh, I wonder if I will ever prepare for Christmas again."

She did not. It was her last Christmas here.

It is difficult to tell from the diaries whether she, her family and friends knew how ill she was. It may be they thought it was a temporary illness. It may be they knew she had "galloping consumption," which in those days was accepted as doom. It almost seems as though they did know, for on Dec. 25 she wrote: "Christmas Day. How many sad and aching hearts today."

Yet, ill as she was, she was still concerned with doing things for others. On Dec. 26 she wrote: "worked all day to get things ready for the Sunday school tree. Unable to attend, so spent the evening alone. (Andrew took Lilly to the program). Bob came down for a little visit afterward.

Dec. 28, 1879. "Today I received baptism and connected myself with the Presbyterian Church. Ceremony performed here, owing to storm. Little Bessie Nourse was also baptized."

There were no entries for New Years Eve, 1879, and there are no other fresh, new pages in a diary dated 1880. Perhaps she did not wish to make any further record. Perhaps she did not have the strength.

Nellie Tate loved the outdoors, and during the bright winter days when she felt able to go, friends would take her for a cutter ride. On one of those pleasant afternoons, Alec Butterfield called for her with Bob Pike's cutter.

At that time, Alec was 16 and was working for R.D. Pike. His mother's death the day before his 15th birthday had left him heartbroken. He quit school and got a job. He had done well in school and Col. Wing and Bob Pike both urged him to finish. Bob Pike promised to arrange work for him after school and evenings so he could continue in school, but Alec wouldn't listen.

Alec had been a member of Mrs. Tate's Sunday School class, and attended the many little parties she gave for the children at her home, with games, lunches and candy making.

That nice winter day Alec helped carry Mrs. Tate to the cutter and put her comfortably among the warm robes.

Andrew asked if she would like him to drive, but she smiled at Alec and said, "No, Alec can drive for me."

They started up the old military road, but hadn't gone far before Alec noticed she was tired. When he asked her how far she wished to go, she replied she would like to go home.

The road was narrow, with no possible place to turn around. Alec got out of the cutter, lifted the back of it as well as he could, talking constantly to the horse, so it would not be startled, he pulled on the reins and pushed on the cutter until he had it headed toward town. He drove her home, and helped carry her into the house. It was the last time she was able to go for a drive.

Recently, Alec, now 94, was telling me of his fine memories of Mrs. Tate, of her home, her musical ability, her kindness and the great pleasure the children had attending parties she gave for them. When he finished, he thought a moment, then summed up the life of Nellie Tate truthfully and simply in one sentence, saying "She was one nice woman."

A band of pirates lived on Oak Island during the 18th century. I first came across a reference to these pirates in a story recorded by G.F. Thomas in his magazine, *Picturesque Wisconsin*, Vol. I, No. I June 1899. He said the story was told to him by a former resident of

Montreal, Canada, who claimed to have read it when a young man, in a book published in Montreal and on file in the public library there. The book was called *The Twelve Apostles.*

The story supposedly gave a true account of the adventures of a band of pirates known as the Apostles and their chief, who in the latter part of the 18th century, made their rendezvous among the Apostle Islands, and upon Oak Island in particular. There they found shelter in a rocky cavern and were protected from sudden attacks by the rugged shores. Oak Island also has the highest point of land which the pirates used as an observatory post to see their prey approaching. . . Their victims were voyageurs with loads of valuable or furs, traders on their way to distant posts with Mexican silver dollars, which were much used in the fur trade.

For a time these pirates met with wonderful success, for they not only robbed the traders and voyageurs, but set upon a party of wealthy Frenchmen, who were on their way to open up the newly discovered copper mines at French River on the north shore. The pirates killed all of the party except the mining engineer, whom they held prisoner, hoping to use his knowledge in their future operations.

The little vessel, which had belonged to the French party, was remodeled by the pirates into a warship. Eventually this proved to be the means of discovery and capture of the entire band.

Friends of the missing Frenchmen engaged a voyageur to search for them. He soon discovered the remodeled boat anchored in a little bay on the mainland, about opposite from Oak Island, probably what is now known as Frog Bay.

The voyageur looked no further, but hastened to LaPointe with news of the discovery. Immediately a volunteer force was organized by the citizens, many of whom were skilled in battle from serving in the Canadian frontier wars. They manned a flotilla of six bateaus with complete armament and started for Oak Island. The pirates were taken by surprise and captured without the loss of a man.

After a short delay at LaPointe, the pirates were taken to Montreal for trial and all were executed except the chief.

This much of the story sounds as though it might be fact, but woven into the story is a romance, with the mining engineer as the hero, and the heroine a maiden called Madeline, by the white inhabitants, and "Light of Day" by her adopted father, a great medicine man of the Ojibways, who resided in a birch bark wigwam at LaPointe.

The engineer, who went to Montreal with the captured pirates, discovered the pirate chief was his own brother, and through various strange circumstances, was able to save the chief from execution. As the happy ending, the engineer married Madeline.

Later on in the Vaughn library in Ashland, I found an old book with pictures showing various points on Oak Island described as pirate's look-out. The story of pirates on Oak Island is a persistent one, and perhaps it is a fact which was later used to build a story of fiction, by someone who had explored the islands during the 18th century, somewhere between 1775 and 1800.

If anyone would like to hunt for pirate treasure on Oak Island, I can offer them a good reason for doing so. In the 1700's, the pirates had no place to spend their loot in this part of the country. They had to hoard it until they accumulated enough to take the long journey down the lakes and the St. Lawrence River to the cities of Montreal and Quebec. Since they were captured before they could do this, it is logical to suppose that the treasure the pirates collected is still hidden on Oak Island.

After the pirates were removed from Oak Island, it was unoccupied until the advent of the wood burning steamboats. At that time, William Knight had a refueling station on the island and sold hardwood to the passing steamers. Eventually, the island was logged and finally it had a king. His name was Martin Kane.

Hermits among the Apostle Islands were no new things. Joseph McCloud, lawyer, district attorney, real estate agent, lived alone on Basswood Island, as caretaker of the quarry. Robert Pugh, a schoolteacher, also spent years alone on Basswood. Wilson, the best known of the hermits, gave the island both his name and his title.

Thanks to an article written by John B. Chapple, and first hand information given by Mr. William Flake, there is quite a lot of information on the King of Oak Island, Martin Kane.

He was born at Winona, Minnesota. He never went to school a day in his life, but without a formal education, he had learned how to figure and could figure rapidly without the aid of pencil and paper. The family moved to Ontonogan, Michigan when Martin was a child. When he was nine years old, his father, who was a well digger by trade, but an explorer and gold prospector by choice, went to Colorado to prospect and Martin never saw him again.

While living in Michigan, Martin met and married Ann MacAlister of Duluth. They moved to Bayfield, spent a summer on Oak Island and some time on Sand Island. Mrs. Kane went to visit relatives on the west coast and liked it so well, she persuaded Martin to join her there. During World War I he worked in the shipyards at Seattle and built a nice home for them. When his wife died, Martin left his job and his home and returned to the place he liked best in the world—Oak Island.

Martin set up housekeeping for himself in the saw filing room of an abandoned building of the Stearns Lumber Company. He used the old blacksmith shop of the lumber company for a storage shed. Thus established, he soon became known as "The King of Oak Island."

The King never owned a foot of land there. He had possession of his subjectless kingdom by "Squatter's Rights." He said if anyone objected, he would move to another island. But no one ever did. What was there to object to?

For years, Martin had no clock or calendar in his home. He would know when Sunday came around because more trolling and pleasure boats went by the island. Later he did get a clock and a calendar so he would know the right day and about the right time to take his fish out to Booth's boat, which stopped by the island to pick up his catch.

He had a small garden and his diet of fish was supplemented with bear and venison steaks. He usually had a dog or two, which enthusiastically chased the bears. One night he heard the dogs after what he thought was a bear and yelled at them to "let him go!" When he went out in the morning, he found that the dogs had captured a coyote. He took the coyote to town and collected a $20 bounty.

When his supply of salt or whiskey was gone, Martin would come to Bayfield. He was a happy whiskey drinker, not a mean one, like Wilson, the Hermit. Martin was a pleasant, independent man, asking aid from nobody as he went about his work of earning a living from his setlines and gill nets. He gave, rather than asked. Many a wayfarer stopped at Oak Island to find warmth and food at Martin's shack. In fact, as I inquired for information about Martin, people said, over and over, "He was a nice old guy," and told of a meal at Martin's, or a humorous incident, quite often connected with his drinking. He always seemed to be able to find his way back to Booth's dock and if he appeared to be a little off course, the dock crew would fix up a place for him to sleep until he was able to navigate himself and the boat.

Martin Kane was sociable, kind and welcomed people to his island kingdom. He made enough money from his small-scale fishing to supply needs, which the wilderness could not provide. If having everything he wants makes a man a king, then Martin Kane was the genuine article.

Martin Kane, King of Oak Island, built his boat, *The Dreamer* entirely by hand. Every plant and rib was cut from island timber with a broad ax and finished to the proper size. To get good planking, he would cut a tree from both sides with a broad ax, until one plank, just the right width, was left. He used the Dreamer until she was smashed beyond repair during a storm while tied to Booth's dock in Bayfield. Some of the planking may be floating under the dock to this day, but part of it, like a prodigal, drifted home. Months after the boat was destroyed, Martin picked up a piece of the Dreamer's wreckage on the beach at Oak Island. Later he had a boat called *Quarry Bay* named after the bay on Presque Island where he got the boat.

His winter fishing was risky. Twice he fell through the ice and had to save himself by carefully rolling out onto the solid ice. At one time he lost what to him was a fortune of about $400 or $500 worth of nets when the ice carried them out. Often he would fish and get a little money ahead for nets, then lose some of them.

Due to his limited diet, Martin developed anemia. He grew weaker and weaker. Finally, with almost his last strength, he hitched his dogs, Rex and Schnaps, to a sled, crawled onto it and told the dogs to go. They pulled the sled across treacherous ice, some of it only an inch thick, to the home of Otto Kuntz, near the Pageant Grounds. Mr. Kuntz took him to the hospital in Ashland, where he spent several weeks recovering from the worst of anemia. After that he took hypos of liver extract, administering the shots himself.

Had it not been for a tragic air accident, Martin Kane's life on Oak Island might have been made easier by the importing of the comforts of civilization. In the 1920s, Dr. Leslie B. Joslyn, of Maywood, Illinois, bought Oak Island. He was a surgeon for the C&NW Railroad. He had no intention of removing the king; instead he was delighted to find him there. As the trip to Oak Island from Maywood took about 16 hours, Dr. Joslyn planned to build an airport there, so he could fly to the island direct. He planned to build a hay fever haven, and he sent Maywood Boy Scouts there on outings, which he financed. At one time he attempted to stock the island with goats and pigs, but the winter weather, or the bears, got them.

William Flake came to Oak Island to plan and help build the airport. Mrs. Flake, who was matron at the Joslyn clinic in Maywood, came occasionally too, and became acquainted with Martin. But all the big plans for Oak Island came to nothing when Dr. Joslyn was killed in an air crash in 1933.

Martin Kane died on Sept. 20, 1947, and the King of Oak Island was laid to rest in Calvary cemetery at Bayfield. Royalty could not have had a finer service than was given the King of Oak Island in the Requiem Mass at Holy Family Church with music by the grade school choir, Sister Rose Angela at the organ and the rites of the church administered by Father Damian.

Mrs. Flake, believing that a person as kind and distinguished as Martin Kane should have a tombstone to mark his grave, collected the sum of thirty dollars around town, getting 25 cents here and 50 cents there with a final donation of $10.00 from John Chapple to complete the purchase of a tombstone. Thus, the grave of the King of Oak Island was marked, and will remain so for years to come.

The last time I was on Oak Island, Martin Kane's little home was rapidly falling apart. Nature eliminates the traces of civilization quickly. Wild raspberries had grown up around the little cabin and had pushed their way through the floor. I could see that soon there would be no trace of Martin Kane's home. I ate a few of the raspberries and decided I had better do something so Martin Kane would be remembered. Therefore, this has been written. Preserved in the State of Wisconsin Historical Society, this paper transferred to microfilm, will probably last longer than Martin's granite tombstone. Readers over 100 years from now will know that once there was a King of Oak Island. His name was Martin Kane.

The Toonerville Trolley had nothing on the Bayfield Transfer Railroad. It ran, on an erratic schedule, from Bayfield all around the town of Russell. The depot was the building which is now Booth's office and not infrequently people will come to the ticket window and ask me for a ticket to Buffalo Bay. I only wish I had them to sell. I'd take a ride myself.

On April 23, 1898, this item appeared in *The Bayfield Press:* "Next Monday morning at 6:35, the Bayfield Transfer Ry. Co. will start its first regular train on the road between here and Buffalo Bay and will continue running the same, making three round trips daily except Sunday. They expected to start today but were unable to do so on account of the caboose not being finished on time."

Steam locomotive of Bayfield Transfer vintage located in the Town of Russell. (Photo: BHA)

Of course, no respectable train should run without its caboose, but once the Transfer got started, it became so popular that Sunday trips were added. In fact, the next year this item appeared in the Red Cliff News of *The Bayfield Press:* Feb. 18, 1899: "The Bayfield Transfer has put on an extra train for Sunday afternoon which enables anyone that wishes to attend our Sunday School to get here before the opening hour. The train does not leave until the close of Sunday School. Everyone is invited to come and spend a pleasant hour with us."

During the summer, baseball games were played at Red Cliff, and the kids in Bayfield would walk out to them, knowing perfectly well that the crew of the Transfer would give them a free ride back.

H.C. Hale was general manager of the Transfer. He was a great baseball fan and went to the games at Red Cliff regularly. But one summer he was stricken with smallpox. At that time, the treatment was isolation and each community had a "pest house", where smallpox victims were placed. Rich, poor, young or old, if you had smallpox, to the pest house you went, and Herbert Hale, manager of the Transfer Railroad was no exception.

The pest house was located along the Transfer tracks, about a mile from town. Each Sunday, after the ball game as the train headed back to Bayfield it would slow down near the pest house and blow the baseball scores with its whistle. In this way, Mr. Hale, feeling well enough to lean from the pest house window, could keep up with the games.

Incidentally, I have wondered who took care of the people in the pest house. Surely they weren't left there to care for themselves. Does anyone know?

When the crew of the Transfer realized the speed of the new train, the time of departure from Bayfield was changed from 6:35 to 6:40 AM The train arrived in Red Cliff at 7 AM There were also special trains for any occasion. Nov. 4, 1905, an auction at Red Cliff was advertised in Bayfield with: "Free ride to Red Cliff. Train leaves at 1 PM and returns at 5." On May 21, 1909, *The Press* reported: "Special train tomorrow at 1 o'clock to see steam stump pulling machine at Feldmeiers' farm."

Nov. 10, 1905–"Work on the extension of the Bayfield and Western Railroad to Cornucopia is progressing nicely. Over 100 men and 16 teams are on the work and it is confidently expected that trains will be running into Cornucopia New Year's Day. Good!"

In the spring of 1906, a crew of Austrians repaired the Bayfield Transfer tracks. They had a standing order in town for 35 loaves of rye bread each day.

In July, 1909, the Transfer, unjustly accused, was exonerated when *The Bayfield Press* reported: "The report that Joe Abidash of Red Cliff has been run over by the Bayfield Transfer train and had both legs cut off, proved that somebody lied."

The Bayfield Transfer Railroad had a sort of cousin named the Washburn, Bayfield and Iron River Railroad, locally known as "The Battle Axe."

June 29, 1901 *The Ashland Press* reported: "The remains of John Copic passed through the city last evening on their way to Dorchester, where they will be interred."

The Bayfield Press immediately replied: "Jack returned from Dorchester Monday night, the liveliest looking corpse we ever saw. He went to Dorchester to attend the funeral of Andrew Reat, who was killed last week on the Battle Axe Ry."

Probably the most exciting time ever had aboard the Transfer occurred in Nov. 1908, when a bunch of Red Cliff citizens attempted to clean out the train crew. It sounds like something from a western movie. At that time the sawmills were running full blast at Red Cliff and the mill workers would come into Bayfield on Sundays for a little relaxation. On this particular day they did not relax, but drank to the point where their fighting blood was stirred.

The Press reported: "They made things unpleasant for the other passengers with abusive language and Conductor Hoefle gave them a severe calling down. This was not sufficient and he had to be after them every minute. Finally, just as the train was pulling out of Roy's Point the men pulled off their coats and went after Hoefle.

Things appeared rather black for him until John Lambert, the engineer, seeing what was happening, climbed back over the water tank and, using a monkey wrench for a weapon, assisted Conductor Hoefle in quelling the disturbance.

The disturbers of the peace were put off the train, suffering several painful bruises, the result of sudden and forceful contact with Lambert's monkey wrench and Hoefle's fists. When the train arrived at Red Cliff, it was discovered that Mr. Lambert had a bad cut under one eye and Mr. Hoefle had a sore chest. The ringleaders were arrested and sentenced by Judge Atkinson to six months at hard labor."

The story does not mention that the train was stopped for the battle. Apparently it just ran on by itself while the engineer climbed over the water tank, monkey wrench in hand, to get into the fight.

There are still a few souvenirs of the Transfer lying around, such as rusted spikes and cracked timbers. Recently while walking the old road near the tracks I found a Swamproot bottle (empty). This old remedy of the lumberjack days was a cureall, especially for the liver. Even if the cure was not permanent, the high alcohol content would give a temporary glow of health.

Though the Bayfield Transfer Railroad departed from Bayfield long ago, it still runs in miniature in the home of Lloyd Church, former Bayfield resident. For the town on his railroad he has rebuilt early Bayfield. He is also a photographer, and this year his Christmas card showed the Island View all lighted up, and people looking into the window of Frank Boutin's store. The boarders in the old LaBonte House must have been having a fine time, for every light in the place was on.

Recently I sent Mr. Church the measurements of Booth's office, the depot of the old Transfer Railroad, so he can build it to scale. Next Christmas I hope for a card with the Transfer pulled up at its depot and people with their arms filled with Christmas packages getting aboard, heading home to Buffalo Bay.

Benjamin Bicksler

Benjamin & Nancy Adaline Pike and children. circa 1862. (Photo: BHA)

B.F. Bicksler arrived here in June 1856, on the side-wheeler *Superior*. Nazaire LaBonte was on the same boat. Fate did Mr. Bicksler a great kindness in bringing him here, for the next year he was in love with one of the prettiest girls who ever lived in Bayfield.

In James Peet's diary, the entry for July 8, 1857, says: "Brother Warren and Bicksler took me in a boat to Br. Pike's house in the woods, some five miles distant."

Now, at this late date, is not time to start questioning B.F. Bicksler's motives in guiding the new minister to Pike's house. But since Benjamin F. Bicksler and Nancy Adeline Pike were married on Oct. 17, 1859, it is only natural to wonder if at least part of his reason for rowing five miles wasn't to see Adeline.

Their wedding ceremony took place in Pike's little log house where the north and west branches of Pike's creek meet. There was such a storm that October day, that the Rev. Wheeler could not get from the mission at Odanah to perform the ceremony. The Rev. James Peet was no longer in Bayfield, since he had left that spring for Oneota, Minnesota. It took three men to perform the ceremony; Judge McCleod, Mr. Mandelbaum, and one other, whose name has been forgotten. S.S. Vaughn, who had a store in Bayfield, sent out two wreaths for the bride and her bridesmaid, Miss Worthy McElroy.

Benjamin Bicksler was a dark, serious looking man. Adeline, who had one of the prettiest, gayest faces ever seen in Bayfield seemed a direct contrast to him. In a family picture, a serious looking little boy, the "spitting image" of his father, is standing between his parents, who are seated, and on Adeline's lap is a fat, laughing baby girl, who looks exactly like her mother.

Prefabricated houses are not a new thing. B.F. Bicksler was building them right here 83 years ago. *The Press* for July 15, 1871 says: "Our friends Bicksler and Perinier framed a house for a Frenchman living on Madeline Island, taking it over on a scow and finishing it in four days. They are not only fast, but good workmen."

B.F. Bicksler was a man with a thoughtful mind, who enjoyed debating with the Bayfield Lyceum group. The subject of debate reported in *The Press* for March 25, 1871, was: "Resolved, that $200,000 be voted by the county of Bayfield to aid in constructing a railroad from Bayfield to Puget Sound. Affirmative: F. McElroy, R.D. Pike, and Nelson Boutin. Negative, A. Whittlesey, William Knight and B.F. Bicksler." As usual, *The Press* , probably because of the limited number of out-of-town subscribers, did not report which side won. They figured everybody in town knew.

The Bickslers lived part of the time in Bayfield and part of the time in Ashland. Just what the dates are, I don't know, but in 1872, when the Wisconsin Central Railroad was coming into that village, B.F. Bicksler was there and *The Ashland Press* reported on June 22: "Bicksler has recently completed a building on Front Street which will be occupied as an office building by the W.C.R.R. engineers."

And in November 1875, they were still in Ashland, for *The Press* said, "Bicksler is the lucky man this week. It's a nice boy and both mother and child are doing well. It's a growing time with Ashland."

Mr. Bicksler had a furniture store in Ashland for several years, but he is best remembered over there as a man who built their first courthouse.

When B.F. Bicksler died January 29, 1885, he was buried in the Pike's Creek cemetery. The *Salmo News* which was published in *The Bayfield Press*, June 18, 1909, has this to say about it. "The large monument in Pike's cemetery which marked the resting place of Mr. Bicksler was recently moved to the Bayfield cemetery, where the remains of Mr. Bicksler were moved some time ago. This is the last monument to speak of to be moved, but we understand there are still two or three graves in this cemetery, perhaps the friends or relatives of which have moved away and if they knew the condition, would move them to the Bayfield cemetery. Then this beautiful place on the hill, which belongs to the town of Bayfield, and with its beautiful foliage and evergreens, could be made into a beautiful park. Then, to honor our good citizen, who has gone to his reward, and who gave this piece of land to the town, we would suggest that it be called, "Pike's Park."

The old account is correct. The grove of evergreens in the old cemetery is one of the most beautiful around here. It belongs to A.O. Milligan now, and it is well pruned up and as beautiful as ever. If you walk up there you will see the old graves, now empty, as far as anyone knows. If two or three people were left behind, their graves are unmarked.

Standing on the bluff on the east side of the old cemetery there is a good view of Pike's Bay and from the west side the backwater of Pike's Creek looks like a small lake. I don't know why they didn't keep the cemetery there and build a road into it from the foot of Salmo hill. Does anybody know why it was moved?

Robert Pugh

ROBERT PUGH ALSO ACTED AS caretaker of Bass Island. He was born in Canada in 1835 and came to Bayfield in 1873. He walked through the woods from Pike's Bay to Buffalo Bay where he was employed as a teacher at the government school. He was still teaching there in 1878 for The Press, on March 13 of that year, says: "a call from Mr. Pew yesterday. His school children at Buffalo Bay are taking their annual sugar making vacation and his school is adjourned until they return from the bush."

Mrs. R.C. Goodwin of Matteson, Illinois, writes: "Robert Pugh was the school teacher who changed a perfectly good French surname Gauthier to Gokee, because he did not know how to spell it. My father, who just recently passed away, went to school to this man. He told me last summer how Mr. Pugh carried him around on his shoulder when he started school."

Mr. Pugh, who spelled people's names phonetically, found that his own name received the same treatment. In all accounts of him, I have found his name spelled Pew. But his tombstone, incidentally one of the finest in the cemetery, spells it Pugh.

He is remembered too, for the large white building he owned where the Standard Oil pumps now stand. This house finally got into a dilapidated state and was known for years, in fact until it was torn down, as "Castle Gardens."

When Mr. Pugh died on May 3, 1908, *The Press* said, "He was a venerable old man, respected by all who grieve to learn of his death."

Since the Brighams had a farm on Bass Island, I wrote to Lloyd, now of Sheboygan, to see what he could remember about these two old caretakers of the quarry there.

He replied: "I am answering your letter with some misgivings. You know, of course, that things seen through the eyes of youngsters quite often seem bigger than they really are."

My recollections of Mr. Pugh (I always thought it was spelled Pew) are somewhat vague. He owned some land on the west side of Bass Island, south of a little bay or cove, at the south end of Col. Rudd's farm. (Bayfield history readers may remember how Col. Rudd refought the Civil War all by himself on the bank corner). I believe he was at one time caretaker of the quarry at the south end of the island and lived in the same house that burned down over Judge McCloud's head. I cannot place in my mind whether Mr. Pugh or McCloud were first to stay there, but I think it was Mr. Pugh. Neither of them were on the island at the time that my father had a logging camp there, at the water's edge. I think both of them were gone. To the best of my knowledge, Mr. Pugh died in Ashland in St. Joseph's and it must have been before 1910 as that was the year my father had his camp there.

I can tell you a story about that house, but I cannot, for the life of me, say for certain whether Mr. Pugh or Judge McCloud was there at the time. On one of our trips past the island in a row boat (and we had to row as well as my father) we stopped there to visit. We were invited into the house to talk, and there was a fire in the stove. That would make it in the fall of the year, and I was quite small, so it would have been considerably before 1910.

After awhile, my father smelled something burning, like old wool, and as the conversation had been about the cat that was missing, it jolted our host's memory. He jumped up and with an exclamation opened the oven door. Out came the cat and beat it for the lake, pretty well done and not much hair!

We left soon after, but on our return trip, stopped again.

"Do you know," he said, "I haven't seen that cat since. I guess she's afraid she will be shut in the oven again."

"Dad" Davis

"DAD" DAVIS HAD PERSONALITY. MANY of you who knew him will laugh and say, "Wow, did he!" Others who read the story of "Dad's" encounter with the Snow Snake which appeared in these columns last winter may have some idea of what he was like. Jokes were his great pleasure in life. He was Justice of the Peace and proprietor of The Davis House. Although, as Bob Pike has written, "Ma Davis was not only proprietor, but in my book she was one of Bayfield's Greats."

That she was, and one of the best cooks who ever lived here, if not *the* best. I have been told that salesmen who had business in Ashland always managed to come to Bayfield to spend the night, so they could eat Ma's good meals and swap stores with Dad. If cooking is an art, then Ma Davis was a great artist. But her work was done behind the scenes, and Dad, out in front, got the laughs. It's just one of the quirks of human nature that nobody quite remembers a meal that it took Ma Davis hours to prepare, but they remember in complete detail a joke it took Dad Davis five minutes to tell.

She was complimented in this item, which appeared in *The Press* July 2, 1909: "Sam Meyer of St. Louis, Mo., was here Thursday and filled up on whitefish. He says: "I have often eaten what purported to be fish, but never struck the genuine article until I found it at the Davis House, Bayfield. I know of several St. Louis parties who are headed this way, and more will come when I tell them about your fine air, beautiful scenery and delicious fish and fruits."

Dec. 12, 1913, Dad put over a land deal that got a lot of attention. "Dad Davis informs *The Press* this week that he has purchased an entire section of land giving the description of same as Sec. 38, township 49 range 17 west. Now, Dad, you tried to fool us, but we know that land of yours lies just 2 1/2 miles northwest of Outer Island. We compliment you on your energy in securing this valuable tract, despite its one drawback of a covering of fifty feet of water."

It was inevitable with Dad playing tricks on people that they would play a few on him. Shortly after a new law was passed about inspections of hotel rooms, a stranger showed up at the Davis House and said he was a hotel inspector. Accompanied by Dad, he went through each room in the hotel, ripping open the freshly made beds, pulling off the sheets and throwing them on the floor, saying they were an inch too short and would have to be replaced. He found a lot of things wrong and overturned as much furniture as he could. Then he gave Dad a short period of time to make the extreme changes he said were necessary. They let Dad stew for several days before they told him the hotel inspector was another practical joker.

Shine Miller remembers the night that he and Johnny Sayles decided to have a car race up main street. Johnny, who lived at the Davis House and was like a son to them, since they had no children of their own, drove Dad's car, an Oakland. Shine drove a Chevrolet. In those days it was a big thing to see a car, to drive one was wonderful, and to have a race almost unheard of in this country. The race took place at 11 o'clock one summer night. It was to begin at the city dock, go up Main Street and with the speed they had attained by then, they expected to make the hill by Stark's store and race on up to Frank Stark's house. There were a lot of hay fever patients around and they lined up to watch this exciting event.

Left: Ma Davis. (Photo: BHA)
Right: The famous Davis House

The race got off to a good start, and when the cars reached the corner by the Standard Oil station, they were going all of 40 miles per hour. Then the unexpected happened. The policeman, seeing them coming, ran out into the middle of the street, waved his arms and tried to stop them. Naturally, at that terrific speed, they could not stop, besides it would have spoiled their run for the hill, so they flashed around him, a car on each side. But the policeman knew them, he caught them later and arrested them. They had to appear in Dad Davis' court.

Dad was very formal, he asked Johnny, "Were you racing?"

Johnny said, yes, he was.

Dad asked, "How did you make out?"

Johnny said, "I lost."

Judge Davis gave his gavel a terrific thump on the table and said, "I fine you ten dollars for letting a Chevrolet beat you!"

Judge Joseph S. Atkinson

JUDGE JOSEPH S. ATKINSON SERVED as Justice of the Peace in Bayfield for thirty years. He first came to Bayfield in 1872. Previously he had served all through the Civil War.

His war record shows that he enlisted at Portland, Maine on October 31, 1861, in Company E, 13th Maine Infantry Volunteers. He served three years and re-enlisted on February 1, 1864, at Matagoda Bend, Texas. When the war ended, he was mustered out at Savannah, Georgia, on August 20, 1865, after almost four years of service.

He married Martha Maria Price at Portland, Maine, on January 14, 1868, and about 1870, they came to Michigan Island where Mr. Atkinson was assistant lighthouse keeper for a year and a half. Then the family came to Bayfield.

Not only was he Justice of the Peace for 30 years, but in the spring of 1911, he had the honor to receive the first appointment by Gov. McGovern to the office of Judge of the newly created Third Municipal Court.

In response to my request for information about her father, Mrs. E.A. Clowater (Carrie Atkinson) has written: "I can tell you that he was a great lover of music. He played the fife in the fife and drums corps all during the Civil War. When people young and old became weary climbing "Cooper Hill" they would get as far as the retaining wall in front of our house (now the Van Duser home) and sit down to rest as they listened to him play on his fife accompanied by my sister, Louise, on the piano. . . I still have his old fife among my most valued possessions."

"My parents were noted for their hospitality. Dad homesteaded some land about eight miles from Bayfield. I was a very small child when I lived on that homestead, but I well remember one very cold, stormy night after we had all retired, we heard a rap on the door. My father got up and opened the door to be greeted by a strange Indian. Father invited him in, gave him a warm meal and made him comfortable for the night on an improvised bed on the floor. Space and accommodations were limited in that little old log house. Next morning when he was leaving, he was very profuse in his words of gratitude. However, his gratitude did not end with those words. It expressed itself in a very tangible form when we were supplied with meat during the remainder of that season."

Judge Atkinson had a very dry sort of humor. Without changing his expression at all, he would make a remark that would set everyone laughing. Mr. Wilkinson recalled one of those remarks the last time I saw him. Black Jack McDonald had come to town and met up with Jack McKay. They met in McCamis' saloon and for some reason, now forgotten, got into a fight that grew to terrible proportions. It finally ended when McKay's face was jumped on until it was hardly recognizable. The two men were arrested and brought before Judge Atkinson. "What is the charge?" he asked. "Assault and battery", was the reply. He sat silently for a moment looking at McKay's battered face, then said quietly, "I don't know about the assault, but I can see there is no question about the battery."

Being Justice of the Peace in Bayfield for 30 years he must have become accustomed to odd requests and situations. Out of many *Bayfield Press* items referring to Judge Atkinson, I have picked this one to illustrate that point. It appeared in the paper January 25, 1896, and is as follows: "William Marquette, a man about 53 years of age, struck town last Saturday with about $50 in money. Saturday night he felt like playing a little game of draw.

He had very poor luck for when Sunday morning came, he was busted. He stopped at the St. James while in town and cast his eyes on the cook, Mary O'Hare, who is 54 years of age, for the first time. It was a case of love at first sight and arrangements were made at once for the wedding Sunday evening. At 7:30, Judge Atkinson was called in and joined the couple in the holy bonds of matrimony. This is probably the quickest case on record, only acquainted 3½ hours when married. Mr. Marquette has a valuable homestead on the Cranberry, where he took his new bride. They left by stage Monday morning."

Judge Atkinson, after 39 years in Bayfield, died on September 13, 1911. *The Bayfield Press* said: "All Bayfield residents were grieved Wednesday morning to learn of the death of Judge Joseph Atkinson... In his death, the Harbor City loses a good citizen, a splendid resident and official.

The (Orlonzo) Flanders Family

SOME TIME AGO, I ASKED Ruth Flanders to send me information for a story about her father for the Bayfield history collection. She did better than that. She wrote the story herself, much more effectively than I could have done, for she wrote with the inspiration of years of affection for her father. She said: "I found it very hard to write about one who was so close to me without making it too personal for publication. I hope that this is a fair picture. I wish it were possible to include more of the power of his personality, but that is not a tangible thing that will go on paper."

By Ruth Flanders

In the summer of 1873, Mr. and Mrs. Orlando Flanders and their one-year-old son embarked on a great adventure. They had been married several years and had moved as many times from one town to another in Iowa, and then to Fayetteville, Arkansas. But this move was different, for they were going on a long journey to a wild country in the north woods.

Mr. and Mrs. A.J. Milligan, parents of Mrs. Flanders, had gone to northern Wisconsin to work for the government as Indian farmers on the Red Cliff reservation. They had written back about the invigorating climate and the healthy atmosphere on the shores of Lake Superior. Best of all, there was an opening for a schoolteacher on the reservation.

So Mr. Flanders, his wife Jennie, and their small son Charlie, started for Wisconsin. The only way to get there was by train to Duluth, several days in a day coach, and then by boat to Bayfield. Red Cliff was then a mile nearer Point Detour than the present town, a beautiful and isolated spot. Finally they were settled on the reservation under the special protection of Old Chief John Buffalo, whom they found to be a very fine and helpful friend.

However, when winter came the lake froze over; the boats stopped running; the big snows came, the roads became impassable and the only way out was over the ice by dog team. Mrs. Flanders often described her feeling as if she were in a bottle and someone was pushing in the cork. It was pioneer life, but they were young and they came from pioneer stock. Where was there a better chance to take root and grow up with the country?

Mr. Flanders learned to speak some Chippewa and many of the Indians spoke English so they spent the winter lonely, but not too uncomfortable. In the spring on a trip to Bayfield, Mr. Flanders found that Mr. Frank Boutin Sr., was badly in need of a bookkeeper and his business was a thriving one. He shipped fish and furs and his store supplied the needs of the countryside. So Mrs. Flanders finished the school term and Mr. Flanders commuted the four miles between old Red Cliff and Bayfield on horseback. As soon as the school term was finished, he moved his family to Bayfield where he lived for almost fifty years until his death in 1922.

Those winters when there was no railroad nearer than Duluth, were long and trying. Mail had to be brought overland or by dog team on the ice once a week and supplies had to be brought in before the lake froze. The story was often told about the hardware storekeeper who refused to sell a keg of nails because he wouldn't have any left. Once Mrs. Flanders suddenly realized in mid-winter that her last pair of shoes were wearing out. When she tried to get a new pair, there were none to fit and she had to wear paper in the soles and rubbers to keep warm the rest of the winter.

At the end of one of those early winters after their son had been drowned off the Boutin dock, they decided to return to Iowa. They left Bayfield with the last boat in the fall, but returned with the first one in the spring. Mr. Boutin was glad to get him back, and that was the only time they moved from Bayfield.

In 1887, Mr. Flanders and Mr. Frank Herrick, in partnership, bought the Leihy General Store with a dry goods department opening on Broad Street, and a grocery and butcher department on Rittenhouse Avenue. With its kerosene lamps, its pot-bellied stove, its dark cellar for winter vegetables and apples, its barrels of sugar, white or brown, its kerosene pump with a tank in the cellar supplying the light for most homes, its warehouse on Broad Street stocked with feed for the cattle, it was a typical country general store, though the building was large and never crowded. There, for many years, the people of Bayfield came and went, leaving their stamp on Bayfield's life.

Because Mr. Flanders spoke Chippewa and the Indians felt that he was their friend, he carried a great deal of their trade, wrote their letters, often interpreted for them, was a go-between between them and the Indian agent, carried their accounts until they got their allotments, shipped their furs and in many ways made their life easier.

One of his daughters was shocked one day when an Indian came into the store badly intoxicated. He had a month's pay and was in a spending mood. Mr. Flanders sold him everything he could, and kept suggesting more. After the Indian left, the daughter asked, "Why did you take all his money when he was so drunk he didn't know what he was doing?" The answer was, "I can send these things to his wife in the morning. She can bring back what she doesn't want. He won't get home with any money and this way his family will at least eat for awhile."

There was always a cat that lived in the store. She earned her way by keeping down rats and mice, especially in the warehouse. One cat learned to sit up and beg as well as any dog. She never made a sound when she wanted anything, but just sat beside it and begged. The cheese was in a box of wire netting with a roll door, which could be heard all over the store. This cat loved cheese and every time the box was opened, she ran as fast as she could to beg for a piece. Mr. Inglis passed through the store between his office and home once or twice every day, just to pass the time of day and get a nibble of cheese for himself and the cat. They were great friends.

The school board consisting of Dr. Hannum, W.W. Downs and Mr. Flanders, often met behind the stove in the store and many of the town's problems were threshed out there. Sometimes on a stormy winter day when business was lax, you might even find a checker game going on there. The board might be drawn on a piece of wrapping paper and the men would bet pennies and nickels, but it was a good game. The three or four chairs were seldom empty. Among the regular callers was Mr. Bigger, a Methodist minister, who seldom missed a morning during his ministry in Bayfield. He came to read the Minneapolis Journal and discuss the news of the day. Another who liked to read the Journal and join in the discussion was Father Casimir, the Catholic priest. In spite of their differing views on religion, he and Mr. Flanders enjoyed and respected one another.

Old Dick, a big black stallion, was the delivery horse and Mr. Luick was delivery man for many years. They were certainly an important part of Bayfield at that time. In summer when the flies were bad, Dick wore a net for protection, but the flies bit his legs until he couldn't be trusted to stand without being tied. So Mr. Luick took two pair of overalls and made him pants, and with a straw hat with his ears sticking through, he made quite a picture, but he was much more comfortable. Mr. Luick made the rounds of the homes of the regular customers early each morning to take their daily orders. When he returned to the store, everyone available was very busy until those orders were put up and he was back on his rounds. Every housewife must have her supplies in time for her noon dinner. Quite different from cash and carry and serve yourself of today, but without telephones and automobiles, life was different.

Prices were different, too, eggs ten cents a dozen, often in trade; Lions coffee, strong enough to suit anyone, ten cents a pound, three pounds for a quarter. The best grades of coffee were twenty-five cents a pound. Salt pork hooked from a barrel of brine was ten cents a pound, excellent for seasoning. Calico was five cents a yard, ten yards to a dress. Any cotton dress material at twenty-five cents to fifty cents a yard was too high priced to sell.

Most of the business was done on credit. The sawmill was in full operation in the summertime and the logging camps in the winter. These were Bayfield's largest payrolls. The logger's families lived in town and had little cash until the men came to town and drew their pay. Then, if they could get past the saloon—one on most corners of the business section—and get home before their money was gone, the grocery bill was paid and they were ready to live on credit for another season. In spite of these conditions and prices, the store made a comfortable living for the two families with five children each.

The firm of Flanders and Herrick dissolved partnership in 1899. Mr. Flanders took over the business and soon afterward sold out the groceries and put in what he called "Queensware" in modern language, china. He closed out his business and retired in 1908.

Mr. Flanders was a quiet man, who never wasted words, but he had no trouble expressing himself well when the occasion demanded. He had a keen sense of humor though you seldom heard him laugh, but oh!, the twinkle in his eye! When his family was growing up he had a rowboat especially built for them. It was rather large and built so that under ordinary circumstances, it could not be tipped over. In the fall of one year a friend who lived on Bass Island asked to borrow it for the fall and spring months and Mr. Flanders let him have it. When summer came the boat was still on the island. Every time the man came to town, Mr. Flanders asked for the boat, but it was always too rough, or he wanted to paint it, or something. One day Captain Vorous, who piloted the *Barker*, reported that the boat had come as far as Roy's Point, but had been left there, so that it wouldn't be found in town. Bessie Flanders took her cousin and went to Roy's Point on the Dalrymple railroad and brought the boat home. In the meantime, the borrower came into the store and told how sorry he was that he couldn't get it home, the channel was too rough that day. When Mr. Flanders told his wife about it she asked, "Did you tell him he was lying?" The answer was, "No, he knew he was lying, I knew he was lying, and he knew that I knew he was lying, so why tell him so?"

This humorous little item appeared in *The Bayfield Press* 86 years ago this April. "If anyone wants to borrow anything of you now, you can tell them 'It's Lent already.'"

Mrs. Flanders was a charter member of Bayfield Presbyterian Church and Mr. Flanders was very regular in attendance and support until he later became a member and an Elder in the church. Because he was a good bookkeeper, he was Treasurer of the church for a long time, as he was of so many organizations to which he belonged. His family grew up in that church and look back now in its influence as an important factor in their lives.

Mr. Flanders never lost his faith in the future of Bayfield. He was very much interested in small fruit farming and spent much time in bringing help from the Wisconsin Horticultural Society and in helping organize the Fruit Shippers Association. He spent much of his time during the later years planting and tending his orchard, testing different kinds of fruit and berries to see which were best suited to the climate and which were the best shippers. He always believed that some day there would be a "Lake to Ocean Waterway" and that then, Bayfield, with her natural protected harbor would become an important port, and so a city. How slowly men's dreams are realized.

Mr. Downs, town lawyer and O. Flanders with businesses on opposite sides of Broad Street at Rittenhouse Avenue, were the best of friends. Both were Presbyterians and Mr. Downs and his wife sat in the seat directly in front of the Flanders' family pew. Mr. Downs always slept through the sermon, and if he was not awakened he would snore until he attracted the attention of the entire congregation, but the next day he would tell you more of the sermon than most people who were apparently awake.

When Mrs. Downs was there she kept him from getting noisy, but there came a time when she went on a visit. Mrs. Flanders took over and when he approached the danger point she poked him with her fan or her glasses case. One Sunday, Mrs. Flanders wasn't able to be in church and it was up to Mr. Flanders to carry the responsibility. You can imagine the suppressed giggles in the Flanders' pew when Mr. Down's head began to drop forward and Mr. Flanders slid down in his seat. Another nod, another slide, then a quick kick and both men suddenly sat very straight in their seats. This lasted a few minutes then it began all over again. After this had gone on during the entire service, it was almost impossible to keep the children within bounds, but the men showed no sign that anything had happened and they got the full content of the sermon. Mr. Downs fully appreciated this help, for he was much embarrassed by his inability to stay awake.

Dr. Hannum, Mr. Flanders and Mr. Downs were life-long friends. Dr. Hannum died in August 1922; Mr. Flanders followed within a week, and Mr. Downs a few months later.

Dr. Henry Hannum

Dr. Hannum and son Frank. circa 1905. (Photo: BHA)

The title of this story should be, "Dr. Hannum was a wonderful man." Almost everyone who had anything to add to Dr. Hannum's story began with that sentence. It was repeated to me so often, I finally knew I'd never be able to write anything that really expressed Dr. Hannum's kindness, patience, humor, his love of his town and his people.

In simple words: Dr. Hannum devoted his life to Bayfield.

When I asked what Dr. Hannum looked like, no one seemed to remember, exactly. They said he was big, and that he was usually smiling. The final answer seemed to be found in the description given by Mrs. M. DeMars: "He was the kindest looking man you could imagine."

Though the memory of his physical appearance has dimmed, no one who knew him has forgotten the kindness in his face.

Henry Hannum was born March 11, 1855, ninety-nine years ago next month. He was a descendant of old puritan stock. His ancestors came from England and located in Dorchester, Massachusetts in the early part of the sixteenth century. He graduated from Rush Medical College in February 1881, first located in Ben Oak, Kansas and came to Bayfield in 1882.

Before he got to Bayfield he stopped in Ashland long enough to have Thanksgiving dinner with the Fifields. And through the years he continued to be their good friend and visit them. *The Bayfield Press* of Dec. 1, 1905 reports: "Dr. and Mrs. Hannum spent Thanksgiving in Ashland as guests of Mr. and Mrs. Gov. Fifield. Twenty-three years ago Dr. Hannum partook of Thanksgiving cheer with Mr. and Mrs. Fifield, it being his first appearance in these parts."

When Dr. Hannum arrived here, he stayed at the LaBonte House (now Greunke's) and had an office in one of the rooms. He was well established in the affections of the town by October 1883, when he went to North Bloomfield, Ohio and married Kittie Sheldon. When they returned, they lived in a small house on Front Street.

Everyone agreed that Kittie Hannum was beautiful. She had dark hair, dark eyes, a clear skin and lots of energy. She began at once to take an active part in the small doings of the town. They were a sociable, friendly couple, who enjoyed playing cards. *The Bayfield Press* for Feb. 7, 1891, reports that Dr. Hannum won high honors in Progressive Whist (then the popular game) at a delightful evening party.

In March 1884, five months after their marriage, Dr. Hannum was so well liked here that people thought his birthday called for a celebration. Here's what *The Press* wrote about it. "A goodly number of Dr. Hannum's married friends treated him to an old fashioned surprise party, the occasion being his 29th birthday. It proved a genuine surprise, and was thoroughly enjoyed by all."

About 1885, he decided it was time to have his own house and built the one now owned by Roy Smith. It was a comfortable, homey place, with a parlor organ in the front room. Company came and went. "I spent many pleasant hours in their home" one of their friends commented, and it well sums up the constant hospitality of the Hannums.

It was in this house their first child, Leila, was born in 1886. She had hardly grown out of babyhood when she was stricken with diphtheria, which was then a much-feared disease, with no dependable remedy. In fact, a common remedy used by the mothers of that day was a small sack of horrible smelling asafetida tied around a child's neck. The little girl was stricken just at the time the old sewer pipes of the city were being dug up and replaced, and some people thought germs from the sewer digging caused her illness. Friends of the Hannums watched anxiously as the doctor put all his skill and knowledge into trying to save his child. But at that time, medical knowledge, even reinforced by a father's love, was not enough, and their baby died.

A year or so after Leila's death, a son was born to the Hannums. They did not have another child, and naturally young Frank Walter Hannum became their pride and joy. They were a devoted family. Everyone knew it, and Currie Bell, writing in *The Bayfield Press* in March 1889, kidded Doc about it a little, saying "Dr. Hannum could not stand it any longer, so he took Sunday evening's train for St. Paul, where Mrs. Hannum and little Frank are visiting. After visiting friends a few days they all returned, and the doctor is happy once more."

Year after year *The Bayfield Press* had items which began, "Dr. Hannum reports the following births this week." There were usually about four, sometimes as high as six, but let's cut it down to two and multiply by 52 weeks and then 40 years. That would add up to about 4,000 babies Dr. Hannum delivered. It is probably a low figure, for Dr. Hannum not only took care of Bayfielders, but went to Washburn, LaPointe, Red Cliff and the general countryside, wherever he was called. He was a progressive doctor, and recorded the births, too. Until then, no one had bothered much about that. If you were born, you were here, and that was all there was to it.

Many of the birth notices are enlivened by a touch of humor. Whether Currie Bell, or Dr. Hannum supplied it, is not known now; but they were great friends, and both possessed a fine sense of humor. Here is one of the notices. "April 12, 1890. Cyrus O. Greenlaw and wife have a son born the 10th day of April. Weight 8 pounds. He looks like his dad and says he wishes the mill would start so he could get a job."

Continuing the story of Dr. Hannum, lets see what also he did besides delivering and recording the births of an estimated four thousand babies. A few news items from *The Bayfield Press* of 1890 and 1891 give us some idea of his many activities here.

March 15, 1890. "Dr. Hannum tells us of a cat, that to his certain knowledge has made night and day hideous under his house for three weeks, and during that time could have had nothing to eat but sawdust. The doctor unearthed the feline the other day, and although but a shadow of its former self, the cat is stall able to navigate. Does this prove that sawdust is life sustaining, or that a cat has nine lives, or what?"

Dr. Hannum took pride in his home and his yard and enjoyed making improvements in them. On May 10, 1890, *The Bayfield Press* says, "Dr. Hannum has erected a barn, (incidentally, a very good barn, which has since been remodeled into Ed Smith's house), put a bay window on his house, is prepared to do the same for anyone who says it is not a thing of beauty and a joy forever, and has also graded his lot."

Some of the affection the town felt for him is expressed at the end of this little news item. July 6, 1890. "Miss Mattie Hannum of Stillman Valley, Illinois was among last Saturday's arrivals and will spend the season at the residence of her brother, our one and only doctor."

It must have been generally known that the Hannums hoped their only son would follow in his father's footsteps, for on July 26, 1890, a small item said, "Mrs. Dr. Hannum and the heir apparent to the doctor's case of surgical instruments visited in Washburn."

When accidents happened, Dr. Hannum had the confidence of interested bystanders as well as the confidence of his patients. We find that fact publicly acknowledged in *The Press* October 18, 1890. "J. R. Copic was injured at the fire last week. While running with the hose cart, he tripped and fell nearly in front of the Fountain House (a hotel where Johnson's Food Shop is now). The downhill impetus gave the cart speed which did not allow the boys behind to stop it in time, and it passed directly over his side and chest. Dr. Hannum was right on hand and Mr. Copic was taken to his residence. Examination showed three rib fractures. He is out again, and while still feeble is still in the ring. He has been under Dr. Hannum's treatment, which accounts for his being around so soon."

Dr. Hannum has been described as "always smiling", "always jolly", a man who "saw the sunny side of life and was a friend to everybody." His remarks on the topics of the day nearly always brought a smile, if not a hearty laugh from his listeners. He had a great deal of humor and loved to tell jokes and funny stories. He laughed, and made others laugh. Even when he did such a simple thing as go to Ashland, *The Bayfield Press* reported, "Dr. Hannum lent the radiance of his smiling visage to the people across the bay."

Once the crisis was over, and the turn for the better taken, Dr. Hannum would offer laughter to his patients as a spirit restorative. Mrs. Myrtle Judd Nourse recalls his treatment of her husband, Laurie Nourse when his leg was injured, became infected, and he was laid up for a six week siege. She writes, "The pain was overcome, and Laurie found time passing slowing as he was compelled to sit with his leg uplifted to ease the throb. Dr. Hannum met me and with the usual smile he wore he chuckled and remarked, "Tell Laurie this is the time to learn to smoke. It's great for the nerves."

Laurie understood the implication, for it was well known that a Nourse had never puffed from his mouth any kind of smoke bearing device and Dr. Hannum's cigar and corn cob pipes were never out of his reach."

Joe O'Malley remembers his first sight of Dr. Hannum in 1890. Joe was about seven years old then and lived in a house on Front Street. He was standing outside where about a hundred or more people were watching a fight between Fred Herbert and a man named Consolver.

In those days when anyone started fighting, people stood around and watched, letting the fight take its course. So it took its course of blows and blood until Herbert bent down to pick up a big rock to crack Cons Oliver's head open. But Consolver, not wanting his head cracked open, pulled out a knife and stabbed Herbert seven times.

That ended the fight. Some of the non-combatants picked up Herbert and carried him to Dr. Hannum's office, which was then on the lot between the Odd Fellow's building (Andrew Tate's drug store) and Alfred Iverson's home.

Dr. Hannum sewed up the wounds efficiently, while Joe and a gang of kids got up on a fence that ran beside his office window and watched.

Later Dr. Hannum's office was moved to the present location of the Express office. On Aug. 29, 1891, *The Press* reported, "Dr. Hannum's new office is going up with a vim."

Wherever the office was, an endless line of patients made their way to it and Doc went to see those who were too ill to come. "He never refused a call." That was another sentence repeated over and over as people told me about Dr. Hannum. Joe O'Malley recalls that Dr. Hannum prided himself on never sending a bill and, as a result, many people called him, but didn't pay him. He vaccinated Joe for 50 cents and that must have been one of his good collecting days, for Joe paid him cash and still has the receipt to show for it.

Dr. Hannum's birthday was a well-remembered occasion. Here's *The Press* report of it in 1891. "Last Friday night a number of Dr. Hannum's friends who learned that he had just passed another birthday, gathered at his house with malice aforethought. They bombarded the door with a large quantity of chairs and finally forced an entrance. When the doctor found himself powerless, he gracefully yielded to the inevitable. His self-invited guests then added insult to injury by insisting upon his acceptance of a handsome plush uphol- stered chair. The guests then acted just as though they had come to spend the evening, and a very pleasant evening it proved to be. Mrs. Hannum was equal to the occasion too, for after a period of sociability, she set before her guests bounteous refreshment. Say, Doc, you didn't for a moment think your wife, being forewarned, was forearmed, did you?"

Logging accidents were one of Dr. Hannum's problems. He had to be ready to treat, with what little equipment there was in those days, the people who were crushed by falling trees, rolling logs, who had been half drowned in the mill slips, ripped by saws and those just badly banged up in lumberjack fights.

Here is a case that was too late for treatment. It happened February 1, 1906. Maybe some of you remember it. "Bert Steinke received injuries at Green's Squaw Bay camp yesterday afternoon, from which he died while being brought to town for medical aid. He was engaged in top loading and was caught between the logs and badly crushed. He was brought to town at once, and it was not known he was dead until he was taken to Dr. Hannum's office. He breathed his last just before reaching the office. A wife, with a little babe, two weeks old, is left without a husband."

Runaway horses caused many of the injuries he treated. Here is one of his cases. July 1906. "Joe Howder sustained quite serious injuries Thursday afternoon near his farm seven miles west of town. Mr. Howder was driving down hill with a large load of hay when the neck yoke strap broke, allowing the wagon to run down hill at great speed. Mr. Howder was thrown from the wagon, but the extent of his injuries was not thought to be fatal. He was attended by Dr. Hannum."

Runaway horses caused Dr. Hannum other troubles, too. May 28, 1909. "Rittenhouse Avenue was the scene of excitement at 11 AM when a heavy team of work horses belonging to George Green ran away. In their dash they collided with Dr. Hannum's rig in front of his office and came in contact with a hydrant near the Davis House and broke away from the wagon. They were stopped at the corner of First Street and Washington Avenue."

Besides taking care of his many patients, Dr. Hannum did numerous other things for the good of the town. He acted as health officer at a salary of $5 per month. He served on the library board. In 1906, with William Knight, he presented a resolution to the town board that $300 be appropriated to fence and grade the Carnegie Library grounds. This resolution was approved and levied.

The fence was necessary to keep cows out of the yard, and probably out of the library itself, as they went everywhere and people took cover. The holes where that old iron fence fitted into the sandstone wall can still be seen. Naturally William Knight, who Bayfield history readers will remember was a shooting enemy of cows-at-large, teamed up with him on this resolution.

Dr. Hannum was president of the school board. And, incidentally, some of the teachers roomed at Hannum's home. Charlotte Lamoreaux, of Ashland, was one of them. She became engaged to John Anderson, who was assistant cashier at the First National Bank here. The Hannum's gave an engagement party for them and Kittie had the dining room beautifully decorated with paper streamers from the ceiling. Somehow a lighted candle touched them and that was the end of the decorations, but fortunately, not the end of the house.

In 1908 Dr. Hannum was elected president of the Ashland, Iron and Bayfield Counties Medical Association. In February 1909, he was appointed physician for the Red Cliff Indian Reservation. He was a member of the Wing Hose Company, Bayfield's fire department, and acted as company treasurer.

Dr. Hannum was a Mason, a Thirty-second degree Mason, and was master of the lodge here several times. Many newspaper items about a Bayfielder's illness ended with the words, "doing nicely under the care of Dr. Hannum." The same phrase could apply to the endless number of civic committees and organizations Dr. Hannum worked for. Before I started to write Dr. Hannum's story, I had one definite instruction from everybody. It was, "Don't forget to write about Molly!" And I haven't.

Molly was a small sorrel horse, with a white face and light colored mane and tail. She was as well known as Dr. Hannum, and seemingly endowed with the same kind understanding and devotion to duty. She lived about 25 years, and when she got too old and tired to take Doc on his rounds, he saw that Molly had a comfortable retirement. He would never let her be disposed of. She lived out her life in the nice barn behind his house.

Children used to come to the barn to pet and feed her. Bud McQuade remembers he used to feed her ground corn from a pan, after her teeth got so bad from age she could not eat firmer food. Other kids used to curry her and naturally, they all ran around the barn making noise. But though Molly's age was great and she would certainly have been justified in kicking them occasionally, she accepted their noise, their attention with the currycomb, and their food, very amiably.

Fred Bloom wrote this about Dr. Hannum. "He never refused to go to a sick person if it was in any way possible to get there. I was asked to get him one time for a neighbor at 5 AM in winter and there was lots of snow; but what is now Highway 13 was used for hauling supplies to the lumber camps and was good traveling. I used skis to get there, then trotted most of the way to town. Got to Doc's house about 7:30 AM before breakfast and told him of my errand and road conditions. All he said was, "Sit down." and went out to the barn to feed Molly, a horse as faithful as himself. Then we had breakfast and were off. We got to the road leading homeward and left the horse and cutter. It was then I gave him his first lesson in skiing, and I think his last. After helping him up a few times, he said he thought he could do better walking, but never a grumble."

After Molly retired, Dr. Hannum did not replace her. Cars were considered fairly reliable by then and he bought a little chain drive Buick.

Typical of Bayfield, he had a lot on the books. It was suggested that if I wanted something really startling for this story, I should find out how much Dr. Hannum had on the books when he died. One woman said, "Some people never had their births paid for, and they never paid him for the births of their own children."

But whether babies were delivered free, or paid for, Dr. Hannum had a great affection for children, and they for him. They took care of Molly for him, rode in his buggy, and later in the chain drive Buick. Naturally, a lot of children were named after their doctor.

Lloyd Church wrote, "Concerning Dr. Hannum I seem to remember him more for his box camera than for the lancing of abscesses, patching up sawed off thumbs, and setting broken bones, with which we kids kept him rather busy. His consistent picture taking and the very good blue prints he produced should make a perfect pictorial record of Bayfield around the turn of the century."

If Dr. Hannum's kindness can be measured by his attitude toward youngsters, he was most kind. Many of his pictures were of kid activities; two of which he made of a home made, hand-powered automobile I struggled with about 1901 or 02. It was my fascination for Dr. Hannum's camera, and its works, that resulted in a life hobby of photography for me that has never ceased its pleasure."

After his own son, Frank, had grown up and was in college, children still played in Hannum's yard. This item appeared in *The Bayfield Press* in the summer of 1909. "Talk about cherries! Dr. Hannum is growing some with six trees, from which he harvested ten bushel, besides feeding the usual number of birds and small boys."

Sometime in the early nineteen hundreds, Dr. Hannum had a stroke which left one of his hands helpless. He had to walk with a cane, then, and one foot dragged a little. But that didn't stop him from going on calls, or his old friends and patients from wanting him to come. By then, other doctors were available and there was a hospital in Ashland. But people kept right on calling Dr. Hannum because their confidence was not in the strength of one of his hands, but in his knowledge, experience, and especially because they knew he cared what happened to them.

He still never refused a call, and went on all of them regardless of weather. Kittie Hannum told Myrtle Nourse of the anxious hours she had put in waiting for his return from the long and lonely trips he made to see his patients, especially after his stroke, and at night. But she always put absolute confidence in Molly to bring him home. She always, in later years, met him and helped him at the barn to unharness Molly and get her into her stall.

Dr. Hannum used to relax by sitting quietly, playing solitaire. The quiet shuffling of cards, the possibilities of red on black and black on red seemed to rest him. He nearly always played after coming home from lodge, or social functions, no matter how late the hour. After Currie Bell retired from newspaper work, about 1908, he used to spend much time in Dr. Hannum's office, where the two old friends would play cards, if no patients demanded the doctor's time.

Shortly after the stroke, Dr. Hannum went away to receive some special treatment. This departure left one of our local matrons, who was expecting a baby, almost frantic. It was pointed out to her that Doc was ill, that one of his hands was incapacitated, that other doctors were available, but she paid no attention. She paced around the house saying she would not have anyone else, and finally declared that if Dr. Hannum did not return, she would not have the baby at all. Fortunately, since the baby's arrival was only a short time away, Dr. Hannum returned, and gave a safe delivery into the world to one of our prominent citizens.

I didn't write this story about Dr. Hannum. It was written by Ruth Flanders, former Bayfield resident, now of Portland, Oregon. She did such a good job, it would be a shame for me to add or subtract a word.:

Dr. Hannum and William Knight were good friends and Ruth Flanders reports that when they came here, "they were both young and single." They were quite an addition to the social life of the town and mothers with eligible daughters found them very interesting. It wasn't very long, perhaps a year or so, before Dr. Hannum returned to Ohio for his bride. The doctor soon returned to Ohio for another member of his family. From the same home that he had gotten his bride, he brought Molly. Molly was a colt, which his father-in-law had raised for him, and she became as much a part of Bayfield as the people who lived there. Summer or winter, rain or snow, hail or sunshine, Molly and Dr. Hannum were always available. When automobiles came, Molly took it easier, but was still useful, for she was needed when snow came and roads were impassable for cars. When she died, there was an obituary in *The Press* that read like that of a human. And she was almost human.

Living today in the city, where very few doctors will make house calls, I often think of the long night rides he made behind old Molly to relieve pain, even though he knew he would never receive a cent of pay. Medical men today recognize the value of psychology in healing, confidence in one's doctor and a feeling of ease in his presence, are considered important factors. Dr. Hannum probably wouldn't have called it psychology, but he often used it. He was known for his ability to tell a good story, and for the fun of them he could always produce. He fully believed there was no medicine like a good laugh, and he always brought one along. But he wasn't a comedian, and could be as serious as anyone when the occasion demanded it.

He never worried a family unless it was really necessary, and so, often kept his own counsel. I remember one home where a baby was born early one evening. The child was dressed and put in a basket beside the kitchen stove. The mother was resting and the house had quieted down. Dr. came into the kitchen and began to talk to the grandmother, and he told one story after another. Time passed and the grandmother began to wonder why he did not go home, but he had another story to tell. She made some coffee and thought that then he would go, but he had another story to tell. She considered asking him to go, but he still had another story to tell. Finally, he got up, made an examination of the baby and said, "He'll be alright now," and went home to bed. Then the grandmother wondered why she hadn't known that he was not just wasting time, but his stories were to keep her from worrying while he watched the child.

I am sending a copy of a picture I have that was taken at Frank Hannum's fifth birthday party. I have had the original since I was six years old. The children were all from four to perhaps ten years old. There is one little boy I can't name. Perhaps someone else can. (If anyone can name him, please let us know) The picture was taken in the Hannum yard and the buildings in the background are the back of the Island View Hotel. I was very ill the summer I was six years old and this is one of the small gifts Dr. Hannum brought me when I was getting well.

Doctor was always active and interested in civic affairs. He, my father and Mr. Downs were the school board for many years. They were the best of friends and worked together with enthusiasm and understanding. They spent many hours working out the problems of the schools, when their only pay was the satisfaction for work well done, and the meager thanks of the public.

One fact that has shown me Dr. Hannum's sagacity pertains to my birth record. Many people whom I have known have had a hard time to prove that they were born, in this day when birth records are so important. Many are hunting every record, making affidavits and going to considerable expense and trouble to obtain such records. The last time I was at Bayfield I was able to go to the County Clerk's office and in a few minutes time, and for a very small sum, I received a certified copy of my birth record. All this because Dr. Hannum registered births he attended, when no law required it, and few doctors, whether in towns or cities, bothered to do so.

He was a small town doctor, but he was a man with a keen mind and kept up with new methods as long as he practiced. How he would have enjoyed it if he could have had antibodies, inoculations, blood transfusions, etc., and what use he could have made of them.

He practiced efficiently for about fifteen years after paralysis badly damaged the use of one side. He still made night calls, and calls into the country, even when he had to take a driver, because he would have been helpless in case of mishap, or too much snow on the road.

Bayfield never had very many people, but she always had a few of the best.

In spite of his injured hand, Dr. Hannum mastered the chain drive Buick. Kids loved to ride in it with him. Bud McQuade remembers one day when he was standing beside the Iverson building, he saw Doc come around the bank corner in his Buick and start up the hill. Cars went slowly in those days, and Bud suddenly decided to ride with him, ran across the street, grabbed the side of his car and jumped in. Naturally, an object shooting toward the side of his car caused Doc to swerve, and the car narrowly missed going in the ditch before he could stop it.

Bud says, "But even then, Doc didn't scold me. He just talked to me so nice, and explained why I shouldn't do things like that."

During the busy years of Dr. Hannum's life, his son, Frank, was growing up to be as fine a man as his father. He graduated from Bayfield High School with the class of 1907. There were two boys and one girl in that class. The custom was for each graduate to give an oration. Frank's subject was, "The U.S. of the Future."

In 1909, he won the Illinois State Fencing Tourney, while attending Chicago U. Frank graduated from Rush, his father's alma mater and became an eye, ear, nose and throat specialist.

Whenever he came home to visit, Bayfielders would appeal to him to remove their tonsils. As Frank seemed to have his father's kind disposition and, like him, did not refuse a call, he took out many tonsils here, operating on dining room or kitchen tables, whichever was handiest and where the light was best. Gladys Knight, now Gladys Hale, was one of his patients, having her tonsils removed in the dining room of the house now belonging to Russell Valentine.

When I first asked for information about Dr. Hannum, one of my questions was, "What did Bayfield do for him, or to him." Here's an answer.

Dr. Hannum worked hard on the fire department He was a member and treasurer for years. When the fire alarm wound up, he would jump into the little two wheeled cart pulled by Molly and be off to the fire. He was the hydrant man, so even though the stroke incapacitated one hand, he could still manage the hydrant with no difficulty. It never occurred to him or to any members of the department that he should quit, just because of the loss of one hand.

But a yak stiff appeared and changed everything. If any of you have been so fortunate in life that you have never encountered a yak stiff, here is a definition of one. He has his mouth wide open, yakking criticisms, while his hands are stiff at his side instead of being lifted to help.

At one of the fires, this yak stiff made the remark, "Too bad they don't have a few more cripples like Doc Hannum on the fire department."

Doc either heard the remark, or some other yak stiff repeated it to him. He was deeply hurt. In fact, the word used at the time was heartbroken. He resigned from the fire department and, in spite of the persuasion of all its members, he would not change his mind.

But if Doc felt bad, the fire department felt worse. They had a fund of fifty or sixty dollars, which they had contributed themselves to be used in case a fireman was injured. They knew Doc was badly injured, for all injuries are not physical. Carl Wasmuth, James Long and Ingvald Larson were appointed as a committee to buy a farewell gift for him. They got a beautiful Masonic ring, a box of LaZora cigars, the kind he always smoked, and then found they had a nickel left. Determined to spend every cent of their fund for Doc, they took the five cents and bought a small cotton sack of P.A. tobacco.

Jim Long remembers the emotional moment when they gave Dr. Hannum his gifts, and he said, "I'll wear the ring, and I'll smoke the cigars, but when I die, I'll still have this package of P.A."

And he did.

His death came in 1922 after a second stroke. He is buried beside his small daughter in the Bayfield cemetery. A large gray monument stands there, placed where the morning sun shines on it, and when it does, the monument is no longer gray and dull, but full of reflecting light. That sort of expresses Doc. He was a plain looking man, but the light of his personality shone with so many warm reflections that now people don't remember just what he looked like. They saw and remember only what he was. And "Dr. Hannum was a wonderful man."

Johnny Sayles

Johnny Sayles, front left. L-R, High
school teacher, Blair Sherrick,
Jimmy O'Connell, Ray LaBonte,
unknown. (Photo: BHA)

NOBODY'S FORGOTTEN JOHNNY SAYLES. NOT yet they haven't. They haven't forgotten his piano playing, his recitations, or the fact that Joe O'Malley called him, "The Agent." But here's something maybe you don't remember about Johnny. He was a champion roller skater in his youth. A clipping from the *Duluth News Tribune*, dated Dec. 1905, forty-eight years ago this month, has this to say about him. "Little Johnnie Sayles pleased two audiences at the Temple roller skating rink yesterday with an exhibition of trick and fancy skating which would have done credit to an older performer. The little fellow is only 11 years of age and made a great hit with the women in the audience, who presented him with a large bouquet in the afternoon. He does a number of difficult stunts and is exceptionally graceful on his skates."

Johnny was good at entertaining. His recitations covered most anything humorous and practically everything, Robert Service wrote, including, "The Shooting of Dan McGrew," and "The Cremation of Sam McGee." His Swedish dialect version of "Barbara Fritchie" was probably Bayfield's favorite. But there are some intriguing lines from two of his recitations that can't seem to be fitted into anything published. Does anyone remember the rest of this one? "You'll never be drowned on Lake Champlain as long as you stay on shore." And how about the one, which ended, "I'm in the jail house, here to remain. Your ever loving husband, Muklus McLaine."

There have undoubtedly been better piano players than Johnny, and certainly worse ones, but there has never been another one just like him. He played by ear entirely, and when he sat down at the piano, he never lacked requests nor an audience. His two specialties were *Kitten on the Keys*, and *Maple Leaf Rag*. He liked to play *The Winter Blues* too, since he had been a member of composer Eddie Fortier's Novelty Four, Bayfield's favorite orchestra in the 20's when the Shimmy Dance was popular. And no story of Johnny would be complete without mentioning his dog, Caleb. Caleb was sort of a setter, an amiable rover, who liked everyone, but Johnny best, of course. When Johnny was cashier at the First National Bank, Caleb used to sleep on the floor of the cashier's cage. In one of Caleb's efforts to lie as close to Johnny's feet as possible, he leaned heavily on the burglar alarm switch.

This was before the bank was remodeled and, at that time, the switch was on the floor, connected to a loud bell over the clock in front of the bank. When Caleb lay down, the bell began its awful clang. People stopped on the street, turned around, looked hopefully, but not too expectantly at the bank door, thinking they might see a burglar run out with a sack of cash in each hand. But when no fleeing burglar appeared, someone said, it being the de*Press* ion thirties, "Well, who's got money in the bank, anyway?"

No one admitted they had any, and the hopeful expressions faded. By then, Caleb had been pulled off the switch and the alarm was over. Temporarily over, that is. Caleb seemed to develop a liking for the switch. He lay on it frequently and just as frequently, the alarm went off. But after the first time or two, no one paid much attention. People on Main Street laughed and said, "It's only Caleb," and went on about their business.

Johnny died Dec. 13, 1943, ten years ago this month. He's got a nice white tombstone in Greenwood cemetery. But he's got another one too, at Siskiwit Lake. The Cochrane Hunting Gang, which Johnny belonged to, had a shack out there. Hi Hanson built concrete steps down to it with a members name on each step. After Johnny died, Hi put a star by his name. Johnny would like that marker especially. And one hundred years from now, when some committee starts pawing through these papers to rewrite Bayfield's history for our town's 200th birthday, here's something I'd like to say to them. We've had a lot of nice people in Bayfield. There's a good bunch here right now, in 1953. But... too bad you couldn't have known Johnny.

Jake Oeffinger

JAKE OEFFINGER WAS A MAN who had humility, the word that gets kicked around so much nowadays. He had humility and great kindness. Jake was born in Germany in 1835. How and when he crossed the ocean and came to Bayfield is lost in the past, but he lived here, a bachelor, loved and respected for many years. He died on March 16, 1908. His tombstone had the German inscription "Ruhe Seiner Asche" which, as interpreted by Gus Weber, means, "Rest his ashes."

Joe O'Malley remembers Jake very well, and his first remark about him was, "He was a kind old man." Jake was a carpenter and used to saw wood too, getting $1.25 for hand sawing a whole cord, but he earned his own living and was independent. Once he gave Joe a sack of apples and ten cents. In those days that was a splendid gift, a dime having great value. Joe remembers going home, believing he was one of the richest kids in the world.

Other people said, "Sure, I remember Jake. He was a small man, with a sharp goatee and he usually carried a buck saw under his arm."

Mrs. Kranzfelder remembers him well. When her son, Leonard, was a baby he liked to run away, and since his mother was too busy to chase him constantly she tied him to the clothes reel, so he could run around, but not escape. Naturally, he was mad, and cried and kicked his heels. In a few minutes Jake burst in the back door, angrier than the crying child. "How can you tie the boy up like that?" he demanded.

Mrs. Kranzfelder explained that she didn't want to risk losing her son, but Jake would not be pacified. Finally she agreed to untie him if Jake would watch him, and from then on Jake toted Leonard to various jobs and took care of him until he was able to go around by himself.

One of the best revelations of the town's feeling for Jake is shown in an item in *The Bayfield Press* dated November 15, 1906. "A goodly number of Jake Oeffinger's friends gave him a surprise, it being his 70th birthday. Jake was called out to one of the neighbors and when he returned found his snug little house filled with people, baskets and presents. Jake had hardly collected himself when Gretchen came in and made the hit of the event by her old fashioned curtsey and the German speech to Jacob, presenting him with a birthday cake. Then followed such a good time that everybody felt young again. . . "

And, another person who should go down in Bayfield history is Hans Austad, born in 1860, died in 1943, whose tombstone says, "He willed his estate to Bayfield." He was a man with no relatives. Bayfield was all he had, it was both his home and his family.

Joe Hardy, the intrepid fisherman of Devil's Island may not be buried here, at least his grave is not marked if he is, but it doesn't matter much because his fame is still spread by word of mouth. He was called, 'The famous fisherman and dauntless sailor of Devil's Island.' He fished, as they did back in those days in a sailboat called *The Witch of the Wave*. One time after his boat capsized and he had floated about in the water of cold Lake Superior for about 36 hours he was found clinging to the boat in an almost insensible condition. But when he revived enough to speak, his only answer to the inquires of the rescue party were: "I have lost three days of blamed good fishing."

Tourists used to want to stop at Devil's Island to visit with Hardy Joe. Here's what he was doing in June 1890. "Joe Hardy has put in a pond net near Devil's Island that is 70 feet deep with pond sticks 84 feet long and a capacity of 100 kegs per day. Who has a better?

And on January 3, 1891, this item appeared in *The Press*. "Captain Joseph Hardy and his sloop, *Witch of the Wave* was in port Tuesday with a goodly load of fresh fish. It's a cold day when Hardy Joe can't make port."

Henry Johnson Sr., was one of the rugged old-time fishermen, too. Ole Frostman remembers a story about him. During the 1953 herring season, when Ole was mad at himself for not going out in stormy weather to lift herring nets he said, "I wasn't taught to fish like this. I was taught to fish like the old timers, to go out and fish and let the weather drive you in, and to follow the rule, 'go up to the buoy and if you can't catch it the third time, go home'." Then Ole recalled the morning on Rice's Island when Henry Johnson, lunch bucket under his arm, was walking down to the dock with his partner, Albert Larson. Albert looked up at the sky where storm clouds were gathering and said doubtfully, "It looks pretty stormy up there, Henry."

Henry glanced up, shifted his lunch pail, spat decisively and answered, "Hell, Albert, we ain't going up there." He kept right on walking to the boat.

The item about Henry Johnson brought forth two more stories of his courage and endurance. Old Frostman recalled the herring season when the nets Henry Johnson was lifting got caught in the boat propeller. Henry took off his heavy clothes, tied a rope around his waist, went into the water with a knife in his hand and cut them loose. I will remind former Bayfield residents, now living in milder climates, that in December Lake Superior is icy cold and apt to be rough.

Joe O'Malley remembered the terrible fire that swept through some buildings located where the root beer stand is now. Captain Peterson was trapped upstairs in one of the buildings. People could hear him screaming, and wanted to save him, but didn't know how, as it was feared the wall would collapse from the weight of the ladder. When Henry Johnson arrived at the fire, he did not hesitate a moment. He grabbed a ladder, threw it against the wall, climbed it, went through a window and came back down with Captain Peterson over his shoulder.

Joe "O'Malley also remembers a story his mother used to tell about Joe Hardy, "the dauntless fisherman of Devil's Island." The O'Malley family and Joe Hardy were fishing from a camp on York Island. They fished as late as they dared, but when the lake started to freeze, they knew it was their last chance to get off.

At that time all fishing was done from small sailboats and they loaded their equipment and people into one of them. The boat was filled to capacity with two dogs standing up in the bow. Joe Hardy looked at the heavily loaded little craft and as he cast off said, "Well, here we go, to hell or to Bayfield."

Mrs. O'Malley, a woman of firm religious convictions was shocked and frightened by his words, feeling that because of them they would all go to the bottom.

But God had more understanding of Joe Hardy than did Mrs. O'Malley. The trip was made safely and as they approached Bayfield, they saw a crowd gathered to watch the little sailboat make its way through the forming ice. Friends hands helped them onto the dock, and Mrs. O'Malley lived for many years to tell the story.

Dr. Pickett

P EOPLE STILL RECALL DR. S.L. Pickett, his many kindnesses to them and how he exhausted himself caring for others during the influenza epidemic of World War I. I regret that I do not have enough material to write a full-length story about this good doctor, but I did find one item in the Bayfield Progress of March 20, 1917, which told of the difficulty he had in making a call on one patient.

It is as follows: "Dr. Pickett was summoned to attend a case at Cornucopia Friday. Securing the team and driver from the livery, he made the trip and was caught in the snowstorm. The already bad roads were very quickly blocked and the doctor on his way back home soon was stalled. It finally became necessary to cut loose and leave the sleigh, thereafter now riding and now leading the floundering horses, the two men succeeded finally in reaching a house in the settlement late Friday night, both they and the horses being just about all in. Not until Sunday afternoon were they able to come from the settlement into the city."

This blizzard was called, "The worst snow storm in forty years." Two storms dropped four feet of snow and the Progress said, "Many a time in future years the residents of this North Country will hark back to this period and it will undoubtedly find a permanent place in local annals under the title of *The Big Snow.*

The snowstorm came on Friday and the streets could not be cleared until Wednesday. Many will remember how the streets were plowed in those days. The Progress described it this way: "Late Wednesday afternoon, the wind having subsided, Mayor Wachsmuth sent out the big snow scraper and the streets were cleared for travel. Two teams in trio and four in pairs, a total of fourteen horses, were required to drag the plow. The same performance was repeated Saturday."

The engine of the *Bayfield Scoot* attempted to plow the track at the depot and ran off the rails. On Saturday three locomotives from Ashland were able to shove a plow over here.

Magnus Halvorson came in on skis from his home at Sand Bay. It took him 7 hours to go 12 miles.

Andrew Kordius, a farmer from the Town of Russell, tried to drive his horse to the home of a neighbor. "On the way the animal played out entirely and died in the snowdrift in which it became hopelessly mired and floundered itself into exhaustion."

It was a tough March in 1917, but worse was to come in April. In the spring election that year, Bayfield was voted dry by a count of 173 to 128. After discovering this startling fact I rushed to find some old timers and asked, "What was it like when Bayfield was dry?" And I received the answer, "It never was!"

To settle the question of when the bridge fell down, I include this item from the *Bayfield Progress*, Sept. 14, 1911, which says: "The wooden bridge fell today of its own weight about half past ten o'clock and lay in a heap at the bottom of the ravine park, fifty feet below. Mrs. Jelinek had just crossed the bridge as it fell. Petitions had recently been presented for building a new bridge and by coincidence, City Clerk Long was phoning a bridge contractor at Grand Rapids, Minnesota, about the bridge contract likely to be let and as he hung up the receiver, he heard the crash. The simple jar of the telephone collapsed the rotten old shell. Charge it to Long."

Cars did not seem expensive today when I read in the Progress that Frank Boutin paid $6,000 for his Pierce Arrow touring car in 1913.

Among some interesting short items is the description of LaPointe in the summer of 1894. "The white tents are so numerous that the island looks as if an army were encamped here and they are coming every day. People are learning that Madeline Island is one of the healthiest spots to be found anywhere."

In August 1906 the register of the Old Mission Inn on Madeline Island showed that 200 guests dined there one Sunday noon.

Also, in August 1906, Madeline Island had a newspaper. The first number of *The Mirror* with Mr. Mills as editor was published. It was an 8-page paper and was later enlarged to 12 pages.

Bass Island also has its place in history. A story in *The Press* says, "The Bass Island quarry was the first to be opened on Lake Superior and the stone from it has proved of superior quality, especially in fire tests, being the only stone that successfully withstood the great Chicago fire in 1871."

A better late than never Happy Birthday to Washburn, which was 75 years old last June. June 16, 1883, *The Press* said, "The owners of the land adjoining the railroad property at McClellan have been busy during the past week laying out a town site at that point. We are informed that they have decided to name the new town Washburn in honor of Ex-Governor Washburn."

Lon Wilkinson

A.H. "Lon" Wilkenson. (Photo: BHA)

THE TIME WORN PHRASE, "LOCAL Boy Makes Good," can be truthfully applied to A.H. "Lon" Wilkinson. He will celebrate his 79th birthday on July 23, and his 79 years have been filled with innumerable civic jobs well done.

He was born on a farm near Stewart, Iowa, and when seven years old, came with his parents to Wisconsin, traveling in a covered wagon. They lived at Cumberland for four years and then moved to the village of Bayfield in 1886.

Lon Wilkenson's early life here was not one of luxury and ease. His parents were poor and the responsibilities of life were soon imposed on the oncoming generation. After obtaining what education he could at the Bayfield schools, he was forced to seek and secure his first job as handy man in the mill yard. When he was seventeen, he became assistant bookkeeper in the offices of the R.D. Pike Lumber Company, and when he was nineteen, entered the employ of the Lumberman's Bank at Bayfield. He furthered his education by an intensive course of study he mapped out for himself, which included banking, taxation, and transportation.

When the Lumberman's Bank was reorganized as the First National Bank in 1904, he became its president. He held this position until he became Collector of Internal Revenue for the District of Wisconsin. This job he held from 1921 to 1933.

He was married in 1902 to Lillian Tate, daughter of Andrew Tate, Bayfield's pioneer druggist.

During the 35 years he lived in Bayfield, he has a record of public service that has been equaled by very few. At the age of 22, he was elected Treasurer of the Town of Bayfield and at the age of 25, was elected without opposition as Treasurer of Bayfield County. As president of the bank he was the first one whose assistance was asked in pioneering new projects. It was in this position he learned of the bitter experiences and hardships of the pioneering farmers. His public labors to solve agricultural problems became so well known that three different Wisconsin governors appointed him to serve the state at agricultural meetings and projects.

In 1916, Mr. Wilkinson was drafted to run for the position of State Senator. *The Bayfield Press* said, "Mr. Wilkinson did not want to run for the office, but when he was finally convinced by the heaviest kind of pressure that his district demanded that he should run, like the true patriot he is, he took off his coat and entered the arena."

His campaign was conducted largely by his friends and he was elected for four ears. Then he went to work and made an outstanding record. In 1919 when he was elected chairman of the Joint Finance Committee of Senate and Assembly, he established a record by completing all state budgets by April 1. His acquaintance with the struggles of the farmer in Northern Wisconsin caused him to lead the fight in rebuilding the Farm Mortgage Association Law. This law aided the development of improved and unimproved land and was so successful that it was used as a basis for national legislation.

Also, while in the Senate, he became interested in the disposition of war surplus explosives. The method being used by the Federal Government of dumping them into the Atlantic Ocean was to him wasteful. He was delegated to take up the matter with the Secretary of the Interior and, as a result, acquired free of charge a large portion of these explosives. He then succeeded in creating a Land Clearing Department in the College of Agriculture and the surplus explosives were used for over eight years in clearing land, saving the farmers of this state, and other states which adopted the plan, many thousands of dollars and it put into cultivation thousands of additional acres.

At the close of the First World War, Mr. Wilkinson devised the first Soldier's Bonus Plan in the Unites States, providing for an immediate cash payment to all war veterans and secured an additional appropriation to make certain that all returned veterans would be assured of an education. Thus, the Bayfield boy, with little formal education, who started out in the mill yard, did his best to get education for others. His plan was later adopted by a number of other states.

We haven't space to list all the committees and organizations Mr. Wilkinson has worked for, but it would be safe to say that the organization closest to his heart is the Sons of the American Revolution. He organized the Wisconsin Society in 1936 and was elected Vice President of the National Society in 1939. This society works quietly, but effectively, to promote all patriotic efforts. They stress the correct use of the American flag and try to keep alive the spirit of the American pioneers.

Naturally, we are most interested in Mr. Wilkinson's life in Bayfield. Perhaps the type of work he did for the town can best be revealed in his speech on the subject, "What the Town Needs", which he gave to the Commercial Club in 1909, when he was President. In fact he had been president since the club was organized in 1906.

Too bad we didn't heed the advice given in the first paragraph as reported by *The Bayfield Press*. "It has been wisely suggested that the town purchase the "big ravine" and it has been opposed for no particular reason and never done. The town and county now own practically all of the property to the town line and no doubt the balance could be secured at a very small cost per acre. The timber along the banks is being cut off and already you can see land slides and I have no doubt that the money spent in five years taking care of the wash in the spring freshets would more than pay for this property. Unless this is done' the cutting and washing along the banks will increase, and the town will annually be paying for it in one way or another, and it ought to have the consideration of the town improvement committee."

"One of our largest items of trade during the summer months to the retail stores comes from the islands and I want to call the retail merchants attention to the fact that the town does not furnish a suitable landing for gasoline boats in which most of this trade is carried. Last summer these boats were compelled to land in the mill yard and most of you are familiar with the walk to the business section. I have seen times when one had to cross a mud hole a foot deep to get up town. It seems to me as a matter of pride a small landing ought to be furnished with suitable approaches. Along this same line I believe that a telephone service can be established between here and LaPointe, which would be appreciated by people coming there during the summer as well as those making their homes there. This matter belongs to the committee on harbor...

I have past the point where I believe that you can build a town by waiting for somebody to do something. It must be built by the men in it, and I know that the business men in Bayfield can do things if they only will."

Like any Bayfield citizen, Mr. Wilkinson often found himself chairman of a committee. He was appointed chairman of what turned out to be one of the biggest Labor Day celebrations ever held here. It all started with a plan to get Freddie Beal, who by beating Strangler Lewis out on the West coast had become the champion wrestler, to come to Bayfield. When Freddie was working his way up in the wrestling world, he often came here, liked the town and the people and told the committee he would come to their celebration and wrestle for nothing. They engaged a wrestler from Chicago to tackle Freddie for the sum of $75 and expenses. But no sooner had the deal been set than outsiders said, "How is Bayfield going to get a big-time, well-known wrestler like Freddie Beal to go there? It's all a fake."

The talk got so loud and disparaging that even the committee was affected by it. Mr. Wilkinson telephoned Freddie, who assured that he would be here. Thereupon, trusting his word, Bayfield immediately offered to donate $1,000 to charity if Freddie Beal did not show up.

On Labor Day the town was packed. Ten thousand people came and ate every scrap of food available. Expenses began to mount and the committee called a hurried consultation. Bert Bracken said, "I have a little game called 'Jingle Board' put away somewhere. If I can find it, I can set it up and run it for awhile to get some money for the committee."

The committee agreed with enthusiasm. Bert found the game, set it up, and it had become very popular when John J. Fisher, city attorney, happened to push through the crowd to see what the great attraction was. His legal eye at once detected a gambling angle to 'Jingle Board' and he hastily informed the committee of that fact. But by that time, Bert had raked in $250, and that seemed to be enough to meet the increased expenses, so they quit.

In the meantime, three platforms had been built, one by the hotel, one by the bank and one by the Standard Oil station. Different acts were staged on each platform, at the completion of which each act went to another platform, so the crowd; packed on Main Street, saw the whole show.

Among these acts was a dancing act led by George Gordon, and a show put on by Al Harveaux, wearing his famous Frog Suit. Freddie Beal and the Chicago man wrestled on the platform on the hotel corner, and Freddie threw the other wrestler out of the ring. He was battered and mad, but everyone else was happy and thought it was one of the best celebrations ever held here.

Mr. Wilkinson was chairman of stage shows for the first Frolic, one of the all time social and money raising events of Bayfield. He said, "I remember for the first Frolic I had Agnes Fiege and Herman Sense assisting with the stage shows. We ran a show for one hour on the big stage. We opened with just enough show to run one night, which made it necessary for us to find and rehearse a show for every night as we went along. It was a remarkable thing that we finished on Saturday with more show than we could use. . . "

That, in a way, is typical of Mr. Wilkinson. He started out working in the mill yard, a poor boy, with little education, but what he had, he used, and by constant study, added to it. He applied that same formula to all the activities of his life, whether he put on a show for the Frolic, or salvaged explosives from the government. Mr. Wilkinson took whatever was at hand and began to build, and the things he built he can be proud of. That is why this story has the title, *Local Boy Makes Good.*

Colonel Isaac Wing

Colonel Isaac H. Wing.
Wing was one of Bayfields
prominent citizens who spent
his winters in Washington DC.
Wing's home was located in
Block 89, lots 5-8 and was the
former funeral home. He died
on August 27, 1907. (Photo:
BHA)

WITHIN THE NEXT FEW WEEKS, *The History of Bayfield*, which I have been writing, will be completed. If anyone knows of a special incident or story, which should be included, please let me know before I write "The End."

Naturally, in my research I have run across stories, which seem best forgotten, and I have left them out on purpose. Also, some good Bayfield citizens have been left out, or mentioned only briefly, because I couldn't learn enough about them to make an interesting story. Many good people lived here, minded their own business, went quietly to work, to church and social affairs. Among these people was Col. Isaac H. Wing. He was one of our best citizens and will always be remembered because Port Wing is named for him. A wealthy man, and a bachelor, he lived a quiet life at his home on First Street.

Col. Wing gave generously to many causes. The Wing Scholarships, which are awarded each year at Washburn High School, were given by him. To his own college, Boudoin, he gave $50,000. To the Swedish Lutheran church here he gave two lots and $100. The beautiful brass altar rail in the Episcopal Church is the gift of Col. Wing. At the beginning of the Spanish American War, he equipped a company, Company K., of the Fourth Wisconsin Volunteers, which were afterward known as the Wing Guards. Their armory in Bayfield was Wing Hall, which later became the Memorial Hall and belonged to the Civic League. Though he is not buried here, he gave Bayfield the present cemetery. It was given in 1888, ten acres for the city cemetery and he also gave five acres to the Catholic Church. A list of twenty names was submitted and Greenwood was the name chosen for the city cemetery. Like the other Bayfield pioneers he had great enthusiasm for hunting, fishing and camping.

Another person of interest was Birdsey B. Wade. If he lived here today he would be Bayfield's entry in a TV quiz show. He was a graduate of Hamilton College and Columbia Law School and had been a prominent lawyer in New York. His health began to fail and he tried Colorado then finally came to Lake Superior, settling in Bayfield in a broad verandah cottage picturesquely located on the outskirts of town. The interior of his house was a transformation from the wilds of Lake Superior to a student's room at Yale or Harvard. While at home to his friends, books were his constant companions. He was a great reader and his mind was a storehouse of historical and scientific lore. He was always consulted by any one desiring information, which required an extensive knowledge of books. He managed R.D. Pike's complicated interests and held numerous county offices, but in August 1892, his health failed completely and he died at the age of 51.

Other people did at least one thing, which attracted my attention. For instance, Captain Boucher did something dangerous, yet comical and easily visualized today. The account appeared in the Bayfield Progress, September 16, 1909. "Captain Boucher of the tug *Fashion* while attempting to pull a bolt that stuck out from the Independent Fish Company dock being a heavy man fell overboard into the water. Lucky the engineer was on deck, for hearing the splash and seeing the predicament the Captain was in, he lost no time in tossing him a line and pulling him to safety. The Captain says he likes a bath once in a while, but prefers not to fall overboard to get one. It was a narrow escape. This story also furnishes a moral for us marine-minded citizens. If you want to pull nails out of docks, don't pull toward the water.

Mr. J.H. Shippey made a remark that is often made by Bayfield citizens as they return from traveling. June 10, 1915, the Progress reported: "Mr. J.H. Shippey, who has a farm on Hermit Island, returned from a business trip to Monmouth, Illinois. He has been gone about two weeks and remarked that he came home to get a good drink of water."

Incidentally Mr. Shippey had a nice, small farm on Hermit Island and was the Island's second hermit. He located there after domestic troubles and farmed and did a few odd jobs for "The Hermitage" summer hotel. At that time, tourists could spend a week at "The Hermitage" for only $10.

I liked a poem written by someone initialed D.L.S. in the *Bayfield Progress* May 8, 1917, titled *An Appreciation of the Bayfield Men's Club*. There are many lines, but these are some of the best:

> *"And what is the aim of the Bayfield Men's Club*
> *To make earth turn round Bayfield Peninsula as hub*
> *To make city and country and all that near lies*
> *A haven of bliss and unique paradise.*
> *But to accomplish this patriots must enlist*
> *Imperative it is that e'en slackers assist*
> *So Bayfield Men's Club all heroes should join*
> *And help the noble cause with service and coin.*
> *In deed we may be proud the Bayfield Men's Club*
> *Will never one moment the Civic League snub."*

Chapter 3

The Harbor City
Times & Tones

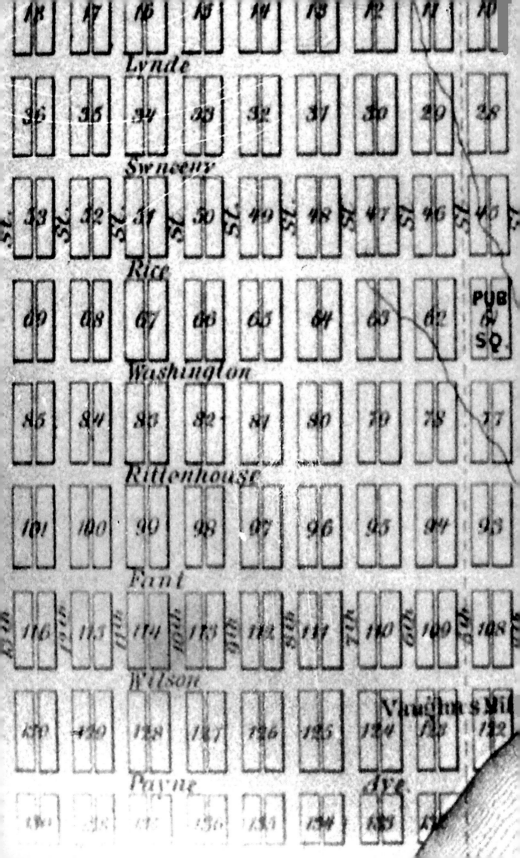

Lynde

18 17 16 15 14 13 12 11 10

36 35 34 33 32 31 30 29 28

Sweeny

53 52 51 50 49 48 47 46 45

Rice

69 68 67 66 65 64 63 62 PUB SQ

Washington

85 84 83 82 81 80 79 78 77

Rittenhouse

101 100 99 98 97 96 95 94 93

Fant

116 115 114 113 112 111 110 109 108

Wilson

130 129 128 127 126 125 124 123 122

Vaughn's Mill

Payne

Ave.

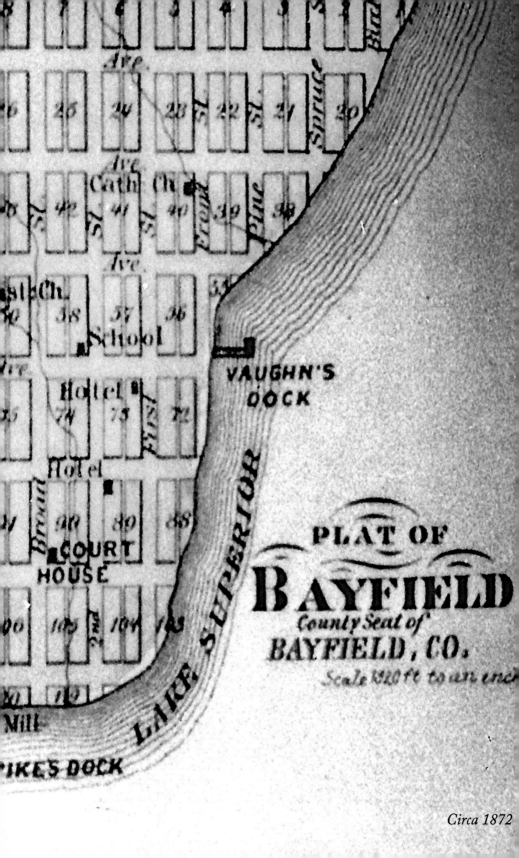

PLAT OF
BAYFIELD
County Seat of
BAYFIELD, CO.
Scale 1320 ft to an inch

Circa 1872

The Chronological History of Bayfield

March 24, 1856. Party of nine men arrive from LaPointe and on the shore in what is now known as lots 11 and 12 in block 88, they cut the first tree and commenced building a log cabin on what is now lot 2 block 89.

March 26, 1856. First cabin is completed.

March 27, 1856. Mr. John M. Fram arrived with Major Wm. McAboy and others.

March 28, 1856. Major McAboy, a civil engineer, commenced surveying and laying out the town of Bayfield.

March 29, 1856. The hauling of timber for the pier was commenced.

March 31, 1856. The first crib for the pier was sunk and the pier was completed about May 1.

May 8, 1856. The first family, that of John C. Hanley, arrives on the schooner *Algonquin* and this schooner is the first boat at the Bayfield dock.

June 16, 1856. The *Lady Elgin* is the first steamer to arrive at Bayfield. On the steamer were the engineer and carpenters to build a sawmill.

The Lady Elgin.
(Photo: BHA)

July 27, 1856. The Propeller *Mineral Rock* arrived with the engine and machinery for the sawmill. The mill was built on the west half of block 121. This mill was finished and commenced cutting lumber about September 1, 1856.

Jan. 12, 1857. The mill was destroyed by fire.

The latter version of
S.S. Vaughn's Mill circa
1880. (Photo: BHA)

July 1857. A new sawmill built which commenced work on August 28, 1857. The first dwelling was erected by John C. Hanley on lot 1, block 74.

April 9, 1857. Henry M. Rice writes to Admiral Henry W. Bayfield to tell him the new town on Lake Superior has been named for him. The first provision store was erected in lot 11, block 73 by S.S. Vaughn who commenced business about the first of October 1856. A hardware store managed by Joseph McCloud opened September 1856 on lot 11, block 56.

October 1856—post office established with Joseph McCloud the first postmaster.

First school opened December 1856 in the upper room of Mr. Vaughn's building on Lot 11, block 73. It was paid for by subscription and taught by Miss R. McAboy. A second school was opened October 1857, also by subscription and was taught by the Rev. James Peet. It closed about April 1, 1858.

At the Centennial planning meeting many suggestions were made for observing Bayfield's 100th birthday in 1956.

Should Bayfield look 100 years old, or 100 years young? Some people thought a whole Centennial Summer was too long for the men to wear beards and the women long dresses. But a special costume is needed. It was suggested that men wear plaid vests and women matching stoles or blouses. Do you like that idea? Have you a better one?

We thought Bayfield might have a "family" party on March 24, 1956, Bayfield's true 100th birthday. This would probably be a picnic supper. People would wear their costumes for the first time and get used to seeing each other in them. What kind of party should it be and where?

The idea of the Centennial running for 8 or 10 Sunday afternoons was generally accepted. Each one would have a different theme such as: Religion in Bayfield, Strawberry Sunday, Regatta, Teen-agers Today, Apple Pie Picnic, Homecoming and—what ideas do you have?

The next meeting will be June 6th at the library. We hope everyone in town will be there with new ideas and ready for action. Even if you've never been on a committee before, don't you think that once in a hundred years you should be? Serve now and be exempt on Bayfield's 200th anniversary!

But for those who cannot come, and for former residents too far away to attend, this blank is printed. Please send in your ideas.

Here are suggestions for the Centennial Celebration and costumes.

Here are suggestions for raising money before and during the Centennial.

Here are names and address of former residents who would like to receive Centennial programs.

Bayfield Shows Good Growth; Many Businesses & Trades

OCTOBER 5, 1856 THERE WERE in Bayfield 112 persons, of which 17 were women and 22 were children.

March 4, 1858 there were in Bayfield 30 families.

36 children under 5 years old
18 over 5 and under 15 years old
61 adult males
37 adult females
152 Total
Of these 33 were unmarried males and 7 were unmarried females.
There are some six or eight other persons of whom their residence at Bayfield is uncertain. They are now absent from the place.
When the census of Bayfield, Wisconsin, was taken March 4th 1858 there were found:

2 Merchants
1 Grocer
No one who gave his occupation as a Rumseller
2 Clerks
14 Carpenters
1 Blacksmith
17 Laborers
4 Teamsters
2 Agents
1 Civil Engineer
1 Dealer in Real Estate
1 Missionary
3 Painters
1 Gentleman living on the interest of his money
1 Millwright
1 Machinist & Engineer
2 Hotel Keepers
1 Post Master
2 Mail Carriers
1 Butcher
1 Fisherman
Several with no particular occupation
23 Members of the Lyceum
2 Members of the Temperance Society
2 Church Organizations
16 Dwellings Finished
2 Stores
1 Restaurant
1 Grocery

4 Liquor Shops
2 Hotels
1 Boarding House
1 Office
5 Shops
1 Sawmill
1 Church
1 Warehouse (so it was written)

The first work was commenced on the Bayfield Town Site March 24th 1856, which was the building of a log shanty by nine (9) men and was finished on the 26th.

Mr. John M. Freer came with his team from Superior and brought Mr. McAboy, who commenced the surveying March 28th.

The hauling of timber for the dock was commenced on the 27th of March and the cribs sunk the 30th. About the 8th of April part of the men went to cutting wood for steamboats, soon after which Mr. F. McElroy and son of LaPointe were engaged to work with their teams, one horse and yoke of oxen.

The first family (J. Hanley) came from Superior in the Schooner *Algonquin* and landed at the pier May 8th, which was the 1st boat at the dock.

The *Lady Elgin* was the 1st steamboat and arrived June 16th, 8 o'clock AM The Prop-Manhattan arrived July 7th, and the Steamer Superior arrived July 8th. The Mineral Rock (Propeller) arrived with the mill engine July 27th.

Mr. Caho and his men arrived. Mr. Hanley erected the 1st frame house July 16th.

The 2nd family was Mr. Wymonds, which arrived July 5th, 1956, in AM and Mr. A. (Anzi) J. Day's family arrived the same day PM

The building of the hotel was commenced December 25th 1956 and foundation laid March 16th 1857.

The mill burned down Jan. 12th 1857.

Perhaps it has been forgotten that the files of *The Bayfield Press* were destroyed in the 1942 flood. That is why we are having difficulty assembling material for our 1956 centennial celebration.

This week we are indebted to Mrs. Maude Kranzfelder for the information that the old town hall was located where the dry cleaning establishment now stands. We are also indebted to Connie Dahl for a book of old pictures and information about Bayfield County. The book has a fine picture of the community building in its prime, with the clock in the tower showing quarter of two on a long forgotten summer afternoon. The old cannon is standing in the yard. Whatever became of the cannon? Does anyone know?

Bayfield Kitsteiner is still missing, too.

Bayfield had a gay celebration when it was thirty years old. And it had an even bigger and better one when it was fifty.

News of the semi-centennial comes from A. H. Wilkinson of Milwaukee, former president of the First National Bank here (now the Washburn State Bank). He has always been an enthusiastic Bayfield booster and was president of the Commercial Club when it sponsored the fiftieth anniversary celebration. He acted as master of ceremonies and has sent us the original congratulatory telegrams, which he read on that occasion.

It was a wonderful party. Nearly two hundred people, dressed in their elaborate best, attended a banquet at 8:30 PM on the evening of March 23, 1906 at the Island View Hotel. Why it was on March 23 is not clear, but perhaps it was because everyone wanted to be up at midnight to sing Happy Birthday. At any rate they believed that 8:30 was the proper, leisurely time to start a banquet. The bountiful dinner served was 75 cents a plate. Does anyone remember the menu? Toasts were given by prominent citizens, old timers talked, and afterward there was a dance to music donated by the Zenith orchestra.

Those present who were in Bayfield when the first trees were cut on the site of the new city were: N. LaBonte, Robert and William Morrin.

In the reception room there was a display of relics, all of them past the half-century mark. What were the relics and what became of them? Anybody know?

We do know that Charles Bartleme had special 50th anniversary souvenirs for sale that night. But what were they? Did anybody buy one?

The thirtieth anniversary was celebrated at the Island View Hotel, too, but it was a different building then, in some downtown location. But whatever it was the citizens of the young city enjoyed a banquet and ball there on the night of March 24, 1886.

The Iron River Pioneer had this to say about the fiftieth anniversary: "On the 24th of this month Bayfield will be 50 years old and the Commercial Club of that city is taking steps to properly celebrate the anniversary. For a town of its age Bayfield is not so large, but it has rejuvenated to beat the band in the past year or two and is setting a pace which indicates beyond a doubt that rheumatism and other afflictions of old age has not fastened itself upon Bayfield county's oldest city."

And *The Ashland Press* said: "The good people of Bayfield will celebrate their fiftieth anniversary this evening. Elaborate preparations have been made. There will be a big banquet and much speechifying. Bayfield is one of the prettiest towns in northern Wisconsin. It has a lot of good people and it is an enterprising city. The 50th anniversary celebration has the good wishes of Ashland."

The telegrams which Mr. Wilkinson read on that occasion, and which he so thoughtfully saved, are all dated March 23, 1906, and are as follows:

"Congratulations to Bayfield's anniversary. Sorry I cannot be with you."

Hannah Austrian was a member of the Julius Austrian family, formerly of LaPointe. For sometime Mr. Austrian was governor-general of all the country west of Ondossagon to Superior. He came over from LaPointe for the founding of Bayfield on March 24, 1856.

The Commercial Club of the City of Duluth extends congratulations on your fiftieth anniversary and wish you continued and increased prosperity.

Commercial Club of Duluth. H. O. Eva, secy.

Ashland sends congratulations to its older, but more beautiful sister city across the bay. May prosperity ever shine on you abundantly.

Burt Williams, mayor

To Bayfield, the mother town of Bayfield county, greetings. The city of Washburn extends its congratulations on your fiftieth anniversary, and hopes that prosperity, always obtainable by united action, will keep pace with the years to come.

William H. Irish, mayor

The Daily Press is glad to know that Bayfield is fifty years old, and hopes that like Methuselah, it will live to be a thousand. All Ashland joins with the *Daily Press* in congratulating Bayfield on being a live city, a city of good people, at its fiftieth anniversary.

Guy M. Burnham, Editor *Daily Press*

Accept my hearty congratulations on this memorable occasion. I cannot be with you with spirits, but am there in spirit.

Lawrence M. Dickerson.

LaBonte's Early Bayfield

Bayfield's front street looking south toward Houghton Point. Circa pre- 1886. (Photo: BHA)

VERY FORTUNATELY, N. LaBONTE, ONE of our pioneers, took time to write an interesting account of early Bayfield. H.C. Hale read it to 200 assembled guests at the Island View Hotel the night Bayfield's 50th birthday was celebrated. Now, with our town's hundredth birthday coming up, let's read it again.

"Mr. Toastmaster, The Bayfield Commercial Club and Ladies and Gentlemen: We are here this evening, as you all know, to commemorate Bayfield's fiftieth birthday, and I am duly grateful and exceedingly happy to be in your midst this evening, and at the request of the club, to make an accounting of the fifty years just past, which were spent here; and in order to prepare you for the ordeal, it might be well to remind you that I am not an orator of note, and if I should chance to hear someone say, "that man LaBonte is a cracker jack of a talker," don't you think for a moment I will believe it.

If you are prepared for the worst, I will proceed. I am one of a family of eleven: (five boys and six girls) and the son of Francis and Angeline LaBonte. I was born at Quebec, Canada, April 6, 1836, and lived on a farm adjoining the city from childhood, until I departed for Bayfield, which occurred when I was twenty years of age, taking passage at Detroit on the side wheel steamer Superior. Captain Sweet commanded the boat.

I am not sure, but believe the folks around felt pretty bad when I left, and I have heard since, that lots of people in Canada cried when they learned I had quit the country; and it was said I was a brainy man and it was a shame to see me go and that it would be hard to replace me. I cannot say whether they ever replaced me or not.

Among those who were fellow passengers with me for Bayfield were Benjamin Bicksler, Frank Davidson, John T. Caho (who built the first steam mill here), and a Mr. Wyman and Steadman. Our boats cargo consisted of a little of everything, including a lot of cattle for Ontonagon, Michigan, but on account of a heavy sea that prevailed, we were unable to make that port and came on through to LaPointe, Wisconsin, then a stirring village and headquarters of the American Fur Company, where we arrived June 9, 1856, being enroute four days, as I remember it. The boat did not stop at Bayfield for the reason there was no dock here at that time.

I was anxious to continue on to Superior, but my cash was running low and when I struck the captain for a ride to that port on the strength of my good looks, or pay fare on the installment plan, and all I could scrape up was 17 cents, the captain in a gruff way said, "You walk, you pea soup."

I never liked Captain Sweet since.

The following morning, in company with those mentioned, I came over from LaPointe to Bayfield in a row boat, which landed us at the present site of the Dormer Boutin Fish Company's plant, where there was a dock being built owned by a Mr. Charles Childs, of Sault St. Marie, who sometime afterward sold the same to H.M. Rice, C.P. Rudd and S.S. Vaughn, and was afterward known as the Vaughn docks, until sold to W.F. Dalrymple.

The only building here was a log house located where M. Ryders store now stands, built and owned by the Bayfield Land Company for the accommodation of the men employed by this concern. The company consisted of H.M. Rice, Pres.; John D. Livingston, Rittenhouse, Davidson and Payne. There was not a woman here, and it makes me lonesome to make this statement."

We continue N. LaBonte's own story of the early days in Bayfield.

"That part of the town lying on the flat was covered by a scattering growth of small Norway pine, with an occasional large white pine; and the only thoroughfare was a trail leading from the dock site (near the present Booth Fish Co.) to the log house mentioned (near Burtness Hardware). The hills, now dotted with buildings, were covered with mixed woods, mostly hard wood.

I found employment here with the Bayfield Land Company on a mill that was building on the site upon which now stands the R.D. Pike Lumber Company's mill. (Southwest of the present depot.) The mill was completed and operating in October of that year and about two months afterward burned down, after which I turned my attention to cutting cord wood which was sold to the steamers for fuel.

In the spring of fifty-seven, I, with others, started to cut out the Bayfield and St. Paul stage road as far as Yellow Lake, a distance of about 140 miles. The balance of the route to St. Paul was by way of Wood River to Sunrise over logging roads. Sunrise, fifty miles from St. Paul, was a junction where the St. Paul stage met both the Bayfield and Superior stages and took their freight and passengers.

It required six days to make the trip from Bayfield to St. Paul and the fare was $20, meals extra at 50 cents each and lodgings the same.

From this time, until about 1860, I cut cord wood, logs and made fish barrel staves of clear white pine that was so plentiful at that time.

On April 4, 1861, I was married here to Miss Matilda Davis, Father John Chebul officiating.

In the summer of '61, I went to work in the Red Cliff sawmill, the property of Uncle Sam, which had just been built under a contract with the government, by Col. John Banfield. I worked there for twelve years in the capacity of sawyer, filer, and scaler on a salary of $3 per day. My family and myself resided there about half of this time and the balance of the time in Bayfield.

Six men, including myself, constituted the mill crew and the capacity of the mill was 6,000 feet per day, which was measured, marked and piled as fast as it left the saw. My neighbor, Commodore Bob Inglis, was engineer in this mill part of one season. Bob was a good mechanic, a trim, good looking fellow and, of course, was a favorite with the maids on the reservation and I never found out why he quit that good job and pleasant surroundings so soon. I am told Bob likes the girls yet, but of course one must not believe all he hears, and allowing that it is the truth I cannot blame him, for I like the girls myself.

The mill was sold to Duluth parties after operating twelve years, after which I built and kept a summer boarding place known as the LaBonte House at Bayfield, which house was open to the public for many years.

I raised a family of four children, two daughters Mrs. N. Bachand and Mrs. D.E. Church (later Mrs. M. DeMars), who are both here with their families at the present time, and lost a son at the age of six and one half years and also an infant daughter.

(Mrs. M. DeMars attended that 50th anniversary dinner and heard her father given the account of his pioneer life in Bayfield. When asked if she remembered any special details of the dinner she laughed, and recalled that the 200 dinner guests drank the first pots of coffee so quickly that more had to be made. In fact it was bad. Grounds flowed out of the pot and settled down in the cups like a quicksand bottom. Thanks, Mrs. DeMars for remembering something so typical of Bayfield. In this town, a bad cup of coffee deserves to be remembered for fifty years.)

My health has always been good and, as far as I know, I am a better man than my wife today. I am seventy years of age, have lived here fifty years and expect to live here fifty years longer, at the expiration of which time, if politics are too corrupt, or conditions just don't suite, I shall move West and grow up with the country.

Seven months after Bayfield's fiftieth anniversary, Nazaire LaBonte died. The date was October 20, 1906.

Thomas Bardon of Ashland, one of the oldest white settlers on Chequamegon Bay, was grief stricken at the loss of his old friend. The pioneers were going one by one and feeling it deeply, he sat down to write a tribute to them.

"The death at Bayfield last Saturday morning of Nazaire LaBonte, removes one more of Lake Superior's oldest inhabitants... When that gallant soldier-citizen of Bayfield, Captain R.D. Pike, died last spring, Mr. LaBonte attended the funeral, as the sole survivor of the old band of Bayfield settlers who located there long before the Civil War... The taking away of Mr. LaBonte leaves no one in his class of old settlers that I can now remember in Bayfield. . .

It will be fifty years next July 5, since the writer first saw Bayfield. I was a small boy on the old steamer Iron City, in charge of our parents, moving from Kentucky to Superior. Our boat first landed at LaPointe, the first Wisconsin town I ever saw, where we found several Indians sitting on a pile of steamboat wood. The lake boats all burned wood in those days. These Indians wore blue and red blankets and were the first Indians I had ever seen.

Our steamer towed a scow from LaPointe over to what was then called Bayfield, a few houses and a clearing in the woods on the hillside. On the way across from LaPointe my father missed my older brother Jim, from our boat and was frantically hunting for him, when the mate pointed out the missing youth, he having slid down the fender of our boat and was riding in the scow, where he remained until we reached Bayfield, about dusk in the evening.

These lake towns had no railroads in those days. When navigation closed you were frozen in until spring. When the Pike shingle mill blew up at LaPointe and killed Henry Smitz and others (May 17, 1869) and wounded many, the nearest doctor to be reached was at Ontonagon and Dr. Ellis was sent for in a small boat and came and returned home the same way, as he then resided at Ontonagon. No roads except snowshoe trails over which a weekly or semi-monthly mail was carried on a man's back. In summer, a Mackinaw boat or canoe was used.

It will be forty years ago next November 4, since Martin Beaser was drowned in Ashland Bay. November 4, 1866, he was returning here from LaPointe when he lost his life by the capsizing of his sailboat. The tender thoughts of old pioneers came up of all who have gone ahead of us on the trail, and are now in their eternal camp. This colony of dear old timers are all together in the other world, awaiting the final coming of old friends.

We, too, who came half a century ago, in the order of things must soon join the departed associates of our boyhood. The land of snow and ice and often of starvation, of desolation, of fish and fur, of privation and hardships, of frontier suffering and exile, of the few and scattered log hut settlements, is today changed. The Hudson Bay and Northwest Fur companies are here no more. The smoke of the wigwam has died out. Snowshoes, steel traps, blankets and pack traps, dog trains, moccasins and leggings are no longer the style. The French voyageur and missionary live only in history.

Today the sun shines on prosperous cities and happy people. Farms, factories, mines and railroads are now where the muskrat and Indian held away. The church and school bells ring where the sound of the tom tom was heard. The locomotive supplants the moose. The big steel steamers have driven out the bark canoe.

But the fond recollection of old days and old friends will cling to us as long as life lasts. Now new innovation can kill that law of old customs so deeply rooted in the hearts of the pioneers of early days on Lake Superior. We learn to love and respect the old pioneers. They stand as sentinels pointing back to the days of early history of our state. We cherish the memory of the old pathfinders who first blazed the way in this, then remote from civilization, wilderness. Their lives and deeds are their monuments. When they pass away, the good they did remains with us. The surviving pioneers will call the roll. How many will be recorded as absent. Their voices are forever hushed.

Nazaire LaBonte was the last to ferry over the dark river and go from us forever.

Nazaire LaBonte Stories of Bayfield

(Photo: Scott Hale Collection)

MARCH 1955: AS WE APPROACH Bayfield's 99th birthday, which will be the 24th of this month, it is interesting to read or re-read an article written by Nazaire LaBonte, which appeared in The Press on Feb. 13, 1903. I have condensed it some, because similar paragraphs were in the story Mr. LaBonte wrote for Bayfield's 50th anniversary party. The Fiftieth Anniversary story reappeared in this column last year, when Bayfield was 98 years old.

"There wasn't much here when I first set foot on the townsite, that is true, but those who were here lived and worked in great hopes. . . There were but two shanties constructed of logs and these were located on the site now occupied by the bank and adjoining buildings. One was used as a sleeping room and the other as a cook shanty. These were the only buildings in existence at that time and they were in the midst of a dense forest. Great Norway pines sighed and moaned at their very doors.

When I became well enough acquainted with the English language (Mr. LaBonte was French), to glean from the conversation of the few inhabitants that here was to be built a large city, I could not see for the life of me how it was to be done.

George Stark was here at that time. (In fact his son, Frank Start, was the third white boy born in Bayfield and the Starks have resided here ever since.)

The first frame building was put up in August 1856. In September, S.S. Vaughn put up a store building on the site of *The Press* building (now the Harbor Theater). John Hanley was overseer of the work of clearing the townsite.

I was personally acquainted with Wilson, the man who was known as the Hermit of Wilson Island. He was residing on the island when I came here. He was a cooper by trade, worked hard and saved his money. He was a bright old man, and good company when not drunk, but he had queer ways. He had no time for Indians and would not allow them to land on his island. When he saw a canoe making for his shore, he would take his rifle, walk to the beach and warn them off. He was a hard drinker, and a most desperate man when under the influence of liquor. When he had to go to LaPointe in the fall for his winter stores, the first thing to find its way into his boat would be whiskey. I believe, however, that he possessed greater wealth than that found after his death, but that he had it buried.

Lots in Bayfield down here on the flat sold in '57 and '58 for $300. Those further back for a little less. Those who wanted to build were given a lot. But if they wanted two lots, the second was $300. . .

The finest thicket of timber in this section was where the townsite of Washburn now lies. Very few of the early settlers picked up any timberlands, although they could have had all they wanted for $1.25 an acre. They didn't think it was worth anything, in fact it wasn't at that time, but we now see the mistake of our lives.

The Nourse building was built in 1857 and was the first building in which religious services were held. The first street opened was from the present bank corner to the dock. It was not opened straight to the lake, but went one block east then one block north and then east again to the present Booth dock.

In 1856 on Christmas morning, it was 40 degrees below zero. We had much colder weather in those days than we have now.

When I first came here there was a small stream running down Rittenhouse Avenue to the lake, a branch of it coursing its way to the lake down Broad Street. One night we had a terrible rain storm, almost a cloudburst, and this stream, which came from the big ravine took a straight shoot for the lake and is still running in that bed in the alley between Second and Broad streets.

(Not any more, Mr. LaBonte, and we hope it will never take a straight shoot for the lake again.)

It was not as hard to get provisions as some people might imagine, although the early spring, before the opening of navigation saw some of the people on pretty short rations. We had to get our winter supplies in the fall and if they gave out before the boats arrived in the spring, we just had to fast. If it had not been for the trading between here and St. Paul, there would have been considerable suffering, but this helped out wonderfully.

In the spring of '56, the work of cutting a road through to St. Paul was commenced. As soon as this road was finished, there was considerable amount of winter trading both ways. The people here who had teams would start out with a load of fish and return from St. Paul with provisions. . . but it was an awfully disagreeable job, for in those days we had nearly twice the amount of snow during the winter that we get now. Four or five feet on the level was not uncommon. Everyone here had snowshoes for it was impossible to get anywhere without them. This 200-mile stretch of road was covered by the stage in six days as a general thing, but the traders had a longer siege of it.

I remember one spring, and I believe it was in '63 when there wasn't a drop of liquor in town and the boat that was to arrive with supplies, the *North Star,* was two weeks overdue. I tell you there was lots of wailing and gnashing of teeth. Some of the old topers were nearly crazed for want of it. A barrel of whiskey would have been worth a small fortune at that time.

One of the settlers here had a barrel of whiskey into which he had put several quarts of wintergreen berries. The last of the whiskey was used up just a few days before the scheduled time for the arrival of the first boat in the spring. But when the boat failed to get here on time, there was a general scramble for the whiskey-soaked berries and I believe if it had not been for them, some of the settlers would have died. When the boat did arrive, the sufferers were all at the dock and two-thirds of them were three sheets in the wind before the gang plank was out."

Well, now in 1955 I can report there has not been a whiskey shortage since 1863 (except during a brief moonshine era). There is no shortage of wintergreen berries, either, but I doubt if anyone in this day and age would pick several quarts of them and pickle them in whiskey.

Does anyone know the purpose of this? Were they used as appetizers? Medicinal purposes? Surely not a large dish of whiskey-soaked wintergreen berries for dessert! Does anyone have the recipe? If so, in the interests of further historical research, please forward it.

Bayfield Advertising in 1858

WHAT WAS PROBABLY BAYFIELD'S FIRST advertising effort, appeared in 1858, a little paper bound booklet called, *Bayfield, Lake Superior*. It reveals that Joseph Mc-Cloud was the real estate agent here. The Hotel Bayfield had pleasure yachts and teams for the accommodation of visitors. Page 2 says, "The channels of entrance into the bay are wide and deep, making it one of the safest and most commodious natural harbors in the world. The surface upon which the town of Bayfield is laid out is most admirably adapted to health, convenience and beauty. That portion of the plot south of Washington Avenue and east of Fourth Street is level and dry bottom land. From this area the surface rises gently in north westerly, westerly and south westerly directions to the confines of the place from the higher portions of which numerous springs rise furnishing an abundant supply of excellent water.

"The buildings in the town are generally larger and more spacious than in most of the new towns on the lake. During the past year a Methodist church was built and it is contemplated to erect an Episcopal and a Presbyterian church this season. For the encouragement of settlers, the owners of Bayfield lots have determined to sell them very low, to those only, however, who will improve. This is the true policy and by this means, speculators, the curse of every new country, are prevented from monopolizing property to the detriment of the interests of the town.

"There are still thousands of persons in the East who look toward Bayfield with a disposition to emigrate. Perhaps they mete out from year to year a bare subsistence. The year rolls by, and if they have enjoyed the right to labor during the bulk of it they have accumulated but little. Imagine some of these persons on their own fare, the plow in their grasp and fortune before them. What, then, would be the result of their labor? Houses, plowed land, fences, farms would grow under their hands, with half the labor now given to procure a living and every day's work would be for themselves and would add to their own personal wealth, to say nothing of the yearly rise in their property. In grading the streets of the town, a lump of very pure copper ore weighing several pounds was picked up. The summer tour from Bayfield to St. Paul has repeatedly been made. The Messrs. McCloud drove over it on several occasions in the light wagon in the spring and fall of 1857. Let those who reside in the city and cannot find profitable employment come here and raise their food out of the bosom of the earth. Government land in Bayfield is $1.25 per acre. We assert that a good farmer or mechanic failing to succeed in Bayfield is almost an impossibility, in fact we would like to hear of one.

The settlement of Bayfield is unlike that of most other towns. Emigrants from the Atlantic cities and from most points come here principally on steamboats and have brought with them all the conveniences and comforts of civilized life; indeed, many of the luxuries were in about one weeks time, without toil, danger or exposure, transported to their new homes and in a few months they were surrounded with the appendages of civilization and the blessings of law and society. . . Settlers can embark either from Cleveland, Detroit, or Chicago with his house, store, furniture, goods, cattle, etc., and in four days be landed at Bayfield. We mean good-sized houses. Some are 16 x 25, two stories high. Freight on lake boats are low, the rate from New York to Bayfield is $1.00 per hundred pounds.

It would astonish Aladdin, even, were he to see how quickly houses are erected and occupied nowadays, and then for him to look at a stump machine clearing a stump or tree from the ground in a few minutes. . . Who would go to Kansas, Nebraska and other out of the way places where there is no timber to build even a log shanty with, where the wind in winter ranges fearfully across the lonely prairie. Ah, my readers, if you want to feel the keen, cutting blast, settle in a prairie country. A few winters ago, we remember two trains of cars being shut up in snowdrifts in Illinois. Settlers, do you want a magnificent climate, land of marvelous fertility, no chills, fever, ague, damp and disagreeable weather, sloppy walking and keen cutting winds, constant political agitation, etc. Then emigrate to Bayfield and enjoy the Lake Superior atmosphere. . . Why should the climate of Lake Superior second to none in healthfulness and already proved to be like that of Upper Egypt, not be mentioned to the invalid to whose suffering frame it would impart new health?

Evaluations of Bayfield 1890

*A*s *WE ARE* IS THE title of an article published in The Bayfield County Press Saturday, June 28, 1890. And there are two subtitles, *Bayfield as the summer of 1890 Finds Her,* and *Notes of Progress for the Past Decade.*

Here is Currie G. Bell's review of the ten years between 1880 and 1890:

The enumerators of the census of 1890, the eleventh taken by the United States Government, are now hard at work and in the course of a few weeks, we may hope to know something of the results. In the meantime, there are many sections of our country in which these returns are awaited with almost breathless interest. In many places the decade just past represents the most vigorous period of their growth. Such is indeed the case with Northern Wisconsin. Bayfield County has received no small part of her growth within ten years. It is our purpose to review briefly the history of Bayfield County for this time and to note her present status.

The census of 1880 credited this entire county with a population of less than 500 souls and they were then living almost entirely in the village of Bayfield, 23 years old. Bayfield was then uniquely handsome. It's whitewashed houses, scattered irregularly on the flat and the hills reminded the traveler approaching by water of the pictures of quiet out-of-the-way places in foreign lands. No railroad had as yet penetrated thus far, and as the winter season approached, our merchants had to stock up for a long spell of cold weather and loneliness, as they well knew that when the boats stopped, all their supplies not already on hand must be packed in from St. Paul.

The Changes Of Ten Years to one who has watched are marvelous. The population of the village of Bayfield itself is estimated to be about 3,000, of the town of Bayfield, 6,000 and the entire County, 20,000. In 1880 there was but one polling place in the county. In 1883, it was divided into four towns, Bayfield, Mason, Drummond and Washburn, each of which has several large sawmills which make the principal part of her business. They are owned by Bigelow Bros., S.G. Cook and Co., and the C.C. Thompson Company.

The Brownstone Industry has been born, bred and taught to walk and brought to years of discretion within the last decade. Previous to 1880, Cook and Hyde had operated to a large extent on Bass Island. Since the advent of railroad facilities, this business has developed to enormous properties on the mainland. The Bayfield Brownstone Company, owned by Col. E.F. Drake of St. Paul, and Captain R.D. Pike of Bayfield, put in the first plant and were soon followed by the Prentice and Hartley quarries at Houghton and Cook and Hyde's plant near Bayfield. The Ashland Brownstone quarry on Presque Isle, which was for sometime managed by William Knight of Bayfield, is a product of later times. The quarry is now owned in Chicago and represents a capital of $6,000,000. It's facilities are being largely increased and another season from 300 to 500 men will be given employment on Presque Isle. The company will, this season, build a large dock at Bayfield to be used for winter shipments. They have selected Bayfield for these shipments because they can be made from Presque Isle to their docks here for a period of from 30 to 90 days in the fall after the close of navigation at the "Soo" and all other Lake Superior ports.

The City Of Bayfield, the county seat of Bayfield County, has met with a steady and encouraging growth since 1880. Her whitewashed houses have been remodeled and a large number of tasteful modern residences built. Externally it would be hard to recognize the Bayfield of 1880, could it be placed along side of its successor of 1890. Bayfield fortunately escaped the boom of 1888. Real estate, while never flighty, has always been firm. Since 1880 the Booth Packing Company has established its Lake Superior packing houses at this place and we are the headquarters of the largest fish packing industry on Lake Superior. Pike's mill has been greatly enlarged and its capacity doubled. The Bayfield Box Factory established in 1887, has recently been purchased by Messrs. Downey, Fischer and Pike and under the management of Mr. Downey will ship boxes to all parts of the west. On the first of January 1890, William Knight opened the doors of the Lumberman's Bank, an institution which has been long needed and is now doing a flourishing business. Bayfield has five churches, each of which worships in its own edifice. The Sisters of St. Francis conduct an orphanage and boarding school, which has increased to such an extent that an additional building will be immediately erected. Our public schools have outgrown their primitive environments in 1885 and a handsome high school building was erected during the following year. In the fall of 1887 the free high school system was adopted under the authority of the State Superintendent and was the first school of the kind in Bayfield County. Two graduating classes have already received the god-speed of their alma mater. The high school building has been adopted by the state inspector of high schools, Prof. W.F. Parker, as the model for all similar buildings in Wisconsin. The wants of amusement lovers are supplied by the Grand Opera House fitted up by Robert McCamis. The Island View Hotel, erected in 1887 at a cost of $20,000 has lately been entirely refinished and refitted and under the control of the Island View Hotel Company will be no small factor in our business interests during the summer. In this brief glance at the progress of Bayfield and Bayfield County for the past ten years, many things have been only slightly mentioned, any one of which deserves a separate article to do it full justice. In future issues we hope to enlarge upon many of these interests. Our purpose has been to show that from the small fishing hamlet of 1880, Bayfield has now grown to be the center of large and permanent business interests."

And just to recall how proud Bayfield was of her new high school, here are two more items.

May 24, 1890, "We notice that the school board has been improving the school ground by the planting of numerous trees the past week. It is a cold day when our board doesn't think of some improvement in school matters."

They not only planted trees, they planted them so well that they grew for over sixty years. A few of them had to be removed in the spring of 1952, when the new gym was built.

May 31, 1890. "Prof. W.F. Parker, Wisconsin Superintendent of Free High Schools, has decided to recommend the Bayfield High School building as a model to all school boards needing similar accommodations and has secured plans and specifications of the same with that end in view."

Bayfield's Brass Cannon

WHEN THE SOLDIERS CAME TO Bayfield to defend it during the Sioux scare, they brought a small brass cannon. They left it here when they went away. Several years afterward, the state held a public auction and the cannon, which it had received from the national government, was condemned as worthless and left standing on the boulevard, still intact in its original wrappings with the ammunition in its original packages.

It remained there undisturbed until one Fourth of July several Civil War veterans were overcome by patriotism. They removed the wrappings and celebrated the day by firing off all the cannon's ammunition.

When the Bayfield Rifles went to the defense of Ashland during the Ashland War, the cannon went with them and no doubt its formidable appearance helped keep the peace during the ten days our Rifles stayed there.

From that time on, the cannon took an active part in Bayfield's history. It developed the qualities of Mary's little lamb, for everywhere that Bayfielders went, the cannon was sure to go.

It became traditional for the cannon to boom at sunrise on the Glorious Fourth. Its thundering tones were used to spread the tidings of political victories and defeats. It was fired with great joy when Bayfield high school students defeated Washburn students in a debate on the subject, "The removal of the county seat was unwise and detrimental to the county."

Whenever there was deep emotion in Bayfield, our cannon gave voice to it.

When General Sherman came to visit Bayfield after the Civil War, the cannon was wheeled rapidly down Main Street and waited for the General on the dock, with its deep voice saluting the hero of the famous march through Georgia.

When General Grant died, the cannon spoke solemnly, being fired at timed intervals all during the hours of his funeral, paying tribute for Bayfield to the memory of a great soldier and statesman.

The cannon was rushed to the depot to greet the first train on Oct. 12, 1883. The fire, smoke and noise it made on that happy day were recorded in accounts of that event.

When the cannon was not occupied with patriotic and general celebration duties, it stood peacefully at the entrance of the courthouse grounds and was admired by passers-by. It appears in many of the old pictures of the courthouse.

Lloyd Brigham was the one who discovered that a tomato can filled with mud fitted the cannon nicely. One of these cans, when fired, sailed over the high pointed steeple of the old Presbyterian Church and thumped down on main street in front of what is now Andy's market. Fortunately, nobody's head interfered with its landing.

Miss Lila Stark gave the history of our old cannon in her graduation oration. At that time, the cannon was badly worn from its strenuous duties in Bayfield and had been moved to an obscure place in the rear of the courthouse. She called for its restoration, pointing out that it had been remounted twice, and could be again. A couple of worn out wheels didn't mean the cannon was done for.

Her appeal was evidently answered, for in World War I, the cannon was taken to the Armory and stored there by the Home Guard.

In March 1923, the cannon was discovered in the basement of the Armory, which by then had become Memorial Hall and was owned by the Civic League. It was decided at a League meeting that the cannon should remain in the basement until it could be given a fitting and permanent place on the Memorial Hall grounds.

But in January 1924, Memorial Hall burned to the ground. What became of our cannon then? It was evidently not destroyed, because the furnaces in the basement were not. If you ask along main street, the opinion seems to be that it went to World War II.

Well, going to war is an honorable thing for a cannon to do. But our cannon was old, eighty years old, and sadly worn from booming out Bayfield's emotions through those eighty years.

That's why we're sorry it went as scrap.

Bayfield News Items

H ERE ARE SOME BAYFIELD NEWS items, which appeared in The Ashland Press on April 28, 1877. Bayfield items: David Cooper had built a neat and substantial fence around his residence. Col. John H. Knight has put his fine grounds in order, built a new fence, and slicked up generally. (There was a reason why they built those fences...Cows!!!) The schooner Mary Ann came into the harbor from her winter quarters near Raspberry Light Wednesday. The ice in the harbor broke up on the 17th. On the 18th the first fishing boats of the season, sent out by N. and F. Boutin, left for south shore fishing points.

Captain R.D. Pike got up steam in his mill last Saturday and saluted the villagers with the whistle. The schooner *Marco Polo*, which was sunk at Vaughn's dock last winter by the ice, has been raised and hauled out. The schooner *Maple Leaf* is loading for Isle Royale and north shore fishing grounds with nets, salt, fish barrels, etc. Captain R.D. Pike's new tug, the *Mocking Bird*, was launched Wednesday. The tug has been fitted up in good shape for business, and will be quite an addition to the Bayfield fleet. Bob Inglis has cleared the dock for business and opened up his office for the season. Bob finds time to attend to business with his usual promptness, notwithstanding his new boy.

The fishing season has commenced in earnest. N. & F. Boutin will put in six-pound nets at Bark Point this week, and several at other stations. They will employ upwards of fifty men this year, several pound nets and about 2,000-gill nets.

The Bayfield Rifles have made progress in their drills this spring and intend to celebrate the 4th this year in better style than ever. They will visit Ashland and take part in the grand opening ceremonies of the Wisconsin Central railroad, if any "doings" are had on that occasion.

(Bayfield history readers will remember on New Year's Day 1873 the Bayfield Rifles went to Ashland and saved the city from being wrecked by the railroad workers. Now, 4 years later, they were equally ready to go to Ashland and celebrate with the citizens and the transient railroad workers.)

The hotel is nearly ready for the grand opening. The new landlord, William Knight Esq. takes hold of the business as though he had followed it all his life, and has already demonstrated that he is the right man in the right place. Mr. LaBonte and family have been engaged to take charge of the internal arrangements of the house, and will keep it in first class style.

1890-91 News Files

THIS IS NOT STRICTLY BAYFIELD history, but all of these news items appeared in The Bayfield Press in a State News column in 1890-91. To me they revealed the appearance and character of some Wisconsin citizens. What came before, or what happened after these incidents, is lost in the past, but from them I concluded that:

Beards were nice, but a hazard. "A strange accident occurred to George May, a farmer residing a few miles southeast of West Bend. While stooping over a feed cutter in motion to oil the machine, his long beard caught in the gearing and pulled out by the roots, considerable skin going with it."

Teaching required more than book learning. "Lizzie Dunbar, a 16 year old girl teacher at Darien, used a four pound school bell to keep an overgrown boy from breaking up the school. She pounded him over the head until he was helpless, and the admiring citizens presented her with a diamond ring and a toilet set in admiration of her disciplinary skill."

Some people believed in direct action. "Charles Barker's place near Eau Claire, one of the most notorious pinery dens in that section, was burned at 4 o'clock the other morning. It was supposed it was set on fire by the inhabitants of the neighborhood. The occupants, ten women, barely escaped. The place has been a nuisance this spring and a scene of continual fighting and robbery."

Some were publicly outspoken. "Ervin Lober, a bachelor aged 66 years, died in Milwaukee the other day from the heat. . . Ervin was highly educated, aristocratic, poor and dissipated, too lazy to work and too proud to beg. Scandinavian friends both supported and buried him."

Some received disappointments. "The kind hearted sheriff of Pierce county telegraphed to Circuit Judge Bundy from Ellsworth to know whether he could take the prisoners in his jail to the county fair. Judge Parish, who was sitting for Judge Bundy, replied that he had better keep the prisoners in jail."

Horseplay was popular. "E.M. Boyer of Michigan has begun suit in the United States Court against Price County, this state, claiming $25,000 damages by reason of a charivari to which he was subjected at Phillips. The county clerk of Price County, the chairman of the county board and others united in disturbing him with discordant sounds and also squirted water into his house through hose owned by the company."

Conservation unnecessary.

And a spade was called a spade. "Lottie Morgan, who had been living with Johnny Sullivan, a Hurley politician, for the past three years, was murdered at Ashland the other night. Her body was found the next morning in Sullivan's saloon, her head having been split with an axe. The diamond in her ears and one on her fingers were undisturbed."

Women were unpredictable then, as always. "Will Johnston and Bob McKeon indulged in a fifteen round prize fight in the open street in the Sixth ward at Eau Claire over a lady's hand. . . In the fifteenth round, Johnston was knocked out by a blow between the eyes. . . The girl has discarded them both."

They were strong. "Mrs. Dahlman, the muscular lady from Belle Plain, who knocked her husband out in one round, was fined $5 and costs by Justice Howard."

Unpredictable. "Louise Alwart, aged twenty years, committed suicide in Manitowoc rather than marry an aged man her parents had selected for her."

Mysterious. "A handsome woman, giving her name as Minnie Lloyd, died at Janesville. The name was evidently assumed, but she refused to reveal her identity."

Determined. "While James Stephens and wife of Dodgeville were out at dinner, their daughter, Jennie, aged about 20 years, eloped with Henry Lewis, brother of Evan, "The Strangler." The old folks were much opposed to Lewis."

Efficient. "St. Croix County has a female superintendent of schools, Miss Wright, who is said to fill the office better than any male superintendent that ever held it."

And the men had a few quirks, too. "A chapter of the Owl Club is to be established at Janesville. The peculiarity of the organization is that at each annual election, a man is selected by secret ballot who is obliged to marry during the year."

One of them 'cried wolf'. "Fritz hack, a middle aged farmer of Washington township, had been in the habit of locking himself in his bedroom and playing suicide by firing a revolver to bring his wife to terms after a quarrel. So the wife and children paid no attention when he did it the other day. After three hours, they broke in and found him lying unconscious with a fatal bullet hole in his chest."

One was stubborn. "Twenty-five masked men surrounded the residence of a young man named Mortimer at Palmyra and bombarded the building with stale eggs. A few days ago Mortimer was notified to leave town, but refused to do so. The home of a married woman to whom Mortimer was accused of having been too attentive, was also visited and stormed."

One could manage a woman. "A newly married young farmer living at Greenbush near Sheboygan has hit upon a novel, but effective, scheme for getting his wife out of bed in the morning. He fills the stove with damp shavings, lights them and then shuts the damper in the pipe. By the time he reaches the barn, she is effectively smoked out."

One died for love. "A Foolish Old Man. William Oliver, a respected farmer of Poygan, killed himself by taking a dose of carbolic acid the other day. He was a widower, aged 70 years. The cause of the suicide was said to have been the refusal of a woman to become the third Mrs. Oliver."

And one had better luck. "Israel Love, aged 80, was married for the sixth time at Beloit."

On Wisconsin.

Navigation Open & Closing

THIS MONTH BAYFIELD WILL BE 99 years old. Also, in this month of March, the ice may or may not go out of the bay. Chances are that it will not, for as the following record shows, it went out in March only twice in 31 years. For the benefit of those who like to guess at the departure date of the ice, this table is reprinted. It first appeared in The Press in 1888 with the statement: "The Press is indebted to Andrew Tate, one of Bayfield's first settlers, for this chart showing the opening and closing dates of navigation since 1857."

Open	Closed
May 20, 1857	Jan. 6, 1858
March 20, 1858	Dec. 24, 1858
April 10, 1859	Dec. 26, 1859
April 15, 1860	Dec. 17, 1860
April 17, 1861	Dec. 22, 1861
April 19, 1862	Dec. 31, 1862
April 10, 1863	Dec. 20, 1863
April 18, 1864	Dec. 22, 1864
April 22, 1865	Dec. 23, 1865
April 17, 1866	Dec. 29, 1866
April 20, 1867	Dec. 23, 1867
April 29, 1868	Dec. 24, 1868
April 19, 1869	Dec. 25, 1869
April 15, 1870	Dec. 27, 1870
April 8, 1871	Dec. 15, 1871
April 28, 1872	Dec. 10, 1872
May 5, 1873	Dec. 6, 1873
May 4, 1874	Dec. 26, 1874
May 13, 1875	Dec. 18, 1875
May 7, 1876	Dec. 16, 1876
April 17, 1877	Jan. 28, 1877

March 3, 1878	Dec. 26, 1878
April 21, 1879	Dec. 17, 1879
April 24, 1880	Dec. 1, 1880
May 2, 1881	Jan. 4, 1882
April 10, 1882	Dec. 26, 1882
April 25, 1883	Dec. 19, 1883
April 27, 1884	Dec. 19, 1884
April 27, 1885	Dec. 8, 1885
April 24, 1886	Dec. 16, 1886
May 2, 1887	Dec. 26, 1887
May 5, 1888	

Does anyone have a record of the opening and closing of navigation in the Bayfield harbor that will bring this chart up to date?

There was always rivalry between Bayfield and Ashland over the opening and closing of navigation. In the winter of 1881 and the spring of 1882, editor Stevens of *The Bayfield Press* and Sam Fifield, editor of *The Ashland Press* exchanged bits of humor on the subject.

The first exchange which appeared in *The Bayfield Press* the first week in December, 1881, was more triumphant than numerous. *The Press* stated: "*The Ashland Press* states that the bay was closed by ice there December 2. Well, here we haven't even seen any ice on the bay yet, and don't expect to for some time to come."

The Ashland Press could not deny their bay was frozen solid. Instead, they tried to make their ice appear to be a valuable commodity, which Bayfield did not have by replying: "And what a fix your town will be in next season—no ice for mint juleps and the boys so thirsty."

The record shows that the Bayfield harbor was not closed by ice that year until Jan. 4, 1882, a month and two days after the Ashland harbor was closed. And it was not until January 28, 1882, that *The Ashland Press* reported: "After this day teams will go on the ice all the way to Bayfield. A road is being staked out."

In this day and age of rapid transportation we do not feel the deep concern over the coming or going of the ice that the pioneers did. Ashland had a railroad in 1882 and Bayfield was to get one in 1883, but a boat was still a lifeline to the little towns. Our main concern now is for the fishermen, who either want it solid, or want it out of the way.

In Aril, 1882, *The Ashland Press* said, "It's a blarsted lie they have been telling on over at Bayfield during the past week, that we 'stand on the end of the railroad dock every day and swear at the ice.' We do it at home by our own fireside and blast a man who doesn't."

The Ashland Press reported later: "The *Manistee* arrived at Bayfield last Saturday evening on her way down the lake, her first trip of the season. She did not attempt to push her way through the ice floes in our bay which the plaguing northeast wind has kept from sailing out for some days."

The Bayfield Press said: "Sam, we wish you would take a pole and shove that ice out of the way over there so that the boats can run."

The Ashland Press replied: "We would gladly do it Bro. Stevens, but the fact is we have too much regard for the ice. It cools us off when we feel like swearing. It acts that way on some people, you know."

Kids Print Their Own Election Ballot

BOYS WILL BE BOYS, IN any day or age, and if this boyish prank had succeeded in 1891 all of the members of the Bayfield Town Board would have been less than seven years old, which certainly would have set an all time record for youth in government.

Maybe it proves that people don't read ballots very carefully. Anyway, Currie Bell's editorial version of the affair, which appeared in the Bayfield Country *Press* for Saturday, April 11, 1891, is as follows:

"Young Man's Ticket.
About noon of Election Day the following ticket with the above head was sprung upon an unsuspecting public and anxious candidates:
For Supervisors–
Donald C. Bell, Chairman
Ray Eccles, Supervisor.
Martie Gleason, Supervisor.
For Treasurer –
Douglas Knight.
For Clerk –
Eddie Williams
For Assessor –
George Currie
For Overseer –
Harrison Mussell
For Justices –
Frank Hannum, two years.
G. Feldhausen, two years.
Sy Greenlaw Jr., one year.
For Constables –
Norman H. Van Horn
Homer Stahl.

Chairman Bell did not discover the change in the political sky until about one o'clock when he was shown a copy of the ticket. He was noticed within five minutes making a beeline for his residence, closely followed by Judge Wade, who is said to have lost several pounds of good solid avoirdupois in his haste. Mr. Bell is said to have rudely torn a lusty shingle from his woodshed roof and planted it in no uncertain terms upon the first pair of pants ever worn by the new aspirant for mayoral honors. Several erstwhile happy homes were turned for the nonce into abodes of wailing and gnashing of teeth. Ed. Eccles and Ex-Sheriff Van Horn had affecting and effective interviews with their young hopefuls.

It is thought that had this ticket been put forth early in the day, it would have changed the complexion of the entire election. As it was, the complexions of several of the candidates were for a time of an ashen hue. The ages of these candidates ranged from three to seven years, and most of them were the heirs-apparent of the regular nominees." *The Ashland Press* had the last word and got the last laugh with the following: "Currie G. Bell has been elected mayor of Bayfield about seventeen times, but last Tuesday he was threatened. Early on Election Day, a ticket was sprung which came near upsetting things. It was his son, age 7, and some other lads who had tickets printed and were right in the field to win. Currie quelled the riot with a shingle."

Poem of Bayfield Summer

This week we will interrupt our stories of the Bayfield pioneers to reprint a timely poem which was published in *The Bayfield Press* in February 1908. The author isn't given, but the fact that it appears in February may be a clue. It sounds like it was written by some poor city slicker eager for summer to come so he could once more escape from the concrete canyons and return to Bayfield.

By the Shining Big Sea Waters

In the early days of summer
When we bask in pleasant sunshine
And enjoy the cooling breezes
On the shores of Lake Superior
When our pine trees all are glorious
In the richness of their verdue
And all nature seems rejoicing
In the beauty of the landscape,
Then it is the summer tourist
In his land of heat and sunstroke
Suffering sadly with hay fever
Packs his grip-sack in a hurry
Buys a ticket straight for Bayfield
Levels that land of scorching sunshine
And prepares to spend the summer
In this land of bracing breezes
In this land of health and brook trout
In this pretty Harbor City
On the shores of Gitchie Gummee.
And he seeks the Island View House
Or it may be at another
And engages board and lodging
For six weeks, and maybe longer.
Then he lies him down to Shep's or Louie's
And invests in fishing tackle
And he seeks a guide next morning
Joe Petite, or Henry Dennis
Whom he hires to be his pilot,
Pilot to Onion or Sioux River
For he wants to go afishing
And wage war among the brook trout.
But he dreams not of the brush wood,

Nor of sand flies or mosquitoes.
And the good guide does not tell him.
When the shades of night are falling
Homeward comes the conquering hero
With a goodly string of brook trout.
Does he tell his friends and neighbors
That he bought those speckled beauties
Of a dark skinned little native?
No, he keeps that precious secret
Safely locked within his bosom.
And he speaks not of mosquitoes
Neither tells he of the sand flies.
Thus the happy days of summer
Glide away, as is their custom.
And the peaceful summer tourist
Sails about among the islands,
Eats and sleeps and lives in comfort.
Grows at length quite fat and hearty
And he knows no more hay fever.
When the light frost herald autumn
Then he takes his journey homeward
And his children do not know him
And they run to find their mother
And they tell her that a bummer
Or perhaps a tramp is coming
Thus he meets again the dear ones
Vowing that another summer
Shall behold them all together
In the healthy town of Bayfield
In the pretty harbor city
On the shores of Gitchie Gummee.

Bayfield News Items

W HEN WILDLIFE GOT OUT OF hand, or even threatened to, Currie Bell made note of it in the *Press* on Feb. 16, 1884:"Several deer have been seen near town during the past week. The law prohibits the killing of deer at this season unless they attempt to bite you." Aug. 10, 1901. "While out berrying the first of the week, near A. Turnquist's farm, Fred Berger hearing what he supposed was a fight between his dog and another canine, went to his dog's assistance and taking hold of the nose of what he supposed was a dog, he discovered that it was a lynx. He immediately let go his hold and the lynx took to the woods with the dog after him. The dog was badly lacerated, but will come out all right. Fred was lucky enough to get out of it without a scratch." June 28, 1902. "Elmer Beebe, while wheeling in from his homestead last Monday morning, encountered a mother bear and two cubs and the former gave him something to think about for a few minutes.

Mr. Beebe was riding along slowly when two cub bears came out of the brush in front of him and started down the road. He did not get frightened at this but instead took after the little ones and was becoming quite interested in the chase when a noise behind him attracted his attention. He turned to look, but was not at all pleased with the sight he saw, for here was the mother bear coming down the pike at a rapid pace and getting uncomfortably close.

It was now a case of the pursuer being pursued and what was fun a few minutes before had now grown to seriousness. Mr. Beebe said perspiration started in small rivers, his hat raised about four inches and the cold chills played tag up and down his spinal column. His hands began to shake and the bicycle ran over snags and into ruts and through every mud puddle in the road, but the bear kept on coming and his only salvation seemed in keeping the machine going.

He was about to give up in despair and let the bears breakfast, when the cubs, to his delight, trotted off into the brush and the old bear followed. Mr. Beebe says at one time during the race the bear was within a few feet of him. Bayfield's birthday was noted in *The Press* as follows: March 29, 1884. "Last Monday, March 24, was the 28th anniversary of the birth of Bayfield. The old girl has got lots of vitality and is fast developing her latent resources."

And on August 16 of that same year *The Press* said, "They all notice it. Notice what? Why that there is not a town in the northwest where law and order prevails to a greater extent than in the Harbor City, and for much of which we have to thank our efficient police force." In 1885 Currie Bell took note of the arrival of spring with the following: "The trees are putting on their summer clothing in a most distracting manner. The prevailing color is light green."

And on June 23, 1888. "Three years ago *The Press* was laughed at for advocating the advisability of having a livery stable in Bayfield. Today the town boasts for two, well equipped with horses and carriages of all kinds and both report business good."

Currie was generous in giving space to club meetings. Dec. 12, 1896. "The Oak Island Fishing Club is holding daily (or nightly) meetings. Fish bait, herring, nets, dog teams, etc., are the topics of discussion. Parties wishing to secure *large* fish in carload lots are requested to correspond with the secretary, F.D. Miller 244½ Large Catch Avenue, Telephone, call 2-1-2, Oak Island Branch.

Jan. 20, 1900. "Bayfield now boasts of being the terminus of five great railway systems: The Omaha, The Bayfield Transfer, The Bayfield and Great Western, The Bayfield and Western, The Washburn, Bayfield and Iron River. All aboard for China and Japan, via the Pacific coast."

And speaking of trains, *The Press* reported this happening in the issue of May 4, 1901. "The incoming passenger train that arrives here at 10:45 was brought to a sudden standstill the other night before reaching the depot. As the train came around the curve, coming into the depot, the engineer saw what he supposed was the lights on the hind end of the caboose standing on the main track near the depot. He immediately put on the air, stopping the train so suddenly that the passengers were thrown from their seats. You can imagine how the engineer felt when he discovered that the lights that caused him to stop were some colored lights that Ole Reiten had put up in front of his place of business on Broad Street and lit them that night for the first time."

Letters to the Editor

THE FIRST NEWSPAPER WAS PUBLISHED in Bayfield in 1857. It was the *Bayfield Mercury*, and didn't last very long.

There was a *Bayfield Press* which began Sept. 24, 1859, but that didn't last either.

The paper we all know of is *The Bayfield County Press* , which was started in 1870. Probably from the moment it started, Bayfield citizens began to write "Letters to the Editor." Through the years, letters on every conceivable subject appeared usually signed by fancy names such as Observer, Sympathizer, Socrates.

Here is a letter with some strong feelings behind it, which was published on Washington's Birthday, Feb. 22, 1890.

"Editor *Press:* Last week's fire it is claimed by some of the wise ones showing that Wing Hose Company only needed a good foreman. I grant it, but to manage a fire in our village he would have to be superhuman to please the foremen–protem who always turns out to a fire and have more to say and more orders to give than anyone man who may be Foreman. They will not join us and help us keep up the company and practice. As a rule, even when we are out for practice, they stand on the sidewalk and croak, either ridiculing or finding fault with us. There is an extra cart in the town house, which I would like to see manned by these self appointed foremen and fire marshalls, etc., and let them practice and work as well as talk. My opinion is that the fire company should not be disturbed in their work by anyone not in authority, and I would request that at the next fire the police keep the crowd from meddling with the fire apparatus and firemen or arrest them, the same as is done in every city."

Members of Wing Hose Company

SIXTY-FOUR YEARS HAVE PASSED SINCE that letter was written and now we can laugh at it; because people in Bayfield don't act like that anymore. Do we?

Some of the most violent letters concerned cows. If the rage of the citizens against cows had ever been converted into action, there wouldn't have been a cow left in Bayfield. Here's a letter published Aug. 10, 1906.

"To the citizens of Bayfield: "Lord" Cow, for many years in possession of all vacant lots about the city has assumed control of the public highways and thoroughfares. Something must be done. Strangers coming to the city are pleased with the beautiful shade trees and excellent position of our little city. But, they also make remarks as to the condition of our streets, the presence of the cow being shown in every street in the city. Cows are sensible creatures. They use the sidewalks. People are not sensible because the cow made them so. People use the streets to walk on. Not long ago several young ladies were standing in the doorway of one of our leading stores, when lo and behold, one of our sensible cows came walking down the sidewalk, evidently out for a stroll and enjoying the fine Lake Superior breeze. Being perfectly fearless, the cow paid no attention to the young ladies and they found it necessary to retreat into the store in order not to intrude upon "Her Majesty's" private property–the sidewalk. Gentlemen, walking along the street, when you meet the cow, step aside and politely take off your hat as she passes. . . "

And in 1910 someone who called himself "Resident voter" got mad at the police force. Here are the most interesting excerpts from his letter to *The Press* .

"With our taxes above the safety mark, as they have been for several years back, and in spite of that, the town never had sufficient funds with which to improve our streets and highways as they should be improved, does it not appeal to the average taxpayer that we might dispense with the luxury of two full-grown and full-paid policemen these days? There is never a time during the year, with the exception of two or three months during the summer that a 15 year old boy could not do all that is required of our two policemen and at any rate, all that they do, whether required by the superiors to do more or not. . .

In the writer's opinion, which is shared by man, it is a needless expense to keep two officers. . . put a big fur overcoat on some good strapping boy at about $40 per month and you will never know the difference."

And someone who signs himself Observer didn't like an article published in the old Bayfield Progress in 1910. His comment recalls the historical aspects of early Bayfield plumbing, for he says about the disliked article, "If I could find nothing better to fill the space occupied by it, I would just say, this is clean toilet paper, and let it go at that. I have lived in this old world nearly seventy years and this is the first time I ever attempted to write an article for a newspaper, and I find myself in the same position as the stammering applicant for a railroad ticket who told the agent he guessed he'd have to go by freight, because he couldn't express himself!

Don't be so modest Observer. You can express yourself all right!

Deer Hunting

B AYFIELD AND DEER HUNTING HAVE been synonymous since the town was founded 100 years ago. At first, hunting was a necessity. The settlers needed meat. The diary of the Rev. James Peet for Jan. 5, 1858 says, "George Day shot two moose in woods lately, so we have a piece of meat for our table."

But as civilization came, bringing many kinds of food, and conservation laws, hunting, instead of a necessity, became a sport. This sport still has many enthusiastic participants in Bayfield.

Like any sport, it requires meets to plan strategy, to discuss past victories and the cause of failures. That was just as true 73 years ago as it is now. September 29, 1883, *The Bayfield Press* had this to say: "The Order of United Deer Hunters held their semi-occasional meeting in Andreas Jewelry store last Tuesday evening. The meeting was well attended and the exercises were very entertaining."

Seventy years have changed a lot of things, but not deer hunters. With a change of meeting place, that same item could be a report on a United Deer Hunters meeting and entertaining exercises, which took place last night.

Fifty-one years ago, deer hunting was headline news in *The Bayfield Press* when this humorous, yet truthful article, *Some Timely Hints on Deer Hunting* from the Northwestern Sportsman was reprinted.

"Get a gun. Most any old kind will do. Then get some of your friends to go along, because if you should accidentally shoot one of them, his relatives won't make so much fuss as strangers.

The first real point to remember when you get into the woods is that you are the only man in the woods and everything else you see is deer.

Now some people would have you believe that deer always look like the photographs in The Sportsman, but don't you stand for that. Deer look like most everything else. Even cows have been known to look like deer. Pine stumps look just like big bucks.

Don't take any chances; shoot every time your finger strikes the trigger. If you see an old black hat sliding along through the brush, take a crack at it. A buck probably hooked it off the clothesline.

It's funny how the deer try to make themselves look like hunters. Why, I expect that most of the old cunning fellows are growing scarlet hair this year in imitation of hunter's jackets.

Of course, there will be other hunters after deer, but they won't come into your territory. So if you see the brush move, empty your gun into it and you'll get something. . .

You are out after deer and you can't afford to take any chances. If some other fellow is foolish enough to dress himself up to look like a deer and then come prowling around the woods where you are, it's his funeral, not yours.

But then, deer are curious creatures. It is remarkable how much a deer resembles a man, especially in the woods. I know this is so, for I once saw one coming toward me and I thought it was a man and so lost a good shot. Deer are smart. They have been seen walking on their hind legs so they wouldn't get shot for a man.

If there were any distinguishing features about a deer, I would tell you, but as I have said, they look so much like everything else, you simply have to shoot at all things in order to get one.

Another really important thing is to learn to shoot well, not because it is difficult to kill a deer, but because through this promiscuous shooting, you might just wing some regular hunter and he might get angry and show you up for what you are."

On March 14, 1891, *The Bayfield Press* presented this problem, which was solved by deer hunters. "Two hunters killed a deer and sold it in the woods. They had no way of weighing it, but knowing their own weights, one 130 pounds; the other 190 pounds, they placed a rail across a fence so that it balanced with one on each end. Then they exchanged places, the lighter one taking the deer on his lap and the rail balanced again. What was the weight of the deer?

This is the time of year to get a deer, get a rail, get a fence and solve this problem. Does anyone know the answer?

Sam Fifield's Story of Apostle Islands

Samuel S. Fifield was born in Maine in 1839. Fifield was an influential newspaper owner but is most remembered as a politician serving in the State Assembly (1874-1876), State Senate (1877-1881) and then as Lieutenant Governor from 1882 to 1887. Camp Stella at Sand Island was often a site in which he found refuge. He died in 1815. (Photo: BHA)

I HAVE BEEN FORTUNATE IN RECEIVING from Mrs. Margaret Brooks of Milwaukee a newspaper clipping giving a very interesting story of the Apostle Islands. It was written by S.S. Fifield who founded The Bayfield Press and later became editor of The Ashland Press .

The exact date of the article is not known, but it was written sometime after 1890. Its flowery language is partly due to the style of the times, but probably it is mostly due to the fact that Sam Fifield loved and enjoyed the islands so much he could hardly find enough adjectives to describe them.

The article is as follows, "Along the south shore of the Great Northern Sea, the scenery, while of entire different mould, is no less interesting and pleasing than that of the bold shores of the north. From Duluth to the Sault Ste. Marie, there is a great variety; from the peaceful isles of Chequamegon to the rugged cliffs of the Pictured Rocks. There are wild mountain ranges with their wealth of minerals that fade away into the gray haze of the northern sky, as they roll inland to the height of the watershed. They are crowned with dense forests through which wind crystal streams and brooks, and the song of the waterfall keeps time with the beating waves and the sighing winds. It is a wonderful panorama that unrolls as one sails along the green shores, with their beautiful bays and inlets–Nature's flower-decked parks, swept and trimmed by the summer gales.

But of all the charming spots that gladden the eye and heart, there are none that equal the magical islands of the Apostle group. How lovely they are, reflecting their brilliant foliage in the glistening waters that kiss their brownstone shores! A cruise among them for a few days even, and one becomes enchanted with their romantic beauty. And then there is such a variety in their wonderful formation that one never tires of their society. They seem to welcome one with their sheltering arms, safe harbors in all weather for all craft that visit them.

Almost every island has its own peculiarity, its bit of romance or its own curiosity to exhibit. Sailing among them they bear a considerable likeness to each other, but close inspection dissolves the illusion, for they differ very materially.

They are mostly rock-bottomed, their foundations being old Postdam sandstone, of the age of trilobites, which geologists claim to be the first evidence of life on the globe. If their theory be correct, then our isles are as old as life itself in any form, in this great mysterious world of ours. In these sandstone layers there are wonderful caverns shaped by the ceaseless waves that, during centuries, have carved them into magnificent grottoes and halls, connected and supported by grand arches and columns, requiring but a slight stretch of the imagination to transform into the ruins of some of the grand old cathedrals of the old world. Some of these "Nature pictures" are grand beyond conception, especially the group along the northeast face of Devil's Island, the outer sentinel to the north, where a bright light at night guides the sailor on his way.

This island from its exposed position receives the full force of the sea when the Storm King reigns, hence to a greater extent than the others of the group its rocky base is honeycombed into these wonderful forms. Here, with a small boat, one can, when the sea is calm, row hundreds of feet under the island, passing through vaulted chambers, supported by numerous pillars and arches, fine specimens of Nature's masonry, lighted by circular and gothic windows cut through walls of variegated stone. Truly some of the carved columns it is hard to believe Nature's work, so much do they resemble the work of man.

Devil's Island is owned by Uncle Sam and is reserved as a lighthouse station. On the north end, a temporary tower has been erected containing a light of the fourth order. Two steam fog horns are in position for service, one always being held in reserve. A fine, substantial brick residence shelters the lightkeeper and his family, which includes two stalwart assistants. On the southwest side and near the south end of the island nearly a mile distant, is the lifeboat station, a trail through the woods from the lighthouse leading to it.

During severe gales, the spray from the surging sea among the rocks below dashes over the tower, and at no point on the great lake can a grander view be had of a storm at sea. The island then resembles a leviathan ship, around which the sea rushes with terrific force, sending its foaming spray high into the air with an almost deafening roar, as though the world's artillery was engaged in a terrible battle beneath and around it.

"Four miles southeast of Devil's Island lies Rice's Island, its nearest neighbor. It is low, irregular and heavily wooded, extending from N.E. to S.W., four miles in length, an angle in the center forming a safe harbor on the southeast short. The extreme southwest point is a long sand and gravel reef, dropping into deep water a quarter of a mile from its base. The harbor is one of the most important fishing stations of the Booth Packing Company. There is a dock and warehouse, while scattered along the sandy beach is a number of rustic huts, the homes of the fishermen. This station is occupied all the year round, in winter by gillnetters, who fish on the outside reefs, using dog teams with which to haul in their catch.

Rice's Island is named after the late ex-United States Senator, Henry M. Rice of Minnesota, who purchased it years ago from the Government and to whose estate it still belongs.

It is designated on the charts as "Rocky Island." The soil is very poor, though there is a good spot on the east end where Mr. Rice had a clearing made in 1858, with a view to planting fruit trees, but the enterprise was soon after abandoned.

Close by Rice's, which shelters it from the north and west is Willey's Island, named after the Senator's life long friend, Dr. Samuel Willey, who died at Bayfield in 1872. Dr. Willey entered the island at the Government land office at the same time Senator Rice did and had it improved by clearing up a small farm. It was occupied and tilled by the veteran fisherman, John Smith, whose son, born on the island still lives near by on Rice's, following his father's calling.

The farm was deserted years ago and nature has covered it with a forest of "second growth." The soil is excellent for small fruits and vegetables and there is just enough of it, about four hundred acres, to make a good farm. It is heavily timbered with hard and soft woods and well sheltered from the storms, having an excellent harbor on the northwest side.

Willey's Island is called "South Twin" on the government charts but all our state maps designate these two as Rice's and Willey's and one seldom hears them spoken of in any other way and generally coupled together as "Rice and Willey's."

Northeast of Willey and distant four miles is "North Twin" a low flat piece of sandstone, covered with a coarse sand-gravel soil upon which is a thick growth of balsam, cedar, white birch and poplar, with now and then a ragged knurly hemlock, bent and twisted by the storms of many years.

This island has but few attractions, though its northern point, storm beaten and bleak, forms an interesting and rugged rock picture. It is sort of a halfway mark between Devil and Outer Island lights. Its isolation is such that it is seldom visited.

"East of North Twin and on a parallel north line with Devil's Island is the third largest of the group, Outer Island. Here, upon its extreme northern point is located the finest lighthouse on the upper lake. It is a round brick tower painted snow white, 78 feet high, which with land elevation, places the light 130 feet above the lake level. The light is a white flash of the third order and in clear weather, is frequently seen at Grand Marais 47 mils away on the north shore. At the base of the tower and connected with it by a covered way is the red brick dwelling of the keepers, a neat and tasty building.

Five hundred feet west of the tower the fog whistles are located, one of which is never silent when it is foggy weather, for this is a rough and dangerous coast with reefs of glacial boulders which line the northern and western shores. The elevation of the bank at the lighthouse is 52 feet from the water level and this is reached from the dock below by two separate flights of stairs containing over 100 steps each.

The dock is a solid crib, facing northeast and carries but four feet of water. There is a lifeboat house and a warehouse at the landing. Seen from the lake the tower and its cluster of buildings present a beautiful picture.

Outer Island differs from its associates in being almost entirely free from sandstone outcroppings, its banks being chiefly boulders and gravel supporting from thirty to fifty feet of red clay. The surface is a deep alluvial soil covered with a very heavy growth of sugar maple, birch and hemlock. There is, on the southwest end a small grove of Norway pine and a few small groves of white pine are to be found on the east side. The island contains about 15 sections of land, all fair farming land, capable of raising all kinds of root crops and grasses. If cleared of its timber, it would make a fine dairy country; in fact, would support a good-sized colony of farmers.

One drawback is the fact that there is no good harbor on the island, though one might be made by building a small breakwater in the little sandy bay at the south end, where a long reef extended southwest affords some natural protection from northeast gales. Outer Island is the nearest land on our coast to the North Shore and the sailor crossing, overlays his course for its friendly beacon, which is also hailed with delight by the crew of every storm-tossed vessel, seeking refuge among the Apostles.

Immediately west and five miles away is Cat or Hemlock Island, laying northwest by southeast four miles in length by about one mile in width. Unlike its neighbor, its shores are of solid stone, the northeast exposure being largely undermined with caverns, many of which are wonderful.

Twenty-three years ago, the largest cave known among the islands was one of this cluster, but the entire roof fell in during a terrible gale in September, 1873, and since then, the waves have beaten it into a shapeless mass of rocks.

The writer of this article visited this cave in 1870 with a party of jovial companions on board the yacht *Minne V* which sailed into it and tied up at "Table Rock" upon which all landed and partook of a fine picnic dinner. This rock was located in the center of the cave and was a solid round islet. At that time there was a circular cone in the roof of the chamber about twenty-five feet in diameter, through which a hemlock tree, fully twenty inches through was growing, the roots of which were embedded in the seams of the little island. The cave proper was about 50x90 by 40 feet high. There was plenty of room for the little steamer and the scene of that strange picnic with its romantic surroundings will always remain a vivid one.

The soil of Hemlock Island is cold and poor. It is covered with a dense hemlock forest scattered through which is some white pine of poor quality. Near the northwest end there is a small sand bay, which affords a fair shelter in a northeaster, and at the south end a sand spit runs for a quarter of a mile in a half circle forming a basin, the shore of which is lined with a beautiful grove of Norway. On the bank of this little harbor, beneath the shadows of the pines, is nestled a lonely cabin, the home of a fisherman–the only sign of life.

"Directly west of Hemlock (Island) lies a group of three very pretty islands, viz: Ironwood, Otter and Manitou. This group is separated by deep channels from one to one and a half miles wide. They are heavily wooded and possess a good soil. They are all well protected form the sea and in time will be settled. One of these, Otter, better known by the local name of Hardwood, is nearly round, and contains about 1,000 acres; the soil is rich and covered mainly with hardwood through which are scattered groves of "sugar pine."

Manitou is a rather low island, its shores being mostly of hardpan and gravel, though there are some sandstone exposures on the northwest side. This island lies northeast by southwest and on the southwest presents one of the greatest curiosities of the south shore, "The Little Devil." This strange formation is composed of clay and hardpan, resting upon sandstone boulders rising to a height of sixty feet above the sea at the end of a rocky reef, extending nearly across the channel, which separates it from its parent island. Though exposed to the fury of the elements for ages, it stands like a giant sentinel, guarding the reach before it. In length it is probably 500 feet, in width not over 150 at its base and 20 at its top in its widest place. Its crest is crowned on the north end and center with a few scattered evergreens, with two or three weather-beaten hemlock trunks, and on the south end by a series of hardpan cones, which afford an excellent rookery, for one of the two great families of gulls which rear their young on this coast. Seen from a distance, this remarkable islet greatly resembles a modern battleship with powerful ram and monitor-cased batteries. On a bright sunny day, the illusion is complete.

South by east of the last named triplet lies Presque Island, the second in size and the queen of them all. This beautiful island derives its name from a narrow peninsula extending south from the main body a mile and ending in a circular knob, "nearly an island" or in the French "pres-qu'ile." The government chart calls it Stockton Island, but it is never spoken of locally except by its old French voyageur title. The island contains upward of half a township; is heavily wooded, mostly with hemlock and pine. There is a fine maple and birch grove on the west end and a large cedar swamp and cranberry marsh in the center of the south tier of sections.

The island lays almost east and west, is about eight miles in length by an average of three miles in width. There are three excellent harbors, two on the south side and one east of the "knob." All are deep sandy bays, affording good anchorage and ample shelter. Presque Isle is founded on a rock and a good solid foundation it is, too.

At the southwest corner of the main island is located the quarry of the Ashland Brown-stone Company, one of the leading quarries on Lake Superior. Here, half way up the side of a steep brownstone bluff, which rises 90 feet in height, the works are located, surrounded by quite a village, all belonging to and a part of the plant. The company has put in a breakwater affording a safe harbor for their tugs and scows and extensive stone docks lined with steam derricks and tramways give them every facility for handling their product. The stone is the same as is quarried at other locations among the islands and on the main land, of excellent color and quality. The south side of the island is quite low, near the center a mere strip of sand beach, back f which lies the big swamp, half a mile wide and over a mile long. From the north side of the swamp, the land gradually rises to an elevation of from 40 to 50 feet. The peninsula is a narrow neck of sand covered with scrub pine and blueberry bushes. The knob is a pile of broken sand rock, crowned with a thick growth of balsams, white birch and poplar.

The bays are famous fishing grounds, both for netting and bobbing, and there is always a colony of fishermen on the island, winter and summer. The north shore of the island is a high steep bank of clay with gravel and frequent outcroppings of sandstone. It is a bold shore devoid of reefs and with but one small bay near the west end.

But it is the east and northeast end of grand Presque Isle that gives it prominence. Here is a most wonderful collection of natural curiosities. For nearly four miles the shore presents a high wall of solid brownstone cut and carved into fantastic shapes with caves and grottoes, arches and columns, and wide riffs into which the sea rushes like a maelstrom during stormy weather; the roar of which can be heard miles away. No pen can describe this wonderful scenery; it is simply grand and beautiful.

There are many prominent features such as "Lobster Point", a great arm of sandstone shaped like a lobster's claw: "Trip-hammer Point", an immense brownstone trip-hammer; "Silver Cascade", a very pretty feathery waterfall in a moss covered dell bordered wit evergreens; "Lone Rock", a beautifully molded islet nestled in a charming little cove: "The Sphinx", a wonderful stone photograph of the Egyptian original: "The Anvil" and the "Hammer of Thor" which guards the entrance to "Split Rock", a deep chasm 190 feet deep with perpendicular walls 50 feet high into which a good sized yacht can be run and completely hidden; together with hundreds of beautiful points all of great interest to visitors.

This upheaval of sandstone is undoubtedly the greatest on the south shore; certainly the most interesting. One has not seen the "Wonderland" of the islands if Presque Isle has been passed by.

"Southeast of Presque Isle lies Michigan Island with its satellite, Gull Island, the home of the second family of our graceful sea birds. Michigan Island light is one of the oldest stations on the upper lake; is a fixed white light of the three and a half order, visible for twenty miles. The tower is of the old fashioned round white style such as are often seen on the north Atlantic coast, built of stone and brick with a one story stone cottage at its base. The south end of the island upon which the light is located is a bold headland 85 feet above the sea, which with the tower, 44 feet in height, gives the lantern an elevation of 129 feet. At the base of the bluff, reached by a flight of stairs containing 99 steps is a plank walk leading to the life boat house. The light is the coast guide to Chewamic point via the south channel.

Michigan Island is three miles long and a mile wide, with deep clay soil covered with a mixed growth of timber. It is a pretty island with clean sand beach shores. In 1867, Mr. Pendergast, then lightkeeper, started a nursery near the tower and was quite successful with apples, plums and cherries, as well as small fruits. When he resigned in 1873, the nursery was distributed among his friends at Bayfield and Ashland and nothing now remains of his once beautiful garden except a few scattered cherry trees.

Gull Island lies northeast of Michigan, to which it is connected by a long rocky reef, over which there is seldom but little water. The island is a huge gravel drift thrown up by the sea. About two acres of it is covered with a stunted growth of mountain ash and willows. There is a low marsh in the center, containing a thick growth of wiregrass. The most of the island is a coarse gravel bed, though on the south end there is a bunch of red clay covered with scraggy bushes. The island is an immense rookery and here every year thousands of young gulls are reared. It is a great sight to witness the flight of these birds when disturbed. They rise in a cloud containing many hundreds and their plaintive cries can be heard a long distance from the shore. The island is sometimes occupied by fishermen who feed the gulls from their cleaning tables. They become quite tame under these circumstances, especially the young ones. Near the center of the east side there is a lonely hut and a few abandoned net reels. If it were not for the gulls, there would be little of interest attached to this barren and worthless spot.

Taking Devil's Island as our starting point, we have now described the northeastern part of the group which is much more numerous than the original twelve, containing double the number. How they received the name they bear is not recorded, but perhaps the early missionaries wishing to give them a pious turn, dubbed them the "Twelve Apostles." Investigation shows that Jonathan Carver was the first to give them their title in print, recording them in his book of early travels in the northwest as "Twelve Apostles."

Again taking Devil's Island as a guide, we run southeast four miles and enter a beautiful bay on the east side of Bear Island, one of the most imposing and interesting on the western side of the archipelago. It is nearly round, laying north and south, a high ridge running through the center attaining an elevation of 200 feet near the north end. It is three miles long and two wide, and with the exception of a lonely, deserted clearing on the west side is covered with a forest of hemlock and pine. The entire west side is a high clay drift, the banks steep with many boulders at their base. The East side is lined with a brownstone ledge 25 feet high, cut and carved into many curious features by the rolling seas from the north and northeast to which it is fully exposed.

"Pipestem Bay", the bay mentioned, is in nearly the center of the east coast line and has been cut out of this stone wall, in fact it has been beaten back inland by the great storms of the past centuries until it forms a beautiful circular basin half a mile across, which has in turn been filled with great drifts of white and amber sand, washed and separated into different grades, from grains the size of peas to drifts almost as fine as flour. There is also on the north end of this little bay a small drift of white and amber colored gravel, some of the stones of which are clear and quite brilliant.

Another curiosity is a great brownstone bathtub filled with water three feet deep. This is kept constantly fresh through a wave-worn channel running into the lake. The stone is an immense flat layer of rather soft sandstone, which the sea has gradually hollowed out to its own level, leaving a hardened rim, which forms the tub. It is fully 50 feet long and 20 feet wide.

The sandstone along the south shore of the bay is worthless for quarrying, as it is of many colors, much of it laminated and all more or less filled with gravel stones and agates. There is some that might be used on the extreme north end of the island, but it has broken into great blocks, which have tumbled into the sea in a chaotic mass.

On the extreme south end of the island, a sand spit runs out several hundred feet, fringed with Norway pine and water maples. It is an ideal campground with good protection on each side. It is known as "The Bear's Tail."

"Seven miles southwest of the head of Bear Island is Sand Island Light, a fixed white light of the fourth order, on the extreme northern point of Sand Island. This light is the guide to the northwest channel from the open sea. Outer Island light bears on Devil's Island light and Devil on Sand Island light, thus marking the outside course around the islands.

This lighthouse is modern in style and consists of an octagon tower 37 feet high attached to a story and a half dwelling, all built of variegated sandstone, quarried from the rocky point upon which it stands. The site and building is one of the beauty spots on our coast. From the tower, the view is indeed grand, the great sea stretching away to the north and west where the blue outline of the north shore can be seen from thirty to thirty seven miles distant. East and Southeast lie the islands spread out in a beautiful panorama, their green shores casting shadows upon the clear channels which surround them, forming a most interesting and charming picture. As the light is on the main course for all the craft which sail the lake, there is a grand procession of them constantly passing. On a bright summer day one can find no more beautiful spot from which to lazily watch the ships pass by.

Sand Island possesses many treasure in the way of natural art. On the extreme western point is "Grand Arch" a most wonderful structure. It has been photographed and painted by artists of high and low degree and is quite familiar. Bierstadt, the great American landscape painter, who visited the islands in 1878, was so pleased with it that he sketched it and afterward formed the subject of one of his little landscape gems.

The west side also possesses the largest and most perfect cave, known as "Trout Cave" to be found among the islands. This cave is entered through three circular openings rising out of the sea, just large enough to admit a small boat. Within the chamber expands into magnificent proportions, the valuted roof being fully thirty feet above the water. It is lighted through an oblong window high up one side and in the center, one can stand on a miniature island of stone and cast a line into the dark pools after the gamey brook trout which in the months of July and August, are frequently taken there.

On the west shore there are two excellent harbors, one near the lighthouse, where there is a good substantial pier, behind which is kept the government lifeboat, and the other at O'Malley's bay. Both afford good protection from the north and northeast. On the east side there are also two good arbors for all except northeasters, one at Justice's bay and one at Eat bay. These two beautiful harbors are separated by a long peninsula of solid sandstone rising to a height of 35 feet, the northeast exposure of which contains many beautiful caverns. In East bay is perhaps the most wonderful piece of natural rockwork to be found on the coast, "Temple Gate." This structure rises out of the water 35 feet high in the form of an arch, through the center of which extends a cross piece of stone. The sides are irregular columns of masonry laid up in courses and supporting the arch, which forms the top and is composed of several layers of soft variegated stone in the crevices of which a few balsam and spruce bushes seem to thrive. To crown the whole on the top nearly over the center of the arch, the bleak and barkless trunk of a pine tree, fully 30 feet in length, stands as a signal staff.

There is a settlement of Swede and Norwegian fishermen-farmers on East bay which bids fair to increase the numbers and prosperity for Sand Island contains much rich soil for farming which only needs clearing and improvement.

Sam Fifield (front left) with the steamer Stella at Shaw Point, Sand Island. Circa 1890
(Photo: Scott Hale Collection)

On the south side of the island there is an excellent harbor at Shaw's Landing, upon which is located "Camp Stella" where for the past 15 years, the white tents have been pitched and a happy party have enjoyed their outing every August. Captain Frank Shaw has a good snug farm at this point where he has been for the past twenty years engaged in fishing and farming. The nearness of Sand Island to the mainland makes it more desirable for settlement than any of the other islands and it is justly a favorite place with sportsmen and campers. The island contains nearly 3,000 acres most of which is good soil and fairly well timbered.

"Five miles southwest of Sand Island lie the last two islands to the westward, Steamboat and Little Steamboat. Steamboat is designated on the chart as Eagle Island. It is small and is covered with balsam, poplar and birch. Little Steamboat is a bunch of hardpan clay and a reef of boulders and gravel, with a covering of evergreens, the whole together having an area of less than one acre. These islands lie close together having an area of less than one acre. These islands lie close together and were without doubt originally one. A reef extends from them far to the westward and is a favorite fishing ground, especially for winter, 'bobbing' through the ice.

(Is it true that Little Steamboat Island sank during a terrible fall storm, and if so, what year?)

York Island lies directly east of Sand and about two miles distant. It is low and sandy and thinly wooded. A fine sand beach bay occupies two-thirds of the north side, and there is an old fishing station on the east end.

Raspberry Island is a high knob containing about 300 acres, and lies on the northwest steamboat channel. On the southwest point is located a white flash light of the fifth order, which is elevated in a tower on the frame residence of the keeper, 77 feet above the lake level. This light is a guide to vessels passing through the channel and ranges with Sand

Island light. At the foot of the bank there is a lifeboat dock and boathouse, from which a long flight of stairs leads to the top.

Raspberry Island is very inviting in appearance. In the clearing in which the lighthouse is located, there is a fine lawn and an excellent garden, with small fruits and flowers and it is a charming place to visit.

Southeast of Raspberry lies Oak Island, fourth in size and of the greatest elevation, its hills rising fully four hundred feet above its companions and affording an excellent landmark far out at sea. In crossing the lake from the North Shore, the first land seen is the hazy outlines of Oak. The island has high, bold shores, and is heavily wooded in which hardwood predominates. The soil is red clay and the foundation sandstone which outcrops on the east side, where "Oak Head" a great brownstone point, is the single scenic feature.

On one of the hills there is an exposure of lean magnetic iron ore, the only mineral known to exist among the islands. In old times, Oak Island was quite an important point as there was a wood yard established there where wood was furnished steam vessels, which in the early days used it exclusively for fuel on Lake Superior.

The west side forms the east shore of the northwest channel. The banks are high clay drifts, wit deep water to within a stone's throw except at the south point, where a long circular sandbar runs out into the main thoroughfare for over half a mile.

While Oak Island is a fine large island, no one seems to like it well enough to make a settlement upon it, and with the exception of lumbermen who, in the winter, occasionally put in a camp to cut saw logs it is entirely deserted."

(In later years there was some one who liked it well enough to live there. He was Martin Kane, King of Oak Island. It would be nice to have a chapter about him in the Bayfield history. Who knows where he came from, when, or why he chose to live alone on Oak Island? If I can gather enough information about him, we will have a chapter on the "King.")

"South by east of Oak is Wilson or Hermit Island. In every large family there is always some particular one selected as the beauty, and so it is with the Apostles. Wilson is the beauty of the family. It lies east and west at the base of the two main channels separated by Oak, a snug, brownstone-bottomed oval and oblong island with a bouquet of evergreen and hardwood forest crowning its banks. In all there is about 800 acres of it and every acre good soil except on the east and where the outcropping brownstone presents its bold face to the sea. Here on a great ledge that extends inland for half a mile or so is located the Excelsior Brownstone quarry, belonging to Mr. Frederick Prentice. This property is considered one of the best brownstone properties on the lake, as the stone is of first quality and practically inexhaustible. Near the quarry on a projecting point of stone forty feet above the sea, Mr. Prentice has built a summer residence known as "Bark Cottage" it being completely shingled with cedar bark, an idea retreat, its verandas facing the east and a vista that is a dream of beauty, a poem in itself. A fine, natural lawn, a high flag staff from which "old glory" floats to the summer breeze, a romantic windmill and rustic seats and shade trees are the settings, which adorn and embellish this lovely spot.

Near the west end and facing south there is a large grove of second growth birch and maples intermixed with stately balsams, whose perfect spires rise above them like steeples. This spot was once a garden surrounding a small log hut, the home of "Wilson, the

Hermit." He was a strange old man, silent and grave with no companions or friends. He seldom left his island place where he worked away alone in the summer tilling his garden and attending to the wants of his chickens and dogs, of which he had a large number, the latter savage brutes in whose love he found his only solace. In winter he made fish barrels, for sometime in his life he had learned the cooper's trade.

He came to LaPointe in 1841 and for a time worked at his trade in the American Fur Company's shop. He was evidently a hard drinker and his personal appearance indicated that he had endured many hardships. Soon after he located in LaPointe, he and Judge Bell, then in the prime of life, fell out, and the result was that Wilson got the worst of the encounter and swore he would never live where he was not the "best man." Soon after, he went to Wilson Island and built his cabin, remaining there until his death. He soon became sullen and ugly, allowing but very few to visit him and, on several occasions, it is said that he used his gun to drive away unwelcome meddlers.

Wilson was a well educated man, and it was told the writer in 1870, by one who knew the lonely old voyageur well, that he had been in the employ of the American Fur Company since a very young man, having enlisted with Ramsey Crooks as a hunter, and made the overland trip to Astoria, enduring all the hardships of that ill-fated enterprise. He came through to Lake Superior from a trading post on the Missouri when he came to LaPointe. That he had a hidden history is quite evident, for he could never be prevailed upon to speak of his early home.

For many years he purchased his supplies at Bayfield, always paying for them in specie, mostly in Mexican silver dollars. He came there once or twice a year to transact his business, remaining only long enough to load up his boat with his goods. Because he always had money for all his needs, rumors among the people living in Bayfield and LaPointe attributed to him some dark crime by which he had come by it unlawfully, and many wild stories were told of him which had no foundation in truth. It was our informant's opinion that he had but little money and that his savings from his service as hunter and voyageur and from the sale of his barrels was all he had.

In 1861, he was found dead in his cabin where he had undoubtedly been murdered as everything had been overturned, evidently by parties in search of his wealth. Judge Bell, as county judge, had his body brought to LaPointe and it was buried in the old cemetery, where he sleeps in an unmarked and unknown grave.

When Judge Bell searched the premises he found a shot sack in the clock, which had been overlooked containing 35 Mexican dollars, all the money ever known to have been discovered, though parties for years after his death searched the premises, literally tearing his home to pieces in search for his gold.

In looking over the site of the Hermit's home not long ago, we found the decaying foundation of his root-house and could discern by outlines in the soil the place where his cabin stood. He chose a beautiful spot in which to hide himself from his fellow men and where for many years he alone was master. And from this, the story of Wilson the Herman, the island takes its name.

"A little west of south (from Wilson Island) two miles distant is Basswood, or as commonly called, "Bass Island." It is another beautiful member of the Apostles, nearly twice the size of Wilson. It is noted as being the site of the Superior Brownstone quarry, the first to be opened in this district, in 1869. For the past two years it has been worked but little, though the lessee, Captain W. H. Singer, has it well equipped with machinery and will resume business when the times improve.

Col. C. P. Rudd has a farm near the center of the island on the west side and near by is the homestead of Judge McCloud, who for many years has lived alone on the island, leading an almost hermit life.

Basswood is timbered like the rest, with perhaps more hardwood than is usually found. On the southeast side a quarry was started by Duluth parties in 1890, but after spending considerable money in building houses and clearing, the property was abandoned.

Bass Island has its natural curiosity to present as well as the reset in "Profile Rock," located near the north end, a most striking and interesting feature. There are also a number of rock pictures along the northeast exposure where the waves have left their impress upon its foundation walls.

Last comes fair Madeline, the most noted of all. It lies to the southwest of the rest, its trend being northeast and southwest 12 miles long and an average of three in width. Its foundation is a poor quality of brownstone, which shows in numerous ledges along its shores, that in general are of clay drift, full of boulders, steep, ragged and irregular from the washing rains and heaving frosts. The southwest end forms the north side of the south channel at the entrance to Chequamegon Bay, opposite Chewamic point and light which is a red flash light of the fourth order.

Madeline Island will some day be settled by farmers. The soil is good and will support quite a community. Of course, like all the islands, it is heavily wooded; hence its improvement will be slow and not until all the most valuable timber is exhausted, for it is not mostly held for its timber values. The surface is gently rolling attaining in places an elevation of 150 feet, but generally speaking it is only rolling enough for good drainage. Its northwest coast is the lowest and quite straight, with but one shallow sandy bay, while on the east side, the coast line is broken with two deep bays, one Big Bay extending inland over a mile and a half, bordered with a beautiful sand beach, lined with a scattered fringe of Norway pines. This is a famous blueberry patch and the Indians gathered hundreds of bushels of them here every year. Back of this bay is a lake nearly two miles in length, filled with small, swampy islands, the shores lined with fragrant pond lilies. The water is quite deep in places, but darkly covered with tamarack root, just such water as the Pike family thrives in. Through a bayou, at the extreme northeast end of the bay, the lake finds an outlet. The bay and lake is often visited by sportsmen as it is good duck ground in season and there are plenty of pike and perch for the angler in June, while later in the season the pond lilies are plenty. At the head of the lake there is a cranberry marsh where the Indians gather their supplies of the delicious fruit.

Between Madeline and Michigan there is a dangerous reef of boulders along which in winter the fishermen catch the Mackinaw trout with hooks through the ice. In early days when the fish were more plenty than now, the Indians used to go there for their winter's supply, camping out in great numbers and following the reef with their holes across the channel to Michigan Island which they called "Bug-a-da-by-Minis", or hook and line island.

"Madeline Island figures in history as the first site occupied by the Ojibwas when they emigrated from the St. Lawrence Valley in Canada to Lake Superior according to the best authorities about four hundred years ago. They chose the island as it afforded them protection from their dreaded enemies, the Sioux, into whose territory they had come to make themselves a home, having been driven from their own land by the fierce and bloody Iroquois, and for the further reason that there was an abundance of fish in the channel which could easily be taken with their crude nets and spears.

It was also the site of the first white settlement on our northern boundary. Ancient LaPointe has figured extensively in the history of the northwest. Here all the great fur companies of history have in their day had trading posts and received recognition from the governments under which they lived.

As early as 1718, the Northwest Fur Company established a post there and the government of New France occupied the southeast point of the island with a fort, which was garrisoned by a company of French regulars. This fort was built by Captain St. Perrie in 1718, who was in command until relieved by Siedn De Linclot in 1726, who was sent there by his government to negotiate a peace between the Ojibwa and Sioux.

When the French were succeeded by the British, Fort St. Perrie was abandoned and it became a trading post. When the United States, after the war of 1812, took possession of the country, Michael Cadotte was in possession of the old fort as a trader.

In 1818, John Jacob Astor made LaPointe headquarters for the northwest trade of the American Fur Company. It was under this rule that LaPointe reached the measure of its greatness. The population reached high water mark in 1830-5 about 2,500 souls, traders, voyageurs, half-breeds and Indians.

Bishop Baraga, during the year 1834, founded the fist Catholic Mission at LaPointe and in 1835 built the old church that still stands as a monument to his zeal. In 1835, the Rev. Sherman Hall established a Protestant Mission at "Middle Port" halfway between the village and the old French fort and the old Mission house as well as the little church in the village, built in 1836, still remain to mark the field of his labors.

The American Fur Company wound up its affairs in 1857 and since then, LaPointe has gradually wasted away. The buildings at the old fort long since disappeared and now the once garrisoned camp from whose flagstaff floated the Lilies of France is a deserted waste.

There are four cemeteries at LaPointe where the dust of Christian and Pagan mingle together. In one of these near the old Catholic church, John W. Bell, "King of the Apostle Islands" sleeps soundly, while at the "old Catholic burial ground" at Middle port the dust of old Chief Buffalo, whose forefathers first brought life to the inland wilderness mingles with the mother earth. On a hillside nearly half way between the old Mission and Fort Point is the lonely Protestant cemetery where many Protestant settlers of the early days lie deserted and forgotten; while near the site of the ancient French fort on the bank where the waves beat their requiem is deposited the dust of soldier, trader and voyageur, who were laid to rest nearly two centuries ago.

Of the later history of LaPointe, much of interest might be written, but it is not essential. It was the capital of the first county organized on our shore of the great lake, the county of LaPointe, and later, when absorbed by the counties of Bayfield and Ashland, it also retained the seat of government of the latter until 1874 when it was removed to the city of Ashland, thus ending its political importance.

The LaPointe of today is, however, very interesting to the visitor and in summer is a favorite camping ground. The village is the seat of justice for the Town of LaPointe, composed entirely of islands with a population of 300 souls. There have been quite a number of summer cottages erected on the site of the ancient village during the past few years and it bids fair to become a summer resort not only for strangers who seek our invigorating climate, but for our own people as well, who love its rustic simplicity and romantic associations."

(Some readers will undoubtedly ask, 'Why did he skip Long Island?' It is probably because even at that time it wasn't considered a real island, but a point. It did not become an island until sometime in the 1820s. When Mr. Fifield did refer to what we now call Long Island, he called it Chewamic Point.)

Travel by Horse

THE BAYFIELD HISTORY WOULD NOT be complete without mention of a hard working friend of the pioneers—the horse. Bayfield was not a covered wagon town, it was a lake town, built by steamboats, sailboats and even rowboats, but on the small farms, the big logging camps and for land travel, the horse was essential.

It is not surprising that a lake town developed some seafaring horses, as recounted from this item in *The Bayfield Press* January 9, 1897. "Napoleon Rabideaux took a logging team from Rice's Island to Oak Island, a distance of ten miles, on a cedar raft 11' x 24' last Sunday during the heavy northeast snow storm. The raft was towed by rowboat and guided by a pair of oars in the stern. When opposite Hardwood Island, the raft came very near going to pieces. It was taken ashore, repaired and the balance of the trip was made without accident.

Horses were also ice travelers. On Sunday, January 28, 1900, the first horse to cross on the ice from LaPointe that winter came hitched to a sleigh by a rope 50 feet long.

And the horses didn't always make it. April 6, 1906, *The Press* reported: "Tuesday, R. J. Russell lost a team of horses and sleigh through the ice while crossing from Bayfield to LaPointe. There were several passengers along and all succeeded in escaping, although one lady, Mrs. Bently, had a close call owing to her efforts to save the children in the sleigh. This is the first accident of the kind this spring. There will be others if you don't keep off the ice!

Seventy-three years ago the fishermen stayed out on the islands winter, as well as summer, and the hardworking horses plodded around among the islands, gathering the catch. Jan. 26, 1884 this item appeared in *The Press:* "Fish are cash these days, being worth five cents a pound on the ice. Teams are making weekly pilgrimages among the islands, picking up fish caught at the several stations."

Civilization was coming fast in 1886. A carriage road was being thought of. On July 24, 1886, *The Press* said: "The Washburn Bee is advocating the building of a carriage road connecting Washburn and Bayfield. The idea is a good one, although three years old. *The Bayfield Press* advocated this over three years ago and have built the road along the bay shore to Sioux River, with the understanding that the people of Washburn would build north to the same stream and then, if the county could not be persuaded to build a bridge across that stream, the two towns should unite in doing so."

As early as 1871 R.D. Pike and J.A. McClusky formed the Bayfield, Superior, Duluth Stage Co. Stages of that line carried freight and passengers. (Photo: BHA)

Before the carriage road was built, the only way to go to Ashland was by boat in the summer or on the ice in the winter. On Bayfield's twenty-first birthday, March 24, 1877, Sam Fifield wrote in The Ashland Press: "A very pleasant ride on the ice with genial companions was our experience last Saturday. We found the beautiful little village all there without spot or blemish. We were kindly greeted by its many warm-hearted citizens and felt, as we always do, perfectly at home. Bayfield contains many courteous friends that it is always a pleasure to meet, and if our neighbors did but realize it, it is one of the features that make Bayfield so popular as a resort. A stranger, when he visits Bayfield, is always entertained handsomely, and we were not surprised to hear one of our companions express himself, "I am surprised to meet so many well informed, fine, genial and courteous people in so small a village. I feel perfectly at home already." Exactly, and it is one of Bayfield's best recommendations."

There was nothing deluxe about horse and wagon travel. *The Ashland Press* described this trip made by Mrs. Davis in 1874. "Mrs. E.C. Davis returned from a visit with friends in Winona. She cam via the Duluth route through the storm of last Saturday and Sunday and was much fatigued from the journey. Between Superior City and the Brule station the road was so badly drifted that the driver was compelled to stamp the snow down for the horses until he became so cold and exhausted as to be obliged to lie down under the buffalo robes and Mrs. Davis drove the team 16 miles herself arriving at the station after nightfall. The horses had all they could do in some of the drifts to draw the sleigh its length without stopping to rest."

Thirty-one years later, there still were no snowplows and the stages were having rough going. Dec. 1, 1905, *The Press* said: "The Cornucopia stage left that place at 6 AM Thursday and arrived here at 5 PM the same day. The trip is usually made in three hours."

In April 1906, Dr. Anderson went to Cornucopia on horseback and reported the road in very bad condition with "patches of sleighing, then wheeling, then mud, then profanity."

"While stepping out of a two seated buggy, George Sawyer, Bayfield resident, was run down by a dray and badly injured. The accident took place at the corner of Second Street and Rittenhouse Avenue, near the St. James Hotel. Mr. Sawyer had just alighted from the rig and stopped to speak to the driver when he was struck by the hub of the front wheel of a single dray, which came suddenly around the corner. The force of the contact threw him to the ground and the back wheel ran completely over him, inflicting very painful, if not serious, injuries. He was taken to the boarding house of Mrs. Arseneau on Front Street, where he received medical attention. He was then taken to an Ashland Hospital. Eyewitnesses state that a little more care on the part of the driver of the dray would have averted the accident, as they state the dray was driven too fast around the corner."

July 30, 1909. "Quite a little excitement was created on Second Street Monday at about 1:30 PM, when a heavy work team belonging to the Bayfield Mill Company engaged in a wild run down the street. The team got away from the driver on top of the hill at the corner of Rice Avenue and Second Street when the planks on the wagon slid forward striking the horses. This so frightened them that they started on a mad dash down the hill and were only prevented from doing themselves greater damage by colliding with a tree at the corner of Second Street and Rittenhouse Avenue. Andy Gavin, the driver, was thrown from the wagon. The horses tried to turn down Rittenhouse, but could not make the turn. They ran into the ditch in front of the pharmacy and then up on the sidewalk across the street before straddling a tree. The wagon overturned, the driver was thrown about 20 feet, but was only scratched. The horses ran so fast that when they hit the tree the harness of one horse snapped like strings and he was stripped of every vestige of harness.

The late A. H. Wilkinson wrote this account of his experience with a runaway team. "The team was a fine pair of bays from Nelson's livery. One of the horses liked to run away and was usually controlled with a choker bit. The other horse would run with him. A new barn boss did not know about the runaway horse and gave him to me with an ordinary bridle. I drove out back of Pike's Bay. Theodore Wieland rode out with me. It was a nice day in late fall. The ground was frozen solid. Everything worked fine until we reached the top of Pike's Bay hill on our way home, then everything happened. The team broke into a run and we made the rest of the way to the edge of town in about two minutes. Theodore climbed out over the back of the buckboard and dropped to the ground without being badly hurt. It was late in the afternoon and quite dark. As I neared the first turn into town, I saw a team with a wagon ahead of me. The road was narrow, but I pulled the team over to pass the wagon and when the buckboard dropped partly over the side of the embankment, I floated out into space, landing in the bottom of the ravine on a brush pile. The team ran on, but failed to make the next turn. They straddled an electric light pole, bumped their heads together and the fun was over. Those who saw us said it was quite a show. It was talked about for a long time."

Horses were a hazard to the first automobiles, and vice-versa. In another account of the early day cars, Mr. Wilkinson has written as follows: "A story printed in *The Press* several years ago gave me credit for bringing the first automobile into Bayfield County. I believe that statement is correct. It was a model T Ford shipped in from Minneapolis, after snow time, in the spring of 1909... It was necessary to ship in your own gas, oil, and grease, and if your car needed repairs you just had to get down and get under. With the roads as they were then the old machines gave plenty of trouble. I have another record. I changed tires thirteen times and patched eleven inner tubes one night while driving from Washburn to Bayfield. My old friend, Frank Burlingame, who liked to cuss was with me. It was a great opportunity for him to express our feelings. I believe horses gave early drivers more trouble than any other one thing they had to contend with. Whenever a team of horses saw one of these monsters coming toward them on a narrow road they simply became unmanageable. The only thing to do was to stop the car and lead the horses up to it. It was no use trying to drive them, but by leading them they would quiet down, and by doing this, the first drivers avoided causing many serious accidents.

Albert D. Anderson of Ashland sent the account of the first automobile to come to Bayfield. The car belonged to Dr. W. T. Rinehart, of Ashland. On July 21, 1903, it made a "quick" trip to Bayfield to deliver *The Ashland Press* with news of the death of Pope Leo. Chauffeur Edwin Reynolds of Minneapolis, was at the brake. The time it took: Ashland to Nash, thirty minutes; Nash to Washburn twenty-two minutes; stayed in Washburn forty five minutes; Washburn to Bayfield, fifteen miles of corduroy roads, sand and hills, sixty minutes; stopped twice for teams; was in Bayfield thirty minutes. This is the first time an automobile was seen on the streets of Bayfield. (Fifty-four years later you can hardly park.)

Return trip–Bayfield to Washburn thirty minutes; Washburn to Nash twenty minutes; Nash to Ashland fifteen minutes. This car got up to a speed of forty-five miles an hour on good roads.

Roads and Horses

ON FEBRUARY 23, 1883, THE Bayfield Press said proudly, "Bayfield has two very fair carriage roads extending up and down the bay for several miles. The one leading to Red Cliff, 5 miles up the bay, being so far as beauty is concerned, one of the handsomest drives in the country.

In October 1905, it was expected that the new wagon road around the head of the bay between Washburn and Ashland would be completed in another month.

August 31, 1907, *The Press* reported: "The wagon road from Bayfield to Washburn is in fine condition, baring two or three places near Houghton Point. It is a beautiful drive along the lake shore and is well patronized these fine days."

Every family did not own a horse and tourists arriving by boat enjoyed short scenic jaunts with horse and buggy, therefore, the livery business became a thriving one. June 28, 1890, *The Press* said: "C. L. Willey has opened a livery barn near Rittenhouse Avenue and Second Street. He has a comfortable two-seated carriage, besides numerous single rigs and a good outfit of horseflesh. Give him a call."

During a February thaw in 1907, the livery business boomed. "Last Sunday was one of the warmest days we have had since last November and was a banner day with the liverymen of the city. Many people took advantage of the pleasant weather and every available livery rig in the city was in use. Several parties drove up from Washburn and spent the day in the Harbor City."

To change your mind is not strictly a woman's privilege. June 11, 1909 *The Press* had this item: "Peter Edlund last year decided that Bayfield was too small for his business and removed his livery outfit to Ashland. This week he decided to return to his first love and has rented his old stand, the A.B. Sayles barn on First Street."

The horse and buggy days imply a time of serene, plodding horses. However, there were times when horses were more dangerous than horsepower, and much more unpredictable.

The following items taken from *The Bayfield Press* illustrate this point.

September 21, 1906. "August Turnquist's delivery horse got away from its driver Monday morning and took a run down Rittenhouse Avenue. When opposite Turnquist's store, it ran into Kranzfelder's delivery wagon, throwing it to the sidewalk. Mr. Turnquist's little boy, who was standing on the sidewalk, was struck by Kranzfelder's wagon and his leg broken above the knee. He was taken to an Ashland hospital. Turnquist's delivery wagon was badly smashed."

July 19, 1907. "T.J. Stevenson of Minneapolis, "Father of Cornucopia," had a rather peculiar accident Monday night while enroute to Cornucopia. The team Mr. Stevenson was driving was frightened by a large bear, which stood in the highway, and they backed off a log fill, throwing Mr. Stevenson out of the rig and into a puddle of water. One horse, which had fallen back into the buggy smashing it considerably, was extricated with difficulty."

October 9, 1908. "In a mad rush down Second Street and Fant Avenue last Sunday evening, a heavy work team belonging to A.J. Mussell caused considerable damage. The driver was; just in the act of driving into the alley entrance on Washington Avenue between Broad and Second Street after returning from the days work at Red Cliff, when the horses became frightened and started on a wild gallop down Washington Avenue. The team swerved into Second Street and dashed down the hill as far as Fant Avenue. Here they turned onto Fant Avenue and started east. They were unable to make the corner and collided with a railway switch, the wagon rebounding clear across the street and striking a tree. The driver, Steve Rockwood, was thrown out and the team, breaking loose, continued its wild run. Reaching First Street, the team barely cleared several trees and finally wound up colliding with a small tree. One horse was thrown and entangled in the harness. Here they were found later and released. It is astonishing the speed a team like this can obtain, as the wagon collided with such force against the railway switch as to twist the iron rods completely out of shape, and itself, although a heavy lumber wagon, was thrown about 15 feet. The driver was thrown a distance of 30 to 40 feet from appearances, although it is thought by some that he was dragged while holding the reins. He, however, cannot tell, as the accident happened so quickly he knows very little about it. When found the driver was lying beside the railway tracks, covered with blood and badly hurt, his injuries consisting of scratches, bruises and an injured side."

October 23, 1908 *The Press* had an editorial complaining because the wagon box from the wreck had not been removed from Fant Avenue, saying, "Very, very neglectful, indeed we might say extremely neglectful. Why isn't it removed?

Early Cars and Roads

WITH THE ADVENT OF AUTOMOBILES came a demand for good roads, or, at least, passable ones. Facts had to be faced. A car could not go where a horse could and people who owned cars were determined to have a place to drive them. In March 1909, the *Duluth Herald* reported: "An automobile road along the south shore of Lake Superior is a possibility. The Bayfield Commercial Club is trying to interest Duluth and Superior enthusiasts in the project. Duluth autoists have been handicapped thus far by a lack of suitable country roads; the proposed road would offer one of the finest automobile driveways in the Middle West. It is contended the expense would be light, for the road would closely follow the lake shore almost the entire distance and little clearing of trees and stumps would be necessary. The Bayfield Commercial Club has taken the trouble to have a committee traverse the route with a team, and according to the report, there are several roads, which could be utilized, and these, with strips of beach adapted to teams and automobiles would hold the cost of improvement to a minimum. Scenically, the ride would beat anything offered in the state, aside from short drives, like Duluth's boulevard. If the road could be brought to a proper stage of perfection, it might develop into one of the most famous speedways in the west."

Two years later, in July 1911, the McHenrys decided to try to drive from Duluth to Bayfield. The Progress gave this account of their trip: "Last week George A. McHenry, Mrs. McHenry and their son, Allan, went to Duluth and purchased a fine $1,900 Cadillac automobile. They decided to return via the highways of Douglas and Bayfield Counties, leaving Duluth on Friday with Harry Bergher of Duluth as chauffeur in charge... Before reaching Brule, they encountered some of the old fashioned corduroy roads built of poles and logs such as our grandfathers used to tell us about, the logs being nearly afloat in places... The first night they were welcomed at the camp of Lawyer Stone of Chicago. Harry and Allan stayed by the machine enjoying a fine rest in its upholstered seats O.K. They decided to take a short cut to Herbster and Cornucopia, but although they were directed on what they supposed was the right road, after traveling some distance, they landed in the yard of a settler and a little boy had to cut down a number of bushes and young trees to turn the auto around... Presently the road led down a ravine and there being no chance to turn around and too uncertain as to attempt further progress up an uncertain hill in the night, the boys decided to stay with the machine for the night while Mr. and Mrs. McHenry walked in seven miles to Herbster where they found rest and refreshments of which they felt much in need.

Sunday morning, after getting help to pilot the machine over that hill and some mucky roads, they landed in Cornucopia. Someone directed them to Bayfield via Washburn, instead of by the settlement and it was no doubt a mistake for when they struck the sand beds of the blueberry barrens, the sand in places let the machine in clear to the hubs, necessitating in one instance the getting of a team to help them out of the difficulty. It was learned afterward that the clutch was not working just right to assist them, which was easily adjusted when discovered. Such a trip should be taken by the supervisors of both counties. It might spur them to carry along those planned boulevards or county highways to and from the Twin Ports to Bayfield."

The next year in September 1912, four cars went from Bayfield to the State Fair in Milwaukee. The autos all bore the pennant "Bayfield" and H.C. Hale's car had "Bayfield, Biggest, Badger Booster." A carload of fruit and other farm samples from Bayfield had been sent down earlier. H.C. Hale, wife and daughter, Margaret, left Saturday morning at 4 o'clock. B.J. Bracken, wife, Mr. and Mrs. J. Long, and Freddie Wachsmuth left at 5 o'clock. Frank Boutin and wife, sons Dode, Hilliard and daughter Dorothy left at quarter to seven. H.J. Wachsmuth and wife left the next morning. The Bayfield Progress had this report: "By wireless we learned that all was well until near Butternut. Mr. Hale's auto skidded into a ditch and fortunately Frank Boutin arrived on the scene and pulled his machine onto dry land. We learned of no other serious mishaps except two or three blowouts, which were soon repaired, and all arrived at Marshfield in the evening, leaving Sunday after a good rest. It was reported by a later dispatch that H.J. Wachsmuth went 210 miles the same day with his J.K. Case car, which would mean that he must have spent Sunday night in Marshfield."

To travel the roads at all you had to buy a guidebook. This route from Ashland to Marengo was published and copyrighted in 1912 by M.C. Moore. At Ashland, set speedometer at .0 with City Hall at left. Go out with trolley, following same out of city. At 6.8 miles, bear slightly left. Caution for dangerous sharp descent and ascent. Must have chains if at all wet. At 7.1 miles, bear right at fork and go over White River dam. Dangerous high clay causeway. At 11.0 miles, go 90 degrees left leaving wires. Frame house at right just before turn. Go straight ahead to end of road. When the speedometer showed 16.8 miles you should be in Marengo and if you were the station would be at your right. If you were not there you would have to do the best you could.

By 1915, a law had been passed saying there should be guide signs on the roads, but there were continual complaints from lost motorists that guide signs had never been put up.

Lumbering

The Henry Wachsmuth saw mill, circa 1920. In 1904, R. D. Pike sold this sawmill to Henry Wachsmuth, a German immigrant. Sam Vaughn, R. D. Pike and Wachsmuth employed thousands of hardy lumberjacks, teamsters, sawyers and local merchants for nearly 75 years. (Photo: BHA)

THOUGH THE GREAT LUMBERING INDUSTRY of Wisconsin is not far in the past, a mere fifty years or so, a lot of it has already been forgotten. The annual arrival of thousands of men in a community is recalled by this item from The Bayfield Press in November 1906.

"It is estimated that close on to 2,000 men have arrived in Bayfield this fall to work in the lumber camps in the surrounding country and that about 300 have come in to participate in the herring fishing."

There were giant trees, giant logs and giant loads of logs. *The Bayfield Press* reported all of these. Feb. 28, 1891, "Martin Gleason, who is scaling at Sutherland Bros. camp on Sec. 32, T51 R 5 W gives the scale of a tree cut last week which is the largest so far reported in Bayfield county. Mr. Gleason calls the tree, "The King of Bayfield County." The scale was as follows:

Butt	16 feet long	1,780 feet
Next	16 feet long	1,530 feet
Next	16 feet long	1,280 feet
Next	14 feet long	980 feet
Next	16 feet long	800 feet
Next	16 feet long	500 feet
Total	94 feet	6,870 feet

It took awhile to grow trees like this, longer than a man lives. March 8, 1890: "It is estimated it requires from 125 to 150 years of forest growth to perfect a merchantable pine tree."

May 3, 1907, "The largest log ever sawed in the Wachsmuth Lumber Company Mill was cut Thursday evening. It was one of the largest logs ever seen in this vicinity and measured

16 feet in length, five feet across the butt and four feet across the top. It scaled 1,500 feet of lumber. It was found necessary to use an extra chain and small engine to haul the log up into the mill and it required the united efforts of ten men to handle the log on the log deck."

March 12, 1909. "What was probably the largest load of logs that was hauled in this vicinity this winter was taken to the landing Thursday at W.J. Laughren's camp. The load scaled a trifle over 11,000 feet and was hauled to the landing by Bert Soper with a team weighing thirteen hundred. Oscar Jeffers scaled the logs."

Feb. 23, 1906. "The largest load of logs hauled this winter was by Ben Conlon at Arcie McPhee's camp, 128 logs."

Feb. 1884. "The first sale of this season's cut of logs that has come to the notice of *The Press* was made this week by George B. Best to Sheriff and Son, consisting of 4,000,000 feet on White River and Outer Island. Price–$10 per thousand.

Snow was essential to the loggers. Not too much, but just enough. Sometimes it was one way, sometimes the other. January, 1906 *The Press* had this notice. "Loggers want no more snow. The snowman is requested to take due notice and govern himself accordingly."

In January, 1908, there was not enough snow. Small loggers were ceasing their operation because of the lack of snow. They had not been able to make even ice roads to haul on. Not enough snow had fallen to cover the ground. Signs of spring had already been reported in late January. A flock of wild geese went north. Bushes budded out and a buttercup in full bloom was picked in the ravine and placed on display at the Pharmacy. The ice harvest was in danger.

About January 31 that year three men were caught in the loose ice between Bayfield and Presque Island. They had been employed in logging on the island and had quit their work, starting to town in a sailboat. A few miles away from the island they encountered an ice floe, which packed in around their boat so tight they couldn't move. The weather was mild and the ice chunks, which held them, were in such poor condition the men did not dare to attempt to cross them. They had no food or fuel aboard, but in an old bailing can they burned what spare clothing they had with them to keep from freezing to death. They stayed there three days, until a cold spell one night came to their relief. The ice formed solidly enough to hold the chunks together and the men dared to walk across it to Bayfield.

Of course, the Bayfield Transfer kept busy hauling logs to town to the mill. The Progress had this item on August 4, 1910. "Word was telephoned in about four o'clock from the Transfer crew hauling logs for the Wachsmuth Lumber company that the Raspberry bridge was burned and that the train is on the other side, unable to come in."

I searched through the files further to find out how the Transfer got to town, but its arrival was never reported, so maybe its still out there.

Logging Accidents

THE ACCIDENTS IN THE LOGGING camps and in the work related to logging were terrible. There were so many accidents at the camp on Presque Island in the early 1900's that the Bayfield Progress commented on it. When the camp manager came to town, he explained there were bound to be accidents where so many men were gathered for such a large logging operation.

He was right, for as I searched further I realized that many of the men must have been incompetent. In one case one of them suffered from such delusions that he jumped down the stack of one of the tugs and was burned and smoked to death. Among the wandering, homeless groups there were, of course, others. Young men moving West, saving money for a good start in life. Some were learning the logging business, getting ready to start camps of their own.

Some of them were killed in the accidents. Some survived their injuries with the crudest home treatment. John Buza was one of these. March 8, 1890, *The Press* reported: "John Buza, who was so seriously injured two weeks ago on Presque Island was in town this week and seemed not much the worse for his hurt. It will be remembered that he was injured by a falling limb which made a scalp wound some five inches in length and that he was unconscious for about 48 hours. Frank Bell, in whose employ he was, succeeded with such appliances as he had at hand in bringing the man out all right. Pretty well done."

Ed Johnson was employed at Cowie's camp in 1902 and one day in June was struck a glancing blow on the shoulder and chest by a great hemlock tree as it came crashing to the ground. His fellow workers made a stretcher and started for Red Cliff. In the meantime, a telephone message was sent to Bayfield for a team and rig to come out. The men carried the injured worker for a mile and a half before they met the team. He was taken to the train to be sent to Washburn to the hospital. As the men were about to lift him onto the train, Dr. Hannum advised them to leave him here, as his time for this world was short.

He was removed to a hotel, where he died in a few minutes. His name was all that was known of him and he was without friends and relatives. He was asked where his home was and about his parents, but he waved the inquiries off and would say nothing. *The Press* could only say of him personally, "Johnson was of medium height, dark complexion and wore a mustache." That description would have fitted many a lumberjack.

Lon Stevens was another stranger who lost his life here. In June 1906, while he was working on the boom at the R.D. Pike Lumber mill he was drowned in the mill slip. He was pulling on the rope, which took the logs up to the chain, which carried them into the mill when his foot slipped, and he fell into the water. He went down once and on coming up, got across a log. Only one person saw him fall in and after seeing him get onto the log, supposed he was all right and went about his work. Glancing around in a moment or so, he was startled to find that Stevens had disappeared. He immediately notified the mill authorities. The mill was shut down and they recovered the body. Dr. Anderson came and worked ¾ of an hour, but it was no use. Again, as in the case of Ed. Johnson, *The Press* knew nothing of his family or where he came from and could only print briefly, "Stevens was a small man, about thirty years old."

There are countless graves of unknown lumberjacks in this part of the country. They came and went leaving only one great mark to show they had been here—the disappearance of the timber.

The sight and smell of a forest fire can still be recalled by many local residents. June 24, 1910, *The Press* said, "The past week the lake has been covered with smoke from the forest fires that are on the south shore.

On July 5, that year Cornucopia was threatened with destruction by a forest fire. Fanned by a strong south wind it was sweeping down on the little village. A call for help went out to the Settlement. The men fought their best, but the fire approached to within a mile of Cornucopia and a call to Bayfield for help was made. Booth Fisheries sent their steamer *Barker* out and picked up a load of refugees, bringing them into Bayfield.

All roads had been cut off by the flames and the only means of escape was by water. Then came the miracle that saved Cornucopia. The wind, which had been south, switched to southwest. A great feeling of relief was experienced by the weary fighters. The wind continued in that direction until a heavy downpour of ran came that night and put the fire out completely. It rained heavily for two solid hours. The next day the *Barker* took the refugees home.

Robert Morrin saws the last log in the Henry Wachsmuth mill. Wachsmuth closed the mill in 1927. (Photo: BHA)

Scenes From Bayfield's Logging Camps

(Photo: BHA)

Bellanger Settlement Loggin Camp. (Photo: BHA)

Railroad trestle leading to the
Squaw Bay camp. (Photo: BHA)

The Squaw Bay
Camp(Photo: BHA)

The Toonerville Trolley in
the township of Russell,
served as a spur line to
the mills in Bayfield and
Roy's Point.
(Photo: BHA)

Steam Jammer. (Photo: Bob Nelson)

Lunch Time (Photo: BHA)

Inside the Pike & Wachsmuth Mill

(Photo: BHA)

(Photo: BHA)

(Photo: BHA)

Chapter 4

The Fountain City
Faithful

The Diary of Reverend James Peet

GLIMPSES OF PIONEER LIFE IN Bayfield are revealed to us by the diary of the Rev. James Peet, Methodist minister, pastor of the first church in Bayfield.

On July 6, 1857 he left his wife and fifteen months old son in Superior and came on the propeller *Iron City* to Bayfield. The fare was three dollars. It was hot that day, but the boat left Superior in the cool of the evening. It stopped at Oak Island to take on wood (for fuel) and from there towed a raft of logs into Bayfield, getting to town about noon.

July 7, 1857. He stayed at the home of William S. Warren and notes: "Our little church building is progressing finely." He also records that on July 7, 1857 Bayfield had about 35 houses, shops and shanties and perhaps 250 inhabitants. This was quite a change, and a remarkable growth, for the little town, since his visit a year ago, when Bayfield had only three or four log shanties.

Photo: BHA Inc.

July 8. Brother Warren and Bicksler took me in a boat to Br. Pike's house in the woods, some five miles distant. (This house was on Pike's Creek, somewhere near the Red Dam.)

On July 12 he preached a sermon in the unfinished church, using a carpenter's bench as a pulpit. Perhaps he meant the carpenter's bench to be symbolic. But perhaps then, as in the future, he just took whatever was available and made the best of it. At any rate there were 31 present in the morning to hear his sermon and 20 people attended the evening service.

The Methodist Episcopal Church of Bayfield was legally organized on July 14, 1857. The trustees were B.F. Bicksler, Elisha Pike, and John Jacobs of Bayfield and George Newton and R. M. Pease of Superior.

By July 15, a little over a week after he had arrived, the new minister was getting well acquainted in the small town. He subscribed to the *Bayfield Mercury*, the thriving newspaper of the community, paying 50 cents for three months subscription. He took note of agricultural progress with the words: "Strawberries ripening."

And then, "The Methodist conference at Winona, July 30, 1857 set off LaPointe County by itself, and I was placed in charge."

This was a large territory for one man in a day when traveling was done by boat or on foot. But if it scared him he didn't show it. He simply went to work.

He shared a worry common to ministers. Finances. His diary reports that for the year ending July 31, 1857 "My table expenses have amounted to $218.21. Fuel $18.27. House Repairing $15.75. Total amounts $252.23, being $2.23 more than my estimate."

The Methodist Episcopal Church, Circa 1880.
Photo: BHA Inc.

He also had something in common with Job. His Aug 31 entry says, "I have a 'bile" under my arm."

As we read through the diary of the Rev. James Peet, first Methodist minister in Bayfield, we begin to wonder what he looked like, and if his friends ever called him Jim. He was a strong man, certainly, or he could never have covered his large parish as he did, on foot, on snowshoes, in a row boat or a sailboat, depending upon the season and the weather. He went to see his flock, however scattered they might be, and no matter what exertion it cost him. He was evidently warmly welcomed and popular, for when the people of Bayfield enjoyed themselves with picnics and camping parties he shared their enjoyment.

Here is his diary entry for Sept. 2, 1857. "A company of us went to Preskeel Island, 15 miles distant for whortleberries (Blueberries). Had a strong wind and fine sailing. Our company camped out on the lake shore, but the little sand flies were so bad we slept but very little."

Thursday, Sept. 3 1857. "Saw the sun rise from the lake, then went out with some fishermen to see them take up their nets. They got some four or five barrels full. Then we picked berries awhile and at 11 o'clock we started for home. Had a strong head wind and a rough sea and had to 'tack about' a great deal to get home. I enjoyed the sail best I ever did any in my life."

The next day, Sept. 4, there came dramatic news. The steamer *Lady Elgin* went aground off "Shagwamagon" Point. Evidently people from Bayfield went out to help the grounded ship, for Mr. Peet went out in a small boat and stayed aboard all night.

On Sept. 5, his old trouble returned. "I have another "bile" under my arm."

He left the *Lady Elgin* and went to LaPointe, a distance of three miles. From there he crossed to Bayfield. The *Lady Elgin* got off the sand bar shortly afterward and he left on it that night for Superior. The boat fare was still three dollars.

Sept. 15 found him busy in Superior, packing up his household goods to move to Bayfield. While there he received word that the Rev. Thomas Elder, Presbyterian minister at Bayfield, had died on Sept. 7.

Sep. 19. Mr. Peet and his family left for their new home in Bayfield on the *Lady Elgin*.

The Sept. 30 entry is familiar to every Bayfield generation. "Heavy Northeaster. Geese flying south. Temperature 54 degrees."

Oct. 13, 1857. Mrs. Peet was taken "in labor" about 2:30 AM and about 4:45 PM presented us with a boy, our second born, which weighs when dressed 8 pounds, is 20 inches long, its arm 7 inches long. Named Robert Charles Peet.

Oct. 14. Went to Elisha Pike's to get his daughter Adaline to come and stay with us for a few days. Bought 5½ bushels of potatoes from him for $5.50.

Oct. 24. The steamer *North Star* brought in a bill of winter provisions, which cost $80, and the freight on the same was $7.62.

Oct. 25. Rowed boat over to LaPointe and back. 18 persons attended prayer meeting.

Nov. 9. Began school with 13 scholars.

Nov. 14. Bought 21# of beef of Mr. Nourse, $2.50. 5¼# suet of Mr. McElroy for 94 cents.

Nov. 18. "This day I am 29 years old."

Methodists, on Nov. 18, 1953 it will be 125 years since the Rev. James Peet was born. He did a lot for your church. Why not have a special observance of his birthday?

Nov. 25. Singing school held at the hotel as the teacher, Mr. Nourse, had been hurt in a runaway. (The hotel was on the corner now occupied by Johnson's Food Shop. It was run by Mr. Bono.)

Typical of a Wisconsin winter is the Nov. 27 entry. "We are nearly all sick with bad colds."

But in spite of colds, boils, the smallness of the town, the hardships of traveling about his parish, he was hopeful. On Nov. 29 he writes: "I think there is some prospect of a little revival of religion in Bayfield."

Dec. 4. A meeting was held at Mr. Vaughn's store to organize a Lyceum (An organization for lectures and debates.)

Dec. 7. I counted 23 fishing boats on the bay this morning. Good hauls, I understand.

Dec. 8. The Lyceum met in the schoolroom.

Dec. 12. Br. Pike brought his son and daughter down today to board in my family and go to school. Adaline is to work for her board, and for Roberson he is to pay $4 per week. I got 30# of fish of Mr. Davises fishermen today.

Dec. 18. The Lyceum met and discussed the merits of a grog shop over and above the practice of bottle drinking at home. This (not surprisingly) attracted the largest audience ever assembled in Bayfield, 80 were present.

Dec. 21. The mail left for St. Croix Falls, 200 miles through the woods.

On Christmas Day the Hon. H. M. Rice gave the Rev. James Peet lot 11, block 40, evidently as a Christmas present. He built a house on that lot. Is there a chance that the house is still standing, or even part of it, long since converted to a woodshed? Does anybody know?

The 1858 diary of the Rev. James Peet, pioneer Methodist minister at Bayfield, begins with the happy promise of a house for himself and his growing family.

Jan. 1. Friday. Mr. Nourse's team and Mr. Davis helped me haul timber to my lot for house foundation.

Jan. 2 Accounts for Aug. 1, 1857 to Jan. 1, 1858.

Expenses	$787.77
Receipts	730.85
I now owe.	$ 56.95
Bal. due me is	167.00

Jan. 3. Major McAboy starts through woods for St. Paul today. I preached in my schoolroom in the morning to 18 persons, in the evening to 13 persons.

Jan. 5. George Day (Indian) shot two moose in woods lately. So we have a piece of meat for our table.

Jan. 7. 10 below to 11 above zero. Ice closed over the bay last night. Several persons crossed on the ice to LaPointe.

Jan. 8. Mail from St. Paul. Bishop has recalled one-fourth missionary appropriation because of late financial crash. Our mission treasury is in debt.

Maybe we've forgotten the strictness of those early days. We are reminded by his entry of Jan. 10. "There has been considerable Sabbath breaking today by skating and other amusements on the ice of the bay. Oh when will men learn to fear God?"

Jan. 12. Mr. Caho's steam mill of Bayfield burned down. (This was the first mill built in Bayfield. It was somewhere below the present depot. It burned two months after it was built, but was rebuilt the next year and cut about 1,000 feet a day. Later Mr. Vaughn bought this mill and moved it to Ashland.)

Jan. 14. 16 above zero. Mr. Austrian's team crossed on the ice from LaPointe to Bayfield and returned. First team to cross this winter.

Jan. 23. Mail arrived on a dog train from St. Paul. 42 above. Meltin.

He would hardly have been human if there wasn't an entry in his diary like this one:

"Jan. 26. Discouraged, no conversions, constant headache, tired."

There is reason for him to be tired, for it is evident that he gave his best to his parish, sparing himself not at all. Entry after entry is similar to this one. "Preached at Bayfield in the morning to ten people. Walked to LaPointe in the afternoon and preached to six. Preached again in the evening in Bayfield to seven. . . "

In addition to this he taught school, chopped wood, kept fires going, carried ashes, worked on the church and the church lot, shoveled snow and even made his own ink.

Here is his recipe for ink: 1½ oz. extract of logwood in 1 gal. of boiling water. 24 grains of bicarb of potash. 12 grains of prusiate potash. Stir well.

His family must have had the simplest food, with few variations. It is evident that the moose George Day shot was a real treat. The house was small, yet it held himself, his wife, two small boys and two boarders. In that little space he prepared lessons for his 13 scholars, wrote three sermons for each Sunday, and handled his domestic accounts. He was expected to be normal, cheerful, full of encouragement for those who needed it, ready to comfort those who were hurt, able to lead all those who would follow. We have already discovered he was strong physically. His mental strength must have equaled his physical strength.

Jan. 27, 1858. A large mail arrived. An arm full of papers, some as old as the previous April.

Jan. 29. I closed school, terms of my engagement expiring so boarders went home.

Within a week he was using the time he had spent teaching school for calls throughout his parish.

Feb. 5. Mr. Warren and I walked to LaPointe on the ice. Three miles in 33 minutes.

Feb. 7. Preached in Bayfield in the morning. In the afternoon at LaPointe to 17 persons in the "Old Protestant Mission Chapel." In the evening at Bayfield.

Feb. 8. Went to Bad River Indian Mission. Called on 6 or 8 Indian families with Wheeler.

Feb. 9. 14 degrees below zero. Traveled road on ice from Bad River to Bay City and Ashland. Preached in Bay City in Doctor Ellis's house in evening to seven adults, and four children, which I suppose was the second or third sermon ever preached in that place.

Feb. 10. 24 below zero. Doctor Ellis promised to give three lots in Bay City for a church. (Bay City was laid out in the fall of 1856 by Dr. Edwin Ellis. It included about the east third of the present city of Ashland.) Walked on ice 16 miles from Bay City to Bayfield in 6 1/2 hours.

Feb. 11. 18 below zero. A man found frozen to death on ice between Bayfield and LaPointe, result of Sunday rum selling and drinking. The man had his six-year-old boy with him wrapped in blankets on hand sled. Child survived.

At last this long-walking man got a ride. On Valentine's Day, Feb. 14, 1858, he says, "Mr. Nourse took me and Br. Warren to LaPointe with his cutter on the ice."

Feb. 15. Bought lumber for my house to be hauled on ice by Nourse team. Bought of Pike 2700 feet inch boards $22.00. 20 pieces 2 x 4 12 feet long, 8 pieces 2 x 4 18 feet long, 5 joists 2 x 8 16 feet long, 15 joists 2 x 8 18 feet long, altogether cost $18.00. 3000 shingles cost $9.00.

Feb. 16. Paid 20 cents for two months dues at Lyceum.

Feb. 18 must have been very cold, for the prayer meeting was held in the minister's kitchen. Seven persons attended.

Feb. 24. Business and pastoral calls at LaPointe. Left deed of M.E. church lot Bayfield with recorder of deeds at LaPointe.

Feb. 26. 56 above. Walked to LaPointe in the afternoon, preached, took supper at Mr. Maddocks's, then returned to Bayfield for the evening preaching.

There was no doctor in Bayfield, so he had to do the best he could when sickness struck. On Mar. 1 he "received medicine to doctor my little boys who are both sick with colds, and Br. Warren's boys who have dysentery."

March 6. I received mail from Superior and Chicago, very old mail; some of it dated the previous April. But no matter how old it was, it was mail and good to have. All of the inhabitants of the small, new town must have rushed out when word came that the tired dog team had appeared at the edge of the forest. They must have waited excitedly, impatiently for the mail sacks to be opened so they could receive word from relatives and friends, who were shut away from them by a dense, snow-filled forest and a frozen lake.

The new house was progressing. Mr. Peet notes that he had been working on it since Feb. 25 and was "also beginning my boat."

Mar. 14. Got lost in fog going to LaPointe. 40 above.

Mar. 18. Laid lower floor of house.

Mar. 21. Ice broken up. 31 above. Could not get to LaPointe.

Mar. 24. Today the anniversary of the first settlement of Bayfield was celebrated with a substantial picnic dinner. Two years old today. Dance in evening.

That was probably Bayfield's first birthday party. If they marked the occasion the previous year, when Bayfield was one year old, we have no record of it.

Mar. 31. My son, Olin Fisk Peet is two years old today.

The big day finally came. On April 2 the family move into the house which the Rev. Peet had built from foundation to shingled roof in just a little over three months.

April 20. Too rough to row my boat to LaPointe.

On that same date came one of the happiest events of the year. The evening began quietly. There was a meeting of the Lyceum. But the meeting was broken up when the first boat of the season arrived. The *North Star* came in at 9:00 p.m.

"Broken up" was probably the exact phrase. The people must have been sitting quietly at the Lyceum meeting, listening to some serious discussion, when suddenly through the dark, windy April night came the sound of a boat whistle. They undoubtedly sprang up, rushed for the door and ran down the street to the dock to greet the boat that was bringing them food, clothes, news of the outside world.

On April 22 the second boat came in. The propeller *Iron City* arrived and its crew and Bayfielder's danced on board in the evening.

April 28. "Spring flowers in the woods." But there were forest fires, too. "Cleared brush off church lot to avoid its catching fire from the one in the woods."

May 4. A steamboat came into LaPointe this p.m.

May 12. Borrowed $10.00 of Mr. Julius Austrian for a few days. Bought 23 pounds of ham for $4.14. Found box of books at LaPointe warehouse brought by *Lady Elgin* for $9.00 freight from St. Paul, for I [had] left my library in St. Paul two years ago when I moved to Superior.

May 21. North Star arrived bringing the Presbyterian preacher, Mr. McKee.

June 12. Paid Mr. Austrian $12.50 full amount of what I owed him. H.M. Rice gave Mrs. Peet one lot in Bayfield.

June 13. McKee preached excellent sermon to 37 persons in our church. Bible class organized. McKee is teacher.

June 23. Bears are very numerous in woods on this part of Lake Superior.

July 2. Left deed of our lot with Mr. J.W. Bell of LaPointe to be recorded.

July 5. Monday. Went in company with a large number of citizens to Shagwamagon Point to celebrate. Turned back on account of head wind and in new warehouse held celebration in the evening.

July 8. In the evening I went to church for prayer meeting, but God and I were alone there.

The diary of the Rev. James Peet for 1858 continues, telling of his hardships, as, unsparing of himself, he served the people of his wilderness parish.

July 31. Preached in Mr. Oliver's vacant house in Ashland. Twenty persons. Walked through the woods in rain one mile to Bay City. Toothache. Severest pain.

Aug. 2. Sailed my boat from Doct. Ellis's at Bay City to Houghton (Point) stopping there with Sis. Maddocks's family. (The Maddocks had moved there from LaPointe.) Four or five families there.

Aug. 4. Having been towed from Houghton to LaPointe by Mr. Maddocks's large sailboat dined with Mr. Austrian and called on a sick colored man there.

Aug. 10. Picked 10 or 15 quarts of whortleberries at Onion River.

Aug. 15. Called on colored sick man at LaPointe. Fear he will die. (He did, soon, and was buried by a Catholic priest Aug. 18. 1868.)

On August 30 James Peet started building again. The little house just wasn't large enough, so he had to construct an addition to it.

Aug. 31. Fourteen years ago today (when he was 15 years old) I commenced seeking the Lord publicly 1500 miles from this place.

Sept. 21. Spent the day pasting newspapers on the inside of our house.

How much wind and cold did those thin newspapers keep out? If we could find the house he built would any of those old papers still be on the wall? Would any of them be the old *Bayfield Mercury*?

Oct. 1. Mr. Drew is Indian agent at Bad River or Odanah Mission. There are about 12,000 Chippewa's in vicinity of Lake Superior, 5,000 of whom are under Drew's jurisdiction. 1200 are supposed to live at Bad River reservation. 22 bands of Chippewa's are paid at Odanah this year, about 2,000 persons.

Oct. 10. Our youngest child baptized. Robert Charles.

Jan. 16, 1859. I had a very good time preaching at Bayfield to 13 persons. Both myself and congregation wept some. Walked to LaPointe in the afternoon through very hard snow and windstorm and water on the ice. But did not preach, so stormy.

Jan. 21. Walked to LaPointe with Rev. Wheeler. Paid one dollar for getting boots mended. Tax on Bayfield lot $1.23. Left watch with Mr. Bell to be fixed.

Feb. 10. All school children went to LaPointe on a sleigh ride.

Evidently during the hard winter months James Peet was pressed for money, for he notes on Feb. 17, 1859, "bought one gallon of vinegar of S.S. Vaughn on credit, 40 cents.

But money or no money his labors in his parish did not slacken. On Feb. 18 he walked to Houghton Point on snowshoes and stayed overnight at Maddock's.

Feb. 19. Walked from Houghton to Odanah. Snowshoes blistered both feet. Part of way waded half knee deep in water over ice. Stayed at Wheeler's overnight.

Feb. 27. Preached to 15 persons at Bayfield, afternoon 6 at LaPointe. A good time. Nearly all of the LaPointe people leave this week for the woods to make sugar.

It is evident the little town felt no need for discrimination because of race or creed. Mr. Peet, Methodist minister, enjoyed taking tea in the afternoon with Catholic friends. He was a dinner guest at a Jewish home. He got meat from Indians, called on a sick Negro and shared his church with Presbyterians.

He evidently considered them all God's children. But he could be displeased with them, too.

The winter of 1859 was a long one, much longer than the winter of '58. Eleven and a half feet of snow fell. Shoveling and firing must have been constant. The ice stayed in the bay until the middle of May.

Over sixty years later Eddie Fortier would write a song for the Bayfield Frolic expressing a feeling common to people in northern climates, his still popular, *Winter Blues*. Sometimes when a town gets shut in on itself a virulent type of "cabin fever" sets in. The month of March can drag and be a tough one.

We can understand then how this hard-walking, hard-snowshoeing, hard-house building, hard-preaching preacher could finally write, toward the end of March:

"My very heart is sick over Bayfield's wickedness. But very little righteousness in the place. My rebukes, etc., have brought upon my head their hatred and curses. Even Brother Warrens' influence is bad and unreliable. He dodges all responsibility. For five or six weeks the scholars have been so absorbed with dancing that it has been a serious drawback to the prosperity of the school and the nearly whole of Bayfield population has been in quarrels and gossiping broils for nearly two months passed.

On April 15 he writes: "Very stormy. Mail carrier has not returned. Five days overdue. A dispatch has been sent out with some provisions to meet him."

By April 18, when winter still held Bayfield in with a tight, unbroken fence of snow and ice everyone must have been sick of the sight of everyone else. The Rev. Peet, being human, was not immune to that feeling. The discouraged man writes: "As far as visible fruit is concerned I fear I have bestowed ministerial labor in vain at Bayfield and that I shall be called in judgment to witness against this people."

But in spite of the discouragement and the severe ness of the seemingly unending winter he kept going. On April 24 he walked the five miles out to Mr. Pike's and preached to his family and hired men, seven in all.

April 30. Snow still three or four feet deep in the woods. Ice not yet broken up in the bay.

On May 6 the *Lady Elgin* made it to LaPointe, but couldn't get through the ice to Bayfield.

It must have been hard for the little cluster of people standing on the Bayfield shore to see the boat from the outside world come into LaPointe, then fail to cross to them.

May 9. Mr. Pike started to Bayfield on horseback, but turned back on account of deep snow.

But on May 11 came a welcome spring sound. "Heard frogs sing."

Sometime between May 11 and May 15 the local ice must have broken, for on May 15 he reports: "The *North Star* got within twenty miles of Superior, but turned back on account of ice and left her passengers at Bayfield."

One of his first projects for spring was a garden.

May 17. At LaPointe. Went to "old fort" and got some garden plants.

May 19. Mr. Maddock at Houghton gave me ten apple trees.

Then on May 21 one of the cows, that plagued Bayfield from its beginning until cars drove them decisively from the streets sometime after 1910, attacked little 18 month old Robert, tossed him six feet into the air and bruised his head considerably. The child recovered.

May 27, 1859. The leaves are getting green.

But with his garden started, his house and boat finally finished, he was called away. And he went, as a good missionary would.

June 5, 1859. Took passage on *North Star* with my family for Superior and my new home to be at Oneota, Minn.

Whether the Rev. James Peet visited Bayfield again, whether he ever again saw the house he had labored so hard to build and had so carefully lined with newspapers, we do not know. But we do know of two things that happened after he left here.

On Aug. 7, 1859, his third boy was born. Weighed 8 pounds when dressed, 22" tall, with dark hair.

And we know too, that on Dec. 29, 1859, four days after Christmas, Robert, the little boy who was born in Bayfield, died of scarlet fever.

Certainly, here is a man who did not have to ask in the words of the old hymn, "Will there be any stars in my crown?" The Rev. James Peet must have lots of stars. We know how he earned them in Bayfield.

Have you been wondering about Mrs. James Peet, wife of Bayfield's first resident minister? Wondering what she was like? How she dealt with the hardships of pioneer life?

Thanks to Gil Fawcett, "The Old Timer" on Radio Station KDAL's *Diary of Duluth* program, we know something about her.

Mrs. Peet was a small delicate appearing person, yet she was the first white woman ever to travel "The Old Military Road" the hazardous trail through the woods from St. Paul to Duluth. She was expecting her first child within a few weeks, but that didn't stop her from going with her husband to his parish in the wilderness.

They made the trip about the middle of February 1856. It took nine days; and eight nights were spent out doors in a bitter twenty eight below zero temperature. She rode on a crowded sleigh, surrounded by barrels of flour, pork, books and personal effects.

Here is an excerpt from the diary she kept of the trip:

"About four o'clock in the afternoon we upset our load and were detained half an hour. I got wedged in between the load and a tree when the sled overturned and they had to cut down the tree to get me out. I would have been crushed to death had the sleigh and horses gone six inches further, but luckily I was extricated unhurt, for which we were all thankful."

Six weeks later, in Superior, Mrs. Peet gave birth to her first son, Olin Fisk Peet, who on March 31, 1858 celebrated his second birthday in Bayfield.

In her 1856 diary Mrs. Peet wrote this description of Superior and Duluth. "There were just three buildings in Duluth and two of them were saloons. There were three families in Superior and only one horse, which belonged to the Rev. Ely, who made the trip with us."

On Sept. 19, 1857 when Mrs. Peet, her husband and their fifteen-month-old son stepped off the *Lady Elgin* onto the Bayfield dock it must have been a pleasure to see this thriving new town, where there were about 35 homes, shops and shanties and perhaps 250 inhabitants. At that time little Bayfield was bigger than Duluth and Superior put together.

Mrs. Peet outlived her husband, later married Charles Jones, and when she was eighty five this happened to her:

She was a passenger on the first train over the new branch of the Soo Line from Minneapolis to Duluth. On the evening of Aug. 1, 1912 this train pulled into the Sixth Avenue W. Duluth Station. A band was there and a large crowd was shouting and waving flags. Little Mrs. Jones thought the celebration was all for the new train. But when she stepped down from the Observation car a representative of the Duluth Commercial Club presented her with a huge armful of American Beauty roses and the waiting crowd burst into cheers.

A moment of complete astonishment was replaced by deep emotion. Then Mrs. Jones managed to wipe the tears from her eyes and wave to the spectators. Later, at the Lenox Hotel, the crowd called her to the window of her room, where she stood, with her little black bonnet bobbing and her arms full of roses. She freed one hand from the large scarlet bouquet and waved a white handkerchief to the crowd, while the band played in her honor.

Duluth loved this little woman, who was known affectionately in the annals of their pioneer days as "The Little Lady of the Lonesome Trail." And surely the pioneers of Bayfield must have loved her, too.

History of Bayfield

ON JULY 28 THE FRANCISCAN Friars will officially celebrate the completion of 75 years In Bayfield. This immediately brings to mind a question. When were churches started in Bayfield? Which one was first? Where did they build them? Who preached? Who listened?

Actually the Catholic Church was the first in the Chequamegon Bay region. Their work for Christianity began when Fr. Claude Allouez landed at Chequamegon Point Oct. 1, 1665, 288 years ago. But until 1860 headquarters for the Catholic priest, who served all of the surrounding territory, were at LaPointe. That year Father John Chebul moved the church headquarters to Bayfield and in 1861 had completed a frame church and rectory.

It has been said that in 1858 a small Catholic Church was built on Lot 8, Block 40 of Bayfield. Catholics, is this right?

There isn't much question but that the Methodists had the first church in Bayfield. We know that on March 10, 1857 a board of trustees was elected for the purpose of building a Methodist church. Two hundred eighty five dollars were subscribed. The church was well started by July 12, 1857. But what date was it completed and dedicated? Methodists, where was it?

July 17, 1857, the Rev. Thomas B. Elder, a Presbyterian minister, arrived with his family at Bayfield, and on Aug. 16 organized the Old School Presbyterian Church of Bayfield. Mr. Elder lived less than two months after his arrival. He died on Sept. 7, 1857 and was succeeded eight months later by the Rev. Wm. McKee, who arrived on May 21, 1858. A Presbyterian church was built in 1859 and received considerable aid from the Hon. H. M. Rice, founder of the town. Presbyterian, where was this church? What happened to it?

The facts are nice to have, but the wonderful thing to know is that the people of Bayfield wanted churches. It was one of their first concerns, once the town was founded. The desire for churches continued with the growth of the town. Other denominations came and now, almost a hundred years later, the churches of Bayfield can all be pointed to with pride. From the lake a view of the cross-topped church spires marks the town as one with a firm belief in Christianity.

What was it like to be a minister in the new little frontier town of Bayfield?

Thanks to Hamilton Ross, of LaPointe, we have a fair idea of what duties and hardships were the lot of a pioneer minister here. Mr. Ross has furnished notes from the 1857, 1858 and 1859 diaries of James Peet, who was the first Methodist minister in Bayfield, and pastor of the first church here.

A. H. Wilkinson of Milwaukee has also contributed to the account of James Peet by sending information which Ed. L. Peet, son of the minister, copied from his father's writings for Mr. Wilkinson on Feb. 23, 1904.

In the Rev. James Peet's own words we learn how he happened to come to Bayfield.

"In the later half of the month of June 1856, (three months after Bayfield was founded) Mr. Elisha Pike of Bayfield township, LaPointe County, was up to Superior on business and called on me, desiring a Methodist preacher to come and preach to the people in the region about LaPointe. I accompanied him and spent a week on LaPointe County with Mr. Pike and two Indians in a small boat.

Bayfield, at this time, had but two or three houses and they were temporary log cabins in which the workmen were living who were building the dock."

He later learned and recorded this bit of Bayfield history, although he was not here at the time it happened.

Feb. 8, 1857. Mr. Warren came from Bad River and preached. This was probably the first regular sermon in Bayfield. Mr. Warren moved to Bayfield after this and on March 9 reorganized the Methodist Class. The next day a board of trustees was elected for the purpose of building a church. It now became a legal "Body Corporate." A subscription was started and $285 was pledged for a Methodist church to be used for a schoolhouse. . .

And there was a further generous stipulation made by the Methodist trustees. It was "to be open to any minister of an authorized church.

The Catholic Church

The Catholic Church, center. Father John Chebul moved the Catholic Church headquarters from Lapointe to Bayfield in 1861. The original Church and rectory are shown here. (Photo: BHA)

The Catholic Church was the third church to be established here. In 1860 Father John Chebul arrived at LaPointe, but soon moved his headquarters to Bayfield and began to build a church. In 1861 a frame church and a small wooden rectory were completed and became the center for Catholic missionaries in this region.

Father John Chebul was an unusual person. You would know that from his picture which shows he was a bearded man with eyes set wide apart and a serene ex*Press* ion. He holds a pair of metal rimmed glasses, as though he had removed them briefly for the photographer, but intended to put them right back on and go to work.

Father Chebul was remarkable for his linguistic talent, speaking fluent English, French, German, Slavonic and Chippewa. He came from Austria, well acquainted with the luxuries and elegance of the old world, but on the frontiers of America, he was completely at home with the pioneers. He was highly esteemed by both Catholics and Protestants while he lived in Bayfield. A man of charm, intelligent conversation an great physical endurance, he was always a welcome guest.

A letter to the Leopoldine Society of Vienna, Austria, written in 1861 by Bishop Baraga, says: "In LaPointe, Father John Chebul is very active. God grant that he may not exhaust himself prematurely. He has a very extensive and difficult mission. Last winter (1860-61) he was called to a sick man who lived 90 mils from LaPointe. There was no other way to make the journey thither and back again than on snowshoes. It took him six days to go and he was obliged to sleep in the woods every night. As he did not know beforehand how far it was to the sick man's village, he took provisions along for only three days. He had to eat very sparingly, therefore, and suffer hunger besides enduring the hardship of the journey."

That one incident characterizes Father John Chebul. It would never had occurred to him not to walk 90 miles through a trackless forest in the middle of winter to offer comfort to the sick. If he grew hungry during his strenuous travels it made no difference. He went anyway.

February 4, 1871 *The Bayfield Press* reported: "The Rev. Father Chebul of the Catholic church arrived last week and held services on Sunday, which were largely attended by his parishioners, who were rejoiced by his return. He has, by his energy, built a commodious and beautiful church at Duluth and recently turned it over to a successor who will watch its interests in that growing town. Father Chebul left Superior Thursday morning, arrived at Pine Lake on the stage at 3 o'clock Friday afternoon and came here afoot, 27 miles, arriving at 11 the same evening. When Fr. Chebul came he was presented with a purse of $90, which was not only from Catholics, but from members of other denominations."

The churches at Duluth and Bayfield were not the only ones he built. In February, 1871, *The Press* noted that Father Chebul, missionary in charge of Bayfield, Superior and LaPointe, was taking steps to have the "old church" at LaPointe repaired and had also built a chapel at Odanah. His mission field was large. He covered most of it on foot.

St. Patrick's Day, 1871, Fr. Chebul celebrated Mass and administered the Holy Sacrament to several persons on Bass Island. The people there lived at the quarry, which was one of the first to be opened here. Fr. Chebul went at the request of Mrs. Monaghen, grandmother of the first child born on Bass Island, a boy, appropriately named, Bassiah. Little Bassiah was three months old in March 1871, had two teeth at that time, said papa and mama quite plainly, had a nice smile and weighed 22 pounds. Does anyone know anything more about little Bassiah?

January 1872, found Fr. Chebul still traveling on foot through the woods, building up his missions. *The Bayfield Press* said: "Father Chebul held services here on Sunday late, but for the next three weeks will be absent, as he is going into the interior to visit the Lac de Flambeau and Lac Courterill bands of Chippewas. He left last Tuesday in company with several Indian guides and packers."

Feb. 17, 1872, *The Press* reported: "Fr. Chebul returned home last Saturday after a few weeks absence among the interior Indians. He walked from Superior to this place in two days so he could hold services Sunday. He is looking hearty and we are glad to see him back again."

The Holy Family Catholic Church. Circa 1920.
(Photo: BHA)

"He walked from Superior to this place" does not really convey what a terrible walk it was. It is hard to imagine, for there are no roads today as bad as that first road hacked through the woods to Superior. It was called "the tote road" and that is about all it was. It coincided with the rough trail to St. Paul as far as Moose Lake, then took a westerly turn to Superior, a distance of about 70 miles. Station houses were built at Pine Lake and Brule. It had another decided drawback. *The Bayfield Press* reported: "Wolves are plenty on the new Superior wagon road."

During that same February of 1872, Henry A. Sweet, prominent Bayfield citizen, because exhausted during a storm while he was walking from the Brule station to the Pine Lake station and was frozen to death.

On Sunday, April 13, 1872, Father Chebul preached the first Catholic sermon on the townsite of Ashland and organized a Catholic Society and Sabbath School at the residence of Antoine Perinier.

Father John Chebul spent about 12 years in this territory. Sometime between 1872 and 1874 he left, but there were persistent rumors that he was coming back. In June 1874, *The Ashland Press* reported hopefully: "We understand that the Rev. Fr. John Chebul is to be returned to the Bayfield Catholic Church. He is the most beloved by his believers or any priest who has ever had charge of the missionary work in this section of the state."

Whether he came back or not we do not know, but let's hope that he at least came back to visit the people who were so eager to see him again. He evidently continued his missionary work in the lakes region, for this hard working, long-walking priest died about 1901 at St. Ignace, Michigan, where he was undoubtedly as beloved as he had been in Bayfield.

*The Catholic Sisters
of St. Francis
Convent.
(Photo: BHA)*

Father John Gafron and Casimir Vogt

O N OCTOBER 13, 1878 FATHERS John Gafron and Casimir Vogt of the Franciscan
order, arrived in Bayfield on the steamer Manistee. They went to live in the small
frame parsonage Fr. John Chebul had built. The two priests began to study the Chippewa
language taught by Father Martin Ferrad S.J., who was here collecting additional material
for his Chippewa dictionary. Their progress was rapid. On Christmas Day they preached
their first sermon in Chippewa. It was short, but genuine Chippewa.

Father Casimir soon started the Catholic school. He bought what was known as the
Moore residence and a small house adjoining with 6 lots and remodeled them into a
residence for the sisters.

In the fall of 1879 the first Franciscan sisters came from Joliet, Illinois, and commenced
teaching. In 1880 they opened a small boarding school for Indian children, supported by
collections from the lumber camps. Two years later the government gave some assistance
with a contract for a limited number of Indian boarding and day scholars. This was of
great help. The sisters donated their services, not even taking any sum for their wearing
apparel.

Fr. John Gafron and Fr. Casimir Vogt had all of northern Wisconsin as their mission, as
far south as Chippewa Falls and St. Croix Falls with the exception of Superior where
Fr. Verwyst was stationed. They covered their large territory on foot and, of course, went
on snowshoes in winter. At one time 111 missions were served from Bayfield. Thanks to
Father Chrysostomus Verwyst, who wrote "Indian Missions of the Lake Superior Region"
we have much information about these missions and the priests who started them.

To attend these scattered missions, which were mostly small Indian settlements, required
a great deal of physical endurance. Fr. Casimir and Fr. John traveled on foot and in their

Franciscan habits, which did not make the going any easier as they waded rivers, climbed fallen logs and made their way through trail-less forests.

The Wisconsin Central Railroad was running into Ashland at that time, but had not yet come to Bayfield and was of little help to them anyway, as most of the missions were inland, far from any railroad and often without even wagon roads to them.

Usually one or two Indians would go along as guides and to help carry some of the equipment. They slept where they happened to be when night came, in the open, or, if conditions were favorable, in a poor tent, a lumber camp, or an Indian wigwam.

When one Father started on these distant trips, which generally took from six weeks to two months, the other Father would attend the home district, Bayfield, LaPointe, Bad River, and Ashland, which of course, gave him a chance to rest up, as these places were all within easy walking distance, not more than forty miles at the most.

Father Casimir or Father John, one or the other, was always on the road winter and summer, not letting the bitter cold of Northern Wisconsin or the deep snow stop them. In the spring and fall the chilling rains made the traveling bad too, for their heavy Franciscan habits would be soaked and had to dry on their backs as they walked. Father John Gafron, who was otherwise of a strong constitution, broke down and contracted an illness, which brought him to a premature death. Father Casimir survived, but his health was impaired by the years of hardship and the misery of foot travel.

Naturally this travel was dangerous. One night Father Casimir making his way to a lumber camp to collect for his Indian missions, was surrounded by timber wolves, and no doubt would have been torn to pieces and eaten, had he not carried a lighted lantern. The wolves accompanied him for two miles, circling him, waiting for him to fall down or his lantern to go out so they could close in. Fortunately he walked steadily and surely and the small flame burned until he reached the camp.

On another occasion he met a huge bear at night in the woods not far from Flambeau Farm. Once in the early spring he was lost in the woods when the water was high in the river bottoms and had to wade many miles through cold, knee-deep water between Big Bend and Flambeau Farm.

Another time Father Casimir and his Indian companion John B. Denomie got lost in the woods in winter and had to sleep near a fallen log where they built a fire. The next morning Father Casimir said Mass on an old pine stump in the open air. Once Father Casimir and his Indian guides were lost and after walking all day in the woods found they had circled back to the logging camp where they had spent the previous night.

Father Casimir preached to the men of the logging camps, many of who were Catholic. He heard confessions at night and held Mass the next morning in the logging shanty.

While alternating on the easier job of attending the "home" missions, Father John Gafron broke through the ice as he walked between LaPointe and Bayfield and was almost drowned.

These are only a few of the hardships the two pioneer priests suffered as they made the rounds of their little missions, offering their faith and the comfort of their church to all who would accept. They were weary as they crossed the swollen rivers and ice bound lakes. They were cold and often hungry and in the summer the plague of mosquitoes and other insects hummed in their ears and stung them as they journeyed through the forests. But they let none of those things stop them.

Catholic Missions and Priests

THE TWO PIONEER PRIESTS, FATHER John Gafron and Father Casimir Vogt, held services at Courtes Oreilles, generally four times a year, taking turns coming all the way from Bayfield on foot.

Father Christian A. Verwyst, who also attended the missions from Bayfield in 1878, left Bad River on September 24, 1878 in a birch bark canoe paddled by two Indians, Haskins and Waiekwa-Gijig, who took him as far as Ashland. The next day he went to Silver Creek (now Highbridge) by rail. From there, accompanied by three Indians, Wawieiash, Andjigijig and Joe LaPointe, who was one of the best of the Indian guides, he traveled partly on foot, partly by canoe to Pakwewang, an old Indian trading post about 20 miles from Courtes Oreilles. Mass was said there on Sept. 29, 1878.

Wawieiash went on to Bellil Falls, 24 miles down the Chippewa River to acquaint his relatives with the fact that a "Black-gown" had arrived in Pakwewang, the first one ever seen there. Several Indian women started from Pakwewang, traveling mostly on foot, to hear Mass and have their children baptized.

During the Mass the people knelt with their backs to the altar, as the seats were close to the wall on three sides. Father Verwyst, noticing this comical incongruity of position, explained that they should kneel facing the altar, which they did. Some pinery men also attended this service, chewing tobacco and spitting on the floor, showing by their rudeness that they were less civilized than the Indian women.

Flambeau Farm, situated at the mouth of the Flambeau River where it empties into the Chippewa, was one of the missions attended by the Bayfield priests, Father Casimir and Father John. They traveled the 200 miles to this mission on foot, using snowshoes in winter. Four times a year regardless of weather or hardships, they made this trip and built the church there. Trade River mission was also founded in 1879 by these priests who came the 200 miles from Bayfield.

Father Casimir, in 1879, finished the small church in Ashland, which was begun in 1874 by the Rev. Schuttelhofer. But until 1882 when a small room was built for the priest, Father Casimir slept in the belfry or steeple of the church. He must have been uncomfortable there, cold in the winter, pestered by flies and insects in the summer, yet he wrote about it cheerfully saying, "Completing a round of mercy to the sick and dying I hid to my belfry home which the swallows and sparrows had already claimed for their own. The belfry is seven feet square and the mattress on the floor is the only furniture. I sat on the mattress and by candle light memorized a sermon which I hope to deliver in Chippewa tomorrow."

Father Casimir kept a crucifix and the conjugation of Chippewa verbs on the wall.

When the village of Hayward was begun, about the year 1882, Fr. Casimir took note of it and said Mass there for the first time on March 22, 1883, in the home of Joseph Caho. In July he began to build a church at Hayward and traveled from camp to camp to collect funds for it. By November of 1883, this church was sufficiently furnished so the first Mass could be said in it.

In 1884 the city of Washburn was laid out. A mission was started there attended by the priest from Bayfield. In the back of the church a small bedroom was built for the priest. It was a mean, impoverished little building, only roughly papered with thick building paper and had a small coal stove, the upper part of which was about the size of a soup bowl. Soft coal was kept in the shed, which adjoined the bedroom. One night the priest was almost suffocated by coal gas escaping from the stove.

Once, in the winter, Fr. Firmatus went up Sioux River where he was called by someone who was ill. After he had attended the person, a farmer brought him to the railroad tracks at Sioux River, at that time a solitary place without a depot, gave him a lantern, a few matches and drove away and left him.

Fr. Firmatus, alone in the cold, dark winter night moved around to keep warm. When he heard the train coming he began to light the lantern to signal it to stop. He tried to light a match quickly, but failed. He kept on trying, but the matches went out until with the last match he succeeded. If he had failed the train would have gone by and he would have had to walk the tracks to Bayfield.

Pioneers, Priests & Missions

FATHER JOHN GAFRON, PIONEER PRIEST at Bayfield, once made a trip of more than 300 miles on snowshoes to serve the little missions in the wilderness.

When *The Bayfield Press* wrote of Father John it was with words of praise. Dec. 7, 1889, *The Press* reported: "Fr. John Gafron has been down the line this week looking after the spiritual interests of his people at Odanah and other points. Fr. John labors constantly for the good of the cause which he represents."

March 1, 1890, this item appeared in *The Press*. "Father John Gafron visited Ashland Wednesday. In the forenoon of that day, which it will be remembered was one of the coldest and most blustering of the season; he made a trip to LaPointe in the face of a biting wind. Father John is a priest who faces all inconveniences in the pursuit of his calling. Men of his stamp among the clergy make their profession a power among men."

By 1890 the mission in Bayfield had progressed enough so that an adequate residence could be built for the priest. Brother Adrian of St. Louis, a noted architect, drew plans for the new residence.

But even with his interest in the plans for a new house and the prospect of having a sound roof over his head, Father John, as always, put first things first. On May 2, 1891, *The Press* said, "The Mission held at the Catholic church in this city last week was a success in every particular. Father John and the Jesuit Fathers are deserving of much credit in bringing back to the fold many a stray sheep."

W. Feldhausen built the new residence for the priests in the summer of 1891. The building was 50 x 38 and consisted of a basement and two stories. The basement in brownstone, the remainder brick. All the material, as far as possible, was native to this country. Col. Rudd furnished the brick, Captain Pike the brownstone and F. Fischer the lumber.

Oct. 17, 1891, *The Press* had this item. "Thirteen years ago last Tuesday, Fathers John Gafron and Casimir Voigt arrived in Bayfield on the *Manistee*. The anniversary of their arrival was selected for the blessing of the new Franciscan residence."

The women of the church had been busy too, during those 13 years. The school started by Father Casimir and taught by the Franciscan sisters was flourishing and Nov. 24, 1888 *The Press* noted: "Several sisters from St. Joseph's hospital in Ashland are in Bayfield taking charge of the branch hospital." The first patient in this hospital was named Hanson. He was brought in from Frank Boutin's logging camp and *The Press* said vaguely, "he has some sort of fever." The Bayfield hospital was called St. Mary's and in January 1889, had seven patients.

By 1891 the church had many workers. September 5 of that year *The Press* reported: "the Catholic Fair, which was held last week, closed Saturday in a blaze of glory having been the most successful ever held in Bayfield. The ladies of St. Mary's Society, who are the originators and promoters of these annual fairs, are deserving of great credit for the pains taken to make this the success it was. The total receipts were $900.68, the expenses $80.08 leaving net receipts $820.60."

It must have been a satisfaction to Father John Gafron to see the church he had labored so strenuously for growing so vigorously. His hardships in establishing the missions had worn him out and in July, 1897, he died in Ashland. In writing of the passing of this pioneer priest, *The Ashland Press* said: "Father John saw that there were many difficulties to be overcome in this new work, but nothing could make him discouraged. He had an aim and was going to attain it. Of course, the first thing that had to be done was to master the Chippewa language. This he did so perfectly that the Indians themselves said that he spoke better than any in the Chippewa nation. Fr. John was a pioneer missionary at Bayfield. On one of his journeys, he caught a severe cold while crossing a river. This cold, which developed into pneumonia, he never recovered from, and was, perhaps the cause of his death. When his health failed completely he was obliged to go to Memphis, Tenn., but as soon as possible he was back at his missionary work. He labored four years more, but was then taken ill again and went to St. Louis. When a call came from a person skilled in the Indian language, Fr. John volunteered to go to Ashland, but it was too strenuous for him and he lived only six weeks."

The work which Father John and Father Casimir had begun so well was carried on. Father Odoric Derenthal and others also walked the swollen rivers and over the ice bound lakes as far as 600 miles in a circuit of Indian missions served from Bayfield, eating what they could find as they went, wild rice, rabbits, porcupines and muskrats. Many of the little missions they started grew into parishes with priests of their own. At last the Catholic church was firmly established in the northern Wisconsin wilderness.

Civilization made travel easier, new materials made churches more comfortable and beautifully decorated, but the value of the spirit of the missionaries who founded them remains greater than all their material gains.

Thousands of students were in the Holy Family Catholic School system. Circa 1918.
Right to Left:
1st row: Roger O'Malley, Fred Gordon, Daniel O'Connell, Wally Boutin
2nd row: 1st unknown. Mike McQuade, Jimmy Sexton, Anthony Bearing
}rd row: Walter Copick. Laurence Williams. Jimmy Richards, Ray Gonia
4th row: Art Duquette, Robert Cadotte, Carl Meyers. Alex MacClaen
5th row: George Bressette. Emma Gay, Genevieve Murray. Alex Kranzfelder
6th row: Lena Vallincort, unknown, unknown, Jane Neveaux
7th row: Annie Morio, Ruth Boutin, Teresa Bear
8th row: Guy Stewart, Lloyd Lamoreaux, Lawrence Hoefle. Leo Gonia, Frank Roy, Father Norbert, Hike Deragon, Sister Cordulla
(Photo: BHA Inc.)

Bayfield's Buildings

Bayfield Norske Evangelike Lutheran Kirkke. aka Bethesda Lutheran Church. Founded as a congregation on December 6, 1893, the new church building was dedicated on March 28, 1897. (Photo: Burt Hill collection)

Swedish Lutheran Church. This church was completed in November of 1889 and dedicated on September 29, 1891. The building was located on Manypenny mid-way between 7th and 8 th Streets. (Photo: BHA)

Bayfield Presbyterian Church. The Reverend Thomas B. Elder organized the "Old School" Presbyterian Church in 1857. The first church was constructed in 1859. (Photo: BHA)

Washington Avenue School. Completed in 1871 this school served the students until 1885. It was thereafter utilized as the cities Town Hall and lasted as such until the early 1900's. (Photo: BHA)

Bayfield Central School. Completed in November of 1886-razed in 1943. (Photo: BHA)

Bayfield "Lincoln High". Completed in November of 1895 this school still exists as the core building around which the current Bayfield School District revolves. (Photo: BHA)

L-Front- Dennis .J. Etsell- Hardware Store. R-Front- Ervin Leihy- General Merchandize
R-Back. August Turnquist Building. (Photo: Burt Hill Collection)

July 4, 1906.

L-Front- Dennis .J. Etsell- Hardware Store. R-Front- Ervin Leihy- General
Merchandize
R-Back. August Turnquist Building. (Photo: Burt Hill Collection)

Expanded view of central
city Bayfield. Front- Bayfield
Lumber Company, Mid-Left is
Washington Avenue School
House, Mid-Right is Island
View Hotel, Back is Holy Family
Catholic Church. (Photo: BHA)

Bayfield County Press and John Fiege Cigar store. The original Bayfield County Press building was of wooden frame construction, by Samuel S. Vaughn. The building burned and was replaced by the present day Bell Building in 1892. Back right, Jim Chapman Hardware store, circa 1886 and home of the Bayfield County Press in the 1950's and 1960's. (Photo: Burt Hill Collection)

(Photo: Burt Hill Collection)

Broad Street. Circa 1890. (Photo: BHA)

L- Methodist Episcopal Church. R- William Knight residence. Circa 1900. (Photo: BHA)

The Fuller home was built for General Allen C. Fuller and his second wife, Mary, having originally come to Bayfield in hopes of curing his first wife and daughter from tuberculosis. After their deaths, he married Mary Wiley, a widow, and built this fine home for their summer cottage. (Photo: Jerry Phillips)

Chapter 5

Politics & Chicanery

Courthouse History

This building was constructed by Benjamin F. Bicksler of Ashland at a cost of $15,000.
Bayfield County offices and records were held in private buildings until the building was
completed in 1874. In the early 1880's County officers included John McCloud- Justice
of the Peace, John Gonyon-Sheriff, Louis Bachand-Clerk, Nelson Boutin-Treasurer, Joel
D. Cruttenden-Register of Deeds, W.J. Herbert-Clerk of Court, B.B. Wade-District Attorney,
Orlonzo Flanders Superintendent of Schools and Elisha Pike was coroner. All resided in
the Town of Bayfield, then registering over 1000 law abiding residents. (Photo: BHA)

T HE FIRST COURTHOUSE IN BAYFIELD was built on the corner north of the present
Omaha depot. It stood there until a cold morning in February 1883. The account of
its loss was given in The Bayfield Press on February 17 of that year. "Wednesday morning about 6 o'clock the courthouse in this village was discovered on fire. The alarm was
speedily given, but the fire had gained such headway that it was beyond all control and
in a very short time, the entire structure was a seething mass of flames. Grave fears were
entertained that the county records might not escape uninjured owing to the fact that
the tall chimney on the south side of the building fell on the vault, but as soon as the
fire had burned out, the vault was opened and its contents found in safe condition. The
court records were destroyed also the contents of the country clerks and treasurer's offices
and the library of the Bayfield Lyceum, a collection of choice works of history, biography,
travel and fiction. The cause of the fire is unknown. The Bayfield courthouse was a large
two-story structure located on the corner of Broad Street and Fant Avenue. It was erected
in 1873 at a cost of between $8,000 and $10,000 and was insured for $3,500."

Immediate preparations were made for a new courthouse and on March 3, 1883, this item
appeared. "The temporary courthouse is finished and ready for occupancy. It will cost in
the neighborhood of $700."

A new brownstone courthouse was planned on some land, which had been given to the village for a park by H.M. Rice, founder of Bayfield. Mr. Rice agreed to let the site be used for the county courthouse, with the provision that the property should revert to the original owner when not used for county purposes. This provision later became a great talking point for Washburn in their fight to get the courthouse.

Saturday, June 23, 1883, *The Bayfield Press* said: "The contract for the new courthouse was awarded to Messrs. Cook and Hyde of Milwaukee, who agreed to have the building up, enclosed and offices and vaults of the county clerk, treasurer and register of deeds ready for occupancy by the first of November at a cost of $21,000. The building will present an imposing and pleasing aspect. A magnificent spring of pure, soft water not far from the plot with sufficient head to convey water to the highest part of the building will be utilized and it requires no great stretch of imagination to see the Bayfield county courthouse ground converted into a handsome little park spouting numerous fountains at no far distant date."

Sat. Sept. 8, 1883. "The cornerstone of the new courthouse was laid by the Masonic Society assisted by members of the Ashland lodge who came over on the "N. Boutin." A sealed box containing records of the lodge, of the county, copies of the daily papers, a copy of *The Press* and several coins were deposited in the stone. Dinner was served at the Island View."

July 5, 1884. "The bell for the new courthouse is in running order and now peals out the hour in tones that may be heard for miles."

Incidentally, this bell has its own little history. Weighing 1,500 pounds, it was brought from Ashland to Bayfield on a barge. As it was being loaded onto a wagon at the dock, the team became frightened, probably by the sidewalk engineers, and ran away. They ran so fast and it happened so suddenly that they got way out of town and ran into the woods before they stopped and the bell could be recovered.

In 1833, when the courthouse building was being remodeled it was given to the Young People's Society of the Federated Church. During the Christmas holidays of 1933, the boys of the society under the supervision of the contractors, removed the bell from its place in the courthouse, laid the beams and hung it in the church. Breaking its silence of many years, the bell rang out again and is still heard on Sunday mornings in this year of 1957, almost 73 years after it was first heard in Bayfield.

July 12, 1884. "This week Bayfield County's new brownstone courthouse was completed and turned over to the county."

July 19, 1884. "The star-spangled banner waved from the top of the courthouse this week in honor of the first term of the court held within its walls."

From then on the courthouse was in constant use. It had uses, which we do not associate with courthouses of today. Parties were held there and in April 1888, Mrs. Frederick Fischer's funeral was held at the courthouse. Does anyone know why this was done?

Improvements were constantly being made and on April 4, 1891, *The Press* reported: "The courthouse is now lighted by electricity adding much to its general appearance and usefulness for evening sessions."

The Bayfield Press also remarked proudly that it was "the only brownstone courthouse in the country outside of Milwaukee."

How Washburn Stole the Courthouse

The Bayfield Courthouse with the old bell tower In all her glory.(Photo: BHA)

THIS ARTICLE BEGINS A SERIES on a subject that in Bayfield can have only one title, "How Washburn stole the Courthouse."

Before I begin, I would like to express my thanks to two people who gave me a great deal of assistance with this controversial subject, Charles M. Sheridan of Washburn, who had already done much research, and Paul Robinson, editor of the Washburn Times, who made available to me the old volumes of the Washburn News.

Before we get down to the fine points of courthouse stealing, it is best to find out how a county named Bayfield came into existence.

The first known inhabitants were the Chippewa Indians. Before the year 1490, they left their ancestral home near the Gulf of St. Lawrence and, guided by a sacred seashell, moved up the river into the vast wilderness eventually to be named North America. For a time they stayed at what is now Sault St. Marie. Then these Indians split into three divisions and the Chippewa proper continued westward until they came to what today is Long Island. Here, about 1490, they built a settlement. Eventually, missionaries and voyageurs brought the first touches of civilization and the wilderness was named and divided into counties.

The territory which included Bayfield county had five different names before it was set apart as an individual unit. It first belonged to the county of Michilimackinac, created in October 1818. In 1825, it became part of Chippewa County. When the territory of Wisconsin was organized all of this region was included in Crawford County. In 1840, an act of the territorial legislature of Wisconsin created St. Croix county which included all the northwest section of the state. In 1845, LaPointe County was created form part of St. Croix County, and included what is now Ashland and Bayfield counties. From 1845 to 1858, the village of LaPointe on Madeline Island was the county seat of LaPointe County. It was moved to Bayfield in 1858 and two years later, a new county called Ashland was created. In 1866, another county was "born" and named after the first settlement in it, which was the village of Bayfield founded in 1856.

Bayfielders, not wanting to go to Madeline Island to conduct county business succeeded in getting the county seat away from LaPointe in 1858. LaPointe naturally did not like that and retaliated by voting to become part of Ashland county, a step they soon regretted since it was difficult for them to reach the county seat in Ashland.

This item appeared in *The Bayfield Press* in January 1891, "The residents of LaPointe are agitating the question of being annexed to Bayfield County. It takes them the best part of three days to get over into their voting precincts in Ashland County, which they think rather expensive for the suffrage privilege."

No story of Bayfield and LaPointe counties would be complete without mention of Judge John W. Bell, commonly called King of the Apostle Islands.

Almeda Johnson, in her valedictory address to the Bayfield High School graduating class in 1909, described the LaPointe situation as follows:

"Fifty years ago, all legislation concerning this northern section of Wisconsin was carried on in a small box like structure at LaPointe on Madeline Island through the strong and mighty hand of Judge John W. Bell, commonly called the "King of the Apostle Islands." When Judge or "Squire" Bell first took up his residence at LaPointe, he established a bakery, but later turned his hand to the cooper's trade, carrying it on quite extensively. Probably because of the part he took in the business life of the town, and partly because of his strong personality, he became the one prominent man in the politics of the day. The people all looked up to him and he ruled quite autocratically. A story is told of his marrying a couple and later divorcing them. A lawyer, chancing to visit this region, heard of Judge Bell's action and engaged in conversation with him on the subject.

"You can't divorce that couple," the lawyer said.

"I can," maintained Judge Bell and a heated discussion began.

At last the lawyer demanded, "Well, if you can, prove it!"

Judge Bell replied, "I can do it because I have done it!"

The lawyer withdrew, admitting this was quite conclusive proof. Many such stories of court life could be told, which show that the proceedings there were both original and interesting. . . if not always legal.

In a booklet by G. F. Thomas, son-in-law of King Bell is this little item: "Squire Bell did all the business and in the early days, the records and legal documents required little room. Squire Bell was always elected to hold several offices, in fact all that the law would allow, then he would do the business for his friends holding the other offices, most of whom were not capable of doing it themselves."

Thus the background of Bayfield County indicates that anything could happen, the boundaries could be changed, the county seat could be moved, and even that it flourished under one-man rule.

With Bayfield as the county seat, it flourished, too, as is indicated by this item in *The Bayfield Press* December 9, 1882. "Bayfield County, town and village is entirely free from debt, a fact that parties looking for new locations had ought to take into consideration."

Washburn Plans to get Courthouse

WASHBURN WAS FOUNDED IN 1883, the same year the new courthouse was built here. Its sawmills gave it rapid growth and by 1892, it was larger than Bayfield.

Washburn then began to cast covetous eyes on the courthouse. What followed Charles M. Sheridan has described as "a rough and ready, no-holds-barred, feud over the moving of a county seat, a wild campaign that has no counterpart in the history of Wisconsin's various county seat removals. Highhanded tactics were used, coercion was practiced, money was spent freely, the law was ignored or evaded and Washburn finally won a victory over Bayfield at the polls by a 500-vote margin. To cap the climax the actual moving of the county records and courthouse furnishings from Bayfield to Washburn was done by a caravan of horse drawn wagons in a carefully planned final stroke that combined stealth, force and persuasion. Arrival of the caravan in Washburn precipitated an all night celebration that will always be a high point in the city's history. So bitter were the feelings aroused by that campaign of 1892 and its outcome that it was not a safe topic of conversation between Bayfielders and Washburnites for many years. . . "

The first step was taken by Washburn at a town election in the spring of 1892. A committee was appointed to hire an attorney and get the movement to change the county seat under way. A committee member, John Jacobs, was sent to Eau Claire to hire either Mike Griffin or H. H. Hayden, prominent attorneys of that city. Griffin was a delegate to the National Republican Convention which was busy nominating Harrison for President, so Jacobs retained Hayden.

Attorney Hayden was trying an important case in the United States Court, but became so interested in the county seat removal that he succeeded in getting his case adjourned and turned his complete attention to the courthouse matter. His interest was stimulated by the contention of his friendly rival Judge Bailey, that a county seat could not be changed under the laws of Wisconsin. As an example, he offered an unsuccessful attempt in Barron County in 1873. Hayden, with the same legal spirit Judge Bell had shown in LaPointe County, said it could be done. He proceeded to prove his contention.

The night before Jacob returned to Washburn, Attorney Hayden had a stenographer working all night preparing petitions, which had to be circulated as the first step in the movement. When sufficient signatures of free-holders or property owners were obtained Hayden arranged for a special meeting of the county board and the petitions were presented. The board then had the duty of ordering that the question be submitted to a vote of the people, but opposition to the movement had sprung up and had power enough to force an adjournment of the board. The opposition hoped they could campaign against the move and get some of the petition signatures canceled.

However, just the reverse happened. Hayden was pleased at the action, for the margin of necessary signatures had been small and he hoped to obtain more during the interim. To obtain these signatures, the Washburn faction divided up a five or ten-acre plot of ground into 25 foot lots and "sold" the lots at $1 each. Purchasers then, of course, were property holders and could sign the petition asking for a change of the county seat. An urgent need for money was felt by the Washburn faction and it was suggested that a piece of real estate belonging to some of the supporters of the Washburn movement could be "sold" to the town government for $3,000 for use as a poorhouse site. Walter S. Rait, who had been chairman of the movement until that time thought that was going a little too far, announced his fear of such a procedure and resigned.

The other committee members knew they were taking a chance but had been told by their attorney, Hayden, that money was needed to continue the fight. They elected a new chairman and proceeded with their plan. The town board bought the "poorhouse site" and the $3,000 went into the fund for the county seat fight. Naturally the newspapers of the county had jumped into the battle. *The Bayfield Press* and Iron River Times were on one side, favoring retention of the courthouse in Bayfield. The Washburn Itemizer was violently for Washburn and the Washburn News also fought for the courthouse in Washburn, but took vigorous sideswipes at the Washburn Itemizer, its rival. It was a general free-for-all of individual citizens, newspapers and lawyers.

Washburn Stole Courthouse

A FTER WALTER S. RAIT HAD resigned as chairman of the "Courthouse for Washburn" movement and had left town, The *Iron River Times* commented as follows: "In him (Walter S. Rait) was embodied more real, modern, practical vim than in any two dozen citizens at that burg. He was the life and essence of the movement having for its objective the removal of the courthouse from Bayfield to Washburn this fall. Now that he is gone, the bottom has virtually fallen out of that scheme, as nobody particularly desires the change except a few grasping bankers in Washburn who have some real estate on hand that they wish to sell at inflated prices to some uninitiated sucker. The people of Bayfield county cannot see any particular reason why they should tax themselves $100,000 for the mere purpose of making a few bankers in Washburn still more bloated than they are now. Iron River and the other towns in the county will vote solid against this robbing scheme. If the courthouse was moved at all, Iron River should be the place, but there is time enough yet."

When the county board met after its six weeks adjournment the petitions for removal were so strong that the board was forced to order the question be voted on at the November election. The real fight began then and Washburn started with a vigorous campaign.

Two factors in the election were accepted. Washburn would vote solidly for and Bayfield solidly against the courthouse removal. These were the two largest centers of population in the county and Iron River, the third largest was doubtful and became the very center of the fight for votes.

Many odd situations arose. There was a fair held in Iron River shortly before the election with the prize of a bedroom suite to be awarded to the woman who received the most votes in a popularity contest. The two principle contenders for this honor were the wives of a hotelkeeper and a liveryman. Madame Hotelkeeper favored Washburn for the county seat and Madame Liveryman favored Bayfield and the victory of the former became of great importance to the Washburn cause.

Attorney Hayden suggested that a sortie be made into this doubtful Iron River territory. A special train was chartered and three carloads of Washburnites descended on the fair at Iron River. With the help of their votes, Madame Hotelkeeper won the contest and the bedroom suite by a large margin. A public meeting was held to boost the Washburn cause with speeches by Hayden and some of the others.

The psychological effect of Madame Hotelkeeper's victory was all that had been expected. Jacobs recalled years later that when the votes were counted, it was found that every Iron River vote had cost the Washburn fund about $15.00."

On October 8, 1892, the Washburn News made this statement concerning the Washburn side of the case: "Since Washburn has come into prominence very many throughout the county expressed the conviction that it would be far better having it the county seat and a constantly growing sentiment in favor of the removing from Bayfield to Washburn exists. In view of this fact, the business men and workers of Washburn have come to an understanding and make a proposition which will furnish the county a good, commodious courthouse, one which will be ample for the needs of business for many years, the finest county government to be found in northern Wisconsin and a new jail, light, dry, healthy and of ample size, a credit to the people. All this will be done absolutely free of expense to Bayfield county outside of Washburn. The building offered is now used by the high school. It will be remodeled and enlarged in any way needed to fully meet the needs of the county. The present courthouse stands on ground to which the county has not title. The Washburn people will deed to Bayfield county and become its property in fee simple."

A letter writer to *The Bayfield Press* commented that the building Washburn was so anxious to donate was "ill ventilated", had been abandoned for school purposes and further, that Bayfield county had been burned out of one wooden courthouse and would not like to repeat the experience.

"Where Are We At?" asked an article in *The Bayfield Press* in 1892, and continued. . . "What does Washburn offer as a compensation for deserting the present quarters occupied by the county. She offers a building and grounds which according to the figures of her own paper, *The Washburn News*, are worth only $2,000. The building is constructed of wood, so poorly ventilated and heated that it has been abandoned for school purposes. It has not a fireproof feature about it and is not as large as the present county courthouse at Bayfield, which the Washburn News claims is already too small for the purpose of this county. Toward construction of receptacles for county records and county jail the people of Washburn offer the paltry sum of $6000. Figures cannot lie and in removing to Washburn, the county would throw away $60,000 to get $8,000. Even if the present quarters were one-fourth as good as they are, the removal would be a case of jumping from the frying pan into the fire. It would be much as though a lady were left an interest in a comfortable estate on condition that she lived upon the property, yet should desert it to marry an actor because he offered her a silk dress, a set of diamonds, and had a drooping mustache, classical features and could smoke a cigarette."

The Iron River Times said, "We have county buildings which, with a little additional expense, would answer our purpose for many years to come. The buildings are fine, being furnished with water and all the modern convenience and are worth in the neighborhood of $50,000. Now Washburn asks that we quit this town and these buildings and move the seat of the government over to that burg, a distance of about 13 miles, not toward the center of the county and no more accessible to any part of the county except the people in that immediate city, that we erect there enough county buildings which will cost us (if these we have are not large enough and cost $50,000), say $70,000.

Now is it true that in consideration that four-fifths of our county is yet undeveloped that it would be a good policy to move our county seat 13 miles and expend from $65,000 to $75,000 in the building of county buildings? The question is, "Can we afford it?"

The people of Washburn are nice people, although we think a little selfish and we would like to please them and would be willing to grant them almost anything in reason, but we cannot see the expedience of shifting our seat of government of this new county one cog further around the shore. Wait until the county is older and more developed and, if Washburn grows accordingly, when the time comes she can have it, but if the town in the more central part of the county, and that town is more accessible today, by all odds, should grow and develop in the future as in the past, then Washburn will not be in it. So we say, let us wait. The time has not come for Bayfield to change the county seat."

Special correspondence to *The Iron River Times* said: "It is not any secret that a resolution was adopted by the county board which favored the removal of the county seat from Bayfield to Washburn and to discuss the question fairly two questions are pertinent. What right has Washburn to the county seat and how much better will it be for the taxpayers to have it in Washburn than Bayfield? First, Bayfield is an old village, platted and laid out in 1856, while Washburn was an unknown quantity ten years ago. The business men of Bayfield, as a rule, are all pioneers, who came many years ago when Bayfield county was a howling wilderness, who by their pluck and perseverance have opened up to the outside world a chance to come in and make this, our county, what it is today, and it is by their efforts that Bayfield county has as fine a courthouse as almost any in the state.

"Washburn is a village of chance. That great company of Chicago, St. Paul, Minneapolis and Omaha Railroad made her what she is and is responsible for her birth and a vast majority of the taxpayers of Washburn never paid one cent of the $40,000 or $50,000 of the tax which went to build the present county courthouse.

The cry is that Bayfield is too far from the center of the county. What higher prerogative has Washburn? She, like Bayfield, is on the very eastern line of the county and only a paltry ten or eleven miles nearer the southern line. How much nearer, my western or southern friends, is Washburn than Bayfield? If this cry of distance is justifiable... let's put the county seat in the geographical center of the county, which will satisfy the most exacting."

"There is still another phase to the question. Washburn says she doesn't want the taxpayers of Bayfield County to help her build another courthouse if she gets the county seat. Do not be misled my friends. A class of scheming sharpers like those in Washburn who will, because they think they have the power, voluntarily cause the county to lose $48,000 (the cost of the present county courthouse) will not, if they have the power, hesitate to vote an appropriation of $100,000 to help them perpetuate that power in Washburn.

Voters, have you confidence enough in them to trust them not to put this additional tax on you, already overburdened with taxation? Still another phase, the taxable property of Bayfield is mostly non-resident pineland from which the county tax is derived. An appropriation made in order to build a new courthouse at Washburn would necessitate bonding the county, such bonds running at least ten years. On whom would the payment of such bonds fall? Not on the millionaire pine landowners, for their pine would be gone, but on the men who have little homes scattered over the county. They, my friends, the poor men, will have to be the burden and not the rich pine landowners. Look to it that this is not done."

Washburn had one good talking point for moving the county seat. It is summed up in one sentence, which appeared in a Washburn newspaper. "Bayfield has never offered to secure for the county a deed to the property there."

To the contention that Bayfield County would lose a $50,000 property by moving the courthouse, the Washburn News said sharply, if ungrammatically, "Bayfield County has no $50,000 property to lose. It don't own any property in Bayfield. It has made some very good improvements on property of a well-known private citizen of that beautiful little burg, though no $50,000 worth by any means. The county has no title to the property and cannot get one. Common sense would dictate that if a better property in a town twice as large and more conveniently located can be procured and a good title given the county change should be promptly made. That is the proposition Washburn makes. Should the county seat ever have to be removed from Washburn, the county could secure by sale the value of its property to aid in the erection of new buildings elsewhere."

As Election Day came closer, the fight grew hotter. Washburn News, Nov. 5, 1892. "Bayfield offers nothing for the retention of the county seat except that if the county seat remains at Bayfield, the citizens of the county will be invited to put $5,000 county money into a new jail. If the removal is made, Washburn will build the jail free of expense to the county. Net saving to the county on the new jail alone, $5,000 in cash."

The Bayfield Press took a soothing attitude. Nov. 5, 1892. "The contest between this city and Washburn has not been as acrimonious as might have been expected. Bayfield people believe that if the rest of the county want to take the county seat away from her after county buildings have been provided her in this city, well enough. But public opinion is certainly coming our way. The fight over the county will be close. No one can correctly predict the results."

But Washburn was taking no chances, and was quite frankly buying votes. *The Iron River Times* said: "C. H. Flynn of Washburn was in the city Thursday night, coming over, he said, authorized to spend $500 in the interest of moving the county seat, but saw that we did not want his money. Well, that is the kind of people we are, Brother Flynn, We vote our convictions. You can't beat us."

On the night of the election in which the county courthouse was at stake, station agent Dickerson kept at his post at the telegraph office until three o'clock Wednesday morning and returns were transmitted to the opera house where they were read by George Packard to a large cows. F.V. Holston assisted in receiving the messages at the depot. The crowd at the opera house was good-natured and as up to the morning, the situation was decidedly mixed, neither of the parties went into ecstasies.

The results of the election were hard to determine. Although it was held on November 8, when *The Press* came out on November 12, it had this item: "On the question of removal of the county seat, Bayfield and Iron River gave 1,031 votes against the removal, 242 for the removal and three blank. The most persistent inquires of pilgrims from Washburn cannot elicit even the information that the county seat removal question came up in the election in that town in any way, manner or shape. Even the courtesies accorded one newspaper to the other has been denied *The Press*. Whether it was lost and Washburn hates to own it, or whether the people of that burg have not yet ceased to roll their victory as a sweet morsel is a matter unknown to the people of Bayfield and we may, until further advice, claim that the vote is in favor of this town."

Finally, all the votes were counted and it was learned that Washburn had won by a margin of 500 votes. As usually happens, the vote in each town was not completely solid. In Bayfield, 41 people voted for Washburn and in Washburn, 51 people voted for Bayfield.

Before the county seat could be moved, it was necessary to have a gubernatorial proclamation. Governor George W. Peck signed the proclamation on Friday, December 2, 1892.

When the Governor stepped outside the capitol at Madison to make an oral proclamation, his secretary dispatched a telegram to Washburn. All was in readiness there and when the message arrived, a cavalcade of eight teams and wagons set out for Bayfield and a crew of Washburnites left for Bayfield on the train.

In the meantime some of the Bayfielders who were fighting to the last ditch had obtained an injunction to prevent moving the courthouse and were trying to serve this injunction on County Clerk, John Froseth. Froseth, who was in sympathy with the Washburn faction immediately left Bayfield for Washburn and there he hid in the attic of the Washburn brewery. As he peered through a cobwebby window in his attic-hiding place, he caught glimpses of the Bayfield citizens who had followed him to Washburn and were searching for him with the injunction. He hid until dusk, which the injunction was useless, as then Bayfield was no longer the county seat.

When the Washburnites who had set out by train arrived in Bayfield, they pretended they had come on a good will tour and rounded up as many of the Bayfield faction leaders as they could and proceeded to entertain them at the town's liquor marts. A few of the Washburnites quietly left and went to the courthouse, locked the doors and detained all Bayfielders who might spread word of what was happening and told the county officers to start packing their records and office furniture.

Most of the county officers were in sympathy with the Washburn faction so were ready to assist with the move. The cavalcade of eight teams took a devious path through the back streets of Bayfield and pulled up at the back door of the courthouse. The records and furniture were loaded and, under the cover of darkness, the Bayfield county courthouse went on the road, bound for a new county seat.

In their greedy enthusiasm, the movers even took the clock out of the courthouse tower, but that was going a little too far, and though they held onto it for two years, it finally had to be returned at county expense.

When Washburn people saw the teams rounding the turn in the road a mile from town, they lighted a huge bonfire across from the town hall. That was the signal for an all night celebration. A public meeting was held and everyone connected with the undertaking was called on for a speech.

Attorney Hayden was as happy as could be. He had long been at odds with Judge Bailey over the possibility of moving a county seat, and now he had proved himself right, although the proving had involved the expenditure of $7,000 or $8,000 and "a few minor legal infractions."

County officers were established in the town hall and plans for a new courthouse were underway, as Washburn immediately forgot about the "fine building" they had promised to donate as a courthouse. The new structure was completed and occupied in the spring of 1896.

Of course there was talk of fighting the election, but on November 26, 1892, *The Bayfield Press* said: "That there are good and sufficient reasons for fighting the recent election in this county is an indisputable fact. But will it pay? The small property owners will have ample reason to squirm on tax paying day for several years to come without adding to their burden by litigation of this character. As far as Bayfield is concerned, looking at it from a financial point of view, she has recovered a $60,000 property from the county seat.

Property of that character never goes begging in this county and the day may not be far off when it will be evident to all that Bayfield has the best end of the bargain."

Washburn bragged and gloated. The following correspondence from Washburn appeared in the *Ashland Daily Press* headlined, "Washburn, November 11. "The people here, irrespective of party, are talking of holding a grand celebration in honor of the great victory of Washburn over Bayfield. The county seat comes to us as easily as knocking persimmons off a tree with a pole. Iron River was practically the only friend Bayfield had in the fight. We wish to give that city a pointer, which is not to expect to ever win the prize from us. Some Iron River people seem to think that they will grow enough to win from Washburn with the help of Bayfield, but they will have to grow some first. As for Washburn, it is alright and we are happy."

The Iron River Times said: "Iron River was naturally against the removal of the county seat for reasons given in the columns of the *Times* repeatedly before. Once when our people make up their minds it takes good arguments or plenty of money to change them and, as they had not the arguments, they had to use money and we predict that the 183 votes that Washburn got out of the first ward or precinct of Iron River cost them $10 each and we are of the opinion that this is a conservative estimate."

The *Washburn Itemizer* said: "The county seat fight is over. Washburn was successful and is under no obligations to Iron River... The People of Iron River will now have time to study over the county seat question, but it is too late for them to come in out of the wet."

The Washburn News tried to calm things by saying, "While the fight on the county seat has been spirited and earnest, there is no feeling on the part of Washburn, and the News hopes there is none on the part of Bayfield. It was a contest fairly won."

In a lengthy article *The Bayfield Press* replied: "It will require a large amount of gloss for the people of Bayfield to look with unforgiving eyes upon a movement which was started by the (Washburn) News and its coterie of real estate speculators and was carried to a finish by the free use of money, buying votes at $10 a head, colonizing illegal votes and prostituting the county to every method of corruption. As to the position of Iron River in the result, *The Press* sees but one course for it to take, and that is the course that every town outside of Washburn should have taken from the outset, if any of them propose to get anything at all of their fair share of county representation... What in the name of common sense we ask, can Iron River, or any other town that wants a fair deal, do except fight Washburn and the *Washburn News* and the county seat ring?"

In addition to fighting other papers and other towns, the two Washburn papers, the *News* and The *Itemizer*, fought each other. The *Itemizer* wrote: "Our friend of the *News* is mistaken in his opinion that the *Itemizer* does not want him here. We should consider it a misfortune to have him retire from the business. Some good man might come in his place." *The Bayfield Press* reported their controversies under the headline: "They Love Each Other."

As an aftermath of the courthouse fight, every little town suddenly wanted to become a county seat. Drummond and Mason wanted to have a county to themselves. The town of Bayfield wanted to become a county and use the vacant courthouse for a county seat. It was argued the expense of running a county government would be no larger than for a township. An Ashland county division was proposed. Iron River wanted to be in a new county, and if there had been force enough to put all these plans in effect, Washburn would have been all alone, the county seat of Washburn.

Aftermath of Courthouse Move

The courthouse later transformed into Bayfield's City Hall. The Bayfield Canon from the civil war time period guards the courtyard. (Photo: BHA)

A FTER A FEW YEARS, WASHBURN began to long for peace and quiet and wanted to come out of the doghouse. September 14, 1895, the Washburn News said: "The railroad bids fair to unite the towns of Bayfield and Washburn in the bonds of brotherly love. There has been altogether too much fighting between the towns of the county for either or any to prosper as much as they might, but from now on it looks like a steady pull for Bayfield county from all hands. It goes without saying that all will be benefited by such a pull and to outside towns that have in times past looked with delight on our little scraps will now look with fear and trembling on the prospect of us working unitedly for this side of the bay, and well they may, too."

After the change in favor of Washburn had taken place, Bayfield paid H. M. Rice $1,500 for his equity in the deed and the old courthouse property came into the hands of the town.

The project of establishing a Normal school in the northern section of Wisconsin was under way and Bayfield was anxious to have the authorities use the courthouse building for this purpose. But the building would have to be remodeled for a school and Superior, offering better inducements, was the location chosen, and the Normal school has now become Superior State Teachers College.

It was talked of converting the building into a high school, which was badly needed here, but some influential men of the time knowing the cost of remodeling and refitting and building an addition, would be more than the cost of a new building and in the end not satisfactory as a school, forced abandonment of this plan. They built the new high school a block further up the hill, not realizing that the day was coming when people would moan and groan about walking up there. For in those days, every one did not have a horse and walking was taken for granted.

In Almeda Johnson's valedictory address to the class of 1909, she refers to these men who held out for a new school as follows: "They have been severely criticized for doing so, by those who were not as far seeing as themselves. Besides the practical side of the question, their defense was that some day in the future this northern peninsula, together with the Apostle Islands may form a county with Bayfield as the county seat. Men of a later day have appreciated this step in advance for they feel that should the question come up in the legislature it will be looked upon with more favor than it otherwise would, since there would be no expense for necessary buildings. Many of the men who have fostered this project may not live to see the day when Bayfield will enter upon her second career as county seat, but the younger generation will not forget nor fail to appreciate the action of their forefathers."

In August 1907, there was talk of turning the building into a hospital. It had been used for a town hall, but was much larger than needed for that purpose. It was finally remodeled for a vocational school, but was abandoned for that. It was then remodeled for use as a community building and city hall, but a few years ago it was completely abandoned and now (1957), has deteriorated to the extent where it seems it will never be used again. Built of solid sandstone it would be costly to tear it down, but eventually it will be done, and who knows what will replace it on the square block of land which was set aside for a park when H. M. Rice planned the city in 1856.

The courthouse controversy was the subject of debate for many years. Sadie Bailey Smith, former resident, has sent me a program of a public debate, which was held by high school students on Friday evening, April 19, 1895. The subject: Resolved that the removal of the County Seat from Bayfield to Washburn was unwise, unreasonable and is detrimental to the county. Bayfield naturally took the affirmative with Henry Stall, Maud Bisbee and Ernest Brigham as their team. Washburn had the negative with Peter Savage, Albert Oscar and Nels Oscar as their team. Miss Blanche Dunbar and Mr. Percy Inglis furnished an instrumental duet and Messrs. R. E. Bailey, Ernest and Earl Brigham were a banjo trio.

The debate was won by Bayfield and the students ran down the hill to the old cannon that was in the courthouse yard and fired a victory salute.

But winning the debate did not bring the courthouse back. The bitterness, which the controversy aroused, lasted for years among some of the participants, but died with their passing. The coming of the automobile, which could not be foreseen in 1892, forced the building of roads which made such a difference in travel that placing the courthouse a few miles one way or the other could no longer be a great issue. The courthouse move did cause a rivalry between Bayfield and Washburn, the last traces of which still show in high school athletics. Though the young athletes of today may not know why the struggle between Washburn and Bayfield is so great, it is because they are still fighting for a courthouse.

Chapter 6

Community Spirit

The Civic League

THE BAYFIELD CIVIC LEAGUE IS the oldest civic organization for women in Bayfield, and we will review some of their history. Of course there have been many other women's clubs and groups through the first hundred years of life in Bayfield, mostly church groups and social groups.

The Pleasant Hours Club was giving "dramatical entertainment" back in 1876. The Macabees flourished about 1900. In February 1908, *The Press* noted: "The ladies of the Macabees enjoyed a sleigh ride to James Stewart's camp at Raspberry Bay. Mr. Stewart treated the ladies to a supper that made their home cooked meals look like thirty cents."

This seemingly rash statement by *The Press* had no repercussions, for though the women of Bayfield had become known as excellent cooks, the fame of lumber camp meals had spread far and wide until a meal at a lumber camp had become a real treat. However, as I thought it over, it seemed to me that after riding to Raspberry Bay on a horse drawn sleigh in February, almost any kind of food would have looked good.

In the 1900's women were getting restless, tired of housework, wanting to vote, and above all to get rid of the bustles, hoops and the voluminous hampering garments they wore all the time, whether at a party, cleaning house, fishing in one of the streams, or even in swimming. Some daring women had already discarded their skirts in favor of gym bloomers, which were almost as large and weighty as skirts, but were a step toward freedom.

About 1902 there was a Federated Women's Club in Bayfield, which had as one of the features of it's yearly programs, a debate on the subject, Resolved: That bloomers are more hygienic than skirts. The affirmative was taken by Mrs. Mary Rowley and Mrs. H. Anderson. The negative was taken by Mrs. Marion Andreas and Mrs. A. Packard. There is no account of who won, but the debate was a bright arrow, pointing the direction women were going. They were casting off clothes by the pound. From bloomers to slacks, to shorts, to bikinis, took them less than 50 years.

Inventors were discovering that anything that lightened a woman's housework, if patented, was as good as a gold mine.

Another sign of women's break for freedom was evident as early as March 29, 1890, when this item appeared in *The Bayfield Press*. "We hear that several young ladies in town are learning shorthand. This is evidence that they intend to know pretty well how to take care of themselves."

The Bayfield Civic League was organized on March 1, 1913, following a horticulture meeting held in the town hall. Twenty-eight ladies were present. Mrs. A. H. Wilkinson was elected the first president. The object of the League was the cultivation of higher ideas of civic life, the promotion of sanitation, outdoor art and the general welfare of the town.

The first thing they did in the interests of sanitation was launch a vigorous, all-out attack on flies and partly defeated them, though it was a tough battle, since most of the citizens had barns which housed a horse, cow or both, and naturally attracted flies. DDT was of course unheard of and the women fought with swatters and an educational campaign.

They also instituted a clean up day, cleaned vacant lots, placed rubbish cans throughout the city, installed a drinking fountain on main street, fixed up a public rest room in the Flanders building and insisted on a curfew ordinance.

As two major projects, they decided to improve the big ravine and make a park, which would be a pleasant place for picnics, and build a small pavilion at the lakefront where people could sit and wait for boats, or just sit and enjoy the view.

The ladies handled the first part of the pavilion project with certainty, getting bids for the construction, but then when the bids were in, they fell into great confusion. Peter DeBraie said he would build the pavilion for $230.00 and furnish all the material, or the League could furnish the material and he would do the work for $4.00 per day. William Sinclair said he would build the pavilion for $254.25. Which was the best deal? Would it be better for Peter DeBraie to build at $230.00, or would William Sinclair have better material and workmanship for $254.25? Or should they get the material and pay $4.00 a day for the work?

This problem became so weighty that it was moved and carried that a committee of businessmen be appointed to confer with the League executive committee. Five business-men, H. J. Wachsmuth, Carl Johnson, H. C. Hale, A. H. Wilkinson and W. H. Weber were appointed. The result was that William Sinclair got the job and built such a fine substantial pavilion for the ladies that it is still in good condition and regular use today. The money to build the pavilion was borrowed from the bank, the first time, but not the last, that the Civic League would go into debt to support a project they believed in.

The Bayfield Civic League continued its good work. September 8, 1913, a committee of ladies was appointed to see the businessmen in regard to having hitching posts placed for the use of farmers, who, of course, came to town with teams. Mrs. Bigelow, Mrs. Bovee and Mrs. Turnquist were the committee members. The businessmen recommended the building of sheds for the horses.

The receipts for the League's first year were $479.67 and the disbursements were $469.99, so they had $9.68 to start with in 1914. In July of that year, they had seven picnic tables and benches in their park in the ravine. Grills had been built and they had tiled the bubbling spring at the first big bend. It was a park thoroughly enjoyed by the public. In a letter from Mrs. John J. Fisher on the League's 25th birthday is this paragraph, "Some of my happiest memories are of those gatherings when we women would 'pick up something,' telephone to our husbands, then take our baskets and our children and go to the ravine, where we would have dinner ready when the mill whistle blew at twelve o'clock. I believe it is something that always stayed in our minds, these happy, informal gatherings that we have enjoyed with our friends in 'God's great outdoors.'"

At the League social held on Washington's Birthday in the town hall, "a number of gentlemen spoke very encouragingly and assured the ladies that they all stood ready to cooperate in every way, and that they felt the League was a factor for good in the city and that it would increase in strength and good work as time went on." Little did the 'gentlemen' know at that time all the projects the League would undertake, and how hard said 'gentlemen' were going to have to work to assist them.

In June, 1914, Dr. Pickett offered to furnish side lights for the little pavilion at the water-front, and his offer was gratefully accepted.

The voices of women were becoming heard in the affairs of the city. On October 12, 1914, the League petitioned the mayor and council that hereafter when library board appoint-ments were made that ladies be chosen to fill at least one half of the membership of this board. They not only got on the board, but for many years they supported the library and kept it open, paying $25.00 a month to Mrs. Robinson for acting as librarian and $10.00 a month to Mr. Lewis for janitor service.

The League applied their feminine talents for cooking to money raising and have done that through all their years of activity. In fact, if the thousands of dishes the League members have washed and dried at their fund raising events were stacked up they would reach into the clouds, and if this stack ever toppled, there would be a flying saucer for everyone.

The following menu was adopted for the dinner the League served on November 30, 1914. Chicken pie, boiled ham, brown and white bread, pickled beets, dill pickles, baked beans, mashed potatoes, apple pie, cheese and coffee. Using their age-old prerogative of changing their minds, the women, at the next meeting, voted to revise the menu and have rolls instead of bread, celery and cranberries instead of dill and beet pickles. It sounds equally good either way.

The women had always taken good care of their homes and their families. Now they began to take care of the refinements of the town and extended their protection and concern to animals. In the winter of 1914, as cold weather came on, the women posted warning notices that horses must be blanketed during cold weather. Two scoundrels, who did not blanket their horses, were caught by the League Humane Committee. The ladies "spoke to them." What they said is not recorded, but never again in the minutes of the League was there a report of an unblanketed horse.

On October 22, 1915, the Civic League served a dinner to the Rotary Club of Superior. 105 men came from Superior and 29 Bayfield men attended. Each paid 50 cents for his dinner, making a total of $67.05, because someone put in an extra nickel.

The expenses of the dinner were as follows: 75# fish–$6.00; 36 dozen rolls–$3.50; roasting the beef–50 cents, groceries–$3.95; 31# roast beef–$5.30; draying–$3.00; roll of table-cloth–$1.25; gasoline and can–45 cents; work–$1.00; music–$3.00; broken dishes–50 cents, making the total expense of $28.81, so the League had a profit of $38.24–pretty good for a 50 cent dinner.

Dec. 12, 1915, the League visited Kranzfelder's meat market at 2:30 PM where Mr. Felty gave a very interesting and helpful talk on the different cuts of meat and how to buy, after which the regular meeting was held at the library.

Since their founding, the League had been buying chairs, tables, and dishes, which had reached a total value of $200.00, so they insured this property for three years, the premium being $3.60.

The Chautauqua was sponsored by the League in 1916. The League operated a dining room and sold meals during the time the Chautauqua was here. League members went to work in the dining room at the courthouse at 6:30 in the morning. The series of meals they served cost $4.00. When the financial reports on the dining room were read, it was discovered the receipts were $159.35, the disbursements $160.85–net loss, $1.50. However, the Chautauqua had brought some culture to the town, the League members had enjoyed working with the entertainers, and the entertainers had enjoyed the town, praising the scenery and the beautiful moonlight on Chequamegon Bay, so this brought some conso-lation to the weary League members.

The interests of the League were varied. In November 1916, Att. John J. Fisher spoke to the League on the signing and execution of legal documents, and it is well he did, for the

League was to do a great deal of note signing and property owning during the coming years.

In February, 1917, the Men's Club asked the League to cooperate with them in fitting up the basement of the library for club purposes. The League thought the men ought to be encouraged to do this and offered to give them $100.00 as a starter for their project. It was a good idea at the time, and is still an idea that is periodically brought up and talked about, for it was not done then, and never has been done, although the large library basement has tempted many organizations with its possibilities.

During 1917, among the programs given was one on *The Use of the Check and How To Draw One*. Another was *Why We Should Conserve Food*, the latter becaue it was during the years of World War I.

The League members were not only money raisers; they did a great deal of physical work on their park project. In 1917 Mrs. Ross, who was chairman of the park committee at that time, said the committee spent only 60 cents for labor, and did the remainder of the work themselves.

In 1917 the minutes of the League record: "On account of war activities, did not try to do too much in way of raising money, except for war purposes, but left that opportunity for organizations in war work." But they did do a few things, such as sponsoring the movie, *Womanhood, the Glory of the Nation* at the Princess theater, and as a result had $15.45 to turn over to the Red Cross. They had a program on war foods and how to prepare them and then had a war food sale, using the approved recipes. They adopted a French war orphan named Marcella Prene.

On March 30, 1918 the League had an eatless, chargeless social at the home of their president at that time, Mrs. H. Hannum. Twenty-five ladies were present, and without anything to eat, or even a small cup of coffee to drink, they still had a very good time. To add a cheerful note to the wartime grimness, they sponsored a community sing. This was so successful that it was decided to have one once a month during nice weather.

With the terrible war finally over, the ladies settled down to listen to some first hand reports of the conflict. Harold Powell spoke to them on "Life in the Navy." Corporal Ray Close spoke to the ladies also, thus very fairly giving the Army and Navy the 'equal time', so often demanded on television today (1957).

In March 1920, began one of the most interesting chapters in the life of the Bayfield Civic League. They began to think of buying the old Armory (Wing Hall) and making it into a community building. On March 16, they had a special meeting with an attendance of 35 at the library for the purpose of discussing the following questions. 1. Shall the League purchase the Armory? 2. Shall the school be allowed use of dishes at the Junior Prom? 3. Shall the League serve lunch at the Easter Ball?

The dish question was considered first, since it seemed to be the easiest to dispose of, but such was not quite the case. At first a motion was made and seconded that the school *not* be allowed to use the dishes because they hadn't paid for the use of them at the Prom back in 1918. But before the motion could come to a vote, the ladies relented and said their dishes could be used. They decided with no wavering to serve lunch at the Easter Ball.

Then, "A full report on the findings of the committee on the Armory proposition was given by the chairman, Miss Hannah Nelson." Roll was called in order that each member might be given an opportunity to express a personal opinion. All expressed themselves in favor of the proposition. H. J. Wachsmuth and J. P. O'Malley explained the business details of the proposition. By a unanimous vote it was decided that the League incorporate and purchase the Armory. What the purchase price was the League minutes do not say. Maybe someone will remember. The League borrowed $4,000 from the bank to put the building in good shape.

They had lots of plans for raising money. Mr. Sharp, who owned the Princess theater at that time, made them a proposition offering 60% of the net proceeds of the 6 reel movie *Pollyanna* on the condition that the League sell as many tickets as possible. The League accepted, the members got out and sold tickets and they also had special music to go with the show, since music of some kind was always a necessity with the silent pictures.

The original plans for remodeling the Armory were too expensive, but it was decided to excavate, fill in the grounds, have the basement walls put in, also a large chimney and fireplace, and to have the building painted.

The members of the GAR were invited to share their personal belongings in Memorial Hall, as the Armory was renamed, in other words, to make it the home of their organization.

There were numerous donations to the Memorial Hall fund. A rummage sale was held. At first there was some doubt about having this, but when it was reported that there was nothing in the laws of Wisconsin to prohibit or govern a rummage sale, it was held, and rummage sales have been thriving in Bayfield ever since. A Harvest Festival was held, and all members who had gardens saved some of their produce to sell at this festival. Boxes were placed around town for contributions.

The first League meeting to be held in their new home, Memorial Hall, was on May 24, 1920. The Senior high school class offered to give their class play for the benefit of the hall. The hall was rented to the Red Arrow Jazz Orchestra for a dance on June 2, 1920. Price for the evening, $18. The Blue Mound Jazz Band rented the hall on a 35-65% basis. Eddie Fortier's Novelty Four had a dance on June 18 and paid the League $20.00.

A sink, sewer and waterworks were installed. A Timberman's Dance was given with the receipts $25.00. The movie, *The Girl from Outside* brought in $27.00. The $4,000 the League had borrowed from the bank was all spent on remodeling and $3.14 besides.

In 1920 the Frolics began, probably the most fun Bayfield ever had, and they were certainly the greatest money raisers in the history of the League. Doortenders were appointed for afternoon and evening during the week before the Frolic, so no one could get in and see any part of the preparations.

The late A. H. Wilkinson wrote this about the Frolics, "I remember for the first Frolic I had Agnes Fiege and Herman Sense assisting me with the stage shows. We ran a show for one hour on the big stage. We opened with just enough show to run one night, which made it necessary for us to find and rehearse a show for every night as we went along. It was a remarkable thing that we finished Saturday with more show than we could use. After the stage show we had sideshows and booths selling many things. Hannah Nelson handled the merchandise. We were blessed with fine weather and the show caught on with the people and they came in droves. By Saturday night, the place was so packed we were turning them away. Robert Inglis said it cost him ten cents to get in and twenty-five dollars to get out."

The first year the Civic League Frolic took in $4,613.72, the disbursements were $2,300.63, giving the League a nice net profit of $2,313.09. $2,000 were immediately turned over to Mr. Pine, former owner of the Armory, which saved the League $10.00 interest.

October 11, 1920 the League decided to have a woodcutting bee at their hall. Everybody was to invite everybody and a lunch of baked beans, sandwiches, cake and coffee was to be served.

That winter the hall was rented to the city basketball team.

When the time came to install the furnace, a large group of local businessmen went down and did the work, donating their labor.

The dances brought the League a problem. At the meeting April 25, 1921, a motion was made and carried that in the future, cheek to cheek dancing; the shimmy and "any other undesirable dances that might be invented" would not be allowed in Memorial Hall. Placards were put up to this effect.

May 26, 1921 a working bee was held on the grounds. The yard was thoroughly raked and grass seed planted. Then, with the grounds so neatly fixed, it was voted that they should not be rented at any time for lunch counters or peanut stands.

August 1, 1921, in making plans for the second Frolic the League decided that gambling games with no returns should be eliminated, which was a pretty fair thing to do, especially when the ladies were so eager to make money. They also decided there would be no jitney dances. The price of the dance would be decided on by a committee.

Mr. Turnquist donated a goat to be given as a prize during the Frolic. Mrs. H. J. Wachsmuth was appointed to take charge of the goat. If this seems to you like a startling and wild choice for a goat tender, as it did to me, recall the barns of the Wachsmuth Lumber Company, where the goat probably went to reside with the horses until he was awarded as a prize to some lucky winner. But whoever won this goat evidently would not take him as a gift, for after the Frolic since it seemed impossible to dispose of the goat in any other way, the League decided to return him to Mr. Turnquist at once.

The League made a decision not to book any entertainment where the bulk of the receipts were to be taken out of the city, at least not until the hall was paid for.

A community picnic was held at Dalrymple Park. The League furnished coffee, cream and sugar, with each member paying 10 cents into a fund for this purpose. Each family brought their own lunch and one lemon for each member of the family.

The League held an informal discussion on the advisability of hiring the Ashland orchestra again to play for dances in the hall, as many unfavorable criticisms of the orchestra had been made. What the orchestra did or did not do the minutes do not say.

The ladies of the League had high standards, and felt there should be no shirking of obligations. Mrs. Donald C. Bell, who was president at the time, called attention to the fact that very few of the League members had been present at the funeral of Miss Della Olson, one of the League's most faithful members, and that in the future, on like occasions, more consideration should be shown on the part of every member. This was written into the League minutes so it would be remembered.

H. J. Wachsmuth was still doing his best to help the League. He offered to send them dry hardwood at the same price as the green hemlock they had ordered if the League would get volunteers to pile it in the basement. They agreed, but at the next meeting gave Mr.

Wachsmuth a rising vote of thanks, for he had not only delivered the wood, but had it piled neatly in the basement for them.

In November 1921, the League sponsored an Armistice Day parade, accompanied by bells and whistles and there was an afternoon program. The hall was kept open all day for those who wished to attend and bring their own lunches. The League served coffee.

Paul Johnson donated four loads of pine stumps to help keep the building warm through the winter.

The League suddenly discovered that back taxes, amounting to nearly $100, for 1918, had not been paid. It was suggested that since Company D (Home Guard) was using the building at that time, the bill be sent to the state, but in the meantime the League paid the taxes, so that no one could buy tax titles on their treasured property.

At the New Years Eve dance, four cases of pop called "Lovitt" were donated to the League. Does anyone remember ever drinking this particular beverage?

The story of the Bayfield Civic League is continued. Late in 1921 the Men's Club seemed to abandon the idea of fixing up the library basement. In spite of the fine business advice they gave the ladies, they trailed them in activity. Now they came forward again, sending Dr. Harris to put their best feet forward and speak well for them in their persistent search for a basement they could call home. They now wished to fix up the Memorial Hall basement with a concrete floor, a bowling alley, billiard and pool tables, a shooting gallery and a kitchen and dining room for the Civic League.

All of these improvements would be made in the Ladies new hall, but the financial responsibility would be assumed almost entirely by the men. The ladies liked the idea, but were not hasty, perhaps remembering the library basement, which had never been remodeled, though the ladies had offered $100 and lots of encouragement. They appointed a committee to think about the idea some more.

The men then had a meeting to plan the formation of an Athletic Association for themselves, and evidently felt the need of good food to sustain them during the strenuous feats they were planning, for they requested the League to serve them a lunch. The ladies promptly agreed to do this.

It was decided that Junior parties at Memorial Hall should close at twelve, and that there should always be a League chaperone present, but the young people could have a choice of chaperone from the League members. Therefore, it must go without saying that the youngest and most lenient League members were always chosen for this duty.

By this time the Bayfield American Legion had grown into a thriving organization and was given free use of the hall.

In February, 1922, there was a big storm and the condition of the roads were so bad that Mrs. D.C. Bell, president, announced that the entertainment of the Salmo Club would have to be postponed.

About this time a small fire was discovered in the hall. It broke out under the fireplace during a dance. According to findings made by a committee of men, including Paul Pedersen, fire chief, the cause of the fire was an overheated fireplace. It was February, and the leaping flame in the big fireplace must have looked good to those coming in from the cold outdoors. They kept throwing in the wood, making the flames leap higher and higher until the chimney got too hot.

March 13, 1922, the roads were evidently in good condition again, for the Salmo Club was welcomed to the Federation of Women's Club with a big party given by the Civic League. It was a good day for a party, warmed by bright spring sun, the snow was melting a little and a large assemblage of League members turned out to welcome the Salmo Club members, who appeared with every one of their members present.

At that time, Mrs. Leadbetter was the district president of the Federation. A letter from her was read emphasizing that it was the duty of country women to make living conditions on farms more attractive for women and children, in order to bring back to the county the populations lost to city jobs during the war. They didn't sing "How You Gonna Keep 'Em Down on the Farm," but they did sing a song "Salmo", composed by Mrs. D.C. Bell, which began "Salmo, the little club of human kindness. . ." The tune was "Irene." The history of the Salmo Club was read, it had also been founded in 1913, the same year as the Civic League. The Salmo Club began with four members who met for companionship. Mrs. Stensvad, who was present, was one of the original four members.

A solo *Main Street* was sung by Mrs. Grover Boutin, accompanied by Mrs. Joanis. The words to this song are of local interest, evidently being all about our Bayfield main street. The music was composed in part by Miss Hazel Crawford. Does anyone have a copy of this song?

The program closed with *Farewell Salmo,* sung to the tune of *Cherie.* It began "Farewell Salmo, you're nice, just as nice as you can be. . .and it ended, "Salmo, farewell, three cheers, Federated Salmo."

March 27, 1922, Mrs. Stewart donated a flagpole for the yard of Memorial Hall and in 1956 the League, still very flagpole conscious, donated the fine steel flagpole at the city dock. It was dedicated during the Centennial Celebration and the Centennial Time Capsule was placed in the concrete at the base of it.

In April 1922, the League gathered a list of names of the Bayfield boys, living and dead, who took part in the Great World War, which unfortunately in later years, had to be renamed World War I. The list was to be placed on the walls of Memorial Hall.

Being a strongly feminine organization, the League was anxious to get the kitchen remodeled, and they did. The men helped all they could by donating labor. The biggest donators of labor were O.M. Nygaard, 24 hours; James Gundry, 16 hours; H. L. Erickson, 32 hours; Bill Weber 8 hours, and Charles Vincent, 12 hours.

There was dance after dance in the old hall and many parties for young people, well chaperoned by League members. But as the crowds grew their exuberance grew and in April 1922, it was necessary to ask the council to appoint a special policeman to act at all affairs held at Memorial Hall.

The Legion asked if they could convert the upper north end of the hall into clubrooms, but the League felt that the hall should not be partitioned off, that it should remain one large room to be used by everyone, so the request was unanimously voted down.

Again in September 1922, it was necessary to discuss police protection at the hall, especially during dances. The crowds were big and fun loving, but. . .in January 1920, the Prohibition amendment had gone into effect becoming the unintentional foster parent of the Moonshine Era with its rumrunners, stills, and bathtub gin. Liquor, which had once been confined to saloons where no lady would set foot, now was defiantly poured into silver hip flasks, became a necessity at parties, made millionaires out of bootleggers.

The nice old-fashioned phrase used by the ladies, "lips that touch liquor shall never touch mine" became a great big joke. By the time the amendment was repealed, 13 years later, it was far too late. Syndicates of gangsters formed during the Prohibition Era moved on to new activities. Alcoholics Anonymous moved in for salvage.

But the League met this bad drinking situation by petitioning the council for a special policeman for outdoors and turned over the policing inside of the hall to "our responsible businessmen." The men were to throw the unruly out the front door to the outside policemen who would take them to jail.

My dad, Doug Knight, being on call as one of "the responsible businessmen" was requested to throw out an unruly character after the ladies had politely asked him to leave and he had boisterously refused. He threw him out, all right, but his clothes were ripped to shreds, which he claims he does not remember, but my mother remembers perfectly, most likely because she had to do the mending.

That fall the League discussed whether or not they should have the community fair on the upper or lower floor of the hall. They finally decided to use the upper floor for everything except cattle and poultry. The animals were to stay in the basement.

All during these years the League was doing welfare work. If people were burned out, the League was there, ill, the League was there, temporary financial hardship, the League was there. Reading page after page in their minutes, listing donations made by this comparatively small group of women, it would seem as if all the baskets they gave in their welfare work alone were placed side by side, the end would be but a faint pin point on the horizon. It is amazing that a group of women in a small town could raise so much money and spend it so well and thoughtfully for the benefit of the community. At one time they paid $250 for a piano for community use. They raised $75 for x-ray equipment for the Sanitarium. They worked hard to get a county nurse, sending a committee before the county board.

Again in 1922, Mr. Wachsmuth was on the job for the League. They thanked him for his generous price on wood and also for having the wood piled in the basement free of charge.

And that big hall took a lot of wood. It was finally decided to have just one meeting a month during January, February and March. Previously they had met twice a month. They requested the Legion to meet on the same date, thus a lot of wood was saved.

The League turned down the proposition to sponsor the Chautauqua again at a cost of $1,100, as they had in 1916. They had discovered they made more money on Frolics and had to give no guarantee. The Frolics were also more fun, since everybody got into the act. One of the outstanding performances of the Frolics, still recalled by many, was the wild man act put on by Bostic Gordon, locked in a cage in Memorial Hall basement.

Feb. 12, 1923, the fireplace in Memorial Hall, in spite of repairs, was still defective. The Civic League received an order from the fire marshal to repair it at once. They also planned to purchase fire equipment for the inside of the hall. Mrs. M.B. Johnson, Mrs. John Englund, Mrs. Rowley and Mrs. Belle Leihy were authorized to get prices on two axes, one wrecking bar and 100 feet of hose and a faucet. The committee reported at the next meeting that the equipment would cost about $20. But on motion it was decided to postpone the purchase of fire equipment indefinitely. Was $20 too much? Did the League strain at a gnat (fire equipment) and swallow a camel (the Frolics)? That doesn't seem possible. They just weren't too worried, evidently, for the committee who was to see to the fireplace repair had nothing to report at the next meeting.

In the League notes there is reference to the old cannon, which came to Bayfield with the troops during the Civil War and remained to play a lively part in Bayfield history. The minutes say "An old relic of the Civil War, a cannon, which has been stored in our basement, then received discussion. The question as to whether the cannon was to be disposed of as junk on motion was settled in this manner. That the cannon remain in its present place until such a time in the future when a permanent place be given it on Memorial Hall grounds."

April 9, 1923. The Senior Class of the high school wanted to decorate the stage scenery. The League decided to allow the class to calcimine provided they put on two coats and a League committee work with them. Miss Hannah Nelson and Mrs. E. R. Mitchell volunteered on this committee.

In May, 1923, the League decided to put a veranda on the east side of the hall, a nice porch where people could sit and look at the lake. They did so. The bill for lumber and William Sinclair's labor came to $1,146.00 and provided a porch 110 feet long, 16 feet wide supported by brick foundations. The First National Bank donated the bricks.

In 1923 the Frolic became much fancier. Miss Hazel Melcher of New Richmond, Wisconsin, was hired as manager. For $200 and expenses she took over the entire management of the main show from 8 to 9 o'clock and the various side shows for five nights. She also furnished free $200 worth of costumes, enough for 8 dances.

The League spent weeks getting ready for the Frolic. The mayor was petitioned not to allow any outside lunch counters or concession come into town for the five-day event. Special police were appointed and the fire department placed the chemical cart and large hose within easy reach in case of fire. The Delight orchestra of Ladysmith was hired at a cost of $342.50, this sum including board. The Frolic took in over $2,000 but the expenses had grown larger each year, as new features, attractions and extra days were added. The expenses came to about $1,500 and the profit, therefore was $500.

The community fair was held again in 1923 and here in the League minutes is an item, which, with variations, has been repeated countless times through the years in the minutes of all Bayfield organizations. "Mr. Hauser was voted a letter of thanks for flowers donated for sale for the Memorial Hall Fund."

Nov. 26, 1923, the minutes reported: "A straw vote was taken on our next U.S. President, resulting in a majority for Calvin Coolidge."

In 1924 came the Indian Pageant. The League went to work. They decided that the members would devote 144 hours of work on the pageant between January and August.

The Apostle Islands Indian Pageant. Circa 1924. (Photo: BHA)

The League planned to have a Masquerade Ball on February 12, 1924, but they didn't have it at their hall for one cold night in January, it burned to the ground. It happened during a Girl Scout Party. If the League had purchased their fire equipment it wouldn't have made the slightest difference for when the fire did start, it swept the wooden hall in such a brilliant, consuming blaze that the people at the party barely escaped. Many of them fled without hats or coats, but all lives were saved. Any fire equipment the League owned would have been lost with the building.

The League members were dismayed, of course, but they were not defeated. They went right on with their plans for the Masked Ball, having it at the Pageant Inn and made a profit of $37.90.

After the fire, which destroyed their hall, the League met with 55 of their members present and were unanimously in favor of rebuilding. They received numerous offers of places to meet. Solly Boutin, to comfort them and inspire them to go ahead and rebuild, gave them a gift of $100.

A check for $8,000 for insurance was received and plans for rebuilding were debated frequently. In the meantime, work continued on the Indian Pageant. The Flanders building (where the Standard Oil station now stands) was rented by the Pageant Corporation as a costume shop and those who could, devoted time to sewing for the Pageant. Those who could not sew folded Pageant literature.

The League decided to make pillows, stuffed with excelsior, to be rented at the Pageant. They ordered 750 yards of oilcloth, which would make 1,500 pillows.

They also decided to write a cookbook, the Pageant Cookbook, still in use in many homes today. Prices for printing cookbooks were submitted, the highest was $1,000, the least $639.75 for 1,000 cookbooks. The Bell Printing Company then gave them a really good deal, 2000 copies for $686.70. The League sent a check with the order, getting a 10% discount, and borrowed the money from the bank, evidently not wanting to touch their insurance money.

From the rental of their pillows at the Indian Pageant the League cleared about $80.

**APOSTLE ISLANDS
INDIAN PAGEANT**
Bayfield, Wisconsin
August 1st to 21st, 1924
SEASON TICKET

№ 541　Price $3.00
Tax Included

Pageant ticket.
(Photo: BHA)

About this time the cannery was getting started in Bayfield and the League loaned half of their insurance money to the cannery, which they felt would help the farmers and would put a new payroll in the community.

Rebuilding the hall was uppermost in the thoughts of the League members. A rough estimate of the cost of a Natio-Tile stucco finished brick trimmed building was given as approximately $13,900. Gravel and stone were already being hauled to raise and repair the basement walls of the burned building.

The estimate of Tomlinson and Eagan for a new building was $25,000, but as the building couldn't be put up in time for the Pageant, a motion was made and carried that plans be dropped for the present.

The League wanted to put a temporary roof over the basement of the hall, which could then be made usable as a one-story structure, but this would not comply with the requirements of the Industrial commission, and the League decided not to spend the money on a temporary room.

The League gave thought to buying two other buildings in town for remodeling. Mrs. Turnquist offered her brick building, then occupied by the Farmer's and Merchant's State Bank and the Sense Grocery store for $12,000. Ed Baldwin offered his Lake View property for $4,000, payments on any terms the League wished.

After inspecting the two buildings, League members decided the Turnquist building would cost too much to make into a hall. They still considered Mr. Baldwin's building, feeling it was nearer the kind of building they wanted. Eventually a vote was taken. Seven members wanted to buy and twenty didn't. It is just as well they bought neither, for the Turnquist building burned and was swept completely away in the 1942 flood. Baldwin's building, a wooden structure on the corner of Washington Avenue and Front Street, burned to the ground.

The League turned their thoughts to the vocational building, the old courthouse, built in 1884, thinking it might have possibilities, but the desire to rebuild was strong. It was decided to have a mass meeting at the Princess Theater on May 15, 1925.

At this meeting, H. J. Wachsmuth made the Civic League the best proposal they ever had. He would furnish all the lumber at cost. The lumber company would donate about $2,000 worth of brownstone for a front and all the iron bracing and timbers could be gotten from the old mill at about ⅓ of the regular price. The League, at that time, still had $4,000 of their insurance money for a start. When all costs were figured, it would be necessary to borrow between $10,000 and $12,000. After much discussion a standing vote was taken. Three people were for rebuilding. Fourteen people were against it. If there were any other League embers among the forty people present that day, they did not vote.

The League minutes say: "It seemed that the members have not the courage to assume such a vast debt." The secretary was asked to send Mr. Wachsmuth a note of thanks for his kind interest and offer.

You may think, "Why didn't they take that proposition, then we'd have a nice community building, surely all paid for by this time. But if you were suddenly asked to help raise $12,000 would you vote to do it or not?

Mr. Stanghor, who built Lakeside Pavilion, wanted to buy the League property, but they didn't want to sell it. If they had he would most likely have built the pavilion there, which might have been nice, except we would then have no public park. Also, being a wooden shell it was not usable in winter and was just as subject to fire as the old building.

Even with all the confusion about rebuilding, the League did not neglect their work at the library. On Oct. 29, 1925, they met there to have a mending bee for books. More than 100 books were mended and 150 new books were accessioned and put on the shelves. Baked beans, cole slaw and coffee were furnished. Workers brought their own sandwiches and cake.

The League allowed the Band Boys to flood the old Memorial Hall basement for an ice skating rink and the boys used the money received from admittance charge to pay for their band uniforms and lessons.

Then the League began to give away what was left of the hall. In 1926 they gave one of the furnaces to the library, to replace one, which had given out there.

At the January 26th meeting, Mrs. Whiting spoke urging the League to look into the social morality of the city. At that time there was a person of undesirable moral character here (he has since departed). Though the League wished strongly to have him leave, it was not until the October 10, 1927 meeting that the members held an open and determined discussion of ways to get rid of him. Since there seemed to be no way to dispose of him (short of murder, which naturally was not considered by the League ladies), the matter was referred to the ordinance committee.

In April 1928, some more of Memorial Hall went. The city was given the stone foundation for filling in the city dock. It could no longer be built on and had deteriorated to the point where it was an eyesore. The city removed the stone and filled in the basement.

The League then had their ground plowed, leveled and seeded. In 1930 they spent $300 for landscaping, making it into the beautiful little waterfront park we have today, preserving that section of the shoreline so it could not be used for commercial purposes and would always be open to the public. Since that time they have spent a large amount with generous donations from the Hauser's to help them and the little park has become a beauty spot for the town.

The League considered buying the present Iverson building when the Power Company moved out, but did not. The old pageant Inn was considered, but not purchased. It, also, was an old wooden building, since torn down, and the land made into an attractive land-scaped parking lot by Mr. and Mrs. V. Greunke.

In May 1922, several elm trees and one evergreen were planted in the city by school children and civic organizations in honor of the George Washington Bi-Centennial celebration. The trees were purchased by the Civic League and the Bayfield School and were planted along Broad Street from Rittenhouse Avenue to the library. Mrs. John Kranzfelder, representing the League, threw in the first earth around the pine tree. Lillian Hanson represented the high school, Billy Sayles grades 7 & 8, Betsy Iverson grades 5 & 6, Miriam Walstad grades 3 & 4, Robert Hadland, grades 1 & 2, and Merlin Fisher and Leon Nelson helped plant the pine tree.

In February 1932, the Nelson building, now George Joanis's tavern, was considered as a community building, but was dropped form the list of prospects. That year the League gave the city $3,000 of their insurance money to remodel the old courthouse with special clubrooms for the League.

Labor expenses were met by funds from the state unemployment relief, since the WPA Era had been reached. Not much new lumber was needed, as in wrecking the interior nearly enough lumber of excellent quality was obtained. H. L. Erickson and William Morrin were in charge of remodeling. Between 10 and 20 men worked each day, each man working a three-day shift three times a month. The first League meeting was held in their new rooms on May 8, 1933.

And then as years pass what was once new becomes old. The new community building became the old community building. The Junior Civic League was the first to move out, taking their worldly goods to the library where they built an attractive kitchen. The Senior League followed suit, abandoning their rooms completely. The high school got a new gym and fled the premises. The city council held out a while but at last they fled, too, trailing the ladies from the decrepit, obsolete building to the library and they took the elections with them. Even the nice, sea-gull type of bird on top of the building didn't fly right any more (and still doesn't) and the neighbors were forced to use other methods of telling which way the wind was blowing.

The building had turned into a white elephant, or rather a pink elephant, for it is built of pink sandstone. With or without a drink, this dilapidated pink elephant was perfectly visible standing forlornly in the center of town. No one knew what to do with it until recently (1957) Leon McCarty decided he wasn't afraid to tackle it. He bought it from the city to be used as a factory, and there was rejoicing at the prospect of having it back on the taxroll and a payroll added to the city.

In March 1957, the Bayfield Civic League celebrated their 44th birthday with a luncheon at the Hotel Bayfield. Mrs. Roy Okerstrom, who has served as League president longer than anyone, a total of 16 years, presided. After 44 years of doing good deeds for Bayfield, their spirit still thrives, reflected in the constantly growing beauty of their park and in the brightness of the Christmas lighting, which they provide for the community each year.

The Commercial Club

W AY BACK IN THE SUMMER of 1909, the Bayfield Commercial Club published some facts about Bayfield. Check them over, and see if they are still facts today.

Bayfield the harbor city with a population of 3,000 is located on the Bayfield Peninsula rich in stone, timber and land value.

Bayfield has two railroads, the C. St. Paul M. & O. Ry from the south and the Bayfield Transfer Ry, with its line running along the lakeshore and across the peninsula. Plans are now being made to extend this line to Superior and Duluth.

Bayfield has 3 sawmills with a capacity of 530 thousand feet of lumber in 24 hours, besides lath and shingles.

Bayfield is now building a complete box manufacturing plant with a capacity of 20,000,000 feet of box lumber annually.

Bayfield is the home of the Lake Superior Towing Company with a fleet of boats for handling scows and rafts of logs from any part of Lake Superior.

Bayfield, with its large fishing industry furnishes you with Lake Superior whitefish and trout caught around the islands. The fall herring pack employs hundreds of men.

Bayfield has a brownstone city hall.

Bayfield has one of the largest and best-equipped fish hatcheries in the United States.

Bayfield promises to become the center of the most profitable fruit-growing region in the country. July strawberries, August cherries, and certain varieties of apples, commanding the best prices in a late market.

Bayfield Peninsula is protected from frosts by reason of being nearly surrounded by the deep water of Lake Superior. State frost bulletins give the same frost condition as southern counties in Wisconsin as to dates of spring and fall frosts.

Bayfield's Commercial Club secured the development of a steam stump puller for clearing land at a minimum cost.

The *Bayfield* Peninsula soil survey is now being made by the U.S. Agriculture Department.

Bayfield is exerting her best efforts to secure a complete and modern road system for her farmers.

Bayfield Peninsula is a natural grass producing country.

Bayfield fruit growers have set 125 acres to strawberries this season.

Bayfield will need 700 berry pickers next season.

Bayfield has a public library erected at a cost of $12,000 with 4,660 volumes.

Bayfield owns its own water and light plant, furnishing pure water and service at a minimum cost.

Bayfield is the gateway to the famous Apostle Islands.

Bayfield has a daily boat service among the Apostle Islands.

Bayfield is situated on Lake Superior, the largest body of fresh water in the world.

Bayfield has a new city dock, located near the center of the town, built for the exclusive use of passenger boats of all kinds and for the accommodation of pleasure seekers.

Bayfield's Athletic Association owns its ballpark and athletic field.

Bayfield Peninsula land values are constantly increasing, giving a safe and profitable investment for capital.

Bayfield harbor permits the construction of docks at which the heaviest draught boats may land for one half the expense necessary for other lake ports.

Bayfield Peninsula has over 40 miles of well-protected lake frontage.

Bayfield's First National Bank owned by its citizens has resources of $326,189.38 on April 28, 1909.

Bayfield has two newspapers, two lawyers, two physicians, one dentist, two large first class hotels, three cigar factories, five groceries, three dry goods and clothing stores, one clothing store, two confectioneries, one millinery, one drug and jewelry store, two meat markets, two shoe stores, three barber shops, opera house, two liveries, one furniture store, two hardwares, two tailor shops, two blacksmith shops, cement block plant, planing mill, one plumbing and repair shop, and numerous small hotels, restaurants, bakeries, etc.

Bayfield is healthfully located and has an exceptionally low death rate.

Bayfield has a complete and modern telephone exchange.

Bayfield's streets are lined up on both sides with beautiful shade trees.

Bayfield's wooden sidewalks are fast being replaced by cement walks.

Bayfield has a well-organized Commercial Club to whom you can write for information.

Bayfield's bonded indebtedness is $20,000 on the entire township comprising 100,000 acres.

Bayfield is favored with natural scenic advantages and offers many attractive spots for campers, boaters and recreation seekers.

Bayfield is noted as a mecca for hay fever sufferers. The lakeshore and island shores are fast becoming dotted with summer homes.

Bayfield's harbor is said by the government engineers to be the best fresh water harbor in the world. Protected shores, and surrounded by the beautiful Apostle Islands.

Bayfield's post office receipts in 1898 were $2,545 and in 1908 were $4,110. The receipts in 1908 do not include receipts in sub-stations created in the past six years at Cornucopia, and Red Cliff, which mail is handled through the Bayfield post office.

Bayfield's public schools are excelled by none in the great state of Wisconsin. Has free high school, manual training and domestic science departments.

Bayfield has one parochial school and children's' home.

Bayfield has seven churches.

Bayfield has an efficient fire department.

Bayfield Wants; Woodworking plants, brush factory, gasoline boat factory, glove and mitten factory, steam laundry, dry dock, canning plant, pickle factory, nursery, creamery, boat livery, more summer homes, more farmers, more fruit growers.

Watch The Peninsula Grow. The Tuesday Club

Most of the Bayfield history so far has been about men, their boats, their fishing, their baseball, their town building, their pioneering and their speechmaking. It is high time to write about the part women have taken in the history of our town. This was brought to mind when I learned that the 48th birthday of the Tuesday Club was on May 7th. This is the oldest active women's club in Bayfield. Many thanks to Mrs. Donald C. Bell, of Minneapolis, who sent the following Tuesday Club history.

"The Tuesday Club was organized on Arbor Day, Friday, May 7th, 1909.

Due to the fact Mrs. Alfred LaBonte of Ashland was visiting her folks, the George McHenrys, before moving with her husband to Detroit, Michigan, Mrs. A. H. Wilkinson entertained at a bridge luncheon in her honor. After partaking of the excellent food, the hostess passed paper and pencils and a questionnaire on *Names of Trees* (it being Arbor Day.) The prizes were small elm trees, ready for planting. Having won one, I planted it on Father Bell's (Currie Bell) grounds, where the Fruit Association is now located. (Now part of Allwood.) It did very well for many years. When that land was sold to the Association, it evidently was removed.

We later played bridge and enjoyed such a pleasant afternoon that Mrs. McHenry said she thought we should form a bridge club and meet twice a month. All present were in favor of this, and Mrs. Wilkinson was nominated as President. Several said they did not like Friday for club day so it was decided that Tuesday was most suitable to all and we would name it the Tuesday Club.

Those present were (as near as I can remember) Mrs. A. H. Wilkinson, hostess; Mrs. Alfred LaBonte, honored guest, Mrs. George McHenry and her mother, whose name I cannot recall, also a guest; Mrs. J. P. O'Malley, Mrs. John Kiel, Mrs. Theo Wieland, Mrs. Herbert Hale, Mrs. Donald Bell, Miss Edith LaBonte.

Agnes Kiel did not decide to join the club that day, and did not do so until some time later. I cannot remember whether Edith LaBonte became a member or not. As a result, I guess Greta (O'Malley) and myself are the only charter members who are living, unless Edith LaBonte was a member, and Mrs. T. Wieland may still be living." (Does anyone know?)

Others who joined the club through the years were: Mrs. Frank Boutin, Mrs. John Kiel, Mrs. Wm. Bassett, Mrs. Douglas Knight, Mrs. Wm. Weber, Mrs. H. G. Mertens, Mrs. O. L. Shepherd, Mrs. H. J. Wachsmuth, Mrs. John Dady, Mrs. H. Sense, Mrs. G. B. Thompson, Mrs. F. M. Herrick, Mrs. Stanley Hale, Mrs. F. Bigelow, Mrs. Percy Inglis, Mrs. Ed Mitchell, Miss Anne Padden, Mrs. Roy Okerstrom, Mrs. I. B. Iverson, Mrs. Leon McCarty.

During their 48 years, the Tuesday Club has had only seven presidents. They were: Mrs. A. H. Wilkinson, Mrs. D. C. Bell, Mrs. Herman Sense, Mrs. D. S. Knight, Mrs. I.B. Iverson, Mrs. Roy Okerstrom and Mrs. Leon McCarthy.

The Tuesday Club is a club of friendship. Through 48 years of meeting on Tuesdays, strong friendships have developed. It has never showed signs of breaking up. No one ever got mad and quit. No one ever got tired and left because it was simply and honestly a club of friends who enjoy each others company. During the early days, it was partly a sewing club, but the members found that darning their husband's socks while they visited was quite boring and they switched entirely to bridge.

One Monday evening each month the ladies had a dinner meeting and invited their husbands. Husbands and wives added their bridge scores together and the winners got sterling silver salad forks.

Mrs. Bell remarked in her recent letter that she and Don had won eight of them through the years. But the lion's share of these salad forks were won by a couple whose name I will not mention. She was not a club member, but they were invited often to make an even number for bridge. The salad forks cost about $3.00 and the couple went home with fork after fork, much to the dismay of the members. My mother and dad, by a stupendous effort or an unusual piece of luck one evening, managed to win a fork, which to this day is referred to by all of us as the Tuesday Club salad fork. Anyone eating with us who has a fork that does not match anything will now know it is our one and only Tuesday Club salad fork.

Though the Tuesday Club is not primarily a money-raising club, they have managed to do many good little deeds. During World War I, they adopted a French war orphan, have given magazine subscriptions to the library and Pureair Sanitarium and have donated for special civic and individual needs.

A picnic luncheon had been planned by the Tuesday Club members for their anniversary, but due to the fact that Mrs. Roy Okerstrom was in the hospital, the celebration was postponed until she is able to attend.

Chapter 7

Fun & Festivities

Baseball in Bayfield

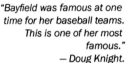

"Bayfield was famous at one time for her baseball teams. This is one of her most famous."
— Doug Knight.

Top L-R. Ed Miller, George Gordon, Douglas Knight, Manager, Jim Long, Glasphell LaBonte, Harry Arseneau. Front L-R. Irvin Day, Nels Brigham, Hillard Boutin, Francis (Dodie) Boutin, Roy Southmayd. circa 1906-1909 (Photo: William Knight Family)

N OW THAT THE BASEBALL SEASON is well underway and Bayfield High School has succeeded in beating Washburn High School, it is a good time to recall a game that made the fans furious back in July 1909.

The Bayfield Press said: "Despite the fact that the Washburn baseball team came to this city last Sunday well padded up with hired outside players, they were unable to hold their own with the locals in what promised to be a splendid game. The game, however, came to an abrupt end in the 5th inning when Washburn refused to play anymore. This was not surprising, however, as it was evident they came here with a "card up their sleeve" intending to either carry off the honors and all bets or forfeit the game and play even. The Washburn team had a strong line-up. . . but strong as they were the locals were better and after the first inning Washburn didn't have a show. Washburn quit, forfeiting the game 9 to 0. It is rumored that the local Athletic Association will, in the future, bar the Washburn aggregation from the local ground, which is conceded by the fans as just procedure considering the action of the Washburn team."

Though the strong feeling over the courthouse deal colored most Bayfield and Washburn affairs, a letter describing this ball game, written by A. Fan, makes Washburn seem very dishonest, or Bayfield very naive and trusting. It is as follows: "The most sweet scented case of welching that ever came under the writer's observation was shown by one or two of the members of the so called Washburn baseball team. This welch act was evidently by a pre-arranged plan (and I will say right here that some of our Bayfield sports are dead easy.) These would-be sports from Washburn came up here with a wad to bet on their team and were eager to cover all the gilt our boys had. Our boys were willing, a little too willing, I think, for had they been a little bit better educated in the game, they would have seen the coon in the stone heap, for these astute gamers from Washburn so worded the conditions in all their wagers that the Bayfield boys who laid any bets on the game hadn't as much chance to win as these same Washburn sports have of going to heaven. They (the Washburn sports) stipulated as one of the conditions in each bet that the game must go nine innings and if the game broke up in a row before that number of innings were played, that all bets should be declared off. How astute! And how gullible our sports were! Why at any time up to the last half of the ninth inning all these dead game sports from Washburn had to do, if the Bayfield team were so far ahead as to preclude any chance of the Washburn team winning, to protect their best was to start a row and quit playing (which they did). But if they were able to beat the Bayfield team, they knew that the Bayfield boys would not under any condition start a row for any such a purpose. Sweet-scented artists? In the tin horn game I allow."

None of this fighting or letter writing discouraged the Bayfield fans even slightly. The very next week a petition was circulated and generally signed asking the Omaha to run a special train to Hayward and return to accommodate the baseball fans who wished to witness the game between the Bayfield Hayward clubs, which was to be played at Hayward.

Baseball also became part of a pool game. June 11, 1909, *The Bayfield Press* said: "The votaries of the pool table at the Commercial Club Rooms have invented a new game which they call Bottle Baseball Pool. It is a fascinating game and calls for the exercise of more head work on the part of the respective teams than has anything as yet been played on the table."

Doug Knight and Baseball

Douglas Knight in his playing days at the University of Wisconsin. circa 1909. (Photo: William Knight Family)

NATURALLY I WAS VERY PLEASED when I came across an item in *The Bayfield Press* telling of a baseball game my dad, Doug Knight, played in. The game was between Bayfield and Ashland in August 1908, one of the years he was a player on the University of Wisconsin baseball team.

The Press said, "Rube" Knight, who covered first during the first six innings of the game went into the box for the locals in the seventh for a "little practice" as he called it. And say! The fun he had with those Ashland batters was certainly amusement for the large crowd. They came to bat and returned to the bench as fast as they came. Only one hit was secured off Knight and that was secured off a slow ball, which Knight threw to see if the batter could hit it. As the batter told afterward, he happened to hit the ball by shutting his eyes and slamming away, hitting the ball to the right garden. . . the final score 20 to 7 for Bayfield."

Since my dad is more apt to talk about what the Braves are doing than his own exploits on the baseball diamond, I am very grateful to Walter Harris of the Antiaircraft Artillery and Guided Missile Center of Fort Bliss, Texas, for sending me an article about those baseball days. Mr. Harris has been writing some articles to be used as permanent documents of the State Historical Society.

In 1909, Doug Knight was elected Captain of the University of Wisconsin baseball team. Mr. Harris reports further events as follows: "In the fall of 1909, as the result of negotiations between the University of Wisconsin and Keio University (of Japan), a series was arranged overseas.

Said Prof. E. A. Ross in a talk before his sociology class as the Badgers were preparing to leave: "American ideals have been introduced to Eastern countries more quickly through baseball than through ordinary channels; and when Doug Knight hurls his curve ball past the bat of Japan's leading swatsmith, and then rifles a three-bagger beyond a Jap outfielder's reach, he will, in reality, be giving messages of American progress to the people of the Far East."

Then, looking at Doug Knight, Prof. Ross said: "Good luck to you. . . Captain Knight. You and Admiral Perry are rated as ambassadors without portfolio."

A Madison sports writer, in covering this unique Japanese event, referred to Doug as "one of the stars last spring in the Western College world, popular among the players."

Wisconsin had only 13 players when arriving aboard the ship Aki-Maru at Yokohama early that fall. These youngsters, on the water for 17 days, were out of practice. . .

As a gesture of good will on the ball field before the first game, Yukichi Fukuzawa, son of the Keio University founder, presented Doug Knight with a huge wreath of flowers, tied with the colors of Japan and the United States. . .

One game lasted 19 innings with Doug Knight pitching the first 16 and also poling a home run. The Japs won that day. But the next afternoon, Wisconsin offset this defeat by winning 4 to 1, and acquired four other victories in a nine-game series, thus finishing the best. Allowing only three hits in one nip-and-tuck battle, Doug lost to the Japs on an infield error. . . When in need of a day's rest as pitcher, Doug played at first base.

In his home town at Bayfield a year later, Doug started the correspondence which resulted in a Keio University barnstorming tour within the United States; and in the spring of 1911, when the Japs landed at San Francisco, Doug Knight was there to meet them and to direct the tour activities. The first game for the Orientals was against the University of California at Berkeley. . .

At Ashland on Saturday, June 10 (1911) Keio won 5 to 4. Ashland's pitcher, Gordon, hit a Jap on the head, causing him to leave the game on a stretcher; but a few days later, at Superior, the same Oriental was in Keio's line up, able to hit and field as of yore.

Thousands of red-hot Chequamegon Bay fans were in Fairmount Park at the corner of West Sixth Street and Cemetery Road on Sunday, June 11, for the final game with Keio. Hundreds were sardined along the first and third-base lines as play started.

On the mound for Tom Uptehgrove's Ashland club was young Bill Snow, one of four all-time-local greats, who was destined to be a foremost Northern League pitcher. The shrewd Frank Asplund, developer of pitching immortals, was behind the plate with Antoine Starr as short, Schlitz Weiss at second, Frank Sidlo at first, Paulie Binsfield in left field, Harry Nord in center and fleet-footed McBride of Odanah in right field.

Stocky little Bill Snow of White River, pitching superbly and holding a one-run edge until the eighth inning, weakened on the fag end, walking one Jap and yielding a base hit.

The Japs tied the score. Excitement was intense. Manager Uptehgrove, gambling to a big extent, asked Frank Sidlo to stop a rally in the 10th inning. Sidlo was unable to make Upte happy. He was pounded. Keio scored two runs on him, winning 3 to 1.

The hearts of many Ashlanders were damaged that day. There was some consolation for players who had performed brilliantly. Fielder Paul Binsfield, for instance, acquired three hits out of five trips to the plate. Asplund, Starr, Sidlo, Snow and McBride each got one hit."

The "Big Ravine" ball park on a typical Sunday afternoon in the 1930's. Players Tommy "June" Thompson, Tots Cadotte, Joe Deragon, Andy Polaski, Sam and brother "Sticker" Newago, played teams from Ashland, Madeline Island, Cornucopia, Washburn and the famous Superior Blues.
(Photo: BHA)

Bayfield Celebrations

T HE EVE OF THE BAYFIELD Centennial Celebration is a good time to recall other celebrations and entertainment, which have been held in the Harbor City.

In July 1872, the great Conklin Brothers circus and animal show came to Bayfield. It was the first circus to visit this part of Lake Superior. The tug Fero ran two special excursions from Ashland to Bayfield for the performances.

In 1890, as today, the church supper was a popular way to entertain and to raise money. On September 13, 1890, *The Press* reported: "The Ladies of the Presbyterian Church gave an old fashioned New England supper at William Haskin's store Tuesday evening of this week. Supper was served from six to ten and in the early part of the evening, the ladies had many more guests waiting to be served than they could find seats for. A reporter of *The Press* dropped in again about 8:30 and found the tables still comfortably filled with every prospect that they would continue so until a late hour. Real old-fashioned baked beans and chicken pie that makes our mouth water even now to think of it, seemed to be the favorite dishes. The chicken pie roosted too high very early in the evening and latecomers were obliged to content themselves with the humble, but soul-satisfying bean. Even beans were at a premium before ten o'clock. The ladies who served were attired after the style of our great grandmothers and the transformation of dress to a century back was so complete that it was difficult to recognize the wearers. Social gatherings of this kind have now become quite the rage and they certainly add to the attractiveness of life and aid a good cause. And now the ladies are again attractively attired in the styles of their great grandmothers to celebrate Bayfield's 100th birthday.

The large scale, all-out type of celebration has always been popular in Bayfield. In fact the Labor Day celebration in 1906 was so big that it wouldn't fit into one day, and parts of the program had to be cut out. *The Press* gave this account of it. "Three train loads of passengers from Washburn and Ashland and hundreds brought here by the steamers Skater and Barker comprised the representation of those two cities at the Labor Day celebration in Bayfield. The number of visitors from outside was considerably more than anticipated. All means of transportation were overtaxed and many who wanted to come had to be left behind. It is estimated that close to 1,000 people arrived by land and by boat. The parade was the largest ever seen in Bayfield and owing to the length of some of the events numbers of others had to be abandoned."

Arthur Fiege won the greased pole climb, and must have been declared champion, for he also had won it at the Fourth of July celebration that year. George Glazier of Washburn was first in logrolling.

The Bayfield Cornet Band was great on parades. Any old occasion was good enough to start them off and for no special reason; they went on parade one September evening. *The Press* had this account. "Last Tuesday night the Bayfield Cornet Band paraded our principle streets for about two hours and furnished the inhabitants of this otherwise quiet burg with a large amount of good music. They first visited the editor's residence, but not finding him at home, they moved down to Col. Wing's house and after they had discoursed a few sweet strains, Manager Williams presented the Colonel with a handsomely framed photograph of the band. The Colonel accepted the gift in a few well-chosen remarks and later accompanied this thanks substantially with a check for $25.00. After parading around the street for a few minutes, the boys next stopped in front of Banker Knight's residence and Manager Williams in a handsome speech presented Mr. Knight with a similar photograph, referred to him as the first banker in Bayfield and wishing him success in the enterprise. Replying briefly, Mr. Knight invited the boys inside. At this point, the reporter, not being a member of the band, lost sight of them for a few minutes, but their looks of satisfaction as they came out of the house showed that Mr. and Mrs. Knight had received them in a very pleasant manner. Serenades followed at the residence of Mrs. Lay, in honor of her niece Miss Fox, who is visiting here from Detroit, Michigan, the home of undersheriff Van Horn and the residence of Mr. and Mrs. M.B. Conklin who were celebrating their silver wedding."

And in 1924, the Men's Club did not need a program for their meetings. Their talented members provided the entertainment. *The Press* report is as follows: "The Bayfield Men's Club had a bimonthly banquet followed by an impromptu program. Forty-three members were present. Joe O'Malley, president, gave a rendition of a dance number, which leads us to believe he lies about his age. Bill Miller put on his famous war-whoop dance all togged up in a gaily-colored bathrobe and carrying a hatchet covered with gore. Dr. Mertens gave two French dialect readings; Kenneth Ellis recited *Last Show in Plunkville Texas.* Johnny Sayles amused everyone with his Swede dialect rendition of Barbara Fritchie. Shine Miller pulled his popular peg-leg number and Don Bell killed the session with his basso rendition of *Annie Laurie.*"

Bayfield Celebrations and Entertainments

A MONG THE PAST EVENTS ENJOYABLY celebrated in Bayfield was the 100th anniversary of the President. The Bayfield Press reported it on May 4, 1889. "The 100th anniversary of the inauguration of the first president of the United States was celebrated in a quiet way by the patriotic citizens who were aroused from their slumbers by the booming of the cannon, a salute of 13 guns being fired at daylight as a salute to the day and the many flags that were flying in the breeze.

The courthouse, R.D. Pike's residence, the store of Mrs. Ley and *The Press* office displayed the ensign of liberty. The store and residence of Andrew Tate were completely hidden by stars and stripes. Fronts of stores of Miss Lizzie Fox and Mr. Barch were most tastefully draped with folds of the red, white and blue, while the starry banner was to be seen in every available spot. The same may truthfully be said of the residence of Col. Cruttenden, which was a marvel of beauty and which displayed the traditional hatchet artistically festooned with the national colors and showed Rice's taste and patriotism.

The bells of the city were all ringing at 9 in the morning accompanied by a chorus of tugs and a mill whistle. The Catholic Knights of Wisconsin met at the Catholic schoolhouse and marched to Christ Church (now Holy Family) where special services were held. In the afternoon, Wing Hose Company turned out on parade for the first time in their new parade uniforms. The hydrant near *The Press* office was tapped and a stream of water thrown through three lengths of hose and over the top of the flat staff on C. T. Andreas' jewelry store.

Of course the kicker was there and declared that neither the waterworks, hose or company was any good, but the test convinced the majority that Bayfield has good fire protection as most cities of several times its size.

Last, but by no means least, worthy of note was the gorgeous display of patriotism, town pride and bunting made by the proprietors of the Island View Hotel. The like was never before seen in this town and seldom in any. Words utterly fail when we attempt to describe the magnificence of the decorations and we must sum them up in one word: **Superb**."

Back in the spring of 1908, Bayfield had some outstanding entertainment. The Episcopal Church ladies gave a home talent play called *The Spinster's Return*. The members of the cast were the ladies of the *Young Ladies Single Blessedness Debating Society*. . . and a few male friends.

The cast included: Mrs. George Packard, Mrs. C.R. Rowley, Mrs. A.G. LaBonte, Mrs. M.B. Johnson, Mrs. C.J. Vorous, Miss Gertrude Owens, Mrs. C.T. Andreas, Miss Gladys Knight, Miss Lila Stark, Miss Edna Vorous, Miss Mae Conlin, Mrs. H. Sense, Miss Hannah Nelson, Mrs. Marie Saunders, Mrs. R.E. Johnson, Mrs. Fitzgerald, Mrs. S.L. Boutin, Mrs. Roy Southmayd, Mrs. B.P. Hill, V.S. Lambert, Grover Boutin, Clayton Ryder, Leonard Bailey, Mattie Rowley, Helen Boutin, Doris Stark, Rachel Lambert, Marguerite Hill, Arden Saunders, Gerald Andreas, Sherwin Johnson and Russell Rowley.

As might have been expected for such an outstanding event the Wing Opera house was packed. Each number was greeted with terrific applause. Arden Saunder's *Pop Goes the Weasel* made a hit, as did Gerald Andreas' poem. The Spinster's orchestra carried the house and they certainly rendered some fine selections. There was a specialty number "The

Dutch Kiddies", a song and dance in Dutch costumes by the Misses Grannis (Mrs. J. P. O'Malley), Dodge, Fenton, Bean, Townsley, Florence Boutin and Mrs. Southmayd. This was a very pretty number and was loudly applauded.

In 1890 the ladies of the Methodist church cleared about $30 for their parsonage fund with an old-fashioned "Krazy" supper at William Haskins store. Supper was served from six to nine and in the early part of the evening, the ladies had more guests waiting to be served than they could find seats for. Food was placed on the table in dishes suitable for the occasion. Sugar was served on a large platter, corn beef in a milk pitcher, milk in a beer bottle, pudding in a baking powder can and delicacies were served in other "Krazy" ways, too numerous to mention.

The Press made this note of a picnic, in October 1905. "Last Wednesday evening a party of young people enjoyed a corn roast at Pike's Bay. They report having a lovely time and from appearances, although things were very dark when they arrived home, we agree with them."

In 1908 the Bayfield Girls' Basketball team provided much entertainment

4th of July

Fourth of July Parade–1906.
(Photo: Burt Hill Family)

THE FOURTH OF JULY HAS always been well celebrated in Bayfield. Sometimes the celebration was large, sometimes not. Sometimes there were little notations in The Press that Judge Tate was the first to have his flag flying on the Fourth of July. Incidentally, this flag of Andrew Tate's was the first one to fly over Bayfield. It was hand made and flew for the first time on the 4th of July 1858. It was gone for many years, but has now come home again: not to fly, it's too old for that, but it will be on display all during our Centennial Celebration.

In 1872 a Bayfield item in *The Ashland Press* reported: "The schooner *Maple Leaf*, Captain Larson, gave an excursion trip among the islands on the Fourth and many of our citizens participated. The weather being pleasant and the vessel commodious, the ride was enjoyed by all. Mr. McElroy favored the excursionists with one of his characteristic speeches which was attentively listened to, notwithstanding he frequently mentioned the name of "the

Great American Philosopher" Horace Greeley, who by the way is doomed to visit Salt River in November.

In the evening another party got aboard the Keyes and made a short, but pleasant trip to Red Cliff and returned, after which they adjourned to meet at the residence of S.S. Vaughn where a few hours were enjoyed in the social dance.

Regular salutes were fired during the day, and in fact to make a long story short, the Fourth of July was observed in fine style at the Harbor City."

In 1878 the celebration was a little larger. *The Bayfield Press* recorded: "The Fourth of July passed off very pleasantly in Bayfield. At four o'clock in the morning the noisy little brass cannon under the charge of the Bayfield Rifle Company woke us by pouring volley after volley out on the morning air. *The Press* answered their salute by firing off a half bunch of firecrackers. At nine o'clock the Rifle Company and those of our citizens who wished to go, got onto the big scow belonging to Captain Wheeler, which was gaily decked with flags and evergreens and were towed by the steam yacht "J.C. Keyes" over to LaPointe. When nearing LaPointe, the riflemen fired several salutes to the citizens of the ancient village who responded with cheers.

The soldiers paraded the streets and then visited the old historical Catholic Church and graveyard, and from there went to Mr. George Stahl's store where someone said, "Here's to health, wealth and prosperity" and the rest of the crowd cried, "Ho!"

After having visited almost everything of interest in the old town, the company fired several farewell salutes with cannon accompaniment and returned to Bayfield where ice cream, cake and lemonade were set out in the big drying house to satisfy the cravings of the inner man. . . (There was baseball in the afternoon.)

In the evening, the Rifles gave a ball at the Smith Hall which was the largest attended of anything of the kind in Bayfield for several years. All went merry as a marriage bell, and they didn't go home til morning.

Out of doors the sky was filled with fireworks, Mr. James Chapman and other citizens giving us fine exhibitions. The streets were filled with young men escorting their ladies to the ice cream saloon, or going down by themselves to see how the new public fountain at the foot of Washington Avenue looked in the dark. Takeing it all in all, it was the most pleasant Fourth of July Bayfielders have enjoyed in a year."

In 1883 Captain Pike took all who wished to go on an excursion on one of his barges. In 1885 he repeated the excursion and over 600 people went.

In 1889 the celebration of the Fourth featured a baseball game between the fats and the leans. The combined weight of the fats was 1,779 pounds.

In 1890 *The Press* reported the Fourth as following: "The day we celebrate has come and gone again. The day opened with that perfect weather which is known only in Bayfield. At daylight the booming of cannon made sleep impossible and from an early hour the streets were full. Hon. S.S. Fifield and 500 excursionists arrived by boat at 10:30 and every train brought large crowds.

The grand procession took place at 10 a.m., headed by the band and consisting of a wagonload of the prettiest girls one could wish to see, dressed in red, white and blue, representing the states of the union.

The address by Gov. Fifield was listened to with deep attention and interrupted very often by prolonged applause. Owning to the dilapidated condition of *The Press* force, we are unable to give the full text of the address this week, but with the Governor's permission it will appear in our next. At the conclusion of the speech, three cheers and a tiger, together with the proposition to make the speaker our next governor were given.

The game of lacrosse was hotly contested, being won by the Buffalo Bay Indians to the tune of $35, the vanquished side receiving $15. A handsome display of fireworks and a grand ball concluding the day's amusements."

"July 4, 1891, dawned upon the small boys and patriotic citizens of Bayfield as perfectly as could be wished. The small boy and the cow bells were abroad at an early hour and staid citizens were perforce patriotic at the first booming of the cannon... Joe O'Malley got third prize as a ragamuffin. Philip Boutin came in third in the boat race.

At 3:30 the Washburn and Bayfield teams, escorted by the Bayfield Cornet Band, proceeded to the ball park... The score was 21 to 3 in favor of Bayfield. A noticeable feature was the absence of the usual wind bag who knows more about the rules and the plays than the umpire, captains and managers combined. The entire game was played with a courtesy both on the part of the visitors and home team worth of remark. The umpire was not even called upon to endanger his life... Fireworks from the verandas of the Island View in the evening were very fine."

Are any of your friends Calithumpians? You don't think so? Well, think again. In 1905, Bud McQuade was the best Calithumpian in the Fourth of July parade. Theodore Ernst won the sack race, Don Bell won the running broad jump, the greased pole was climbed by Art Fiege, a tug of war boat race was won by J. B. O'Malley and Charles Bartleme.

4th of July celebration at 2nd and Rittenhouse. circa 1912. (Photo: BHA)

Chapter 8

Events to Remember

First Train to Bayfield

The Bayfield depot and rail
yard. circa early 1900's.
(Photo: BHA)

I T WAS A GREAT DAY when the first train came into Bayfield. That wonderful event took place on Friday, Oct. 12, 1883, seventy years ago next Monday. Mrs. M. DeMars was at the depot when that first train came in. Maybe some more of you were there, too. But if you were not, here's what happened.

(In 1953, May (Marietta) LaBonte-DeMars was the oldest living Native of Bayfield. Eleanor Knight interviewed Ms DeMars for the article. Marietta's link to Bayfield history starts with the arrival of her father Nazaire LaBonte who arrived in 1856. Mother Mathilde Bono-LaBonte, wife of John B. Bono, were proprietors of the Bayfield House, the city's first inn)

On the morning of that day Conductor Hickey's construction train was at Austrian's clearing. (This is the clearing on the Bayfield side of Dunkel's farm). But even from that distance he promised to have the track in and his train at the depot ere the setting of the sun. Naturally, all Bayfielders were excited over this railroad, which would connect our town to the outer world. All day long the workmen were surrounded by an anxious throng of men, women and children, who were wrought up to a high pitch of anticipation.

They followed the men along the curve of the bay as they worked, noting each tie that was laid, each rail that was fastened in place. As the day wore on, the trainmen and tracklayers seemed to imbibe a portion of this Bayfield spirit and redoubled their efforts to reach their goal. And they made it. The last tie went in, the last rail was spiked to it and then, after a suitably dramatic pause, the train started down the tracks to Bayfield. It came slowly, making the proud moment last, and as the hands of the clock pointed to the hour of 4:04 PM the train halted in front of our depot.

Then the Bayfielders really let go. The star spangled banner was flung to the breeze. The old brass cannon, which came forth on all-important occasions, boomed away with bursts of smoke and flame. The whistles on the steam vessels in the harbor began to blow, uniting with the blasts of the locomotive whistle. The bells of the churches and schools were rung in one prolonged salute that echoed and re-echoed from hilltop to hilltop. But even that wasn't enough noise to greet this new train. The throats of the excited throng pealed cheer after cheer. That was a big day of impromptu celebrations, and it was followed by a big night of more celebrations.

At last Bayfield had a train. At last the day of the long, cold winter walks and rides to Ashland were over. And *The Bayfield Press* reported this effect of the train upon Bayfield: "Bayfield falls into line and adopts the new standard time. Pike's mill, which has so long regulated time in this burg, has been forced to throw up the job and now toots according to railroad time. The school bell also joins the chorus and all things are lovely and fair to look upon."

Mrs. DeMars remembers that for years people met the train every night. It came in at eleven o'clock and the platform was always crowded with train meeters. A stranger arriving would look down from the steps into a large circle of delighted, interested Bayfield faces. It was disconcerting to the shy, a heady welcome to the bold.

People were overjoyed to have this train replace the old stage, which after 1878 had run to Ashland every day during the winter. Four horses pulled a big sleigh filled with straw, where the passengers huddled for protection from the cold. It went down the road to Houghton Point then onto the ice and across to Ashland. It was easier in the summer when the trip was made by boat. The old *Eva Wadsworth* ran a regular schedule. Knowing this we can understand how wonderful it was for Bayfield to have a train, a train that ran regardless of season or weather.

But riding on the train had its hazards too. Maybe the engineer was as new as the train. Anyway he had a little trouble with it. One morning the train going south met with an accident near Onion River. The engine broke loose and ran about three miles before the engineer discovered the rest of his train was missing. He then reversed the engine and ran backward at a high rate of speed. For some unknown reason he failed to see the cars in time to check his iron steed and crashed into them under full steam. The result was a number of scared passengers with badly jerked necks. But no one was seriously hurt.

Mill Yard Fire

NATURALLY, THROUGH THE YEARS, THERE were fires in Bayfield. And, of course, there was a mill yard fire. Almost every sawmill town in Wisconsin had one or two. I am not going to write about all the fires and have chosen the mill yard one for several reasons. It was not as horrible as the fire, which took the life of Anton Miller. It did not put as many men out of work as the Kurz-Downey box factory fire, but the mill yard fire was so packed with drama and hairbreadth escapes you would think it fiction if you saw it on television.

For instance, the owner of the mill yard, H.J. Wachsmuth, was returning from Ashland by boat. It stopped at Madeline Island and there he discovered the mill yard was on fire. As the fierce southwest wind tossed the boat high on the waves, he could see the blaze, then lost track of it as the boat sank in the trough. It was an agonizing trip for him, for it looked as though the mill he had bought only two years before was completely gone.

The Washburn fire department was sent for and came up on the afternoon train, bringing their fire hose. Dynamite and gasoline blew up on the fish docks, and lit the fuse to more dynamite, long piles of slabwood lay behind the powerhouse. If it had caught fire, the powerhouse would have gone and without water, the flames would have consumed the town. Finally, and dramatically, the northeast wind, which has so often been the villain of the story, went to battle with the southwest wind, defeated it, and saved the town from destruction.

Shine Miller saw the fire start that memorable day, Sept. 5, 1908. It was a small one, and as the mill yard often had small fires and maintained their own fire department, he did not think it would amount to much. But even as he watched, the southwest wind caught the flames and threw them in all directions. Shine was on the tug *Emmett* in what is now Halvor Reiten's slip and as he saw the fire spread, he ran the Emmett over into what is now Kuehn's slip, hitched it onto one of the wooden tramways and pulled it down, hoping to stop the fire there, but it was useless. By that time, lumber piles had caught fire and wind, strong wind, carried burning planks through the air, filling the slips with them until the water was covered and flamed as brightly as the land. By that time, Jacob Johnson had joined Shine on the *Emmett* and they rescued two men caught on the end of one of the slips, which was piled with burning lumber.

The Bayfield Press reported: "The largest fire in the history of the Harbor City, the largest in extent of the burned territory and in valuation of destroyed property broke out in this city last Saturday afternoon shortly before four o'clock and burned until late in the afternoon of the next day. The Harbor City in its fifty years of life has been extremely fortunate in the matter of fires and at no time has it experienced a fire in which the loss was greater than $15,000 until the fire of last Saturday.

This last fire was not wholly unexpected by the citizens, but it was not surmised that it would cover so much territory. A crew of men put out small fires in the lumber yards Friday and as the wind was blowing real hard and everything in the lumber yards was extremely dry, it was expected that small blazes would occur, but it was thought these could easily be subdued. However, a spark from the burner of the mill set fire to several piles of lumber at the foot of Second Street and before the mill hand were able to get water to it, it had gotten beyond control and an alarm was sent out. The fire department responded with alacrity, but not soon enough to check the flames, which by this time had spread to ten lumber piles and also numerous piles of dry slabs. A section of the tramway was also burning. As soon as it became generally known that the fire was in the mill yard, the citizens became very excited, realizing that if the flames could not be controlled, the powerhouse would burn and the city would be doomed. However, though the flames got beyond the control of the department, a fortunate change of wind was of great material value in saving the pumping station from destruction. If this had been destroyed, the water supply would have given out and the city would have been at the mercy of the fire demon." Most every native, or Bayfield resident of several years, has seen these strange battles of the northeast and southwest winds. The most violent one I ever observed was during the floods of 1953. Since I was unable to get out of the car due to the tons of rain and hail that were falling, I witnessed the battle from start to finish. As far as I know, the southwest wind has never won. This is, no doubt, due to the fact that the cold northeast wind is the heavyweight.

But, at the time of these battles, scientific reasoning is "thrown to the winds" and the best thing to do is to get out of the way of both of them. The story of the great mill yard fire in Bayfield on Sept. 5, 1908, is continued from last week with this report from *The Bayfield Press* .

"The fire had gained such headway by the time the department arrived, and the wind was blowing such a gale, that the fire soon was beyond control and spread rapidly to the adjoining docks and lumber piles and soon the entire eastern and southern lumber and fish docks were a seething mass of flames. The heat was terrific and several firemen were completely exhausted and were taken to places of safety. Citizens also lent all possible aid and bucket brigades did splendid work in saving adjoining property from destruction.

Although there was no danger from a spread of the fire into the business district from flying sparks, there was eminent danger because of the heat, several buildings catching fire which were quickly put out, however. Heroic efforts were made by both the fire department and the citizens to save the icehouse and contents owned by J.M. Eagen and the buildings and dock of the Jacob Johnson Fish Company, which places were right in the path of the flames.

The Jacob Johnson Fish Company later became the Solomon Boutin Fish Company. Pictured here are the The Elsie Nell and the H. R. Roy. (Photo: BHA)

But the wind was blowing such a gale that the fires on these places soon got beyond control and rapidly advanced upon the remaining lumber dock to the east. The fire department then became aware that it was useless to further endeavor to stop the flames and confined their efforts to protecting the pumping and lighting station. Immediately behind the station were long rows of dry slabs used for fuel, which, had they caught fire, would surely have brought destruction to the power plant. In eminent danger of being blown up by barrels of gasoline in the Jacob Johnson Fish Company buildings, which were stored there with some dynamite, the firemen fought back the flames, heedless of the danger surrounding them. At about five o'clock the first explosion occurred, the gasoline going up, little damage resulting, however, and shortly before six o'clock the dynamite blew up, no harm resulting.

A call to the Washburn fire department for aid resulted in a company of fire fighters with hose coming up from that city on the 4:50 train and their attention was immediately given to extinguishing the flames nearer the sawmill of the Wachsmuth Lumber Company. Here they did good work, and when Sunday morning came, the flames were entirely under control and practically all the docks were saved. Too much praise cannot be given to the local department for their splendid work in saving the power plant and confining the flames to the lumberyard.

Losses were as follows: "Stearns Lumber Company, of Odanah, Wis. $60,000. Their timber was on the Wachsmuth docks and was practically all covered by insurance. Wachsmuth Lumber Company, $40,000. $30,000 of this was in lumber with only $18,000 insurance on it; the other $10,000 was in car tracks, tramways and docks.

Jacob Johnson Fish Company, $10,000, covered by $3,300 insurance. They lost the entire outfit of nets, fish boxes, packing boxes, freezer and dock. New officers were opened in the Turnquist building. The company plans to rebuild. J. M. Eagen, $3,000. This was his icehouse and contents and there was no insurance. He plans to rebuild a much larger and more substantial icehouse. Bayfield Lumber and Wood Company, $2,800 covered by $2,000. This was for lumber. Two months previous this company lost its drying sheds in a fire.

W.J. Lackren and the Independent Fish Company each lost $2,500. Mr. Lockren lost his entire logging outfit, which was on the Independent Fish Company dock and had no insurance. Independent Fish Company lost its shed, icehouse and fishing outfit. Had partial insurance. Captain John Pasque and Ole Hadland lost their gasoline launches valued at about $700 each. No insurance for either one of them. Boutin-Johnson Lumber Company lost about $600 in destruction of a logging camp outfit and booms. Other losses amounted to $200.

The trams and the lumber piled on the docks were burned, but the docks were left intact due to the large amount of sand on them, which protected them from fire.

W.J. Lackren's logging operation and site of the Independent Fish Company. Circa 1899. (Photo: BHA)

First Airplane

THERE WAS AN AEROPLANE BUILT here back in 1897. It didn't fly, but everyone had a good time thinking it might. Mike Gordon was there the day it tried to fly; and fortunately for Bayfield's history collection he remembers the whole thing.

John Bjorge built the plane, and he built it for a good reason. He got tired of pushing his potato crop to town in a wheelbarrow. His farm was seven miles from Bayfield in the direction of Sand River. There were no roads then, and his path to town was just a path, winding through pine stumps.

We don't know at what point he put down his wheelbarrow, straightened his aching back, sat down on a stump to wipe the sweat from his forehead, looked up at the sky, and thought how nice it would be if he and the potatoes could fly over the pine stumps instead of wheeling around them. But at some time he must have had the thought, for he went to work and built a plane in the hayloft of his barn.

The plane was his own design. The frame was made of light saplings and was attached to curved runners, which were well greased with lard so they would glide along the ground when the plane landed. The wings were of heavy canvas, which had been dipped in some kind of oil to stiffen them. But besides stiffening them, it had made them sticky, like fly catching material. There was no motor. The plane was to be hand propelled.

When the day of the trial flight arrived, people came out from town to watch. The door of the hayloft was opened and the waiting spectators craned their necks up for a quick look at the strange contraption, then stood back, way back, not knowing what the thing was apt to do when it flew out of the hayloft door.

A helper said to Mr. Bjorge, "Hadn't we better get a block and tackle, lower it with a rope?"

"It will fly down," Mr. Bjorge said, and gave his plane a final push.

Well, in a way, due to the law of gravitation, it did fly down. But crashed would have been a better word. It landed on its well-greased runners, but did not glide away. The sapling frame sprang apart, as though life had returned to the young trees. The wings bent, touched the ground and bounced a little, as though trying their best to be airborne. Then even the most hopeful spectator had to admit he was looking at a wreck, a wreck, which would never fly.

There was a long moment of silence before the men moved closer, touched the wreckage with their toes, lifted up pieces and let them drop, then shrugged off their disappointment and went back to town to tell about it.

Mr. Bjorge pulled the wreckage into his barn where it remained for years. He continued to push his potatoes to town in his wheelbarrow. But as he walked he must have had the satisfaction of thinking, "Well, I tried."

And six years later when the Wright brothers flew at Kitty Hawk he had the further satisfaction of knowing that he was right, it could be done.

The Ashland War & The Bayfield Rifles

The Bayfield Rifles, Bayfield's local militia. circa 1872. Comprised mainly of Civil War veterans that had moved to Bayfield, seven soldiers from the township actually participated in the Civil War. Frank Artisho and George La Rush died on the battlefield. The Bayfield Rifles organized in 1871 and numbered up to sixty-five "call-to-arms" members. Robinson Derling Pike was Captain, Sheriff John T. Gonyon was 1st Lieutenant, Commercial Fisherman Duffy Boutin was 2nd Lieutenant, and Attorney B.B. Wade was the First Sergeant. (Photo: BHA)

ONCE, WHEN ASHLAND WAS IN trouble, little Bayfield went to her rescue.

It happened during the "Ashland War." The war began on December morning in 1872 when Captain W.W. Rich, engineer in charge of construction of the Wisconsin Central Railroad, which was being built into Ashland, got orders to shut down all work, pay off the thousand or more men who were employed in clearing a way through the forest for a railroad, and transport them, and all others who desired to leave, out of the country. The railroad was in bad financial trouble.

Sam Fifield tells us what Ashland was like at that time: "I wish I could give you a vivid word picture of the conditions existing on Ashland's town site in 1872, the organization of society out of a rough, strange human element, a mixed population rapidly brought together, of rough railroad builders, a camp-following of bad men and bad women, sprinkled with a goodly number of brave and true pioneers who came to make for themselves new homes."

When the order to shut down work came, naturally the whole community was upset. It was late in the season. The bay was nearly frozen over so no boats were running. There were no wagon roads and no railroads. The only way out was to walk the trail through the woods to Superior, eighty miles away.

Besides the shock of having no work, the men felt dissatisfaction over the date for which they were to be paid off. Rich had orders to pay the men to the day work was suspended, keep them in camp, feed them and then transport them to Duluth-Superior.

This plan went along alright at first. But when Rich arrived at what was known as "Kelly's Camp", the men demanded "pay-to-date." But Rich could not do this. He had only enough cash to pay them to the date when work stopped.

The men attacked the paymaster and tried to seize the money. Rich pulled a gun and stood them off until he, the paymaster and their guard could get to their sleigh. They got a head start, but were pursued into Ashland. When they got there, they notified the only law officers, a deputy sheriff and a constable.

Chairman Sam Fifield ordered the saloons closed before the advance guard from Kelly's camp arrived the next morning, which was New Years Day, 1873. But the saloonkeepers only closed their front doors. The back door trade was brisk.

The leading businessmen and the solid citizens had a meeting and sent railroad engineers Dunbar and Wanzer to Bayfield with a letter signed by the local town board asking for help. In this way Nelson Boutin, who was sort of a twin sheriff for both Bayfield and Ashland Counties, was notified of the bad situation.

In a letter written to Mrs. A.H. Wilkinson in 1904, Sam Fifield tells how he sent to Bayfield for rescuers: "I ordered Sheriff Boutin to come to Ashland with a posse sufficient to protect the entire city from a drunken mob of railroaders. Captain W.W. Rich, chief engineer of the Wisconsin Central Railroad, dispatched six or seven teams to Bayfield in charge of Captain Wanzer early on the morning of the first, and returned with 42 men of the Bayfield Rifles armed and fully equipped under the command of Captain R.D. Pike. Arriving at midnight, they remained ten days. The Company was of great service in keeping the peace and in protecting property, especially of the railroad company."

Sheriff Nelson Boutin arrived at Ashland about midnight with Company D of the Bayfield Rifles and our good old cannon, which used to stand in the courthouse yard. They marched up from the ice and Sheriff Boutin took immediate and firm charge of the situation, closed all the saloons, placed guards and sentinels on Second Street and the company stayed on duty until everything was settled. The railroaders left for Superior, on foot, mostly.

We don't know which members of the Bayfield Rifles made up Company D, who left their New Years dinners armed themselves and went to the defense of their neighboring village. But A.H. Wilkinson has sent the muster roll of the entire Bayfield Rifles, written by their Captain R.D. Pike on September 10, 1873. Forty-two of these seventy five men went to the Ashland War. Here are the names. Some of them are still familiar.

Robinson D. Pike, Captain age 36; John T. Gonyon, 1st Lt. 34; Duffy Boutin, 2nd Lt. 26; Birdsey B. Wade, 1st Sgt. 33; Sol. Boutin, 2nd Sgt. 25; W.J. Herbert, 3rd Sgt. 22; W.L. Portock 4th Sgt. 22; J.L. Turner 5th Sgt. 28; Edward Boutin 1st Cpl 45; Nelson Drouilliard 2nd Cpl, 44; G.W. Carrington 3rd Cpl. 24; Fred Herbert 4th Cpl. 20; Louis Bachand 5th Cpl 22; Benjamin Albano, 27; J.S. Atkinson 38; Rolla Baker 39; Edward Boutin Jr. 20; Nelson Boutin Jr. 20; J.N. Burgess 23; Peter Buschman 32; Ira Butterfield 18; Richard Carrington 21; J.D. Cruttendon 45; Thos. Carmady 31; John C. Carlson 35; John Drouilliard 22; Henry Dennis 25; Antoine Denomie 25; Simon Denomie 21; Henry Denomie 30; John A. Davis 23; Charles Goslin 19; Eli Godin 24; George H. Heather 25; Edward Harris 20; Martin J. Hickey 23; William Haskins 25; David Hart 39; John H. Hanson 20; George Hoefle 43; George Hoefle Jr. 19; Gustav Jansen 24; Nils Larson 37; N. LaBonte 40; William LaPointe 25; Henry LaPointe 37; Edward Maloy 24; Robert Morrin 29; William Morrin 37; Michel Moreau 37; John McCloud 43; Antoine Moiseant 31; William Niquette 22; Alonzo G. Pride 20; John Phillips 25; H.H. Picard 25; J.L. Patrick 25; Peter Richards 35; J.T. Sharp

27; William Scuffles 25; A.H. Sliter 24; L.L. Sargent 29; Antoine Soulier 27; Andrew Tate 43; T.J. L. Tyler 45.

Ashland People Stormbound at Bayfield

D RIVING 20 MILES ACROSS THE ice with a mule team would seem a pretty rugged way to get to a dance, but back in 1876, they thought nothing of it. In fact, they thought it was fun. The Ashland Press gave this account of their hilarious good time on March 4, 1876.

"Without exception, the gayest season of merriment has just closed at our sister city of Bayfield. On last Friday night, there was a grand masquerade and dress ball given at Bayfield and Ashland responded to the stirring invitations by sending over three double teams and one single loaded with the liveliest party of fantastic, outlandish Ashlanders that ever vibrated a brogan on a ball room floor.

The twenty-mile ride over the frozen bosom of majestic old Lake Superior was more romantic than Sheridan's far famed 20 into Winchester. The party reached their destination under flying colors and with the din of cowbells suspended from the necks of the mule team, which were elaborately decorated for the occasion.

After partaking of a hearty supper served by mine host Stark, the party assembled at the courthouse (this courthouse was opposite the present depot) where the dance took place. Here was met the brawn and the beauty of Bayfield and the merry ones of both villages commingled in special conversation while the gallant lords lent an ear to sweet warbling and received beams and smiles of their companions.

"On with the dance, let joy be unconfined," was the order of the evening and was prolonged until 5 o'clock the next morning, merely taking time out to partake of an excellent supper.

A violent northeast snowstorm commenced Saturday, which made it impossible for our people to return, and with the storm the solid fun began.

Captain Smith generously threw open his spacious hotel, which has been closed all winter, for the accommodation of the visitors. In the evening the parlors were illuminated and the scene was one of mirth and rapturous enjoyment and the second dance was held in the large dining hall that evening.

Monday the storm still raged and in the evening, the jolly faces were again marshaled and really the liveliest dance of all was participated in. The Bayfield ladies turned out in greater numbers than upon any previous evening.

The outside readers of *The Press* may suppose it is hard to find a real, genuine lady in dress and manner in this western wilderness, as they term it. You may look through the Grand National Kaleidoscope and you will not find more refined or hospitable ladies than in Bayfield. Here they may be found attired in all the modern paraphernalia of their Eastern cousins. You can hear the rustle of exquisite colored silk, listen to their musical voices and mirthful laughter and the sweet perfume floating above them magnetizes and charms the very atmosphere around you. The fashion plates of Madame Demorest need not be viewed, nor Godey, or Peterson, consulted. The Bayfield ladies attired in their fashionable toilettes would be termed connoisseurs of fashion by any Paris modiste.

Tuesday morning the storm being over, the party started homeward, reaching our charming city of the Chequamegon with the unanimous vote that one of the most pleasant and lively enjoyments they ever participated in was ended.

Too much praise cannot be accorded our Bayfield friends for their untiring exertions to add to our comfort and enjoyment. Nothing was left undone to make us comfortable and happy. Many of the party accepted cordial invitation from friends and shared the comforts of their homes during their stay.

Special mention is justly merited by Mr. A.C. Hayward and daughter Mattie for their kindness in edifying the party with choice music. That prince of good fellows, Wm. Knight, Esq., and Messrs. Smith, Stark, McCloud, Tate, Cooley and others with the kind attentions of the Bayfield ladies have placed the party under lasting obligations.

The Ashland guests, one and all, return their heartfelt thanks for favors and attention shown and will ever relate the many kind recollections of a good time enjoyed with their friends in Bayfield.

Sioux Uprising

I N 1862, WITH THE WAR Between the States in its second year, the Sioux decided to take advantage of the government's preoccupation with this war, and staged a mass uprising. Bayfield was six years old then, and growing slowly, but it was still a frontier village, cut off from the world by the surrounding wilderness. Many of the young men had gone into the Union Army. Only the older men, the women and children were left.

Means of communication were poor. No one knew just where the Sioux were, what they were doing, or if things were really as bad as they were rumored. Then, on August 18, 1862, the terrible New Ulm massacre took place. After that, there was no doubt of the deadly intent of the Sioux. This entire Minnesota town was wiped out. Eight hundred men, women and children were murdered there by 650 Sioux, who were mounted and armed to the teeth with rifles our own government had given them to shoot buffalo.

A wave of fear swept through Minnesota and Wisconsin. The little frontier towns pleaded for soldiers to protect them. Through the influence of H.M. Rice, Bayfield's founder, who always had the town's welfare at heart, parts of two companies of soldiers, consisting of about 65 men, were sent here to protect Bayfield.

These soldiers had fought in the Civil War, been taken prisoners, and had been confined in Libby Prison. They had been exchanged for Rebel prisoners with the understanding that neither the federals nor the confederates would re-enter service against each other.

They were a sorry looking bunch when they arrived here. They had almost starved to death in notorious Libby Prison and the long trip from the south and up the rough lakes had not improved their condition any.

But if Bayfielders were dismayed at the sight of this weak looking group, who were sent to protect them, they did not show it. Hospitality came first. Bayfield did its best to make them comfortable. They were given the Chapman warehouse for a barracks. This was a two story building located about one block south of the present depot, near the foot of Broad Street. (This building was afterward enlarged and used as a woodenware factory by H.O. Cook and Arthur Esperson in the early eighties. It burned in 1899.)

After a few hearty Bayfield meals, the soldiers began to regain their strength and turned with a right good will to the defense of Bayfield.

Every available man in town pitched in to help them build two forts. One was on the lot between Valentine's and Walstad's homes. The other was where the Episcopal Church now stands. Trenches were dug for hollow logs, which would carry water from higher up in the hills. Provisions were placed in the forts and all firearms in the little village were put in good order. Bayfield got ready to fight the Sioux and expected to win. The Chippewa here were friendly and were just as worried about a Sioux attack as anyone else. They were ready to help defend the town and themselves, since the Sioux were their traditional enemies.

But, as it turned out, there was no fight here. The Sioux were fully occupied in Minnesota, pillaging, slaughtering, and fighting. The forts were not needed. But, as if to fulfill its destiny, the one next to Valentine's present house, was afterward used as a slaughterhouse by Ervin Leihy. Robert Morrin was chief executioner.

During the time the soldiers stayed here, the plat around the present depot was used as a parade ground. It was a usual sight to see them out drilling. Bayfield people liked to stand around and watch them march to the brisk beat of a small drum.

While these soldiers waited here in suspense for news of Union victories and defeats, they decided to publish a newspaper. They had no printing press , so used foolscap, pen and ink. They called their newspaper the *Republican* and had correspondents who were fighting in the war write to them of the progress of the Union Army.

Here is an excerpt from one of their papers: "We already have several correspondents of whom we are proud, seeing in them the futures of our country and state. It must be apparent to any thinking mind, that when the war closes, the destinies of our Republic will rest with the private soldier of our noble army. Then let us ask: Are we competent to undertake the task? We drill day after day, and week after week, that we may be confident in the day of battle. Shall we not then use some of our leisure moments in preparing for the great battle of civil life?"

While these soldiers were stationed here, one of them, Andrew McConnell, who had fought bravely in the Civil War, and had almost starved to death in Libby Prison, was accidentally wounded, and died in peaceful Bayfield. Andrew McConnell was a private in Co. E 30th Reg. of the Wisconsin Volunteer Infantry. He died July 29, 1863, and was buried in Pike's Bay cemetery. When the cemetery was moved about 1909, his body was taken with the others and placed in Greenwood cemetery.

He was the only casualty of the Sioux scare in Bayfield.

Sioux Scare at Superior

I T IS INTERESTING TO SEE what was going on up at Superior at the time of the Sioux scare in 1862-63. People were just as scared in that little frontier village as they were here, probably more so, as Bayfield had the idea they could make a last stand on Madeline Island and take advantage of island fighting the way the Chippewa had in the past. But at Superior, they had no such chance. If the Sioux came out of the forest there was no way for their victims to escape.

The Sioux tried their best to turn the Chippewa against the whites. Little Crow, Chief of the Minnesota Sioux, sent messages to Chief Hole-in-the-Bay, head of the Chippewa around Superior. But the Chippewa did not get enthused about teaming up with the Sioux, since they were traditional enemies and had driven the Sioux back to the plains in the first place. One of the decisive battles in that drive was fought at the Brule River in 1842, twenty years previously. In that battle, the Chippewa victory was due to Chief Buffalo's brilliant strategy in sending two flanking forces to the west bank of the river, where they fell upon the rear of the Sioux and drove them into Minnesota.

The people of Superior, instead of building forts as they did at Bayfield, decided to fortify the Quebec pier, Superior's first steamboat dock, planking up the warehouses on the dock and making them as nearly fireproof as possible. Every man between 18 and 60 had to take a turn at daily guard duty.

The Superiorites wrote to Washington, pleading frantically for soldiers. But by the middle of September, none had arrived. The people grew desperate, for they knew when the lake froze over, the Indians could come in from the forest and trap them, there being nothing but plain white ice to flee on, and out on the ice they would make good targets.

Finally, in late October, guns and ammunition arrived by steamer and Superior breathed a little easier, hoping that soldiers would follow. But none had come by late November; the lake was ready to freeze and the little town bravely made their plans for a last man fight. Then, when the hope of help was almost gone, a boat whistle was heard in the harbor. Into the dock came the Sea Bird, and on it were soldiers of Co. B of the 18th Wisconsin. These soldiers, like the ones at Bayfield, had been fighting in the Civil War. They had been captured at Shiloh the previous spring and had been traded back for rebel men.

The fortified pier was not large enough for the populace and the soldiers, so the soldiers were taken into Superior homes and all through the winter of 1862-63, everyone pitched in and built a stockade of logs which would house all of them. Funds for it had been sent by the war department.

Superior felt more secure with its new fort, but the barking of a fox, or the hoot of an owl, the usual Sioux signals, could send the whole village on a stampede to the stockade.

One night in May 1863, when it was rumored that the Sioux would surely attack, all the people got into the stockade and guards were put out.

Then occurred the only tragedy in this war of nerves. The guards were uneasy, tense. When they heard a strange sound in the woods, one of them shouted, "Halt, or I'll fire!"

Twice he challenged, as a figure approached, and when the figure did not halt or respond, the guard fired. His shot was followed by a woman's scream.

The guards ran out to the edge of the forest, and in the gathering twilight, the heart-broken guard who had fired, knelt beside the body of young Godfrey Schaar, a pioneer who lived outside the settlement. The boy had been leading his family to the stockade for safety and was walking slightly in advance of them. In the summer dusk in his frontier clothes, with a canoe paddle over his shoulder he had resembled a stealthy Indian. Evidently, because he knew the soldiers so well, he thought they had recognized him, were joking, and he paid no attention to the command to halt. The soldier who fired the shot was so grief stricken, he died. The boy's father, his mind unhinged by grief, died a recluse.

In the Douglas County Museum, they have a drum; a drum that was carried by August Schaar, who marched in the Superior home guard before the soldiers came, a drum which his slain son, Godfrey, had delighted to play.

And in the meantime, the Sioux, indirect cause of this tragedy, were being pursued by General Sibley, who finally forced them so far westward that the little Lake Superior settlements were out of danger. In the late summer of 1863, the Sioux surrendered.

The Early Bayfield Railroad System

The Bayfield Train Depot. Receiver site of the Chicago-St. Paul-Minneapolis & Omaha Wisconsin Central, and the Bayfield Central. (Photo: BHA)

(Photo: BHA)

The Bayfield Transfer railway tracks as they pass Washington Avenue on the immediate lake front. (Photo: BHA)

Burt Hill and his children enjoy the scenery on the flat rocks that are still located north of Washington Avenue. (Photo: Burt Hill Collection)

"Old 154" of the Chicago, St. Paul, Minneapolis & Omaha line. The building in the rear is the famous "First and Last Chance" saloon. (Photo: BHA)

Southern exposure of the Bayfield rail system. Timbered logs supported the economic health and welfare of Bayfield for nearly 80 years. The mill pond that fed the S.S. Vaughn, R.D. Pike, and Henry Wachsmuth mills began far south of the present day "coal dock" site. (Photo:BHA)

Where the Bayfield Tramway system intersects with the Bayfield Transfer tracks at the waterfront. Circa 1900. (Photo: Burt Hill Family)

The Scoot at Third and Manypenny. Left to Right, Bill Burns (Engineer), Ed Hoefle (Brakeman), Abe Lord (Express), George Maxien (Fireman), John Touney (Conductor) (Photo: BHA)

The "Badger". Photo circa 1897. The Wisconsin Conservation Commission had a regulation size Pullman car designed, constructed and outfitted for the special distribution purposes of the fry and fingerlings to streams and lakes. The arrival of the railroad in 1883 served also to relay fingerlings from the Bayfield Fish Hatchery" to inland, Lake Superior and Lake Michigan waters. (Photo: Burt Hill Family)

Chicago, St. Paul, Minneapolis and Omaha Engine #136. (Photo: BHA)

Bayfield as a mill town. (Photo: BHA)

The central city mill yards, encompassed most properties south of Manypenny Avenue. (Photo: BHA)

Family outings followed the old tracks south to picnic sites. (Photo: BHA)

The lakefront track system running north. The Bayfield Opera House, Bayfield Hotel and Island View Hotel are evident. (Photo: BHA)

The tramway system utilized in the Bayfield mill yards, extended out into Lake Superior with the further development of the Bayfield Transfer Company. Shown here, as taken from the present East Dock park, is the Solomon Boutin Fish Company and the north bound railway course to Booth Fisheries area and then on to the Roys Point and Red Cliff mill. (Photo: BHA)

Chapter 9

Potpourri

Cows Caused Hectic Days in Bayfield
Historian Reaches into Bag Of History and Legend And Comes up with a Good Tale

This week we are indebted to Mrs. Maude (Harry) Kranzfelder for the information that the old town hall was located where the drycleaning establishment (Bayfield Cleaners) now stands. We are also indebted to Connie Dahl for a book of old Bayfield County. This book has a fine picture of the Community Building in its prime, with the clock in the tower showing a quarter of two on a long forgotten summer afternoon. The old cannon is standing in the yard. What ever became of the Bayfield cannon? Bayfield Kitsteiner is still missing, too, although a faint clue has been uncovered.

Now it's floods. But way back then it was cows.

Cows were the number one problem in Bayfield for years. An ordinance restraining them was passed in 1904, but no one paid any attention to it. The cows, with large, clanging, locomotive-like bells roamed the streets and yards, disturbing the peace, frightening the timid, and even injuring people. One little boy was knocked down on Main Street by a cow. His collarbone was broken. They put him on the train and took him to Ashland to the hospital, but didn't bother to corral the cow.

Remarks and protests about this situation were bitter. Some people claimed the cows in Bayfield had more sense than the people, for the cows walked on the sidewalks, and people walked in the streets. Tourists, arriving from cities, were upset and frightened by this peculiar situation.

Most yards were enclosed by high fences to keep them cow free for family use. It was necessary for the city to enclose the library grounds with a protective cow fence.

In fly season the cows sensibly gathered on the old wooden bridge, which preceded the present iron one, and standing there in groups of fifteen or twenty, let the breeze blow the flies off of them. This was annoying to people who wanted to cross the bridge.

The cows also liked to rest on the wooden sidewalks, which were raised from the ground on stilts. That made things difficult too, as women wearing long skirted dresses, were not able to climb over them. One of the highest sidewalks was in front of the Wallis Durham residence and as the breeze from the lake was particularly nice there, the cows enjoyed the sidewalk very much.

There are stories of people being forced into stores on Main Street by herds of cows moving leisurely along the sidewalk. This, of course, is what gave rise to rumors that the merchants were protecting and encouraging the cows.

Cows versus people was a lengthy battle. Eventually a cow pound was established under the bridge that spanned the ravine creek between the library and the fire hall. This was a fairly high, long bridge. It was cool and shady beneath it, with plenty of room to confine cows and fresh water for them in the creek. The owners could claim their impounded animals for the payment of one dollar per head.

But even this scheme did not work well. Owners seemed satisfied to pay a dollar or two for the privilege of letting their cows range through town all summer, instead of having to provide pasture for them.

The cow was queen in Bayfield, and continued to be for at least ten years after the ordinance against her was passed. But there is one case where she got the worst of it.

This particular cow belonged to a man named Hunt. Her name has been forgotten, but she had long horns and at night she used them to unhook the cow gate across the front steps of the William Knight residence. After the gate was unhooked she would enter the yard, generously leaving the gate open for other cows to follow. Once inside she liked to stroll around, clanging her bell, eating what appealed to her.

Mr. Knight warned her owner, but it did no good. Finally the end of his patience was reached. The bell clanged under his bedroom window just once too often. He got out of bed, loaded his twenty-two, raised the window and fired.

The cowbell pealed wildly, circled the house and diminished in the dark distance. It was not until the next morning the course of her flight was traced. She had rushed out of the yard, down the front steps and across the street to the Presbyterian Church yard where she dropped dead.

Mr. Knight paid the owner $35. That was a fair price for a cow in those days.

Animals in Bayfield

RECENTLY SIG ANDERSON GAVE ME a dog tag dated 1890, 65 years ago. This tag had suddenly jumped out of the grass into Thor Palm's lawnmower and stopped it. If the old dog, or his owner, can identify this tag by giving the correct license number, it will be returned.

The dogs of Bayfield's history have been a mixed blessing. They were friends and nuisances, loved and despised. The first reference to Bayfield dogs appeared in James Peet's diary on Jan. 23, 1858, "Mail arrived on a dog train from St. Paul."

The first dogs to come to Bayfield were work dogs used for transportation, and one of the most famous of them all was Nourse's Dash." When he died in the early 1890's, he received an obituary in *The Press* , which stated, "The dog named 'Dash' was connected with many stirring scenes of the early settlement as a carrier of the U.S. mail and as an express messenger. Dash became a noted character. About train time it was customary to harness him to his sled or wagon, attached to which, he would lie down and sleep until the whistle of the locomotive announced the approaching train. At that instant he would be on his feet and ready to meet it. In the winter when the mail was carried on the ice between here and LaPointe he was almost invaluable, and he has often been the means of saving valuable mail from destruction. One day Mr. Nourse was returning from the farm with a load of hay. Dash was missed from his usual place at the front. Mr. Nourse stopped the team and called to him. After a short time Dash was seen coming over a hill dragging with him the whip which had accidentally fallen from the load. . . "

I have also been told that when Dr. Hannum's horse "Molly" died, she received an obituary in *The Press* , but I have not been able to find it. Does anyone have it?

However, I did find another story about a Bayfield horse, who confronted by his iron counterpart, succumbed. It was recorded on March 15, 1907. "A. J. Mussell, the first of the week sustained the loss of a very valuable horse. The animal was used in the logging business along the line of the Bayfield Lake Shore and Western Railroad to which line

Mr. Mussell recently built a four-mile spur. The new logging engine, which is being used to haul logs made a run over the line. The horse was near the track and upon hearing the whistle blow, jumped up and fell dead. Mr. Mussell places his loss at between $300 and $400."

And a Bayfield man, confronted with evidence of progress, had a much more sensible reaction. Nov. 17, 1905. "Emil Schlunt, who has been driving delivery for F. Stark, left Monday for Ohio where he has accepted a position in the automobile factory."

Mr. Mussell also had a cow that received notice by *The Press* , which said, "A. J. Mussell was rather inclined to believe that milk had reached a pretty high place Thursday morning and if it continued to maintain its position, it would be considerably difficult to obtain. In other words, Wednesday night Mr. Mussell's cow took a notion to explore the upper story of the barn and took a promenade up the stairs. Yesterday morning she was milked in the loft and it was found necessary to build a slide, fasten a rope around the cow's neck and let 'er go. She's down now, and milk is once more normal."

During Bayfield's first fify years, the animals ran at large and people accepted it as normal. They fenced in themselves, and all public property. Stakes where cow protection fences were built can still be seen today on the library wall and the wall at the Russell Valentine residence. After the first fifty years, someone came to the startling conclusion that the animals should be fenced in and people should run at large. Naturally, such a revolutionary idea met with opposition, and *The Press* began to be filled with letters on the subject, for writing letters to *The Press* was a very popular pastime. Some of the letters were violent, some humorous and some vulgar, but perhaps these two will show the trend of the times.

June 22, 1906. *Impressions of a Newcomer.* Arriving at the Bayfield station one sunny day this spring, the first thing that attracted our attention on alighting was the multitude of dogs running at large. Upon inquiry, we learned that these (best friends of mankind) were used as beasts of burden in the winter by the fisher folk and otherwise, but during the summer were turned loose and allowed to forage for themselves. Proceeding up Broad Street, we walked to the corner of Rittenhouse Avenue and Second Street where the pretty little bank of Bayfield is located and, upon endeavoring to cross the street, were nearly run down by some cattle with locomotive bells attached to their necks which seem to roam the streets in uncountable numbers and unlimited freedom. Alarm clocks are useless in this summer resort for as soon as dawn comes, the tinkling of the many bells attached to these bovine creatures makes an alarm which one has to hear in order to appreciate. . . The residences are pretty, but have to be surrounded by high fences and with padlocks on the gates. Sidewalks, outside the very center, are useless, on account of broken planks, etc., and on the whole, while our impression of Bayfield was that it is one of the prettiest towns on Lake Superior, still, we shall always remain im*Press*ed with dogs, cows and cowbells.

Two years later the ordinances had some teeth in them and Judge Atkinson's court was filled with disobedient cow owners. *The Press* reported June 5, 1908, "The fines recently imposed on some transgressors of the ordinances by Judge Atkinson has taught the cow owners that it is more profitable to obey than disobey. Since a special police was placed on the force this spring, whose special duty it is to see that there is no roaming at large of cattle and swine, and to dispose of stray untaxed dogs, the streets have been kept fairly well cleared and as a result, property throughout the city is more beautiful in appearance and can be kept so much more easily than during the reign of Sir Dog and Madame

Cow... The beauty of the Harbor City would be greatly added to if the residences could take down the fences enclosing their property and give proper care to lawns and gardens and it is to be hoped this will be done now that the ordinances are being enforced."

Finally with the help of the ordinances, the automobile, which needed the streets more than the cows and the pure food laws, conditions were reversed, the animals were confined, the fences came down, yards and gardens bloomed, the people were free to run at large and it's been that way ever since.

Movies in Bayfield

THE FIRST MOVIES TO APPEAR in Bayfield received no wild welcome. They were silent, they flickered (in fact they were called Flicks), and the action was fast and jerky. They were viewed with suspicion, too. Being of celluloid, they might catch fire, explode, or do some other dreadful thing. It was doubtful if people should risk their eyesight and the danger of fire to see one. However, operators persisted in showing moving pictures. This article appeared in The Bayfield Press on Nov. 27, 1908. "The moving picture show being conducted every Monday, Tuesday and Wednesday evening of each week by P.J. Bestler at the Island View Hotel is enjoying large patronage. The pictures being shown are fine in every respect, clear and sharp and do not hurt the eyes, avoiding a great deal of the flickering so common with motion picture machines.

"The pictures being shown have never been shown in this city before, and every Wednesday night there is a complete change in the program, thus affording new entertainment to the patrons each week. The machine in use is Edison's latest improved Kenetiscope and has been proven absolutely fireproof, being equipped with special attachments to prevent any catastrophe from that source. The Island View Hotel equipped as it is, is one of the safest buildings in the city, having 12 exits from the large dining room in which the motion pictures are being shown."

The Island View Hotel and the patrons with 12 exits to choose from came safely through the winter. Movies became popular and the next fall, September 1909, the *Bayfield Progress* reported: "Sand Bay items: A moving picture show was at the schoolhouse Friday night. Guess we're "up to date" now. The same show was at Raspberry Sunday night."

In July 1912, Bayfield and the Apostle Islands became the scenic background for the work of a movie company. They spent the days out among the islands, posing on rocks, jumping into the lake, and the nice summer evenings were spent on the wide porch of the Davis house, looking over main street, where local people enjoyed visiting with them.

In July, 1912, the Bayfield Progress wrote this account of their arrival: "Through the medium of the Essany Moving Picture Film Co., branch of the great wizard of invention, Thomas Edison, who is at the head of the Motion Picture Patent Co., of which the Essany Co. is a part, decided that there was something worth while among these islands, not only beautiful, but worth showing to the world its various phases in way back historical and legendary lore.

"On Saturday night last when the train arrived, it brought a bunch of 13 or 14 active producers and photographers of the Essany Company to start the work outline above and they have been busy getting located in hotels and rooms, quite a problem as the summer tourist season is just starting in. Theo. W. Wharton, producer, and wife and photographer David Hargen are at the Davis House. Others are: Francis X. Bushman, William Walters, Harry Mainhall, Bryant Washburn, Frederick Wulf, Al Tracy and the Misses Martha Russell, Helen Dunbar and Ruth Stonehouse. They have chartered Gov. Fifield's *Stella* during their stay to facilitate their transportation among the islands."

During their stay here, Carl Johnson's planning mill caught fire and the Essany Company sped to the scene and set up their cameras. Actors went into the burning buildings and jumped through windows as the cameras turned. The Progress reported: "There was a comical side to the Johnson fire, even while the fire was raging and the firemen were playing on the flames. The Essany Film Company members who were here taking views and making story films among the Apostle Islands were down to the fire and improvised a rescue or two with dramatic effect by some of the participants while the machine turned out a roll of film. Manager Wharton says they often take advantage of a real fire upon which they can make up some story by eliminating or adding to as the case may be."

Francis X. Bushman became one of the great movie stars. Recently I wrote to him to ask if he remembered making movies among the Apostle Islands and received this reply:

"So sorry I can't help you out regarding *Neptune's Daughter.* That we made the picture there, yes. That Harry Cashman, our character man, played old Neptune, and because he spent so much time in the cold water, he returned home to Chicago and died of pneumonia. Martha Russell was my leading lady and Ted Wharton was the director.

"Having made so many pictures and kept no records, I can add no more. When one shoots one or two pictures a week for more than four years, the period becomes a montage."

"Further, I have lived my life a bit different from most. As each day's experience passed, I turned the page and pasted it down. I lived for the day only. Again, sorry I couldn't be of some help. . . "

Humorous Items

MANY ITEMS HAVE APPEARED IN The Bayfield Press , which, though not of great historic value, are thought provoking. The arduous days of spring housecleaning are recalled by this poem of 1878.

Housecleaning time will soon be here
Then the poor man in mortal fear
Away from home a week will steer
And sadly drop a silent tear
And then imbibe some lager beer
Or gaily swallow whiskey clear
Or gently swig his rum
And when the cleaning is all done
With muddy boots he'll homeward run
His nose resplendent as the sun
Declaring he's had lots of fun.
And when he steps up on the floor
His wife will meet him at the door
Take that you brute she'll gently cry
And gaily hit him in the eye
At that he'll heave a doleful sigh
And say he feels almighty dry
And start out on another high
As quick as a cat can wink its eye.

In March 1909, one lady didn't wait for spring. She cleaned house early. "In a frenzied fit of anger Wednesday p.m., Mrs. D. Emmons, who has had charge of the Emmons restaurant, which is run in connection with the saloon, obtained an axe and demolished the entire interior, fixtures, stove and all. A warrant was promptly sworn out and served and she was taken before Judge Atkinson to answer the charge. Judge Atkinson imposed a fine of $100, which was revoked, however, upon her promise to leave town, which she did."

Are these items true, or was the editor short on news and long on space? Nov. 18, 1871. "Mr. Ache, who is well known here, has been unkind enough to name his daughter, Belle."

March 23, 1872. "A corset is on exhibition at Duluth which has squeezed three females to death."

Feb. 4, 1871. "There is an old lady living less than 50 miles from this city who firmly believes that more men marry than women."

This instructive note appeared May 11, 1872. "An old toper being asked one day why he persisted in drinking replied, 'Dry makes me drink and drink makes me drunk and drunk makes me dry again." The explanation was considered quite sufficient."

June 23, 1883. "A victim of the flowing bowl took a tumble into the bay from the dock Wednesday morning, only resulting in strengthening his aversion to water."

Some of the ads were interesting.

April 22, 1910. "For sale, a forty gallon caldron kettle, just the thing for making soap or boiling."

Anyone interested in making 40 gallons of soap this spring?

July 1, 1910. "A revolving folding bed wardrobe bureau and writing desk combined, with beveled plate glass mirrors, as good as new, will be sold at half its cost."

Undoubtedly this thing was as good as new. It was too confusing to operate. While attempting to climb into the revolving folding bed you would probably find yourself shut up in the wardrobe bureau, frightened half out of your wits by your unexpected triple appearance in the beveled plate glass mirrors.

This ad was simpler. "Wash and be whiter than snow. Baths at Pines."

Hackmetack, a lasting and fragrant perfume, sold at Flanders store for 25 and 50 cents. "Pride of Bayfield" was a coffee sold only by Fred Fischer.

August 29, 1885. "Notice: From now on there will positively be no credit given to anyone. I have reduced prices and will sell only for cash and nothing but cash. No one need ask for credit, not even my own mother. J. H. Hanson."

The used car business was just beginning.

April 6, 1909. "Three seated automobile surrey for sale. I need the money and will sell cheap. Machine in good shape. 22 h.p., 2 cylinder engine."

March 18, 1910 the Salmo news reported: "Harvey Nourse was giving his new auto a trial last Wednesday and as soon as the road dries up a little more, he will be able to go some between here and town." April 29, 1910. "A. H. Wilkinson is expecting his new automobile to arrive today. It is a 25 h.p. Ford touring car."

The Bayfield Press had already predicted that the gasoline motor would bring progress.

Oct. 1, 1909. "Automobile delivery of rural mail is not an improbable addition to the postal service."

Feb. 4, 1871. "A dance occurred at Oak Island on Monday evening in which the elite of that place participated."

The Oak Island social register was lost during a severe northeast storm, so we do not know who the elite were, but we are glad they had fun dancing out there over 85 years ago.

July 12, 1890. "Mrs. John McCloud gave a progressive peanut party last Saturday evening."

That might be an idea for the centennial. Does anyone know what a progressive peanut party is?

August 2, 1907. "And now comes the prediction by a Michigan prophet, he who predicted the Spanish American War, that in the next five years, there will be a world wide war in which the United States will pull out the victor."

The Ashland Press had some interesting items, such as this one in 1872. "That horrid redheaded fellow, who accidentally stepped on a lady's dress the other day in front of our office, tearing the skirt off and exposing an Ashland lady in her bustle, has not been arrested yet. He never even apologized to the lady. Our police should attend to their duties more closely and nail all chaps when committing such ungentlemanly acts in public."

And in 1878 the Superior Times printed, "One of the oldest settlers of LaPointe seeing the name Psyche on the hull of a yacht the other day spelled it out slowly then exclaimed, "Well, if that ain't the biggest way to spell fish."

Colonel C.F. Rudd & Politics

(Photo: BHA)

POLITICS! POLITICS! POLITICS! SOME-
BODY IS always getting excited about
them. But what must have been one of the
most entertaining political reactions ever
seen on the streets of Bayfield took place
after Abraham Lincoln's election in 1864.

The entertaining reaction was Col. C.F.
Rudd's. He lived in Bayfield for about 40
years, apparently because he liked the town
and had a lot of fun here. He lived a happy
bachelor life in a small house built on the
lots between the homes of H.D. Winbigler
and Fred Meyers. The back yard was filled
with eggshells, the results of his quick, frying
pan meals. He was still here about 1900. My
dad knew him then, and remembers him as
a pleasant, elderly man, rather stocky, with a
leisurely walk.

The Rev. W.B. McKee, Presbyterian minister, who came to Bayfield on the *North Star*
May 21, 1858, knew him too. He gave an account of Col. Rudd's political frenzy in a letter
written to the Bayfield Commercial Club when they celebrated the fiftieth anniversary
of our town.

Mr. McKee must have been standing on the bank corner, looking, listening, laughing, and
if he was there, it's a cinch that everyone else in town was there too.

Here is Mr. McKee's version: "A laughable incident occurred in the first night after the
news of Lincoln's election was received. Col. Rudd, of Kentucky, was the sole actor in
it. The Colonel had a fondness for Bayfield and cash enough to sustain him in what
appeared to be an aimless and easygoing life. He was genial and entertaining in his way.
He was a strong democrat and equally strong in his southern characteristics. It was a
foregone conclusion with him that Lincoln would be defeated; but when his election
was assured, the Colonel's spirit broke from its natural bounds and found relief only in
the most boisterous denunciations of the president-elect and the Republican Party. He
took in an unusual quantity of Skit-a-wa-bu and went forth rampant, simulating the
passes and movements of the pugilist, sending detonations of his voice through the town.
He strode back and forth on the street between Vaughn's store and Teemeyers building
(between Iverson's and Meyers Drug Store). He exhibited the civil conflict in pantomime.
He was the South, and the North was not a "patchen" to it, and would be annihilated. The
North was ignorant, uncultured, and rooted. "One Southerner was equal to two Yankees
and could wallop them." This was an utterance I heard him repeat over and over. As the
firewater was doing its work he did the vehement raging and continued his lonely carouse
until after midnight."

So that is how the Civil War was re-fought on our main street in 1864. The South won. . . temporarily. But in the end the knockout punch was delivered by Skit-a-wa-bu.

The Winter Blues

THIS IS THE TIME TO recall one of Bayfield's favorite songs, *The Winter Blues.* A lot of people can still sing it, the chorus, at least. But just to record it for Bayfield's history collection, here are the "Cold Words and Air by Eddie Fortier."

> *1. Winter, winter, that is the time I fear.*
> *That time is drawing near.*
> *With its ice and its snow*
> *And there's no place to go.*
> *Winter, Winter, that name makes me freeze.*
> *I would not care*
> *If I had underwear*
> *All I've got are BVDs.*
> *2. Winter, Winter, if you were here a day*
> *And then go miles away*
> *As it is you are here*
> *'leven months in each year.*
> *Winter, Winter, that name makes me sigh*
> *Now this isn't bunk*
> *Why I feel so punk*
> *I could lay right down and die.*
> *Chorus:Because it ain't no joke, my duds are old*
> *I'm dead broke, my feet are cold,*
> *Looking thin, I'm almost in,*
> *I'm blue, hungry too.*
> *When I hear that North wind whine,*
> *There's a chill runs up my spine.*
> *Good-bye, summer. I've got the winter blues.*

The song was published by John Olk, of Bayfield, who had a drug store here for many years in the building now occupied by Burtness Hardware.

Eddie Fortier, who now lives in Minneapolis, has the copyright and on the cover of the sheet music is a picture of Fortier's Novelty Four, which in the twenties was Bayfield's favorite orchestra. The four members were: Mike Carlson, John Westerlund, Johnny Sayles, and Eddie Fortier. The cover also has a very chilly blue and white picture of a man with no overcoat standing in the snow. He is holding his ears. The snow is clinging to his spats. His breath is a white cloud as he looks at a thermometer registering twenty below. Some of you probably still have that old sheet music.

The song's got cold sentiment all right, but the words were good for a laugh to the fun loving Bayfielders who thirty years ago crowded into Memorial Hall (it used to be where the lake front park is) night after winter night and danced to it. They whistled it as they went home afterward, walking up the snow covered hills, and probably got the meaning of it a little better when they went into their houses, found the fires had gone out and the wood boxes were empty.

Yep! Those were the good old days. But this "winter blues" stuff requires a little thought now. We don't walk up the snow-covered hills any more than we have to. We get into cars, well-heated ones, and ride. Cars don't get put up on blocks for the winter anymore.

And after stepping out of a well-heated car and making a quick dash into the house, if we should find the furnace was not working, there would be an outcry, "The furnace didn't switch on! Call the power company!" There would be no snowy trek out to the piles of slab wood from the millyard, which used to flank each Bayfield home.

So times have changed. But Bayfield still likes, and always will like, *The Winter Blues*. It's a good song.

Snow Snake

A LOT OF YOU REMEMBER DAD Davis, the rotund, genial proprietor of the Davis House. But do you remember Dad's account of the snow snake? In case you don't, and for those who were too young to either know Dad or hear the story, it is now repeated. Dad wrote it in reply to an article telling of the experience a man down in central Wisconsin had with a snow snake. Dad's authoritative account of this creature was published in the *Superior Telegram* in 1908 and also in The Bayfield Press .

Dad says: "I saw your report of the fight between I.T. Elliott of Rhinelander, Wis., and the Snow Snake, and I want to congratulate the doctor upon his narrow escape. The reporter who wrote up the affair evidently is not entirely familiar with its habits.

Another correction I would like to make is that Northern Wisconsin is not entirely the home of the reptile. Had the reporter secured an interview with Mr. Gene Shepard, also of Rhinelander, much valuable information as to the peculiarities of this venomous snake could have been elicited. It is a well-known fact to all old lumberjacks that about a month after the first appearance of the snow snake in the fall, there begins to grow upon the tail of the snake a hard, stony substance. As winter advances it increases in size until it is nearly as large as a baseball.

For many years I was at a loss to know what use the snake had for his appendage. But about five or six years ago, Mr. Gene Shepard and myself ad occasion to go up to the northern part of Minnesota in quest of a female Hodag, has a companion to the male Hodag captured by Mr. Shepard and now in his possession. One night while camping on the north shore of Lake Winnebegoshe, and after having eaten our supper we were sitting before a rousing fire smoking our pipes when our attention was aroused by a muffled tapping or drumming apparently coming from the lake.

Our curiosity was aroused, and slipping on our thick clothing we went forth and cautiously approached the lake. We parted the thick bushes that lined the lake and to our astonishment, out upon the lake about ten rods from shore a sight met our eyes that seldom if ever was seen by the eyes of man. There was a space of perhaps a half acre as smooth as ice could be with the bare exception of a large, round lump of ice apparently three feet high and about the same in diameter. Upon the top of this lump of ice was coiled the largest snow snake I ever saw.

His head was raised about a foot from the center of the coil and to the swaying motion of the head, he was beating a rhythmic measure upon the ice upon which he lay. Stranger still, gliding around upon the glossy surface of the ice were about 20 or 25 couples of snow snakes enjoying themselves much after the fashion of a lot of boys and girls on a skating rink.

After looking for a moment, Mr. Shepard grasped me by the arm and whispered in my ear: "Say, Dad, we have got to get out of this at once. If those snakes had any suspicion that we had looked upon their secret method of enjoying themselves, our lives would not be worth a straw, for they would immediately leave the ice and pursue us and either sting us to death with their poison fangs, or beat our brains out with their tails." We hurried back, packed up and struck out for the woods. We walked until daylight the next morning before we stopped, fearful that they might be on our trail.

But fortunately for us, they did not discover our near presence. To the active brain and great knowledge displayed by Mr. Shepard, I solemnly believe I owe the privilege of telling this seemingly preposterous tale.

Unusual Wedding

(Photo: BHA)

W HO HAD THE FIRST WEDDING in Bayfield? We don't know that, but we do know who had one of the most unusual weddings.

It was unusual for several reasons. The guests didn't know they had been invited to a wedding. The minister suffered considerably, and the best man was the best man, in one sense of the word.

The groom was Robert Inglis, one of Bayfield's prominent citizens, (the house now occupied by the Bainbridges was his), and the bride was Margaret Walton, great-aunt of Mrs. Wallis Durham. The ceremony took place on the steamer *Japan* enroute from Ashland to Bayfield on August 26, 1891, sixty-two years ago last month.

The bride and groom, being of middle years, evidently wanted a quiet wedding, so they did not announce their plans. Mr. Inglis simply invited some unsuspecting friends to take a boat ride to Ashland, as it was his custom to do quite often.

A pleasant trip across the bay was enjoyed and the steamer was held at the Ashland dock, until E.A. Inglis, who was to be the best man, arrived on the night train from St. Paul.

The Captain of the *Japan*, Robert Smith, was to give the bride away, and in the capacity of host he "extended every courtesy which his magnificent steamer could afford, to add to the eclat of the occasion."

Well, maybe eclat is the word. The dictionary says it means "a striking effect." Certainly a striking effect was present in this ceremony.

The striking effect began when a hard storm sprang up shortly after the *Japan* left Ashland. The boat rocked fearfully, but the surprised wedding guests gathered around and the wedding started as planned. When the clergyman asked the groom if he would take, cherish, etc., the groom, thrown off balance by a particularly high wave, lurched forward and struck the preacher amidships, doubling him up. The clergyman rallied from this and extracted an affirmative answer from the sea-tossed groom, and put the same query to the bride. Another lurch of the ship sent her crashing forward, her fair head hart sport against the minister's shirtfront, giving him quite a jolt.

The minister was a hardy man, used to difficult situations, but being pounded in the stomach in the midst of a rolling sea was too much for him. He grew pale and had to adjourn proceedings while he leaned over the rail. When he felt able to, he finished the ceremony.

There was a delightful wedding repast, but all of the guests were too seasick to partake of it. Only the best man, best to the end, managed to drink the bride's health as he held fast to a halyard.

When the boat finally landed and they crawled out onto the Bayfield dock, they weren't the gayest wedding party in the world; but they were probably one of the happiest landing parties in history.

Bayfield Compliments

B AYFIELD HAS BEEN THE SUBJECT of many complimentary accounts printed in outside newspapers. One of them appeared in The Ashland Press July 17, 1875. "Bayfield as a pleasure resort still attracts the attention of the fashionable of the outside world. The editor of *Forest and Stream* writes that he could fill a hotel four months in each year with friends writing about Bayfield and the Lake Superior resorts. We can assure him that if he will send them along they will be properly cared for, that Smith's fine hotel has all the accommodations necessary for their comfort while the fishing and resources for pure, unadulterated pleasure are unbounded.

Pleasure boats for sailing, row boats for exercise, drives for invalids, walks for lovers, bowers and rest of the weary and the good things of life for those who enjoy healthy livers abound. There is no place equal to Bayfield and its surroundings on the continent for beautiful scenery, pure water and life giving climate. Come and see us you tired and weary laden, you seekers after pleasure and health and you will find our words true in every respect. Elegant steamers sailing the Great Lakes will land you safely at our docks and a warm-hearted people will make your stay pleasant and agreeable. No tourist can die happy unless his eyes have drunk in the beauty of the Apostle Islands and his heart has beat with the fullness of joy experienced in viewing the lavish works of nature that greet one on every hand."

Seventeen years later, on July 16, 1892, the *Lincoln Daily Call* had this to say about Bayfield. "It is a beautiful and quiet little town of about 1,500 population, which is visited every summer by a few of the best people in the country, but it is not one of those crowded resorts that demand an unlimited expenditure of money and impose annoying rest-destroying social excursions. At Bayfield, you can come as you please and go as you please. You can do as you please and dress as you please. At the Island View Hotel you can have large rooms and all the delicacies of the season at the same rate as is charged by first class hotels elsewhere. There is no lack of the best kind of society, but you need not be in it and have it unless you wish. There is no place in the whole country where one can feel such a delicious sense of freedom and of rest and such an exhilarating sense of physical renovation as at Bayfield." Sixty-six years have passed since that was written. Is the truth still in the story? For many years, until the railroad came in 1883, the docks were Bayfield's front doorsteps. June 20, 1891, *The Press* said, "It is now a good many years since one could speak of going down to the dock in Bayfield. Away back in ancient times when the *Mayflower* and craft of that ilk plowed the blue waters of Lake Superior, there probably was a time when going down to the dock meant only a trip to the foot of Washington Avenue. Year by ear, however, the dockage facilitates of Bayfield have increased."

The article continued, telling of the many Bayfield docks used for freight, fish and lumber. But by 1909 Bayfield felt the need of a new and special dock, a city dock. Feb. 26, 1909, *The Press* said, "As spring approaches, the city dock question looms up more important than ever. It is a well-known fact that at present there is no free dock in the harbor. The only landing facilities, which are now on hand, are at the lumber docks and the fishing docks, neither of which afford a suitable landing place for the excursion steamers and small pleasure craft which are so greatly utilized by summer tourists. There is at present a very suitable location at hand for a city dock, this being at the foot of Rittenhouse Avenue. Here an "L" shaped dock could be erected at a small cost, which would be the means of affording a splendid landing place and an excellent place for safety during storms.

By June of that year the city dock was becoming a reality. *The Press* reported: "Building of a new city dock at the foot of Rittenhouse Avenue will soon be commenced. . . Commercial Club members and others have subscribed toward the building of the dock. The town will make up the balance." H.J. Wachsmuth was the largest contributor to the fund for the dock. He gave $1000. A.H. Wilkinson, Theodore Ernst and Kransfelder Bros. were next, each giving $475. It didn't take long to build this first city dock. By the end of July *The Press* said, "The new city dock is now doing business and island dwellers say it is one of the very best improvements made here in years. It certainly adds greatly to the appearance of the bay front and renders access to all parts of town easy and free from obnoxious surroundings."

The Faces of Early Bayfield

Back Row: Florence Thompson, Margaret Moore, May Gleason, Mina Jath, Edna Flanders, Kate Mussel; Front Row: May Jones, Reta Wachsmuth, Gertie Burt, Margaret Felthauser. (Photo: BHA)

Left to Right: Harry Welty, unknown, Nels Brigham, Ed Miller, Shine Miller Glasphel LaBonte, A.G. LaBonte, Douglas Knight, Harrison Mussel, Herbert Hale, Joseph P. O'Malley, Unknown. (Photo: BHA)

Group Portrait of Young Ladies: Ollie Herrick, Bessie Flanders, Grace Atkinson, Lillian Jones, Blanche Thornton, Carrie Atkinson, Maude Thornton (Photo: BHA)

Group Portrait of Young Ladies: Top: Josie Shaw, Lulu Shaw, Georgia Bell LaBonte; Bottom: Anna May Shaw Hill, Luella Jones, May Jones - July 1889 (Photo: BHA)

Chippewa Indian Peace Committee, 1845: Upper Left: Frank Roy, Vincent Roy, E. Roussin, Old (Frank) Do, Peter Roy, Jos. Gourneau, D. Geo. Morrison (Photo: BHA)

The Messengers: Upper row from the left- Vincent Conyer- Interpreter, Vincent Roy J., Dr. I. L. Mahan Indian Agent, no name given, George P. Warren- civil war veteran, Thad Thayer. Lower row-Messenger, Na-ga-nab, Moses White, no name given, Osho'gay—head speaker, Nay'-qua-as'- Head chief of LaCorre" Oreilles (Photo: BHA)

Bayfield's Early Movers & Shakers. (Photo: Jeannette Southmayde Casparri).

Chapter 10

Shipwrecks, Sailors & Lake Superior Stories

The Storm of 1905

SCARCELY TWO MONTHS AFTER THE Sevona went down on York Island reef and the *Pretoria* went down at Outer Island, the lake was swept by another violent storm. This was worse than the September 1905 storm for it carried snow, like the blizzard, which took the Lucern.

The storm began on Monday, November 27, 1905, and before midnight reached a terrible violence of snow, wind and towering waves, which lasted through Tuesday and until Wednesday forenoon.

Damage was done to shipping all along the lake. At Duluth the big steel steamer *Crescent City* went on the rocks. Fortunately her crew escaped. The steamer *Mataffa*, ore-laden, trying to make entrance to the Duluth harbor was thrown against the pier and nine of her crew of twenty-three were lost. The *R. W. England* went ashore near Superior entry. Her crew was rescued. The *Isaac L. Elwood* sunk in the Duluth harbor. The schooner *Constitution* broke loose from the steam barge *Victory* near Copper Harbor and drifted helplessly until she was picked up near the Porcupine Mountains by the steamer *Moore* and was towed to Bayfield.

Men who had sailed the lakes for years said they had never experienced a storm of greater fury.

In Bayfield, the herring fishing fleet remained safe in port. The greatest loss was to time and nets. But in spite of all precautions the storm struck with such force that four boats were lost, three in the collapse of boat houses and Captain Charlie Russell's gas boat, *Madeline,* was struck by a log while in the slip at Booth's dock and sank. She had been leased by Captain Ben Peterson for the herring season.

Damage was done to slab docks not loaded with lumber. The boathouse belonging to F.V. Holston was completely destroyed and two boats were lost with it. The railroad tracks along the shore were damaged. Wm. Knight lost his naphtha launch, and though it was felt the engine, one of the best of its size, might be saved, the boat was a total loss.

On Thursday afternoon, November 30, when the storm was well spent, the first mate and four seamen of the big steel steamer *William E. Corey,* arrived in Bayfield in a small boat and reported that the *Corey* was beached off the northeast end of Michigan Island on the Gull Island shoals.

The *Corey* was the largest of the steel boats comprising the fleet of the Pittsburgh Steamship Company. She was their flagship, having been launched the previous June and was considered the finest boat on the lakes in 1905. She had been light bound for Duluth when she struck the rocks.

A wrecking outfit went out to work on her, confident that she would be released unhurt. *The Bayfield Press* reported that there was not a cent of insurance on her, and if she should go to pieces, the company would be out $475,000.

A week later the big *Corey* was still on the reef and it was known that the bottom was badly damaged. Four steamers and three tugs pulled on her Wednesday, December 6, but their combined efforts could not move the big boat one inch. Dynamite was used to blast out rocks under the boat.

Finally on Sunday, December 10, the *Corey* came off the rocks with such a fearful rush that it almost caused disaster to her rescuers.

Able Seaman A.L. Mattson gave this eyewitness account. "I was on the big steamer *William E. Corey* when it was pulled off the rocks at Gull Island Sunday morning. The *Douglas Houghton* had a line fast to the *Corey*. The *Marina* had a line fast to the *Houghton*. The *Gladiator* had a line fast to the Marina, all pulling for all they were worth. Only one vessel, you see, had a fast line to the *Corey*.

"The *Manila* had a separate line fat to the *Corey*, but was not pulling at the time, having stopped to coal up. The *E. G. Crosby* and the *Edna G.* lay by for emergencies. Suddenly the big vessel started with a rush. The effect on the three vessels pulling was the same as if you were pulling on a rope, the further end of which was tied to a tree. The rope breaks and suddenly you fall on your back.

"When the *Corey* started with a rush, of course the *Douglas Houghton,* which was pulling with all its might, also started with a rush. The *Marina,* which was pulling on the *Houghton,* started with a rush. The tug *Gladiator,* at the end of the procession, also started with a rush, but its wheel happened to be turned wrong and it ran directly athwart the *Marina,* which butted into it and nearly turned it over.

Mr. Smith, in charge of wrecking operations, gave orders for the master of the tug to cut his line, which he did, just in time to escape being swamped. For a short time the tug and its crew were in great peril.

"An idea of the extent of the injury to the *Corey* may be inferred from the fact that you could go down into the hold and see daylight through the side of the bottom forward."

So the *Corey* was rescued from Gull Island shoals in the early winter of 1905, and it may be she is still on the lakes. Does anyone know?

The Christopher Columbus

June 12th 1897. The Christopher Columbus at the North dock. Note the Booth tug T.H. Camp at right. (Photo: BHA)

THERE ARE STILL MANY PEOPLE in Bayfield who remember the great whaleback steamer, *Christopher Columbus*. When this great boat was first built, it was on exhibit in Duluth. People went up to see it and paid about $2.00 for the privilege of going through it. Mrs. Ida Hoaglund was one of the people who went from here, and she remembers that day very well.

In September, 1897, an *Ashland Press* item said: "Bayfield is to be congratulated on being the only town on Chequamegon Bay to welcome the big whaleback steamer, *Christopher Columbus,* to her port."

And on September 25, 1897, *The Bayfield Press* reported a visit of the Christopher Columbus that was long to be remembered here. The headlines said, "The Balloon Went Up."

"Fully 8,000 excursionists visited Bayfield last Saturday and Sunday. The two largest crowds that ever visited in Bayfield were landed here last Saturday and Sunday by the big whaleback steamer *Christopher Columbus.* Sunday was the last trip for the Christopher and closed the most successful season in her existence.

"On Saturday the *Chris* landed at the Dalrymple dock with over 2,000 people on board. She remained at the dock one hour, during which time the excursionists took in the sights of our town.

"Professor Deer made an attempt at an excursion while in the harbor. The balloon was held on the windward side by 15 or 20 men, but when ⅔ inflated, a heavy gust of wind caught it and piling the men in a heap, the balloon swept the dock, knocking over the hot air flue and was set on fire. The men immediately let go the guy ropes and the large airship blew over into the water where the flames were extinguished. Considerable excitement prevailed, causing two ladies to faint, but fortunately no one was injured.

Sunday the airship was repaired and when the *Chris* was lying at the dock at Bayfield during the hour's stop the ascension was made. The balloon was inflated with hot air upon the forward deck, and additional staff being erected to hold the canvas in place during the process.

It took about 15 men to inflate the balloon and a dozen men held it down as its constantly increasing size doubled its efforts to get away.

Suddenly there was a signal. The men on the guy ropes released their hold and the balloon shot upward. It was one of the prettiest aeronautic performances ever seen.

Suspended from the bottom of the balloon proper was a parachute. Suspended from the parachute was a trapeze, and as the balloon left the dock at the rate of a mile in about 11 seconds, Professor Patsy J. Deer was seen hanging by his feet from the bar. An instant later, he reversed his position and held on by his teeth.

It seemed an incredibly short time until the balloon was up in the air between 3 and 4 thousand feet, when the Professor pulled the string and let the parachute off. Down it shot with the Professor dangling at the trapeze. Inside of three hundred feet, the parachute opened like a huge white canvas umbrella and soared slowly down to terra firm. A good many people thought the descent, even at this was too fast for comfort.

Deer landed a few hundred feet back from the lake in Bayfield, safe and sound. The balloon, now the size of a hen's egg, was rapidly emptying of its hot air. . . It turned bottom up and came down in the top of some trees. Ten seamen from the *Chris* were waiting for it and picked it up, bringing it on shipboard and the vessel immediately pulled away."

Sinking of The *Friant*

The Friant in her days as a transport and passenger steamer. Circa 1923. (Photo: BHA)

I T IS 30 YEARS AGO last Wednesday, January 6, 1925, since the *Friant* went down. Recently Captain Shine Miller was asked if he had any comment to make before the *Friant* sank again in the history column of *The Bayfield Press* , and he said, "I'm glad I wasn't on her!"

We're glad too, Shine, real glad!

Halvor Reiten, half owner and fireman on the boat stayed below trying to keep up the steam until the water rose to the grates and put out the fire. But when he crawled onto an ice-glazed, rocky shore, he was "dressed like a gentleman."

The *Friant* sank during a hazardous attempt at all winter fishing on Lake Superior. The crew had no illusions about the difficulties and hardships they were facing when they made the attempt. Lights, and other aids to navigation had ceased the middle of December. They planned to set nets out from the north shore in open water, about ten or fifteen miles run from Two Harbors, which would be their headquarters. It was not likely they would see any other boat, except possibly a fish boat. They knew if the *Friant* was disabled, or had to run in a northeaster, there was no shelter closer than Two Harbors, or a fifty-mile run to Duluth. Ice all along the south shore ended any expectation of shelter there.

But nine men went, a hand picked crew, who were willing to take chances to earn a living. For back in 1924 there was no unemployment compensation. You either earned a dollar or went without.

The crewmembers were Captain Shine Miller and Fireman, Halvor Reiten, owners of the tug *Thomas Friant*. Sherman Bolles of Ashland was the engineer and the others were fishermen Charles and George Jones, Andrew Hanson, John Anderson, and Thomas and Emery Jones, all of Cornucopia.

The *Friant* was a large tug, built of wood, 111 feet long, with an 18-foot beam. It carried 140 pounds of steam and had transported freight and passengers between Duluth and

Bayfield all during the summer of 1923. Captain Shine Miller had intended to use the *Friant* to bring a party of Bayfielders to Ashland on a New Year's Day excursion, but ice formed so the trip could not be made.

(Just for the history record, let's set down the fact that the bay was open for the first time in the memory of any white settlers in 1878, and that year, Ashlanders came over in the tug *Eva Wadsworth* to pay a New Year's call on Bayfielders. Bayfield tried every year after that to repay the call, but were not able to do so until 1932. On Jan. 1 of that year, despite a northeast gale and a snowstorm, such as had not visited the region before that winter, the boats *Nichevo* and *Byng II* crossed the bay. And as the "Squibber" wrote in *The Ashland Press* , "Outstanding in the program on Friday was a promise that was made. It was a promise exactly the same as one made (by Bayfield) 54 years ago. And it will be kept. On the next New Year's Day that Chequamegon Bay is free from ice, Ashland will visit across the bay."

Recently, when it looked as though the trip might be made in 1954, a few Ashlanders said doubtfully, "But how can we come? We haven't got anything to come in."

Don't worry about that Ashland. Bayfield's got lots of boats. If necessary, our hospitality will extend so far we'll come and get you.")

When it was realized the *Friant* was not needed for a history-making voyage to Ashland, it left for Cornucopia to pick up the fishermen. There they loaded nets, bedding, food, clothes and other winter gear aboard. By night ice was forming in Corni Bay and they pushed out to the edge of it, about two miles, so there would be no danger of freezing in.

The next morning the tug started for Bark Point. It was a bitterly cold January morning. The lake was steaming so there was little visibility and the boat ran into thin ice, which it could cut easily. But then an odd thing happened. Rats began to come up from below decks. As they jumped out of a hole in the galley, Tom Jones clipped them on the head with a poker. "Rats desert a sinking ship" is a well-known saying. But how did they know enough to start deserting before she was even hit?

The boat soon met heavier ice and finally drift ice. A large chunk pounded into the *Friant* with such force it punched a hole in the after port side. It happened about noon, just as the *Friant* rounded Bark Point.

It was decided to turn back and seek shelter in Bark Bay. The turn was made and they got inside within an hour. The weather was growing worse every minute. The temperature was dropping and finally sank to a low of twenty-three below zero. The *Friant* began to freeze in. The crew working frantically in spite of the cold managed to list the boat on her side enough so they could patch the hole in the hull. John Anderson was lowered over the side and worked on the patch in the freezing water.

The crew thought the *Friant* was sealed in for the winter for sure. Plans were made to walk ashore on the ice the next day. The men from Cornucopia said they would come out, watch the boat and take care of it through the winter. But about 1:30 in the morning the ice around the boat could be heard breaking up, and by 3 AM the tug could move again. That afternoon they got out of the bay and headed for Port Wing. The patch on the side held perfectly watertight.

Three miles of thin ice were encountered. Then, about nine miles from Port Wing, a heavy sea struck. By 3:30 PM they were in trouble. The *Friant* started leaking through a new hole in the starboard side, about amidships. A chunk of ice had probably crushed through there and stuck until the heavy seas washed it loose and let the waters pour in.

Everyone got busy with pumps and pails, but the water gained on them rapidly. Hampered by ice, cold and wind, they fought a hard, but losing fight in the middle of Lake Superior.

Halvor Reiten remembers vividly that struggle to save the sinking *Friant.* He stayed in the fire hole trying to keep up steam so they could maneuver, and maybe save the boat. As the waves tossed the *Friant,* he was thrown off his feet time after time into the dirty, coal-dust filled water that was rising around him. Coal rolled out of the bunkers and he and the coal were tossed around "like peas in a rattle" as he described it. He couldn't shovel any longer, but kept grabbing lumps of coal and throwing them into the boiler, hoping the steam would last. Finally, the crew yelled at him to come up. It was hopeless. By then the water was up to the grates and the fire sizzled out as he left.

He was soaked with coal-blackened water and knew if he didn't get dry clothes he would freeze to death in the life boat. He ran to the cabin and found that the water had not reached the top bunk where his best suit was. He grabbed it and waded out through floating kitchen utensils and some fresh made donuts where were drifting around. Finding a sheltered spot he changed clothes and got ready to abandon the *Friant* dressed in his best.

In the meantime, Charley Jones and Shine Miller had been working on the lifeboat. It was a good, new one, but was covered with canvas and the canvas and ropes, which held it, were stiff with ice so they could hardly free them. Working as fast as they could they broke the boat loose and lowered it. They took the compass from the pilot house. Then the nine men got into the small open boat and headed into open Lake Superior. They were midway between the north and south shores, but knew they stood no chance in the drift ice around Port Wing. The north shore was their only hope, though it was 12 miles away and they had to row against a strong, northeast wind.

As the crew rowed away they looked back and saw the *Friant* settle in the waves. She went down on an even keel until water was almost half way up the pilothouse. Then with a rush, the stern rose thirty feet in the air and she dove to her final resting place, 70 fathoms below. In case any former Bayfielders, who have moved inland and become landlubbers, have forgotten, a fathom is six feet. Therefore, with 420 feet of water over the wood boat, they knew there was no hope of ever raising her, of ever recovering their fishnets or personal belongings.

The means of their livelihood were gone, and there was no insurance, since all marine insurance expired in the winter. There was no insurance on the equipment, either. Back in 1924 the *Friant* was valued at $10,000 and the equipment at $6,000. Shine and Halvor had just purchased the tug that fall.

The rowing was hard against the bitter January northwest wind. The crew managed to change places at the oars a few times. Charley Jones of Cornucopia stayed at his oar the whole way. The strong head wind blew spray over them, which immediately froze. As Halvor said, "We were like turtles, each one in a shell of ice." But this ice around them did form a windbreaker, which protected them some.

When they were seven or eight miles off the north shore they sent up flares. Later they were told the flares had been seen, but people who saw them thought someone was just out shooting fireworks, celebrating something. Though why anyone would be out on Lake Superior in January in a northwest gale shooting fireworks was never explained very clearly.

The shipwrecked crew hoped that if their flares were seen, the big fire tug at Two Harbors would come out to pick them up. But it never came. The crew of the sunken *Friant* rowed steadily against the wind and freezing spray from 4 PM until 11 PM In those seven hours they went twelve miles. Shine later told Don Bell of *The Bayfield Press* , "If every man on the crew had not been a real boatman, we would not have escaped so fortunately."

But they were all boatmen, trained to the ways of Lake Superior, toughened to the hardships it could inflict on them. And they made it. They landed about 5 miles west of Two Harbors.

But once the shore was reached, they were faced with a new problem. The beach was rocky, and completely ice coated. A rough cliff rose above it. Yet, they couldn't stay where they were so they cut nicks in the ice and climbed the cliff, knowing that if they slipped, it meant at the least a bruising fall down the rocks and into the icy water.

Climbing and encouraging each other, they made it to the top. A short distance away they found some fishermen in a shack who, with immediate sympathy, took them in, built up a roaring fire and put on a big camp coffee pot. They were fed, got dried, but there were no accommodations for nine men to sleep, in fact it was badly crowded with all of them standing in the little shack, so toward morning they walked about a mile to a small depot on the branch line of a railroad, where they could get a train to Two Harbors.

There was a big box stove in the depot and they sat close to it. Shine remembers that they did not speak at all, just sat there, heads down, exhausted. And as they sat, a man came in. Shine remembers one outstanding thing about him. He had on a big, warm overcoat, a great contrast to their wrinkled, shrunken clothing. The man unbuttoned the warm overcoat and stood beside the box stove, holding his hands out to its warmth, as he looked over the dejected survivors. Then, with no greeting, he suddenly launched into a forceful exhortation, which ended, "That will teach you a lesson! Lead a better life!"

Halvor remembers that for emphasis the man jumped up and down as he preached.

After the sermon the man fastened his comfortable warm overcoat and left them. They never found out what denomination or sect he belonged to, but it was quite evidently one, which believed in berating the afflicted, instead of comforting them.

The train finally came. They got on and rode into Two Harbors. There they received material comfort, at least. A restaurant owner heard of their plight. He had been shipwrecked once himself; and he took them all to his restaurant and cooked them a hearty meal, refusing to take any money for it.

The men caught a train to Duluth, and then came on to Bayfield where they found a warm welcome waiting for them. Bayfield had first heard about the loss of the *Friant* by telephone. But Walt Barningham remembers the startling way he heard it. When he went to school one cold January morning, Heinie Kranzfelder was there ahead of him. In those days, Heinie was tinkering with an astounding new thing called radio. He had built himself a crystal set with earphones and had succeeded in getting a broadcast from Duluth. On it he heard the news that the *Friant* had sunk. His schoolmates were so impressed with this achievement, that Walt still remembers it.

The survivors of the shipwreck were given a "welcome home" party in Hank Fiege's garage, now the Viking Motor Co. The next morning the men from Cornucopia walked home, 19 long, snow-covered miles. That was an era when cars were up on blocks for the winter. There was a stage running at the time, but it could only carry one or two, and as none of them would ride and leave his friends to walk, they all walked home together.

The *Sevona*

The Sevona being salvaged after sinking with the steamer Ottawa by her starboard side. (Photo: BHA)

IT WILL BE 50 YEARS September 2, since the *Sevona* went down. Seven men lost their lives and from the Pretoria, which went down in the same storm, five men were lost. The Bayfield Press, in reporting this disaster, said the storm, which swept Lake Superior, was the worst since 1873.

The *Sevona* left the Allouez docks at West Superior Friday night, September 1, 1905. The boat was in charge of Captain D.S. McDonald and had a cargo of about 6 thousand tons of iron ore on board. There was a heavy sea running when the boat cleared but the Captain thought nothing particular of it until he was outside of Outer Island. There the wind and the waves became so terrible that he concluded to turn back and seek shelter among the islands.

Captain McDonald was lost, so it cannot be told exactly what happened, but it is supposed that he was headed for the West side of Sand Island, but got in too close and struck the reef which projects out from Sand Island about 1½ miles from the lighthouse.

At 5:45 Saturday morning, the big boat was battling its way through the high seas to shelter when there was a terrific crash. The crash was closely followed by two others and then the boat came to a stand, badly broken at the center.

The waves pounded the broken ship until she gradually sank onto the rock and seemed solid.

The whistle was blown for help until the rising water put out the fires in the boilers. Then rockets were sent up, but no one saw or heard the distress signals.

Fifteen minutes later, at 6 o'clock, with another mighty crash, the *Sevona* broke in two at the fourth hatchway.

The forward end of the vessel seemed to be still solid on the rocks but the stern gradually sank into the water. When daylight came, there was no let up of the wind on the stern section of the wrecked ship, [the Chief Engineer] ordered one of the boats lowered, and in this he placed four women, Miss Kate Spencer and Miss Jones of Erie, Pa., Mrs. William Phillippie of Buffalo, and Mrs. Cluckie of Bay City, Michigan. Then, with six of the crew he got into the boat himself and left the wreck.

For five hours in the small boat they battled the waves and finally, one large wave lifted the boat and set it high and dry on the beach at Little Sand Bay. *The Bayfield Press* said, "More than once the men thought they would have to give up, but their courage was kept up by the ladies, who nerved them to further efforts and they finally landed safely."

At the same time, Boat No. 2 containing six of the crew, put off, but they handled the boat so badly, the people in the first boat thought they had surely been drowned. But in less than an hour, the wind and weaves drove them ashore at the West Bay of Sand Island.

There were seven men left on the forward end of the *Sevona*. They had absolutely nothing to leave the wreck in after the other boats left. It was impossible for them to reach the after end of the boat after the crash, as huge waves were going clear over them.

Those who reached shore at Little Sand Bay in the engineer's boat made their way to the logging camp of Napoleon Rabideaux and were taken care of. The engineer, after being rested and refreshed started for Bayfield with a teamster from the camp, and it took them nearly all day Sunday to get here, as the heavy wind had felled many trees across the road.

The *Sevona* struck the reef at 5:45 a.m., Saturday and it was not until Sunday evening that the exhausted teamster and chief engineer Phillippie arrived in Bayfield to report the wreck of the *Sevona* and ask for help for the seven men who had been left stranded on the forward end of the wreckage.

A half-century has passed since the *Sevona* went down on the rocky reef between Sand and York Islands. Chief Engineer, Wm. Phillippie, one of the survivors, brought the news of the wreck to Bayfield and gave *The Bayfield Press* a vivid description of the terror and suffering they experienced in the shipwreck.

He said, "The sea got so high that the Captain concluded to run for shelter and it was shortly after we turned that we struck.

Shortly before this, I received a signal from the Captain to check the speed, but after she struck I received no more signals and I stopped the engine. There were three distinct shocks and crashes when the boat came to a stand and broke in two.

We blew the whistle for help until our fires were put out.

The vessel broke in two as soon as we struck, but there was a portion of the starboard side railing hanging and I don't know why the Captain didn't try to come aft. Of course, it was almost impossible, but they might have made it for almost ½ hour after she broke. It may be that he thought the forward end would stand the sea, as it seemed to be hard aground. I don't know why.

I wanted to go forward with our lifeboat and try and pick them up, but we couldn't and I didn't want to lose the people I had. If there had been only one of the mates or even a sailor after to take charge of the other small boat (which was also launched from the stern with six men aboard), they might have gotten them off, but every sailor on the vessel was forward and cut off. Those in the rear were deckhands and oilers and knew nothing about managing a rowboat."

Miss Kate Spencer of Erie, Pa., another survivor gave *The Bayfield Press* this first hand account of the wreck of the *Sevona*. "It makes me shudder to talk or think of the terrible experience through which we passed.

About three o'clock in the morning, Captain McDonald knocked on our door and told us that he was going to seek shelter and for us to secure all breakable stuff in a place of safety, as when the boat put about she would toss badly. It was only a short time before the Captain came to our stateroom again and told us to dress. This we did, and a little later two sailors came and accompanied us to the after end of the boat. We were instructed to put on life preservers, which we did.

No one seemed to be especially frightened, but at 5:45 a.m., came the terrible crash, which broke the vessel in two.

We got into the lifeboat at that time, but the Captain and the men could not come aft owing to the break. He called to us through a megaphone, "Hang on as long as you can!"

We did so, but the sea was pounding so hard that we finally got out of the small boat and into the large vessel again, all congregating in the dining room, which was still intact.

The big boat was pounding and tossing, now a piece of the deck would go, then a portion of the dining room in which we were quartered. During all this time, the men forward could not get to us.

Finally at 11 o'clock everything seemed to be breaking at once and by order of the Chief Engineer we took to the small boat again. One by one we piled into the boat, leaving six men behind us. I never heard such a heart-rending cry as came from those six, "For God's sake, don't leave us!"

They cried so two of the men who were in our boat got out and helped the six men get the port boat over to the starboard side so they could launch it. These men then left in their boat and our men came back to our boat and we put off.

It was a terrible fight to keep the small boat afloat, and to the skill of Second Engineer Adam Fiden we certainly owe our lives. He is an experienced skuller, and kept our boat right when oars on the side were practically useless. We knew we were in danger, but we obeyed his orders implicitly and he finally landed us safe and sound."

Chief Engineer William Phillipie's Account of the *Sevona*

A CALM AND FACTUAL ACCOUNT OF the sinking of the Sevona was made by Chief Engineer William Phillipie to the Duluth officer of steamboat inspection. The adjectives are left out. It is a simple and clear report made by a good ship's officer.

"The Steamer *Sevona* left West Superior at 6:03 PM Friday, September 1 (1905) and all went well until 3 o'clock AM Saturday, September 2 when I was called by the second engineer pursuant to instructions from the Captain. The *Sevona* was then about one hour's run past Outer Island and owing to the heavy seas, was put about and headed for shelter.

At 5:05 AM, a signal for half speed was received in the engine room and answered. In about ten minutes the steamer ran aground, seeming to strike three times, as I felt three successive shocks. From that time until I left the ship, no official communication passed between the Captain and myself.

Immediately after the ship struck, the members of the crew who were on the after part of the ship and consisted of two engineers, three firemen, two oilers, four deckhands, two cooks and one porter, lowered both metallic lifeboats into the water. . .

I believe that the captain, pilots, wheelsmen and watchmen could have come aft if they wished to any time within 20 minutes after the steamer struck bottom, but I believe they thought themselves safe in the turtle back. It was possible to take a lifeboat from aft forward any time within one half hour after the steamer went aground. After that time, I consider it would have been impossible, due to the heavy seas, which had increased steadily. . .

After the lifeboats had been lowered, I beckoned to the men who were on the forward part of the steamer to come aft and thought their failure to do so was caused by a feeling of security on their part. While I did not hear the Captain say it, the crew aft reported to me that the Captain had shouted through the megaphone to "hang on as long as you can." This we did, and until the houses were going to pieces.

During the period of waiting five hours, men had to be kept in the lifeboats in order to keep them from being destroyed by collision with the ship's side.

We were compelled to leave the ship as seas were breaking over the after part of the vessel. The pilothouse and Texas had also been destroyed, but the forward part of the ship's side was in the same position as it was shortly after we struck bottom.

Eleven persons were in the boat I came ashore in, seven of the crew and four women passengers. I do not believe the presence of the passengers interfered in any way with the saving of the lives of the men who were drowned.

Neither of the lifeboats attempted to go to the assistance of the men on the forward part of the ship for the following reason. When it became too late for the men forward to come aft it was impossible to take a lifeboat forward. However, I believe that had the men equipped themselves with life preservers and jumped into the water, it would have been possible to pick them up. As they made no attempt to do this or to communicate with the people aft, I assumed that they felt more or less secure where they were.

I believe that all the men drowned were on the forward part of the vessel when the lifeboats left. However, we did not see them, as they had sheltered themselves beneath the turtle back deck.

The *Pretoria*–The *Sevona* Sinkings

About 11 hours after the *Sevona* sank near Sand Island, the *Pretoria*, in tow of the *Venezuela*, foundered and sank off Outer Island. Both sinkings occurred in the terrible storm, which swept Lake Superior on Sept. 1, and 2, 1905, fifty years ago last week.

The *Pretoria* and the *Venezuela* were loaded with ore. At eight o'clock on the morning of September 2, about two hours after the *Sevona* broke in two, the storm snapped the towline between these boats at both ends and the line fell into the water. The *Venezuela* ran for shelter and the *Pretoria* lay helpless in the heavy seas.

By four o'clock in the afternoon, the *Pretoria* had drifted to within a mile and a half of Outer Island. The anchors were thrown out. They caught and held so that the boat was at the mercy of the waves, which pounded open, the seams and at 4:35 p.m., the *Pretoria* went down.

Before the final plunge, ten members of the crew got into a small boat and headed for shore, but the high waves overturned them.

Captain Smart of the *Pretoria* said in a statement to *The Bayfield Press:* "When the *Pretoria* had arrived within 1½ miles of Outer Island, I saw that it was in bad shape, but thought that it might possibly stand it if I threw out the anchor, and I knew it would go to pieces if it went ashore.

When it began to sink, we were forced to take to the small boat and started for shore in the heavy seas. At last a gigantic wave struck us and we were thrown overboard, some of the crew being thrown 10 feet in the air. At one time or another, every one of the ten men were clinging to the overturned boat, but they dropped off one by one and only five of us reached shore and were sheltered in the lighthouse."

I asked Captain "Shine" Miller, who is old enough to remember these things, although you would never guess it from looking at him, why the *Venezuela* was towing the *Pretoria* in the first place. He explained that the *Pretoria* was a barge, and in those days it was a common practice to have these barges loaded with ore towed down the lakes. I also asked why the *Venezuela* ran off and left the *Pretoria* to sink and he said, "To save themselves." The third question, which must have occurred to anyone looking at a chart of the islands— When Captain McDonald had the *Sevona* at Outer Island, why didn't he run into the lee there, instead of going all the way back to Sand Island?

"Shine" explained that many captains had no knowledge of the islands as far as traveling among them was concerned, and probably Captain McDonald's intention was to get back to Sand Island so he could take the lighted steamboat channel along the mainland shore.

When Chief Engineer Phillippie reached Bayfield with news of the wreck of the *Sevona*, the tug *Harrow*, under the command of Captain Anderson, went out to endeavor to rescue the seven men who had been left on the forward wreckage. But when the tug reached the scene of the wreck, nothing but the stern of the *Sevona* remained. The bow had been entirely swept away.

Shine Miller and Martin Benson, who were aboard the *Harrow* launched a lifeboat, as it was impossible for the *Harrow* to go very close to the wreckage due to the large dead swells that were rolling. They rowed to the stern of the *Sevona*, where Shine grabbed the ropes left dangling when the two lifeboats were launched and pulled himself on board. It was hoped that all or some of the seven men had found a place of safety on the stern when the bow was swept away, but when Shine searched, it was quiet and empty, all seven of them were gone.

On Monday, Captain John Pasque went out to Sand Island with the *R. W. Currie* and there at the West Bay of Sand Island found the six men who had set out in the second lifeboat. The wind and waves had driven them ashore less than one hour from the time they left the wreck. They said that none of them had even tried to row or handle the little lifeboat. They had just clung to it until the wind and waves tossed them ashore.

That was one of the strange twists of the wreck. The stern, from which the two lifeboats had been launched and all 17 had escaped, remained afloat and weathered the storm until rescue came. The forward end, where there was apparently no lifeboat or means of escape for the seven men, was gone. The six men in the NO. 2 lifeboat who were deckhands and oilers, weren't even able to launch the boats by themselves, and knew nothing about navigation, had piled into the little boat and drifted ashore safely. The Captain and other officers who were forward, and would have known how to launch and navigate a small boat, were drowned.

The bodies of Captain McDonald, Nels Severson, wheelsman, Louis Darwin, first mate, and one unidentified body washed ashore at Sand Island. Justice Dars was instructed to go out there and hold an inquest. Shine Miller remembers that when they went out to pick up the bodies, Frank Shaw called him aside to say he had found a dollar bill near Captain McDonald's body, and showed him how he had placed the bill under the Captain's head. Later, more money washed in, but what became of it is now forgotten. A search was made for the three remaining bodies with no success.

On Tuesday, Isaac Alskog, a fisherman at Outer Island, found four of the bodies from the wreck of the *Pretoria*. He came to Bayfield and notified the authorities. The tug *Fashion* went out Tuesday evening and brought them in.

The eight bodies recovered from these two wrecks were brought in to Bayfield and placed in one of the buildings on the waterfront until relatives could be notified. Whether the other four bodies were ever found or not, I do not know. Does anyone remember?

Sevona and *Pretoria* Stories

SINCE THE STORIES OF THE wrecks of the Sevona and Pretoria appeared in The Press last fall, further items of interest about them have been collected.

The late James Long reported that 11 of the bodies of the victims of these two wrecks were recovered. He also said that Captain McDonald of the *Sevona* was a "regular old sea-dog" and knew the lake well. McDonald had been in a previous shipwreck and in a life preserver, managed to paddle some distance from the wreckage, in fact he had gotten so far away that a rescue vessel passed without seeing him. Using his seafaring knowledge, he figured it would come back on the same course and he might be picked up. Saving his strength he floated in the water as quietly as he could. When the ship came back, he attracted attention and was saved. He lived for many more years and sailed the lakes until he went down with the *Sevona*.

Captain Smart, who was cast ashore from the wreck of the *Pretoria*, lost his life little more than a year later. This item appeared in *The Press* Sept. 28, 1906. "The body of Captain Smart of the barge *Mantanzas*, who was accidentally drowned or murdered at Ashtabula was recovered. Ashtabula is one of the toughest lake ports on the chain of lakes and foul play is feared. Captain Smart was one of the five men who were rescued from the wrecked *Pretoria* off Outer Island last fall and was in Bayfield about two weeks ago.

In May, 1906, Captain Pasque went to the scene of the *Pretoria* wreck and with the tug *Currie* succeeded in raising the 1,200 pound steam pump from a depth of 52 feet. He also brought in one of the masts, about 100 feet long and nearly two feet through.

In May, 1908, Captain Reid of the Reid Wrecking Company, Superior, purchased the wreck of the *Sevona* for $5,000 and in July of that year, the tug *Salver* cleared away the wreckage. The company got the two boilers valued at $10,000 each, besides a large amount of machinery and tons of plate from the hull. The two boilers were nearest the surface with about 12 feet of water over them. When the wreckers were through there was at least 20 feet of water over the highest part of the wreck.

In July, 1909, *The Bayfield Press* said: "We notice by the Ashland and Duluth papers that the wreck of the Steamer *Sevona* near Sand Island is again to be removed. It is evident that these papers have not been very well posted upon this matter, but if they will look over their last years files they will probably find that the Reid Wrecking Company removed every vestige of the wreck last summer."

A letter from Edna Lane Sauer, daughter of Ed Lane, veteran lighthouse keeper at Michigan Island says, "The storm of 1905 will always be a vivid memory of mine. We were living on Michigan Island at that time and were packed and ready to go to town for the opening of school. The storm seemed to gather force with each passing hour and we feared the *Barker* would not be able to stop for us. Captain Vorous was in charge and late in the afternoon, he managed to get us aboard.

"We were in the cabin on the upper deck and because of the heavy rolling of the boat, had to sit on the floor. I recall that Mrs. Joe Lambert, Ruth and Kay had chosen that day to make the trip around the islands, so we were not alone in our misery and fright.

"The *Barker* followed the south channel and the trip took many hours. Father took his turn at the wheel to relieve Captain Vorous and it was long after dark when we arrived in Bayfield.

J. C. Chapple in his writings mentions that the Labor Day storm when the *Sevona* went down was the worst storm he had ever encountered.

He arrived in Bayfield to go to Madeline Island but the storm was so bad no boats would cross the channel. One of his children was ill on the island and he offered a boatman $50 to take him across but no one would take him.

Wreckage from the *Sevona* was used by Governor Fifield of Ashland to build a cottage on Sand Island called the Sevona Cottage and it comfortably housed many of the guests who visited the famous Sand Island resort conducted by the Governor and his wife, Stella Fifield. Is the Sevona cottage still standing?

Bayfield Boats

SINCE BAYFIELD WAS FOUNDED IN 1856, Bayfield and boats have gone together as inevitably as cream and sugar. Most of the settlers came by boat and the fare from Cleveland to Bayfield on either steamboat or propeller was only $20. The deck, or steerage passage was $11, the time three to four days distance including stops along the route, about 950 miles. In 1858, the Lake Superior line had fast steamers making a run from Cleveland to Detroit, Mackinac, Sault, Munising, Marquette, Portage Lake, Copper Harbor, Eagle Harbor, Ontonogan Bayfield and Superior City, round trip eight days.

Mrs. Ellet's *Rambles in the West* written sometime between 1856 and 1858, says this of Bayfield: "The situation of the town is picturesque and the appearance of its buildings present quite an imposing appearance. The Bayfield hotel is one of the best-built and commodious hotels on the lake. Here we recommend every traveler to spend a few days and enjoy the fine fishing and sailing on its beautiful bay."

In May 1889, *The Bayfield Press* recorded that the first boat to run between Bayfield and Ashland was the *J.C. Keyes* owned by Chapman and Knight. It was followed by the *F.C. Fero* owned by S.W. Tanner. When the Wisconsin Central Railroad was first started, the only boat at Ashland was the small tug, *Minnie V.* owned by S.S. Vaughn. Later on came the *Eva Wadsworth* probably the best-remembered boat on the Ashland-Bayfield run.

Marine news at Bayfield in 1871–The Propeller *Winslow* lands at Bayfield from Duluth with a cargo of 6,000 barrels of flour, the first shipment of the season."

July 1871. "a large party of Wisconsin editors coming via Marquette on the Str. (Steamer) *India* arrive at Bayfield, among them the writer (Sam Fifield) and his wife. Mr. Vaughn gives them an excursion on his yacht Minnie V down Ashland bay where a pound net is lifted for their inspection."

July 1871. "Gov. Austin of Minnesota and a party of fifty ladies and gentlemen arrive at Bayfield on the Propl. (Propeller) *Nashua.*"

July 1871. S.S. Vaughn takes a scow load of lumber to Ashland on the 19th with which to build the first house. Sets a crew at work clearing up his land, now Vaughn's division. This house was the first erected on the townsite upon revival of the place and in 1890 was part of D.G. Sampston's residence."

The Captains of the lake schooners had many interesting stories to tell. July 4, 1877 *The Press* reported, "Captain Bunker of the *Marco Polo* had an admiring crowd gathered around him as he sat on the deck spinning yarns last Sunday."

July 11, 1877. "The town was thronged with promenaders admiring beautiful Bayfield yesterday while the *Peerless* was lying at the dock. A number were so taken with the place that they concluded to remain and go no further."

A letter from a Chicago tourist in July, 1877, contains these fine compliments to Bayfield: "The buildings present a very attractive appearance to any stranger and I have heard several remarks how much like a city of taste and refinement Bayfield is compared with other lake towns. Each house is surrounded by fine grassy lots and a fountain spreads its cooling spray in a majority of the yards. The inhabitants are very social and have none of the roughness and rusticity usually found in the little country villages they all having become quite refined from associating with tourists and pleasure seekers who annually visit the village. They all endeavor to make a stranger's visit pleasant. I can assure the most doubtful that if they wish to find rest and quiet and to recover from too much exhaustion, that the best place to go is to this charming little village of Bayfield."

We have been associating with tourists for the seventy-eight years which have passed since that letter was written, and so we Bayfielders are now very, very refined, in fact we can't hardly be refined no more.

Many interesting boats have visited Bayfield. *The Bayfield Press* recorded this visit in September 1895, sixty years ago. "Last Thursday morning the people of Bayfield enjoyed a treat which will long be remembered by them. Owing to the kindness of Col. Wing, arrangements were made to have the steamer *North West*, the largest passenger steamer on the Great Lakes, to stop at our port in order that our people might enjoy, equally with those of Washburn and Ashland, making a tour of this grand floating palace. At about seven o'clock the heavy sonorous whistle of the *North West* was heard and was promptly answered by a salute from the cannon. The grand boat moved to our pier as easily as a small boat would make a landing. As soon as the gangplanks were lowered, people were welcomed aboard and roamed at will from boiler room to pilothouse. (This great boat was fast, traveling at the rate of 22 miles per hour.) The *North West* remained in port about two hours then pulled out for Washburn. As the grand boat left the dock, she repeatedly received farewell salutes from the cannon and the deafening reports of dynamite blasts from the rocky embankment where the new railroad is under construction."

Don't you wish this was now instead of 1905, fifty years ago this month? "The Chequamegon Bay Transportation Company will make a special trip to Isle Royal with the steamer *Skater* the latter part of September for a ten day trip, providing a party of 30 can be secured. Will feed and sleep party on the boat, which will anchor in the numerous harbors, giving ample opportunity to visit different points of interest. Fare–$2.00 per day, including board."

More on Bayfield Boats

M ANY MARINE ITEMS APPEARED IN both the Ashland and Bayfield papers as the years passed. From the time the first canoe pulled up on the beach of Chequamegon Bay until the first train arrived centuries later, the boat was the fastest and most comfortable means of transportation.

June 22, 1872, *The Ashland Press* had this item. "The *Keyes* is now carrying passengers between Ashland and Bayfield for 25 cents each. The *Fero*, we believe, charges 75 cents." In this present day when business men make sure their prices are competitive, it is hard to understand how the *Fero* got away with it. Does anyone remember the *Fero?* Was it faster, more luxurious, or did it have better accommodations for a ride across the bay?

The sailboat was a regular means of transportation. In July 1877, *The Press* said, "Last Sunday was a grand turnout day for sailboats. We counted 18 in sight of *Inglis'* dock at 3 in the afternoon." But steamboats were fast becoming the business boat, replacing the schooners. During the week of July 31, 1878, there were 14 arrivals of steamboats at the port of Bayfield.

In 1884, Bayfield's local marina consisted of 4 steam tugs, two schooners, two yachts, and 50 or 60 fishing smacks.

Even as late as 1890, it seems evident that the steam engine was not completely trusted. Sails and steam were often combined on a boat so that when horsepower failed, wind power was available, and it was lucky for the *Hunter* that this was so. May 31, 1890, *The Press* reported: "The steamer *Hunter* when 2½ miles out of Duluth Wednesday was disabled by the breaking of her lower connection strap whereby her piston went through her cylinder head. Being fortunately supplied with sails, she returned to Duluth and is undergoing repairs."

August 21, 1886. During the past two or three weeks, the night clerk at the Island View Hotel has visited all the incoming lake steamers and notified the passengers desiring to land that sleeping accommodations were not to be procured. It is safe to presume that the number turned away exceeds several hundred and the influx still continues.

If you would like to know what Bayfield looked like then, this description of the town is given in the Northwestern Lumberman magazine September 1885. "What is Bayfield, anyhow? A little village occupying not a large area on the whole. The streets are smooth and the sidewalks good. On either side of the streets are maple trees boxed in and the boxes are whitewashed. There are 30 feet deep ravines right in the village and from one of these ravines that reach up into the hills, is taken a supply of pure spring water. There are fountains whose waters, as they fall, make a silvery clink in the basins which adds to the quiet, lazy, peaceful spirit that prevails."

By 1906, the gasoline boat was replacing the sailboat for commercial fishing. In August of that year, the gasoline boat *Superior* took a large party of men to Duluth where licenses were taken out for the running of gasoline boats. Those who secured licenses were Jacob Johnson, Louis Moe, John Nelson, Henry Johnson and Ira Russell. Those who secured a license also secured one to carry passengers on their boat.

In October 1905, a barge was burned. *The Press* reported: "The barge *Noquebay* which loaded lumber here last week caught fire at noon Monday when 20 miles outside of the islands and was burned to the water's edge. The *Noquebay* was in tow of the steamer *Lizzie Madden* and left Bayfield Sunday morning for Bay City, Michigan. The crew was at dinner when the fire started in the donkey boiler room in the forward end of the boat and, when discovered, the flames had attained such headway that it was impossible to check their headway and the *Madden* started at once for Presque Island where the burning boat was beached in a sand bay on the east side of the island in 12 feet of water. Captain C. H. Flynn, of Duluth, arrived in the city Wednesday and went out to the burned boat on the tug *Fashion*. As soon as he hears from the owners he will remove it and bring it to Bayfield. The boat will probably be raised and a scow made out of it.

In August 1906, a sailboat was lost. *The Press* gave this account. "Captain Russell Angus of LaPointe suffered the loss of his large sailboat this week in the northeaster which came up suddenly Monday afternoon. The Captain had a party of 22 pleasure seekers on board who were enjoying a sail along the south shore. Upon the storm's approach, the party landed near Little Girl's Point and the boat was anchored, but the wind was so strong the anchor chain broke and she was driven ashore. The excursion party walked to Odanah where they took the train for Bayfield, arriving here at 10:30 Tuesday night considerably disappointed over the outcome of their trip."

Whether or not the following is a marine item may be debatable, but certainly it had its foundation on water. The story appeared in *The Press* January 8, 1898. "A saloon has been established on the ice road in the middle of Chequamegon Bay about half way between Washburn and Ashland. The building was moved on last week. It is said that being beyond the harbor line the city license of $500 cannot be collected. It is near the dividing line between Ashland and Bayfield counties, but the government only has jurisdiction and a government license only is required."

Early Boats and Fishing

The tug Bayfield tied along-side the Finn McCool circa 1920. The Finn McCool rests on the bottom of Lake Superior outside the old south mill pond. (Photo: BHA)

Now that the ice is about to leave Chequamegon Bay, as it has each spring through more centuries than man can count, it is a good time to look back a short distance, not more than 100 years, at some local marine items. Spring in Bayfield is always a time for launching boats, new boats, rebuilt boats, or at least overhauled and newly painted boats. In May 1909, the new tug Bayfield was launched. The officers were: Captain Einar Miller, Mate C. Nelson, Chief Engineer Wm. Duquette, Assistant Engineer, George Perkins.

June 25, 1909, *The Press* said: "Commodore Inglis thinks the people of Bayfield have been remiss in their duty toward a matter considered of more than passing moment by all lake cities. He says it is customary for all such cities to present a set of colors to boats named after the city. The Lake Superior Towing Company's new boat *The Bayfield*, has in this respect been slighted, and it is up to the citizens to take steps to the end that this ancient custom may be properly observed.

The tug was promptly given a set of colors, which Captain "Shine" Miller still has. In case anyone living away from the lake does not know what a set of colors is—it is made of up three flags, the Stars and Stripes, the Union Jack and a flag with the name of the boat on it. The tug *Bayfield* was a powerful one, 100 feet long, 19 feet wide. She worked hard on Lake Superior for forty years. Then, one day in Port Arthur, a friend of Captain Miller's pointed out the *Bayfield* to him. She had completed her years on the lake without loss or accident, then tied to the dock had sunk, dying peacefully and quietly of old age.

The tug Bayfield under construction, circa 1909. (Photo: BHA)

Spring in Bayfield also means fishing. The conversation does not change much in the fish business. It follows one trend. . . "Where are the fish?"

This item appeared May 30, 1891, but it might easily have been heard yesterday. "J. H. Olson came in from the fishing grounds this week. He reports gill net fishing as very poor, and attributes it to the fact that the fish seem at times to change their locality and not that they are fished out. Under the circumstances, it is hard for the fishermen to find them. He thinks the fishing will be better under the pond net system, the season for which will soon be inaugurated."

Seventeen years later the fishing was still going strong. June 19, 1908, *The Bayfield Press* had this item: "Ole Hadland, who is fishing at Bear Island, reports a most extraordinary catch of whitefish in one lift one day this week. The big catch being made in one net consisted of 5,170 pounds of whitefish. He says that even then he did not get them all, as he could not carry them, and left about 700 pounds. The Steamer *Barker* brought in a load of 14,000 pounds of whitefish and lake trout. Fishing has been good in the vicinity of Bayfield and the Apostle Islands and that these large catches can be made at this season is evidence that the fishing is improving."

TA. Booth Pkg. Co. tugs, the S.B. Barker and R.W. Currie were also in the business of transporting passengers to and from the Islands and the Isle Royal areas of Lake Superior. (Photo: BHA)

Another year passed and in May 1909, the fishing fleet was getting modernized. Besides the large number of sailboats engaged in fishing, there were 17 gasoline boats. That same month I.R. Chape left for Bark Bay to begin pond net fishing. *The Press* said, "Mr. Chape is entering the fishing business heavily this year, using about 7 nets. Mr. Chape has the only pond net stake driver on Chequamegon Bay that is run by power. The driver was built by Mr. Chape and is operated by a gasoline engine. Mr. Chape now drives his stakes at one half of what it cost him before."

Another year passed, and fishing was good, and plenty of work was being done to keep it that way. On April 18, 1910, Booth's boat, the steamer Barker, left for Cornucopia. She had on board 1,500,000 trout which were planted at York Island Reef. They intended to plant about 21,000,000 trout on the several reefs among the Apostle Islands.

Later that year, on May 6, 1910, the fishing boat *Fram* became disabled west of Sand Island and drifted about on Lake Superior until picked up by Peter Hanson the next morning. Mr. Hanson, in the *Odin* towed the boat to Sand Island. The *Fram* was owned by Nick Olson and was used by him for fishing. He said he was alright drifting about on the lake, but got a little chilly.

Sail Boat Wreck

After reading in last weeks' Press the story of the wreck of Captain Angus' sailboat, Hamilton Ross of LaPointe has written as follows: "I happened to be one of the party aboard her at the time. In fact, Alfred Lathrop of Ashland, and I were on the boat when she broke her anchor chain and came ashore. The storm came up about 10:00 PM, and in a short time the combers were coming aboard. We were both bailing like mad until one tremendous sea hit the boat, and it was then that the chain broke. It was probably a fortunate accident for us. Otherwise the boat would surely have foundered and it is problematical if we could have gotten ashore in the surf.

"The chain broke about midnight. We both grabbed wooden hatch covers, and when we felt the boat ground we went over the side, not knowing what we were going to get into. Fortunately for us we hit a sand beach and waded ashore. Since the night was as dark as the inside of one's pocket, we had to hunt around for some time before we found the house in which the rest of the party had taken shelter.

The "quote" from the old paper is not quite accurate. The wreck occurred off the Montreal River. The house belonged to the Garnich family of Ashland. In the morning we hiked about eight miles through the woods and finally hit the Northwestern Railway at a siding named *Birch.* There was a logging camp there and the cook certainly did himself proud in feeding us.

"Just to make things more complicated, one of the party was a cripple and we had to rig up a chair on poles and carry her the entire distance. Alfred Lathrop and I were excused from carrying her since neither one of us had any shoes.

"Some days after the wreck, the tug *Currie* went down and towed the *Lizzie W.* back. She was repaired that winter and we had many trips in her after that."

"Getting back to your subject of gas engines: I believe I rode in the first gasoline boat in the region in 1898. It was owned in Bayfield by Nelson Bachand and Herbert Hale. I have forgotten her name, but everyone called her the *Crackerjack.*

"Also, in our old family 'log' I ran across an entry of 1901 which recorded that a party of us went fishing over in the Kakagan in Jack Headland's Seagull. I believe that his was among the first of the successful gasoline-driven fishing boats."

Mr. Ross also writes about Admiral Henry W. Bayfield of the British Navy, for whom our town is named. Admiral Bayfield surveyed Lake Superior in 1823 and Mr. Ross says, "The Canadian charts are still based on his work. Last summer when we were up in the Nipigon, we met some Port Arthur men who were cruising around in a sailboat. They had been doing it for years, and knew the waters thoroughly. The *Navigator* of the party told me that, using Bayfield's original charts, every single rock and reef were located with amazing accuracy. And there are plenty of both up there, believe me. So altogether he must have been *some* guy."

Bayfield was well named after this famous Admiral, for as the years passed, many Bayfield citizens became navigation experts as they pursued their business of fishing. This item appeared in *The Bayfield Press* , November 24, 1883. "Sunday F. LeVine and C. Goslin, accompanied by four others arrived from Nipigon Bay on the north shore, where they had been engaged in fishing during the past two months. They came all the way in two open sailboats, three men in each boat, and were nine days on the route. That these men were successful in crossing the lake at this season of the year in open fish boats, speaks well for the buoyancy of the Bayfield fishing smacks and the skill and daring of her fishermen."

March 25, 1904, *The Press* had this item: "John Peterson, the gasoline launch, row and sail boat builder of LaPointe, has turned out five launches and two sailboats this winter. Four of the boats were built for Bayfield people. Three of them are already on this side of the water. They were made for Ole Hadland, John Nelsen, Henry Johnson, and Gus Carlson. The fifth boat was for John Hagen of LaPointe. Agent Jack Hadland will supply the boats with Wolverine gasoline engines and they will be used for fishing purposes this summer. Boat building has become quite an industry on the island. Mr. Peterson is a first class man at this business. Chequamegon Bay's gasoline fleet will be larger than the white squadron of the U.S. Navy this season."

Six years later, boats were not only equipped with gasoline engines, they were getting fancy trimmings. April 29, 1910, *The Press* reported: "An exceptionally well finished boat was launched at Ashland for two Bayfield young men, Leo Nelson and Monge Hygaard. This is a 24-foot pleasure boat, finished with nickel trimmings and an automobile top (canvas and folding) making it an exceptionally attractive boat. The boat is well equipped with an 11 horsepower engine and that it has the speed as well, is indicated by the fact that after it was launched, it ran from the Ashland dock to the Bayfield dock, a distance of 18 miles in one hour and 20 minutes.

The *Manistee*

Hark! What sad news is it you bring
Across the bay to Ashland's shore.
It is the Manistee's gone down
And we shall see her nevermore.

The Manistee and ore carriers traveled similar shipping lanes to the Soo Locks. Photo-pre 1883. (Photo: BHA)

Probably the loss of any other boat that ran on Lake Superior in 1883 would not have caused so much sorrow as the loss of the *Manistee*. She was more than a boat. She was a friend and a lifeline to civilization for the pioneers of the little lake towns.

Although the *Manistee* was owned by the Leopold-Austrian line, she belongs by affection to the villagers. She was the first boat to reach them in the spring, the last to leave in the fall, extending her help to the last minute possible before the ice closed in. Everyone along the shore knew the sound of the *Manistee's* whistle.

Naturally, the *Manistee* could not have achieved this beloved state by herself. She had assumed the personality of her fine captain, John McKay.

More than seventy years have passed since the *Manistee* was lost, but in the little lake towns, many now grown into cities, she is still remembered. Alec Butterfield of the Settlement, now 92, remembers big, genial, freckle-faced Captain John McKay very well.

Mrs. Marietta Demars, now 87, lived close to the dock in Bayfield. When the *Manistee* whistled for a landing, she and a little friend would run, pigtails flying, to see this fine vessel with beautiful staterooms and a parlor, which had a real piano. Captain McKay, who knew and liked everybody in the little ports he visited, would often greet them and one eventful day he asked if they would like a ride. They would, of course. The Captain shouted orders, the lines were cast off, and the great *Manistee* with two little passengers backed from the dock for a trip along the shore to Buffalo Bay.

Stories which do not describe Captain McKay's physical appearance recall his nature. It can be summed up by saying that he was a kind man, a friend to all. John McKay had been a sailor almost from infancy, beginning his career with his father on a sailing vessel. He was mate on one of the finest lake boats when he was 18 and became a master at 20. From that time on he was never obliged to seek employment. His services were always in demand. He was only 40 the bitter November night he disappeared with the *Manistee*.

Captain McKay took command of the *Manistee* in 1873 and ran her one season between Buffalo and Duluth. Then he went upon the route, which pleased him, better than any other, and upon which his life was finally taken, known as the Lake Superior South Shore Route, between Duluth and Hancock.

In December, 1875, one of the old timers stated: "This navigating of old Lake Superior after the first of December is sheer madness and scarcely ever attended with profit and never with any degree of safety."

Yet, the *Manistee* often ran during December and in the spring made her way through the ice to the villages. On May 10, 1876, she arrived in Bayfield from Duluth, pushing her way through the ice, although 10 days later, May 20, seven boats were locked in the ice between the two towns.

Captain McKay liked to pick up a band from one of the small towns and carry it for a round trip to serenade the other villages. July 25, 1877, *The Bayfield Press* reported: "The popular propeller *Manistee*, John McKay, Captain, laid at the dock one or two hours Tuesday evening and a strong band discoursed sweet music to our citizens."

August 13, 1881. "The steamer *Manistee* came into port on Monday with flags flying and the Lindon Cornet Band playing choice and well executed pieces. The *Manistee* is one of the most popular excursion steamers on the lake, and McKay stands at the head of the class among the captains."

And at six o'clock another August morning in 1881 the *Manistee* slipped quietly up to the dock at Bayfield. Many people were still asleep. The railroad had not reached the village yet. Automobiles were unheard of. The drowsy hum of the sawmill on the water front and the clop of horses hoofs on the dirt roads were the only undisturbing familiar sounds.

Then the Calumet Miner's band filed out on the top deck of the *Manistee* and played "some rattling good pieces." The wild sound carried through the swaying white curtains of open bedroom windows. People startled out of their sleep dressed and ran to the dock to be greeted with the hearty laughter of Captain McKay. The *Manistee*, as usual, was crowded with passengers who had enjoyed waking the town.

In August 1877, the *Manistee* raced the *Eva Wadsworth*. *The Bayfield Press* gave this account of it: "Last Sunday forenoon a race took place on the bay between the propeller *Manistee* and the *Wadsworth*. The *Wadsworth* left Ashland with a large scow in tow, which she was to take to Onion River. She had gone several miles over Ashland Bay when the *Manistee* overtook her and as she passed, sounded some less than a hundred whistles of defiance at the little craft. This was more than the gallant Captain Pat could stand, so telling the ladies to hold onto the railing and the gentlemen to hold onto some bottles which seemed to be full of a deep dark mystery, or something else, he stopped the boat long enough to detach the scow, by which time the *Manistee* was considerably ahead.

Relieved of the scow the *Eva* began to tear along at nearly full speed and at the end of 1 ½ miles she had placed herself abreast of her big antagonist and was still gaining. Here the Captain turned and went back after the scow with no other accident than a slight explosion which occurred in the neighborhood of the above mentioned bottles, the cork hitting a passenger in the eye.

Captain Patrick has shown that big boats can't toot at his boat, even if she is little. There was a large party of ladies and gentlemen on board who seemed to enjoy themselves thoroughly. While several ladies and gentleman indulged in a dance on the hurricane deck, greatly astonishing the *Manistee* passengers by their boldness. It was said by those who often travel on the *Wadsworth* that this was the most pleasant trip of the season."

Captain McKay, though the big *Manistee* was beaten, enjoyed the race more than anyone. And it was in this way that the *Manistee* developed her personality and became a familiar and welcome sight in the little lake towns. Many a boat pulled out from the docks leaving passengers who preferred to wait and ride with John McKay on the *Manistee*.

The railroad came into Ashland in 1877 and to Bayfield in October, 1883. It was stretching helpful steel fingers to the other small towns and the lake boats were not under the last minute fall *Press* ure that they had been. In 1883 the steamer *Manistee* planned to go into winter quarters earlier than usual. On Sunday, November 11, she docked at Bayfield on her way to Hancock. It was storming badly, and although Captain McKay made two or three attempts to go out, he remained weather-bound at Bayfield until November 15. The *Manistee* was tied at the blue dock, so called because it was painted blue. It was north of the present Booth dock.

About nine o'clock that evening, the weather seemed to be more favorable and the storm decreasing. The dock was dimly lighted by reflections from the lamps of the *Manistee*. The planks were wet with rain and spray. The *Manistee* strained and squeaked against her ropes as the waves and wind pushed and pulled her.

A little group of people stood clustered together, faces upturned, watching the big boat twisting and pulling, wondering if Captain McKay would take her out. McKay talked to them for a few moments. Then someone put a hand on his shoulder and asked, "Are you going out tonight, Captain?"

As though the question crystallized his decision, he replied, "Yes."

McKay turned and went on board. Some of the *Manistee* passengers transferred to the *City of Duluth*, which was also weather-bound at Bayfield. Only the passengers for Ontonogan remained on board.

One man, who had been going to Ontonogan changed his mind and stayed here. That man was Mr. Hyman of Oshkosh. He often told of being on the dock, ready to go, when a fisherman told him not to. Taking the fisherman's advice, he went to the Island View Hotel to spend the night and lived for many more years.

The *Manistee* gangplanks were pulled up, the lines cast off and Captain McKay blew the signal for departure, not only from this port, but from his life.

The *Manistee* backed slowly out from the dock, turned on her course and except now and then a flash from the lanterns hanging at the mast was lost to view.

The ballad written in 1883 by Mrs. Emma Graham of Ashland says:

> "T-was midnight when they left the pier
> The low, dark pier on Bayfield's shore.
> And little did they think that night,
> They would see that harbor nevermore."

(Photo: BHA)

Actually, it was about nine o'clock when the *Manistee* left and an hour and a half later the steamers *City of Duluth* and *China* followed the same route. At midnight a heavy southwest gale blew up.

It was first reported that the *Manistee* was in Ontonogan, Michigan, where there was no telegraph station, but when the Duluth put in at that port, the *Manistee* was not there.

Two tugs went out to search. One of them found a bucket with "*Manistee*" on it. The other found part of the canvas carried by the steamer.

The first news that reached Bayfield was brought by the Propeller *India,* which arrived in port and reported sighting portions of a wreck off Outer Island.

The sudden fear that the *Manistee* had gone down cast a heavy gloom over the little south shore villages.

And the gloom deepened when the tug *Swain* came into Duluth and reported a veritable field of wreckage encountered about 4 hours out from Cooper Harbor and nearly opposite Eagle River.

A pilothouse was sighted floating around in the weather. The captain mistook it for a boat, gave the usual signal and pulled out, but on approaching discovered his mistake. A little further on were the remnants of a steamer. Tables, chairs, desks, beds, barrels, buckets, bed clothes, mattresses, fragments of picture frames and even small cakes of butter and breadstuffs were seen floating about, dreadful, yet definite evidence of a tragedy on that stormy November night. Bodies were searched for, but none were found.

The steam barge *Osceola* came into Bayfield and reported that she had encountered wreckage. Captain Cummings of the *Osceola* advanced the theory that the *Manistee* had blown up, as he felt sure that if no such accident had occurred, she could have withstood the storm. Also, the *Manistee* had five lifeboats. None of them had come ashore. The pieces of wreckage were small and would not likely have been so broken by the waves or wind.

It was believed that whatever disaster overtook the *Manistee*, it was of appalling suddenness. She had on board a fine crew. There was not an old man among them, and it was believed that in case of a fire or foundering, the boats would have been launched and some of them would surely have made shore.

The Leopold-Austrian line had tugs search constantly from the Apostle Islands to Copper Harbor on the south shore, and from Silver Island to Port Arthur on the north shore, as well as the coast of Isle Royale.

At first the tugmen looked hopefully for lifeboats, and survivors, then, without hope of bodies, but none were found.

The *Manistee* was 16 years old, having been built in 1867 by E.M. Peck of Cleveland, for the Engleman Line, and had been rebuilt several times. She was not overloaded. She had on 100 tons less than she was allowed to carry. Her cargo was grain, flour and miscellaneous items. She had an A2 rating, the highest a boat over five years old could have. Yet, something went wrong and the *Manistee* went down so swiftly that no effort was made to abandon her.

Finally and reluctantly hope for the steamer *Manistee* was given up and vessels coming into the little lake towns lowered their flags to half-mast.

The Bayfield Press said: "All doubts of the fact that the popular *Manistee* went down in the storm of Friday of last week have vanished, and the hope that was indulged in, but uncertain, has given way to the sad certainty that the popular boat and her genial officers have embarked on the seamless shores of eternity."

The Ashland Press wrote: "The Steamer *Manistee* and all her crew is lost beyond a question. This is the saddest event for Ashland people, which has occurred during 1883, which has nearly expired. The *Manistee* has been a regular visitor at our port on her semi-weekly trips during the past nine years and the sound of her whistle has been familiar and recognizable by every man, woman and child among us. That it will not be heard again is like the removal of one of our household gods, but this is the least cause for sorrow."

"The *Manistee* can be replaced by a better boat, would to God she had been before the fatal accident occurred. But John McKay, her captain, and George L. Seaton, her clerk, cannot be replaced in their families, nor in the circle of friends they have made during the time we have been accustomed to see their familiar faces and become a part and parcel of the genial circle which was always to be collected in Captain McKay's rooms when journeying with him.

"George L. Seaton (the purser), was a man in every respect, fit for his position, and was hardly second to his captain in the hearts of the friends they had made on the route. Attentive to business he was always genial, kindly, giving with untiring affability answers to thousands of questions asked by passengers upon all manner of subjects, relevant and irrelevant. He had intended to quit sailing at the end of the season and settle down with his wife and little ones at his home in Iowa. He is done sailing now, and we trust has gone to a better home."

George Seaton's brother offered a reward of $100 for the recovery of the body. Does anyone know if this reward was ever claimed, or if a body from the wreck of the *Manistee* was ever found?

Eugene Prince of Ashland received a letter from Captain McKay's brother saying, "Prince, it is hardly necessary for me to say anything to you or John's warm friends on the lake in regard to the noble fellow, as you were all so familiar with him. Just as you met him from trip to trip, so he was at all times at home with his aged parents and his wife and children. He lived solely for others, cared little for self if he could make others happy. Poor mother and father are completely cast down, and I fear it will be a short time ere they follow their boy. I have never seen father affected before, as he has a peculiar disposition, and I was greatly surprised to see him give way to his feelings. Mother's grief I anticipated, as you know John was the baby of the family. John's wife cannot give up hopes that he will come to her and the children."

Captain Eber Ward of the Ward Line of Detroit wrote: "Among the many losses of valuable lives during the violent autumn gales, none were more felt and brought out more sincere ex*Press* ions of regret than the loss of that big-hearted, generous, John McKay."

There was no exact count of the lives lost when the *Manistee* went down, for no one knows just how many were on board. When people who were known to have embarked on a lake trip did not return, it was presumed they were lost with the *Manistee*.

The *Superior Times* had this story. "It now appears that our city mourns the loss of four citizens by the wreck of the ill-fated *Manistee*. Mr. C.J. Anderson and his wife and Mr. Andrew Lagore and wife took passage on the *Manistee* on that fatal trip for Ontonogan. Their mail and effects were to be held here until they sent for them, not knowing exactly where they would spend the winter when they left here. For some time their friends felt no uneasiness regarding them from the fact that it was reported that all the passengers had left the boat at Bayfield, but their long silence finally induced inquiry and it has been learned that none of the passengers booked for Ontonogan left the boat, and without doubt these people perished with the rest. In the absence of certainty hope still lingers that they may be alive, but it is hardly probable that they are, or someone would have heard from them ere this."

Judging from the records there were at least seven passengers on board, Captain McKay, the purser, 2 engineers, 2 mates, 2 cooks, 2 or 3 waiters, 3 firemen, a chambermaid, a cabin boy and about 15 deckhands.

Almost a year had passed when men fishing on Isle Royale picked up a chair belonging to the *Manistee*.

Several times bottles with messages signed by Captain McKay were picked up along the shore, but no one seemed to believe they were authentic. Captain McKay was not a man to sit writing notes to stuff into bottles when the *Manistee* was in danger.

Almost 14 years had passed when a bottle was found at Onion River. *The Bayfield Press* gave this account of it May 22, 1897. "The following note was found at Onion River the first of the week in a sealed bottle by James Taggart, who was working on the drive (log drive) at that place. "Nov. 1883–Tossed on the storm billows just in sight of Michigan lighthouse. Left Bayfield 11:10 PM We may not survive this storm. Heavy laden and hard to turn in storm. Captain McKay, Steamer *Manistee*."

"Those who have seen the letter and were acquainted with Captain McKay, claimed that the writing resembles that of the captain's of the lost steamer. It was written with a lead pencil and was evidently written in a hurry. It is probably that the bottle which contained the letter was driven upon the beach that fall and has been buried in the sand ever since and that the rafting of logs loosened it from its hidden position. When the bottle was broken open, it fell all to pieces which indicates that it had been sealed for a long time."

So the loss of the *Manistee* is still a mystery. Just when, where or why it was lost, no one knows. A final word is said in the last verse of the old ballad:

> *And now farewell old gallant boat*
> *And all the brave ones that you bore.*
> *Although we'll watch out on the bay*
> *We'll see the Manistee no more.*

The *Lucern*

THREE YEARS TO THE DAY after the *Manistee* was lost, the schooner *Lucern* left Ashland and never made port again. The *Lucern* was an ore-carrying schooner. Her canvas was all-new and she was considered one of the best on the fresh water. She had been towed up the lakes to Ashland by the steam barge *Raleigh*. There she loaded on 1200 tons of iron ore, 130 tons short of her usual cargo.

The *Lucern* left Ashland on Monday, November 15, 1886, in charge of George S. Lloyd, Master, with a crew of nine men. She had a fair wind to start and with her new canvas spread to the favorable breeze sailed out of Chequamegon Bay bound for Cleveland.

Tuesday a storm came up. That day the captain of the steam barge *Fred Kelly*, which was bound for Ashland, saw the *Lucern* rolling and pitching in the wind and waves, and as he watched saw her come about and head for Ashland. He was the last person to see the *Lucern* while there was life aboard her.

The storm grew into a stinging white blizzard. Visibility vanished. What happened aboard the *Lucern* can only be guessed at, for there were no survivors.

It is clear that they fought to save themselves and the schooner and they almost made it. Only two more miles and they would have rounded Long Island and headed into Chequamegon bay and the safety of the Ashland docks.

They were on the right course. Then, for what reason no one knows, they tried to anchor her. The largest anchor, weighing two and one fourth tons, was thrown overboard, dragging 80 fathoms of chain with it. This would indicate that the *Lucern* was not in a sinking condition at the time, but that they were lost. If they had known their position, and if they had been sinking, it is not likely they would have dropped anchor, but instead would have tried to run up on the fine sand beach of Long Island.

Perhaps the anchor held the *Lucern* so securely that the storm beat her open. Water poured in and she began to founder on her anchor. When she began to sink some of the crew climbed the rigging and tied themselves there. This would indicate they knew they were in shallow water and felt they might survive in the rigging. As the *Lucern* came to rest, they clung there in the blinding snowstorm, barely out of reach of the gray jaws of the waves.

When the *Lucern* had not returned to Ashland by Friday, William S. Macks, captain of the barge *Raleigh*, telegraphed to Bayfield and engaged the tug *Barker* to go in search of her.

The *Barker* set out, but her journey was short. She had hardly turned into the south channel when the crew sighted the spars of a vessel rising out of the water near Long Island. Three white blots appeared in the rigging.

As the *Barker* steamed nearer, the tragedy of the *Lucern* became horribly evident. The three white blots were the bodies of her crew, still lashed to the rigging, swaying above the waves that had not quite reached them to tear them down, but had cast spray over them which froze, until they were coated with ice from one to six inches thick.

A small boat was launched from the *Barker*, but when it reached the wreck, it seemed impossible to get the bodies down. The rigging was ice-covered, unsteady, swaying with the waves. No one knew how securely the *Lucern* rested on the bottom, if she would stand upright or roll over. After studying the situation and weighing their chances, two brothers from Bayfield, Ed and Charley Herbert, decided to try the climb. Working together with a great deal of nerve and skill, they went up the swaying, ice-covered rigging to the first body and cut it loose, then to the second and finally the third.

The bodies were not identified, but were buried in the Ashland cemetery. Later, one body was exhumed, proved to be that of Robert Jeffry, second mate, and was taken to Cleveland.

The *Lucern* lay in 40 feet of water and during the summer of 1887, some salvage was made of the wreck.

Quite a few years later, a fisherman walking near Long Island on clear, new-made ice was startled to see the ghostly schooner lying quietly beneath his feet.

To this day the *Lucern* is not forgotten, for the first storm that sweeps in from Lake Superior with stinging snow and waves that freeze each dock post into a silent white blot will grimly remain someone hurrying to warmth and shelter of the words from the ballad of the *Lucern*:

Oh, it must be dreadful to freeze and then to drown
In the storm on Lake Superior, when the Lucern went down.

The *R. G. Stewart* & the *Fedora* Burn

R.G. Stewart circa 1895. (Photo: BHA)

FIRE AND FOG CAN BE as hazardous on the lake as a severe storm. It was a combination of the two which took the *R. G. Stewart*. The *Stewart* was on her way from Hancock to Duluth one mild night in June, 1899. Near the Islands she ran into a dense fog and at 11 p.m., she went aground at Michigan Island, about a mile east of the lighthouse.

The situation did not seem too bad. Sunday morning the crew launched a small yawl boat and put out an anchor from the stern. Then the whole crew went on the upper deck to work at a windlass and try to pull her off.

Suddenly they looked up from their work and made the terrible discovery that the *Stewart* was on fire. Immediately they ran for a hose and got it connected to a pump, but before they could even start the pump, the flames had gained such headway they knew they would have to jump for their lives.

They grabbed several cows, which were on board and threw them over the side. The cows swam quickly ashore and were saved. R. W. Parker, the clerk, got his trunk and threw it overboard. Then they ran for the yawl boat, which was tied alongside, and got into it. George McKenna was the last to get into the yawl and when he jumped in, the boat, overturned.

Some swam for the beach and some clung to the boat. McKenna tried to swim ashore, but went down in a few minutes. One of the crew who had already reached the beach went after him and brought him ashore, but it was too late to revive him.

Those who did not swim clung to the overturned boat, keeping it as far off from the burning *Stewart* as they could until the rope holding it burned away. Then they drifted ashore.

Lighthouse keeper Brown took care of the survivors at the lighthouse until Tuesday when they went in to Bayfield. Captain Pasque went out in the *Eliza* to get the cows.

The bottom was on the rocks as far back as the boiler room and the bow was out of water about a foot. Mate Heatherington and a crew of five came to Bayfield in a lifeboat and telephoned to Ashland for the tug Crosby. The mate said the accident could not have been averted.

The *Weston*, one of the largest freighters on the lake at that time, was carrying 11,000 tons of coal. The *Crosby* took out a crew of men, threw the coal overboard and pulled her off.

The steamer *Cormorant*, of the Edward Hines Lumber Co., was destroyed by fire on Wednesday, October 30, 1907. She was bound out of Ashland to Duluth and had been in Bayfield that morning to drop the barge *Helvetia* at the Wachsmuth Lumber Company dock to be loaded with lumber.

Flames were first observed around the smokestack. Captain McKenzie and his crew did all they could to put out the fire, but it spread so rapidly, their efforts were useless.

As in the case of the *Fedora*, they were running at full speed and the fire had cut off the engine room, so they could not slow down. They headed the *Cormorant* for the nearest beach and, at full speed, crashed on the north end of Bass Island. The crew were able to jump to land and were later brought in to Bayfield.

All that remained of the old lumber carrier was a smoldering hull. It was thought the boilers were not injured and could be salvaged. Later that month when the hull was floated and towed in to Bayfield, *The Press* commented: "The old hull is sort of a relic of the passing of this type of lumber carrier with their old style engines."

Captain C.W. Flynn, who was the sole owner of the boat lost between three and four hundred dollars in cash besides what other articles he had on board. Mr. Parker picked up his trunk when it drifted in and was the only member of the crew to save anything. The Stewart was a total loss and was valued at $10,000 with only $6,000 in Duluth agencies.

Fire struck again when the steamer *Fedora* burned to the water's edge at Red Cliff, September 1901. The *Fedora*, owned by W.W. Brown of Cleveland, was bound to Ashland from Duluth to be loaded with ore. When she was off Bass Island, a lamp hanging in the engine room exploded. Before the pumps could be started, the flames had made such headway that the engineer was compelled to leave his post.

The *Fedora* was running at full speed and no one could get to the engine room to slow her. The wheelsman turned toward the beach at Red Cliff and wrapped in a terrible scarf of flame that trailed behind on the water the *Fedora* crashed full speed on the rocks a short way from shore. Small boats were launched and Captain F.A. Fich with the crew of 16 reached land safely. Nothing was saved but what the crew could carry. The lumberyard, which at that time stretched along the shore to the north of Red Cliff, had a narrow escape from burning.

For many years the name plate of the *Fedora* hung on a building in Red Cliff, but it finally disappeared. She was a strong, well-built boat, so strong that after almost 55 years of buffeting by weather, waves and ice, the wooden ribs still appear above the water near the mouth of Chicago Creek.

It was fog that put the *Charles Weston* on the rocks at Outer Island in May 1907. She was driven off her course by a heavy northeast wind and could not see the lighthouse lantern, which was hidden by fog. Traveling about 12 miles an hour, she ran firmly and forcefully aground at one o'clock in the morning about two miles south of the lighthouse.

The *Ireland* Aground

The Ireland at Bayfield's East dock taking on a load of milled lumber. circa 1906. (Photo: Burt Hill Family)

SHORTLY AFTER THE *COREY* PILED onto the rocks at Gull Island shoals, in 1905, an old sailor informed *The Press* that if captains of carriers were familiar with channels among the Apostle Islands and would use the island's protection, such disasters as had occurred during the two terrible storms of 1905 would not have resulted.

Later in December 1905, a dispatch from Cleveland printed in *The Press* stated that lack of knowledge of the compass was the reason for wrecks. In iron ore regions of Lake Superior the compass deflects 1½ points and sailors not skilled enough to make allowance for the variations may have trouble.

Pittsburgh Steamship Company issued orders to its 70 lake captains to attend a school of instruction in the use of the compass and course corrector.

Captain Field, the expert who was to teach the school said, "It is not the purpose of the school to make navigators out of lake captains. To sail on the lakes does not require the same knowledge that ocean sailing does, but every vessel master should thoroughly know the use of the compass."

Passengers on a lake boat would surely agree with Captain Field on that point.

But, in spite of the school of navigation and the belief of local fishermen that the islands should be havens, not hazards, there was more trouble.

On Thursday, December 6, 1906, the *Ireland* went aground. It was the first of a series of terrible experiences to be suffered by this boat and her crew.

The weather was bad. A heavy northeast blizzard swept Lake Superior. The *Ireland*, a steel steamer, bound for Duluth with a cargo of 7, 600 tons of soft coal, ran aground on Gull Island reef, about the same spot where the *Corey* had gone aground the previous year.

Dense snow and steam from the almost freezing lake hung over the water, so it was impossible to keep the course, and the *Ireland* crashed onto the rocks.

Mate Snoops came into Bayfield in a small yawl boat. Tugs were telegraphed for.

A crew of about 50 local men were hired to throw coal overboard and received the then fabulous wage of $1.00 an hour for their work. 2,500 tons of the *Ireland's* coal were unloaded.

The wrecking steamer *Manistique,* in charge of Captain James Reid, and the tug *Crosby,* in charge of Captain Alton Cornwall, were employed to release the *Ireland.*

The *Manistique* broke a large steam pipe, came into Bayfield for repairs, and Captain Reid reported: "We found that the *Ireland* was on the rocks worse than the steamer *Corey* was last fall, the *Ireland* being on full length. In looking over the vessel we found that although she was not twisted and the tanks on one side pumped alright, those on the other side were all punctured. She also suffered a broken rudder shoe."

Wednesday, December 12, six days after she went aground, the *Ireland* was released at three o'clock in the morning and arrived in Bayfield at 6:30 AM.

The *Ireland* lay in port here, waiting for favorable weather. On December 15, during a temporary abating of the wind, she cleared for Duluth in tow of the *Manistique,* with the tug *Crosby* acting as trailer.

The journey as far as Sand Island, near the spot where the *Sevona* went down, was not difficult. But once the boats left the protection of the islands and put out into the open lake, the gales beat them badly. The waves grew to such height and strength that they washed completely over the crippled *Ireland* and her escorts, carrying away all loose machinery, including the air compressors from the *Ireland.*

Powerful waves snapped the towline between the *Ireland* and the *Manistique.* The *Manistique* disappeared from the view of the anxious watchers aboard the *Ireland.*

The Captain of the *Manistique* could not turn in the storm and to save his ship and crew ran with the wind across Lake Superior. During this wild race, a distance of 140 miles, the steam pipe which connected the derrick apparatus with the main boiler was carried away by the heavy seas, tearing a big hole in the deck and filling the boat with steam so dense it was impossible to distinguish anything more than a foot away.

Saturday morning, battered, iced, and with an exhausted crew, the *Manistique* arrived at Port Arthur, Canada.

On the drifting *Ireland,* the broken towline became entangled with the propeller and this, with the broken rudder, left the big steamer completely helpless. Orders were given to lower the anchor and signal whistles were blown constantly for the *Manistique.* But the *Manistique* could not come.

The condition of the *Ireland's* crew was pitiable. They clung to the deck with icy spray half freezing, the steering apparatus broken, the engines useless, the pumps gone, knowing all the time they were close to the reef that had taken the *Sevona.*

Rescue of the *Ireland*

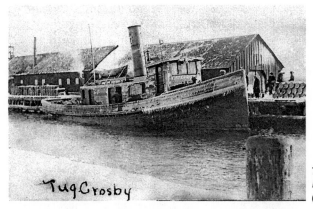

The ice covered Crosby at the A. Booth Fisheries dock circa 1906. (Photo: BHA)

A s THE STEAMER *IRELAND* FLOATED helplessly in the storm the little tug *Crosby,* which had almost been forgotten in the excitement, came up behind the Ireland. It was due to the bravery and unflinching nerve of Captain Alton Cornwall and the *Crosby* crew that those aboard the Ireland were saved.

Captain Cornwall began to fight his way around the *Ireland.* He is credited with saying that he would get every last man of the *Ireland* crew or go to a watery grave himself. Whether he said it, or whether he did not. . . he did it.

Running alongside of the big steamer as close as he dared, Captain Cornwall called to the crew through a megaphone and told them what they had to do. Half numb from the icy wind and spray and the terrible racking of the waves, the crew of the *Ireland* did their best to obey him.

The first person to leave the vessel, the stewardess, and the only woman aboard, was securely tied to a rope and hauled to safety. Then, waiting his chance with accurate eye, steady nerve and good seamanship, the first mate made the terrible leap from the tossing deck of the *Ireland* down to the ice-covered deck of the *Crosby.* One by one the crew followed.

Captain Cornwall made 18 trips around the *Ireland* before he was able to get all of the crew. He made three trips around to get the last man.

Sometimes the little tug rode the waves high above the *Ireland,* and the next moment dropped far below. The seas were so heavy it was hard to control the *Crosby.* Several times she struck the sides of the big steel ship and sustained a broken bulwark and other serious injuries.

One by one, with the knowledge that a slip or poor judgment meant death, each member of the crew made the leap. All but one lived. That one was Andy Dillon, a boy of 18, whose home was in Marquette, Michigan. It was his first trip on the lakes. He had shipped at Ashtabula only a few weeks ago. During the entire battle with the sea he had proved to be one of the coolest members of the crew, assisting in the work of rescue before trying to reach the tug himself.

His jump was accurate, but he landed on a pile of iced-over coal near the engine room. Slipping and struggling down the coal pile, trying to gain a hold, he fell back into the icy water. Several of the crew made a grab for him. One got hold of his coat collar, but being without mittens, his hands could not keep the grip beneath the icy waters and the boy sank to his death.

One of the crew received a broken leg. The wheelsman had fractures of the wrist and ribs, besides being badly cut around the head.

When the last man leaped aboard, the *Crosby* turned and ran for shelter among the islands.

Saturday, much to the astonishment to all, the *Ireland* was reported still afloat. The *Crosby* and the *B.B. Inman* went out and towed her as far as Frog Bay. There, since she appeared to be sinking, they beached her. Later she was pumped out and brought in to Bayfield. A diver went down, cut the towline from the propeller and rigged up a temporary rudder.

A movement was started to recommend Captain Alton Cornwall for a Carnegie medal.

The parents of young Andy Dillon came to see if his body had been found.

One of the rescued sailors got drunk, tried to take over the telephone office, was ejected by force and given 20 days by the local police court.

Again the *Ireland* started for Duluth, but returned to Bayfield the same day, as it was impossible for the tug to handle her in the heavy seas. The *Manistique*, which had returned from her wild trip to Canada, went to Duluth to secure a rudder for the *Ireland*, but met with some mishap and stayed there for repairs.

Finally the *Ireland* made it to Duluth. The balance of the coal was unloaded and she was taken to the ship yard in Superior. By this time it was so late in the season that about a foot of ice was in the channel and the *Ireland* suffered still more damage. Nearly every one of the brackets on her wheel were broken off by the ice and the temporary rudder, which had been put on at Bayfield was torn away.

Steamer *Hoyt* on Reef

O N November 13, 1909, the Steamer *Hoyt* went on the reef at Outer Island. The *Hoyt*, belonging to the Provident Steamship Company, left Duluth bound down with a cargo of over 5,000 tons of ore. She had hardly left the head of the lakes when the engines became disabled. It took 24 hours for the vessel to cover the distance from Duluth to Devil's Island. It took 5 hours more to get to Outer Island. At no time could the *Hoyt* make more than 3 miles an hour.

On this painfully slow trip, a severe northeast gale came up and Captain Ainsworth, master of the steamer, decided to seek shelter behind Outer Island. When he attempted to run around the western end of the island, the *Hoyt* struck a reef and the impact entirely disabled the engines, leaving the vessel at the mercy of the sea.

The reef where the *Hoyt* was stranded was to the westward of Outer Island, about 3 miles from the lighthouse and ¾ miles from shore. The mate, Mr. Chamberlain, and one of the crew got into a small boat and started for the mainland to report the accident and seek help. It took them sixteen hours to reach Red Cliff.

The tug *Bennett* of the Lake Superior Towing Company went out immediately. The tugs *Moose* and *Ferris* and the scows *Limit* and *Interstate*, which were all sheltering in the lee of Oak Island, were mustered in, and after coming to Bayfield the tugs, and also the tug *Helm*, in charge of Captain Kidd, set out for Outer Island to help the stranded vessel.

The tugs reached the *Hoyt* on Sunday night, but the storm was so severe they could only stand by, and made no attempt to free her. By Monday morning they were able to start loading ore on the scow *Limit* but then another storm came up, this one from the west, northwest, and the boats had to seek shelter again.

The crew of the *Hoyt* refused to abandon her, even though she appeared to be in danger of sinking. The bottom was so badly damaged that water rose about 16 feet in her hold. The bow of the boat was in 12 feet of water, the stern in 30 feet.

If the Captain had steered out 30 or 40 feet further from the island, he would have missed the reef altogether. Considerable sympathy was felt for him as it was his first vessel command and everyone did their best to help him. Finally the owners gave up the *Hoyt* and turned her over to the underwriters.

Captain Reid of the Reid Wrecking Company, chartered the tug *Bennett* and after three weeks work, the *Hoyt* was released by the tugs *Ottawa* and *Reid* and was towed to Red Cliff Bay for shelter.

But though the *Ottawa* managed to release the *Hoyt* she did not fare so well herself. The *Ottawa* towed the *Hoyt* to a safe harbor in Red Cliff Bay and was lying alongside. The crew finished their supper and when they came out of the dining room, discovered that the tug was on fire. They got two streams of water on the blaze immediately, but it was no use. Fearing the *Hoyt* would catch fire too, the lines were cut and the *Ottawa* went adrift. The fire consumed the *Ottawa* so quickly the crew could not save a thing. The wrecking equipment, including three diving suits and a turbine pump, was lost.

Captain Reid, who was staying in Bayfield at the Davis House, went out to Red Cliff on the tug Reid. He estimated the loss at between fifty and sixty thousand, insurance about half that amount and none on the wrecking tools. The *Ottawa* was a powerful tug, 420 tons capacity, 151 feet long, 28-foot beam. Her hull finally came to rest on the north side of Red Cliff Bay.

The tug Bayfield went out to help, but it was too late, for the *Ottawa* had already burned to the water's edge. The *Hoyt* was taken to Washburn to coal up, then to Frog Bay to wait for calm weather to go to Duluth. The *Hoyt* was one of the modern lake boats of 1909, valued at $230,000.

The Herring King Burns

The Herring King at Devil's Island. (Photo: BHA)

THE BURNING OF THE BOAT *Herring King* off Sand Island with the tragic loss of her captain, John Gordon of LaPointe, is still remembered by many, for it happened in 1917. Here is the story of the *Herring King*, just as it appeared in *The Bayfield County Press* on Friday, November 30, 1917.

"One life lost, a mother and three small children made fatherless, a financial loss of about $3,000, sustained by the Boutin Fish Company of this city, and a stirring rescue by the tug Goldish of Duluth, in brief sums up the misfortune which fell upon the fishing craft Herring King of the Boutin Fish Company near the Eastern shore of Sand Island between two and three o'clock Thursday afternoon.

The Herring King was in use as a freighter by the Boutin Company, making regular trips to the fishing stations at Sand Island and bringing the product of the lake to the packing plant here. It was manned by John Gordon of LaPointe, as captain, and Clarence Russell, also of LaPointe, as engineer.

According to Russell, shortly after two o'clock they left the Moe station on Sand Island enroute to the Shaw Landing on the same island and were proceeding on their way about a quarter of a mile from shore when the boat became suddenly enveloped in flames, resulting from the ignition of gasoline which came from a broken feed pipe from the tank. It appears the gasoline ran down the boat and burst into flame from the exhaust and before anything could be done to put it out, the entire engine room was in flames. Russell ran out on the aft deck and made his way forward along the gunwale to where Gordon was and the latter, in his apparent excitement, threw the small lifeboat off without either oars being placed in it or a line attached.

This left the two men on the burning boat with no means of escape except by leaping into the icy waters of the lake with the chance of reaching the life boat and shore about nine to one against them. However, Russell jumped and succeeded in getting to the lifeboat and then called to Gordon to do the same, but to no avail, Gordon apparently fearing he would be unable to reach the boat.

The *Goldish*, a fishing craft from Duluth, lying at the Shaw Landing, answered the distress calls and came up near the burning craft, picking up Russell, but not daring to approach too near the *Herring King* fearing the explosion of the big gasoline tank as the flames enveloped it. However, lifebuoys were thrown out to Gordon and he was pleaded with to jump into the water and save himself with one of the buoys if possible. He still continued to cling to the burning vessel, however, and by this time had been driven by the flames to the very peak of the bow to which he was just barely hanging. Finally he dropped off and swam to within about five feet of one of the buoys and then sank out of sight.

"The deceased is survived by a wife and three children, all LaPointe residents. The mother was formerly Elizabeth Nevieux. The children are Cecelia, aged 13, Alex, aged 9, and George, aged 6.

"The *Herring King* burning furiously, drifted out into the open lake through the channel between Sand and York Islands. The boat was followed by Louis Moe with his fishing launch and when the fire had died down considerably, he managed to get a long line attached and towed the burning craft to the beach on Sand Island where she will be salvaged, the possibilities being that the engine can be saved.

"A great deal of credit is due to Captain S.L. Goldish, Duluth, and his assistants, Charles Sjoquist, Two Harbors, engineer and Eugene Michaud, Ashland, deckhand, for the part they played in rescuing Russell and in attempting to get Gordon. Despite the intensity of the heat and flames of the burning craft, they ran the *Goldish* to within 30 feet of the boat and endangered their own lives by running the chance of their own craft catching fire or from an explosion on the Herring King.

Strange Happenings

S TRANGE THINGS HAPPEN ON LAKE Superior and here is one of them. Stella M. Champney in the Detroit News Sunday, May 24, 1931, reported: "There is a story of an earthquake that occurred on the steamer lane between Devil's and Outer Islands on a calm August morning in 1925, an upheaval from below that tossed a 400 foot freighter and the 9,000 tons of ore she carried four inches out of the water and left the crew shaken and bewildered. The story was verified for me by H. Otis Smith, chief engineer on the freighter *John Dunn, Jr.,* the ship that was lifted like a chip by that mysterious subterranean explosion. 'There was a roar like a clap of thunder,' Smith said, 'and the ship rose upward as if the back of some huge monster then settled down again. The water boiled up around the ship in great white churning billows, then spread out in an ever-widening circle as waves will when a stone is thrown into calm water.'

'I ran down to the engine room, thinking something had let go. Everything was in order. An oiler came up from below, his face like chalk. 'What blew up?' he asked. 'Did we hit something?'

'Men swarmed about. Some of them had been thrown out of their beds by the shock. They ran here and there, trying to discover the cause of the subterranean explosion.

'There was no answer. The sea was like glass a moment before it, not a breath of air stirring. It was one of those sultry days on the land late in August, when people seek in vain for a cool place. The *John Dunn Jr.*, a staunch ship, that had ridden out the great 1913 storm without a scratch, was bound down from Duluth with a cargo of ore making about 11 miles an hour when it happened. It was like a bolt from a clear sky.

'Captain N. B. Roach of Marine City was temporarily in command, the ship's regular skipper being ill. 'Say nothing about this,' Captain Roach warned. 'We'll just be laughed at if we report an earthquake out in Lake Superior.'

"So the Lake Superior earthquake was never reported."

And in connection with earthquakes, a sudden subsidence of waves was noticed in Bayfield when the Charleston earthquake occurred in 1886 and a note of it was made in *The Press* .

In the winter of 1887 the ice behaved strangely. *The Press* said on Jan. 15 of that year: "Several times during the past month residents of Bayfield have experienced shocks supposed by many to be genuine earthquake tremors. Severest to date occurred Tuesday afternoon and was so severe as to be felt in all parts of town. Strong buildings trembled perceptibly and considerable alarm was manifested by those residing near the bay shore. The cause of these shocks is due to the expansion of ice between the mainland and the island, but why they should be so much more frequent than ever before since the town was settled is a conundrum that puzzles the old inhabitants."

The wind did strange things, too. May 11, 1889 *The Press* reported: "During a sharp squall one of the most curious incidents was witnessed on Front Street. The wind took a yawl boat belonging to the *Boutin* off from the dock and carried it out to sea nearly 20 rods and dropped it into the lake without shipping any water. After the storm, a boat went out and towed it in."

Some things about the lake are, apparently, predictable. In 1908, Captain Harry Brower, who ran the steamer *Barker* for Booth Fish Company, predicted the early opening of navigation for that year for the following reason. "When the sun crossed the equator the wind was from the south. It has been demonstrated by years of observation that whatever way the wind is blowing at the time the sun crosses the equator that this wind will be the prevailing one for 40 days. The south wind is warm and pushes the ice from the bay." Therefore, he predicted an early opening of Chequamegon Bay, probably by the 15th of April He missed it by one day. That near navigation opened Tuesday, April 14, 1908. The tug *Arthur* was the first boat out.

Strange Happenings on the Lake

S TRANGE THINGS HAPPEN ON THE water and under the water of Lake Superior. Here are two of them. The first tells of the miraculous rescue of a seaman known only as Joe after he was tossed overboard at night during a severe storm. The second one tells of the mysterious reappearance of a dog sled, 21 years after it carried its owner to death beneath the ice.

In October, 1911, the steamer *L.A. Hopkins* was loaded at the Wachsmuth Lumber Company dock at Bayfield with 650,000 feet of lumber for McNeil's dock at Buffalo. The

Hopkins encountered a storm and heavy seas beyond Michigan Island, began rolling, and took on so much water that the engine and pump were shut down.

The Bayfield Progress had these details of the story. "The Steamer *Dinkey* arrived in Ashland Tuesday afternoon with 12 men and one woman that the boat early in the morning saved from death in the waters of Lake Superior. These people, thus rescued by the *Dinkey*, comprised the crew of the Steamer *L.A. Hopkins.* The Captain's story is as follows: "We left Bayfield at six o'clock last night with a cargo of lumber. About 11 o'clock we ran into heavy seas and a heavy squall caused the vessel to nearly capsize. The lumber forward washed overboard, carrying a seaman, who is known as Joe. We thought all was lost.

"The *Hopkins* wallowed in the sea and we started to launch the life boat. It was pretty dark and it dropped into the water with only one man aboard and went adrift and disappeared into the darkness. We started to make a life raft, but the vessel remaining partly afloat we decided to wait until the last minute before abandoning it.

Several times we heard a mysterious hail from the water, but were unable to discover who it was from. It was three hours after the two men disappeared when they suddenly shot up to the ship's side and clambered aboard. Joe had clung to floating lumber and by a miracle; the lifeboat drifted right out to it and Joe was picked up. The two men were able to handle the lifeboat and brought it back. As it got daylight we hoisted signals of distress. A boat passed us. We could see men on deck, but they didn't hear us. Then a second boat came into sight. It was the *Alva Dinkey*. She came near us, but the seas were too high for a rescue. The *Dinkey* poured oil on the water, which quieted the seas and we escaped to her in the lifeboat. We even saved the ship's dog. The engineer and myself own the *Hopkins*. She was not insured."

Captain Einar Miller with the tug *Bayfield* tried to get the *Hopkins*, and started out in a sixty-mile gale from the northwest. He reported the waves were mountainous and he could not find the *Hopkins.* Then the *Hopkins* was sighted by the Steamer *Barth*, downbound, about 15 miles northwest of Ontonogan with the bow still out of water, and on account of the amount of lumber floating, it was thought the cargo was floating out of the hold.

I found no account telling whether the *Hopkins* sank or was salvaged. Does any one know?

The second story appeared in the Progress June 17, 1915, reporting that the sleigh owned by Alphonse Bjorge had been found. After being in the water of Lake Superior for 21 years, it was pulled up in a gang of gill nets. The account was as follows: "Twenty one years ago last March, trout were plentiful at the north end of Madeline Island. There were, at the time, somewhere in the neighborhood of thirty men camped at "Jack Stewart's" and on Wilson and Presque Island, all of whom were bobbing for trout and the catch was good each day.

One Saturday afternoon, just a short time before the ice moved out, there was one of the party, Alphonse Bjorge, who had very poor luck, not catching a fish all day. He saw along the short of Madeline what he thought was a couple of men running on the ice, but which later proved to be a couple of crows. He insisted, however, that it was men, and they were catching many fish, so he decided to go over there the next day and try his luck. Several of the men cautioned him as to the unsafe condition of the ice, telling him that the ice went out along there very often during the night with an off land breeze and when the wind subsided, it froze over again the same night. He did not believe them and in the fact of their remonstrances, started on the perilous trip and had gone but a short distance when he broke through the ice. Although his friends tried every available means to rescue him, their efforts proved fruitless and after drowning his dog in frantic efforts to save his life, he finally sank beneath the ice.

Nothing more was heard of Alphonse Bjorge until last Monday when Andrew Seim was raising gill nets between Madeline Island and Michigan Island and he pulled up the sleigh and part of the dog harness which is in a good state of preservation. Mr. Seim says he is sure it is the same one used by Bjorge, as he can recall the peculiar build of it.

Summaries and the "Old Timers"

Little Steamboat Island circa 1900.
(Photo: BHA)

THIS IS THE FINAL STORY on the early history of Bayfield, which I have been writing. Including this one, the total is 243 weekly stories, which is about equal to three books.

In response to my question about the sinking of Little Steamboat Island, I heard from Shine Miller and Hamilton Ross. Shine remembers the night it sank, or washed away during a heavy northeast storm about 1900. He and Charles Leihy on the tug *Van Raalt* took refuge from the storm in the lee of Sand Island. They saw Little Steamboat before the storm, after the storm it was gone.

Hamilton Ross wrote to the U.S. Lake Survey office for authentic information on the island and received the following report. "Steamboat Island was shown on our original survey of 1869 as a small island entirely above water located just south of Eagle Island. A subsequent survey made in 1902 depicted the island as below water. . . Information given in Bulletin 13 of 1903 states that Steamboat Island consisted of a narrow gravel ridge six inches above water and surrounded by exposed boulders. Bulletin 14 of 1904 describes the island as being worn away, leaving a narrow shoal of gravel and boulders exposed only at low water or rough weather."

Mr. Ross writes further: "I was also much interested in Sam Fifield's remark about the magnetic ore on Oak Island. I had not known of this, but it rather bears out our experience of two years ago when we were checking compass courses on Leo Casper's *Guben* preparatory to setting out for Isle Royale and the Nipigon. We noticed that on a course between the southwest end of Hermit Island and the southeast point of Oak Island the compass was badly "out." If we had followed the true compass course of 23 degrees between these points (relying on our magnetic compass) we would have run smack into Oak Island. The compass showed 27 degrees "out."

"Another interesting (to me) phenomenon is York Island. According to your friend, Henry W. Bayfield's map of 1823-25, there were two islands. One of them he named *York* and the other one *Rock*. Since his time a sand bar has built up connecting his two islands."

"While on the subject of H. Bayfield, his map showed soundings of from 40' to 60' of water between Sand Island and the mainland. Today, according to government charts, the depth averages about 6' or less. This rather bears out the prediction of some physiographers that eventually the two will be connected. Imagine driving your car from Bayfield right out to Sand Island lighthouse!"

Right now, Mr. Ross, I can only imagine it with me in a life preserver and my car on pontoons, but the day may come. Each year the islands change some with a big rockslide or a small new sand bar and, if the depth of the water between Sand Island and the mainland has diminished 54 feet in 135 years the road is a possibility.

As the 1958 herring season approaches, I have made note of two items from the herring season of 1905, which appeared in *The Press* . "This season saw a new departure in the line of herring fishing in these waters in the way of pond net fishing. Heretofore, gill nets have been used exclusively for herring, now large lifts are made from pond nets in shoal water. Later on, when the fish seek deeper water, gill nets will be all the go."

"The tug *Tramp* on Ontonogan, owned by Hawley Bros., will certainly carry off the pennant at the close of herring season if she keeps on at the rate she has been going since the first lift. The banner lift was made Thursday, when she came in with 18 tons. The *Tramp* has done very well, the smallest catch to date, eight tons."

Who will equal the *Tramp* this year?

On August 12, 1915, a homesick "former Bayfield resident" who was living in Tacoma, Washington, took the editor of the Bayfield Progress to task because he didn't write enough about the lake and boats, saying, "Here is a little advice to you, Mr. Editor. Go down to the edge of the lake and wash your eyes, then look out over the water and take in what you can see and go home and write about it, and next fall when the first, heavy northeaster strikes you, sit down and write about it and describe how it impresses you. Certainly you can do that. At night the sound of the wind and the roar of the waves on the shore ought to give you stuff to write about. I would a thousand times rather some winter evening, sit down in Fred Fischer's store and listen to N. LaBonte and see George Stahl spit on the stove until ten o'clock when the store would close than go to the movies and listen to the younger folks chewing gum. Gosh, weren't those glorious days, though? If Captain Pike and Frank Boutin would happen to come in, matters would be interesting."

Taking the old timers word to heart, I went to the lake, washed my face, looked around and have done my best to write about Bayfield. I have written about the northeaster, the wind, the waves. I have also written about the pioneers and their way of life as best I could without actually knowing most of them. The old-timer, exiled in Tacoma, has included the final, homey touch of George Stahl spitting on the stove.

My thanks to all who have helped me, with a very special thank you to Mrs. DeMars. Now, with 243 stories recording the early history of Bayfield completed, I feel I have done my best and can conscientiously write"

THE END

Commercial Fishing Industry of Bayfield

The early Chequamegon Bay and Bayfield commercial fishing Mackinaws existed from the 1830's until the early 1900's. Replaced by gasoline engine and steam powered tugs, these sleek 26 foot long sailboats, supplied many a "planked" whitefish, herring and trout for the fine restaurants on Bayfield's bustling avenues. (Photo: BHA)

Washington Avenue beachhead circa 1899. Shown here is the A. Booth Cooperage building, Island View Hotel, Catholic Convent, and a steam tug tied to the North dock. (Photo: BHA)

Nets drying on the reels at Booth Fisheries. (Photo: BHA)

Crew Apostle Island Bell, W.B Miler. Capt. (Photo: BHA)

Solomon Boutin fish dock circa 1900. Tugs owned and operated by Boutin included the Elsie Nell and R.T. Roy. (Photo: BHA)

Gill nets on the reel. The site of the photo is on the old "Henry Johnson" fish company site. (Photo: BHA)

Booth Boat Yard Located at the beachhead of Washington Avenue circa 1929. (Photo: Courtesy Robert J. Nelson Collection)

Booth Fish Dock. Photo: BHA Inc.

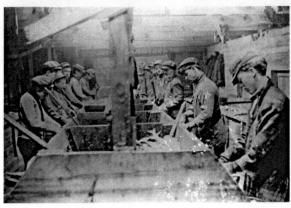

Herring dresser's at work. Circa 1899. (Photo: BHA)

The F.R. Anderson bull gang pulling herring into the picking shed. Circa 1890's. Herring gill nets, 2.5 inch slip mesh, were hand pulled onto the tug deck from sites in Russell Bay, Sand Island and north Madeline Island reefs. "Picked off" by men, women and children in the herring sheds, the fish were then back split, salted into kegs and shipped to the mining towns of the Appalachians. (Photo: Robert Nelson)

Index of Names

H

N

T

U

V

W